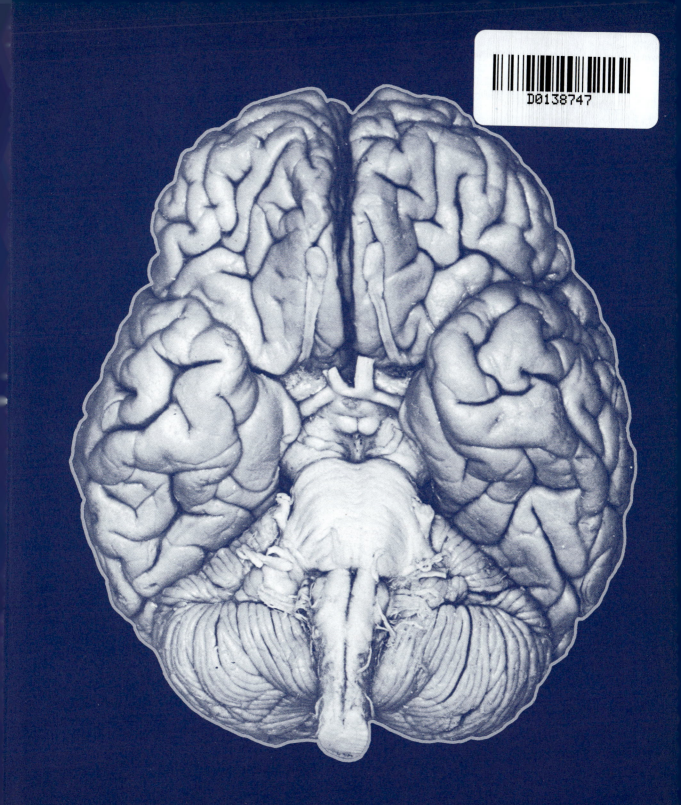

Inferior Surface of the Brain (Actual Size)

Physiological Psychology / *An Introduction*

Physiological Psychology / *An Introduction*

William C. Watson Chicago State University

Houghton Mifflin Company / *Boston*

Dallas   *Geneva, Illinois*   *Hopewell, New Jersey*   *Palo Alto*   *London*

Cover angiograph © Howard Sochurek. Front and back endpapers from Stephen J. DeArmond, Madeline M. Fusco, and Maynard M. Dewey, *Structure of the Human Brain: A Photographic Atlas* (New York: Oxford University Press, 1976).

Printed in the U.S.A.
Library of Congress Catalog Card Number: 80-82838
ISBN: 0-395-30221-8

Contents

v

Part III / *The Major Functional Systems*
              B. The Ancient Subcortical Systems   **213**

Part IV / *Four Perspectives on the Brain*   **289**

Alternative Topical Contents

Preface

This text represents a somewhat innovative approach to the field of the neurosciences. The intent is to present a considerably more comprehensive treatment of current information about the human brain than is usually attempted in an undergraduate text. At the same time, the text remains thoroughly readable and comprehensible to the student with no preliminary training in the biological sciences. A single course in introductory psychology is the only prerequisite assumed.

Innovative Approach   The more traditional topical approach has been set aside in favor of an approach based on an understanding of global brain structure and function. It is the author's conviction that the neurosciences have reached the point where a comprehensive view of psychological phenomena as the direct expression of brain operations may begin to be attempted, and that this approach provides the student with a deeper understanding than can be expected when the focus is on isolated areas of psychological functioning. The focus throughout the text is on neural systems and subsystems and their interrelations in the generation of the phenomena of everyday experience.

As an aid to those who prefer to teach the course in physiological psychology in the traditional manner, an alternative topical table of contents is provided. All of the major topics of emphasis in the traditional course can be conveniently found here.

Flexibility   The text is readily adaptable to a variety of possible approaches to teaching the course, ranging from a solid foundation-course approach to a lighter treatment based on the excitement of recent developments in the field. The first type of course objective may be best met by placing emphasis on Parts I, II, and III, while the second type of objective might be best served by placing more emphasis on Parts IV and V. Some instructors may wish to eliminate whole chapters in Parts II and III, for example Chapter 5 on audition and Chapter 7 on somesthesis. This can be done without impairing comprehension of the rest of the text, since each chapter is designed as a self-contained treatment of a specific area of brain function. The four chapters in Part IV can also be used selectively, depending on the instructor's preferred emphasis.

Art Program   Ample graphic materials have been included to make the subject matter less forbidding than it might otherwise be. The underlying assumption is that a clear understanding of neuroanatomy is a prerequisite to clear thinking about brain functions. For this reason, a good many more, and more complete, anatomical diagrams have been included than is customary in an introductory text in this field, including a brief schematic brain atlas in Appendix B. The student can thus be encouraged to develop a vivid mental picture of the major internal structures and their fiber connections. What the book presents is a somewhat simplified and schematic view of the normal human brain based on materials prepared for my own course over the years through careful analysis of brain atlas materials. For the sake of expository simplicity, certain structures, such as those related to the habenula and pineal gland, have been omitted.

Learning Aids   A comprehensive glossary of technical terms is included at the end of the text. In addition, many terms are defined in the margin on first introduction of the term, and pronunciations are given for troublesome words. The considerable number of unfamiliar technical terms in physiological psychology is apt to be a stumbling block for many students, who especially do not like to deal with words they do not know how to pronounce. As far as possible, references are to articles in journals readily available to the student in the college library, since it is the author's experience that undergraduates seldom find time and motivation to investigate reports available only in a technical library.

Supplements   A Study Guide has been prepared that should greatly assist the student in mastering the somewhat difficult and technical details of the neurosciences. The Study Guide contains fill-in review questions, self-tests containing multiple-choice questions, self-testing essay questions called "Putting It in Your Own Words," and diagrams to aid the student's review of each chapter's content. An Instructor's Manual is also available.

Throughout the text, my policy has been to make clear those areas where controversy still exists, as well as those areas where the facts are still unknown. Thus the student is constantly reminded of the challenge to research in the field, and encouraged to think, rather than to accept in passive fashion a body of predigested information.

I wish to acknowledge the assistance of many who have contributed their time and attention to the preparation of the text, especially John P. Watson, my brother, whose indefatigable attention to details and constant support have been immeasurably helpful. The following reviewers contributed to the development of the manuscript by making valuable suggestions for improvement: Benton E. Allen, Mt. San Antonio College; C. Robert Almli, Ohio University; Herbert P. Alpern, University of Colorado; David L. Avery, University of Arkansas for Medical Sciences; and Daniel E. Sheer, University of Houston. In addition, I want to give recognition to the contribution of hundreds of students, whose questions have been instructive and whose speculations have opened many new directions in my own understanding. To all of these, and to the staff at Houghton Mifflin who have been consistently supportive and helpful, I offer my thanks.

William C. Watson

Physiological Psychology / *An Introduction*

Part I / *A General Overview of the Brain*

We do not often find ourselves astonished by our ability to think, to feel sorrow or joy, to appreciate humor or music, to remember past events, or to plan for the future. We take for granted — even ignore as uninteresting — things that are in fact most remarkable. Only slowly have our eyes been opened to the wonders of biology, particularly the biology of ourselves and the great mystery of our human brain. We appear to be now at a great turning point in human history. New scientific understanding is not only remaking our outer world, but opening up our inner world as well. We are becoming increasingly self-aware. An important aspect of our new sophistication is the realization that all psychological phenomena are the direct expression of the functioning of the brain. If we can come to understand the human brain, perhaps the most intricate and subtle system in the universe, we may come to understand ourselves.

Part I of this text provides a general overview of what is known about the brain and lays the groundwork for more depth in succeeding chapters. It begins with a brief history of efforts to understand what the brain is for and how it works. Chapter 2 examines the brain itself: its structure and components and their interconnections. The reader should seek to acquire a clear mental image of the brain, both its exterior and its interior. Chapter 3 briefly surveys what is known about the nerve cell, or neuron — the functional unit of the brain — also a most remarkable story.

Parts II and III constitute the main body of the text. Part II examines the more recently evolved "cognitive" portions of the brain; Part III addresses the more ancient portions that handle basic survival mechanisms. Parts II and III emphasize functions, rather than structure.

Part IV offers an overview of brain functions from four different theoretical perspectives. Part V reviews current findings and issues in the rapidly expanding field of physiological psychology.

Chapter 1 / *The Discovery of the Brain*

Not until modern times was it recognized that the brain tissues are associated with psychological phenomena. During the 1800s the advent of microscopes revealed that living tissues are composed of individual living cells (the cell theory). At the beginning of this century the neuron — a specialized type of cell — was proposed as the basis of brain function (the neuron theory). Early researches led to the hypothesis that different portions of the brain are involved in different functions (the localizationist theory); other studies suggest that the brain functions as a whole (the antilocalizationist theory). Increasingly subtle research into the function of the different structures of the brain tends to support a modified localizationist theory of brain function.

Until very recent times, next to nothing was known about the brain. Theories about psychological processes focused on two questions: was the soul located in the head or in the heart (Shakespeare refers to the controversy in *The Merchant of Venice:* "Tell me where is Fancie bred, Or in the heart or in the head?"), and, if in the head, in its hollow, fluid-filled *ventricles* or in the gelatinous material of the brain-stuff itself? Curiously, when the head eventually began to seem the more likely site, the ventricles were chosen as the most probable locus of psychic events (Figure 1.1). The brain tissues seem to have been the last place where mental processes might be expected to take place.

Ventricles. **A system of interconnected hollow, fluid-filled cavities within the brain.**

Today the situation is quite changed. No psychic functions whatever are at present attributed to the heart, now universally recognized to be a mere muscle to pump the blood, and none has yet been found for the fluid-filled ventricles. All attention is now focused on the gray matter, the neural tissue, as the seat of consciousness, and a mystery due to ignorance has been replaced by a more sophisticated one: how could this pinkish-gray jellylike substance,

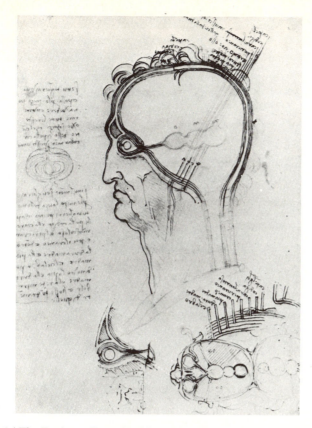

Figure 1.1 / *The Brain as Conceived by Leonardo Da Vinci in 1490.* In this beautiful drawing, one can see three interconnected vesicles in a horizontal row in the middle of the brain, with a channel leading into the first from the eye socket. The result not of observation but of pure imagination, this figure depicts the ventricular theory of brain function popular at the time. The ventricular theory emphasized movement of fluids through these three hollow vesicles, which were thought to produce all psychological phenomena, including consciousness itself. Leonardo later dissected the brain of an ox and recognized his error, but the ventricular theory remained the dominant theory of brain function until fairly recently.

quite uniform in appearance, produce all the varied phenomena of human experience — our moods and our passions, pleasure and pain, imagination and thought, learning and memory, as well as behavior?

Only within the past few decades has significant progress begun to be made toward understanding how our brain works. But the late flowering of the brain sciences is no reflection on the intelligence of those who went before us. The philosopher and mathematician Descartes believed the soul to reside in the tiny pineal gland in the head, proposing no function whatever for the neural tissues, yet he had a brain as good as any today. Our advantage today is not the caliber of our brains, but our possession of the tools and techniques to make the necessary observations. With modern microscopes and the stimulating and recording electrode, we can discover what the naked eye could never discern; with modern methods of chemical analysis, we can examine processes even at the molecular level within neural tissues. Our present understanding waited upon the development of modern research technologies, which grow more powerful, it seems, by the month. We know things about the human brain now that could not have been known even a few short years ago, and a brief review of how we came to this point will provide a useful perspective.

Antique Theories

We know nothing of what prehistoric peoples thought their brains were for, but we do suspect that they sometimes ate them. Many fossilized human skulls are found broken open on the underside, presumably to extract the brain. Early Mesopotamian and Egyptian writings provide few clues to their authors' beliefs about the origin of their thoughts. But about 400 B.C. the Greek physician Hippocrates, author of the Hippocratic oath still honored by physicians today, stated quite plainly what we now know to be the case:

Men ought to know that from the brain and from the brain only, arise our pleasures, joys, laughter and jests, as well as our sorrows, pains, griefs and tears. Through it, in particular, we think, see, hear, and distinguish the ugly from the beautiful, the bad from the good, the pleasant from the unpleasant.[1]

Only fifty years later, however, Aristotle was teaching that the function of the brain was merely to cool the blood, an idea probably suggested by his astute observation that the brains of animals are abundantly supplied with a rich network of blood vessels. So farreaching was Aristotle's authority that his attribution of the human essence to the heart persisted almost two thousand years (Shakespeare wrote the lines quoted above in 1596).

The next entrant in the debate was Herophilus of Alexandria,

[1] Jones, W. H. S. *Hippocrates*, Vol. 2. New York: Putnam, 1923, p. 129.

who supported Hippocrates' position but with the curious twist that the soul resided not in the brain tissues themselves but in the tiny fourth ventricle of the brainstem. Though the rationale behind this notion is hard to guess, it was to dominate speculation thoroughly from that point on. During the fourth and fifth centuries A.D. St. Augustine and other early Church Fathers promulgated a brain theory based on the flow of the ventricular fluids through the three major brain cavities; this was official doctrine for another two hundred years. As late as the middle of the seventeenth century, Descartes proposed a dynamic version of the ventricular brain in which the soul, located in the pineal gland at the rear of the third ventricle, controlled the flow of "animal spirits" through these cavities, producing the phenomena of experience and thought.

The Question of Localization of Brain Function

It was one of Descartes' contemporaries, Thomas Willis, who was most influential in directing attention to the brain tissues. Willis proposed an elaborate theory postulating the gray matter at the surface of the brain (the *cortex*) to be the seat of memory, a group of subcortical structures (the *basal ganglia*) to receive all incoming sensations, and the white matter between to be the seat of the imagination. This widely influential theory was eventually undermined in the next century by Albrecht von Haller, who argued against trying to locate brain functions in any particular portion of the brain tissues. No one again seriously proposed a brain theory based on the flow of cerebrospinal fluid through the hollow ventricles.

One controversy was settled, but another began. Von Haller was only the first in a long tradition of antilocalizationists extending into the present. At issue is whether the brain functions as a whole, each portion fulfilling many functions, or whether various structures of the brain or even regions of the cortex are uniquely responsible for special kinds of operations. Throughout the eighteenth and nineteenth centuries the tide of opinion swung back and forth on this question.

The most dramatic turn in this debate — and a high point in the history of intellectual fads — was the reintroduction of cortical localization into full scientific respectability by Franz Joseph Gall's "science of cranioscopy," known today as *phrenology*. Gall drew maps of the cranium, labelling the corresponding areas of the cortex responsible for particular mental faculties and moral qualities. With the aid of such maps, people's characters and dispositions were de-

Cortex. A type of neural tissue consisting of distinct layers forming a continuous sheet, as at the surface of the brain.

Basal ganglia. A group of subcortical nuclei involved in motor functions, usually the caudate nucleus, putamen, and globus pallidus.

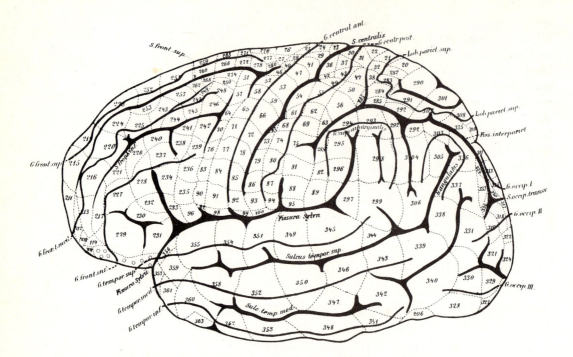

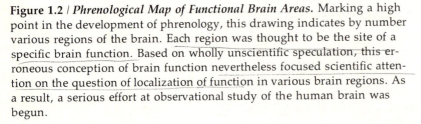

Figure 1.2 / *Phrenological Map of Functional Brain Areas.* Marking a high point in the development of phrenology, this drawing indicates by number various regions of the brain. Each region was thought to be the site of a specific brain function. Based on wholly unscientific speculation, this erroneous conception of brain function nevertheless focused scientific attention on the question of localization of function in various brain regions. As a result, a serious effort at observational study of the human brain was begun.

termined by examination of the bumps and hollows on their heads. Twenty-seven sites were designated on the surface of the brain, each thought to be independently associated with a particular dimension of personality or character. From 1792 to the 1830s the theory and practice of phrenology enjoyed almost universal popularity among professionals and laymen alike (Figure 1.2).

Evidences of Cortical Localization

Fanciful as it was, and based on no observational evidence whatever, phrenology nevertheless served the purpose of attracting scientific attention to the cortex of the brain as a differentiated organ system. The search began for real evidence of cortical localization, and results were soon forthcoming. In 1861 the French surgeon Paul Broca announced the discovery that speech is impaired when damage occurs to a small region of the cortex low along the side of the *frontal lobe* (*Broca's motor speech area*). Four years later Broca found that the effect occurred only when the left side of the brain was affected, an observation that was at the time totally surprising and inexplicable. The door was open, if only ajar.

In 1790 the Italian Luigi Galvani had demonstrated the electrical excitability of nervous tissue in a neuromuscular preparation of a frog's leg with a stump of severed nerve exposed (still a favorite laboratory demonstration in physiological psychology classes). As electricity became better understood, convenient electrical stimulators were developed, and in 1870 a German researcher, Karl von Frisch, reported that electrical stimulation of a particular region on the side

Broca   1861

Paul Broca (*1824–1880*)

of a dog's brain produced muscular contractions on the opposite
side of its body. Four years later an American physician, Roberts *1874*
Bartholow, stimulated the surface of an exposed human brain and
demonstrated the same muscular contraction on the opposite side of
the body, thus establishing the location of the *primary motor cortex*
in the human brain.

The same year, in Poland, twenty-six-year-old Carl Wernicke *1874*
published an important paper describing another area on the left

Figure 1.3 / *The Human Brain, Showing Left Hemisphere Speech Areas.* One
of the first true discoveries regarding brain function came with the observations, by Broca and Wernicke, that there are two speech areas in the left
hemisphere, none in the right. The existence of speech deficits when brain
lesions occurred in these areas supported this finding. It came shortly after
the discovery that electrical stimulation of the cortex of one hemisphere
produced muscular movement on the opposite side of the body.

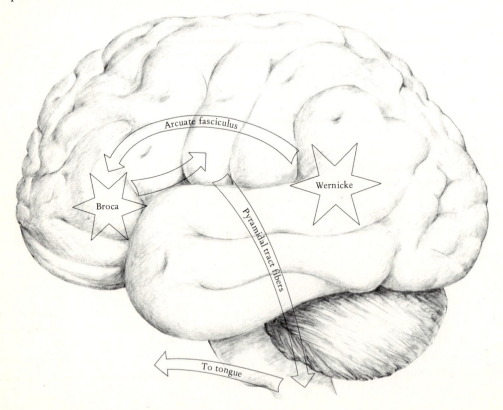

side of the brain where lesions may produce language difficulties. This site was farther to the rear, around the junction of the temporal and parietal lobes, in the region now known as *Wernicke's receptive speech area* (Figure 1.3). Wernicke astutely pointed out that damage to this region of the brain did not disturb the ability to articulate speech, but interfered with understanding it — a highly important observational distinction.

Thus began, about the time of the Civil War, the analysis of the functions of the various portions of the brain, based not on sheer imagination or traditional authority but on increasingly refined observational and experimental studies.

The Discovery of the Neuron

Though low-power microscopes had been in use since the end of the sixteenth century, higher-power multiple-lens instruments capable of revealing the microstructure of living tissues were not developed until the 1800s. In 1838, on the basis of microscopic observations, the German physician Theodore Schwann enunciated the startling *cell theory* that all living tissues, plant and animal, are composed of tiny individual living cells. This was a moment in scientific history fully equal to the American astronomer Edwin Powell Hubble's discovery of the existence of other galaxies beyond our Milky Way System. One of the rare breakthroughs that opens up a new frontier, Schwann's hypothesis was not without opponents and disbelievers.

Though it had been recognized for some time that the nerves Galvani stimulated were composed of many fine fibers bundled together in a cable, the source of these fibers was unknown. It had been theorized that they formed an interconnected network, or "syncytium," extending throughout the brain. With the announcement of the cell theory, however, opinion swung toward the position that these fibers were extensions of a particular kind of living cell: a nerve cell, or *neuron*. In 1891 Heinrich Waldeyer published a summary of studies to date, which led him to the conclusion that nerve cells were indeed independent living units rather than physically interconnected in a continuous network. Thus the *neuron doctrine* was born. The most influential evidence came from the work of Karl Deiters, who painstakingly isolated single nerve cells through microdissection of hardened neural tissues of the brain stem *nucleus* that now bears his name.

Nucleus. Any group of neurons which together fulfill a particular brain function.

The neuron doctrine was further substantiated when the Italian anatomist Camillo Golgi (who himself subscribed to the syncytium theory) developed an ingenious new method for staining slices of neural tissue with silver for microscopic examination. For reasons still poorly understood, this method stains only a small percentage of the neurons in the tissue but stains them completely, in all their extensions, causing them to stand out from the rest while remaining embedded within the complex tangle of other cells. With this lucky discovery in hand, the Spaniard Santiago Ramón y Cajal tackled the vast problem of analyzing the masses of cells called neural tissue, demonstrating beyond question that neurons are indeed independent living cells, and the origin of the long fiber extensions that make up the nerves. In his long career in observational science,

Santiago Ramón y Cajal (1852–1934)

Ramón y Cajal described in minute detail the structure of the cortex and the spinal cord, the retina of the eye, and many other components of the nervous system. In 1906 he shared with Camillo Golgi the Nobel Prize for the Section of Physiology and Medicine.

In the same year Sir Charles Sherrington published his classic work, *The Integrative Action of the Nervous System* (Sherrington, 1906), still available and highly readable. If Ramón y Cajal was the greatest of the early neuroanatomists, Sherrington may have been the greatest neurophysiologist. It was he who first described and named the *synapse*, the junction between neurons where one transmits its excitation to the other. Sherrington also described the chemical nature of this junctional transfer of excitation. Like Ramón y Cajal, Sherrington investigated many aspects of the nervous system, including the neurons of the cerebral cortex, using the light microscope.

Synapse. **The structure mediating the effect of a nerve impulse upon its target cell.**

The Modern Period

Electronic recording and amplifying equipment was introduced in the 1920s, and has become progressively more sophisticated and refined ever since. It enabled E. D. Adrian in 1927 to measure the electrical impulses in the *optic nerve* as a function of stimulation of the eye with a beam of light. In 1931 B. H. C. Matthews recorded electrical potentials from the muscle of a frog during active contraction, demonstrating that muscle fibers exhibit an electrical activity similar to that of neurons. In 1924 the cathode-ray oscilloscope was first used to record nerve impulses, producing a visual screen representation of the electrical activity. Recording of impulses in single nerve fibers still resisted all efforts, owing to the difficulty of dealing with such a slender fiber enmeshed in a cable of similar fibers.

Then came an important discovery by J. A. Young: the giant nerve fiber of the squid, with a diameter of as much as a millimeter. Very quickly thereafter a host of studies were reported on this most convenient find, and much of what we know today about the mechanisms of conduction of the nerve impulse has been learned by studying this remarkable biological curiosity. In 1949, however, R. W. Gerard introduced a micropipette technique for recording impulses from within even ordinary-sized nerve fibers, or cell bodies, using a drawn-glass tube whose ultrafine tip is filled with a potassium chloride solution as electrode. This technique is still used for recording electrical potentials from both inside and outside the individual nerve cell or fiber.

Shortly after Golgi's introduction of his method for staining neurons with silver, Carl Weigert developed a stain that turned the *myelin sheath* coating most of the major nerve fibers a dark blue or black. By causing fiber tracts to stand out from the gray matter (composed largely of cell bodies) through which they passed, this stain permitted the neuroanatomist to trace a nerve fiber's course through the brain. Next A. V. Waller, noting that a severed nerve fiber begins to degenerate (*Wallerian degeneration*), introduced a stain that affects only such degenerating myelinated fibers. These methods made it possible to trace single fibers in their course through the brain-stuff, and thus to begin to establish the anatomical connections that make up the "wiring diagram" of the brain.

A new silver stain method for tracing degenerating nerve fibers themselves (the Nauta-Gygax method) was introduced in 1954, and in 1967 there followed a modification (the Fink-Heimer method) that allowed even unmyelinated nerve fibers to be traced. The development of penetrating electrodes about the same time introduced another method of studying anatomical connections. These electrodes consisted of two fine wires exposed only at their tips to permit stimulation of small regions of neural tissue deep in the brain. A train of brief impulses passing from one exposed tip to the other was found to increase the firing rate of neurons in that region, allowing the behavioral effects, or the neural effects in some other brain region to be observed. By increasing the amplitude of the current, a larger region of brain tissue could be activated. A more refined technique to achieve the same observational purpose became available with the development of the cannula (*can*-yu-la), a slender tube through which a small amount of an appropriate chemical substance can be injected into a specific site in the brain.

Certain chemical substances selectively affect only those neurons involved in a particular neural system, leaving undisturbed those belonging to other systems that may be intermingled with them. Their use yields a more specific and interpretable result than could be obtained through electrical stimulation, which indiscriminately affects all neurons in the vicinity. By applying a tiny electrical potential to such a cannula, moreover, certain chemicals can be injected in very tiny and measurable quantities, making possible a most refined electrophysiological tool of investigation called *electrophoresis* (electro-fo-*re*-sis), or iontophoresis.

When Hans Berger discovered the so-called "brain waves" — rhythmic electrical potentials recordable from the scalp — in 1929, a quite different approach to the study of brain function was introduced. In time, sophisticated electroencephalographic (literally, electrical-brain-recording) equipment was developed with a com-

Myelin sheath. A fatty sheath surrounding many axons, formed by multiple wrappings of the endfeet of a specialized type of nonneural cell.

Electrophoresis. The technique of injecting tiny controlled amounts of chemical substances into specific brain regions by applying a small electrical voltage to the hollow electrode containing the substance.

puter-averaging feature to separate signal from noise. Such equipment made it possible to detect the response of a specific location on the cortex to the arrival of a sensory signal (*evoked potentials*), and neural firing associated with the initiation, and even anticipation, of voluntary movement. Using multiple scalp electrodes for simultaneous recording, the correlated activity of different portions of the cortex can now be detected (even more efficiently as an *electrocorticogram* recorded from the surface of the cortex).

There followed another important advance, the exploration of deep subcortical regions of the brain using permanently implanted electrodes for recording electrical activity in the brain of a freely moving animal, or for stimulating a particular region in order to note the behavioral effect. In its most sophisticated manifestation, the stimulation is triggered from a distance by radio waves. Experimental techniques have also been devised for putting deep-lying nerve cells temporarily out of commission without permanently impairing their function. One is a *cryogenic* (cooling) method; another is the use of a cannula to inject small amounts of drugs, such as procaine, that interfere with normal neural function only momentarily. It is recognized that, with all such techniques, what is being directly affected by the tool is probably but a small portion of a much larger functional system.

Evoked potential. An electrical response recorded from the cortex in response to sensory stimulation.

Electrocorticogram. A record of brain waves recorded from the surface of the cortex.

Tracer Techniques

Other methods of investigating neural connections take advantage of the fact that certain materials tend to be transported along the course of nerve fibers under normal living conditions. By injecting into the brain substances that will be picked up by the nerve cells and transported, and can later be detected in brain slices under the microscope, the course of a nerve fiber can be followed. One tracer method involves the use of natural brain chemicals that have been rendered radioactive, such as by replacing one of their normal carbon atoms with its radioactive isotope. Exposure of a photographic plate will thus occur when the brain slice is applied to it for an extended period. This procedure is called *autoradiography* or *radioautography*. A recently introduced method makes use of radioactive *deoxyglucose*, which is readily taken up into the neuron as a food substance, resulting in the labeling of any metabolic products later transported along the nerve fiber. The genius of this method is that it can be used to assess the amount of activity in the neuron: the more active it is, the more deoxyglucose it will take up. Another method makes use of amino acids, which are linked together to make proteins. Radioactive amino acids injected into the brain are picked up by the neurons in the vicinity, incorporated into new proteins, and sent along the course of the nerve fiber.

Another tracer method is the fluorescence technique. Dyes harmless to the neuron may be similarly taken up and transported along the nerve fiber, and later detected in their new location by examining brain slices under the microscope. One important such dye is Procion yellow, which is not normally taken up by the neuron, but if injected into it will travel to all its cytoplasmic extensions, fluorescing a bright yellow under bluish light. Since the neural membrane is impenetrable to the dye, none leaks out into extracellular space; thus no other neurons are affected, and the injected cell stands out vividly under the microscope.

A recently introduced variant on the fluorescence technique involves the use of the laboratory animal's immune system to prepare tracers which, when injected, will find their way to particular parts of single neurons. Target substances (the *antigens*) are injected into living animals, whose bodies react to them as foreign substances by producing *antibodies*. These antibodies are later isolated from the blood serum of the injected animal, treated with fluorescent material, and injected into the brain, where they react with (attach to) the original target substances, wherever they may be located in the tissues. Thus those portions of the cell will fluoresce most brightly.

Still another tracer technique involves the use of a unique protein substance, *horseradish peroxidase*, which is readily picked up at the neuron cell body, or at the tip end of its nerve fiber, but will not pass through the fiber wall, and is readily transported at good speed along the fiber in either direction. If injected into the region of a synaptic junction between two nerve cells, it will be picked up by both and quickly transported down the entire length of their fibers (in the one case from the fiber tip back to its cell body, no matter how far distant, a process called *retrograde transmission*). Later, brain slices can be treated with chemical stains specific to horseradish peroxidase, allowing the course of a fiber to be traced in either direction from the point of perfusion of the tissues.

The Electron Microscope

Until the introduction of more powerful microscopes it was impossible to visualize such important structures in the brain as the synaptic junction between neurons, or the neural membrane itself. The

resolution of the light microscope is limited because the wavelengths of visible light are too long. The electron microscope, which
uses an electron beam instead of light and electrostatic plates or
electromagnetic coils instead of a transparent lens, came into being
just as its necessity began to be clearly recognized. Its vastly increased resolving power allows these major structures of the nerve
cell (and many more minute structures as well) to be easily brought
into focus.

Figure 1.4 is a *transmission electron micrograph* (the beam passing
through the ultrathin slice of neural tissue). Other techniques produce detailed pictures of the surfaces of submicroscopic structures.
An extreme refinement of this approach is the *scanning electron microscope,* capable of producing vivid three-dimensional images of

Figure 1.4 / *An Electron Micrograph of Neural Tissue.* This is a transmission
electron micrograph of a thin section of a rat's olfactory bulb. By means of
such pictures we are able to examine in great detail minute structures
within the brain, such as the plasma membrane, synaptic junctions, and
organelles within the cytoplasm of nerve cells.

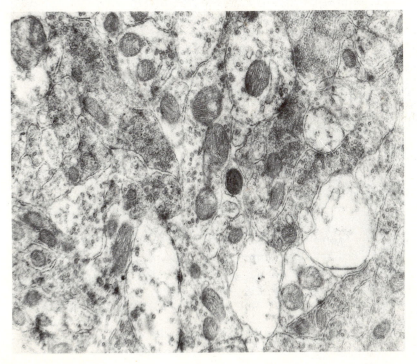

living tissues against their background. A still further refinement, the *freeze-fracture method,* makes it possible to study the interior surface of the cell membrane, incredible as that might seem. The cell membrane is caused to split horizontally at its middle, and its inner surfaces are coated with a thin deposit of metal, revealing their most intimate structure.

Recent Trends

We have come a long way in recent days toward that point in sophistication about the brain where its actual functional mechanisms will be revealed. Much of what has been discovered to date involves anatomical structures and connections, which are an important beginning. Function is often revealed in anatomy. Without knowing what the brain is composed of, it would be difficult to imagine how it works, as the wildly erroneous speculations of the past attest.

Recently the advancing fields of molecular biology and neurochemistry have begun to cast brain function in a new light. The neuron is coming to be looked on not only as a signal transmission mechanism but also as a neurosecretory organ, producing hormones and hormonelike substances that exercise subtle chemical influences on its neighbors. Biochemistry and neuropharmacology have been highly successful in probing the molecular mechanisms underlying neural function, and in disclosing the existence of discrete chemical subsystems, often operating side by side within the brain substance. As will be suggested in Chapter 15, these approaches have come close to answering some of the most perplexing riddles of human nature: its proclivity to psychotic breakdown and to addiction to chemical substances foreign to the body. The mystery of pleasure and pain has begun to yield to the new biochemical approaches with the discovery of natural *peptides* (tiny segments of protein molecules) that operate like morphine in the central nervous system.

Refined analysis of certain portions of the brain, such as the *cerebral cortex* and the *cerebellum,* has begun to clarify the nature of the intricate mechanisms — intermeshing the activities of thousands of simultaneously active neurons — that constitute the fundamental operations of the brain. Simultaneous electrographic recordings from many microelectrodes, both on the surface of the cortex and embedded deep within subcortical gray matter, have suggested a conception of the brain as a single giant megamolecule, a unified

Cerebral cortex. **The gray matter forming the surface tissues of the brain.**

Cerebellum. **A massive structure (little brain) below the occipital lobe and behind the brainstem, involved in motor functions.**

system that may underlie the curious unitary character of the conscious attention, which can flip virtually instantaneously from one preoccupation or concern to another. Astute psychological experiments, such as those conducted with "split-brain" patients (see Chapter 9), confirm the conception of the brain as an integrated system of systems, each subsystem operating autonomously to generate its specific contribution to the operation of the whole neural organism.

At the present moment the neurosciences have moved onto center stage among the classic sciences, and their fascinating discoveries have begun to capture the popular imagination. Thirty years ago the typical researcher in this field was an elderly university professor puttering alone in a small dusty laboratory. By contrast, today the neurosciences are pursued by teams of eager young scientists in well-equipped, brightly lit and spotless laboratories, employing methodologies bordering on the fantastic. Physiological psychology, meanwhile, has changed from an esoteric discipline concerned principally with animal behavior and endocrine functions into a broad foundation on which other psychological disciplines have come to rest. As anyone knows who has tried to keep up with the burgeoning journal literature in the field, reporting discoveries from laboratories in all the major countries of the world, the ancient mystery of the mind, now translated as the study of brain mechanisms, has become as exciting as any detective story. Indeed, that is just what it is, as you may discover in the following pages.

Chapter 2 / *A Short Course in Neuroanatomy*

The anatomy of the brain underlies and reveals its functions. Each major structure is importantly involved in its own special set of neural interaction systems, whose functions would be lost or impaired through damage or removal. The cerebral hemispheres, the most recently evolved portions of the brain, appear to be responsible for the more complex, less mechanical and reflexlike operations, such as thought, and for the subtler aspects of emotion and motivation. The older portions, such as the limbic structures, hypothalamus, and brainstem, still mediate functions we share with very primitive vertebrate forms. Within the cortex itself, there is a degree of localization of function that would not be suspected from the remarkable similarity of cortical tissues throughout. Nevertheless, each cortical region is characterized by its own unique set of input and output relations with subcortical nuclei, and thus participates in a special functional subsystem of the brain. These functional subsystems are themselves integrated into an overall ensemble by the many fiber bundles and tracts coursing between them.

No one has been reported to have seen his or her own brain, even in a mirror, though the opportunity frequently arises in brain surgery. What thoughts would occur if one observed one's own brain in the act of observing itself? We approach this experience when we look into our own eyes in the mirror, for the retina of the eye is in fact an extruded portion of the brain. But the organ with which we think, by means of which we are aware of ourselves and the world around us, is as unfamiliar to us as the other side of the moon. Only the neurosurgical team ever has the opportunity to see it. However, calf and sheep brains can often be obtained in a fresh state from a butcher, and these provide a good suggestion of what **18**

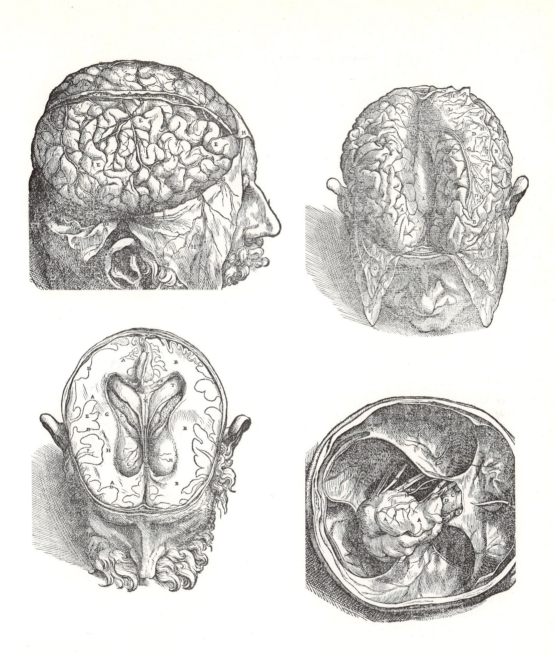

Figure 2.1 / *The Brain as Observed by Andreas Vesalius in 1543*. These drawings represent the first serious attempt to depict the human brain from direct observation, as it might be seen by a surgeon or by an anatomist dissecting it. Note the lateral ventricles in the two hemispheres in the cutaway drawing.

our own brains might look like if we were in some magical way able to get outside them a moment for a look and a touch (Figure 2.1).

But the brains the butcher supplies are in fact only half-brains: the two *hemispheres,* right and left, have been separated. Visible on their *medial* surfaces is the broad band of white tissue, the *corpus callosum* (hard body), whose millions of nerve fibers linked the *cortex* of one hemisphere with that of the other. Many of the fibers, seen in cross-section, are *myelinated,* and the glistening fatty myelin substance gives a whitish appearance to the mass. The rest of the

Medial. Toward the midline of the brain.

Myelinated. Provided with a myelin sheath.

Figure 2.2 / *The Human Brain as Seen from the Rear.* The brain consists of two cerebral hemispheres divided along their entire length by the longitudinal fissure. Each hemisphere might be likened to a boxing glove, with the temporal lobe jutting forward along the side representing the thumb.

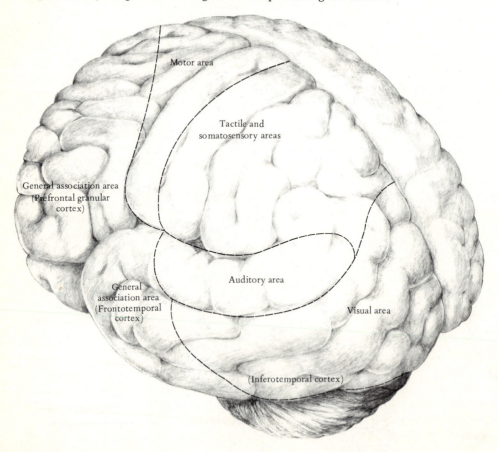

Motor area

Tactile and somatosensory areas

General association area (Prefrontal granular cortex)

General association area (Frontotemporal cortex)

Auditory area

Visual area

(Inferotemporal cortex)

tissue, largely composed of cell bodies and their unmyelinated extensions, appears pinkish-gray.

Figure 2.2 depicts a human brain, the most magnificent structure in the universe. This chapter will be devoted to becoming familiar with it — our own brain, which we will never have the opportunity to see. In lieu of direct observation, we will use pictures and diagrams to describe both its exterior and the parts we would find in its interior if we had the chance to get inside.

The Exterior View of the Brain

Inside its rugged bony case, the brain is the best protected of all our bodily organs. A spongy *arachnoid tissue* forms a protective cushion inside the skull, and the brain itself floats in a bath of circulating cerebrospinal fluid, like a fetus inside its amniotic sack. The surface of the hemispheres is covered with two protective membranes, the tough outer *dura mater* and the inner *pia mater* (tender mother, romantically translated), delicate, gossamer-thin, transparent, and intricately interlaced with tiny blood vessels that give the brain its pinkish appearance. When these membranes are stripped away, we expose the true "gray matter" of the *cerebral cortex,* the surface layer of the brain.

As Figure 2.3 shows, the cortex is deeply infolded, and the cortical gray matter follows the crevices clear to their bottom. The depth of these crevices, or *sulci* (singular *sulcus*) can be seen in Figure 2.4, which gives a cross-sectional view of one hemisphere. It is estimated that, spread out flat, the cortex would cover an area four by five feet (Hubel, 1963), much larger than one might suppose. The white matter visible immediately beneath the cortical gray is composed largely of myelinated nerve fibers carrying signals between the cortex and the gray matter in the interior of the brain. Two large masses of this gray matter can be seen in Figure 2.4, the *thalamus* in the center and the *basal ganglia* (putamen and caudate nucleus) more laterally placed. Between the thalami and the basal ganglia in each hemisphere runs a broad sheaf of fibers called the *internal capsule,* which is the major projection pathway to and from the cortex.

The overall shape of the brain, as Figure 2.2 shows, is something like a boxing glove, the thumb represented by the *temporal lobe,* which juts forward along the side of the head from the *occipital lobe* at the rear. The massiveness of the temporal lobe is apparent in Figure 2.5, a view of the brain from the underside. Note that the tem-

Sulcus. A fissure between two convolutions of the surface of the cortex.

Thalamus. A group of subcortical nuclei intimately associated with the neocortex.

Temporal lobe. The ventrolateral portion of the mass of the hemispheres.

Occipital lobe (ok-SIP-i-tal). The rear portion of the brain, behind the parietal-occipital sulcus.

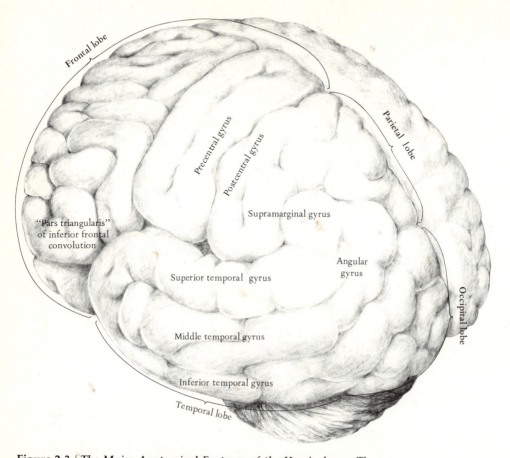

Figure 2.3 / *The Major Anatomical Features of the Hemispheres.* The pre- and postcentral gyri are separated by the central fissure, which also separates the frontal lobe from the parietal lobe. The supramarginal and angular gyri are significant regions within the parietal lobe, having to do with verbal conceptual functions in the left hemisphere, and with imaginal and spatial visualization functions in the right hemisphere. The "pars triangularis" region of the frontal lobe, in the left hemisphere, controls articulation of speech.

poral lobe extends well in toward the center of the brain. From the functional standpoint, the temporal lobe is one of the most interesting parts of the brain, containing some highly specialized areas. Epileptic seizures result more frequently from damage to this portion of the brain than any other. It is also noteworthy that the temporal lobe is found only in the primates, and becomes increasingly prominent and massive as one progresses through the prosimians and monkeys to the great apes, and finally to human beings. (The

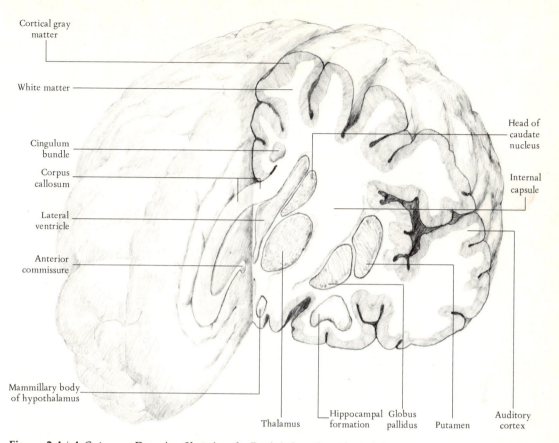

Cortical gray matter
White matter
Cingulum bundle
Corpus callosum
Lateral ventricle
Anterior commissure
Mammillary body of hypothalamus
Head of caudate nucleus
Internal capsule
Thalamus
Hippocampal formation
Globus pallidus
Putamen
Auditory cortex

Figure 2.4 / *A Cutaway Drawing Showing the Brain's Interior.* The left frontal quadrant of the brain has been removed to show the major interior
structures of the left hemisphere. The gray matter of the cortex (shaded) is
only a few millimeters thick in some places. Beneath it is the white matter,
consisting of nerve fibers passing between the cortex and lower structures
and to the opposite hemisphere. Near the center of the brain is the
thalamus, through which the cortex receives all its information. The caudate nucleus, the putamen, and the globus pallidus together comprise the
basal ganglia, important in motor functions. Note the depth of the temporal
lobe and the location of the hippocampus in its most medial portion. *within temporal*

calf, sheep, and pig brains obtainable from the butcher have no
temporal lobe at all.)

The other lobes of the brain are less clearly demarcated. The rear
sector is the occipital lobe. (The slight bony protuberance at the rear
of the skull in human males is called the occiput.) As Figure 2.6
shows, a deep fissure on the medial surface, the *parieto-occipital sulcus,* marks the forward extent of the occipital lobe. Another deep

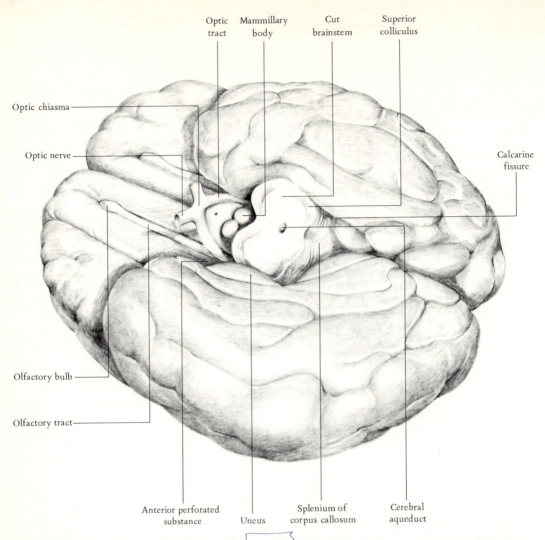

Optic tract Mammillary body Cut brainstem Superior colliculus

Optic chiasma

Optic nerve

Calcarine fissure

Olfactory bulb

Olfactory tract

Anterior perforated substance Uncus Splenium of corpus callosum Cerebral aqueduct

Figure 2.5 / *The Brain Seen from Below.* The temporal lobes in the human brain are massive, extending in to the borders of the brainstem, which is shown transected at the level of the midbrain. Note the olfactory bulbs and the optic chiasma, where a partial crossover of fibers from the eyes takes place before the visual pathway plunges into the brain itself.

Frontal lobe. **That portion of the brain anterior to the central fissure (fissure of Rolando).**

Parietal lobe **(***pa-RYE-i-tal***). The cortical lobe immediately behind the central fissure, between the frontal lobe and the occipital lobe.**

fissure on the exterior surface of the hemispheres, less easily seen, runs diagonally down and forward from behind the *vertex*, or top center of the brain, ending just above the *lateral fissure* that separates the temporal lobe from the rest of the brain. This slantwise fissure passing over the lateral convexity of the brain marks the border between the *frontal lobe* and the *parietal lobe,* and is called the *central fissure* (or fissure of Rolando, for its discoverer; the lateral fissure demarcating the temporal lobe is also called the fissure of Sylvius, for the same reason).

Figure 2.7 should make this all clear. Also note in Figure 2.7 the locations of the *projection areas* for our three major senses — sight, hearing, and touch — and the three *sensory association areas* adjoining them. The projection areas are the major receiving terminals in

sensory

Projection areas. Entry stations in the cortex for visual, auditory, or tactile-somatosensory input.

Sensory association areas. Those cortical areas adjoining the sensory projection areas into which the latter project.

Figure 2.6 / *The Medial Surface of the Brain.* This view is called a sagittal section. The broad white fiber bundle of the corpus callosum, which interconnects the two hemispheres, has been severed, as well as the hypothalamus, the brainstem, and the cerebellum. Above the corpus callosum, and forward and to the rear of it, we see the medial surface of the hemisphere, with the cerebral cortex descending all the way to the corpus callosum in the middle region of the brain. Below we can see the medial surface of a portion of the temporal lobe. Note the position of the cerebellum and the brainstem in relation to the cerebral hemispheres.

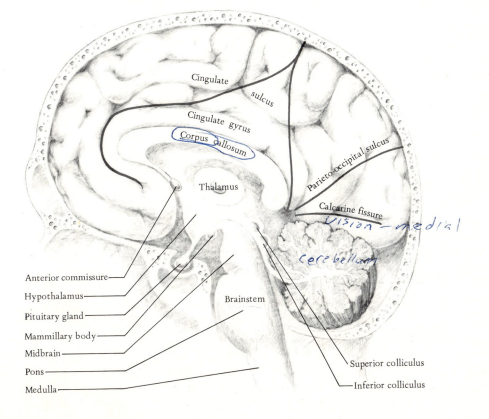

frontal-motor

the cortex for the three types of sensory signals, that for vision lying predominantly on the medial surface of the brain along the *calcarine fissure*, shown in Figure 2.7. The entire cortex lying to the rear of the central fissure (parietal, occipital, and temporal lobes) is devoted to these three perceptual functions, roughly one lobe to each.

The frontal lobe, meanwhile, appears to be more concerned with response processes and goal-oriented activities. The *primary motor cortex*, discovered by Roberts Bartholow, lies just forward of the central fissure, and a massive, recently evolved *prefrontal granular cortex*

Calcarine fissure (KAL-ka-reen). A deep fissure on the medial surface of the hemispheres.

Figure 2.7 / *Major Functional Areas of the Cerebral Cortex.* This overview of the functionally distinct regions of the brain replaces the older maps of the phrenologists. Cortical localization of functions can be demonstrated through stimulation studies in animals and studies of the effect of local brain lesions in human beings. However, localization is not as detailed as earlier speculations would have us believe.

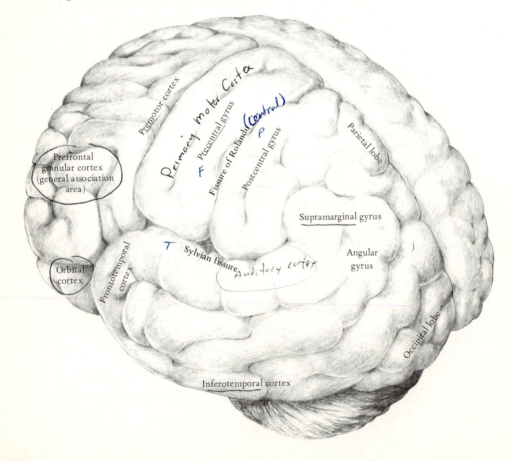

cortex, whose function will come in for considerable discussion, occupies the space behind our bulging foreheads.

A Closer Examination of the Cortex

Over the past two decades it has become increasingly evident that
cortical tissue, long since recognized to be a layered structure, is

Figure 2.8 / *Brodmann's Map of the Cortical Areas, Distinguishable by Their
Microstructure as Seen under the Light Microscope.* Though this map was
drawn many years ago, these numbered regions of the cortex are still used
by neuroscientists in discussing brain function. The occipital lobe (areas
17, 18, and 19 in both maps) is entirely devoted to visual functions, with
visual signals arriving principally along the deep calcarine fissure in area 17
on the lower map. The upper portion of the temporal lobe (areas 41, 42, and
22) comprises the auditory cortex, while areas 3, 1, 2, 5, and 7 comprise the
areas registering sensations from the body surfaces. The motor cortex (areas
4 and 6) is just anterior to this region, in the frontal lobe.

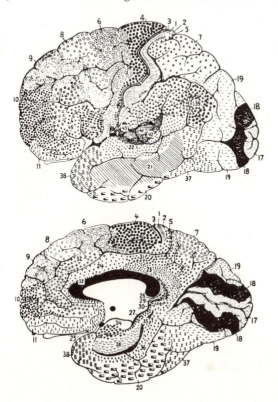

also a mosaic of many hundreds of thousands of tiny columns of neurons oriented vertically to its surface. Each column constitutes a distinct module organized to perform a function different from that of its neighbors. Each such cortical column extends from the cortical surface to the white matter below, and consists of hundreds of thousands of neurons in intimate communication with one another. Though there is only minor interaction with neurons in adjacent columns, each column is interconnected in vastly complex networks with more distant columns (Mountcastle, 1978). On the basis of observational studies of the cortex, the histologist Korbinian Brodmann in 1914 drew his now-classic charts of the visually distinguishable areas of the human cortex (Figure 2.8). His numbered chart is still used as a convenient means of designating cortical regions.

Figure 2.9 illustrates what is known about the input-output relations of the various *cortical layers,* which are specialized regions within the individual column, the module composing the cortical functional organization. Two cortical columns are shown. The one on the right shows no cell bodies, but the origins and destinations of incoming (*afferent*) fibers are indicated. In the left-hand column, three large cortical neurons are represented. The cell soma is somewhat pyramidal in shape. A stout, trunklike dendrite arising from its upper tip or apex runs all the way to the upper layer of the cortex, projecting laterally ascending branches as it goes. The soma of each pyramidal cell also has a brush of laterally extending dendrites, called *basal dendrites.* The pyramidal cells are the principal transmission neurons (sometimes called *projection neurons*), whose axons leave the cortex to enter the white matter below and pass to other regions of the cortex or to subcortical centers. Also shown in the right-hand column are the arrival stations of afferent fibers from various locations.

It will be noted in the left-hand column of Figure 2.9 that specific sensory afferent fibers arriving from their sensory relay nuclei in the thalamus below are received principally in layer IV and the lower part of layer III, where they make synaptic contact principally with a relatively large *interneuron* called a *spiny stellate cell,* which in turn makes "powerful cascading synapses upon the spines of the apical dendrites of pyramidal cells" (Mountcastle, 1978, p. 31). The same pattern is found in the visual, tactile, and auditory projection areas, where sensory signals are first received in the cortex. Note that this is also the level of the cortex where incoming fibers from other cortical regions terminate most densely, as the right-hand column shows. (*Commissural fibers* are those that cross over from the

Cortical layers. Distinguishably different layers in the cortex based on different cell-type composition.

Afferent (*AFF-uh-rent*). Said of neural signals incoming to a given neuron or neural region.

Projection neurons. Neurons transmitting over long distances.

Interneurons. Small neurons whose axons terminate in the vicinity of the cell body.

Spiny stellate cell. A type of neuron in the sensory projection areas of the cortex thought to receive incoming sensory signals for transmission to the local pyramidal cells.

Commissural (*ka-MIZH-ur-al*). Referring to fibers passing between the two hemispheres.

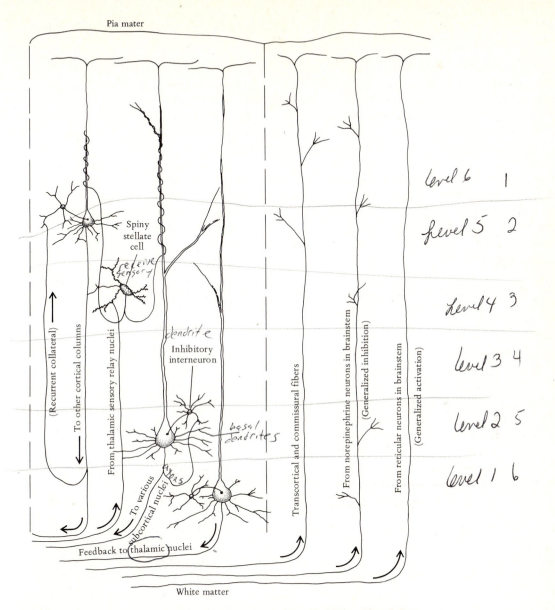

Pia mater

Spiny stellate cell

relay sensory

(Recurrent collateral)

To other cortical columns

From thalamic sensory relay nuclei

dendrite

Inhibitory interneuron

basal dendrites

To various subcortical nuclei

axons

Feedback to thalamic nuclei

Transcortical and commissural fibers

From norepinephrine neurons in brainstem

(Generalized inhibition)

From reticular neurons in brainstem

(Generalized activation)

level 6   1
level 5   2
Level 4   3
level 3   4
level 2   5
level 1   6

White matter

Figure 2.9 / *Major Input-Output Relations of the Cortical Pyramidal Cells.*
This diagram shows two cortical columns extending from the surface of the
brain to the white matter below. Three typical pyramidal cells are shown in
cortical layers III, V, and VI, with a spiny stellate cell receiving sensory
input in layer IV. A small interneuron is shown in layer V serving as an
inhibitory control for its associated pyramidal cell in a feedback circuit.
Output from the cortical columns is principally via axons of the pyramidal
cells, while many types of smaller neurons are involved in processing of
neural signals within the cortical columns.

other hemisphere. *Transcortical* nerve fibers come from other portions of the same hemisphere.) Other fibers arriving from lower brain regions may terminate in all layers, but especially in layer I (see Jones, Burton, and Porter, 1975; Hubel and Wiesel, 1972).

Pyramidal cells projecting back to the thalamus are found in layer VI (Jones and Wise, 1977; Lund *et al.*, 1975), as shown. Those projecting to other cortical regions are located in layer III (Jones and Wise, 1977; Glickstein and Whitteridge, 1976). The largest pyramidal cells, which tend to be found in layer V, project to the basal ganglia, the brainstem, and the spinal cord (Jones *et al.*, 1977; Jones and Wise, 1977; Humphrey and Rietz, 1976). (The thalamus and basal ganglia are shown in Figure 2.4.)

From this brief description it should be evident that the cerebral cortex is organized in a highly specific fashion with respect to its 6 layers. All incoming transmission fibers except those from the norepinephrine nuclei in the brainstem are thought to be excitatory, as are all pyramidal cell axons. Many of the smaller interneurons within the cortical columns (not shown), meanwhile, are inhibitory. Each pyramidal cell may be seen as having two distinct receiving stations — the apical dendrite with its various branches, and the brush of basal dendrites extending laterally and downward from its soma — in addition to its soma surface. Just what the functional differences are between the apical and the basal dendritic domains is still unknown, and the subject of much speculation.

It is characteristic of the pyramidal cells that the axon, before reaching the white matter below the cortex, sends out a collateral fiber (branch) that returns upward to the region of the cell soma, where it synapses with a small inhibitory neuron. This inhibitory neuron in turn projects its axon to the pyramidal cell's soma, forming an inhibitory feedback loop as shown in the left-hand column of Figure 2.9. These recurrent collaterals tend to branch widely into numerous *telodendria* (terminal tips), which make contact with numerous other cells within the cortical column, many of them probably inhibitory. In this manner, it is thought, the pyramidal cell's firing results not only in its own inhibitory control through a negative feedback loop, but also in inhibition of neighboring cortical column activities, a principle called *lateral inhibition*.

This organizational structure appears to be uniform throughout the cerebral cortex. What distinguishes one cortical region from another, then, is not the manner in which it processes information but the information it receives to process and where it sends its results — or in other words, its input-output relations with other brain regions. Each sector of the cortex is closely associated with a particular thalamic nucleus, with which it constitutes a distinct sub-

Transcortical. **Projecting from one local cortical region to another without thalamic relay.**

Lateral inhibition. **Inhibition of surrounding neurons by neural activity in certain sensory receptor fields or cortical stations.**

system within the great thalamocortical system that is the specialization of mammalian brains. We might compare each region of the
cortex to a minicomputer at the service of a thalamic nucleus, with
which it is in private two-way communication at all times. To understand the functional divisions of the cortex, then, we need only
examine the thalamus and its various nuclei and ask what their
special functions are.

The Thalamus

The two thalami are compact clumps of gray matter at the center of
the brain, separated by the vertically oriented third ventricle (refer
to Figure 2.4). They are joined in many, but not all, human brains
by a physical connection called the *massa intermedia*. Figure 2.10 is a
schematic illustrating what the two might look like, viewed from
the left and above, if they were to be dissected out of the brain.
Most of the major nuclei would be visible from this viewpoint. Figure 2.11 shows the left thalamus inside a transparent hemisphere.
Interconnecting channels to their several associated cortical areas
project from each of the major nuclei.

    Note that there are three specific sensory nuclei, the *ventral poste-
rior* and the two *geniculate* (bent) *bodies*, which may be thought of as
relaying to the cortex sensory signals concerned with touch, vision,
and hearing respectively. It should also be noted that both the ventrolateral and the ventral anterior nuclei are associated with the
motor cortex, and may be called *motor nuclei*. The dorsomedial is
another large nucleus in the medial sector of the thalamic mass
whose specific connections are with the huge prefrontal granular
cortex that forms the frontal pole of the brain, as well as with the orbital cortex beneath it. The lateral posterior nucleus and the pulvinar are associated with those regions of the parietal, occipital, and
temporal lobes lying between the regions specifically dealing with
sensory signals.

    The anterior nucleus, at the anterior pole of the thalamus, is func-
tionally distinct from the rest. It will be treated here as belonging to
the limbic system of the brain, rather than to the more recently
evolved thalamocortical system. It projects to the posterior portion
of the *cingulate gyrus* (Brodmann's areas 23 and 29, as shown in Figure 2.8). As Figure 2.10 shows, a band of neural tissues and fibers
runs through the thalamus, separating the dorsomedial nucleus
from the rest. This band, the *internal medullary lamina*, properly
belongs to still another system in the brain, the *reticular system*, associated with the brainstem. Its clumps of gray matter, called the

Geniculate bodies
(*je-NIK-yu-lat*). **The
lateral and medial
geniculate nuclei of
the thalamus, relay-
ing visual and au-
ditory signals re-
spectively.**

Cingulate gyrus
(*SING-gu-lat
JYE-rus*). **That por-
tion of the medial
surface of the
hemispheres that
lies immediately
above the corpus
callosum.**

Reticular system
(*re-TIK-yu-lar*). **An
ancient neural sys-
tem serving to con-
trol arousal, atten-
tion focus, and
states of conscious-
ness, as well as the
various stages of
sleep.**

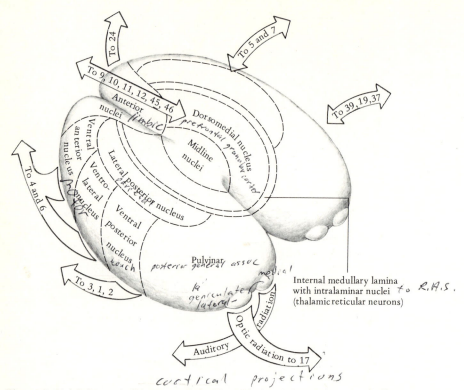

Figure 2.10 / *Schematic Diagram of the Two Thalami.* Here the two thalami are shown connected across the narrow third ventricle (midline nuclei). The motor nuclei (*ventral anterior* and *ventrolateral*) are shown projecting to the motor cortex (areas 4 and 6 of Brodmann), while the *ventral posterior nucleus,* relaying sensory information from the body, is shown projecting to areas 3, 1, and 2, just across the fissure of Rolando from the motor cortex. The optic radiation projects from the lateral geniculate nucleus, and the auditory radiation from the medial geniculate nucleus. The rest of the nuclei shown are association nuclei, neither specifically motor nor specifically sensory in function. The massive *dorsomedial nucleus* is shown projecting to and receiving input from the prefrontal granular cortex beneath the forehead. The equally massive *pulvinar* is shown in intercommunication with the posterior general association cortex. The *lateral nucleus* (frequently divided into *dorsal lateral* and *lateral posterior*) is in intercommunication with the parietal lobe cortex in areas 5 and 7. Thus, each of these thalamic nuclei has its own private area of cortex, and no information arrives in the cortex except via relay through one of these nuclei.

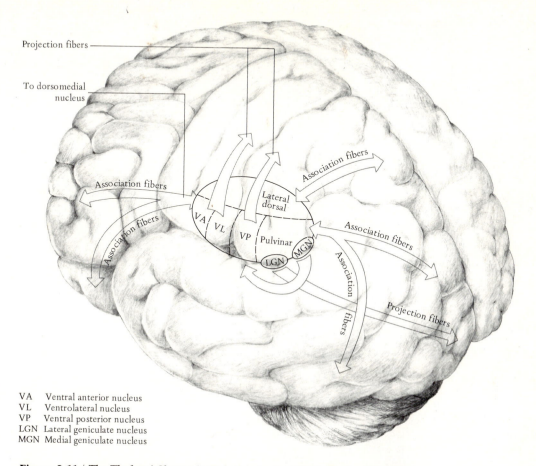

Projection fibers

To dorsomedial nucleus

Association fibers

Association fibers

Association fibers

Association fibers

Lateral dorsal

VA VL VP Pulvinar

LGN MGN

Association fibers

Projection fibers

VA　Ventral anterior nucleus
VL　Ventrolateral nucleus
VP　Ventral posterior nucleus
LGN　Lateral geniculate nucleus
MGN　Medial geniculate nucleus

Figure 2.11 / *The Thalami Shown in Relation to the Whole Brain.* This figure shows the location and approximate size of the thalamic nuclei in relation to the cortex. Situated in the center of the brain, they project to all regions of the cortex and in turn receive input from most. The cortex and thalamus are considered together as a single functional thalamocortical system.

intralaminar nuclei, are closely associated with other reticular-system nuclei bordering the third ventricle in the midline, and called the midline nuclei. Another, deep in the interior of the thalamus, is called the centromedian nucleus. Forming a thin sheet of tissue around the lateral surface of the two thalami is the thalamic *reticular nucleus.* All of these belong to the reticular system of the brain and project their fibers diffusely throughout the cortex. They are concerned with such functions as control of sleep, waking, arousal, and focal attention shift.

This analysis of the major thalamic nuclei suggests that the thalamocortical system consists of three subsystems governing vision, hearing, and touch respectively; a fourth subsystem devoted to organizing motor activities; and two broad expanses of association cortex (one at the front of the brain and the other at the rear, between the three perceptual areas), which, along with their related association nuclei, serve integrative functions.

The Basal Ganglia

The second mass of subcortical gray matter is the basal ganglia, which lie somewhat forward and lateral to the thalami and project

Figure 2.12 / *The Basal Ganglia as Seen from the Rear.* In this schematic diagram the brain has been stripped away, and the two thalami between them have been removed, to show the relative positions of the basal ganglia. The largest nucleus is the putamen. The caudate nucleus has a massive head toward the front and a dwindling tail behind. The tail follows the lateral ventricles into the temporal lobe to the region of the amygdala. The globus pallidus is medially placed and projects medially into the thalamic motor nuclei, forming the common outlet for all three structures. The basal ganglia lie more laterally and more forward in the brain than the thalami.

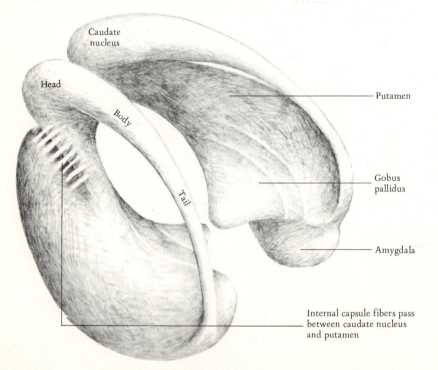

into the thalamic motor nuclei. The most anterior portion is the head of the *caudate* (from the Latin *caudatus*, "having a tail") *nucleus*. It is separated from the more massive *putamen* only by white strands of fibers of the *internal capsule* (see Figure 2.4) that carry signals from the cortex to lower structures and vice versa. These white fibers give the total mass of the two nuclei a striped appearance, and they are often spoken of collectively as the *corpus striatum*.

The third of the basal ganglia is the *globus pallidus* (pale globe), medial to the putamen, which is the sole output station for the entire system. The caudate nucleus fires into putamen and globus; the putamen fires only into the globus, and the globus pallidus projects via two stout bundles to the thalamic motor nuclei and downward into the brainstem. Figure 2.12 depicts these relationships.

The basal ganglia receive their input principally from the motor cortex and from anterior regions, the septal area and the prefrontal granular cortex. Anatomically, they are separated from the thalamus by the internal capsule fibers, through which they receive much of their input. Their functions will be discussed when we consider voluntary behavior.

Other Subcortical Nuclear Groups

In addition to the massive thalamus and basal ganglia that form the central mass of the brain, there are three much smaller clumps of subcortical gray matter that serve as special information-processing centers in the brain. One is the *hypothalamus,* which is situated immediately below the two thalami and joins them in the midline below the third ventricle (see Figure 2.4). Phylogenetically, the hypothalamus is a very much older brain structure than the thalamocortical system. Though relatively tiny, it governs some enormously important biological functions. Further forward, immediately above and forward of the *anterior commissure* (see Figure 2.6), also in the midline of the brain, lie the *septal nuclei*. The third clump — out in the temporal lobe, buried under its medial surface in a protrusion called the uncus — is the *amygdala* (Greek for almond), or, more precisely, the amygdaloid nuclear complex (since a number of distinct nuclei are clumped together here).

Another distinct structure that ought to be mentioned is not a nucleus at all. The *hippocampus* is a curiously infolded cortical structure of very ancient lineage, named for its seahorse shape in cross section (see Figure 2.13). The thin dark line in this picture is composed of the densely packed tiny *granule cells* of the *dentate*

Hypothalamus. The brain region immediately below the thalamus, responsible for numerous basic life-support systems such as hunger, thirst, and temperature control.

Septal nuclei. The two major nuclei of the septal region (medial and lateral).

Amygdala (a-MIG-da-la). A cluster of nuclei located beneath the medial surface of the temporal lobe in the region of the uncus.

Hippocampus. Principal portion of the hippocampal formation, a major structure of the limbic system.

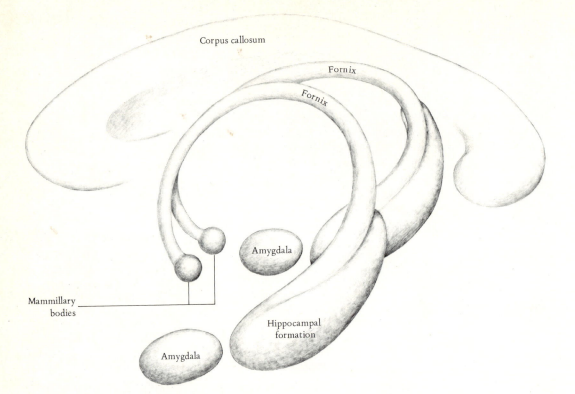

Figure 2.13 / *The Hippocampal Formation, Shown in Relation to the Corpus Callosum, the Mammillary Bodies of the Hypothalamus, and the Two Amygdalae.* The hippocampal formation projects principally via the fornix to the mammillary bodies at the base of the hypothalamus. It has no known connection with the amygdala, although the two are in close physical relation in the medial temporal lobe. Together these two structures — the hippocampus, an ancient cortical region, and the amygdala, an ancient nuclear group — are an important component of the limbic system, which is concerned with such basic functions as mood states, emotional response to experience, and memory.

(toothed) *gyrus,* while the region of larger pyramidal cells at its two ends, enclosing it, is the hippocampus proper. The *hippocampal formation,* as the two are called jointly, projects principally to the hypothalamus via a stout fiber bundle called the *fornix* (Figure 2.13). This structure, together with the septal nuclei, the amygdaloid complex, the broad band of the cingulate gyrus immediately above the corpus callosum, and the cortex lining the basal and medial surfaces of the temporal lobe, constitutes an older system of the brain

Dentate gyrus. **That portion of the hippocampal formation characterized by very numerous, closely packed granule cells, partially surrounded by the hippocampus proper.**

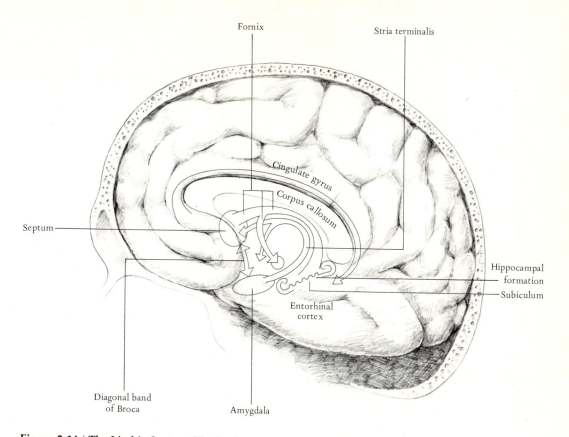

Figure 2.14 / *The Limbic System.* The limbic system consists of three ancient cortical regions (cingulate gyrus, entorhinal cortex, and hippocampus), two major subcortical nuclear groups (amygdala and septum), and the fiber bundles interconnecting them and projecting into the hypothalamus. Shown here is the stria terminalis bundle, which projects from the amygdala and parallels the course of the fornix into the septal region and anterior hypothalamic area.

known as the *limbic system,* now buried under the more recently evolved thalamocortical system (Figure 2.14).

The Brainstem Nuclei

To the rear of the hypothalamus lies the *midbrain,* the enormously important uppermost portion of the brainstem, which serves as the functional interface between the more recently evolved structures of

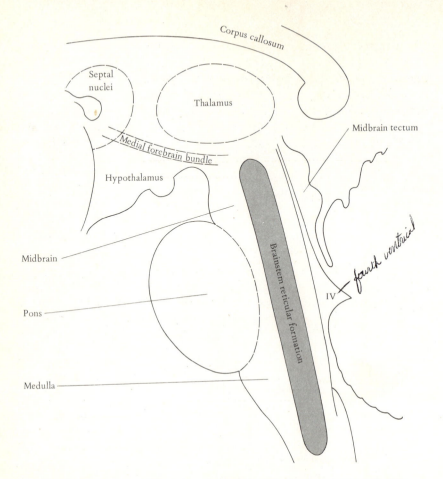

Corpus callosum

Septal nuclei

Thalamus

Midbrain tectum

Medial forebrain bundle

Hypothalamus

Midbrain

Brainstem reticular formation

IV fourth ventricle

Pons

Medulla

Figure 2.15 / *Major Structures of the Brainstem.* The brainstem extends from the midbrain, at the level of the hypothalamus, to the beginning of the spinal cord. Embedded within its neural tissues are numerous distinct nuclei governing various reflex responses, while the reticular formation forms its core. This is perhaps the most ancient neural structure in the brain, appearing to serve as an integrative center monitoring both incoming and outgoing messages to and from the body. The midbrain is shown at the level of the colliculi (forming the tectum), while the bulbous structure of the pons is shown at the level of the fourth ventricle, where the cerebellum is connected to the rest of the brain. The medulla is essentially an enlarged portion of the spinal cord, swollen by the presence of many important nuclei governing vegetative responses. The cord itself contains no such nuclear structures.

the forebrain and the ancient structures of the brainstem below (Figure 2.15). Within its core lie the upper reaches of the brainstem reticular formation, perhaps the most primitive neural tissue in the brain. Known in this region as the *midbrain limbic area*, it is in close communication with the hypothalamus and septum via the *medial forebrain bundle*. In the roof of the midbrain (tectum) are four hemispherical protuberances called colliculi (little hills). The upper two, or superior colliculi, are concerned with visual functions; the lower two, or inferior colliculi, are concerned with auditory functions. The corresponding structure for tactile sensation lies at the base of the brainstem where it joins with the spinal cord, in two structures called the *cuneate nuclei* and the *gracile nuclei*.

Immediately below the midbrain is a bulbous enlargement of the brainstem on the forward or ventral side. This region of the brainstem is called the *pons* (bridge). To the rear or dorsal side is the small fourth ventricle, which is in communication with the central canal running through the spinal cord. To its rear, forming its roof, is the junction with the *cerebellum* (little brain) buried beneath the occipital lobe, which will be discussed at length in conjunction with voluntary and involuntary behavior in Chapter 8.

The pons is below and continuous with the *medulla*, essentially a swollen upper extension of the spinal cord containing numerous nuclei and, in its core, the reticular formation. The medulla is involved in such basic survival functions as breathing, circulation, and digestion. It will be discussed more fully in Chapter 12. The medulla and the spinal cord might be thought of as the brain's interface with the peripheral nervous system, which extends throughout the body and consists of motor and sensory fibers and the autonomic nervous system, also discussed in Chapter 12.

This brief survey of the brain's anatomy will be elaborated on in later chapters that address its specific functions.

Midbrain limbic area. A region in the midbrain with important connections with the medial forebrain bundle and the limbic system.

Pons. The middle of the three structures of the brainstem, between the midbrain above and the medulla below.

Medulla. The lowest of the three structures composing the brainstem, immediately above the spinal cord.

Summary

Anatomically, the brain consists of an enormous aggregate of neurons organized into two distinct types of tissue, cortex and subcortical nuclei. The cerebral cortex may be thought of as a vast mosaic of tiny cortical columns (roughly half a millimeter in diameter at the brain's surface) extending from the pia mater above to the white matter below. Each cortical column appears to process particular informational input relatively independent of its immediate neighbors, but in close association through transcortical fibers with more distant cortical columns, with which it forms an extended neural network.

The concept of localization of functions signifies that certain regions of the cortical sheet, as well as the subcortical nuclei with which they are in communication, appear to be devoted exclusively or primarily to a particular function, such as visual perception, or the initiation and organization of particular patterns of muscular movement. More locally, however, there appears to be great overlap of function in many regions of the cortex, making a concept of strict localization unjustifiable. In the restricted sense, then, we may speak of the occipital lobe as concerned principally with visual perception, of the parietal lobe as concerned with touch and related functions, of the upper portions of the temporal lobe cortex as concerned with hearing, and of the entire frontal lobe, forward of the central fissure as concerned with behavioral processes and goal orientation.

Examining the cortex in detail, we found that it has a laminar structure. Each layer is composed of a particular assortment of neuron types and has a characteristic packing density. These cortical layers were recently found to have characteristic input-output relations with other brain regions. Specifically, transcortical and commissural fibers arise from and project to the upper three layers of the cortex; the fourth layer is in many regions the point of entry for projections from the thalamus — specifically, those from the sensory relay and motor nuclei. Layer V was found to contain many huge pyramidal cells projecting into subcortical nuclei, the brainstem, and spinal cord. Neurons in layer VI project principally back to the thalamus, in part to the same nuclei from which they receive afferent projections, thus forming a direct feedback loop. This simplified model of the very complex cortical circuitry will be elaborated on in later chapters. The thalamus was described as a group of eight major nuclei projecting to the cortex and constituting with it a relatively independent subsystem within the brain, the thalamo-cortical system. These relationships can be succinctly summarized:

Lateral geniculate nucleus and occipital cortex (visual)
Medial geniculate nucleus and temporal cortex (auditory)
Ventral posterior nucleus and parietal cortex (touch)
Ventral anterior and ventrolateral nuclei and the motor cortex (motoric functions)
Dorsomedial nucleus and prefrontal granular and orbital cortices (associational functions)
Lateral posterior nucleus and pulvinar and the posterior association cortex (integrated perceptual functions)

The intralaminar, midline, and reticular nuclei and the centrum medianum are thought to represent an upward extension of the brainstem reticular formation. The anterior nucleus at the forward pole of the thalamus appears to be a part of the limbic system.

The basal ganglia are additional masses of subcortical nuclear tissue lying lateral and forward of the thalamus across the internal capsule. The basal ganglia consist of the caudate nucleus and putamen (which together comprise the corpus striatum) and the globus pallidus, which is the final common output station for the three. It projects to the thalamic motor nuclei and, via another fiber bundle, down to motor nuclei of the brainstem. The basal ganglia receive input from all regions of the cortex, but particularly from the motor cortex, with which they are closely associated in motor behavior.

Among other subcortical nuclei are the hypothalamus, situated immediately below the thalamus in the midline; the septal nuclei, also in the midline but farther forward; and the amygdala in the medial temporal lobe. The hippocampus is a very unusual type of cortical tissue situated in the temporal lobe immediately behind the amygdala. It consists essentially of two different types of cortex, closely apposed: the dentate gyrus, dominated by a layer of densely packed tiny granule cells, and the hippocampus proper, dominated by pyramidal cells and partially encircling the dentate gyrus.

The brainstem proper consists of midbrain, pons, and medulla, in descending order. The cerebellum is attached at the rear opposite the pons, at the level of the fourth ventricle. At the midbrain level is the tectum with its four colliculi and the midbrain limbic area, the latter in close communication with the hypothalamus via the medial forebrain bundle. The superior colliculi are visual structures; the inferior are auditory in function. The reticular formation runs through the core of the brainstem from the midbrain down. The medulla, in turn, contains numerous vitally important nuclei governing essential survival mechanisms. The brainstem as a whole was described as the interface between the brain and the peripheral nervous system, which consists of sensory and motor nerves and the autonomic nervous system.

Little mention has been made of the fiber bundles and tracts through which the various structures within the brain communicate with one another. They will be discussed in conjunction with the functions of these structures in subsequent chapters. We have seen, however, that each region of the cortical mantle is intimately associated through interconnecting fibers with a particular thalamic nucleus, as well as with other cortical regions in its own and the opposite hemisphere. The basal ganglia project through a fiber tract into the motor nuclei of the thalamus, as well as to motor nuclei in the brainstem via a second fiber bundle. The medial forebrain bundle runs longitudinally through the center of the brain between the septal nuclei and the midbrain limbic area, passing through the hypothalamus. All areas of the cortical mantle project into the basal ganglia, though the specific pathways are not fully known. In sum, it can be seen that the brain as a whole maintains a continuous running intercommunication with itself through both discrete and diffuse fiber bundles, which constitute an important part of its anatomy.

Chapter 3 / *The Microscopic View of the Brain*

The basic mechanism of brain function consists of waves of electrical potential shift traveling over the surfaces of nerve cell membranes. Two types can be distinguished. One is a slowly propagating *electrotonic* wave of membrane hyperpolarization or subthreshold depolarization, which diminishes in both amplitude and speed as it travels. The other is a swiftly propagating wave of total depolarization traveling along a specialized structure, the axon filament or nerve fiber; this is the *nerve impulse.* Upon reaching the axon terminus, this impulse initiates the release of a chemical neurotransmitter capable of influencing the rate of impulse production of the second neuron. Inhibitory neurotransmitters tend to slow that rate; excitatory neurotransmitters tend to increase it. Each neuron characteristically receives such influences from many other neurons simultaneously, and in turn exerts its influence on other neurons, frequently many simultaneously through its various axonal branches. Characteristically, local and large-scale feedback and re-entrant circuits between neurons and neural groups are formed in this way. Neural interaction also occurs through electrotonic activity in neural membranes in close apposition, providing an additional means of integrating neural activities.

The focus of this chapter will be the nerve cell, or *neuron.* It has been estimated that there are about 50 billion neurons in the cerebral cortex alone (Mountcastle, 1978). A large percentage of the mass of the brain tissues is composed of the cell bodies of neurons and their fiber extensions, the rest consisting principally of tiny supporting *glial cells* (from the Latin word *gluten,* for *glue*) and blood vessels.

Glial cells. Non-neural cells, greatly outnumbering the neurons, whose functioning they serve.

One of the striking characteristics of neurons is that they all possess fiber extensions of their cell bodies, sometimes extremely long. This fact suggests that it is in their nature to function in great interconnected ensembles, rather than individually. Indeed, they might be called the most sociable cells in the body. Another unique feature of neurons (in mammals) is that, once formed, they never undergo cell division to replace those that die off, unlike the cells of muscle, skin, and many other bodily organs. Most of the cells in our bodies have been repeatedly replaced over the years, but our neurons remain with us to the end. That means that those still there in our heads at age eighty are the very same neurons that were there at our birth, still functioning much as they did eighty years earlier.

Perhaps the point of this remarkable cellular longevity is that it makes possible the preservation of previous learning. Otherwise we might perhaps be perpetually living in the present, unable to recall our experiences of the past or to take advantage of the wisdom they have brought about, and our life would have no meaning or consistent direction. The evidence now suggests that the neurons do learn from experience and retain that learning (see Chapter 16). Perhaps it is only because of neural longevity that our personalities retain their integrity over the years, and that we need not continually relearn those things we must know in order to survive.

The Neuron as a Living Cell

All living cells pursue very similar life processes in their interiors, illustrated in Figure 3.1. The semiliquid material within the cell body (the *cytoplasm*) is enclosed by a two-layer membrane (the *plasma membrane*) and interlaced with a network of membrane-bound channels that function as conduits, collectively called the *endoplasmic reticulum* (internal network). Part of this system — the *rough endoplasmic reticulum* — is lined with *ribosomes,* which are tiny protein-manufacturing stations. Their products and others are packaged in small membrane-bound vesicles in a central depot, the *Golgi apparatus,* composed of a specialized *smooth endoplasmic reticulum.* Also present are numerous tiny *organelles* called *mitochondria,* which are responsible for generating the energy necessary to cellular metabolism.

The neurons differ from all other animal cells in that they have only indirect contact with the circulatory system. They are surrounded by (one might almost say coated with) processes of the glial cells, which form a fail-safe life-support system for them. We might envision the glia as serving the neurons in much the same

Ribosomes (RYE-bo-soamz). Manufacturing stations within the cytoplasm where translation of the genetic code into proteins takes place.

Golgi apparatus. A portion of the endoplasmic reticulum devoted to the packaging of cellular products in membrane-bound vesicles.

Mitochondria. Organelles within the cytoplasm responsible for producing useful chemical energy for its metabolic processes.

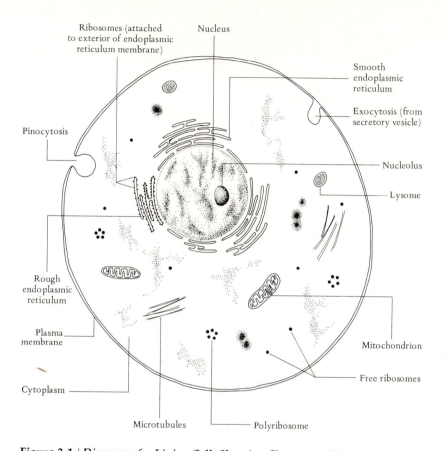

Ribosomes (attached to exterior of endoplasmic reticulum membrane)

Nucleus

Smooth endoplasmic reticulum

Exocytosis (from secretory vesicle)

Pinocytosis

Nucleolus

Lysome

Rough endoplasmic reticulum

Plasma membrane

Mitochondrion

Cytoplasm

Free ribosomes

Microtubules

Polyribosome

Figure 3.1 / *Diagram of a Living Cell, Showing Chromatin (DNA) in the Nucleus, Various Organelles in the Cytoplasm, and Characteristic Membranes.* All living things are composed of units of life called cells. Each cell carries on its life processes within a semiliquid substance, the cytoplasm, bounded by a semipermeable membrane. The cell takes in some materials from the surrounding fluids and excretes others. Within the cytoplasm is a large body bounded by a double membrane and containing the genetic material guiding the cell's functions; this is the nucleus. DNA molecules strung along the length of the chromosomes contain a genetic code which is transcribed into messenger RNA molecules, which leave the nucleus to attach themselves to ribosomes lining the rough endoplasmic reticulum. Here the code is translated into specific protein molecules, many of which are enzymes controlling chemical processes within the cell. Mitochondria are tiny organelles that provide for the energy required for the cell's metabolic processes.

way the placenta serves the fetus, transporting the necessary oxygen and nutrients from the blood stream and carrying away the carbon dioxide and other metabolic waste products of neural metabolism. The glia also provide the neurons with a protective shield that maintains the fluids in which the neurons are bathed ("the internal sea") within the narrow tolerances of optimum condition. Also, synaptic junctions are characteristically enclosed in a protective glial covering to prevent interference from the activities of nearby synapses. Generally smaller than neurons, the glial cells (often called *neuroglia,* accented on the second syllable) are much more numerous.

The membrane surrounding the cytoplasm is an extremely important organ of the cell, corresponding to our skin. A continuous interchange of substances occurs between its interior and the surrounding extracellular fluids, the "internal sea" so carefully monitored by the glial cells. Certain small molecules diffuse passively through the plasma membrane, while others are energetically taken in or expelled from the interior. Very large molecules in the surrounding *extracellular space* may be ingested by a process called *pinocytosis* (cell-drinking) in which a pocket forms in the membrane (through *invagination*), enclosing the desired material, and eventually closes off, so that the ingested material floats within the cytoplasm enclosed in a thin membranous vesicle. The reverse process is called *exocytosis.* In this process, substances are expelled when such a vesicle moves to the inner surface of the membrane, fuses with it, and when the membrane opens pours its contents into the extracellular fluids.

The plasma membrane's permeability, specifically to electrically charged molecules (ions), is an important aspect of the story of the neuron. All living cells actively maintain an electrical charge difference, or *polarity,* between their interior fluids and the exterior fluids. In the case of the neuron this polarity amounts to 60 to 70 millivolts, called the neuron's *resting potential.* It is maintained by continual active extrusion of positively charged sodium ions (Na^+) against the electrical gradient (the tendency of the positively charged particles to diffuse back inside through the membrane). The term *sodium pump* has been coined to characterize this process. Should the sodium pump cease to function, as in cell death, the membrane's resting potential would quickly fall to zero.

Note that positively charged ions are expelled faster than negatively charged ions, such as chloride, which tends to leave the interior negatively charged relative to the extracellular fluids; this is the characteristic state of all living cells.

Pinocytosis (PEE-*no-sye-TO-sis*). Cell drinking. The process through which the cell takes in particles or substances by a local invagination and pinching off of its plasma membrane.

Invagination. An infolding of the plasma membrane to engulf a particle.

Exocytosis. The process through which unwanted substances are excreted by the cell into the surrounding medium.

Polarity. Electrical charge differential on two sides of the plasma membrane.

Resting potential. The polarity normal for a plasma membrane when not under stimulation.

Sodium pump. An enzymatic mechanism through which sodium ions are continuously excreted by the cell against the electrical gradient.

The Neuron as a Specialized Cell

Figure 3.2 depicts a generalized neuron. The stout branching extensions from its *soma,* called *dendrites* (from *dendron,* tree), are in effect antennae that the neuron extends to receive signals from other neurons. Also shown is one slender nerve fiber, the neuron's sole output channel, through which it transmits signals to other neurons; this fiber is called an *axon.* Also shown are the *axon hillock* region of the soma, where the axon exits the cell body, and one of the axon's many terminals making contact with another neuron in a synapse.

If an axon is damaged, such as by a pinch or application of an electric current, its membrane at that point loses its normal resistance to the flow of ions (becomes more permeable), and the electric charge differential between inside and outside (the resting potential) suddenly disappears, due primarily to the influx of sodium ions. We say that the membrane has been *depolarized* at that point. If this happens, moreover, a wave of depolarization spreads along the axon in both directions from the original point, which is in turn restored to normal polarization. This swiftly moving wave of depolarization of the axon membrane is the nerve impulse, technically called an *action potential* or *spike potential.* The ability to conduct such a self-propagating wave along its length is a specialization of the axon membrane.

Such a nerve impulse is initiated at the axon hillock when the membrane of the cell soma at that point is partially depolarized to some critical level. If incoming signals to the neuron cause its membrane potential polarity to drop from about −60 to −50 millivolts at the axon hillock region, that might be sufficient to trigger a spike potential in its axon. The partial depolarization of the soma membrane causes a sudden complete loss of polarity in the first portion of the axon, and this complete depolarization sweeps with great speed and undiminished amplitude all the way to the terminal tips of the axon, much like the burning of a cordite fuse. But the membrane's sudden loss of resistance to the flow of ions across it is only momentary, and active processes such as the sodium pump immediately restore the membrane to its resting potential, ready to propagate another impulse. Until that is accomplished, we say the neuron is in a *refractory period,* absolute or relative, during which another impulse may not be initiated.

The speed of propagation of the nerve impulse depends on several factors. Large neurons tend to have large-bore axons, which propagate impulses much faster and at a more rapid rate (times per

Soma. **The cell body proper.**

Dendrite. **A neural extension designed to receive input from other neurons.**

Axon. **The single output fiber of a neuron.**

Depolarized. **Said of a region of neural membrane when its normal polarity is lost or reduced.**

Action potential. **The nerve impulse, also called the spike potential.**

Refractory period. **The period after propagation of an action potential when the neuron is momentarily incapable (or less capable) of propagating another.**

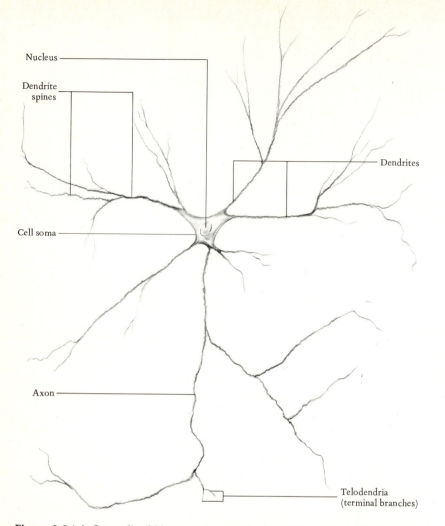

Nucleus

Dendrite
spines

Dendrites

Cell soma

Axon

Telodendria
(terminal branches)

Figure 3.2 / *A Generalized Neuron, Visualized as Floating Free in the Neural
Tissue.* In reality, the neurons are packed together with other neurons and
glial cells in a dense living matrix. Six dendrites are shown extending from
the cell soma, and a single axon is heading toward the upper right corner.
Note that the dendrites tend to branch at acute angles, while axon collaterals tend to branch off at right angles to the main fiber. Also shown are two
incoming (afferent) fibers (the axon terminal branches of other neurons),
one synapsing upon the cell soma (probably an inhibitory fiber), the other
making contact with a dendrite toward the upper left. An actual neuron
might receive many hundreds of synapses from as many other neurons,
both nearby and in distant regions of the brain. By contrast, most of the
other cells of the body have direct contact only with cells immediately adjacent to them. The neurons are thus ideally suited to integrate the activities
of other body cells, and in communication with one another to form the giant
"megamolecule" of the mind.

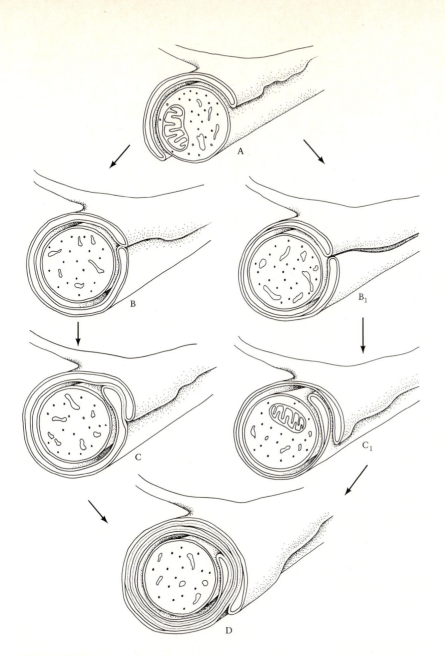

Figure 3.3 / *Myelin Sheath in Six Stages of Formation.* The myelin sheath that surrounds many nerve fibers is formed of multiple wrappings of the end feet of glial cells. It serves as insulation and permits a more rapid (saltatory) transmission of the signal along the length of the axon. At birth, many of our cortical neurons are not yet myelinated and remain nonfunctional until they are. The gradual myelination of cortical nerve fibers marks the progressive development of the cortex throughout childhood.

second) than do the finer fibers of small neurons. It only takes a fraction of a second for the membrane to be restored to its resting potential, and during this time (the neuron's refractory period) it becomes progressively more capable of generating a new impulse. Large neurons may be able to generate spike potentials hundreds of times per second, since they have a very short refractory period. However, they are by no means constantly doing so; their rate of firing changes constantly as a function of the impulses from other neurons incoming to their dendrites and soma.

The axons of large neurons also tend to be surrounded by a fatty

Figure 3.4 / *An Electron Photomicrograph of a Slice of Cortex from a Rat Brain, Showing Examples of Myelin Sheath.* Many myelinated axons can be seen in this electron micrograph. The tissue has been stained to render the myelin electron opaque, hence dark. Some of the axons are severed at right angles to their course, showing their cross section. Others are cut at an angle more closely parallel to their course. In the largest of these, nodes of Ranvier can be seen, where the myelin sheath tapers off rapidly to nothing, leaving the axon bare. Other fibers are shown without a myelin sheath coating. These are either small, unmyelinated axons, or dendritic fibers, or extensions of glial cells. This slice was taken close to the surface of the cortex.

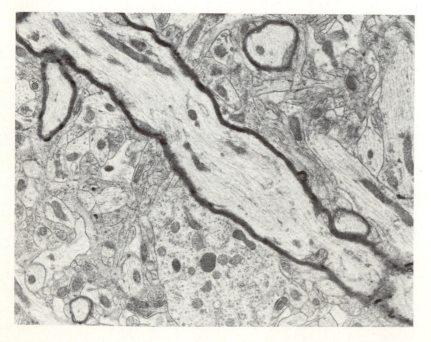

myelin sheath, which serves as insulation much like insulation around an electric wire; few of the smaller neurons (with smaller-bore axons) have such a sheath. The sheath actually consists of multiple wrappings of glial-cell extensions (end feet), which each cover only a few millimeters of the axon's length. Where one glial cell leaves off, another takes over, leaving a small area of axon exposed between them (Figure 3.3). These exposed points along the length of the myelinated axon, called *nodes of Ranvier*, allow for *saltatory* (leaping) *transmission*, which carries the spike potential along far more rapidly than if the axon were unmyelinated. It is as if the action potential moves from one node of Ranvier to the next, rather than progressing steadily along the axon membrane (Figure 3.4).

Neurotransmitter Substances

But the spike potential does not directly stimulate the following neuron. What happens is that each time a nerve impulse reaches an axon terminal in a synaptic junction, it causes a small amount of a chemical *neurotransmitter* substance to be released from the presynaptic membrane into the synaptic cleft (see Figure 3.5). The neurotransmitter substances are stored in the axon terminal in membrane-bound vesicles close to the presynaptic membrane, ready to be released. Their effect, upon diffusing across the very narrow space of the synaptic cleft, is to alter the postsynaptic membrane's permeability to specific ions. A neurotransmitter molecule attaches to a receptor embedded in the postsynaptic membrane, which then "opens its pores" so that certain ions can readily diffuse through (Figure 3.6).

If the effect of this ion flow is to depolarize the membrane (that is, make the interior of the target cell at that point less negative relative to the extracellular fluids), the result will be excitatory, tending to cause the target cell to fire more rapidly. If, on the other hand, the effect of the ion flow through the membrane is to *hyperpolarize* it (make its interior more negative), the result will be inhibitory, tending to reduce the firing rate of the target cell.

An example of such a neurotransmitter is acetylcholine (ACh) (see Figure 3.7). Acetylcholine is the neurotransmitter chemical employed at the *neuromuscular junction*, through which the skeletal muscle cells are caused to contract, and also in many of the synapses of the *central nervous system* (CNS), whose components are the brain and spinal cord. In both of these instances, acetylcholine is an excitatory neurotransmitter. Such transmitters always act to depolarize the postsynaptic membrane, in the case of acetylcholine by

Nodes of Ranvier. **Points between successive lengths of myelin sheath where the axon is bare, providing for saltatory transmission.**

Saltatory transmission. **A rapid mode of transmission in which the action potential leaps from one node of Ranvier to another.**

Neurotransmitter. **A chemical substance released into the synaptic cleft from the axon terminal upon arrival of a nerve impulse.**

Hyperpolarize. **Moving the polarity of the membrane in a direction opposite to depolarization, resulting in increased polarity and inhibition of firing.**

Neuromuscular junction. **The synaptic contact of a motor neuron with a muscle cell.**

Central nervous system. **The brain and spinal cord, collectively, distinguished from the peripheral nervous system.**

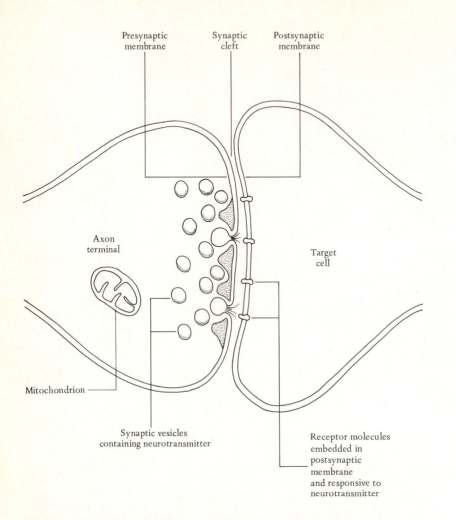

Presynaptic
membrane

Synaptic
cleft

Postsynaptic
membrane

Axon
terminal

Target
cell

Mitochondrion

Synaptic vesicles
containing neurotransmitter

Receptor molecules
embedded in
postsynaptic
membrane
and responsive to
neurotransmitter

Figure 3.5 / *A Generalized Synaptic Junction.* Upon arrival at the axon terminal, the local plasma membrane becomes suddenly more permeable to chloride ions. The ions enter the terminal and cause the synaptic vesicles containing neurotransmitter to move toward the synaptic cleft, to merge with the presynaptic membrane, and to pour their contents into the narrow space separating the two neurons. The neurotransmitter molecules then diffuse across the synaptic cleft and interact with the protein receptor molecules embedded in the postsynaptic membrane. The neurotransmitter molecules are then destroyed or taken up again by the axon terminal for reuse, leaving the synaptic cleft clear for the arrival of the next nerve impulse. This entire process takes place in only a few thousandths of a second.

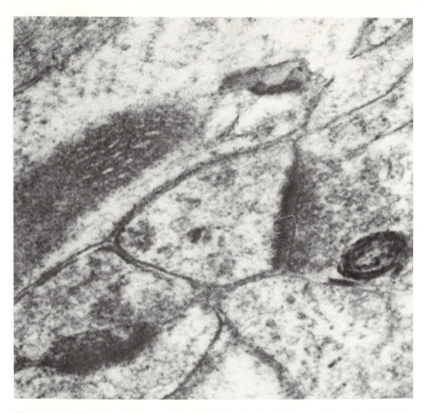

Figure 3.6 / *Electron Micrograph of Rat Cortex, Showing a Characteristic Axodendritic Synapse.* Compare this electron micrograph with the diagram in Figure 3.5. Note the synaptic vesicles in the axon terminal (their presence identifies it as such) just behind the synaptic cleft, shown as a dark area separating the two cytoplasms. The separation between the two plasma membranes is somewhat wider here than elsewhere, and the postsynaptic membrane can be seen to have an electron-dense region immediately behind it whose function is unknown.

increasing its permeability to sodium ions (Na^+) and potassium ions (K^+). However, in some synapses (such as those of the vagus nerve, whose influence is to slow the heartbeat), acetylcholine acts as an inhibitory neurotransmitter. In the heart muscle, it increases the permeability of the postsynaptic membrane to potassium ions, which in turn flow out of the cell, increasing its internal negativity,

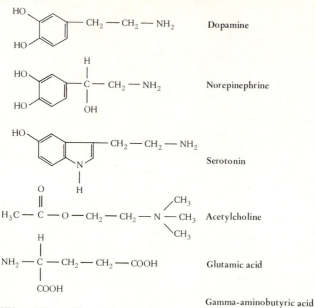

Figure 3.7 / *Structural Formulas of Some Important Neurotransmitter Substances in the Brain.* Serotonin, norepinephrine, and dopamine are known as monoamines and are destroyed by the enzyme monoamine oxidase. They are considered characteristically inhibitory in effect. Acetylcholine is a major excitatory neurotransmitter, both in the brain and in the body, although at the heart muscle, curiously, it is inhibitory in effect. Glutamic acid is another excitatory neurotransmitter widely prevalent in brain tissues, while GABA (gamma-aminobutyric acid) is a principal inhibitory neurotransmitter in the brain. Many other substances now also appear to operate as brain neurotransmitters in certain regions.

hyperpolarizing the membrane, and reducing the tendency of the smooth muscle to contract. Whether acetylcholine is excitatory or inhibitory at a particular synapse depends on what type of post-synaptic receptors are present in the synapse.

For comparison with acetylcholine, a prominent neurotransmitter in the CNS that is characteristically inhibitory in effect is gamma-aminobutyric acid, commonly called GABA (see Figure 3.7). GABA appears to act by opening channels for chlorine ions (Cl⁻) in the postsynaptic membrane. When chlorine ions flow into the cell, its interior negativity is increased, hyperpolarization occurs, and the cell's firing rate tends to be reduced. In some inhibitory synapses, permeability to potassium ions is also increased; they tend to flow out, also increasing interior negativity and producing hyperpolarization. When the membrane is hyperpolarized, it is more difficult for excitatory synapses to bring about the threshold level of depolarization necessary to produce an action potential in the target neuron.

The mechanism of neurotransmitter release at the synapse is dependent on the presence of calcium ions (Ca^{++}). Depolarization of the presynaptic membrane by the arrival of an action potential causes channels for calcium ions to open, and calcium flows into the synaptic terminal. This in turn causes whatever synaptic vesicles are there to move toward the presynaptic membrane and, if enough calcium ions are present, to attach to it, whereupon the membrane opens to allow their contents to spill into the synaptic cleft. If no calcium is present, neurotransmitter substance cannot be released. If, on the other hand, calcium is experimentally injected into the synaptic terminal, transmitter release occurs immediately.

Electrotonic Potentials

The change in the polarity of the postsynaptic membrane produced by the action of the neurotransmitter upon its receptors tends to propagate itself across the target cell membrane in all directions — a wave of depolarization or hyperpolarization that diminishes rapidly in both amplitude and speed, quite unlike the spike action potential of the axon membrane. This *degrading* mode of transmission is called *electrotonic*, and is characteristic of the membrane of the cell soma and dendrites. The electrotonic effect of all the incoming signals to a given nerve cell eventually reaches the axon hillock, and it is this pooled effect, the algebraic sum of all the excitatory and inhibitory inputs at any given moment, that determines the rate of impulse initiation in the target neuron's own axon.

Electrotonic. Referring to a type of traveling wave of polarity change over the surface of a neuron when no action potential is generated.

The Catecholamine Neurotransmitters

Another category of neurotransmitter, the *catecholamines*, has a somewhat different mode of operation. Two prominent members of this group, *dopamine* and *norepinephrine* (see Figure 3.7), appear to be centrally implicated in brain circuitries involving such psychological phenomena as drives, mood states, and emotional expres-

Catecholamine (KAT-a-kol-a-meen). A category of neurotransmitter characterized by possession of the catechol group.

sion. The catecholamines are slower-acting, usually inhibitory in their effect, and appear to operate in part by initiating within the target cell a complex metabolic process that alters its excitability. On attaching to postsynaptic membrane receptors, these neurotransmitters produce two effects: (1) a slow hyperpolarization of the membrane, which is inhibitory, and (2) activation of an enzyme within the target cell, *adenylate cyclase,* that catalyzes the transformation of the energy-bearing molecule, *adenosine triphosphate,* into cyclic adenosine monophosphate (ATP → cAMP), the so-called *second messenger* (the neurotransmitter being the first). This process in turn functions in a complex fashion to set the excitability level of the target neuron. Cyclic adenosine monophosphate by itself, when injected close to the synapse, mimics the effect of applied dopamine or norepinephrine.

After each release of neurotransmitter into the synaptic cleft, it must be quickly inactivated or removed to clear the synapse for the arrival of the next impulse. This is accomplished either by enzymes at the spot, which cause the transmitter substance to be altered or destroyed, or by the re-uptake of the transmitter into the presynaptic terminal for reuse. Interference with either of these processes (such as by antidepressant or antipsychotic drugs) results in a buildup of neurotransmitter at the synapse and an accentuation of the effect of the synapse on the target neuron.

Types of Synapses

Many large neurons in the cortex and spinal cord are encrusted with thousands of synapses and their protective glial coverings. Thus it is clearly not a question of whether a neuron receives a stimulus or not, but the sum of simultaneously arriving excitatory and inhibitory inputs to the cell, that determines whether and how fast a given neuron will generate action potentials. It is interesting to note about incoming inputs that excitatory synapses tend to occur on outlying regions of the dendrites, while inhibitory synapses tend to occur on the neuron soma itself or on the proximal regions of its dendrites. Since they are closer to the axon hillock, the inhibitory influences thus have a certain advantage over excitatory inputs in the determination of the firing rate of a neuron, and can be thought of as exercising a controlling function upon what might otherwise be a runaway electrical brainstorm, as in spreading epileptiform activity.

Large neurons tend to transmit signals over very long distances

Adenylate cyclase (a-DEN-i-late SYE-klase). A chemical important as an intracellular messenger, controlling the neuron's firing rate in the case of some neurons.

Adenosine triphosphate (a-DEN-o-seen). The chemical used by the cells to store and release chemical energy for metabolic processes.

Second messenger. A substance which operates inside the neuron to control its responsivity to stimulation.

through their large-bore, heavily myelinated axons, and tend to be excitatory in their effect. Small neurons, on the other hand, tend to be involved in very local circuits, to transmit over very short distances, and to be inhibitory in their effect. It is convenient to call the first type *transmission neurons* and the second *interneurons.*

A synapse between an axon terminal and a dendrite is termed an *axodendritic synapse.* When it occurs on the surface of the cell soma, it is called an *axosomatic synapse.* Sometimes, however, an axon synapses with another axon, usually close to its terminal; this is known as an *axoaxonic synapse.* What frequently happens is that its excitatory (depolarizing) input to the axon is subthreshold (insufficient to initiate an action potential). When an action potential arrives at that point, the amplitude of the depolarization it produces is reduced, which results in a lesser amount of neurotransmitter being released from the presynaptic membrane.

We have thus far been discussing only synapses at axon terminals. However, synaptic contacts are now known to exist between dendrites, accompanied by the release of neurotransmitter substances. It is also recognized that dendrites in close apposition are apt to be mutually influenced by their electrical activity through the field effects these activities generate. In certain regions of the brain, such as at the surface of the cortex, the tissues are a veritable feltwork of interlaced dendritic and axonal fibers. The electrical interaction, which must be very complex, is beyond the capacity of our present analytic techniques. It will yet probably prove very important to the total functioning of the brain.

Two further points should be made. A very rapid train of impulses along an axon has the effect of hyperpolarizing the presynaptic membrane (because the impulses are arriving too fast), thereby increasing the amplitude of the action potential when it arrives, and thus the amount of neurotransmitter released. This effect is called *postsynaptic potentiation.* Through this mechanism, the effect of the action potential is increased even though its amplitude in approaching the synapse is not.

The second point is that the synaptic effect may be increased in amplitude, as well as prolonged in time, by a very rapid train of impulses if the spike potentials arrive so rapidly that there is not enough time for the neurotransmitter in the synaptic cleft to be deactivated or removed, resulting in a neurotransmitter buildup. This is a mechanism systematically employed in the sensory relay neurons, apparently to insure a high-security transmission of the signal.

Transmission neurons. Neurons whose axons leave the vicinity of the soma to innervate distant regions of the brain.

Axodendritic synapse. A synapse of an axon terminal upon a dendrite, the most usual type of neural connection.

Axosomatic synapse. A synapse of an axon terminal upon the soma of another neuron.

Axoaxonic synapse. A synapse formed between two axons, often close to the terminal of one.

Postsynaptic potentiation. An increase in synaptic effect resulting from the rapidity of arrival of nerve impulses, and unrelated to the amplitude of the impulses.

The Structure of the Membrane

All neural function consists of changes in the electrical polarity of local regions of the plasma membrane. What is known about this structure? Until the introduction of the electron miscroscope, it was impossible to visualize. Since then, electron micrographs of its cross-section have clearly shown the plasma membrane to be composed of two dark layers with a lighter layer in between (Figure 3.8). Until recently this three-layered structure was thought to be composed of a double layer of *phospholipid* molecules (the lighter inner core) coated on both sides with more electron-dense protein molecules (the darker lines), which face the cytoplasm on one side and the extracellular space on the other. It is currently believed that the membrane consists essentially of a bimolecular leaflet of phospholipid molecules whose lipid (fatty, less electron-dense) ends are oriented toward each other, the molecules aligned end to end. The protein molecules associated with the membrane are thought to be embedded within its two external surfaces (Figure 3.6). (The existence of protein molecules embedded in the inner surface, facing the cytoplasm, has yet to be demonstrated.)

Phospholipid molecules. Molecules composed of a phosphate group and a fatty (lipid) group.

In addition to these integral proteins, other proteins are thought to be capable of attaching to and being detached from the exterior membrane surface. In all, several dozen proteins are known to be associated with the neural membrane in the region of the synapse. Speculation is growing that two or three of them participate in the process of synaptic transmission by changing shape upon acquiring a phosphate group (a process known as *phosphorylation*), and thereby either opening pores in the membrane to let ions through or affecting the ionic pump that moves ions across, against their electrical gradient. Whether a similar protein-molecule-mediated process is involved in the wave of membrane depolarization that constitutes the spike action potential is unknown.

Phosphorylation. The process by which an organic substance is changed through addition of a phosphate group.

The classic theory of the membrane potential is that of A. L. Hodgkin and A. F. Huxley (1952), for which they received the Nobel prize in 1963. Hodgkin and Huxley postulated that the membrane potential at any moment is a function of the ionic distributions of sodium and potassium; that these concentrations depend on the degree of permeability of the membrane to these ions, as well as on the sodium- and potassium-pumping action of the membrane (active transmembrane transport); that this permeability is a function of the degree of depolarization, the membrane becoming increasingly permeable as depolarization proceeds; and that the increase in permeability to sodium and potassium proceeds on a

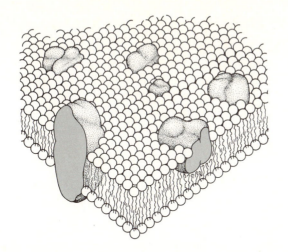

Figure 3.8 / *The Fluid Mosaic Model of the Plasma Membrane, Showing Embedded Protein Molecules.* The phospholipid molecules composing the plasma membrane are here shown oriented with their fatty tails directed toward each other, while their phosphate ends form the exterior of the bimolecular leaflet. The large objects represent protein molecules, presumably operating enzymatically to open or close pores in the membrane to control the passage of ions. These protein molecules are thought to be free to move laterally to different positions within the membrane.

different time course, accounting for the rapid increase in positivity of the interior as sodium ions flow in more rapidly than potassium ions flow out.

A current interpretation has added a few refinements to the theory, but still does not fully satisfy all experimental findings. For one thing, the increase in membrane permeability to sodium ions with increasing depolarization as the spike potential develops is seen as producing a positive-type feedback loop, ever increasing the speed of the ionic flow even as the ionic concentrations are beginning to equalize across that point on the membrane. This interpretation might explain the pronounced sharpness of the spike rise (Figure 3.9). With respect to recovery of the resting potential, it is now thought that since the permeability of the membrane to potassium ions lags behind its permeability to sodium, the membrane is increasing its permeability to potassium ions at about the time the sodium ions have reached a balance. The potassium ions now flow out, quickly reducing the positivity of the interior; the sodium-potassium pump then takes over to restore the ionic concentrations to their previous levels.

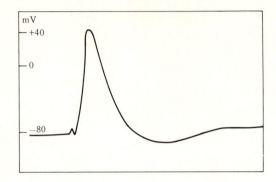

Figure 3.9 / *Spike Action Potential.* The diagram represents the passage of an action potential, or nerve impulse, over a point along the axon. Note that the depolarization tends to overshoot the zero point, causing a momentary positive polarity in the interior of the axon. The polarity is then quickly corrected, returning to resting level at about 65–70 millivolts. During this recovery period (the refractory period), the axon is unable to produce another action potential.

Thus the ion flows that produce the spike potential apparently result entirely from the breakdown of the membrane's resistance to that flow, however it may be initiated. No cell energies are therefore deemed necessary to keep the nerve impulse moving at full amplitude along the axon. Once triggered, the progressive breakdown continues by itself, all the energetic processes occurring in the recovery cycle.

Types of Neurons

Neurons are of many sizes and shapes adapted to their many special functions. The cerebral cortex is dominated by large neurons of a type called *pyramidal cells,* the cerebellar cortex (see Chapter 2) by another large neuron called *Purkinje cells* after their discoverer, and the spinal cord by the large *spinal motor neurons* (or *motoneurons*), whose axons directly activate the muscles. At the other end of the size continuum are the tiny granule cells of the cerebellum, which have been estimated to number 300 billion! (It was previously estimated that there were no more than 10 billion neurons in the entire brain.)

It is neurons of intermediate size that constitute the preponderance of the nerve cells of the brain. These neurons often have

Pyramidal cells (pyr-RAM-i-dal). **Large neurons typical of the cerebral cortex projecting via the pyramidal tract.**

Purkinje cells (pur-KIN-jee). **The large cells characteristic of the cerebellar cortex, inhibitory in their effect upon the subcortical cerebellar nuclei.**

widely ramifying dendritic branches, and axons whose multiple branching terminals arborize in the vicinity of the cell soma. Such neurons may be thought of as involved in integrative functions within their microregion. In the cortex they receive input from other regions concurrently with input to the pyramidal cells with which they are functionally associated. They do not appear to project to other regions. While the pyramidal cells are excitatory, these *stellate* (star-shaped) *cells* are probably largely inhibitory in effect. It is relatively large neurons of this "multipolar" type that predominate in the subcortical nuclei, those masses of gray matter deep in the brain's interior. As we shall see when we discuss the several sensory systems, sensory receptor cells tend to be highly specialized types of neurons (unipolar and bipolar). There is some question whether their output processes ought to be called axons at all.

Stellate cells. Star-shaped neurons prevalent in many regions of the brain.

It should be clear from these examples that the structural units composing the nervous system are highly various, reflecting the complexity of the functions involved and the intricate bioengineering that has evolved to meet their needs.

Neural Circuitries

Throughout the nervous system, neurons are systematically assembled into functional groups, which may be thought of as modules. These modules are in turn in communication with others, forming more extensive interacting systems. When a portion of the brain is damaged, some specific function is apt to be impaired, at least temporarily. This does not mean, however, that the damaged tissue itself was responsible for the lost function. In general, specific brain functions appear to involve widely distributed neurons, organized into interconnected recycling circuitries. Nowhere in the brain are there found master neurons dictating the behavior of their functional group. Instead, there appears to be a pervasive "democracy" and sharing of contributions throughout, with a good deal of redundancy and overlap of functions to provide for fail-safe operation. Yet a case can also be made for localization of functions, since in certain portions of the nervous system the loss of a relatively small amount of neural tissue may result in a permanent specific functional impairment.

Three very general principles can be observed to operate at the level of interaction between the neurons themselves. The principle of *convergence* is represented by the neurons from widely divergent regions of the brain that exert simultaneous influence on a single target neuron through their synapses. The opposite principle, *divergence*, governs the fact that the target neuron may in turn transmit its excitation to numerous other neurons, the targets of its many axonal branches. The third principle is *feedback*, according to which a given neuron is influenced by return signals from the very neurons (or modules) to which it projects. These three principles are illustrated diagrammatically in Figure 3.10.

Figure 3.10 / *The Principles of Divergence, Convergence, and Feedback in Neural Circuitry.* Two excitatory neurons (+) and one inhibitory neuron (−) are shown. In the upper left, numerous axons are shown *converging* upon the single target neuron, some synapsing on its dendrites (probably excitatory), some on its soma (probably inhibitory). In the lower right, the principle of *divergence* is illustrated in the multiple axon terminals going to different neurons, each carrying the same neural message. One of these axon branches is shown synapsing on a dendrite of the neuron in the upper left (excitatory), which in turn projects back an excitatory impulse, producing a *positive feedback* arrangement (a reverberatory circuit, tending to continue its firing). Another axon branch is shown synapsing on the dendrite of an inhibitory neuron, which in turn fires back an inhibitory signal, tending to control the firing rate of the first neuron. This is called *negative feedback*. Most of the cortical pyramidal cells appear to have such a negative feedback circuit governing their rate of firing.

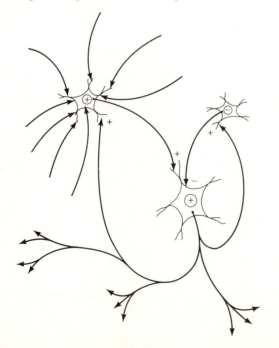

When we speak of interaction between neurons or neural systems, we are usually referring to some form of feedback process (although when the circuits involved are massive and complex, we may speak of *re-entrant circuits*). If the feedback or re-entrant circuits are excitatory, it is easy to see that a self-activating loop may be formed, encouraging prolonged or increased rates of firing. If, however, the feedback or re-entrant fibers are from inhibitory neurons, they will operate as a regulating or control mechanism to prevent runaway firing, as in seizure states, or to eliminate "noise" in the circuitry. Both types of neural interaction can be found throughout the central nervous system, from cerebral cortex to spinal cord. While it is conceivable that local, relatively simple interactional systems of the excitatory type may constitute "reverberating circuits," such as have been postulated to underlie the momentary holding of configurations in short-term memory, more massive re-entrant systems are not considered closed systems, having as they do many points of entry and exit (Mountcastle, 1978).

Re-entrant circuits. Neural circuits forming continuous loops which are more extensive than local feedback loops.

With this conceptual framework in mind, each of the larger anatomical structures of the brain may be thought of as an aggregated conglomeration of much smaller modules such as we have been discussing. Meanwhile, the major fiber bundles interconnecting them may be considered evidence of their joint participation in larger interactive systems. For example, the cerebral cortex itself is a vast mosaic of tiny columnar structures arrayed side by side, operating in relative independence of neighboring columns, each constituting a module serving a specific function within the general function of that particular region of the cortex. In the same manner the various subcortical nuclei toward the center of the brain also appear to contain their own less obvious autonomous modules of interacting neurons, all acting in concert to fulfill the overall functions of that particular nucleus. Meanwhile the white fiber bundles coursing through the brain suggest a brainwide interactive neural system (the giant megamolecule).

Summary

At the microscopic level, the brain is a vast assemblage of nerve cells, or neurons — perhaps hundreds of billions of them — interconnected by their cytoplasmic extensions, the axons or nerve fibers. The nerve impulse traveling along the axon from one neuron to another consists of a swiftly self-propagating wave of depolarization of the axon's membrane. This membrane is immediately restored to its normal resting potential of about 60 to 70 millivolts (the difference in electric charge between the cell's interior and the extracellular fluids) after the passing of the impulse. The wave of depolarization is associated with a sudden localized loss of the membrane's resistance to the flow of electrically charged particles, especially ions of sodium and potassium.

Upon reaching a terminal of the axon at a synaptic junction with another neuron, such a nerve impulse (also called an action potential or spike potential) initiates the release of a small quantity of a chemical neurotransmitter into the narrow cleft separating the terminal from another neuron. Diffusing across this synaptic cleft, the neurotransmitter affects receptors on the opposite membrane's surface, thereby altering its permeability to ions and causing an increase or decrease of its polarity. This change in turn causes a more slowly propagating wave of hyperpolarization or depolarization to pass over the surface of the affected neuron. This is called electrotonic conduction, and such a wave diminishes in both amplitude and speed as it goes, unlike the axonal nerve impulse. Hyperpolarizing influences tend to reduce the target neuron's rate of production of nerve impulses; depolarizing influences tend to increase its rate of firing. The nature of the neurotransmitter and the receptors determines whether the neuron is excitatory or inhibitory in its effect.

A neuron's rate of firing is limited by the refractory period of its axon (the time required for its membrane to be restored to resting potential) and by the time it takes for the synaptic cleft to be cleared of its neurotransmitter substance in readiness for the arrival of the next nerve impulse. The latter occurs either through inactivation of the neurotransmitter by enzymes or through its removal by re-uptake into the axon terminal that released it. These processes, which take a few thousandths of a second, permit some neurons to generate hundreds of nerve impulses per second. However, most neurons' firing rates continually vary, in response to the interaction of many simultaneously arriving inhibitory and excitatory impulses.

Neurons differ greatly in size and in the length and shape of their cytoplasmic extensions. In addition to a single axon, most neurons have many other branching dendritic extensions that serve as receptor areas for incoming axonal fibers. Most large neurons have an insulating myelin sheath, formed of the repeated wrappings of glial cell endfeet. This sheath permits rapid, saltatory (leaping) conduction of the action potential along these axons. Large neurons also tend to have large-bore axons and to transmit over very long distances, while small neurons tend to serve only local circuits. Most large neurons are also excitatory, while most of the smaller "stellate" neurons associated with them appear to be inhibitory. The excitatory neurons tend to synapse on outlying regions of the dendrites of target cells, while inhibitory neurons tend to synapse on the target cell's cell body or on nearby dendritic surfaces. The proximity of the inhibitory neurons' synapses to the point of origin of the impulse gives them an advantage in determination of the target cell's firing rate.

The neurons characteristically function not as independent agents but as part of an interacting group or module. These modules in turn function as elements in larger integrated subsystems within the brain. There are three important principles of neural interaction: convergence, according to which many neurons participate in influencing the firing rate of a given neuron; divergence, by which each neuron through its many axon terminals makes contact with numerous other neurons; and feedback, whereby target neurons, through their own axons, influence the rate of firing of the neurons that affect them. Such interacting neural circuitries may be minutely local self–re-exciting or inhibitory control loops, or vast and complex re-entrant systems characterized by many inputs from other systems. In fact, the entire brain might be considered to be such a re-entrant system, functioning as an integrative whole.

Review of Part I

What may we conclude about the brain at this point? Human history can be traced back some ten thousand years, to the earliest settled village life based on agriculture, animal husbandry, and the beginnings of technology. Presumably it has been at least that long that people have been self-aware and wondered about the source of their intelligence and their consciousness. But it is only within the past few decades of the twentieth century that we have begun to develop a sophisticated appreciation of how our brain works, and can begin to seriously ask the question of where and how consciousness and thought arise. They are reflections of the activities of the brain, whose myriad circuitries of countless billions of neurons flash their incessant signals to one another in endless chains of interaction, all intricately ordered on a blueprint in our genes. We should not let the enormous complexity of these interactions deter us from delving deeper into its mystery, nor need we fear that further analysis will reduce the mind to mechanism. The more detailed our knowledge is becoming, the more fascinating grows the study, each research finding seeming to open more questions than it answers.

We have seen that the neuron is nothing more than a living cell, much like any other. It carries on its own internal life processes, presumably unaware of the grand orchestration in which it plays its part. It is designed to propagate rapid signals along its axonal fiber when appropriately stimulated, blips traveling along its electrically charged membrane, one after another in an unceasing train, toward the synaptic terminal where each releases a few molecules of some chemical stimulus substance to affect the following cell. Each neuron has only one axon, though that axon may branch into a thousand terminal directions to spread its message to others in the same neural network. We have also seen that each neuron reaches out with cytoplasmic arms, the dendrites, to receive signals simultaneously from a multitude of sources in the brain, and integrates their messages upon the membrane of its soma, where they all converge near the axon hillock. There are also regions in the brain where these outreaching dendritic branches communicate with one another.

The single neuron is obviously a highly efficient integrative mechanism. It weighs the balance of excitatory and inhibitory signals, computes their algebraic sum, and acts accordingly in its production of output signals to its assigned network associates. Some of the networks in which a given neuron participates may be very simple and tiny; others may be vast and intricate. Whatever their size or complexity, they too are integrators of multiple circulating messages, all couched in terms of excitation and inhibition, each weighed in the balance, shifting the trend, modulating, controlling. To speak in global generalities, the brain is also characterized by network overlap, fail-safe redundancy, distribution of responsibility among cooperating equals, and no dictator neurons anywhere. More specifically, the brain consists of a great many relatively independent neural systems, which can be studied to learn about their internal modes of operation. This is our next level of analysis. In Parts II and III we will explore each of the major functional systems of the brain, always asking how they ultimately work together to make for the phenomenon of human thought and behavior.

Part II / *The Major Functional Systems*
A. The Modern Thalamocortical Systems

We have seen that the great mass of the tissues of the two hemispheres is preoccupied with perceptual functions based on visual, tactile, and auditory input in its posterior portion, and with the organization of adaptive behavior in its anterior portion. Together, these brain tissues make up the thalamocortical system that evolved with the mammals. Part II is devoted to these more modern brain functions and their neural bases. Part III explores those older structures and functions of the limbic system, the hypothalamic area, and the brainstem, whose anatomy we have already briefly surveyed. With this more detailed examination of the brain's neural organization we may begin to see how the phenomenon of human personality, so taken for granted, could come into existence.

When the first mammals appeared on earth, they introduced a profound change in the organization of the brain, which we have inherited. The new feature distinguishing the mammals is the thalamocortical system, comprised of the neocortex, its associated thalamic nuclei, and the corpus callosum interconnecting the two hemispheres at the cortical

level. With the extinction of the dinosaurs the mammals found themselves in possession of the daytime world the dinosaurs had so long dominated. In their exploitation of the newly available environmental niches, the mammals transferred to their now expanding neocortex functions once handled by lower brain structures. This process (which we call *encephalization*) is most dramatically illustrated in the more recently evolved primates, the monkeys and the great apes, and took another great leap forward with the emergence of the human brain. The older structures of the brain were buried out of sight under the massive new brain forming the cerebral roof.

The enlargement of these portions of the brain seems to have made possible new functions which emerged out of the older functions we share with other mammals. A critical mass was reached, a threshold crossed, and the uniquely human function of symbolic (verbal) language came into being, along with other functions, such as logical reasoning, an appreciation of tonal and color harmonies and the sense of rhythm, self-awareness, and the ability to project long-range future plans and carry them to fruition. This is what makes the study of the modern thalamocortical system so fascinating. When we speak of thought and imagination, decision making, recollection of things past and planning for the future, philosophy, the arts, we are referring to the new capacities emergent in the human thalamocortical system. It is the neocortex and its associated thalamic nuclei that provide us with these emergent powers, the things that make us distinctively human. In this section we will glimpse the mechanisms underlying these truly marvelous new capacities.

Chapter 4 / *Visual Perception: The World Out There*

Through the mechanisms of visual perception, we discern our world to be filled with recognizable objects at known distances. Thus arises, in turn, our sense of spatial orientation. These visual mechanisms include the retinal system, which first analyzes the incoming light pattern; the collicular system, which brings objects to central focus; the geniculocalcarine system, which translates retinal patterns into contour edges in cortical representation; and an intrinsic visual cortex that has become selectively sensitive to patterns corresponding to environmental objects. At each stage in the progression from peripheral (eye) to central (cortical) processing, specific information is lost; it is replaced by another kind of specificity, specificity of interpretation, exemplified by the phenomenon of object constancy. Specific mechanisms provide for such capacities as recognition of an object's distance, color, form, motion within the environmental field, and motion in relation to the self, as well as the subjective stability of the environment despite continuous saccadic (jerking) and smooth-pursuit eye movements and motion through the field.

Consider what happens in normal vision. Objects of interest in our visual field are automatically held in focus, while things on the periphery or in the background or foreground are ignored. The latter two are both out of focus, and, owing to the convergence of our two eyes' line of sight, out of register as projected on their retinas. To see them clearly, we shift our gaze to bring them into central vision, and automatically adjust both focus, to accommodate their distance, and the convergence angle of our two eyes' lines of sight, to bear directly upon the object. All this occurs so automatically and reflexively that we are totally unaware of it. What we are directly aware of is the familiar object, perceived to lie at a precise distance and direction from us and in a surrounding context of other objects — Aunt Matilda on her motorcycle, the leopard moving stealthily through the underbrush, or whatever.

What is so marvelous about this is that we are almost never in any doubt about what it is we are seeing, among the countless billions of possibilities. The mechanism of visual perception is astonishingly definitive. The question is: how does it accomplish such accuracy and dependability?

Perhaps equally remarkable is the speed with which the object is identified as the signals are flashed from retina to brain. This extreme speed allows for rapid scanning of a complex visual field with near-certainty that nothing of importance will be overlooked. Moreover, it can be demonstrated that the eyes "take in" much more than one remembers having seen, and that they sometimes use what might be characterized as logical processes to infer the existence of things not seen at all. In the first case, reminder stimuli may bring back to recall things that were actually observed, but not in central awareness; in the second case, it may turn out that the figure we saw lurking in the shadows was only a fence post. The eyes, as sensory receptor systems, have access to our consciousness and may be thought of as its windows on the world. But it is our consciousness that sees things, not our eyes, and conscious processes are presumed to reside in the brain itself.

In this chapter we will follow visual signals inward, from the living receptor cells in the retina all the way to the most interior regions of the cortex where the experience of seeing is elaborated. In the process, let us see how close we can come, with present-day knowledge, to unraveling the mystery of vision.

Note in Figure 4.1 that the eyeball is remarkably similar structurally to a camera, with a flexible lens in front controlling focus through a change in its thickness, and an iris (the colored portion) controlling the aperture immediately in front of it. At the rear of the eyeball, corresponding to the photosensitive film, is a photosensitive tissue composed of some 130 million tiny receptor cells. Since the mechanism operates continuously when the eyes are open, it is more like a motion-picture camera than a still camera. Moreover, since the information flow is continuous ("on-line" rather than replay), it is most closely analogous to a television camera. The eyeball is an ingenious piece of optical engineering based on stimulus changes. Were we able to immobilize our gaze completely, avoiding the continual tiny *saccadic* jerks called *nystagmus* and thus preventing any stimulus motion across the retina, we would be blind. (This can be demonstrated by a suitable arrangement of mirrors attached to a contact lens.)

Saccadic. Characterized by saccades, sudden swift movements of the eyeball.

Nystagmus. An involuntary jerking of the eyeball.

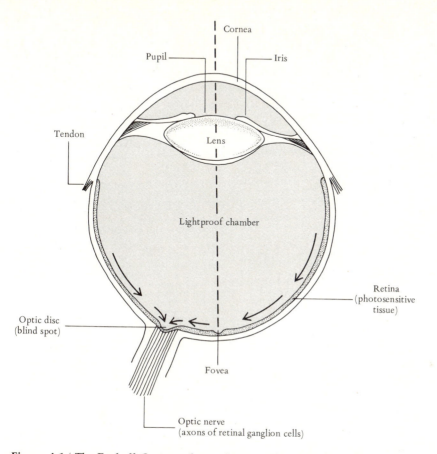

Figure 4.1 / *The Eyeball Compared to a Camera.* The structure of the eye is remarkably similar to that of a camera. In front is an adjustable aperture for the entering light (the iris and pupil), then a focusing lens (flattened by surrounding muscles to increase its focal length), and then a light-proof chamber. To the rear is a photosensitive retina, corresponding to film. However, in operation the eye is more similar to a television camera, since it transmits a continuously changing visual scene into the brain. Unlike the television camera, however, no blur is produced by swinging the camera rapidly from point to point in the scene, thanks to an ingenious mechanism described in the text. Only that portion of the scene projected upon the fovea is in clear focus. Peripheral portions of the retina receive only a vague representation of the world, but they are marvelously sensitive to any motion within the visual field.

The Retina

Contrary to expectations, the photoreceptor units in the *retina* lining the rear of the eyeball are not in the front, where the light strikes first, but in the deepest layer. There are two major types of receptor cells, called *rods* and *cones* for the distinctive shapes of their receptor ends, which face the rear wall of the eyeball (see Figure 4.2). The rods, which are exquisitely sensitive to dim light and serve essentially for night vision, are more common in the periph-

Retina. **The photosensitive tissue lining the interior of the eyeball.**

Rods. **The retinal receptors responsible for night vision and detection of motion in peripheral vision.**

Cones. **Receptor cells, especially in the central regions of the retina, which are differentially sensitive to colors.**

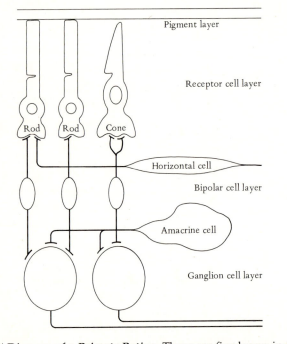

Figure 4.2 / *Diagram of a Primate Retina.* There are five layers in the retina, three for transmission of signals, and two between them for integration. First, in the depths of the eye, facing the rear wall of the eyeball, are the visual receptors: rods for night and peripheral vision, cones for daytime, sharp, foveal vision and color registration. Their excitation is picked up by the bipolar cells, which in turn transmit their excitation to the ganglion cells, whose axons form the optic nerve passing to the brain. Between the receptors and the bipolar cells is an outer plexiform layer where horizontal cells make multiple contacts with the receptors, controlling their responsiveness to light in relation to the activity of immediately surrounding receptors. Between the bipolar cells and the ganglion cells is an inner plexiform layer where amacrine cells make multiple contacts with the ganglion cells and exert control over their firing rate. Signals from the ganglion cells are transmitted to the brain.

eral portions of the retina. The cones are specialized for daytime vision and are differentially responsive to colors, making color vision possible. They are more heavily concentrated in the central region of the retina; at the *fovea,* the point of maximum visual acuity (see Figure 4.1), only cones are found. There are three types of cone receptor cells preferentially sensitive to red, green, and blue light respectively. It was long assumed that we are totally colorblind in our peripheral vision, and that the regions of the retina responsible for peripheral vision were populated exclusively by rods. It has recently been demonstrated (Wooten and Wald, 1973), however, that cones of all three color types are present throughout our peripheral retina. This finding is in keeping with our subjective impression that we do see colors across our entire visual field.

Fovea. **The portion of the retina providing central vision, with maximum visual acuity.**

But the receptor cells do not send their signals directly to the brain, as do some receptor cells in the skin mediating touch. Instead, the retina is a three-layered structure, as shown in Figure 4.2. The neurons that transmit signals to the brain are the *ganglion cells* of the topmost layer (where the incoming light strikes first). In between are the *bipolar cells,* which act as intermediaries. Incoming light penetrates the nearly transparent full depth of the retina to activate the rods and cones. Their response is transmitted by the bipolars to the ganglion cells, whose axons form the *optic nerve,* a stout cable of nerve fibers penetrating the rear of the eyeball and passing to the thalamus, for relay to the visual cortex. Thus we might conceive of the retina as a three-layered cortex (embryologically, it is in fact an extruded portion of the brain itself). Indeed, like the cerebral cortex, it exhibits a mosaic structure, each portion of its surface receiving light stimulation from a different patch within the visual field and processing it in relative independence of adjacent portions.

Ganglion cells. **Third-order cells of the retina, whose axons form the optic nerve.**

Bipolar cells. **Neurons whose input structures extend from one end and output from the other.**

Put more technically, each ganglion cell is said to have its own *receptive field,* corresponding to a small segment of the retina, and to respond to a particular segment of the very broad cone of light entering the eye from the *visual field.* In the foveal region, where vision is most acute, there is one ganglion cell for each receptor cell. Hence each has an extremely small receptive field, permitting a high degree of resolution. By contrast, the receptive fields of ganglion cells in the periphery of the retina are quite large and represent the combined response of many rod receptor cells, permitting at best only a poor resolution. In all, signals from 130 million receptor cells in each retina converge upon a bare million ganglion cells carrying messages back to the brain. Looked at differently, the entire visual field may be said to be divided up by the eye into segments, each segment handled by a different microprocessor in the

Receptive field. **The sensory field to which a portion of the receptor apparatus, or the sensory cortex, responds.**

retina consisting of columns of receptors, bipolars, and ganglion cells.

An additional complication must be mentioned. Between the receptor cells and the bipolars lies a layer of *horizontal cells* that interconnect the receptor cells at their synaptic junction with the bipolars (see Figure 4.2). Another kind of neuron, the *amacrine cells,* interconnects the ganglion cells at their synaptic junction with the bipolars. The function of these two *plexiform layers* within the retina will be discussed below.

This complex layering within the retina strongly suggests that the light streaming in continually from all portions of the visual field is in some way analyzed and transformed into a specific neural code for transmission to the next station in the thalamus. A first great step toward understanding this retinal mechanism was made by Kuffler (1953), who observed that there are two kinds of ganglion cells in the retina of the cat. One type tends to increase its firing rate when light falls on its particular receptive field. The other tends to be slowed, and produces a burst of action potentials when the light is turned off. Kuffler called these responses *on responses* and *off responses.* He also found that a retinal area that produces an on response is commonly associated with a surrounding area that produces off responses to stimulation. Similarly, a receptive field yielding off responses is surrounded by a ring of receptor cells producing on responses. (This pattern he termed *concentric organization.*) The maximum ganglion-cell response occurs when, for example, the tiny central area of the receptive field is entirely illuminated but no light shines on its peripheral field to produce competing off responses. Diffuse lighting of the entire retina produces only a minimal response anywhere, presumably because as many off as on responses are activated.

What Kuffler's experiment made clear is that something about the "wiring diagram" of the retina itself is designed to emphasize contrasts in illumination. Kuffler's findings have since been supported by further experiments (Rodieck and Stone, 1965). Recently Werblin (1972), studying the retina of the mudpuppy, *Necturus,* a type of salamander, found that the horizontal cells in the outer plexiform layer appear to produce *lateral inhibition* — an effect found throughout the cortex — whereby neural activity in one receptive field tends to damp neural activity in surrounding adjacent fields. The effect of such a wiring diagram is to suppress the activity of all but the most active receptive fields of a region at any given moment. Such a mechanism might account for the center–surround organization found by Kuffler in the cat retina. It is of interest that a simi-

On responses. Increased firing of retinal ganglion cells when a light stimulus strikes their retinal field.

Off responses. Cessation of ongoing responses of retinal ganglion cells when a light stimulus strikes their retinal field.

Lateral inhibition. Inhibition of surrounding neurons by neural activity in certain sensory receptor fields or cortical stations, serving to sharpen the signal.

lar contrast-enhancing lateral inhibitory mechanism is found in the monkey retina (a visual system much more similar to our own), as well as in the auditory and tactile sensory systems.

Werblin's analysis of this effect in the retina is very clear. Spreading laterally, the horizontal cells respond with graded electrotonic potentials to the average light intensity recorded by many receptor cells in the local receptive field upon which they synapse. They transmit this signal to the bipolar cells with which they are associated, controlling the latter's response in proportion to the average light level. The bipolar cell's response (also graded) to the receptor cell is thus modified by what is taking place in the surrounding receptors. When light shines only on the individual receptor, and not on its neighbors, its effect on the associated bipolar neuron is maximal. When it shines only on surrounding receptor cells, its response is suppressed, and its effect on its associated bipolar cell is minimal.

In the inner plexiform layer, however, where the bipolar cells synapse upon the ganglion cells, Werblin discovered another mechanism. One type of ganglion cell was found to generate action potentials only when the bipolar cells were "turning on" or "turning off," apparently responding to *change* in retinal illumination in their respective receptive fields. This effect Werblin attributed to the influence of the amacrine cells. Other ganglion cells of the "sustained-response" type are unaffected by the amacrine cells, merely passing on the center–surround light-contrast effect registered in the bipolar cells synapsing upon them. Analysis has shown that ganglion cells that respond to changes in retinal illumination have concentric receptive fields also responsive to change, mediated by the amacrine effect. When the experimental arrangement produces a rapidly changing light situation in the periphery of their receptive field, their response is suppressed. This phenomenon serves to register in the center of the receptive field of that ganglion cell the effect of changes in illumination in its small region of the retina, as differentiated from change over the whole retinal field, which might be the result of the animal's movement in relation to the entire background scene.

Another mechanism of the retina was revealed in Werblin's ingenious experiments. When the general level of illumination is raised — an average registered by the laterally disposed horizontal cells — the receptors' sensitivity to the light is reduced through a photochemical means not entirely clear. Thus the "exposure setting" of the photoreceptors automatically tends to adjust itself within the retina. In the case of the cones, the sensitivity curve was found to shift to a lower or higher sensitivity level in about five seconds, while the rods become inoperative at a certain point as the illumination increases.

Thus the eyeball, operating as a camera, adjusts its exposure level not only by altering the size of the aperture via the iris, but also by adjusting the sensitivity of the photosensitive "film" itself (Dowling and Werblin, 1969; Werblin and Dowling, 1969). While animals show many species differences in their retinal structure, with respect to the basic functions of their horizontal and amacrine cells the vertebrates are probably quite similar.

The Mechanism of the Visual Receptors

A good deal is now known about the physicochemical mechanisms through which the energy of light is translated into a neural signal (Wald, 1968), a process called *transduction*. It has long been known that a nutrient substance, vitamin A, is important to night vision. Wald discovered that a similar substance, eventually found to be the *aldehyde* of vitamin A, is present in the retina. Vitamin A is now called *retinol* in recognition of this association; its aldehyde, produced by its oxidation, is called *retinal*, (Figure 4.3). The actual photochemical substance was found by Wald and his associates to be a large molecule (the "visual pigment") consisting of two parts — a special *isomeric* form of retinal, and a much larger protein molecule called an *opsin*. One kind of opsin (rhodopsin) is found in the rods and mediates night vision; three other opsins are found in the cones, each responsive to a somewhat different portion of the light spectrum.

Light impinging on a photoreceptor cell in the retina has the effect of straightening the "kink" at the 11th carbon atom in the retinal (see Figure 4.3), changing it to an isomeric form that spontaneously dissociates itself from the opsin. This process is followed by a series of breakdown stages that occur automatically, resulting in a *hyperpolarization* of the receptor-cell membrane (how this occurs is not yet known). The original combined photosensitive molecule is then reconstituted. Each receptor-cell tip is thought to contain millions of these unstable molecules ready to be broken down by the action of incident light. A more intense beam of light means that a larger number of such unstable molecules will undergo the same isomeric shift to a more stable form, followed by dissociative breakdown and a greater hyperpolarization of the receptor cell's plasma membrane.

Transduction. The process through which the physical energy of the stimulus is translated into neural energy by the receptor cell.

Retinol. Vitamin A.

Retinal. The aldehyde of retinol, which in association with an opsin forms the visual pigment.

Opsin. A protein molecule attached to the retinal molecule to form a visual pigment, and detached therefrom temporarily in response to an appropriate light stimulus.

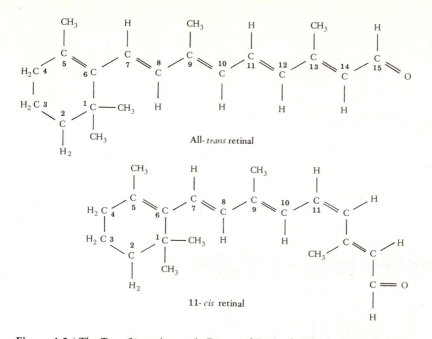

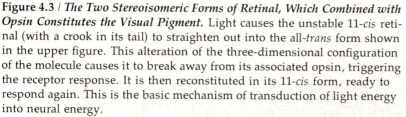

Figure 4.3 / *The Two Stereoisomeric Forms of Retinal, Which Combined with Opsin Constitutes the Visual Pigment.* Light causes the unstable 11-*cis* retinal (with a crook in its tail) to straighten out into the all-*trans* form shown in the upper figure. This alteration of the three-dimensional configuration of the molecule causes it to break away from its associated opsin, triggering the receptor response. It is then reconstituted in its 11-*cis* form, ready to respond again. This is the basic mechanism of transduction of light energy into neural energy.

Perhaps the paradoxical organization of the "inside-out" retinal structure, whereby light passes through the entire depth of the retina before reaching the photosensitive region, is thus clarified. One "reason" for this structure might be that the pigmented epithelial layer behind the retina is the source of the retinol used by the receptors. Retinol is apparently drawn into the receptors by the opsins as needed to form fresh visual pigment. The penalty is a small one: the ganglion cells, lying on the surface of the retinal tissue, have to send their axons across that surface to exit the eyeball together, at a point called the *optic disc* on the nasal (nose) side of the fovea; but these axons are unmyelinated, and hence quite translucent, until they form the optic nerve. Moreover, in the foveal region, where vision is acute, the "columns" of receptors, bipolars,

Optic disc. **The point on the retina where the ganglion cell axons plunge through to form the optic nerve, causing a blind spot.**

and related ganglion cells are all slanted radially away from the center, making this most important point on the retinal surface considerably thinner and more translucent.

Another apparent paradox is the fact that the receptor cells do not depolarize, as do normal neurons, when stimulated; instead they increase their polarity across their membrane. It is this hyperpolarizing effect that is transmitted to the bipolar and horizontal cells. Why this is so is not yet clear. However, neither receptor cells nor horizontals nor bipolars generate spike action potentials; they generate slow, degrading, electrotonic potentials only. At the inner plexiform layer, however, we find more normal neurons. Both amacrines and ganglion cells (the latter are the origins of the optic nerve) depolarize under appropriate stimulation, and the ganglion cells are capable of generating spike potentials. (The amacrines have no axons.)

One simple demonstration of retinal function and structure merits mention at this point. Where the axons of the ganglion cells converge and plunge through the rear wall of the eyeball to form the optic nerve, there are no receptor cells. Thus there is a small region of the eye's receptive field that is naturally blind. We can prove this by waggling a finger about 15 degrees to the side of the point of central focus. (Close one eye, look steadily ahead, and move one finger horizontally in from the periphery until it suddenly disappears.) Because the brain automatically "fills in" for the missing patch of light stimulation, as does the other eye when it is open, one could easily go a lifetime without noticing this blind spot.

Pathways to the Cortex

Each ganglion cell sends its single axonal fiber to the brain to represent visual events occurring in its particular region of the retina, which corresponds to a particular region of the visual field. Light entering the eye from the left half of the visual field passes through the lens and across to the right half of the retina of each eye; light from the right *hemifield* crosses to the left *hemiretina* of each eye. Similarly, what is above the point of focus in the visual field is "seen" by the lower portion of the retina and vice versa, due to the reversal as the light rays cross in the lens. We might say that the visual field is mapped onto the retina in this fashion, and that the map is somewhat distorted in the optic nerve by the denser concentration of ganglion cells in the foveal region. That central region, where object recognition is mediated, is more heavily represented in the signals passing to the brain.

Hemifield. **One half of the visual field to the left or right of the point of fixation of the gaze.**

Hemiretina. **One half of the retina to the right or left of the foveal region.**

Amazingly, despite a stopover along the way in the thalamic *lateral geniculate nucleus*, this retinal map with its spatial coordinates is preserved all the way back to the visual cortex, where each portion of the retina claims its own cortical field. This implies that, during formation of the brain before birth, the right connections were made in the lateral geniculate to insure that its neurons would project their axons to precisely the proper point in the occipital lobe cortex to replicate the original retinal spatial relationships there point for point. The lateral geniculate cells receive about a million ganglion cell axons, and pass on to the cortex approximately the same number of their own. However, this thalamic nucleus is no mere relay point, involving a single synapse. Quite the reverse appears to be true. Much reorganization of the retinal signals takes place here, but the retinal map is faithfully preserved through it all.

After passing over the surface of the retina and exiting the eyeball at the optic disc, the ganglion cell axons pass as a massive fiber bundle under the base of the brain to a point just anterior to the pituitary gland (see Figure 2.5) at the base of the hypothalamus, where the two optic nerves come together to form a crossover point for half of their fibers. This point is called the *optic chiasma* (from *chi*, the Greek letter χ). Here all the fibers from the nasal half of each retina — those that register the lateral half of each visual field — cross to the opposite hemisphere, while fibers from the temporal half of each retina, which register objects near the center of the visual field, remain on the same side of the brain (Figure 4.4). This newly assorted bundle of fibers (now called the *optic tract*, rather than the optic nerve) next enters the brain, most of its fibers going directly to the lateral geniculate nucleus of the thalamus, as shown in Figure 4.4.

Thus the orderly arrangement of fibers leaving the eyeball represents the spatial arrangement of the receptive fields of the retina. That orderly arrangement is preserved in the newly constituted optic tracts, each tract now representing one half of the visual field. All parts of the visual field lying to the right of the eyes' point of focus at any moment are represented in the contralateral, or left, optic tract; the visual field to the left of the point of focus is carried to the right brain. A close scrutiny of Figure 4.4 should make this quite clear: the right hemisphere of the brain looks with both eyes at the left half of the visual field; the left half of the brain sees through both eyes what is to the right of the point of central vision. This ingenious arrangement makes it possible for the whole field to be registered stereoscopically — that is, signals from both eyes being received in the same cortical tissues, with a perfect registration of the two maps from the two eyes.

Optic chiasma. **The crossover point of the optic nerve fibers from the nasal half of each retina.**

Optic tract. **Retinal ganglion cell fibers after they have passed the optic chiasma.**

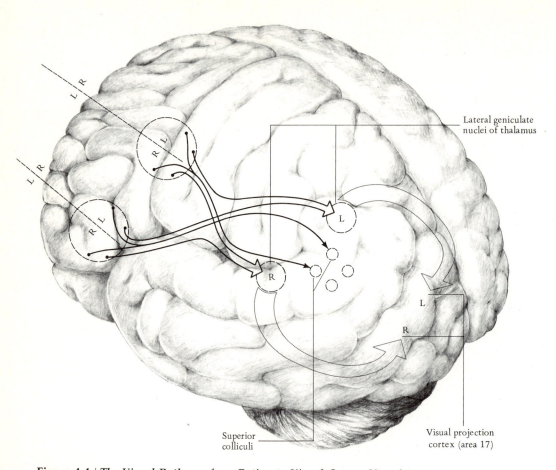

Lateral geniculate
nuclei of thalamus

Superior
colliculi

Visual projection
cortex (area 17)

Figure 4.4 / *The Visual Pathway from Retina to Visual Cortex.* Visual input from the right half of the visual field (R) for both eyes passes to the left side of the eyeball. The left hemiretinae project to the lateral geniculate nucleus of the left hemisphere, which relays the signal to the left visual cortex. Visual input from the left half of the visual field (L) reaches the right hemisphere visual cortex by a corresponding path. This entails the crossover, at the optic chiasma, of those fibers originating in the nasal half of each retina. Visual signals reaching the superior colliculus, however, undergo complete crossover of fibers at the chiasma.

The cortical map is centered along the *calcarine fissure* on the medial surface of the occipital lobe for each hemisphere (refer to Figure 2.6). The lower portion of the retina projects to the region of cortex below the fissure, and the upper half of the retina to the region above the fissure. Central (foveal) vision is represented posteriorly, and peripheral vision anteriorly. If some portion of this visual cortex is destroyed, such as due to a burst blood vessel, there will be a blind spot (scotoma) in both eyes in the corresponding portion of the visual field: in the left side if the damage is in the right hemisphere, below the visual horizon if it is above the fissure, more centrally if toward the rear, and so forth. Here we are referring to the organization of the cortex in area 17 on Brodmann's chart (Figure 2.8), which is the primary projection area, where the signals first enter the cortex, for vision.

Calcarine fissure. A deep fissure on the medial surface of the hemispheres, the site of arrival of visual signals in the cortex of the occipital lobe.

Mechanisms of Feature Detection

Before reaching the visual cortex, the visual signals carried by retinal ganglion-cell axons are first projected onto neurons in the lateral geniculate nucleus of the thalamus. Experimental analysis has shown that they synapse there in precisely ordered fashion.

It is of great interest that, after leaving the lateral geniculate, the entering visual signals have been reassorted in the projections to the cortex. The center–surround organization has now largely disappeared, replaced by a linear organization. Most of the cortical columns that receive the visual signals have been found to respond maximally not to points of light entering the eye, but to such line patterns as narrow slits of light, or dark bars, or straight-line edges between lighter and darker areas. Moreover, the columns in the visual projection area (area 17) are selectively responsive to linear stimuli oriented in a particular way — vertical, horizontal, or at some specific oblique angle — and when these lines are moving perpendicular to their orientation. The visual cortical columns are adapted, in short, to respond to edges and contours in the visual field moving laterally to their orientation. It is readily apparent that this kind of analysis of patterns in the visual field might well underlie our tendency to perceive objects as bounded by their contours, a tendency exploited by artists.

The studies of Hubel and Wiesel (1959, 1963, 1968) represent a classic experimental analysis of the visual system. By recording from electrodes penetrating the surface of the cortex of the cat, they found no cells with a concentric receptive field. The effective visual

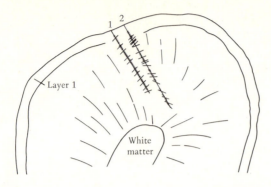

Figure 4.5 / *Preferred Orientation of Linear Visual Stimuli in Different Cortical Columns in the Visual Cortex.* A penetrating electrode (B) is shown passing from the surface of the cortex to the white matter below; the maximal response angle of visual stimuli remains constant to this point. When the electrode is inserted further, into other cortical columns, the preferred stimulus angle changes. Another electrode (A) is shown inserted diagonally so as to penetrate successively different columns; in this case the angle of preferred orientation becomes progressively greater. Such demonstrations suggest that local cortical regions contain cortical columns preferentially responsive to all angles of orientation of visual stimuli.

stimulus was in each case a contour-type linear form. By plunging the electrode deeper into the cortex perpendicular to the surface, it was determined that all cells in a particular cortical column are selectively tuned to respond preferentially to the same linear stimulus orientation and motion. When the electrode was inserted at an angle to the surface, so as to penetrate a succession of cortical columns, the cells encountered had progressively different preferred orientations and motions (Figure 4.5).

Some cells (*simple cells*) respond only when the stimulus is presented to their specific portion of the retina (their receptive field), increasing their firing rate only momentarily as the stimulus moves across it. Others (*complex cells*) continue to fire at a high rate as the stimulus moves across a wide area of the retina, as long as its linear orientation remains unchanged. This finding suggests that for these complex cells there is a *transcortical* (across the cortex) interconnection between columns that respond to the same orientation, making the particular location in the visual field irrelevant.

The same investigators also found *hypercomplex cells* in the adjoining area 18. These cells are peculiar in that they respond maximally only to linear stimulus patterns appropriately oriented but also terminating within the receptive field of their system (a too-

Simple cells. Neurons in the visual cortex selectively responsive to a particular linear orientation of the stimulus within their small receptive field.

Complex cells. Neurons in the visual cortex responding preferentially to a particular linear orientation of the stimulus as it is moved across the retinal field.

Hypercomplex cells. Neurons in the visual cortex responding maximally to linear stimuli of a given orientation, but only if the stimulus terminates within their receptive field.

extended line or edge elicits a reduced response). In the adjoining area 19, they also found cells of a *higher-order complex* type, maximally responsive only to visual stimuli characterized by an angle of particular orientation, especially to angles close to a right angle. Presumably these cells receive controlling input from cells of the hypercomplex type, which may in turn be presumed to interconnect with cells of the complex type, and so on. Each step in this sequence seems to correspond to a wave of excitation passing transcortically forward from area 17 to areas 18 and 19, which appears to translate the retinal input into ever-more-specific representational configurations.

More recent studies have greatly expanded our knowledge of this ingenious signal-analysis mechanism in the monkey cortex. Briefly, in a vertical column of cortex about a millimeter in diameter, comprising some hundred thousand neurons, are found both cells that respond to stimuli received differentially by the two eyes (*ocular dominance columns*) and cells responsive to 18 to 20 different orientation angles (*orientation columns*). To move horizontally across the surface of the cortex is to move from one area of the visual field to an adjoining one. The visual field is mapped into small receptive fields about three millimeters across, which together cover the entire left or right half-field, as the case may be (the right hemisphere covers the left half-field, and vice versa). To move from area 17 toward area 18 is to move from central toward peripheral visual-field representation; upon entering area 18, the map is mirror-reversed and one moves from peripheral toward central field. Presumably this meticulously ordered pattern of input to the cortex from the lateral geniculate nucleus is established through precise genetic coding, and is the same in all monkeys. We doubtless have a highly similar arrangement in our own cortex, permitting instant analysis of the patterns (contour-bounded areas) of our visual field. Significantly, signals from the two eyes retain their independence in transmission to the cortex, allowing for a comparison of what is seen from the two laterally displaced vantage-points.

Ocular dominance columns. Columns in the visual cortex selectively responsive to input from the two eyes which differs owing to the lateral displacement of the eyeballs, and correlated with object distance.

Orientation columns. Cortical columns in the visual cortex selectively responsive to a particular angle of orientation of the visual stimulus.

Mechanisms Underlying Stereoscopic Vision

Binocular input to the visual cortex is made use of for stereoscopic depth perception. (Recall that the signals from the two eyes are kept segregated in different layers of the lateral geniculate nucleus.) The horizontal displacement of the two eyes makes possible simultaneous viewing of the same three-dimensional object from subtly different angles, depending on its distance. In an ingenious experiment, Pettigrew (1972) discovered cortical neurons in the cat that responded preferentially not only to a stimulus with an appropriate linear orientation and movement, but also to a specific disparity in the horizontal positions of two images, one presented to each eye. When the degree of the disparity was changed, by placing a lens in front of one eye or by changing the distance of the visual stimulus, a marked diminution of the response occurred. This finding indicates an inhibitory effect when the two response fields in the cat's retina are "wrong" for that cell. The implication is that visual patterns are multiply represented in the visual cortex, allowing for cells responsive only to a highly specific lateral displacement of the pattern as viewed by the two eyes. In the foveal region this displacement of pattern, a function of the object's distance, can be very critical: as little as two degrees variation turns off a neuron's firing, and in the case of one neuron a change in disparity only one-sixtieth that large — two minutes of arc — was effective.

These were neurons in cortical columns of simple cells. Neurons of Hubel and Wiesel's complex type were found to respond to stimulus patterns over a wider range of the visual field (six degrees), but to be equally specific in their requirement of a certain horizontal disparity in the pattern received by the two eyes. Such a disparity-specific complex cell responds to a visual pattern moving across the retinas of the two eyes in a given orientation (such as a certain oblique angle) only if it is projected from an object at a given distance, so as to produce the appropriate specific difference in lateral position on the retinas at any given moment. Presumably our own visual cortex operates in a similar fashion, its disparity-specific cells permitting automatic and instantaneous judgment of the distance of objects in our not-too-distant surroundings, and thus providing us the rich experience of depth perception. Cues to an object's distance are also provided by the necessary convergence of the two eyes to bring the object to central focus (here there is no disparity effect) and by the lens accommodation required to bring it into clear focus. (At this point the cells responsive to specific lateral disparity would be telling us the distances of other objects in its vicinity.)

Mechanisms Underlying Motion Perception

The feature-detecting cells in the visual cortex that respond to linear stimuli tend to do so preferentially when such stimuli move perpendicularly to their orientation. Many of these neurons have also been found to have specific directional preferences, failing to respond to motion in the direction opposite to their preferred direction. Such a mechanism appears to be the basis of our sense of the directional movement of patterns across the visual field, and perhaps even of differentiation between motion of a pattern and of its background. How, though, do we distinguish between motion in the visual field and the visual displacement of patterns on the retina due to our own locomotion through the field, or by turning eyes or head as we scan the visual scene?

How the visual environment remains subjectively still as our eyes rove about, sampling its offerings, is a question that has always intrigued students of perception. The nature of the problem is clearly seen in the difference between the effect of moving our eye voluntarily and the bouncing scene that results when the eye is passively moved, such as by slight finger pressure on its corner. When we actively turn our head or eyes, some compensation occurs internally and automatically for the shift in retinal pattern that may be expected from such movement. This compensation mechanism, which renders the visual scene stationary, fails to occur when the eyes move due to some external influence. Ever since animals' eyes have shifted from point to point to establish successive visual directions, the brain has been confronted with the basic problem of maintaining the subjective stability of the visual field. The mechanism involved in its solution is unquestionably an ancient one.

It is not surprising, then, to discover mechanisms in the ancient brainstem centers to be involved in the handling of so primitive a necessity. A separate group of retinal ganglion-cell axons travels directly to the superior colliculus of the midbrain tectum — the modern, mammalian version of the *optic tectum* of lizards and birds responsible for all their visual functions. Since the evolution of the thalamocortical system, visual perceptual functions *per se* appear to have become withdrawn into the neocortex and its associated thalamic subcortical nuclei (the lateral geniculates). But other visual mechanisms underlying perception have remained in the midbrain structures, notably those involved in visual tracking and automatic foveal fixation.

The superior colliculus was once believed to be responsible for movement of the eyes, but it is now known that even total bilateral removal of the colliculi does not eliminate eye movements. What an operation of this kind does, in the cat, is to make it impossible to locate small objects in the field and to follow them visually. The animal's ability to localize objects in space gradually improves after the operation, but never returns to normal. Electrical stimulation of the superior colliculus in the monkey, however, has been found to produce eye movements of a specific distance and direction, depending on the location of the electrode.

A study reported by Gordon (1976) did for the superior colliculus of the cat what Hubel and Wiesel had done for the visual cortex: namely, to map out the collicular receptive fields. The experimenters found that most of the collicular cells responded only to moving stimuli in their receptive fields; stationary stimuli flashing on and off had no effect. Most of the cells were also found to be directionally sensitive, specifically to stimuli moving away from the center of gaze toward the peripheral field. Other investigators have found a similar phenomenon with regard to vertical movements: cells responsive to stimuli in the lower portion of the field respond maximally to stimuli moving downward, while those responding to stimuli in the upper portion of the field are sensitive to upward motion. In each case the most effective stimuli were those moving away from central vision, which includes all stationary stimuli as the animal advances through the field, as well as objects (prey) leaving the field and requiring head and eye movement to keep them fixated in the field. (Keep in mind that these studies were done on the cat, a predatory animal.) A similar mechanism might well underlie our own perception of object motion, as well as our own bodily motion through the perceptual field.

Gordon and her associates made another significant discovery: that the cells of the superior colliculus lose their directional sensitivity when the cat's visual cortex is removed. Furthermore, all collicular cells then respond only to stimuli reaching the contralateral eye, confirming the anatomical findings that most of the fibers from the retina to the midbrain do a crossover at the optic chiasma (as shown in Figure 4.4) and that the superior colliculus receives input from the visual cortex. Without that cortical input, the motion-detection cells of the superior colliculus become inoperative. Why this is so is not clear. Also noteworthy is the fact that no similar directionally sensitive system can be found in the colliculus of the monkey (Wurtz and Goldberg, 1972). Monkey collicular cells do not seem to require a moving stimulus — a species difference whose significance is not at present understood. Is it that cats are stalkers and chasers, or simply that the process of encephalization (corticalization) of functions has proceeded further in the primates? Though the question of human collicular function with regard to motion perception is unanswered, studies of the type described above suggest that our visual motion perception may still be dependent, at least in part, on this brainstem structure and its surviving functions.

Bizzi and his associates have implicated another primitive structure — the vestibular mechanism of the inner ear, responsible for the sense of balance — in normal eye-head coordination in monkeys in the course of visually fixing a target through saccadic eye movement (Bizzi, 1976). (A *saccade* is a sudden swift turn of the eyeball whose direction and extent is determined at its start. Such movement is characterized as ballistic, resembling a thrown ball, in contrast with movement controlled from beginning to end.) When signals from the vestibular mechanism are cut off, Bizzi found, the normally finely controlled saccade of the monkey's eyes in fixing on a target exhibit a consistent overshoot, failing to accommodate to the fact that the head is also turning toward the target. Head motion sensed by the vestibular system is also involved in the *vestibulo-ocular reflex*, demonstrated when we turn our head but keep our eyes fixed on a stationary target. The remarkable smoothness with which the eyes compensate for head movement to stabilize our gaze is attributable to signals sent from the semicircular canals of the inner ear to the oculomotor centers in the brainstem.

Yet another ancient brain structure, the cerebellum, is important in the *smooth-pursuit system* whereby our eyes automatically keep a moving target fixed in central vision — an action contrasting strikingly with the sudden-jerk, ballistic saccadic movement. In smooth pursuit, Miles and Fuller (1975) have demonstrated in experiments on the monkey that the *flocculus,* a very primitive portion of the cerebellum, uses visual, vestibular, and oculomotor input to construct a "velocity profile" of the target being tracked, following the saccade with which it was first fixed in foveal vision.

Recently special cells have been found in the visual cortex of the cat that project fibers into a small region of the pons, where they synapse upon pontine neurons responding maximally to a particular direction and speed on the part of the visual target. These pontine cells lie in a region that sends its fibers into the cerebellum. Some respond maximally to single spots, and might be thought of as specialized to follow the flight of a small animal. Others respond maximally to larger textured field stimuli, with a preference for stimuli moving downward or laterally. These cells are presumably specialized for recording the direction of visual movement of the ground or other background features as the viewer animal moves through its environment, thus monitoring its own motion. Interestingly, the pontine cells responsive to visual stimuli in the foveal region, where object discrimination is best, tend to receive their input from corticopontine cells in the visual association area 18, while those responding to visual stimuli in the peripheral field tend to receive their input from corticopontine cells in the primary visual

Saccade. A sudden swift movement of the eyeball in fixing upon a target.

Vestibulo-ocular reflex. The effect upon eyeball turning caused by a turning of the head in the course of fixing the gaze upon a target, the head turning being registered by the vestibular system.

Smooth-pursuit system. The eye-movement control system employed in visual tracking of a moving target.

Flocculus. The midline portion of the cerebellum concerned with postural reflexes.

projection area, area 17. This arangement might be expected if object perception indeed occurs in connection with activities in the visual association cortex.

It is clear from such animal studies that a number of regions of the brain provide the neural basis for visual motion perception. Werblin found the retina itself, in its amacrine cells, responsive in such a way as to distinguish between background motion and the motion of a stimulus in relation to its background. In the visual cortex were found cells specifically sensitive to linear stimuli moving perpendicular to their orientation, and often directionally sensitive as well. In the superior colliculus, neurons were found that respond only to visual stimuli in motion across the retina, most of them maximally sensitive to a specific direction toward the periphery. Cerebellar cells found in the floccular region respond in a precise manner to the speed of motion of a visual stimulus. Other neurons in the pons firing into the cerebellum respond to the movement, either of spots or of textured fields, and receive input from areas 18 and 17 of the cortex. No doubt these and other neurons will be found to belong to a complex integrated system governing not only saccadic target acquisition and smooth-pursuit following but also perceived motion of objects in the field, either local motion across the stationary background or field motion due to the viewer's own movement through the environment.

Mechanisms Underlying Color Perception

How we see colors is a question that has intrigued psychologists for many years. Originally limited to deductions from behavioral data, the analysis of sensory qualities has been revolutionized by the electrophysiological and anatomical techniques that are now making possible solid biological understanding.

Briefly, the postulated existence of three different kinds of cone receptors in the retina has recently been supported, for both human and monkey visual systems, with very comparable experimental results. The technique, called microspectrophotometric measurement, involves passing a tiny beam of light (in reverse direction through a microscope) through a single cone cell extracted from a human or monkey retina immediately after death. By comparing the light absorbed by the cone with equivalent light that did not pass through it, a "difference spectrum" can be obtained, specifying the light wavelengths that had been absorbed and, by inference, the wavelengths to which the cone responded in life. Figure 4.6 depicts

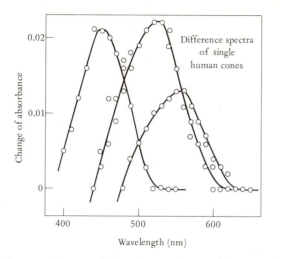

Figure 4.6 / *Response Curves of Three Types of Human Cone Cells to Light of Different Wavelengths (Brown and Wald, 1964).* The experiment described in the text demonstrates that there are indeed three types of color-sensitive receptors in the human retina. One is maximally sensitive to red light (the curve on the left), one to blue light (the curve on the right), and the other to green (the tall curve in the middle). Note, however, that each type of cell responds to a fairly broad spectrum around its preferred color and that the cells' sensitivities broadly overlap. Still unanswered is the question of how those of us who differentiate colors clearly, in countless shades, do so on the basis of just three relatively crudely discriminating types of cone cell. An interesting fact is that with these three cone types the eye can register a great many colors, such as purple and brown, not found in the spectrum of white light.

the findings of these two very comparable experiments, performed nearly simultaneously by two groups unaware of each other's work (Brown and Wald, 1964; Marks, Dobelle, and MacNichol, 1964).

While these results are based on a very small sampling of receptor cells, they are sufficient to clinch the argument. There are indeed three kinds of cone receptors, each maximally sensitive to a particular range of wavelengths of light in areas we subjectively perceive as red, green, and blue. This finding runs counter to the theory that there should be four kinds — red opposed to green and blue opposed to yellow — which had been postulated (the "opponent theory" of color perception). In 1968 the matter was partially cleared up when Gouras, studying the relatively easily recorded signals from ganglion cells in the monkey, found not only concentric organization (center-surround opposition) but also that some ganglion cells respond "on" to red light but "off" to green, and others just the reverse. Still other cells seemed to respond in the simple trichromatic fashion, responding to red, green, or blue light, more or less intensely as the stimulus approached the center of the cell's receptive field.

DeValois and his associates performed an intensive study of color responses in the lateral geniculate nucleus of the monkey (DeValois and Jacobs, 1968). They discovered one group of cells that responds to red by increasing its steady firing rate, and to green by ceasing to fire (red$^+$, green$^-$); another group of cells responds in the opposite fashion (red$^-$, green$^+$). A third group responds with an increased firing rate to a yellow stimulus and a decreased rate to blue (yellow$^+$, blue$^-$), and a fourth group does just the opposite (yellow$^-$, blue$^+$). These cells were termed *opponent color* cells. Another group of geniculate neurons, which either increases or decreases their steady firing rate as stimulus flashes move over the color spectrum, increasing or decreasing their response over the middle range of the spectrum, were termed *nonopponent excitators* and *nonopponent inhibitors*. The typical sensitivity curves of these six types of lateral geniculate cells are shown in Figure 4.7.

Wiesel and Hubel (1966) also studied monkey lateral geniculate neurons, questioning whether they all coded in a center–surround spatial organization as well as being responsive in an opponent-color fashion, or whether spatial and color-coding functions were performed by different neurons. They found that most cells are responsive to both color and spatial factors, but that there are four different types — some maximally responsive to one color at the center of their receptive field and to its antagonist in their surround; some exhibiting concentric organization but response only to one color; some manifesting no center–surround organization but opponent-color response over their entire receptive field; and others exhibiting center–surround organization and a surround unresponsive to the antagonist but always responsive to a longer

Figure 4.7 / *Response Curves of Six Types of Lateral Geniculate Neurons (DeValois and Jacobs, 1968).* Six different types of response to color stimuli can be found at the level of the lateral geniculate nucleus of the thalamus. They are typified by these response patterns. Four of the six types respond oppositely to yellow and blue or to red and green light, whereas in the retina there are only three types of cones responding preferentially to red, blue, and green. At present it is unknown how the opponent-color system found at the lateral geniculate nucleus and at the visual cortex is generated from these three cone receptors.

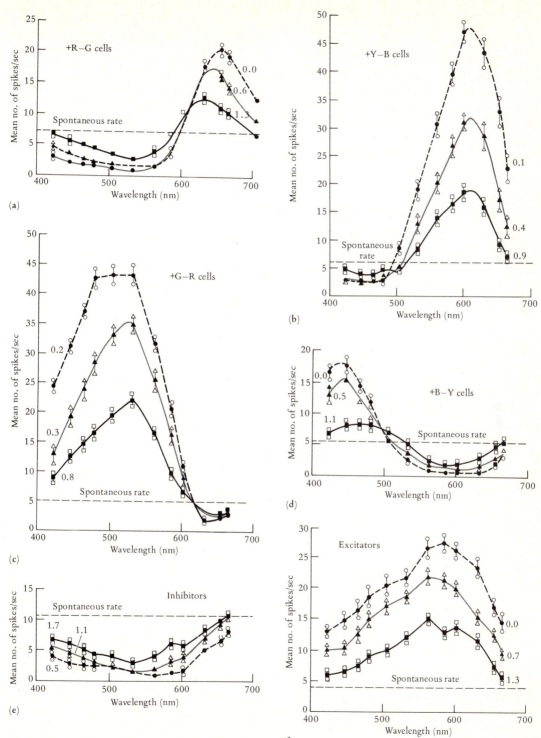

wavelength (toward the red end of the spectrum). The coding system for color at the thalamic level is thus quite complex.

In the visual cortex, Motokawa, Taira, and Okuda (1962) found some cells responding as do the retinal receptors, only to red, green, or blue light. However, they also found cells exhibiting opponent-type responses, and others that conformed to neither the retinal nor the lateral geniculate nucleus pattern. In these studies, microelectrodes were inserted through the monkey skull into the visual cortex to record extracellularly from single neurons.

In sum, it is clear that the cone receptors themselves respond differentially to three portions of the visible spectrum, substantiating the old trichromatic theory of color vision. On the other hand, many modifications are introduced in the ascending pathway from receptor cell to cortex, including a prevalence of opponent red-green and blue-yellow coding at the ganglion-cell and geniculate-neuron levels. The visual cortex apparently makes use of both coding systems. While it is evident that there must be three different cone opsins to generate this spectral preference, they have not yet been differentiated chemically. Nor do we yet have evidence of how their retinal-opsin link happens to be maximally sensitive to breakdown under a particular wavelength of light, or how, when the dissociation occurs, the hyperpolarization of the cell membrane (the receptor potential) is generated.

Some individuals are born with a faulty retina that responds as if its cones could not differentiate colors at all. This type of colorblind person is called a monochromat. Others have difficulty responding to reds (protanopes), greens (deuteranopes), or blue-yellow differentiation (tritanopes). Some people merely have somewhat diminished sensitivity to color, though they are not colorblind. Presumably these visual defects have to do with a failure of the receptors to produce the normal opsins in sufficient quantity.

Where Does Visual Experience Occur?

There is a curious kind of evidence suggesting that, while the visual projection cortex (area 17) may be necessary to perceptual learning, it is not necessary to object discrimination afterward. On the other hand, it does appear to be necessary to conscious awareness of seeing a familiar object. People who have suffered damage to area 17 experience regions of blindness (scotomas) in those portions of the visual field whose patterns are projected to the damaged cortical tissues. When a simple stimulus pattern, such as an X or O, is presented to this blind region, the subject has no conscious awareness of the stimulus but can make an appropriate response to it, demonstrating visual discrimination of the difference (Weiskrantz, Warrington, Sanders, and Marshall, 1974). It must be inferred that those cortical regions that "recognize" the stimulus, presumably including areas 18 and 19, are incapable of mediating conscious awareness of the stimulus in the absence of the area 17 activation. (Signals are sent from the lateral geniculate to areas 18 and 19, as well as to area 17.) As Weiskrantz reports, "When the patient was asked to guess whether a line flashed in his blind field was horizontal or vertical, he 'guessed' almost perfectly, maintaining each time that he was unable to see the stick. This ability might be called 'blindsight' " (Weiskrantz, 1977, p. 345).

It had already been discovered that even a total ablation of the visual projection area in the monkey does not prevent discriminations based on either color or pattern, as long as visual association cortex is spared (Pasik, Pasik, and Schilder, 1969; Schilder, Pasik, and Pasik, 1972). Thus the recognition process, however it occurs, appears to be more closely associated with association cortex, but this apparently does not imply conscious experience of the stimulus.

When the human skull is opened in preparation for brain surgery, stimulation of the cortex with a mild electric current can locate the precise area of difficulty and, at the same time, tell us something about cortical localization of function. If the electrode touches area 17, the patient is apt to report an unformed visual sensation, such as a flash of light or a color. If area 18 is stimulated, the response is apt to be a perceptual image, such as a butterfly — demonstrating the activation of an interpretive function. Furthermore, it has long been known from clinical studies of people with cerebral damage that destruction of the parietal visual areas (areas 18, 19, and 7 on the lateral convexity of the brain) frequently results in *visual agnosia,* the inability to recognize (or name) a previously familiar object. The classic monograph on the parietal lobe function is Critchley's (1953).

Visual agnosia. A neurological disorder characterized by inability to recognize familiar objects by sight.

Luria (1976) has described in great analytic detail the kinds of failure of object recognition that result from lesions of the parietal-occipital visual association cortex. Such patients can characteristically still describe individual features or parts of objects, but fail to combine these individual impressions into complete patterns. A patient shown a picture of a pair of spectacles might first notice two circles, then a cross-bar joining them, and conclude that it must be a bicycle. A picture of a rooster with variously colored tailfeathers might be interpreted as a fire, the tailfeathers seen as flames. A dial telephone might be taken for a clock, or a brown couch for a trunk. An integrative function that normally produces perceptual recognition is missing, though the visual apparatus more peripheral to that region is intact. It is interesting that such patients can instantly recognize such visually unrecognizable objects by touch, and that their intelligence in other respects seems quite unimpaired. Prior to touching the object, their visual awareness is not of a known object — a kind of psychic blindness. We can infer that these posterior general-association cortical regions are in some way critically involved in the phenomenon of visual experience, though just how is not yet understood.

Gross and his colleagues (1972) conducted a most interesting series of investigations of the function of the *inferotemporal lobe* cortex in the monkey, recording the responses of single cells to various stimuli. Certain neurons were found to have a quite astonishing specificity in their preferred stimulus pattern. Such neurons vigorously responded only to specific complex object shapes, even in one case the silhouette of a monkey's hand, as demonstrated by a rank-ordering of the responses of that neuron to a number of stimuli more or less resembling a hand-like silhouette.

Inferotemporal lobe cortex. **The inferior portion of the temporal lobe neocortex, roughly comprising Brodmann's areas 37 and 21.**

It is of interest that many of these cells clearly preferred three-dimensional stimuli, rather than two-dimensional versions of them. Luria's study of patients suffering from visual agnosia also revealed them to be far less capable of object recognition in response to a picture or a silhouette than when the object is presented in three-dimensional form. The same principle characterizes the visual responses of infants (Bower, 1979). Apparently, simpler is not easier: contrary to what is sometimes supposed, visual experience is most vivid when the stimulus is the real object in all its complexity, rather than a simple abstraction. The underlying neurophysiology of our experience of *object constancy* is still unanalyzed, but — despite the "monkey's hand" cell discovered by Gross and his associates — it may be presumed to involve vastly complex neuronal circuitry.

As we move inward from the retina to the lateral geniculate nucleus and superior colliculus, on into the visual projection area, and still further into areas 18 and 19 and the inferotemporal cortex, specific information is lost along the way as the manner of its coding is changed at each stage. However, another kind of specificity begins to enter in — interpretive specificity. By the time we reach the "highest" levels of the visual system, what was little more than mechanical linkage in the periphery becomes meaningful perceptual experience, presumably based on neural connectivities forged

Object constancy. **The tendency of objects to continue to be perceived as of the same shape even though the retinal pattern they present changes when they are viewed from a different position.**

during prior experience. There is no one-to-one correspondence between the response of a receptor cell and anything measurable happening in the inferotemporal cortex. We must obviously think in terms of the concerted activities of great numbers of neurons, both in the ascending channels and spread across the cortical columns in a pattern of interactions.

The visual projection cortex (where scotomas are produced) feeds back to the lateral geniculate nucleus, and appears to in some way modulate its own input at the same time it is flashing signals to its neighboring association cortex (areas 18, 19, 37, 21, and 7, on Brodmann's chart). These areas in turn are in reciprocal intercommunication with two massive thalamic nuclei above the lateral geniculate — namely, the lateral posterior and the pulvinar. All of these structures together comprise the great thalamocortical subsystem concerned with visual functions. It is safe to assume that awareness of visual experience depends on neural activity throughout these immensely intricate interlocking circuitries. As we begin to discover the "wiring diagram," it will be important to keep in mind that momentary visual experience, like all other visual experiences, has a unitary character. The activities of these myriad neurons, or some specific portion of them, issue as a single visual experience of something in the world-out-there — such as a flower, in all its multidimensional qualities of three-dimensionality, color, and form, all contained within the instantaneous visual impression — which passes into the next impression and the next, in endless sequence, on which the attention is focused.

The question is: how do we manage to focus our attention, much as we focus our eyes, on just one thing at a time, damping all other circuits at least for the brief moment that belongs exclusively to that flower?

Summary

Light entering the eye penetrates the retina to the receptor-cell layer in its depths, where the rods and cones are arrayed like a photosensitive film exposing some 130 million points, each responsible for detecting light stimuli in a specific portion of the visual field. The receptors respond only to changes in incident light, due either to the movement of objects within the field or to the observer's movement through a stationary field. The effect of the changed stimulus is to hyperpolarize the receptor-cell membrane. This occurs as the result of breakdown of the visual pigment molecule: rhodopsin, in the case of the rods; for each of the three types of cones, a special opsin preferentially responsive to red, green, or blue light. The hyperpolarization of the receptor-cell membrane is the receptor potential, which, transmitted to the bipolar cells, begins a long chain of neural interactions resulting in vision. The mechanism of transduction itself has been found to be associated with the dissociation of the opsin part of the visual pigment from the retinal molecule, an aldehyde of vitamin A. Once the dissociation occurs (in a series of steps), the visual pigment must be reconstituted before it is again reusable.

Receptor cells and bipolar cells do not, like normal neurons, produce a spike action potential. Their slow, degrading electrotonic potential may be attributable to the short distances signals travel within the retina. The same is true of the horizontal cells, which interconnect receptor cells at the junction with the bipolars, providing for lateral inhibition (contrast accentuation) as well as adjustment of the receptor's sensitivity to flux in ambient light. The bipolar cell synapses with a ganglion cell, a normal neuron that sends its axon through the optic nerve and tract to the thalamus and midbrain, producing spike action potentials. The synaptic junction of the bipolar cell with the ganglion cell is modulated by the amacrine cells, which appear to be specifically responsive to the motion of the stimulus pattern across the retinal fields.

The ganglion cells' retinal fields are characterized by a concentric (center–surround) organization. Some respond maximally when the center of their field is stimulated but are inhibited by light falling on their immediate surrounding receptors; others are just the opposite. Some 130 million receptor cells are served by only one million ganglion cells in each optic nerve. In the foveal region, where vision is most acute, there is a one-to-one relation between receptor and ganglion cell; in the peripheral regions, particularly the far peripheral rod regions, there is a convergence of many receptors upon one ganglion cell. This pattern makes for increased sensitivity to dim light (such as at night) but degraded resolution of the field.

Ganglion-cell axons from the nasal half of each retina cross to the opposite hemisphere at the optic chiasma before passing to the lateral geniculate nucleus with their partners from the other eye. Thus the visual field to the right of the point of central vision at any given moment is represented in the left hemisphere, and all stimuli to its left are represented in the right hemisphere. In consequence, each hemisphere receives corresponding stimuli from the two eyes, permitting stereoscopic depth perception through neurons in the cortex sensitive to the lateral disparity of the input from the two eyes. Upon reaching the geniculate nucleus, these signals from the two eyes are kept separate, synapsing in different layers. Each set relays to precisely the same cortical "map" of the retina in area 17.

At the cortical level, visual signals have a predominantly linear, not concentric, organization of receptive field. There are cortical columns in area 17 all of whose cells respond only to visual stimuli corresponding to the contour edges of objects (bright slits, dark bars, straight edges between light and dark areas) oriented at a particular angle (horizontal, vertical, or some specific oblique angle) and moving perpendicularly to that orientation; these are the so-called simple cells. In areas 18 and 19 especially, columns are found whose neurons all respond maximally to such stimuli anywhere in the visual field (complex cells), or to angles between such linear patterns in a particular orientation (higher-order complex cells), or only to linear patterns of a limited length (hypercomplex cells). At the "highest" cortical level in the inferotemporal cortex, neurons have been found that respond maximally to even more discrete patterns, such as (in the case of the monkey) the silhouette of a monkey hand.

Motion perception and the normal stability of the visual field as the observer, or the eyes and head, moves appear to be mediated by a wide range of interrelated mechanisms. The retina itself has amacrines apparently responding specifically to degrees of motion. The superior colliculus in the midbrain tectum receives a separate set of optic-nerve fibers. The vestibular mechanism and its associated cerebellar region, the flocculus, are involved. The pons receives fibers from the visual cortex, which synapse upon pontine neurons responding maximally to a particular direction and speed of motion of the visual target (these cells appear also to project fibers into the cerebellum). The visual cortex, finally, has many columns of neurons responding maximally not only to motion of linear patterns, but frequently to specific direction as well.

Color perception combines two principles: a concentrically organized tricolor system, based on the three types of retinal cones; and an opponent-color system in which red-green and yellow-blue take the place of dark-light, one color of the pair damping the effect of the other. Individuals whose retinas fail to produce the normal cone opsins have varying degrees and types of color blindness.

Clinical studies of individuals who have suffered damage to area 17 suggest that this cortical region is necessary to the conscious experience of visual perception, though the individual may still be able to discriminate, and behave adaptively in response to, stimuli falling in the damaged region. Damage to cortical areas 18, 19, and 7 in the parietal lobe tends to produce a different phenomenon, awareness of but inability to identify an object, though it may be instantly familiar to the touch. Thus, while the visual projection area (area 17) may be necessary to conscious perceptual experience as such, regions in the association areas of the cortex are requisite to the full experience of discriminative perception.

Chapter 5 / *Auditory Perception: Communication and Event Monitoring*

Auditory perception provides us a means of continuously monitoring events in our environment, from whatever direction, as well as the possibility of language reception and production. Sound waves entering the auditory canal vibrate the eardrum. These vibrations are in turn transmitted, much amplified in force, to the oval window of the cochlea of the inner ear (the auditory receptor system). Hair cells lining the basilar membrane in the cochlea operate as receptors, responding to its motion. Contrary to intuitive expectation, low-pitched sounds are registered at the small end of the spiral tapering cochlear cavity and high-pitched sounds at the large end near the oval window. These pitches are ultimately registered in the auditory-projection cortex atop the temporal lobe (Heschl's gyri) in an orderly progression from the lateral to the medial end, like keys on a piano (tonotopic registration). The ascending pathways are quite complex, a majority of the fibers crossing to the contralateral hemisphere. Sound localization depends in part on the fact that sound waves reach the two ears at slightly different times and intensities, which are then compared within the brain. Some evidence suggests that the human brain at infancy is peculiarly sensitive to speech sounds, which in maturity the left hemisphere is specially adapted to deciphering.

The auditory system might well be considered more important than vision in the human being, owing to the importance of hearing in the development and use of language. Indeed, many deaf people maintain that they would rather be blind.

Sounds arrive at our ears continuously, some loud, some faint, from many directions. Each sound has a unique character, on the basis of which the sophisticated brain can identify the source of each of them, and frequently its precise direction as well. The question we shall ask, and partially answer, in this chapter is how such a thing is possible. In the simplest terms, we can say that the brain "recognizes" the specific pattern of sound-wave frequencies of an astonishing number of sources of sound.

If there is any justification for considering hearing less important than seeing, it is that only certain objects emit sounds, whereas all reflect or transmit light. Thus the sheer number of things that can be heard is smaller than of those that can be seen. On the other hand, vision is handicapped at night, while sound can be heard equally well twenty-four hours a day. Most important is that hearing brings us the spoken word, and for most people *ambient speech* is much more prevalent than printed words.

Hearing, like seeing, is a means of detecting things at a distance. Because sound waves lose much of their force through the inertia of air particles, they do not travel as far as light waves. Our perceptual systems range in scope from vision, the most far-reaching, through sound and smell to touch and taste, which require physical contact with the stimulus. Of all these, the auditory system seems most suited to the task of monitoring occurrences going on around us, in the periphery of our attention, while we focus our gaze and attention on matters of immediate concern. With our ears, in other words, we can keep track of what is going on around us without bothering to turn our heads and look. As we shall see, auditory impulses pass into the reticular system of the brainstem — alerting us to any noteworthy noise — even before they reach the cortex and thus consciousness. By contrast, visual signals go to the cortex first, and then to the reticular activating systems.

In order to understand the auditory system's special mode of functioning, let us first examine in detail its anatomic structure.

Figure 5.1 / *The Ascending Auditory Pathways.* In this cross section through the plane of the ears, the auditory pathways for one ear only are shown. Sounds reaching the eardrum are transmitted with magnified force to the cochlea, a coiled tube along whose length lie the auditory receptor cells. The auditory nerve (2) transmits the cochlear signals to the cochlear nuclei (3) in the medulla. From there, three pathways cross to the opposite side of the brain, while only one transmits signals to the cortex of its own hemisphere. Note that both paths send collateral fibers into the reticular formation before reaching the inferior colliculi in the midbrain tectum. From the colliculi (5) the signals go to the medial geniculate nuclei of the thalamus (6), which relay them to the auditory cortices atop the temporal lobe. High-pitch sounds are registered there at the medial end of Heschl's gyrus.

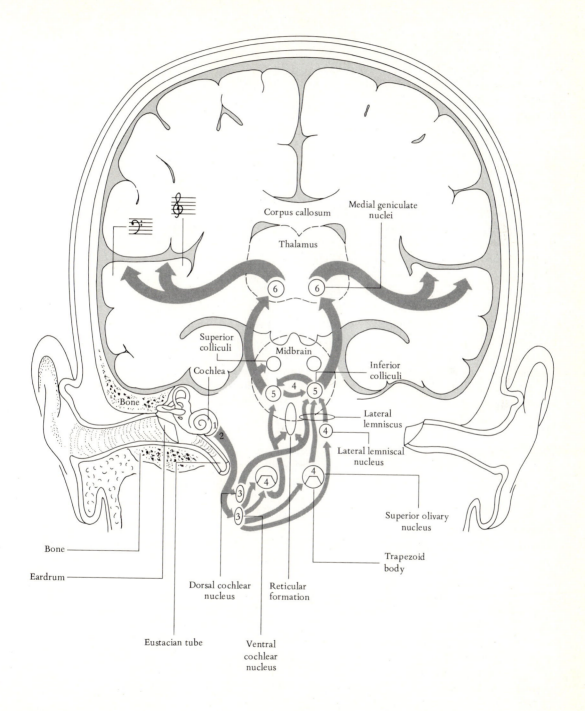

Corpus callosum

Medial geniculate
nuclei

Thalamus

Superior
colliculi

Cochlea

Midbrain

Inferior
colliculi

Bone

Lateral
lemniscus

Lateral lemniscal
nucleus

Superior olivary
nucleus

Trapezoid
body

Bone

Eardrum

Dorsal cochlear
nucleus

Reticular
formation

Eustacian tube

Ventral
cochlear
nucleus

The Structures of the Ear

Figure 5.1 depicts an imaginary cross section through the skull at the plane of the ear. Note that the auditory canal (*external auditory meatus*) extends well into the head below the bony shelf on which the temporal lobe of the brain rests. It is closed at the inner end by the eardrum (*tympanic membrane*), a thin but sturdy sheet of tissue that vibrates in time with the sound waves entering the ear canal. This vibration is transmitted to the inner ear by three tiny middle-ear bones (the *ossicles*), arranged lever-wise in such a way that they greatly amplify the force of the vibrations while reducing their amplitude. At the inner end of this mechanism of three interconnected bones, the vibrations are transmitted to a much more delicate membrane covering the *oval window* of the *cochlea,* a spiral-shaped hollow or cavity within the bony mass of the skull. Inside this fluid-filled cavity in the bone, shaped like the spiral of a tiny sea shell, the auditory mechanism resides. A second membrane-covered opening in the bone, the *round window,* permits the (incompressible) fluid to flow through the length of the spiral chamber and back by another route to the large end, as shown in Figure 5.2.

Consider first the external ear, or *pinna.* Many mammals (deer, rhinoceroses, even dogs and cats to some extent) have external ears that operate as directional horns, turning toward the source of a sound to improve reception. They amplify sound waves from the direction toward which the ear is turned and damp out sound waves coming from other directions. The human ear, like those of primates generally, is relatively immobile and shaped like a very flat horn; its baffles break up entering sound waves in such a way as to give minimal advantage to sounds coming from a specific direction. As any engineer would attest, it is suited to a mode of directional detection quite different from that of the rhinoceros ear (Figure 5.3).

Though quite nondirectional, the human external ear nevertheless serves as a horn, gathering sound waves from a cross-sectional area much larger than the opening into the auditory canal itself. The ear canal into which sound waves are funneled is itself an almost straight tubular passage, slightly swelling at the interior (the very opposite of a horn). The length of the canal prevents sound waves from striking the eardrum at any angle other than that to which it is designed to respond.

The eardrum is attached at its middle to the first of the ossicles, the *malleus* (hammer), which draws it inward under tension into a flat cone resembling the diaphragm of an electronic speaker. The

Oval window. The cochlear aperture receiving sound stimulation from the eardrum via the ossicles.

Cochlea (KOE-*klee-a*). A spiralling hollow tube in the temporal bone housing the auditory receptor mechanism.

Round window. A second membrane-covered opening in the cochlea permitting flow of the perilymph through the cochlear canal.

Pinna. The external ear.

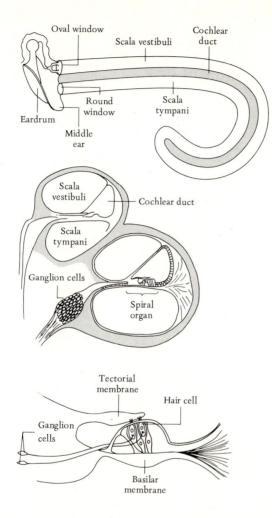

Figure 5.2 / *Cross Section of the Cochlea.* The receptor cells for sound lie along the basilar membrane, which winds through the approximately two and one-half turns of the hollow, spiralling cochlear canal. Vibrations reaching the oval window from the ossicles set the basilar membrane into a waving motion, which is thought responsible for the hair-cell stimulation. Through a still unknown mechanism, the hair cells at the near, large end of the tube respond preferentially to high pitch; those at the far, small end to low-pitch sounds. The cochlear canal is similar to a piano keyboard in that different pitches are registered at different locations (tonotopic registration). The same scale of pitch registration is preserved throughout the ascending auditory pathways to the auditory cortex.

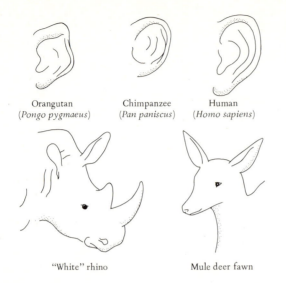

Orangutan   Chimpanzee   Human
(*Pongo pygmaeus*)   (*Pan paniscus*)   (*Homo sapiens*)

"White" rhino   Mule deer fawn

Figure 5.3 / *Primate Ears Compared with Other Mammalian Ears.* The ears of
the primates are of a unique structure, differing radically from those of other
mammals. Primate ears make use of a series of baffles to modify incoming
sound waves. This baffling, rather than turning of the ears toward the sound
source, is the means of sound localization. The extreme form of directional-
horn ears is found in the prey animals. They are able to turn their ears far to the
rear to detect approaching predators. The primates evolved as tree-living
animals, and presumably other selection pressures governed the development of their external ears. In human beings, a sound source can be very
efficiently located with ears stationary, without turning of the head.

malleus is attached to the second ossicle, the *incus* (anvil), in such a
way that both twist with each vibration. The extended arm of the
incus transmits the vibration to the third bone, the *stapes* (stirrup),
whose two prongs in turn transmit it to the oval window of the
cochlear chamber (Figure 5.2). Two tiny muscles, the *tensor tympani*
and *stapedius*, connect the ossicles to the bony wall of the middle-
ear cavity, controlling the amplitude of their movement and thus
protecting against damage to the ear from excessive sound. These
muscles are analogous to the iris of the eye, which closes the aperture in response to excessive illumination.

The cochlea is filled with a fluid, the *perilymph*, which is continuous with the fluid filling the semicircular canals and oval chambers
of the vestibular apparatus. The cochlear canal is divided through
its entire spiral length by an elaborate tissue called the *organ of Corti*
for its discoverer. The receptor cells are located in this structure;

Perilymph. The
fluid that fills the
cochlea and the ves-
tibular system.

Organ of Corti. The
complex structure
in the cochlea re-
sponsible for audi-
tory registration.

called *hair cells*, they consist of two types, outer and inner. The hair cells project tiny cilia into a narrow space beneath an overlying tissue, the *tectorial membrane*. The space above the organ of Corti is separated from the rest of the cochlear cavity by a delicate membrane of single-cell thickness (*Reissner's membrane*); the closed-off fluid (*endolymph*) is slightly different in ionic composition. The *basilar membrane* is the nonneural structure of columnar cells underlying the hair cells.

The Cochlea and Pitch Discrimination

Sound waves transmitted to the cochlear fluids at the oval window are propagated through the length of the spiral chamber to its apical end, where the fluid is in communication with a returning channel to the region of the round window. These vibrations are thought to cause a traveling wave in the basilar membrane through at least two-thirds of its length down the cochlear canal. Movement of the basilar membrane is in turn thought to cause a shearing action of the hair cells' cilia in contact with the overlying tectorial membrane, stimulating them to alter their plasma membrane potential, presumably in the direction of depolarization. This effect at the presynaptic membrane at their base produces action potentials in second-order neurons forming the acoustic nerve.

Comparison of the Auditory and Visual Receptor Systems

The auditory receptors of the cochlea respond to the two variables of sound intensity and *pitch* (number of vibrations per second); the visual receptors of the retina similarly respond to the two variables of light intensity and color. Pitch might be thought of as analogous to color. Though we know something about the mechanisms of the cones' differential response to photic stimulation of different wavelengths, we know considerably less about how the auditory receptors respond preferentially to a given range on the spectrum of sound-wave vibrations (see Figures 5.4 and 5.5). Research on this question to date has sought only to determine how the ear detects the pitch of a single pure tone, or perhaps two, and their interaction effect (beats). We have not yet even begun to ask experimentally how the ear can simultaneously record thousands of pitches in their relative intensities and shifting combinations from moment to moment, which is what ordinary hearing entails.

Research on the auditory mechanism is a great deal more difficult

Hair cells. Receptor cells in the inner ear, both in the cochlea and in the vestibular apparatus, characterized by protruding cilia.

Tectorial membrane. A membrane immediately overlying the auditory hair cells, movement of which is thought to activate them.

Reissner's membrane. A thin membrane in the cochlea separating the perilymph immediately surrounding the organ of Corti from the rest of the fluid (endolymph) in that portion of the cochlear canal.

Basilar membrane. The structure within the cochlea upon which the auditor receptors (hair cells of the organ of Corti) ride, and whose movement causes their stimulation.

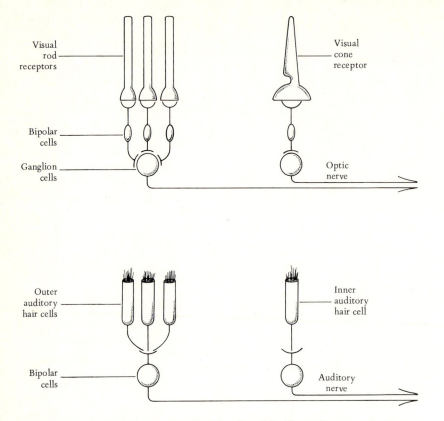

Visual
rod
receptors

Visual
cone
receptor

Bipolar
cells

Ganglion
cells

Optic
nerve

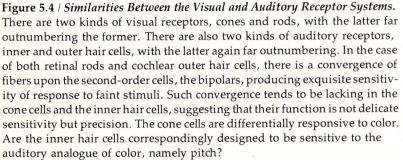

Outer
auditory
hair cells

Inner
auditory
hair cell

Bipolar
cells

Auditory
nerve

Figure 5.4 / *Similarities Between the Visual and Auditory Receptor Systems.*
There are two kinds of visual receptors, cones and rods, with the latter far
outnumbering the former. There are also two kinds of auditory receptors,
inner and outer hair cells, with the latter again far outnumbering. In the case
of both retinal rods and cochlear outer hair cells, there is a convergence of
fibers upon the second-order cells, the bipolars, producing exquisite sensitivity of response to faint stimuli. Such convergence tends to be lacking in the
cone cells and the inner hair cells, suggesting that their function is not delicate
sensitivity but precision. The cone cells are differentially responsive to color.
Are the inner hair cells correspondingly designed to be sensitive to the
auditory analogue of color, namely pitch?

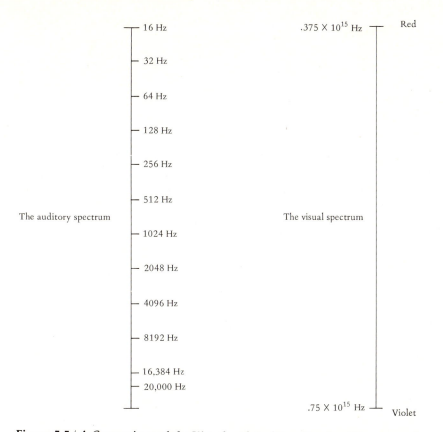

Figure 5.5 / *A Comparison of the Visual and Auditory Spectra.* The range of visible light is only about one octave, the electromagnetic waves at the red end of the spectrum vibrating at about half the rate of those at the violet end. By contrast, auditory vibrations to which our ear responds cover more than ten octaves, from a low of perhaps 16 Hz to a high of about 20,000 Hz. This very extended sound spectrum makes possible an extremely rich sound mix, whereby the practiced ear can differentiate very subtle qualitative differences. For example, we can distinguish the sound of different voices speaking at the same pitch level and volume, and thus can instantly recognize the individual speaking. The same broad range of pitch registration makes possible the recognition of countless unique sound sources, in part by their special sound spectrum.

than research on the retina, since the receptor cells are not conveniently accessible as in the eye, but sequestered within a cavity in solid bone. Nevertheless, evidence of many sorts suggests that low-pitched sounds are registered toward the apical or small end of the cochlear spiral, contrary to expectations, while high-pitched sounds are registered toward the large basal end of the cochlear duct. Moreover, Georg von Békésy, who won the Nobel Prize in 1961 for his work on the auditory mechanism, actually observed a traveling wave along the basilar membrane through openings in the cochlear canal wall, using stroboscopic illumination (von Békésy, 1960), and reported greater amplitude to correlate with low-pitched sounds at the apical end. There is nevertheless a good deal of controversy over how the structure and motion of the basilar membrane or the endolymph are translated into the surprisingly specific pitch preferences of the hair cells along the membrane, or at least in the second-order fibers carrying their message in to the brain.

At the level of the acoustic (cochlear) nerve, the receptive field of the second-order fibers becomes wider with increasing stimulus intensity (loudness). The problem is that the human ear can detect the difference between two tones only a few vibrations per second (Hz) apart in pitch in the range from 50 to 3000 Hz. The observations of physiology do not yet match the measurements of psychophysics. Even if the auditory nerve in question is that of the cat, we are faced with the difficulty of explaining the astonishing capacity of the ear at the highest levels to discriminate differential pitch. How can the broad tuning evident at the basilar membrane level form the basis of the ultrafine tuning found at the conscious or behavioral level? Controversy persists over the precise mechanism by which the cochlear receptor potential is generated, but no theory to date has even come close to answering this question.

The structural arrangements in the cochlea bear a remarkable similarity to those in the retina. The two kinds of receptor cells, the inner and outer hair cells, appear to correspond to the two kinds of retinal receptors, the cones and the rods. The outer hair cells outnumber the inner hair cells about three-to-one (Uttal, 1973). Each inner hair cell, like many of the retinal cone cells, connects to a single second-order fiber one-to-one; the outer hair cells converge as much as ten-to-one on a single bipolar cell of the cochlear nerve (Spoendlin, 1973). The functional meaning of this division of the auditory receptors into two distinct types is still unknown, but the exclusive inner hair cells appear to be, like the analogous retinal cones, in a position to yield a more precise sensory discrimination, perhaps of pitch.

The auditory system also resembles the visual in that, in both, efferent fibers have been found passing out to the receptors from the brain (Rasmussen, 1946), presumably to exert a controlling effect upon their sensitivity. In that we can pick out and follow the sound of a single instrument in the complex of sounds of a symphony orchestra, some such control mechanism appears to be just what is called for. In view of the ears' major function as monitors of events transpiring outside the attention field, it is guessed that such fibers are a part of the auditory attention control mechanism (Galambos, 1956, 1960). These influences arise from the *superior olivary nuclei,* which are the second brainstem way-station along the auditory pathways to the higher centers of the brain (see Figure 5.6). Another efferent pathway descends directly to the first way-station in the cochlear nucleus, which may also exert an auditory sensory control (Desmedt, 1960). More recently discovered is a sympathetic nervous system outflow to the cochlea, which may form part of the alerting system (Spoendlin, 1973). Such a relationship would correspond to the sympathetic system efferents to the dilator muscles of the pupil, which enlarge the visual aperture in visual alerting.

By recording action potentials from single nerve fibers in the auditory nerve (Galambos and Davis, 1943; Tasaki, 1954; Katsuki, 1961), it has been found that fibers tend to respond with increasing rapidity as their preferred auditory frequency is approached, and to drop off abruptly as the pitch rises beyond it (Tasaki and Davis, 1955). As fibers further along the ascending pathways are tested, it is found that this "tuning" becomes ever more specific, indicating further "sharpening" in the neural processing of the nuclei along the way (Katsuki, 1961). How this sharpening occurs is not yet known.

The Problem of Sound Reception

It was once taken for granted that the receptor cells in the cochlea would respond to all frequencies and encode them simultaneously for transmission to the brain. We now realize that neurons cannot fire at rates higher than 1000 Hz, and that we hear frequencies much higher than that. Von Helmholtz (1863) had theorized that the basilar membrane acts like a harp, whose tuned resonators resonate to ever-increasing frequencies toward the basal end. Von Békésy evolved a similar theory that a traveling wave is created in the basilar membrane by the vibrations transmitted from the eardrum, and that the maximum membrane-displacement point varies systematically with the frequency. According to this theory, receptors

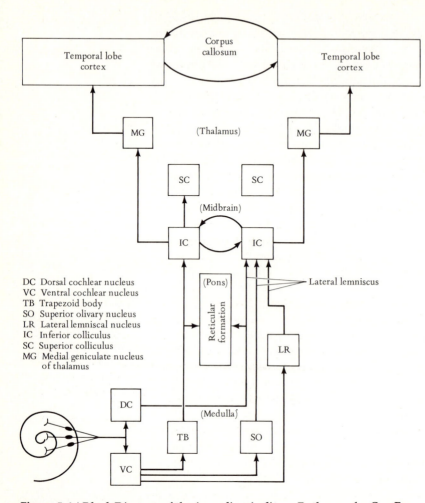

Figure 5.6 / *Block Diagram of the Ascending Auditory Pathways for One Ear.*
This diagram shows the complexity of the auditory interactions. Note the possibility of inter-ear comparison of sounds at the level of the pons (reticular formation), the midbrain (inferior colliculi), and the cortex (corpus callosum). In addition, both ears send their signals to both inferior colliculi, to both medial geniculate nuclei of the thalamus, and to both auditory cortices, although the pathways for only one ear are shown here.

would be tonotopically arranged along the basilar membrane's length, with ever-increasing characteristic firing frequencies as one approaches the basal end. This is precisely what seems to be the case. However, the theory can hope to account only for pitch discrimination up to about 1000 Hz.

Wever (1949) proposed a "volley theory" to circumvent this difficulty. At pitches beyond the capacity of the receptors to record, or the bipolar cells to follow, Wever suggested, other neurons with a slightly different recovery cycle will fill in for those in their refractory period when the stimulus arrives. This appears theoretically possible, but evidence indicates that it probably does not account for frequencies beyond 4000 or 5000 Hz. Thereafter, the Wever theory postulates a strict localization principle: that receptors in the basal region of the cochlea respond preferentially to ever-higher frequencies (but not *at* the frequency of the sound-wave stimulus).

But some believe a curious electrical response of the cochlea, which still defies our understanding, may prove to be the basis of pitch discrimination. The *cochlear microphonic* is a field effect, somewhat similar to the brain waves recordable from the cortex, discovered by Wever and Bray (1938) long before the advent of our refined investigative technologies. Since it continues for a time after the death of the animal, it has been concluded that the cochlear microphonic is not produced by activity of the receptor cells (an electrical rather than a neural response). It is extremely sensitive, responding to the smallest intensity of sound currently measurable. Nor does it fatigue or exhibit habituation on repeated exposure to the stimulus pattern, as do neurons. It is mapped out along the basilar membrane just as is pitch discrimination; higher pitches are produced near the basal end. A reasonable hypothesis is that this electrical response of the total inner ear itself, rather than movement of the basilar membrane, is the stimulus to the receptor cells. This cochlear microphonic theory was proposed by Davis (1965). But how the cochlear microphonic is generated, and how its direct-current fluctuations could cause the neural response that so perfectly reflects it, is unknown.

To fully appreciate the ingenuity of the cochlear microphonic mechanism, however it works, keep in mind that sound consists of an enormously complex composite of pitches, each of which is rapidly shifting. Moreover, the amplitudes of the component air waves within a single sound are constantly changing. The cochlear microphonic — and our hearing — is somehow capable of keeping track of all these pattern transformations, which we recognize as the sound of rustling leaves or the voice of a friend or a stranger. Wever

Cochlear microphonic. **A response of the entire cochlea to incoming sound waves and capable of registering their pattern seemingly without dependence on neural receptors.**

and Bray (1930) found that by amplifying signals picked up from the acoustic nerve in the cat, they could project from a loudspeaker whatever sounds entered the cat's ear!

There is a great challenge to scientific curiosity here. Presumably this entire complex of sound waves is transmitted as a neural coding all the way to the thalamus and cortex without serious distortion. Unlike the visual system, there is no evidence that the auditory signals are recoded anywhere within the ascending system. As far as we know, the sound pattern is transmitted to the cortex in virtually the same form in which it enters our ears, splayed out across the auditory cortex in the transverse gyri of Heschl atop the temporal lobe, like the strings of a harp from one end to the other.

The Ascending Pathways and Primary Projection Area

As Figure 5.6 shows, axons of the bipolar cells of the cochlear nerve, activated by the hair-cell receptors, send their auditory signals to the brainstem via the cochlear branch of the vestibulocochlear (eighth cranial) nerve, which — as its name implies — also receives signals from the semicircular canals denoting head movement. These second-order fibers synapse in the dorsal and ventral cochlear nuclei of the medulla. Note that the majority of the fibers then cross the midline (contralateral pathways), while a minority go to the trapezoid body on the way to the ipsilateral cortex. Note too that both contralateral and ipsilateral pathways send collateral fibers into the reticular formation of the brainstem, and that there is a cross-back at the level of the midbrain inferior colliculi.

The tonotopic registration of pitch in the cochlea is apparently reflected in the arrangement of fibers throughout this ascending system. A parallel tonotopic organization recurs in the primary projection area of the auditory cortex; high-pitched sounds are registered toward the medial end of the transverse gyri, low-pitched sounds toward the lateral exposed end.

Figure 5.7 shows what the brain might look like from above if it were cut through on the plane of the Sylvian fissure, exposing the upper surface of the temporal lobe. Note that the areas receiving auditory signals are differently structured in the two hemispheres, particularly the shape of the *planum temporale* (temporal plane). The significance of this difference will be discussed later with reference to functional specialization of the hemispheres in the human. The transverse gyri of Heschl, forward of the planum, correspond for hearing to the area bordering the calcarine fissure (area 17) for vision.

Planum temporale. **The structure immediately behind the auditory projection area (Heschl's gyri) atop the temporal lobe.**

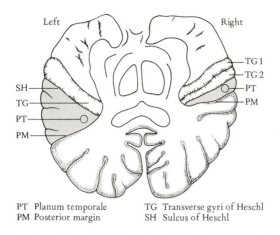

PT Planum temporale   TG Transverse gyri of Heschl
PM Posterior margin   SH Sulcus of Heschl

Figure 5.7 / *Drawing of a Brain Sectioned at the Level of the Sylvian Fissure.* It was long assumed that the two hemispheres of the brain were symmetrical, mirror images of each other. Observation corrected this faulty speculation. The upper surface of the left temporal lobe is frequently strikingly different in appearance from the right, having a significantly larger auditory association cortex. Another discovery was that the Sylvian fissure reaches farther toward the rear in most left hemispheres, tending to turn upward on the right. The functional significance of these differences in the two hemispheres is not yet clear.

It is interesting that this hemispheric difference in the size and shape of the auditory projection area atop the temporal lobe is not uniform. In some individuals the difference is as striking as in Figure 5.7; for others there is little or no difference, and in a rare few the planum temporale is larger in the right hemisphere. It has not been established whether this variation correlates with such variables as left-hemisphere speech representation, handedness, stuttering and other dysphasias, or musical talent. These questions will be discussed in Chapter 9, and in clinical terms in Chapter 15. Throughout the long course of anatomical study of the human brain, this striking hemispheric difference in the auditory cortex went entirely unnoticed, so strong was the preconception that the brain is bilaterally symmetrical.

Mechanisms Underlying Sound Localization

A careful examination of Figure 5.6 will show that there are several points during the ascent of the auditory signals at which those entering the left ear can be compared with those entering the right ear. (Figure 5.6 shows the paths of those entering the system from the left ear only for the sake of clarity.) Comparison is also possible at the cortical level via the commissural fibers. When a sound source lies to the left of us, our left ear receives the sound waves a fraction of a second sooner than our right ear, and the wave phases of all the sound components will be subtly different at the two eardrums. The cochlear nuclei and the superior olivary nuclei will be able to register that lack of synchronization, and thus infer that the sound source is, let us say, on our left. The signal will also be slightly stronger from the ear whose flat horn faces the sound. If there were no opportunity for direct comparison of such differences, this means of sound localization would be unavailable to us.

But subjective experience and psychophysical measurement both demonstrate that sound direction is often more precisely localized than seems explicable on this simple basis. We can also sense that a given sound comes from in front of or behind us, even though such sounds may reach the two ears simultaneously, in corresponding wave phase and equivalent intensity. Comparison of the signals from the two ears would in this case provide no useful information.

Perhaps here our external ear becomes functional. Certain portions of the pitch spectrum of sounds from the rear would be more muffled than others, allowing for a comparison with sound from in front. The brain could quickly learn to utilize this information to differentiate between the two, irrespective of their average intensity and without turning the head. Note that such information, contained in the *timbre* (quality) of the sound rather than its intensity or wave phase, would depend on a transmission system that accurately records the vast complexity of pitches composing natural sounds all the way to the cortex. More subtly, a comparison of the timbres of the sound envelope entering the two ears may provide ample information for interpretation of the precise direction of sounds throughout the compass, provided the head is held stationary. Perhaps blind people tend to hold their heads rigidly to the front in order to make such sound comparison maximally reliable.

Predatory animals' eyes and ears tend to be aimed forward. Prey animals' eyes are located more laterally, enabling them to detect predators approaching from the rear without having to rotate the head completely, and their ears are mobile enough to swing back and magnify sounds from the rear. Primates' eyes are in front facing forward, for stereoscopic depth perception, but their ears are of a quite different sort. The primate ear is designed to capitalize to the fullest on the superior thalamocortical auditory system, which depends not solely on sound intensity or wave phase, but on fine discrimination of the full complex of sound-wave pattern differences as they impinge upon the nondirectional ear horns. Such a thing was presumably made possible by a further elaboration of the auditory cortex rendering it capable of registering the full complexity of such wave patterns, manifested in the human ear's capacity to distinguish the subtle harmonies and discords in music. The delicacy of this mechanism is easily tested by focusing one's attention on some complex sound, then slightly turning one's head, and noting the difference in the sound quality registered.

We might speculate that it is this advanced mode of hearing that permits us to identify people by the sound of their voices — a talent that might have had great survival value for our early progenitors, who traveled in troupes through the tall elephant grass of the African savannah. This ability permitted them to keep in touch vocally, sight unseen, and perhaps thereby led to the development of vocal speech.

Mechanisms Underlying Sound-Source Recognition

As we have seen, visual pattern recognition makes use of a translation of retinal stimulus into a neural code representing linear elements (object contours) as well as lateral movement. No such translation appears to occur in the case of auditory signals. Sound pattern appears instead to be registered in the cortex as a unique complex of frequencies (vibrations per second). Each of its component pitches is registered in its momentary relative intensity, as well as its transformation over time (in fractions of a second).

Research on the auditory cortex has largely been bypassed for other research interests in the temporal lobe. Von Békésy, considering how the broadly tuned signals at lower levels can result in remarkable fine-tuning of auditory pitch such as a musician's, has postulated that lateral inhibition must occur at the cortical level. But there is as yet no direct evidence of cortical lateral inhibition in any of the sensory systems. Simmons (1970) maintains that there is no sharpening of the auditory code beyond the level of the cochlear nucleus. Whatever the mechanism, there is an exquisite registration of the complexity of natural sound at the thalamocortical level. The survival value of such a thing must involve identification of the sources of sounds.

Everything that produces a sound produces a unique sound. It is rare in everyday life for a sound to be mistakenly identified. Each of us learned long ago to identify innumerable sound patterns as originating in some particular creature, object, or event. While we began by having to turn our eyes to identify the source, doing so is no longer necessary for the sophisticated brain. We appear to have stored memories of the precise wave-pattern transformations of all audible events in our environment, making those events instantly recognized by the brain. Moreover, as in the case of visual imagery, we can evoke almost any sound we wish, remembered or imagined, merely by giving thought to it. It seems improbable that the reptilian brain, which never evolved the mammalian thalamocortical system, is capable of such a feat. Instead, frogs and crocodiles, like birds and some insects, seem to have "wired-in" recognition of a very few highly significant sounds, such as the call of the mate.

Recall that the pulvinar, the thalamic nucleus massively interconnected with the auditory association cortex, is greatly expanded in the human brain, and that our temporal lobe itself has considerably extended and fattened relative to that of the other primates. Both exquisite sound-pattern registration and object-sound pattern association are presumably served by this expansion of temporal cortex.

Hemispheric Specialization for Audition

The visual cortex, as far as we know, is not characterized by specialization of function in the two hemispheres. Each visual cortex receives signals from the retinal region of both eyes, and the two half-fields register equivalently, with the same clarity and discriminative power. The hemispheres thus seem to be exact mirror images of each other. In the auditory system we discover something different both anatomically and functionally, in the human brain.

As we noted in discussing Figure 5.7, the temporal lobe is differently structured in the two hemispheres. In the vast majority of brains studied, including fetal brains, the auditory cortex is significantly larger in the left hemisphere, where the posterior margin of the *planum temporale* is angled backward rather than forward (Geschwind, 1968). If we assume that this entire portion of the upper surface of the temporal lobe represents auditory cortex, it is in many cases approximately twice as large in the left hemisphere. This structural difference is presumed to bear on the fact that the speech function and related language functions appear to be centered in the left hemisphere in the vast majority of people.

As we have already seen (Figure 5.6), the bulk of the ascending auditory pathway crosses to the opposite side. Thus the right ear sends most of its signals to the left temporal lobe cortex, where a larger cortical area appears to be available to process them. Does this mean that sounds are louder for the right ear? Apparently not. The differences between left-ear and right-ear hearing found thus far all seem to relate to the language function. As we shall see, *word sounds* are more readily detected by the right ear (left hemisphere), and the sounds of nature by the left ear (right hemisphere). (See Darwin, 1974, for a critical discussion of this issue.)

If sodium amytal is injected into one of the two carotid arteries leading to the brain, one cerebral hemisphere can be momentarily "put to sleep" while the other hemisphere remains normally awake (Wada, 1949). If the left hemisphere is thus affected, the individual usually falls silent and is unable to respond verbally to questions. This suggests that the speech function, curious as this may seem, is controlled in that individual by the left hemisphere. The demonstration becomes unequivocal when it is discovered that putting the right hemisphere to sleep in the same manner leaves the individual's capacity for speech unaffected.

It has long been known that cerebral accidents affecting the left hemisphere tend to disturb language functioning — speech, understanding of others' speech, writing and understanding the printed word, and the like — whereas lesions of the right hemisphere tend to leave such functions intact. This implied specialization of the two hemispheres for specific functions is called *lateralization*. A child normally learns to speak long before lateralization is fully completed. Thus the finding that the right hemisphere understands certain simple commands (Gazzaniga, 1970) presumably indicates a residual language function remaining there. If the left hemisphere is damaged early in life, speech may be acquired or reacquired via the right hemisphere. After lateralization is complete, however, the plasticity of the right-hemisphere cortex appears to be lost, and *aphasia* (impaired language function) is permanent.

The ability to learn and to produce spoken word patterns appears to be found only in the human brain. While natural sounds have great variety, they do not often consist of a complex sequence of contrasting patterns as do spoken words, whose unique temporal transformations are myriad and instantly recognizable. Perhaps the expanded cortical area available in the auditory cortex of the left hemisphere is of importance to the acquisition and retention of a large spoken vocabulary. Could it be that lateralization occurs only when the child's vocabulary reaches such a size that the capacities of the right hemisphere to handle it with ease are outstripped? Is increasing use of the left hemisphere for speech function as the child matures genetically prescribed in its maturational timetable,

Lateralization. **The specialization of the two hemispheres for different functions, particularly language versus nonverbal functions.**

Aphasia. **A neurological disorder characterized by impairment of the ability to speak or to understand language.**

or merely a matter of cerebral convenience? Some brains exhibit little difference between the two temporal lobes (Geschwind, 1976), and there are some individuals in whom speech, even in adulthood, appears to be at least partially bilaterally represented. This issue will be discussed at greater length in Chapter 9.

Audition and the Attention Mechanism

As Figure 5.6 illustrates, ascending fibers from both the dorsal cochlear nucleus and the trapezoid body send collaterals carrying auditory signals into the reticular formation of the brainstem on their way to the midbrain. All sounds entering either ear are monitored, bilaterally from each ear, by this most primitive region of the brain, one of whose functions appears to be to prime the cortex for the reception of stimuli. Thus sounds entering either ear may be monitored for their attentional demand-quality by this activating system, which sends fibers to the thalamic reticular nuclei and from there to all parts of the neocortex, as will be discussed in Chapter 12. This mechanism could govern attention shift as well as alerting or arousal. However, this attentional mechanism in the brainstem is primitive, operating as it does without the refined source-detecting (object recognition) powers of the neocortex. It responds to loudness and suddenness — that is, to the dynamic properties of sound. It should be noted in passing that a similar collateral system is found in the ascending pathways of the *somesthetic system,* which transmits signals from the body involving pressure, pain, or temperature sensations.

   Here again the visual system is somewhat differently organized, since it has no known collateral fibers running directly from the retina to the brainstem reticular formation. In the visual system, the reticular activation underlying arousal appears to follow an as yet ill-defined pathway, perhaps via the superior colliculus (see Chapter 12). By contrast, the *lateral lemniscus* of the auditory system and the *medial lemniscus* of the tactile and body-sensation systems in the brainstem are ancient and well-defined systems.

   Mammals' attention tends to be drawn not only to loud or sudden sounds, but also to sounds recognized as significant or of interest. On repeated exposure, those found to be irrelevant and inconsequential quickly lose their power to attract attention, due to an attention-inhibiting mechanism known as *habituation.* This mechanism is essentially independent of the dynamic properties of the stimulus, which affect the sensory systems in a parallel suppres-

Habituation. Cessation of attention to a meaningless stimulus after repeated exposure.

sive fashion (*sensory adaptation*). Nor does it have anything to do with the fatigue of the receptors. The sensory input continues to reach the cortex, but its power to activate the arousal system and to hold our attention diminishes.

Habituation itself is one of the most primitive mechanisms of adaptive response; it is vividly exhibited, for example, by the sea anemone. In the mammalian brain, however, it appears to make increasing use of sound-source recognition: our attention mechanism tends to suppress response to sounds recognized as coming from an innocuous source. The mechanism is not yet understood, but its importance is apparent. We are continually suppressing attention to countless sounds recognized at the inhibitory level as of no interest. At the mammalian and human levels, it is sounds of *unknown* significance or source that are apt to call attention to themselves. This is presumably a function of the temporal lobe cortex, where such refined sound-pattern identifications can be made.

For many mammals, the olfactory sense (smell) appears to rival or exceed hearing as an alerting device. For primates and human beings, however, auditory perception appears to be the ideal distance receptor for the alerting function. When mammals were small nocturnal creatures living in trees, the auditory system must have played an important role in survival, developing early into a highly efficient warning device as well as a means of locating food, mate, and wayward offspring (Jerison, 1973).

Sensory adaptation. The tendency of sensory receptors to diminish their response to repeated or continuous stimuli.

Audition and Spatial Orientation

Hearing is extremely important to blind people as a means of orienting themselves to their surroundings. Auditory orientation appears to be a very complex process, somewhat similar to visual scanning. The multitude of sounds emanating from events and surfaces in the surround are automatically analyzed for information about their location and distance, allowing the hearer to maintain a continuous spatial orientation relative to environmental things. We know from the experience of the blind, as well as from echolocating animals (bats, some birds, whales) that the echoes of sounds reflected from nearby surfaces are important to such orientation.

In normal situations outside the sound laboratory, we receive a continual barrage of echoes, each containing information from which the brain might deduce the direction and distance of objects, reflective characteristics of surfaces, rebound phenomena, and the like. This aspect of hearing may be most vividly displayed in the cat, a nocturnal animal able to move about smoothly without bumping into things in the forest at night. A cat blind from birth behaves astonishingly normally, orienting itself effectively indoors and out — principally, it is presumed, by means of sound reverberations. The sonar principle — making noise so as to generate information from one's own echoes, such as when a blind person taps a cane — is merely an additional technique superimposed on the deciphering of natural echoes.

A neurophysiological finding of great pertinence to auditory spatial orientation is that the deeper layers of the superior colliculus contain neurons that respond to both auditory and visual stimuli from a similar source (Wickelgren, 1971; Gordon, 1976). A glance at Figure 5.6 will reveal the basis of integrated visual-auditory activity. Fibers from the interior colliculus (strictly auditory) pass to the superior colliculus (heretofore thought to be strictly visual). Most of the bimodally responsive cells of the deeper superior collicular layers are directionally selective in both modalities, firing more rapidly in response to stimuli, both auditory and visual, moving toward the periphery of the contralateral auditory-visual (space) field.

Of great interest is Wickelgren's finding (1971) that the colliculi are topographically organized for both auditory and visual fields. Thus we have the following picture, at least of the cat: the superior colliculus receives fibers directly from the retinal ganglion cells in a retinotopically organized matrix; fibers from the corresponding retinal fields of the striate cortex project to these same neurons; and the tonotopically organized auditory signals find their way to their corresponding cell locations in auditory space as mapped out in the deeper layers of the superior colliculus (the superficial layers are strictly visual). We may guess that blind cats use these subcortical nuclei for their spatial orientation via the auditory modality; the visual cortex may also be utilized in the process. That we know from its sound the direction from which a speeding car is approaching may be attributed to such a collicular spatial orientation; but perhaps our auditory cortex is also spatially organized.

Auditory Object Identification

The ability to recognize a sound as emanating from a specific source implies a capacity to analyze the complex sound-wave spectrum and its transformations in momentary time, as well as to remember the characteristic sound pattern associated with known events. This capacity would seem to necessitate the storing in the brain of some sort of sound template against which incoming sound patterns can be tested for their significance. The very primitive auditory animal may be able merely to respond reflexively to certain relatively simple features of the sound spectrum of an event. In the highly evolved human brain, as we know from our subjective experience, sound recognition may be highly specific (for example, the croak of a toad), determined by both its spectral intensities and its sequential pattern — its transformation in time.

Unlike visual perception, which is characterized by instantaneous grasp of a total pattern, auditory perception involves sequential processing of a series of shifting wave patterns. Sounds have characteristic temporal shapes, brief or extended. Sounds are identified and recognized as familiar on the basis of such transformations. It is the shape of the transformation that is unique; clipped out of context, no natural or speech sounds on a recording tape are recognizable. In recognition of a visual pattern it makes little difference which portion of the pattern is encountered first, but sounds are totally unrecognizable if played backward. It would seem that the auditory system at the cortical level must be organized fundamentally differently than the visual system, specialized for simultaneous processing of information.

Though, under the microscope, the auditory cortex looks much like the visual cortex, there may be quite different neural connectivities within it. The little research that has been done on it suggests some similarity, however. Cells of the on, off, and on-off types are found, as well as cells that respond not to spatial movement of the stimulus (as in the deep layers of the superior colliculus) but to changes in pitch, sometimes in one direction only, or changes in intensity (Whitfield and Evans, 1965; Goldstein, Hall, and Butterfield, 1968). As has been mentioned, there is a tonotopic mapping of sound-wave frequencies from the interior to the exterior end of Heschl's gyrus.

The identification of sound patterns requires short-term memory. Any portion of the wave pattern would be meaningless without the context of the foregoing pattern. This is no less the case with respect to identification of objects and events. Even a thud has a particular temporal pattern, with an indefinite number of identifiable variations. Thus, although the cortex atop the temporal lobe is arranged as a spatial array of neuron columns differing in pitch sensitivity, it is the sequence of their firing that appears to be critical to recognition of the sound.

In the insect and the bird, significant sound sequences are presumed to be genetically coded. In the human being, it seems obvious that auditory perception — recognition of things by their sounds — has developed in association with visual experience. That is, we originally associate certain sounds with their sources by turning to look. It is not surprising, then, that the visual cortex is ultimately linked to the temporal lobe cortex by a broad fiber bundle, the *inferior longitudinal fasciculus,* or that the temporal lobe cortex is in large part a visual interpretive cortex. This anatomical association might have been expected, though we still have little understanding of the specific neural auditory–visual connections of the temporal lobe cortex.

Inferior longitudinal fasciculus. **A fiber bundle interconnecting the occipital and temporal cortical regions.**

In the visual association areas 18 and 19, however, many cortical columns respond to either auditory or visual stimulation (*cross-modal response*). The neural association through which auditory object recognition is learned may be based on this cortex.

Summary

Whereas all things in the environment reflect or transmit light, only certain things emit audible sounds, and sound waves travel limited distances. On the other hand, sound is as audible at night as in the daytime, and one does not have to be looking in its direction — it is omnidirectional. Thus it is a natural means of monitoring events in our environment without specifically attending to them. More important for human beings, however, is the use of sound as a means of communication.

Sound entering the ear vibrates the eardrum, a sturdy membrane closing the end of the external ear (auditory meatus) and kept under muscular tension. The eardrum's vibration is transmitted to the receptor organ of the inner ear (cochlea) by three tiny interconnecting bones, the ossicles, which greatly magnify the force of the vibration while reducing its amplitude.

The cochlea is a spiral, tapering, hollow cavity (named for a seashell, owing to its form) in the bony skull. Extending the entire length of its fluid-filled interior is a membrane (the basilar membrane) which divides the cochlea into two parts, upper and lower. The receptors (hair cells), lined up along it in orderly rows, are activated by motion (a shearing action) of the membrane relative to an overlying tectorial membrane.

The causal mechanism of the hair-cell response is difficult to investigate, since the cells are within a bony cavity and not exposed to observation as in the retina. It is known, however, that the receptors respond to progressively higher pitches from the small end of the cochlea toward the large end (outward in the spiral), hair cells at each point along the basilar membrane responding preferentially to a specific speed of air vibration. It is theorized that, for low pitches, the receptors activate action potentials in their second-order neurons (forming the auditory nerve running to the brain-stem) in time with the air-wave vibrations; to account for reception of higher-pitched signals (beyond the maximum rate of action-potential production), the "volley theory" proposes that the cells respond only to intermittent waves of the series as they overcome their refractory period. A still-mysterious feature of auditory reception is the cochlear microphonic response — the capacity of the cochlea as a whole to act as an effective transmitter of sound, in the manner of a microphone, even after the hair cells may be presumed to be inoperative (after death of the animal).

In the auditory system, as in the visual system, the second-order fibers are bipolar cells. These neurons are the origin of the auditory nerve (the vestibulocochlear or eighth cranial nerve, which, as its name implies, also carries signals from the other inner-ear structure, the semicircular canals, registering balance and head motion). Their axons synapse in the cochlear nuclei of the medulla, from which several pathways ascend to the inferior colliculus of the midbrain for relay to the thalamus and cortex. Here again the auditory system differs from the visual system in that signals reaching the cortex go first to the midbrain tectum (the inferior colliculi) before entering the thalamocortical system. It has been speculated that this suggests an earlier origin for the auditory portion of the thalamo-cortical system. Another difference is that both ipsilateral and con-tralateral auditory pathways send collaterals into the brainstem reticular formation, thus serving as an early alerting mechanism (see the discussion of the arousal mechanism in Chapter 12).

The tonotopic registration of pitch in the cochlea is apparently faithfully preserved along the complex multisynaptic pathways to the cortex, since it is found again in the auditory-projection area atop the temporal lobe (Heschl's gyri), where low-pitched sounds are registered at the lateral exposed end and high-pitched sounds toward the deeply buried medial end. There appears to be a normally larger auditory-association cortex immediately adjacent to the transverse gyri of Heschl in the left hemisphere, and the planum temporale is differently structured on the two sides. In this respect too the auditory system differs from the visual, since there is no known hemispheric difference in the visual cortex. It is speculated that the larger association cortex for audition in the left hemisphere is associated with the typical representation of language in the left hemisphere (lateralization of the speech function).

Unlike visual perception, which is characterized by instantaneous grasp of a total spatial pattern (*simultaneous processing*), the auditory perceptual system deals with a series of wave patterns that shift over time in both intensity and spectral quality (*sequential processing*). Sounds have a characteristic temporal shape, brief or extended, by means of which their source is recognized. Though it makes little difference to recognition of a visual pattern which portion of the stimulus is fixed on first, sounds are totally unrecognizable if played backward. This suggests that the auditory cortex is fundamentally differently organized than the visual cortex. What little research has been done on the auditory cortex to date, buried as it is above the temporal lobe in the Sylvian fissure, has identified cells of the on, off, and on-off types, as well as cells that respond not only to changes in intensity but also to changes in pitch (sometimes in one direction only).

Chapter 6 / *Tactile Perception: The World of Things and Tools*

Tactile perception in the human being is a highly evolved mechanism for the identification of objects by their feel. The hand is an ingeniously devised perceptual system, on a par with the eye and ear, capable of simultaneous tactile sensory (cutaneous) and proprioceptive (muscle and joint) input. The hand is intimately associated with the voluntary motor system, which guides manipulation and palpating. It is also intimately associated with the visual system, through the early learning experience of watching as one manipulates things. The ascending pathways for tactile sensory and proprioceptive input from the hand are similar, relaying in the cuneate nucleus at the base of the medulla. The proprioceptive fibers are principally relayed to area 3, along the posterior border of the fissure of Rolando, and normally fail to reach conscious representation. The receptors in skin, muscles, and joints are mechanoreceptors, activated by mechanical deformation of the peripheral tip of the unipolar sensory neuron, whose cell body lies in the dorsal root ganglia along the spinal cord.

The third great perceptual modality of the thalamocortical system is the sense of touch (sometimes referred to as *haptic perception*), which makes possible the recognition of familiar things. Tactile perception is of particular importance to the primates. Many mammals are covered with fur or very thick skin, and thus have little use for a finely discriminating sense of touch. Rhinoceroses and giraffes have lips so tough and insensitive they can eat thorny twigs without discomfort. Most of the herbivores have hooves with very little feeling. However, some mammals have a highly developed sense of touch in their snouts; notable examples are ground borers such as hedgehogs and voles, and rooters such as swine. Elephants have an exquisitely sensitive touch projection from the tip of their trunk. Raccoons use their front paws in locating food on stream beds without visual assistance and have highly developed tactile perception in these "hands."

Haptic perception. Perception mediated through touch.

127

In monkeys and apes the tactile perceptual system centers in the front paws and involves manipulation — feeling with the fingers as they turn and palpate objects with the fingertips. (In the orangutan, the hind feet are employed in manipulation almost as much as the forefeet.) In the human species, perception centered in the manipulation of objects has achieved a unique place in the total perceptual scheme, in terms both of its competence and its importance in everyday life. Familiar objects are readily identifiable if small enough to fit in the hand so the fingers can close around them and move them to different positions. Shape, weight, and such qualities of the surface as rough-smooth, hard-soft, and the like appear to be the dominant cues. These characteristics are registered by pressure receptors in the ventral finger surfaces and the palm, as well as by proprioceptive signals from the muscles and joints of the fingers (Figure 6.1).

Tactile perception differs significantly from visual and auditory perception in that it is inextricably bound up with voluntary movement, discussed in Chapter 8. Tactile perception arises from manipulating and stroking things, whereas visual scanning involves largely involuntary eye movement and hearing requires no movement at all. For this reason the cortical projection area for touch, in the postcentral gyrus, must be considered in association with the motor cortex of the precentral gyrus. The two regions together constitute the combined *sensorimotor cortex*, illustrated in Figure 6.2.

The Hand as a Tactile Receptor System

The eye, the ear, the nose, and the tongue are each specialized receptor surfaces, which transmit somewhat different kinds of information to the brain. The hand too may be considered a specialized receptor surface, with some very interesting features. First, its basic structure resembles a cup or receptacle, the thumb at one side and the little finger at the other; the middle of the palm forms its base. Its holding or grasping capacity can be altered by bending in of the fingers and *adduction* (turning inward) of the thumb. The most touch-sensitive skin surfaces, on the palmar side of the fingers and thumb, face inward to contact any object grasped. These surfaces are *glabrous* (nonhairy) and have no sebaceous follicles. They are covered instead with tiny ridges formed by microscopic papillae, which provide a frictional surface that also lends itself to microscopic surface deformation under light pressure. This deformation stimulates the touch receptors. Moreover, the skin of the palm, con-

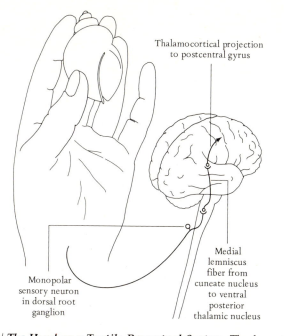
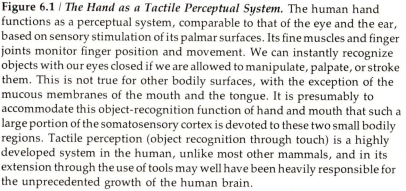

Figure 6.1 / *The Hand as a Tactile Perceptual System.* The human hand functions as a perceptual system, comparable to that of the eye and the ear, based on sensory stimulation of its palmar surfaces. Its fine muscles and finger joints monitor finger position and movement. We can instantly recognize objects with our eyes closed if we are allowed to manipulate, palpate, or stroke them. This is not true for other bodily surfaces, with the exception of the mucous membranes of the mouth and the tongue. It is presumably to accommodate this object-recognition function of hand and mouth that such a large portion of the somatosensory cortex is devoted to these two small bodily regions. Tactile perception (object recognition through touch) is a highly developed system in the human, unlike most other mammals, and in its extension through the use of tools may well have been heavily responsible for the unprecedented growth of the human brain.

trasted with that of the forearm, is exceedingly dense and tough, despite its surface pressure sensitivity, and intimately bound to its subcutaneous structures permitting little lateral movement. Thus the brain can be certain of the precise location of signals sent from the palmar surface.

There are more touch receptors in a given portion of these palmar surfaces of the hand than in any other bodily surface except the lips and tongue. The tips of the fingers, in particular, are densely supplied with touch receptors and thus exquisitely sensitive to touch, their surfaces closely packed with neuron tips specialized for response to pressure. Many of these receptors are *free nerve endings* located in the superficial layers of the skin (epidermis). Others, such as *Meissner's corpuscles,* have their terminal fibers within a non-neural structure, facilitating their firing to a specific kind of stimulus; these are located deeper in the skin (dermis). Still others (*Pacinian corpuscles*) lie in deeper tissues and register "deep pressure"; they are surrounded at their tip by a many-layered ball resembling an onion.

In addition to the touch receptors, there are receptors in the tiny muscles of the fingers and thumb registering their momentary tensions as they manipulate objects, and in the finger joints indicating both the precise position and movement of their bones in the process of manipulation. As Figure 6.3 shows, these neural signals are transmitted to the brain along the same ascending pathway that carries the touch sensations (the *lemniscal system*) and arrive independently in the same location, the "hand" area of the sensorimotor cortex along the fissure of Rolando.

As a first-order generalization, we can say that the hand perceives and identifies things through touching or manipulation on the basis of combined *cutaneous* (skin) and *proprioceptive* (muscle-joint) sensory signals. Both forms of sensory input are increased by finger movement. Squeezing brings into play both deep-pressure receptors and muscle-stretch receptors, which help gauge weight, density, and hardness-softness. Cold receptors may help discriminate wet surfaces or substances from dry ones, and warmth receptors provide further information. By virtue of its manipulative capabilities and greater sensitivity to pressure, the hand can easily recognize objects that might go unrecognized if contact was made with another portion of the body surfaces. In this sense the hand is comparable to the mouth as a tactile perceptual system, and we know that both develop object-recognition skills concurrently in infancy, along with the growth of hand-eye coordination.

In manipulation, the voluntary squeezing pressure put on an object or substance is felt by the muscles and their receptors at the same time it is felt by the skin surfaces involved, usually the ball of the thumb and the tips of the first two fingers. Thus a rubbery substance or object has qualitative specifics that are registered simultaneously by both proprioceptive and cutaneous inputs — specifics subtly different from those of a material that is resistant or mushy. Moreover, we "know" how much muscular effort we are putting into the application of pressure, and are surprised when the thing squeezed is harder or softer than expected. Thus, although we are

Free nerve endings. **A type of sensory nerve ending in the skin and other bodily organs thought to be especially involved in the sensation of slow "burning" pain.**

Meissner's corpuscles. **A type of rapidly adapting nerve ending in the skin, lying just below the epidermis, and sensitive to touch.**

Pacinian corpuscles. **Sensory structures in the deeper layers of the skin and other regions responsive to deep pressure.**

Cutaneous. **Referring to the skin.**

Proprioceptive. **Pertaining to sensory input from the muscles and joint receptors.**

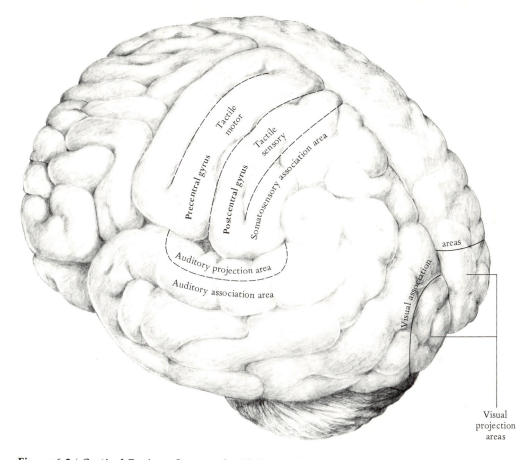

Figure 6.2 / *Cortical Regions Concerned with Tactile Perception.* Tactile perception, being intimately associated with manipulation, palpating, stroking, hefting, and the like, cannot properly be dissociated from the related motor functions. Properly speaking, the tactile cortex consists of the combined sensorimotor cortical regions associated with hand movement and tool use: this means both sides of the fissure of Rolando — both precentral and postcentral — in the middle third of the lateral convexity.

not normally conscious of the proprioceptive signals from muscles and joints, these signals are an important part of tactile perception. The volitional component must also be recognized as an integral part of the tactile perceptual system, with reference to active manipulation for the purpose of object identification, since it is the voluntary act that generates one's expectation of a particular sensory feedback (Held and Hein, 1963).

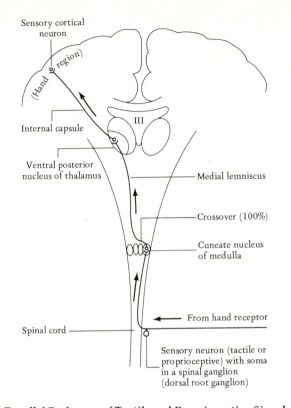

Sensory cortical
neuron

(Hand region)

Internal capsule

Ventral posterior
nucleus of thalamus

III

Medial lemniscus

Crossover (100%)

Cuneate nucleus
of medulla

From hand receptor

Spinal cord

Sensory neuron (tactile or
proprioceptive) with soma
in a spinal ganglion
(dorsal root ganglion)

Figure 6.3 / *Parallel Pathways of Tactile and Proprioceptive Signals.* Sensory input from the palmar surfaces of the fingers follows the same lemniscal system route as do the proprioceptive signals from the small muscles of the fingers used in object manipulation and grasp. This is the modern, rapidly transmitting system, whose first-order fibers synapse only after passing up the cord to the cuneate nucleus at the base of the medulla. After relay in the ventral posterior nucleus of the thalamus, they project to the same region of the cortex. The proprioceptive signals project principally to Brodmann's area 3 along the banks of the fissure of Rolando, as well as to some degree into area 4, the primary motor cortex.

Nowhere is it clearer than in tactile perception that the essential nature of the perceptual process is an active search, rather than a mere passive response process, as was once thought. In trying to identify miscellaneous objects through tactile manipulation with the eyes closed, the individual can be observed to test a series of hypotheses by trying different configurations of the fingers and by squeezing, hefting, rubbing, and the like until the object is sud-

denly recognized for what it is. (A slow-motion film of this process
makes it explicit.) The visual parallel is the scanning of an unclear
or ambiguous stimulus until the *Gestalt* pops into mind (German for
"form" or "configuration," *Gestalt* is used in English to mean "the
configuration perceived").

Once the object has been identified, the active phase is over;
thereafter the response may be quite passive. During manipulation,
however, what we do with our fingers depends on the sensory
feedback we have thus far obtained; in turn, the sensory input
depends on the voluntary movements we make to change the points
of sensory contact with the object. Properly conceived, what is
transmitted to the brain through manipulation is most likely a continuous transformation of the envelope of sensory inputs from all
the sensory surfaces of the hand. In vision, similarly, what is transmitted from the retina is information about the transformations of
patterns of light and dark and color; in hearing, it is the shifting
pattern of sound, considered as a whole, that is transmitted (Gib-
son, 1966).

Experiments on the monkey have clarified some of the neural
bases of sensorimotor function underlying tactile perception in the
hand (Asanuma and Rosén, 1972; Rosén and Asanuma, 1972). Microelectrodes were inserted into the hand area of the motor cortex to
stimulate motor neurons projecting to various thumb muscles.
When the skin of the thumb was stimulated, the afferent signals excited pyramidal cells of the motor cortex whose effect is to move the
thumb in a direction that would bring it into contact with another
surface. That is, a touch on the hand area tends to stimulate reflexive closure of the hand over the touching object — which, as Eccles
observes (1973), could account for the reflex grasp of the infant.

This finding implies that, in addition to the registration in the
postcentral gyrus of sensory stimulation of the skin surfaces of
the hand, there is simultaneous neural input to the motor cortex
of the hand area in cortical columns meaningfully related to that sensory stimulation in the act of object manipulation. This process would
be analogous to the parallel receptive-field organization for visual
and auditory stimuli in the deep layers of the superior colliculus
described in Chapter 5. It also illustrates that the activities of the
motor cortex of the precentral gyrus are functionally integrated with
the activities of the *somatosensory* cortex of the postcentral gyrus,
presumably through the interconnecting *U fibers* running beneath
the fissure of Rolando (Figure 6.4). Presumably these findings pertain no less to the human brain than to that of the monkey.

U fibers. Transcorti-
cal fibers dipping
below a fissure.

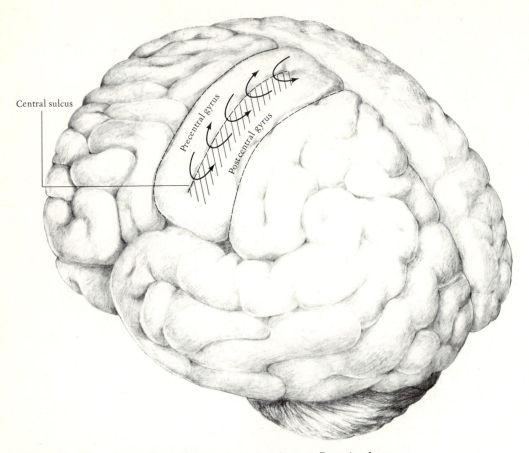

Central sulcus

Figure 6.4 / *Fiber Connections of the Sensorimotor System.* Running between the precentral and the postcentral gyrus are interconnecting "U" fibers dipping below the depths of the fissure of Rolando. These fibers relate the tactile and proprioceptive neural activities of the parietal lobe with the motor activities of the frontal lobe. Evidence suggests that tactile cutaneous areas are interconnected with those motor units whose activity would bring those skin regions into contact, as in closing upon an object. Thus, presumably these "U" fibers keep the two cortical regions in functional relation to each other.

Ascending Pathways and Cortical Representation

The combined cortical sensorimotor system in the human being occupies a broad area of the lateral convexity of the hemispheres, as shown in Figure 6.2. We are concerned here only with the portion receiving tactile and proprioceptive input from the hand region: principally the portion of the postcentral gyrus occupying the middle third of its expanse over the lateral convexity, and the paths taken by that input, originating in the skin surfaces and in the muscles and joints of the hand.

The cutaneous receptors of the hand project signals to the cortex along a three-neuron pathway. (Recall that the corresponding auditory pathway has six neurons, and the visual pathway four.) The first-order fibers extend to the surface of the hand from cell bodies located alongside the spinal cord in the vertebral column, in clusters called *spinal ganglia*. The neurons involved are of a peculiar type — monopolar — with a single extension emanating from the soma which immediately bifurcates, one branch extending to the skin surface and the other projecting into the spinal cord. The branch going to the surface is sometimes spoken of as a dendrite, but in fact functions as an axon; the action potential generated at its tip is self-propagating all the way past the cell soma and into the cord (see Figure 6.5).

Spinal ganglia. Sensory nuclei located within the vertebral column alongside the spinal cord.

Upon entering the spinal cord, these first-order neurons continue up to the *cuneate nucleus* (see Figure 6.5) at the base of the medulla, where they synapse upon second-order fibers that cross over and continue up to the thalamus. Significantly, the cell bodies of these first-order sensory neurons have no dendritic extensions and receive no synapses from other neurons. Thus, like the receptor cells of the visual and auditory systems, they function to generate the receptor potential, rather than to integrate signals. There is no summation of graded potentials leading to a depolarization of the membrane at the axon hillock, as is usually the case. Like the visual and auditory receptor cells, what activates them is only an external physical stimulus, whose intensity is registered in the cutaneous receptors by the rapidity of their production of action potentials. It is because a mechanical deformation of the peripheral tip generates the depolarization of the membrane that these first-order sensory neurons are designated *mechanoreceptors*.

Cuneate nucleus. A nucleus at the base of the medulla forming the first relay station for the lemniscal system from the upper regions of the body.

The tactile receptors of the glabrous ventral hand surfaces include both slowly adapting receptor tips, which tend to keep on producing action potentials as long as the mechanical stimulus (pressure) continues, and rapidly adapting receptors that fire, in the extreme case of the Pacinian corpuscles, only when there is a change in the stimulus. The free nerve endings, which have no specialized nonneural structure at their tips, tend to be very slowly adapting. (These very fine unmyelinated fibers, probably of very primitive origin, are commonly designated *C fibers*.) They are usually found ending in the most superficial layers of the skin. The more sophisticated sensory neurons all tend to have a specialized end-structure facilitating production of the action potential, to be larger in bore

Mechanoreceptors. Sensory receptors responsive to deformation of the sensory nerve tip.

C fibers. Slender, unmyelinated nerve fibers of ancient origin.

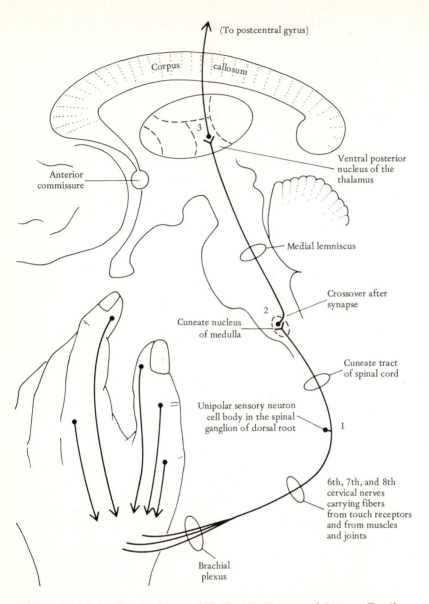

(To postcentral gyrus)

Corpus callosum

3

Anterior commissure

Ventral posterior nucleus of the thalamus

Medial lemniscus

Crossover after synapse

2

Cuneate nucleus of medulla

Cuneate tract of spinal cord

Unipolar sensory neuron cell body in the spinal ganglion of dorsal root

1

6th, 7th, and 8th cervical nerves carrying fibers from touch receptors and from muscles and joints

Brachial plexus

Figure 6.5 / *Ascending Pathway of the Tactile Perceptual System.* Tactile sensory receptors, along with muscle and joint receptors, project into the spinal cord via fibers of monopolar (unipolar) neurons whose cell bodies are stationed in ganglia alongside the spinal cord. Their single-fiber extension bifurcates shortly after leaving the cell, one branch passing to the sensory receptor structures in the skin (or muscles, or joints), the other projecting into the cord and up to the cuneate nucleus of the medulla. Crossover (100 percent) takes place after the first synapse, in the second-order fiber following the medial lemniscus through the brainstem and projecting to the ventral posterior thalamic nucleus for relay to the cortex.

and myelinated (hence more rapidly transmitting), and to be particularly responsive to stimulus change.

The rapidly adapting receptors include the Meissner's corpuscles, which lie just below the epidermis and are often supplied with an end-plate structure, and the Pacinian corpuscles, which tend to lie in the deeper layers of the skin, in muscles, and in the subcutaneous tissue. Other types of nerve ending, such as *Merkel's discs* and the *Ruffini endings* (see Figure 7.3) are also found in the tactile regions of the hand. Each specialized end-structure was thought at one time to mediate a specific sensory modality (pressure, touch, pain, warmth, cold), but there is less certainty today about this "theory of specific nerve energies." Some regions of the skin, such as the external ears and the tip of the nose, contain only free nerve endings but are responsive to the entire spectrum of sensory modalities. It now seems more likely that the various sensory structures serve to improve the sensitivity of the neuron, or provide a characteristic adaptation rate, or some such function, rather than responding to a particular type of stimulation, and that all of them work in an integrated fashion upon arriving in the interpretive centers of the brain (Uttal, 1973).

Upon arrival at the cuneate nucleus in the medulla, the fibers, ascending in the cuneate fasciculus (Figure 6.6), synapse upon the main excitatory neurons projecting to the thalamus and, by axon collaterals, upon inhibitory interneurons, which in turn synapse upon these same projection neurons. This type of inhibition is called *feed-forward inhibition* (Eccles, 1973). These projection neurons of the second order are also inhibited in their firing by interneurons excited by efferents running down from the cortex (Figure 6.7). Some portion of this inhibitory action is of the presynaptic type (see Chapter 3), as Figure 6.7 shows.

The next stop along the ascending pathway is the ventral posterior nucleus of the thalamus, which is in communication with the sensory cortex of the postcentral gyrus, immediately behind the fissure of Rolando. Here the projection neurons upon which the second-order neurons synapse receive excitatory input from the cortex, rather than inhibitory input as do those of the cuneate nucleus. Their inhibition is of the *feed-backward* type: collaterals from their own axons activate interneurons, which in turn send inhibitory influences back to them, as illustrated in Figure 6.7. This mechanism was discussed earlier (Chapter 2) in connection with the pyramidal cells of the cortex.

The effect of the feed-forward inhibition on the cuneate-nucleus neurons is thought to be of the "sharpening" variety, seeing to it

Feed-forward inhibition. Inhibition of neural firing through local inhibitory neurons activated by collaterals of incoming fibers to the neuron inhibited.

Feed-backward inhibition. Inhibition of neural firing through local inhibitory neurons activated by collaterals of the axon of the neuron receiving the inhibition.

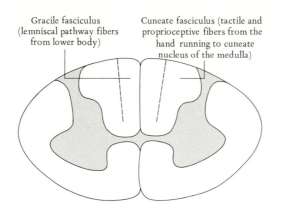

Gracile fasciculus
(lemniscal pathway fibers
from lower body)

Cuneate fasciculus (tactile and
proprioceptive fibers from the
hand running to cuneate
nucleus of the medulla)

Figure 6.6 / *Cross Section of the Cervical Cord, Showing the Dorsal Funiculi of the Ascending Lemniscal System.* Lemniscal fibers from the lower part of the body follow the more medial gracile funiculus (fiber bundle) to the gracile nucleus, while those from the hand follow the more lateral cuneate funiculus to the cuneate nucleus. Note that this more modern lemniscal system is more massive than the older spinothalamic system (compare with Figure 7.2).

that only the fibers carrying the stronger signals are permitted to propagate their signals on to the next station — an effect comparable to the lateral inhibition in the retinal cells and postulated to exist between the cortical columns of all the thalamocortical sensory systems (Eccles, 1973). The effect of the feed-backward inhibition of the thalamic ventral posterior nucleus cells is apparently of the "governor" type, regulating the action-potential output of the cell within certain boundaries. Inhibition of the cuneate projection cells through fibers descending from the cortex is thought to block attention to minor or irrelevant sensory signals from the cutaneous receptors by reducing the firing rate of the cuneate projection neurons.

The excitatory efferent fibers from cortex to the ventral posterior thalamus are thought to constitute the second half of a self-re-exciting feedback loop, an arrangement found in all three major thalamocortical sensory systems.

Proprioceptive signals from the muscles and joints of the hand follow a similar three-neuron pathway to the cortex of the postcentral gyrus. As mentioned, they themselves appear to produce no perceptual experience other than knowledge, sight unseen, of finger position and movement. This knowledge may be demonstrated by a curious illusion. If the first and second fingers are crossed and a pencil is spun between their tips, one's expectations based on the proprioceptively registered position of the fingers are fulfilled, and one experiences no surprise at the resulting sensations. However, if the fingers are held immobile for a moment, such as by pressing them down on a table top, to reduce their proprioceptive output, the spinning pencil between their tips will suddenly feel like two pencils, an interpretation based wholly on learned *cutaneous* expectations.

Figure 6.7 / *Interaction of Neurons at the Cuneate Relay.* This figure shows an intricate relationship between excitatory and inhibitory neurons at the cuneate tactile relay station and at the thalamic level. Neurons in black are inhibitory interneurons. See text for explanation.

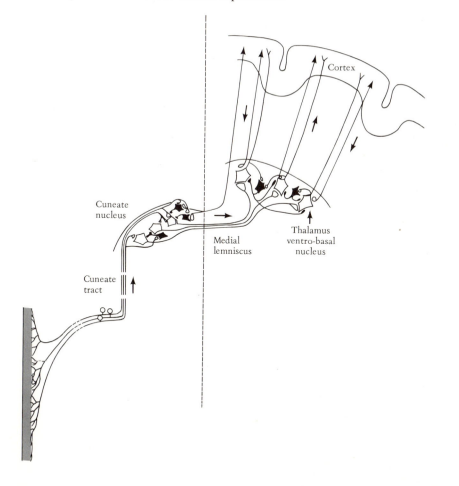

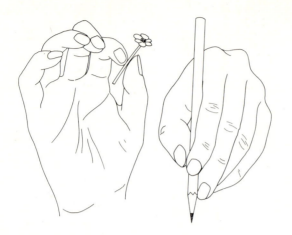

Figure 6.8 / *The Hand as Tool and as Tool Manipulator.* The hand operates as a tool used for countless different purposes. It is also ideally designed as a user of tools of every description, including those for fashioning and perfecting other tools. The human organism would be more seriously crippled without hands than without eyes or ears. It is through the human hand, and the two hands used in conjunction, that human intelligence is implemented. No other species is so marvelously equipped.

Tactile Object Perception

At the thalamocortical level the simple pressure sensations from the skin receptors, coded for intensity by the rapidity of the arriving action potentials, are translated into such perceptual qualities as surface texture, weight, shape, hardness or softness, and the like on the basis of previous experience of such arriving impulses while feeling particular surfaces or substances or manipulating solid objects. Shape, however, appears to be perceived uniquely relative to the proprioceptively apprehended positions of the fingers when these tactile signals arrive. Object perception appears to depend heavily on perceived shape. To understand the mechanisms underlying tactile object recognition, we must look at what occurs during tactile manipulation (Figure 6.8).

An object turned in the hand produces a unique sequence of touch and pressure patterns. Through experience beginning in infancy, these patterns become correlated with a corresponding unique sequence of proprioceptive stimuli arising from receptors in muscles and joints and registering the moment-to-moment conformation of fingers and thumb (discussed in more detail in Chapter

14). This entire system of transformations in neural input becomes correlated with simultaneous visual input characteristic of the size and shape of the object. These combined visual–tactile input patterns presumably form the basis of recognition of the object as familiar — that is, of our concept of the object. Even prior to the acquisition of language, objects of many kinds are perceptually known.

Once an object's feel is familiar through manipulative experience, each voluntary movement of the object in the hand arouses a corresponding expectation of the next pattern of sensory input — the anticipated feel of the object in its new position. It is presumed that such tactile-pattern transformations are integrated with the corresponding visual-pattern transformations in the image or memory of the object, and are normally seldom dissociated. Most research on object perception has tended to treat objects as solely visual phenomena, which is of course an oversimplification. Our images and memories of objects frequently include their feel and their sounds, and sometimes their odor, taste, feel on the tongue, and the like. Where, then, does this integration occur — or, in other words, where in the brain is object memory located?

It is of interest to compare perception in the hand, produced by stroking and manipulation, with perception in the other great tactile receptor system, the oral cavity — tongue and lips, teeth and gums, the roof of the mouth, and so forth. Movement of an object in the mouth is primarily accomplished by action of the tongue, which has proprioceptive receptors in its muscles but no joint receptors. Only receptors in the articulation of the jaw, which monitor its opening and closing, can contribute that kind of proprioceptive information. Object recognition in the mouth is nevertheless second only to hand-touch recognition, even of objects with no distinctive taste or odor, through sensory receptors in the mouth surfaces (especially the upper surface of the tongue) and the receptors gauging muscle tension in the tongue.

A study of the convergence of sensory transcortical signals in the monkey (Powell, 1973) discovered two regions of the cortex that appear to represent end-points of this convergence, one in the prefrontal granular cortex and the other in the inferotemporal cortex (see Jones and Powell, 1970). Recall that the latter is the region where a particular cortical neuron in the monkey was found to respond preferentially to the sight of a monkey hand (Gross, Rocha-Miranda, and Bender, 1972). Unfortunately, a parallel search for object-responsive cells was not conducted in the prefrontal granular cortex!

Given our current state of near-total ignorance of the brain, viewed from the perspective of what we shall no doubt soon know, it may be idle speculation to suggest, on the basis of this evidence, that human object memory is a particular function of the corresponding areas in the parietal cortex of the human brain. Nevertheless, that seems to be the trend of the evidence thus far. Now let us examine another kind of evidence.

Parietal and Temporal Lobes in Agnosia

Agnosia is inability to recognize familiar objects, which may result from damage to the cerebral cortex. In tactile agnosia, the pattern of sensations produced by a familiar object would not be recognizable if manipulated behind a screen, out of sight, though the sensations themselves are undiminished. In visual agnosia, the visual pattern alone is insufficient for recognition. In both cases, however, the object might be instantly recognized if the other perceptual modality were permitted. It thus appears that, although both tactile and visual input are used in object perception, the correlated tactile and visual systems are independent: one can be impaired through cortical damage without the other being impaired. The portions of the cortex on which one perceptual modality depends may not be the portions on which the other depends. Both visual and tactile agnosia occur, however, with damage to the parietal lobe (the general association cortex lying between the tactile and visual cortical centers).

Agnosia. **Failure to recognize familiar objects owing to neurological impairment.**

In the adult, tactile agnosias are more common if damage occurs to the right hemisphere parietal lobe (dominant for perceptual functions); damage to the corresponding region of the left hemisphere (dominant for language functions) might produce merely inability to bring to mind the name of the object — a form of aphasia (Luria, 1966; Denny-Brown and Chambers, 1958). Thus the perceptual and language functions — whose integration under normal conditions is demonstrated by the fact that the object's name is on the tip of our tongue the moment we recognize it — can be localized in two different brain regions as independent systems of neural activity (see Chapter 9). The tactile and visual systems underlying object recognition are also shown to be independent though related systems by the finding that damage to the right temporal lobe, into which visual signals project, often produces visual agnosia for objects instantly recognizable by touch and manipulation.

If the damage occurs to the right hemisphere above and behind the end of the Sylvian fissure (the *supramarginal* or *angular* gyri), the object is apt to be unrecognizable both visually and by touch (see Figure 6.9). If, however, the temporal lobe is intact, the object may be recognized instantly by its characteristic sound (the rattle of a bunch of keys, for example), indicating the independence and neural isolation of the auditory object perceptual system (see Hécaen, 1962).

Clinical findings in the study of the agnosias generally support the impression that object perception involves simultaneous apprehension of the object via several perceptual subsystems — vision, audition, touch, and others. Everyday experience testifies that other

Figure 6.9 / *Areas of the Right Hemisphere Associated with Visual and Tactile Agnosia.* The supramarginal gyrus region and the angular gyrus region appear to be particularly important in object recognition. Damage to these areas is apt to completely block recognition of familiar objects.

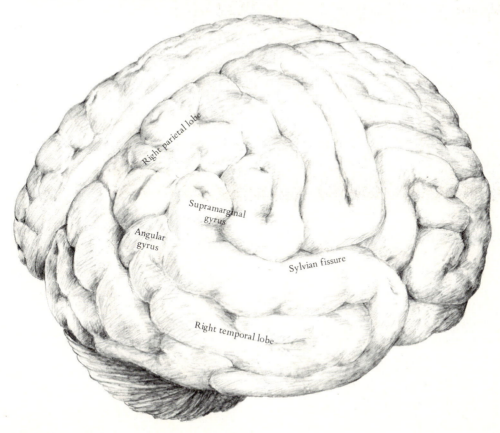

sensory modalities — temperature, odor, taste, pain — may also be embedded within the concept of the object and its mental image. We have already seen that object perception through the tactile system is inextricably bound up with the voluntary motor system. Presumably such concerted activity on the part of several perceptual systems would involve the entire general association cortex of the post-Rolandic brain and its underlying thalamic nuclei (Teuber, 1964), and perhaps the motor cortex as well.

Hands and Tools

Human hands, unlike the forefeet of most mammals, are in themselves tools, marvelously adapted to grasping, manipulating, carrying, throwing, probing, scratching, pulling, lifting, overturning, tapping, patting, fondling, shaking, stroking, and so forth. In our species, however, the hand has also taken on a transcendent function, the skilled use of tools manufactured for its purposes. Manual tools become extensions of the hand — consider the ax, the spear, the knife, the needle for transforming hides into clothing, the pestle for grinding grains, the hoe and plow, and more recently the scissors, the pencil, the typewriter, the golf club and tennis racket, the violin and bow, and so on. In an astonishingly short time, in evolutionary terms, the human brain has evolved the capacity for learning to use tools of every imaginable sort.

It is often unrecognized that, once we have become familiar with tool use, our tools become extensions of our tactile perceptual system. We actually feel the ground we probe with our stick, the grass we cut with our scythe, the ball we hit with our golf club, and the paper over which our pen moves.

Tool use defines the human mode of life. All cultures, from the most primitive to the most advanced, depend on the manufacture and use of tools. Moreover, much of our enjoyment of life involves playing with tools that augment the already remarkable abilities of our hands; and much of our work, in the factory, on the farm, and in the office, represents an exploitation of our hand-tool skills. This capacity requires a brain whose thalamocortical system is capable of coordinating a highly refined motor system under voluntary control and a marvelously integrated visual–tactile perceptual system, which enables the unique structure of the hand to be fully capitalized on as both tool and tool user.

This human use of the hands should be contrasted with that of the chimpanzee, our major rival as a tool user. The chimpanzee did not evolve a hand such as ours, whose fingers can move independently, with a palm perfectly designed to cradle a hand ax or a gearshift knob. While the chimpanzee can be taught to use many manual tools, and in the natural state creates and uses tools, its repertoire is extremely small. Only in the human species have the full potentialities inherent in the tactile system been realized.

Summary

The tactile perceptual system, based on the hand as a receptor mechanism, is in the human being a highly evolved modality for the recognition of objects through manipulation and palpation. It differs from the visual and auditory modalities in that it is intimately associated with the voluntary motor system. Its primary input is from the touch receptors in the ridged palmar surfaces of the fingers and from the tension, position, and movement receptors in the muscles and joints (proprioceptive input), which monitor changes in hand configuration as objects are held and moved within the grasp. Beginning in infancy, object perception develops from the correlation between visual and tactile sensory signals.

The touch receptors in the skin are the terminal tips of sensory fibers whose neuronal cell bodies lie in the dorsal root ganglia within the vertebral column, immediately adjacent to the spinal cord. The centrally directed fiber of these monopolar neurons enters the cord and passes up to the cuneate nucleus, at the base of the medulla, where it synapses with its second-order neuron. This cuneate neuron in turn crosses the cord and ascends to the ventral posterior nucleus of the thalamus, for relay to the postcentral gyrus of the cortex. A similar path is taken by the ascending fibers from the muscle and joint receptors, which provide information on muscle tension and finger position.

In the human brain, the region of the somatosensory projection area in the postcentral gyrus devoted to the hand is very large, in keeping with the importance of the tactile perceptual system. The corresponding hand region of the motor cortex in the precentral gyrus is so organized that tactile stimulation activates motor-cortex neurons that cause the fingers and thumb to close over the touching object, wherever it stimulates the hand surface. This process implies a neural integration between the two cortical regions on either side of the central fissure, constituting a unified sensorimotor system.

Clinical studies of agnosia demonstrate that the general association cortex of the right parietal lobe is particularly crucially involved in visual–tactile object perception.

The tactile perceptual system achieves its fullest development in the invention and use of tools, which are in effect extensions of that system. While other species, such as the chimpanzee, can be taught to use a variety of crude tools, and indeed create and use simple tools in the natural state, the animal repertoire of tool use is extremely limited relative to that of the human being, for whom tool using has become an essential feature of life.

Chapter 7 / *Somesthesis and Self-Awareness*

Such bodily sensations as pain, temperature, and the wide range of distinguishable feelings emanating from our bodily surfaces and interior belong to an older (protopathic) sensory system and are transmitted to the brain by a different pathway from that of the tactile perceptual system. Upon entering the cord, the centrally directed fibers of the unipolar dorsal-root ganglion cells synapse almost immediately, the second-order fibers crossing the cord and ascending all the way to the thalamus (spinothalamic system). There is some question about whether they receive cortical representation in the postcentral gyrus. The prevailing view is that, though there are many types of sensory endings in skin and subcutaneous tissues, they have no direct one-to-one correlation with experienced sensations. Free nerve endings, for example, are apparently capable of registering the entire spectrum of sensory qualities. While visual, auditory, and tactile perceptual systems mediate awareness of the world, the somesthetic system appears to provide immediate sensory awareness of the body, registering conditions on its surface and in its interior pertinent to survival of the organism and its well-being.

It is traditional to define *somesthesis* in a very restricted way as consisting only of touch, pressure, warmth-cold, and pain (and sometimes the vibratile sense). The arbitrary narrowness of this definition is based on an early hypothesis — now in serious question — that each of these sensations is mediated by a specialized sensory receptor. A moment's reflection will reveal that there are innumerable bodily sensations — tickle and itch, wetness, prickle, roughness and smoothness, stickiness and slipperiness, rubberiness, soft and hard — that are just as legitimate as warm and cool. In addition to surface sensations, there is an equally rich variety of internal sensations, such as fatigue, suffocation, nausea, distended stomach or lower bowel or bladder, hunger and thirst,   147 and many more, often described as due to stimulation of *interocep-tors* (receptor neurons in the bodily interior and responsive to con-ditions there).

It is difficult to say where sensation and perception differ. Grant-ing that the distinction is not easily drawn, it will be clearer if we treat somatic sensations not as part of a perceptual system (see Gib-son, 1966) but as feelings in themselves. Such sensations do provide information about external conditions: when the sun warms our skin, we can distinguish its warmth from the heat of a radiator; when the wind brushes the hairs on our arm, we register the effect of the breeze, and perhaps a cooling of the skin similarly inter-preted. Our concern here, however, will be the sensations or feel-ings produced when some portion of the somesthetic system is stimulated.

Interoceptors. Sen-sory receptors within the body that register its in-ternal conditions rather than en-vironmental events.

The Spinothalamic System

Unlike the lemniscal system, the pathways that carry bodily feelings synapse almost immediately upon entering the spinal cord, rather than traveling all the way up to the medulla. This is thought to be a remnant of an older system, associated with primitive segmental animals (such as the worm), each segment of whose spinal column takes charge of its own body region. The first-order neurons are of the same monopolar type, the cell body situated in the dorsal root ganglia alongside the cord, but the centrally directed fiber synapses within one or two segments of its point of entry. The second-order neuron then crosses the cord at that level and travels nonstop to the ventral posterior thalamic nucleus, as shown in Figure 7.1.

The lemniscal system, as we saw in Chapter 6, ascends in the *dor-sal funiculus* of the cord (Figure 7.2), which consists of large-bore, rapidly transmitting, well-myelinated fibers. The ascending fibers of the segmental system, called the *spinothalamic system,* carries bodily feelings along the older lateral and ventral spinothalamic tracts and the spinotectal tract.

There are several distinctive types of nerve endings in the skin and subcutaneous tissues, as Figure 7.3 shows. Note that the *free nerve endings* have no specialized end-structure other than an ar-borization of their terminal portion, while the *Ruffini endings* have a tightly curled terminal section of several branches. The nerve end-ing associated with the hair follicle merely winds around it many times, so that the slightest movement of the hair base depolarizes

Ruffini endings. Sensory receptor structures in the skin once thought to be exclusively re-sponsive to heat.

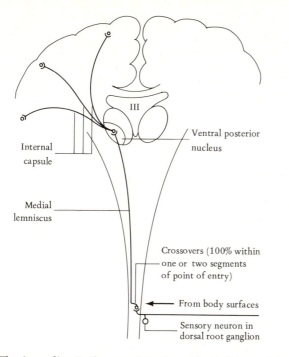

Figure 7.1 / *The Ascending Pathways of the Somesthetic System.* Many of the sensory signals from the body surfaces follow the ancient spinothalamic pathway to the brain, differentiated from the lemniscal system of the dorsal funiculi. These fibers synapse almost immediately after entering the spinal cord. The second-order fibers then cross at that segmental level before ascending to the thalamus. This system mediates the temperature sensations and slow, burning pain, among others. As with the lemniscal system, there is a 100 percent crossover of ascending fibers, the right half of the body being registered in the somesthetic cortex of the left hemisphere.

it. The *end bulbs of Krause* and *Meissner's corpuscles* have a specialized end-structure, as do the *discs of Merkel* and, most spectacularly, the *Pacinian corpuscles.* The more recently discovered sensory end-structure shown in Figure 7.4 is perhaps the most complex sensory organ in the (hairy) skin. The arborization of its terminal fibers results in many specialized end-plate structures within a capsule, and the multiplication of the stimulation so generated makes this perhaps the most sensitive of all the cutaneous receptor structures. As can be seen, its fibers are myelinated clear to their end capsules (Iggo and Muir, 1969).

Most of the peripheral sensory fibers have many terminal

End bulbs of Krause. Sensory receptor structures in the skin once thought to respond exclusively to cold.

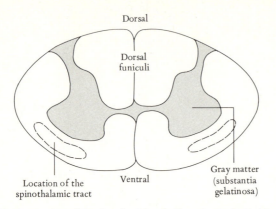

Dorsal

Dorsal
funiculi

Ventral

Gray matter
(substantia
gelatinosa)

Location of the
spinothalamic tract

Figure 7.2 / *Cross Section of the Cervical Cord, Showing Relative Location and Size of the Spinothalamic System.* The somesthetic fibers of the spinothalamic sensory system follow a more ventral and lateral course up the spinal cord than do those of the lemniscal system. Note the much smaller size in comparison to the dorsal funiculi of the lemniscal system. Intractable pain is sometimes blocked by surgically severing a portion of this pathway.

branches. It is unclear just what happens when these many sensitive tips are depolarized at once, but their combined effect is presumably to increase the firing rate of the main fiber passing to the cord. In any case it is clear that each such inflowing fiber is affected by physical stimuli over a rather extensive microregion of the skin surface, which in turn overlaps the domains of other receptors. Current speculation has it that it is the interplay between closely adjacent receptor signals, rather than the discrete signals themselves, that is the basis of fine-point localization of *punctate* stimulation of the skin (Uttal, 1973). The receptor fields of the cutaneous sensory nerves are too large to account for the delicacy of two-point discrimination.

Punctate. **Produced by a point, or affecting only a very local region.**

Not all receptor types are found in all areas of the skin. The external ears and tip of the nose, for example, appear to be served only by free nerve endings, while the fingertips are predominantly served by encapsulated nerve endings. The Krause end bulbs, which look like tiny balls of yarn, predominate at the mucocutaneous junctions of the body surfaces, such as the edges of the lips, while Pacinian corpuscles are common in the internal tissues of the body. There is as yet little understanding of the reason for this distribution. It may be best for the present to think of the skin and other bodily surfaces containing sensory receptors as a single complex receptor system that makes use of a variety of specialized

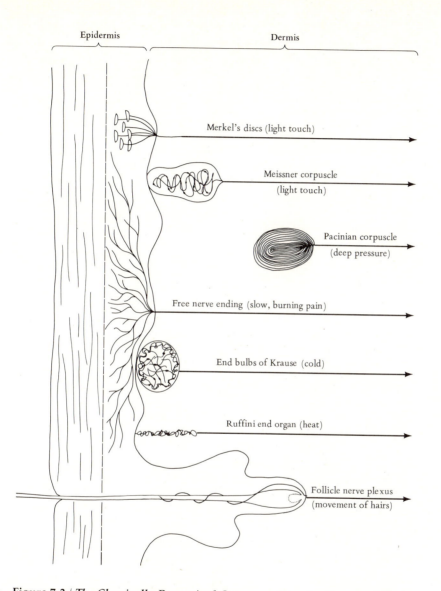

Epidermis   Dermis

Merkel's discs (light touch)

Meissner corpuscle
(light touch)

Pacinian corpuscle
(deep pressure)

Free nerve ending (slow, burning pain)

End bulbs of Krause (cold)

Ruffini end organ (heat)

Follicle nerve plexus
(movement of hairs)

Figure 7.3 / *The Classically Recognized Cutaneous Receptor Types and Their Presumed Functions.* Seven types of receptor end organs are shown in their approximate relationship to the skin surface. To oversimplify a very complex picture, it may be said that the upper three are associated with the lemniscal system, the lower four with the older spinothalamic system. Except for the middle one (free nerve ending), all have a specialized nonneural structure surrounding the nerve fiber tip to modulate its response. Many other intermediate types of nerve endings are also found.

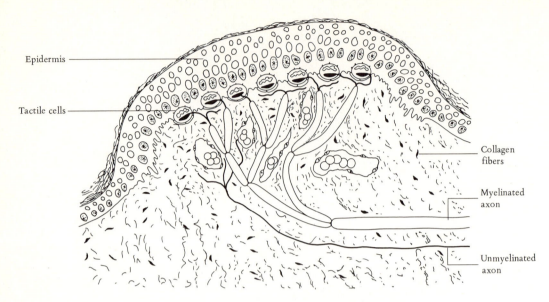

Epidermis

Tactile cells

Collagen
fibers

Myelinated
axon

Unmyelinated
axon

Figure 7.4 | *An Extremely Sensitive Touch Receptor.* This extremely complex receptor, known as an Iggo cutaneous receptor corpuscle, is found in hairy skin (Iggo and Muir, 1969).

and unspecialized types of receptor. It is impossible to say much more at present than that it is the kind of stimulation, rather than the sensory nerve stimulated, that determines the feeling we experience.

Except on the surfaces of the hand and the mouth, these sensory receptors are apparently not organized for the perception of form, as is the tactile perception system. For this reason it is appropriate to treat them as a separate system, whose purpose is to register changing external and internal conditions, and in some cases to elicit reflex responses such as withdrawal from contact, scratching, or brushing away.

Organization of the Dermatomes

A *dermatome* is a region of the skin surface whose sensory fibers arise from a particular dorsal-root ganglion along the spinal cord, approximately one for each vertebra. Figures 7.5 and 7.6 are maps of the dermatomes. Note that there is considerable overlap (often, in fact, more than is suggested in the figures). Incoming fibers from

Dermatome. An area of skin served by sensory neurons at a particular segmental level of the spinal cord.

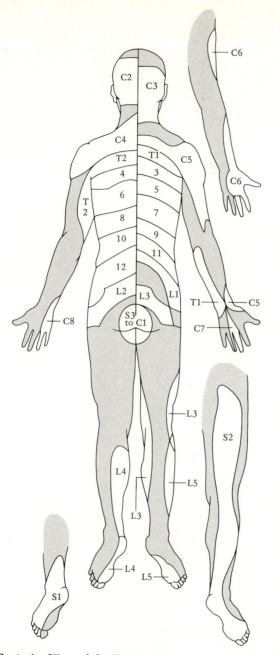

Figure 7.5 / *Posterior View of the Human Dermatomes.* Sensory nerve fibers from various portions of the body enter the spinal cord at different segmental levels, thus very roughly mapping out the body surfaces from head to toe. This diagram shows the regions handled by different segmental levels on the back of the figure.

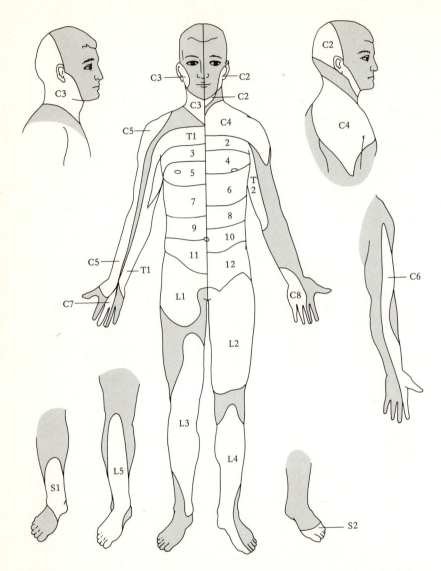

Figure 7.6 / *Front View of the Human Dermatomes.* In this frontal view of the figure, it can be seen that the dermatomes significantly overlap, as shown in the numbered regions of the thorax.

the various dermatomes join to form bundles, the *peripheral nerves,* which are covered with a tough elastic tissue.

In the thoracic region each segmental level of the cord, corresponding to an individual vertebra, serves a corresponding level of the skin of the trunk region. The peripheral nerves that conduct sensory signals into the central nervous system also contain motor fibers that pass out to the muscles in the same region of the body, well insulated from the sensory nerves to prevent crosstalk. The sensory fibers enter the vertebrae via the dorsal roots (toward the back); the motor fibers leave the vertebral column via the ventral roots (toward the interior of the body), the afferent and efferent fibers separating just before the nerve reaches the vertebral column. At levels above and below the thoracic, the peripheral nerves become difficult to trace as they branch and rejoin others, forming interconnected plexuses redistributing the fibers going to the arms and legs.

On their way to the brain, the sensory fibers from the dermatomes appear to maintain their relative positions in the nerves and as second-order fibers passing up to the thalamus. When they arrive there, they map out the regions of the body faithfully. The same topographic representation of the bodily surfaces is then translated into a cortical map of the body along the postcentral gyrus, shown in Figure 7.7. This *sensory homunculus,* which closely matches the *motor humunculus* of the precentral gyrus, maps the body upside-down along the course of the central fissure. It is noteworthy that ascending fibers from bodily sensory receptors cross to the opposite side during their ascent, either in the spinal cord or in the medulla. Thus, for most regions, the left side of the body is only represented by the sensory homunculus of the opposite hemisphere. As we shall see in Chapter 8, the same crossover occurs in the motor system.

The Spinothalamic and Lemniscal Systems Compared

The spinothalamic and lemniscal systems were differentiated by Head (1920), who associated the former with the grosser and more diffuse sensations of touch, as well as pain and temperature, which he called *protopathic* signals. The latter, concerned with precisely localized light touch and pressure, he called the *epicritic* system. These terms are still in use. When the fibers of the protopathic system are severed, loss of sensation results. When fibers of the lemniscal system are severed, deficits in fine motor control occur. This

Peripheral nerves. Bundles of nerve cell axons outside the central nervous system, collectively the sensory, motor, and autonomic nerve fibers.

Sensory homunculus. The map of the regions of the somatosensory cortex associated with sensations in various regions of the body.

Motor homunculus. The map of the regions of the motor cortex associated with movement in various regions of the body.

Protopathic. Referring to the more ancient of the two major ascending somatosensory pathways registering temperature sensations and slow "burning" pain, among others.

Epicritic. Referring to the more recently evolved lemniscal sensory system characterized by fast-firing, highly specific sensory registration.

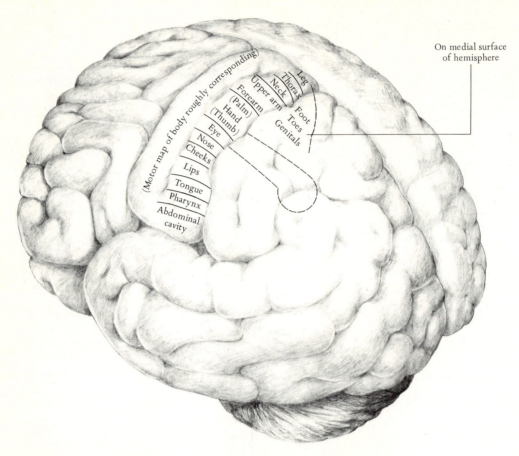

On medial surface
of hemisphere

(Motor map of body roughly corresponding)

Leg
Thorax
Neck
Upper arm
Forearm
(Palm)
Hand
(Thumb)
Eye
Nose
Cheeks
Lips
Tongue
Pharynx
Abdominal
cavity
Foot
Toes
Genitals

Figure 7.7 | *Map of the Points of Somatosensory Representation in the Postcentral Gyrus.* The sensory regions of the body surface (the dermatomes) are mapped out along the postcentral gyrus in an orderly fashion, with the body represented generally in an upside-down position. Note that the lower limbs and genitalia are represented on the medial surface of the hemisphere, while face and hand regions together occupy most of the lateral convexity of the somatosensory cortex. Immediately forward across the fissure of Rolando lies the motor cortex, with the body mapped out in a roughly corresponding fashion. Together these two cortical strips are known as the sensorimotor cortex, since they operate in close conjunction.

observation lends support to the notion that the functions of the lemniscal system are specifically associated with adaptive motor behavior, such as manipulation or climbing a tree. Protopathic sensations, such as warmth-cold and "slow" burning pain, are less relevant to motor behavior than are precise touch and pressure sensations from the skin and the proprioceptive signals from muscles and joints.

There is some question about whether all the sensory modalities of the spinothalamic system find cortical representation in the postcentral gyrus. Pain, for one, has not been demonstrated to reach cortical elaboration in primates, and warmth appears to be mediated at the cortical level only for the surface of the tongue.

In all these respects the lemniscal system appears to be more intimately associated with the more advanced thalamocortical perceptual systems of vision, audition, and hearing, and with voluntary behavior, while the spinothalamic sensory system appears to mediate older sensory functions more closely allied with odor and taste. These older systems of the brain seem less concerned with perception, which involves conceptual representation of things "out there," than with raw feelings and their affective (pleasant and unpleasant) associations and reflexlike motoric response.

The Question of Cortical Representation

It was long assumed that pain and temperature signals enter the cortex along with pressure and touch signals, perhaps simply because we are equally conscious of both sensory modalities, and consciousness was assumed to "reside in" the cerebral cortex. But perhaps awareness of pain and temperature occurs in subcortical regions, as all awareness must have before the neocortex evolved. Before dismissing the possibility of cortical representation of sensations transmitted via the spinothalamic pathways, two possibilities should be considered. Forty years ago Adrian (1940) discovered in the cat a second cortical area where sensory stimuli to the feet are registered. More recently an entire secondary sensory cortex has been outlined in the cat, the rat, and the monkey. In the monkey brain, it lies below the primary somatosensory cortex, just above the lateral fissure (Woolsey, 1958). A *homologous* secondary sensory cortex presumably exists in the human brain, and could be the site of cortical representation of pain and temperature signals.

A second possibility is that the *primary somatosensory cortex* may

Homologous. Having the same relative position or structure.

Primary somatosensory cortex. Brodmann's areas 3, 1, and 2 in the postcentral gyrus, receiving input from the ventral posterior nucleus of the thalamus.

be reserved for sensorimotor integration, while the descriptive sensory modalities — warmth and cold, tickle and itch, rubberiness, slipperiness, stickiness, vibration, and the like — find representation in the *somatosensory association cortex* immediately posterior to the primary projection area along the central fissure.

Penfield and Jasper (1954) made the interesting observation that fully a fourth of all cortical points that yielded bodily sensations in the awake human patient when stimulated were *forward* of the central fissure, in the motor cortex. A significant characteristic of these sensory neurons within the motor cortex was that sensations in a limb produced by their stimulation were accompanied by *a desire to move the limb*, which was not true of sensations resulting from stimulation of a corresponding point in the postcentral gyrus. This, then, is evidence of cortical localization of a different kind of bodily sensation, one accompanied by motivational feelings.

A recent detailed analysis of the somatosensory cortex of the primates has added further clarification. Brodmann (1914) defined four distinct cytoarchitectonic areas (namely areas 3a, 3b, 1, and 2) in the primary projection strip along the central fissure in the postcentral gyrus, moving from the depths of the fissure up over the parietal convexity (refer to Figure 6.2). Using microelectrodes to detect cortical responses to stimulation of body surfaces in monkeys of several species, it was found that each of these narrow strips of cortex contains a complete map of the body, each a mirror image of the next, as is true of areas 17 and 18 for visual fields (see Kaas *et al.*, 1979, for a summary of these studies).

Area 3a, in the depths of the fissure, is principally responsive to proprioceptive stimulation from the muscles, while areas 3b and 1 respond to light touch of very discrete locations on the skin. Area 2, on the other hand, tends to respond only to stimulation of deep-lying receptors in regions containing Pacinian corpuscles. These corpuscles' end-structure resembles the layers of an onion, the nerve fiber tip embedded in the center, and responds only briefly to pressure change. This cessation or diminution of response to applied stimulation is called *sensory adaptation*. For example, we may notice the added pressure on the soles of our feet when we stand up, but only momentarily until sensory adaptation takes place. This phenomenon is very striking with respect to warmth and cold, and to odors, such as our own body odors, which may be very noticeable to others whose noses have not become adapted to them.

The touch and pressure components of the bodily sensations are thus demonstrated to have cortical representation — not only in the

Somatosensory association cortex. The cortical region immediately posterior to the somatosensory projection cortex into which the latter projects.

Sensory adaptation. The tendency of sensory receptors to diminish their response to repeated or continuous stimuli.

hand, but throughout the surface of the skin and its underlying tissues. Whether interoceptors that register visceral sensations also find cortical representation is not clear at present; nor do we know where hunger and thirst, sexual pleasure, and feelings of suffocation and the like find cortical representation, if they do. If we include such feelings as fatigue and its opposite, ebullient energy, among the bodily feelings, it becomes evident that the line between bodily sensation and emotional feeling is difficult to draw. Where cortical localization of sensations is concerned, we are only at the threshold of understanding. Perhaps the most reasonable stand to adopt at the present juncture is to recognize that self-awareness involves feelings registered throughout the body, and that many of these may have no direct cortical representation in the thalamocortical system, but only in older regions of the brain, such as the limbic system, the hypothalamus, or the midbrain.

Summary

The somatosensory system consists of sensory receptors throughout the bodily surfaces and in the viscera, devoted to monitoring the body's state of well-being and specific conditions affecting it. It appears to be through this system that we are directly aware of ourselves in the immediate sense. The system has been largely identified as antedating the evolution of the neocortex, and finds little or no registration there except for receptors for touch, pressure, and proprioception.

The skin as a receptor organ contains a wide variety of sensory endings, each consisting of the tip of a nerve fiber whose cell body resides in one of the dorsal-root ganglia situated close to the spinal cord in the dorsal vertebral column. What distinguishes the different types are the various non-neural structures surrounding the tips, which adapt them to specific types of physical stimulation and adjust their manner of firing. Much less is known about the receptors within the viscera. The exteroceptors' domains overlap, suggesting that it may be their simultaneous activity when a particular surface point is stimulated that determines the sensory quality that is apprehended, rather than the type of sensory receptor. The fact that the external ears and tip of the nose contain only free nerve endings demonstrates that one receptor type is capable of transmitting a variety of sensory qualities to the brain.

The ascending pathways for warmth, cold, and burning pain,

among other sensations, follow a different route than the lemniscal-system fibers, which turn upward on entering the cord to follow the dorsal funiculus to the base of the medulla before synapsing. The spinothalamic-system fibers synapse shortly after entering the cord, and the second-order fibers then cross and follow the spinothalamic tract all the way to the thalamus, where they synapse in the ventral posterior nucleus along with the lemniscal-system fibers. Since the fibers crossed at the segmental level, the left side of the body is felt in the right hemisphere and vice versa.

Chapter 8 / *The Pyramidal System and Voluntary Behavior*

Voluntary, deliberate behavior is a function of the pyramidal motor system, characterized by a fast-firing, rapidly transmitting monosynaptic pathway from cortex to muscles. Included in the system are two massive feedback loops, involving the striatum and the cerebellum respectively, which feed into the thalamic motor nuclei for relay to the motor cortex. The striatum and the cerebellum receive massive input, directly or indirectly, from both the perceptual and motor regions of the cortex, and both structures have been found to become active prior to voluntary movement. Even earlier, a sustained increase in EEG baseline negativity over the cortex of the frontal lobe is associated with anticipation of action and the decision to initiate it. It is proposed that the cerebellar loop is specifically concerned with ballistic movements, and the striatal loop with "slow-ramp" movements. Once initiated, action is controlled by highly complex integrating mechanisms within the spinal-cord motor centers, involving a gamma efferent loop through which muscle tension can be finely adjusted to the requirements of the behavior. This process involves fibers passing to sensory receptors within the muscles, a muscle spindle mechanism, and feedback to the motor neurons with collaterals projecting to the brain as proprioceptive input.

From the protozoan level to the human, animal life gives the impression of voluntarism and purposiveness. Watching *Vorticella* in a tiny aquarium mounted on the stage of a microscope, one can scarcely avoid the conviction that this single-celled animalcule possesses a deliberative intelligence, though there is no brain that could conceivably be doing such deliberating (Figure 8.1). But multicellular animals do have brains, and they get better, though no more obviously purposive, as one approaches the human level. Throughout the spectrum of animal species, goal orientation is perhaps the most striking universal phenomenon, yet only recently have psychologists begun to explore its mechanism.

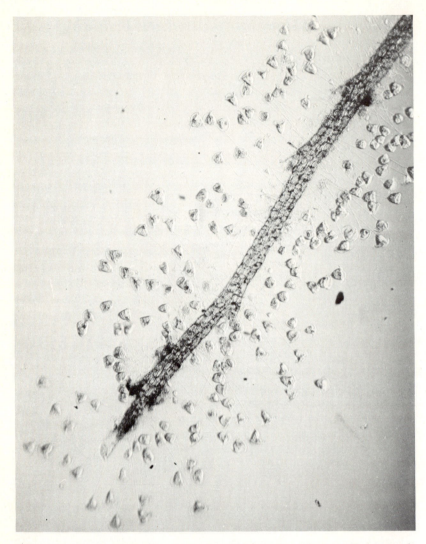

Figure 8.1 / *Vorticella Feeding: Voluntary Behavior in a Single-Celled Animal.*
This pond-water animalcule attaches itself by a long flexible stem, then, by
means of rapidly beating cilia around its top edge, causes a swift stream of
water to flow toward it, carrying various floating particles. They flow by
swiftly and untouched until a preferred food item appears. This mysteriously
pops into the mouth of the *Vorticella,* where it is allowed to spin for a moment
in a tiny whirlpool as further evaluation of its desirability takes place. Then it
is either ejected again into the swift stream or ingested. Anyone watching this
activity through a microscope gains a vivid impression of deliberative choice.
Thus, from the single-cell organism to the human being, selectivity of
response and action decision appears to be the universal manifestation of life.

Reflex response is automatic, "wired-in," and inflexible. Voluntary behavior is the product of deliberative choice, accommodated to the circumstances, withheld until the appropriate moment, and executed with some degree of monitoring and course correction in the process of its execution. This chapter will take a brief look at the nature of this mechanism.

The perceptual mechanisms discussed in the last four chapters were found to be intimately associated with the parietal, occipital,

Figure 8.2 / *The Brain Seen from the Front, Showing the Motor Cortex.* Anterior to the fissure of Rolando lies the frontal lobe of the brain. Within it lie the motor cortex, the premotor cortex, the frontal eye fields, and at the frontal pole the massive prefrontal granular cortex. Each of these regions is concerned principally with behavioral processes, as distinguished from perceptual processes, to which the posterior portion of the brain is so largely devoted. The motor cortex itself (Brodmann's areas 4 and 6) lies immediately anterior to the fissure of Rolando and forms the major source of the pyramidal tract fibers, which project to the spinal motor centers governing behavior.

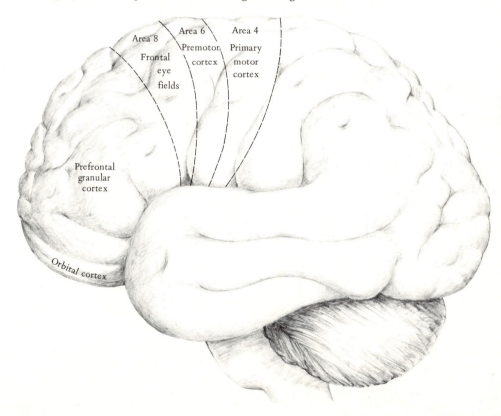

and temporal lobes. The behavioral mechanisms are similarly associated with the frontal lobe, the vast region of the brain anterior
to the central fissure (Figure 8.2). It will be useful to begin by contrasting the character of the information flow into and out of these
two major functional divisions of the brain.

Recall that visual signals enter the occipital lobe cortex from the
lateral geniculate nucleus of the thalamus, which in turn receives
feedback from the same region. Very similar relationships exist between the auditory cortex atop the temporal lobe and the medial
geniculate nucleus, and between the tactile projection areas of the
postcentral gyrus and the ventral posterior nucleus of the thalamus.
Lying between these three cortical projection areas are larger expanses of association cortex, which appear to elaborate the sensory
signals passed to them transcortically from the projection area.
These association areas of the cortex are reciprocally interrelated
with two large thalamic nuclei of their own, the lateral posterior
and the pulvinar (Figure 8.3).

In the frontal lobe, the anatomical arrangements are similar but
the paths of signal flow are different. The primary motor cortex
(area 4) is an output station through which activities generated in
all parts of the cortex appear to be funnelled. Its large *pyramidal cells
of Betz* send their axons directly to the spinal-cord motor centers,
relaying signals to the muscles. Its input, like that of other frontal-
lobe regions, is not new, fresh, incoming sensory information, but
already highly processed information coming from other regions of
the brain. Its principal sources are the ventrolateral and ventral anterior nuclei of the thalamus, which themselves only handle already
well-digested information. It is also in reciprocal intercommunication with the premotor cortex (area 6) anteriorly, and the tactile sensory and proprioceptive regions of the postcentral gyrus posteriorly.
Anterior to the premotor cortex lies the vast expanse of the prefrontal cortex running clear to the frontal pole, which also receives only
highly coded preprocessed information, arriving from all portions
of the posterior regions of the cortex. Below it lies the orbital cortex.
Both of these project massively into the large dorsomedial nucleus
of the thalamus, as well as into the basal ganglia (see Figure 8.4).
With these anatomical relations in mind, we can now consider their
related functions.

Pyramidal cells of Betz. Large neurons in the motor cortex projecting via the pyramidal tract.

The Pyramidal System

With the emergence of the thalamocortical system in mammals, in
addition to a vastly superior visual, auditory, and tactile perceptual

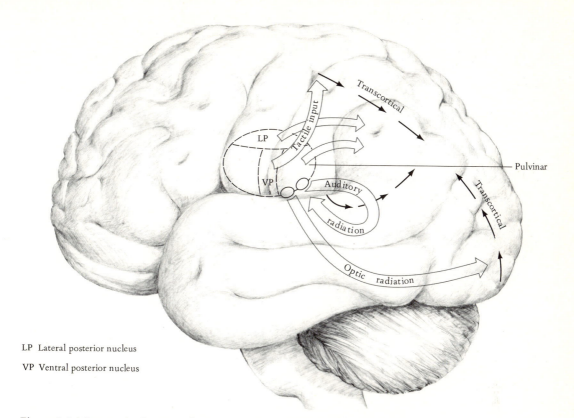

LP Lateral posterior nucleus

VP Ventral posterior nucleus

Figure 8.3 / *Converging Input to the Posterior General Association Cortex.* The posterior general association cortex lies at the junction of the parietal, the occipital, and the temporal lobes, from each of which it receives a transcortical flow of information to be integrated. The posterior general association cortex also receives input from the lateral posterior and pulvinar nuclei of the thalamus, with which it is in two-way intercommunication. Its function would appear to be primarily perceptual and conceptual, the analysis of environmental events with the aid of the symbolic systems, such as verbal language. It represents the "highest level" of integration of the brain's input pathways, preparatory to behavioral response.

system there evolved a new high-precision, rapid-firing motor system to supplement the older, semi-automatic, more grossly organized motor system of the premammalian brain. The newly evolved system has been dubbed by neuroanatomists the *pyramidal motor system* to differentiate it from the older "extrapyramidal system." It appears to have taken upon itself a special portion of the total response tasks of the brain, but there is some dispute about how that set of response tasks ought to be defined. Here we will emphasize

Pyramidal motor system. The voluntary motor system taken as a whole, including some extrapyramidal structures.

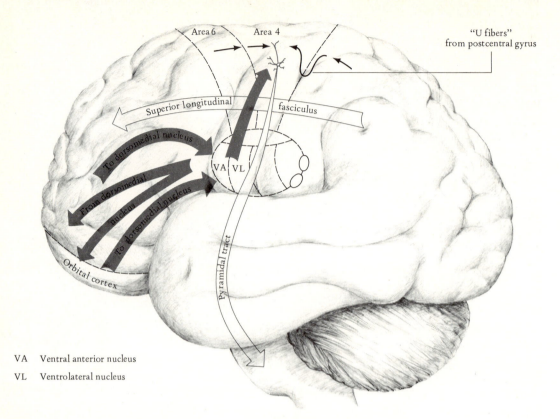

Labels within figure: Area 6, Area 4, "U fibers" from postcentral gyrus, Superior longitudinal fasciculus, To dorsomedial nucleus, From dorsomedial nucleus, To dorsomedial nucleus, Orbital cortex, VA, VL, Pyramidal tract

VA   Ventral anterior nucleus

VL   Ventrolateral nucleus

Figure 8.4 / *Paths of Input Converging upon the Pyramidal Tract.* Sensory information integrated in the posterior general association area is transmitted to the anterior general association area in the prefrontal granular cortex via a massive fiber bundle, the superior longitudinal fasciculus, coursing through the deep layers of the white matter. At that anterior station, information received appears to receive further processing in connection with the massive dorsomedial nucleus of the thalamus. Ultimately it is transmitted to the thalamic motor nuclei, principally through the septum and basal ganglia, for relay to the motor cortex. The motor cortex is the source of the pyramidal tract, the final common output pathway of the entire cerebral cortex. The motor cortex also receives direct communication from the somatosensory area across the fissure of Rolando, transcortically via "U" fibers.

its role in behavior that involves conscious assessment of the requirements of a situation, anticipation of the future, and response withholding until the time is ripe, by contrast with behaviors triggered by some relatively simple releaser stimulus, such as a fly settling on the nose. Both types of behavior make use of the same muscles and spinal motor neurons, but they might nevertheless be quite different in their organization. The former is apt to be more deliberative in character, based on a complex assessment of the total situation; the latter is more unthinking.

It might be best to approach this system first by examining a relatively simple response mechanism, adaptive behavior triggered quite directly by some observation. Imagine that somebody walking in front of you drops a book and you stoop down "spontaneously" to pick it up and hand it to its owner. Incoming stimuli from the visual and auditory receptors produce a perception of the situation, which triggers a decision mechanism somewhere in the brain. This decision in turn initiates a familiar, highly overlearned action program, which is then "run off" by the muscles automatically and autonomously. You don't have to think about it at all. The process of organizing the response will be discussed below. Here we will consider only the *executive function,* once the decision to act has been made.

The Pyramidal Tract

Execution of motor commands via the voluntary motor system makes use of the *pyramidal tract,* whose fibers pass without synapse all the way down from the cortex to the spinal motor centers in the cord. Most of the fibers cross over to the opposite side at the level of the medulla, where they form two curiously pyramidal-shaped ridges on the ventral surface, which give the tract its name. The pyramidal tract contains the axons of most of the giant pyramidal cells of Betz of the primary motor cortex (area 4), as well as many fibers from the premotor cortex and from the postcentral gyrus and parietal lobe. Some 10–20 percent of these axons synapse directly upon the spinal motor neurons, forming a monosynaptic relay from the cortex to the muscles themselves, which provides for an exceedingly quick response.

Pyramidal tract. **The fiber bundle passing directly from the cortex into the spinal motor centers active in voluntary behavior.**

This very fast-acting two-neuron system for initiating behavior was once thought to be peculiar to the primates, and especially pronounced in the human, but similar fast-acting tracts are found in birds; some mammals, including seals and chimpanzees, may actually have more such fibers than do humans. However, this system is unquestionably important to our manual dexterity and athletic skills, as well as such skills of everyday life as picking up a dropped book and handing it to someone in a single deft, graceful movement.

Not all the pyramidal-tract fibers cross over to the contralateral side of the body: 10–30 percent continue down the ipsilateral half of the cord. However, behavioral evidence indicates that it is fair to say that the motor cortex of the left hemisphere controls the muscles of the right side of the body, while fibers from the motor cortex of the right hemisphere control the left side (Figure 8.5).

The Gamma Efferent System

In the primates, the cortical pyramidal cells of area 4 synapse upon two types of spinal motor neurons, called "alpha" and "gamma." It is the large-bore, rapidly transmitting *alpha motor neurons* that directly activate the muscles to produce behavior. Each alpha fiber branches toward its tip to make contact with a number of muscle fibers in a synapse called the *neuromuscular junction*. The motor neuron and its associated muscle fibers constitute a *motor unit*. In the case of small muscles such as those of the fingers, the number of muscle fibers per motor unit is small, nearly one-to-one, insuring precise control. (Recall the parallel situation of the ganglion cells of the retina in the foveal region.) In larger muscles, such as those of the leg, the motor units are much larger, each spinal motor neuron is associated with many muscle fibers, and control is less precise.

The second type of motor neuron, called a *gamma efferent neuron,* synapses not on muscle fibers proper (called *extrafusal fibers*), but rather on tiny *intrafusal* muscle *fibers* within structures called *muscle spindles,* which are embedded among the large extrafusal fibers. The muscle spindles are actually receptor systems designed to respond to muscle stretch. When the muscle elongates, the muscle spindle and the intrafusal fibers within it are also elongated. Wound around these fibers is a receptor fiber, the *annulospiral ending,* which when stretched sends signals back to the motor neuron via 1a fibers to cause it to increase its firing rate (to cause the extrafusal fibers to contract more strongly), thereby relieving the stretch on the intrafusal fibers. Thus there is a feedback loop through which the elongation of the muscle is continually monitored and controlled. What the gamma efferents do is activate the intrafusal fibers to contract, thereby stretching the annulospiral endings at their middle and causing them to activate the alpha motor neuron to faster firing,

Alpha motor neurons. Large neurons in the spinal motor centers whose axons synapse on muscle cells, causing the skeletal muscles to contract.

Neuromuscular junction. The synaptic contact of a motor neuron with a muscle cell.

Motor unit. The group of skeletal muscle cells activated by a particular motor neuron, together with that motor neuron.

Gamma efferent neuron. The motor neuron projecting to the muscle spindle, a sensory receptor mechanism within the skeletal muscles, rather than to the muscle cells proper.

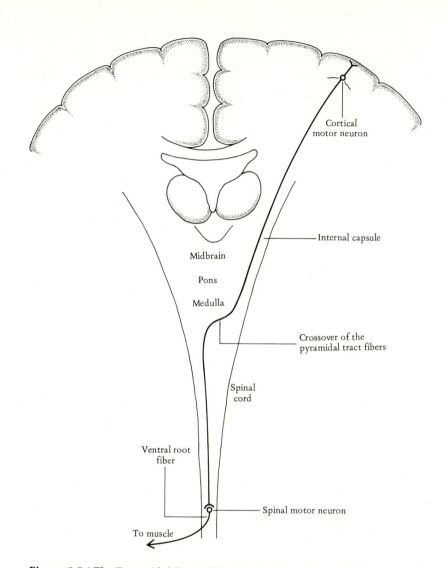

Cortical
motor neuron

Internal capsule

Midbrain

Pons

Medulla

Crossover of the
pyramidal tract fibers

Spinal
cord

Ventral root
fiber

Spinal motor neuron

To muscle

Figure 8.5 / *The Pyramidal Tract, Showing its Two-Neuron Pathway to the Muscles.* The pyramidal tract fibers originate in large projection neurons of the cortex, principally in its layer V and principally from the motor cortex. They descend through the internal capsule, cross to the opposite side at the level of the medulla, then descend as the corticospinal tract to the various spinal motor centers for relay to the skeletal muscles themselves. This extremely rapid-firing and rapidly transmitting neural system evolved with the mammals and is responsible in large measure for all voluntary, deliberative behavior. The pyramidal system is differentiated from the extrapyramidal system, which takes over without much assistance from the cortex when the behavior is so well practiced as to require no attention.

and thus greater contraction of the muscle. These relationships are diagrammatically illustrated in Figure 8.6.

Examination of Figure 8.6 will reveal that what we are discussing here is an ideal *servomechanism* for muscular control. The muscles can be activated either directly by exciting the alpha motor neurons or indirectly by exciting the gamma efferents, which will cause the intrafusal fibers to contract, activating the annulospiral endings to send signals to excite the alpha neurons. If a tendon is pulled, stretching the muscle, the muscle-spindle receptor system is activated to counteract the stretch by a greater contraction force of the muscle. On the other hand, the gamma efferent fibers can, by their level of excitation of the intrafusal fibers, set the level at which this resistance to muscle elongation begins. Thus we can keep an arm extended at a certain height and adjust our muscle tension automatically to accommodate the weight of an object held in it.

Servomechanism. A feedback circuit controlling the intensity of a given function.

This process is interestingly demonstrated in infancy. At six or seven months of age, the infant can support the weight of a small object (as well as the arm's weight) while bringing it to the mouth, or examining it, but it does so with a tremor, indicating that the gamma efferent loop is unsure and adjusting itself. If handed an object, the infant's extended arm initially drops under the weight; then the object is raised back up to the desired level and supported there. This implies gamma efferent stimulation to the muscle spindles to give just enough stretch to the annulospiral ending receptors to activate the alpha motor neurons to exert the needed additional extrafusal muscle contraction. If the main muscle fibers contract too rapidly, the muscle spindles embedded among them will shorten and the annulospiral endings will stop firing, removing that source of stimulation to the alpha motor neuron in question. When the child's arm falls under the weight of the object, the voluntary motor system brings it back up via the pyramidal tract fibers to the alpha neurons, while the desired level is then maintained by adjusting the required "setting" of the gamma efferent loop.

In addition to resisting muscle stretch automatically and setting the desired level of muscular contraction, the muscle spindles — via their annulospiral ending receptors — also signal to the brain what is going on. Collateral fibers from their axons passing back to the alpha motor neurons project up the cord in the *dorsal funiculi* to the cuneate and *gracile nuclei* at the base of the medulla. These are the proprioceptive fibers from the muscles, discussed in Chapter 6 in connection with the tactile receptor systems. The cuneate nucleus handles lemniscal-system fibers from the arm; the gracile nucleus handles those from the leg. From there the second-order fibers cross

Dorsal funiculus (*few-NIK-yew-lus*). The mass of ascending fiber bundles in the dorsal (rear) portion of the spinal cord.

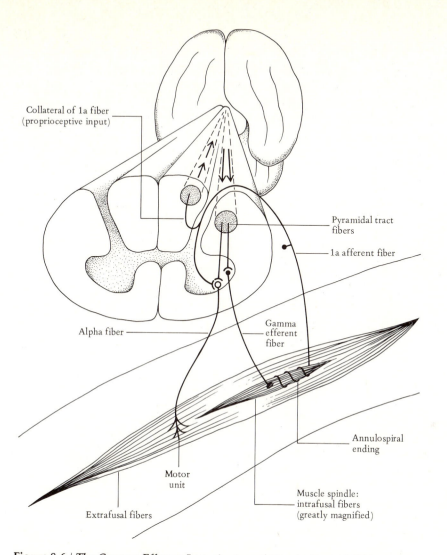

Collateral of 1a fiber
(proprioceptive input)

Pyramidal tract
fibers

1a afferent fiber

Alpha fiber

Gamma
efferent
fiber

Annulospiral
ending

Motor
unit

Muscle spindle:
intrafusal fibers
(greatly magnified)

Extrafusal fibers

Figure 8.6 / *The Gamma Efferent Loop System of Muscle Control.* This motor feedback loop system is an ingenious device for regulating skeletal muscle movement. Within each motor unit of the muscles there are embedded small muscle spindles which, when stretched, send signals back to the motor neuron to increase its firing rate, thus shortening the muscle through contraction and relieving the stretch of the spindle. (The same fibers send collaterals to the brain via the lemniscal system and constitute the proprioceptive input from the muscles.) However, the muscle spindle itself can be caused to contract independently by motor neurons of another kind in the spinal motor centers. Their fibers are called gamma efferents, and their effect is to stimulate the muscle spindle receptors (the annulospiral endings shown), thus providing another means of activating the motor neuron. This is the gamma efferent loop that makes possible the setting of a particular muscle tension, such as for holding an object up against the force of gravity.

the medulla and ascend with the somatosensory fibers in the *medial lemniscus* to the ventral posterior thalamic nucleus for relay to the cortex. Note that signals passing down from the cortex are shown activating the thalamic relay neurons, while other descending fibers synapse in the cuneate nucleus on inhibitory interneurons, which in turn synapse on the ascending second-order neurons. (This inhibitory system is thought to serve the function of habituation to inconsequential sensory signals, so that they no longer elicit one's attention.)

Medial lemniscus. A fiber bundle passing upward through the brainstem carrying signals of the somatosensory system.

In addition to resisting muscle stretch and reporting conditions to the brain, the muscle spindles perform the third function of maintaining *muscle tonus*. The skeletal muscles are characteristically kept under slight tension, through a continual mild activation of the gamma efferent system, even when they are not being used to move the body. Muscle tonus of the body as a whole totally disappears only during the stage of sleep called rapid-eye-movement (REM) sleep, discussed in Chapter 12. During this stage the body goes limp (and, if lying on our back, we snore) due to a severe inhibitory blockade of the gamma efferents as well as the alpha motor neurons. It has been conjectured that this blockade is necessary because we dream frequently during this stage and might otherwise tend to "act out" our dreams.

A controversy over whether normal activation of the muscles occurs solely via the gamma efferents was recently resolved by the finding that alpha and gamma motor neurons are activated by the pyramidal-tract fibers synchronously (Vallbo, 1971). The time it takes the gamma efferent loop to operate brings the excitation influence of the annulospiral ending receptors to bear just in time to make of the spinal motor centers an ideal servomechanism: the input from the muscle spindles arrives after contraction of the main muscle has begun.

The Alpha Motor Neurons

Within the spinal motor centers, the alpha motor neurons send collateral fibers to local inhibitory neurons, called *Renshaw cells* after their discoverer. These cells may in turn synapse upon the cell soma of the same motor neuron, thus operating as a governor of its firing rate. Or they may synapse upon alpha neurons on the opposite side of the cord going to muscles that flex coordinately, as in walking; or upon alpha neurons projecting to opposing muscles within the same member — relaxing the extensors when the flexors are ac-

Renshaw cells. Small inhibitory interneurons surrounding the motor neurons in the spinal motor centers.

tivated and vice versa — to avoid conflicting muscular tensions. Each inhibitory Renshaw cell synapses with a great number of alpha neurons at that level of the cord, and each alpha neuron in turn receives inhibitory input from a large number of Renshaw cells activated by the collateral fibers of other alpha neurons. These inhibitory neurons may also synapse upon other inhibitory neurons, slowing their firing rate and thus *disinhibiting* the alpha neurons to which they project — a form of excitation. Figure 8.7 shows the relations of Renshaw cells in the spinal motor centers. The upshot of this complex interneuronal barrage is that only the more strongly excited alpha motor neurons succeed in carrying through their muscular activation; stray weakly stimulated neurons drop out (Eccles, 1973).

Disinhibition. Liberation of a neuron or nucleus from inhibitory control through inhibitory neurons slowing the firing rate of those neurons acting as inhibitory controls.

Other inhibitory influences arrive at the spinal motor centers from higher regions, either through synapse upon the motor neurons directly (inhibitory fibers) or through activation of local inhibitory interneurons. Some of these arise from the cerebellum, others from the balance organ of the inner ear by way of brainstem vestibular nuclei. Thus it is clear that the spinal motor centers serve as the locus of a highly complex integration of signals, calculated to deliver precisely the right degree of excitation to the motor units under their command. The inhibitory fibers serve to shape the response in the manner of a sculptor shaping a stone, through elimination (Eccles, 1973).

Through the specialized synapse called the *neuromuscular* or *myoneural junction,* the alpha motor neuron finally activates the muscle fibers with which it is associated. The terminal branch of the fiber loses its myelin sheath just before entering a deep groove in the muscle cell *endplate,* a specialized region of its membrane homologous with the neuronal postsynaptic membrane. Here the fiber terminal releases a small quantity of acetylcholine with the arrival of each spike potential, which brings about a momentary depolarization of the muscle-cell membrane. Then the equivalent of the neural action potential travels the full length of the extrafusal muscle fiber, in both directions from the junction. Through a mechanism not yet fully understood, this initiates the lengthwise contraction of the muscle fiber. The traveling wave of depolarization here is not called a spike potential, but a *muscle impulse.*

Endplate. Motor endplate, the equivalent of the postsynaptic membrane at the neuromuscular junction.

The intensity of the muscle-cell contraction is dependent on the firing rapidity of the alpha motor neuron innervating it — that is, how many times per second a muscle impulse is sent along its membrane by the discharge of fresh acetylcholine into the synaptic cleft of the motor endplate. The intensity of the contraction of the

Muscle impulse. The wave of depolarization of the muscle cell plasma membrane which initiates the cell's contraction.

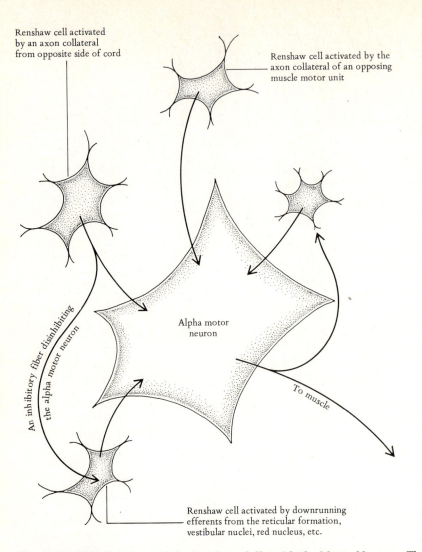

Renshaw cell activated
by an axon collateral
from opposite side of cord

Renshaw cell activated by the
axon collateral of an opposing
muscle motor unit

Alpha motor
neuron

An inhibitory fiber disinhibiting
the alpha motor neuron

To muscle

Renshaw cell activated by downrunning
efferents from the reticular formation,
vestibular nuclei, red nucleus, etc.

Figure 8.7 / *The Relations of the Renshaw Cells with the Motor Neurons.* The alpha motor neurons are the large cells that project to the skeletal muscles, causing their contraction. Here a collateral fiber from a motor cell axon is shown synapsing upon an inhibitory Renshaw cell, which in turn projects back to the motor neuron's soma to slow its firing, a simple negative feedback loop. Above is shown another inhibitory fiber coming to inhibit the firing of the motor neuron while an opposing muscle is active, as occurs, for example, in all arm movement. A third Renshaw cell is activated from the other side of the spinal cord, as in alternate arm swinging. This third Renshaw cell is also inhibiting another Renshaw cell below, causing it to cease its inhibitory influence on the motor neuron. Some of these Renshaw cells exert a powerful inhibitory force to put the motor neuron temporarily out of action, allowing its neurotransmitter supplies to be replenished.

entire skeletal muscle depends, of course, on how many of the motor units composing it are activated, as well as the intensity of their activation.

Unlike some other neurotransmitters, acetylcholine cannot be removed from the synaptic cleft by re-uptake into the axon terminal, but must be destroyed by the enzyme acetylcholine esterase (the suffix -*ase* always denotes an *enzyme,* a protein substance that facilitates a biochemical reaction without itself being changed). There is thus some danger that the neuromuscular junction may run out of its supply of acetylcholine under heavy bombardment of spike potentials because it cannot be reconstituted rapidly enough. This may be one reason why the alpha motor neurons send collaterals to adjacent Renshaw cells to inhibit their own firing. These inhibitory neurons produce a very powerful effect, which may last as long as half a second. In normal behavior, when muscles are not tensed to their maximum, they may thus be put out of action momentarily while their terminals are replenished. The entire motor unit relaxes and other motor units carry on with the task. The number of muscle motor units is sufficiently large that many can be out of action simultaneously without their contribution being missed. Perhaps the often-reported superhuman power of the muscles in emergencies (or under hypnosis) can be rationally explained by this circumstance.

Enzyme. A protein whose biological activity is to catalyze a specific chemical reaction without itself being altered.

The Motor Cortex

The primary motor cortex acts like an obedient servant, taking orders as to what *motor program* to execute and duly executing it. It was once presumed that the premotor cortex anterior to it was engaged in higher-level activity, perhaps organizing the response in a more complex manner. This impression arose because body movements aroused by stimulation of this region appeared to be more complex. However, recent research has refuted this notion. It appears that the stimulating electrode tends to produce bodily movements associated with the larger muscles close to the trunk as it is moved anteriorly into the premotor cortex, and movements of the smaller muscles associated with the extremities as it is moved posteriorly into the region of the central fissure. Thus, while stimulation of area 6 produces grosser movements, this seems to represent not a higher level of coordination but merely a different set of muscles. Current thinking is that the two areas, primary motor and premotor, represent one integrated motor cortical system operating,

Motor program. The neural basis of a particular skilled motor performance.

at the same functional level, as executors of the motor program chosen in some other region of the brain. Note that both regions project fibers into the pyramidal tract, and in almost equal numbers (Figure 8.8).

Traditionally, the premotor cortex has been more closely identified with the extrapyramidal motor system governing more automatic behaviors, and a distinction between the two regions was made on this basis. This too now seems insupportable. As we shall see, older brain structures once thought to be uniquely associated with extrapyramidal motor functions are now recognized as intimately involved in the voluntary behavior of the pyramidal system.

Figure 8.8 / *Major Pathways Entering and Leaving the Neocortex Concerned with Voluntary Behavior.* The primary motor cortex (area 4) and the premotor cortex (area 6) both contribute fibers to the pyramidal tract. Together they represent an integrated motor system executing the orders received from the thalamic motor nuclei.

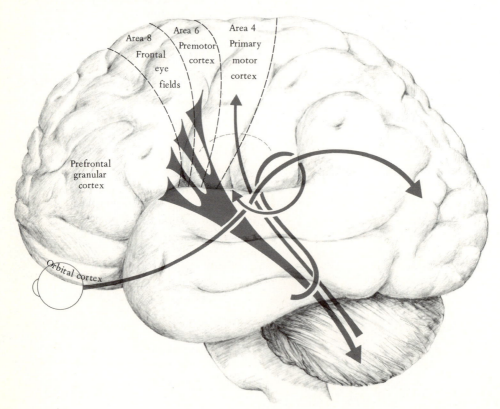

Moreover, section of the pyramidal tract in primates does not prevent integrated voluntaristic behavior (Lewis and Brindley, 1968), and recent studies in the human indicate that damage to the pyramidal tract leads only to a loss of muscle strength and dexterity, principally in manual manipulations. This finding suggests that the pyramidal tract serves in humans to facilitate motor functions, primarily in connection with tactile perception (Brooks and Stoney, 1971). Thus normal voluntary behavior, once associated particularly with the function of the primary motor cortex in the precentral gyrus, is now better understood as a joint function of the pyramidal and extrapyramidal systems, involving the activities of the entire motor cortex, including area 6 of the premotor cortex and the region of the postcentral gyrus as well.

Nevertheless, there are differences in the functional connections of areas 4 and 6, as is dramatically illustrated when they suffer damage. Lesions in area 4 tend to result in a flaccid paralysis of muscles of the opposite side controlled by the damaged portion of the cortex; lesions in area 6 result instead in a spastic paralysis. The former represents loss of normal activation of the spinal motor neurons; the latter involves loss of an inhibitory influence that normally limits their excitability.

The Striatal System

A major input to the motor region of the cortex originates, as we have mentioned, in the ventrolateral and ventral anterior nuclei of the thalamus, which in turn receive a major fiber input from the basal ganglia via fibers projecting from the globus pallidus. Since the motor regions of the cortex project into the caudate nucleus and putamen — together called the *striatum* — which themselves project through the globus pallidus, there is a significant circular feedback loop linking cortex to subcortical nuclei. We have already seen that the motor cortex receives continuous input from other cortical regions. The striatum too receives input from substantially every region of the cortex, one known pathway being a massive inflow to the caudate nucleus from the prefrontal granular cortex and its underlying orbital cortex. Moreover, the thalamic motor nuclei receive input from other regions associated with motor functions, notably the cerebellum (see the next section), and may well integrate this information rather than merely relaying it. Thus the cortical-striatal-thalamic feedback loop is by no means a closed one. It is the con-

Striatum (strye-ATE-um). **The caudate nucleus and putamen considered together.**

fluence of a vast continuous inflow of information, on the basis of which the overt behavior is governed. This loop is illustrated in Figure 8.9.

Figure 8.9 shows that, in addition to the pathway projecting from the globus pallidus to the thalamic motor nuclei, another fiber bun-

Figure 8.9 / *The Basal Ganglia Motor Loop.* The head of the caudate nucleus and the putamen are both shown receiving cortical fibers (from many regions of the cortex, but principally from the motor region) and projecting into the thalamic motor nuclei for relay back to the motor cortex. This continuously running feedback circuit is considered especially important in the execution of careful and deliberate behaviors requiring monitoring and control over the course of the movement. It is balanced by another such loop operating through the cerebellum.

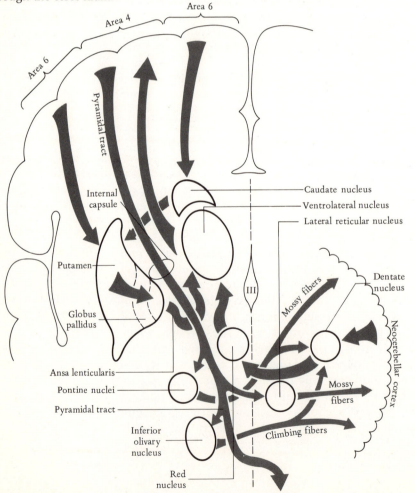

dle projects down into the brainstem motor nuclei, beginning a multisynaptic pathway to the motor neurons in the spinal motor centers. This more ancient system belongs to the extrapyramidal part of the motor system — the part that takes over functions after they have been well learned, and no longer require the attention of the thalamocortical system for smooth operation. Such behavior could be said to be under direct control of the globus pallidus.

The Cerebellar System

The cerebellum has been likened to the cerebrum in that it has a cortex and subcortical nuclei buried in the white matter beneath it (Figure 8.10). However, its cortex has a simpler structure, and a very consistent and orderly arrangement throughout. In the regularity of its intracortical connections, it is approached only by the relative stereotypy of the hippocampal cortex in its relations with the dentate gyrus. This very simple structure marks both as ancient systems. Indeed, the cerebellum is found in the most primitive of fishes.

The cerebellar cortex is essentially a two-layered cortex, the large *Purkinje cells* forming a conspicuous boundary between the layers (Figure 8.11). It receives two kinds of afferent fibers. The *climbing fibers* are so named because, on reaching the cerebellar cortex, each winds repeatedly around the very complex dendritic tree of a single Purkinje cell, in an ascending fashion and making repeated synaptic contacts along the way. Each Purkinje cell receives input from just one such fiber, which exerts a powerfully exciting effect on it. These excitatory climbing fibers arise in the *inferior olivary nuclei* that bulge laterally from the ventral medulla just below the pons (Figure 8.12).

The other type of afferent fiber entering the cerebellum is called a *mossy fiber*. Mossy fibers appear not to synapse upon the Purkinje cells at all (Llinas, 1976), but on the dendrites of tiny granule cells in the layer below. These cells in turn project their axons up into the surface layer, where each one bifurcates to form extended *parallel fibers* passing in opposite directions through the dendritic trees of the Purkinje cells. The Purkinje cells' dendritic trees are splayed out like fans perpendicular to the direction of passage of the parallel fibers. In this manner the influence of a single mossy fiber is brought to bear on a great number of Purkinje cells in succession. Since the mossy fibers each synapse upon a great number of granule cells, which in turn synapse upon a great number of Purkinje

Climbing fibers. Fibers entering the cerebellum from the inferior olivary nucleus, each synapsing upon the dendritic tree of a single Purkinje cell and powerfully activating it.

Inferior olivary nuclei. Large nuclei situated in the ventral brainstem below the pons; the source of the climbing fibers.

Mossy fibers. Fibers projecting to the granule cells of the cerebellar cortex.

Parallel fibers. Axons of the cerebellar granule cells which ascend to the level of the Purkinje cell dendrites, then bifurcate to pass in parallel with others through the array of such dendrites.

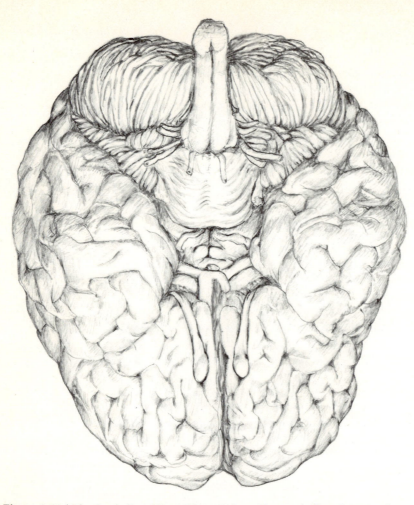

Figure 8.10 / *The Cerebellum Viewed from Below.* The cerebellum is a massive structure in the human brain, as a result of the vast enlargement of the two laterally lying cerebellar hemispheres, whose expansion in the mammals occurred simultaneously with the expansion of the neocortex. The cerebellum is relatively larger in human beings than in any other large mammal and underlies our capacity for remarkable feats of muscular dexterity (such as virtuosity on the violin, piano, or typewriter).

cells, their influence, unlike that of the climbing fibers, is widely distributed. The mossy fibers do not arise from the inferior olives, but from a number of smaller nuclei in the brainstem (the pontine motor nuclei, among others).

There are several types of inhibitory neurons in the cerebellar cortex, and the Purkinje cells themselves are inhibitory. The sole output from the cortex, the Purkinje cells project only to one or another of the subcortical nuclei embedded within the cerebellar white matter. These nuclei also receive excitatory collaterals from

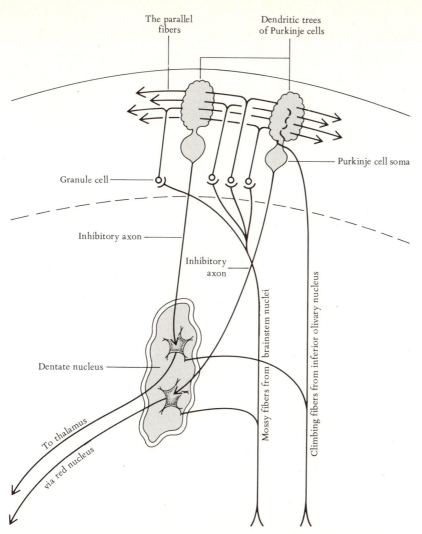

The parallel fibers

Dendritic trees of Purkinje cells

Purkinje cell soma

Granule cell

Inhibitory axon

Inhibitory axon

Mossy fibers from brainstem nuclei

Climbing fibers from inferior olivary nucleus

Dentate nucleus

To thalamus

via red nucleus

Figure 8.11 / *Simplified Diagram of the Cerebellar Cortex and its Circuits.* Two types of sensory fibers (mainly proprioceptive) are shown entering the cerebellum from the brainstem nuclei and elsewhere. Each fiber sends a collateral to a large subcortical nucleus before proceeding to the cortex. One synapses on numerous tiny granule cells (estimated to number in the hundreds of billions), which in turn are the source of the excitatory parallel fibers passing through a series of Purkinje cell dendritic trees. The other makes multiple synaptic contacts with a single Purkinje cell dendritic tree, exerting a powerful excitatory effect. The Purkinje cell axons are the only fibers leaving the cortex to project to the cerebellar nuclei embedded in the white matter, and these are inhibitory. They balance the excitatory input from the collaterals of the mossy and climbing fibers. The only output from the cerebellum is via axons of these subcortical nuclear cells, which in the voluntary motor system go from the dentate nucleus to the motor nuclei of the thalamus.

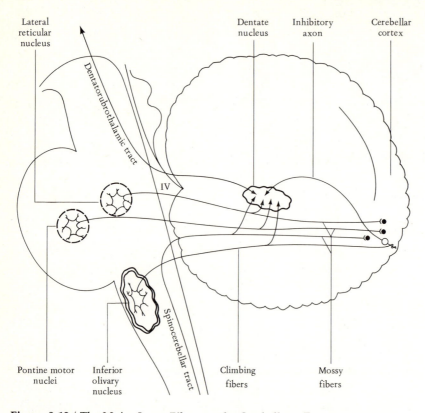

Figure 8.12 / *The Major Input Fibers to the Cerebellum.* Excitatory input to the cerebellum is of two kinds. Climbing fibers synapse on the Purkinje cells, only one fiber to each. Mossy fibers synapse on a great many tiny granule cells whose axons in turn synapse on a great number of Purkinje cell dendritic trees. Both types of fibers send collaterals into the dentate nucleus, which also receives the inhibitory output of the Purkinje cells.

both the mossy fibers and the climbing fibers, and this excitatory influence is balanced against the inhibitory influence of the Purkinje cells. The output of the cerebellum is solely from these subcortical nuclei, which project into the brainstem and, via the *dentatorubrothalamic tract* (see Figure 8.12), through the *red nucleus* and into the thalamic motor nuclei.

Since collaterals from the pyramidal tract synapse upon the brainstem nuclei from which the mossy fibers arise, and upon the infe-

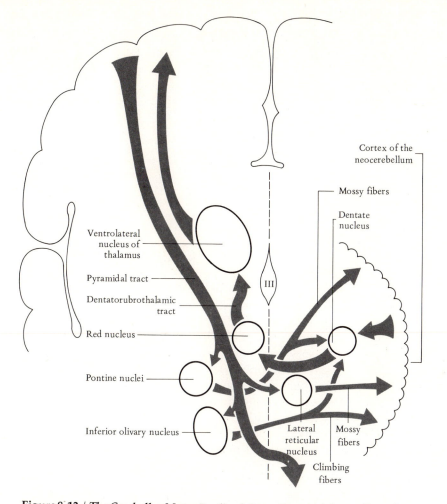

Cortex of the neocerebellum

Mossy fibers

Dentate nucleus

Ventrolateral nucleus of thalamus

Pyramidal tract

III

Dentatorubrothalamic tract

Red nucleus

Pontine nuclei

Inferior olivary nucleus

Lateral reticular nucleus

Mossy fibers

Climbing fibers

Figure 8.13 / *The Cerebellar Motor Feedback Loop.* Pyramidal tract fibers from the motor cortex passing through the brainstem send collaterals to the pontine, lateral reticular, and inferior olivary nuclei, which in turn project fibers into the cerebellum — mossy fibers in the case of the first two, climbing fibers in the case of the inferior olivary nucleus. The output from the cerebellum stimulated by these fibers goes from the dentate nucleus to the thalamic motor nuclei (via the red nucleus of the midbrain). The motor nuclei of the thalamus then relay the signals to the motor cortex, completing a feedback loop. This loop is joined by the fibers of the basal ganglia feedback loop at the thalamic motor nuclei, where the two loop processes are presumed integrated before relay to the cortex and further pyramidal tract firing, which allows for course correction of the action in progress.

rior olivary nucleus from which the climbing fibers arise, here too — as in the striatal system — we have a grand feedback loop. The motor cortex projects to the brainstem nuclei, which project into the cerebellum, which in turn projects to the thalamic motor nuclei, which project again to the motor cortex (Figure 8.13).

The dentatorubrothalamic tract mentioned above arises from the largest of the cerebellar nuclei, called the *dentate nucleus.* "Rubro" refers to the *red nucleus,* a prominent motor nucleus of the midbrain region that acts as a relay point for fibers of the complex extrapyramidal multisynaptic motor system.

The Locus of Action Decision

In an ingenious series of studies by E. Evarts and his colleagues, monkeys were trained to move an arm on cue, and microelectrodes implanted in the brain and in the muscles made simultaneous recordings of activity. It was first demonstrated that cells in the motor cortex become active a very short time before the initiation of muscle movement, indicating that the motor cortex is indeed involved in the circuits initiating voluntary behavior. It was next shown that this is not the case for the somatosensory projection area in the postcentral gyrus, whose neurons begin to fire only after muscular activity begins. This finding indicates that the brain circuits that initiate behavior, as opposed to those that regulate it once begun, do not include the somatosensory cortex.

Since the cerebellum is known to receive proprioceptive sensory input about muscular movement, the same experiment was conducted with simultaneous recording from the motor cortex and the cerebellar cortex. The investigators were surprised to discover that, in voluntary behavior, cerebellar activity also precedes the onset of muscular movement. It had previously been understood that cerebellar function occurred only in response to feedback from the muscles, but this finding indicates that it also has something to do with organizing intended behavior. (See Evarts, 1976, for a complete discussion.)

To complete the story, the study was extended to the basal ganglia. Again, the surprising finding was that the striatal system is active not only following muscular movement, but also prior to its initiation. If we combine these two systems, as shown in Figure 8.14, we can conceptualize the major aspects of the pyramidal system as a whole. When a movement is voluntarily undertaken, it ap-

Dentate nucleus. An important subcortical nucleus within the cerebellar white matter whose neurons project to the thalamic motor nuclei.

Red nucleus. An important motor nucleus in the midbrain region forming a relay station for extrapyramidal pathways to the spinal motor neurons.

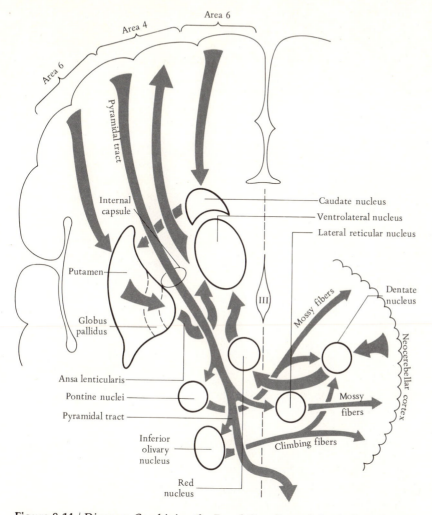

Figure 8.14 / *Diagram Combining the Basal Ganglia and Cerebellar Motor Feedback Loops.* For sake of clarity, only the pyramidal system of one hemisphere has been drawn. It is understood that motor cortex, basal ganglia, and cerebellum all receive sensory input concerning environmental occurrences in the course of a voluntary act. Such input permits adjustment of the system to changed circumstances, as in darting about on a basketball court, at any or all three points. In addition, the brainstem reticular system receives collateral fibers from both the pyramidal tract and the ascending spinothalamic pathways, providing a further opportunity for behavioral monitoring and adjustment of the act in progress.

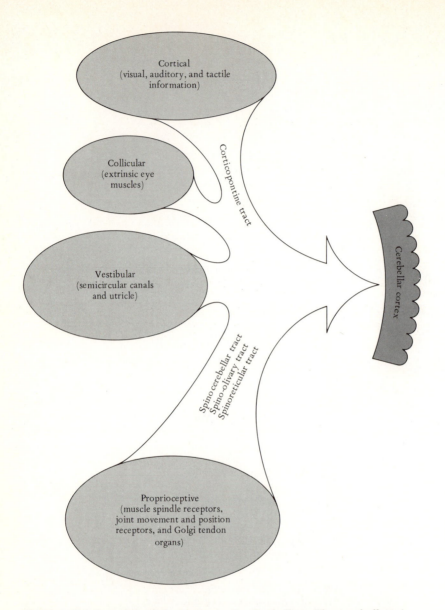

Figure 8.15 / *Overview of the Inputs to the Cerebellum.* The cerebellum is actually a more complex structure than has been suggested. In addition to cortical motor signals, it receives cortical sensory information and, from the body, proprioceptive information via three ascending tracts of the spinal cord. It also receives input from the vestibular system and the superior colliculus, both of which may be significantly involved in voluntary behavior even though the operation of the cerebellum remains below the level of conscious registration.

pears that all the structures and pathways shown in the figure become active prior to the activation of any muscles. Once behavior has begun, new sensory information is generated by the behavior itself: proprioceptive information from muscles and joints, somatosensory information from the bodily tissues and skin, and visual distance-receptor input. Thus, when we stoop down to pick up a book and hand it to someone who dropped it, a motor program with a purposive goal, intended by the brain, is set in motion and then monitored in light of its goal through sensory feedback. We know that both cerebellum and striatum receive input from the cortex about the progress of the action, as does the motor cortex itself via the *U fibers* running beneath the central fissure from the postcentral gyrus to make such monitoring possible (Figure 8.15).

U fibers. Transcortical fibers dipping below a fissure.

As we shall see in Chapter 9, there is evidence that the prefrontal cortex, which feeds into the striatum, is also involved in the initiation phase of voluntary behavior, perhaps full seconds before. An *expectancy wave*, which appears to have something to do with focal attention processes in anticipation of the moment of release of the action program, has been electrographically recorded. The question of the locus of action decision is thus broadened to include the entire frontal lobe as a prospect. But the prefrontal granular cortex is also in intimate communication with the posterior association areas of the brain, via several massive longitudinal fiber bundles, which makes it possible that action decision is arrived at in the perceptual regions of the brain.

It has been proposed that the cerebellum specializes in the control of rapidly executed ballistic movement which "runs off" an intended motor program too quickly to be much altered in the process, as in our example of picking up a book and handing it to its owner. The basal ganglia, on the other hand, have been conjectured to be in charge of more slowly and deliberately executed action programs requiring delicacy and refinement of motor control, such as threading a needle. These two structurally independent systems are presumed to be coordinated in their functions through the juncture of their two great feedback loops at the thalamic motor nuclei (Figure 8.16).

The Vestibular System

Let us turn next to a very fundamental question: how do we keep our balance while walking on our stiltlike legs, or darting around

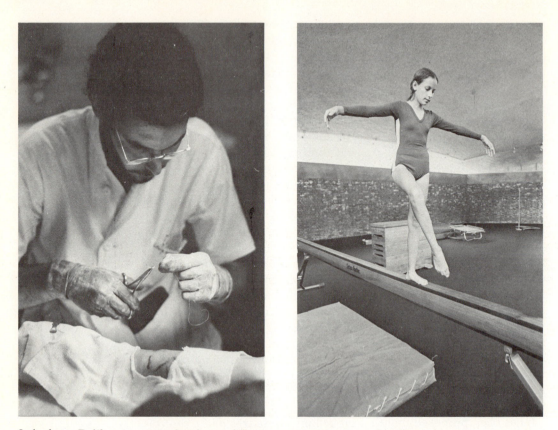

Left photo: Deliberate, meticulously careful movements are executed under the guidance of the basal ganglia, via the striatal feedback loop. Called slow ramp movements, they are the basis of the remarkable human manual dexterity, the basis of all art and craftsmanship, upon which our civilization is founded.

Right photo: It is our vestibular system, with its semicircular canals and utricle deep within the temporal bone of the skull, that makes possible such feats of postural control as we see in gymnastics. The direction of the force of gravity is continuously monitored, below the level of consciousness, to give us stable orientation in space.

on a basketball or tennis court? Our sense of balance underlies voluntary behavior by providing a stable base in bodily posture for its execution, but, like breathing, we tend to be unconscious of its operation under normal circumstances. In large measure, and in the dark almost completely, our ability to maintain our upright orientation is owing to the existence of the *vestibular system*, consisting of

Vestibular system. The inner ear mechanism responsible for sense of balance and acceleration, consisting of semicircular canals and utricle.

It is the cerebellum, that little brain to the rear, that is preeminently responsible for our ability to execute rapid skilled movement of the type called ballistic. The cerebellum is proportionately enormously large in our brain, making us the unrivaled motor-skill specialists on our planet.

the tiny *semicircular canals* and *utricle* of our inner ear, shown in Figure 8.17.

As we saw in our discussion of the auditory system in Chapter 5, the endolymph within the cochlea is in communication with the fluid filling the three semicircular canals in the bone lying adjacent to it. Each of these tubular cavities lies at approximately right angles to the other two, and the three join at a central hollow space, the utricle, filled with the same fluid. Each canal is in effect an independent fluid circuit. As the head turns in any direction, the fluid in one or more of these channels will be caused to flow in relation to the walls confining it. The flow is partially blocked in each canal by a sensory organ called a *cupula,* close to the point where the canal joins the utricle. The sensory receptors in the cupula are similar to the ciliated hair cells within the cochlea, and are stimulated by the pressure of the flowing endolymph.

The utricle also contains a sensory organ, the *macula,* situated on its anterior and medial walls. Here the sensory receptor cells project their cilia into a gelatinous mass containing particles of limestone called *otoliths* (ear stones), which move in relation to the receptors as the head moves, owing to their inertia. Acceleration — up or

Semicircular canals. That portion of the vestibular system consisting of three slender tubes in which the perilymph flows in head turning.

Utricle (YOU-*trik-l*). A hollow structure in the vestibular system containing receptors responsive to movement of tiny particles of calcium carbonate embedded in a gelatinous matrix.

Cupula. A structure at the junction of the semicircular canals and the utricle, containing the vestibular receptors.

Otolith. A particle of calcium carbonate embedded in a gelatinous matrix in the utricle, registering head movement and position.

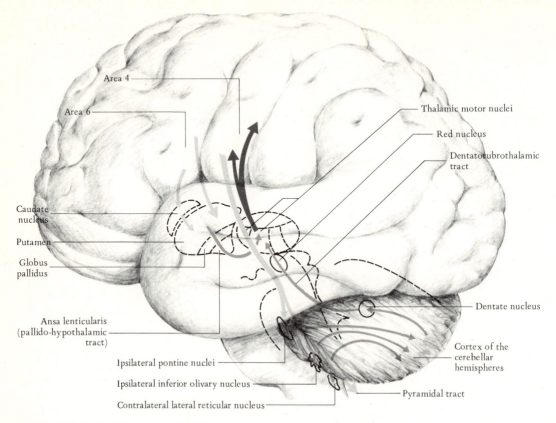

Area 4

Area 6

Thalamic motor nuclei

Red nucleus

Dentatorubrothalamic tract

Caudate nucleus

Putamen

Globus pallidus

Dentate nucleus

Ansa lenticularis (pallido-hypothalamic tract)

Cortex of the cerebellar hemispheres

Ipsilateral pontine nuclei

Ipsilateral inferior olivary nucleus

Pyramidal tract

Contralateral lateral reticular nucleus

Figure 8.16 / *The Voluntary Motor System of the Brain as Seen Through a Transparent Cortex.* Only a single hemisphere is represented. Not shown is the input from the prefrontal granular cortex, which appears to be especially important in projecting behavioral programs into the future in goal pursuit, nor the complex information processing at the final output end, in the spinal motor centers. Note that the thalamic motor nuclei play a pivotal role in forming the final instructions passed to the motor cortex for execution.

down, forward or back, or sidewise — stimulates the utricular receptors, as does tilting the head to change the direction of the gravitational force on the otoliths. This information, along with information from the semicircular canals, is transmitted to the brainstem via the eighth cranial nerve, along with the auditory signals. Some of the signals are transmitted directly into an ancient medial portion of the cerebellum called the *flocculo-nodular lobe.* However, most are projected into four vestibular nuclei strung out along the brainstem reticular formation.

Information from the vestibular system appears to be used by the

Flocculo-nodular lobe. **The older, midline portion of the cerebellum concerned with such reflex functions as balance and postural control.**

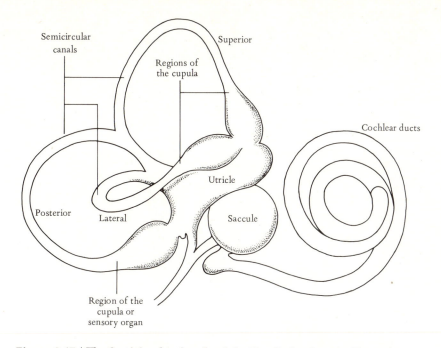

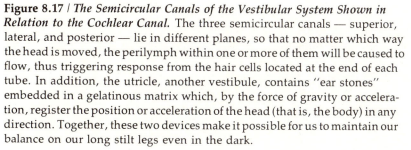

Figure 8.17 / *The Semicircular Canals of the Vestibular System Shown in Relation to the Cochlear Canal.* The three semicircular canals — superior, lateral, and posterior — lie in different planes, so that no matter which way the head is moved, the perilymph within one or more of them will be caused to flow, thus triggering response from the hair cells located at the end of each tube. In addition, the utricle, another vestibule, contains "ear stones" embedded in a gelatinous matrix which, by the force of gravity or acceleration, register the position or acceleration of the head (that is, the body) in any direction. Together, these two devices make it possible for us to maintain our balance on our long stilt legs even in the dark.

brain in the same way the proprioceptive information from the muscles and joints is used: as a means of continuously monitoring the progress of ongoing motor behavior. The vestibular system also has important reflex functions. One involves fibers crossing the brainstem to the contralateral oculomotor centers (nuclei of the third, fourth, and sixth cranial nerves) to control head–eye movement coordination, discussed in Chapter 4. (When the head turns, the eyes do not have to turn so far in their sockets to fixate a peripheral target.) Other vestibular signals, both excitatory and inhibitory, pass to the spinal motor centers governing the "righting reflex," which comes into play when we begin to lose our balance. It is also likely that vestibular signals play a subtle role in our perception of the environment as stable, utricular indications of the direction of gravitational pull providing a sense of the upright. Postural balance, the basis of all skilled whole-body action, is dependent on an intact vestibular system.

Summary

We have seen that voluntary behavior is associated in particular with the pyramidal motor system and pyramidal tract. The pyramidal tract is a feature of the thalamocortical system that evolved with the mammals, supplementing an older multisynaptic pathway to the muscles known as the extrapyramidal system. The motor cortex acts as the final common path through which the manifold activities of the brain ultimately leave it to innervate the spinal motor neurons producing overt behavior. Large Betz cells in layer V of the motor cortex project their axons directly to the spinal motor centers, crossing to the contralateral side at the level of the medulla, where these fibers form two prominent ridges on its ventral surface. The layer V neurons are thought to synapse, for the most part, directly upon the alpha motor neurons innervating the muscles. Smaller cells in the motor cortex, the layer III pyramidals, are thought to synapse on the gamma efferent neurons, which project to the muscle spindles embedded within the muscles. These gamma efferent neurons may indirectly cause muscle contraction by stimulating the muscle spindle fibers, activating the annulospiral sensory endings wound around them. These sensory fibers in turn activate the alpha neurons to greater firing rates.

The gamma efferent loop just described is used to set the level of muscular contraction required, for example, to hold an object at a given height against the force of gravity. It also controls muscle tonus, the constant minimal level of excitation of the muscles that keeps them in readiness for activity. The muscle-spindle fibers also send collaterals up to the medulla as proprioceptive input indicating the state of muscular contraction or elongation.

The alpha motor neurons send their axons to the muscles, where they branch and synapse upon a variable number of the main (extrafusal) muscle fibers; the alpha neuron and its particular set of associated muscle fibers constitute a motor unit. In small muscles with fine control, there are likely to be only a few muscle fibers for each alpha neuron. In large muscles, such as those in the thigh, each alpha neuron is associated with a great many muscle fibers. Activation occurs via synapse in a neuromuscular junction, using the neurotransmitter acetylcholine. The effect of action potentials in releasing acetylcholine at the neuromuscular junction is to cause a muscle impulse to travel over the length of the muscle fiber, much as an action potential travels along an axon membrane. Through an as yet little-understood mechanism, this causes the muscle fiber to contract. The strength of the muscle's contraction depends on the number of motor units simultaneously activated and the intensity of the activation — that is, how many times per second an action potential arrives at the neuromuscular junction.

The alpha motor neurons characteristically send recurrent collaterals from their axons to innervate tiny inhibitory Renshaw cells situated in the spinal motor centers, some of which project to the alpha neuron soma as inhibitory governors of its rate of firing. If a motor unit is activated too intensively over too long a period, the neuromuscular junction is in danger of being depleted of its store of acetylcholine, since this neurotransmitter is not taken back into the presynaptic terminal and thus preserved after its release. The inhibitory Renshaw cells apparently provide a protective mechanism against such depletion by regularly putting the alpha neuron out of action for a brief period while other motor units carry on, thus allowing the acetylcholine store to be reconstituted. At any moment, therefore, even during strenuous muscular activity, some portion of the motor units within the muscles involved are ordinarily resting.

The alpha neurons also project collateral fibers to the opposite side of the cord to synapse on Renshaw cells inhibiting muscles on that side of the body that relax coordinately with a muscle contraction, as in walking, and also to Renshaw cells on the same side to inhibit opposed muscles, such as extensors or flexors in the arm, so as to minimize tension due to conflicting muscular contraction. The Renshaw cells are also inhibited by descending fibers from brainstem nuclei, such as the vestibular, modulating the spinal motor center activities. Thus the spinal motor centers are the locus of an exceedingly complex neural integration nicely adjusted to produce adaptive behavior.

The motor cortex appears to take its orders, so to speak, from the thalamic motor nuclei, which receive controlling input from both the basal ganglia and the cerebellum. Two large feedback loops are involved in the initiation and execution of voluntary behavior. The striatal loop involves input from the motor cortex (and other cortical regions) to the caudate nucleus and putamen, which project through the globus pallidus to the thalamic motor nuclei, which in turn project to the motor cortex. The cerebellar loop begins with the pyramidal tract, collaterals of which branch off in the brainstem to innervate motor nuclei there, which in turn project into the cerebellum. The cerebellum projects a fiber bundle up to the thalamic motor nuclei, which in turn project to the motor cortex, the origin of the pyramidal tract. The two loops join in the thalamic motor nuclei and in the motor cortex. It is conjectured that the cerebellar loop modulates ballistic behaviors — movements too rapidly executed to permit careful control during their execution — while the striatal loop modulates more deliberate behaviors permitting finer motor control. Experimental evidence shows that both these loops become active before the initiation of muscle movement in voluntary behavior, suggesting that the locus of action decision is not in the motor cortex, but in other portions of the brain feeding into it.

The vestibular system provides a fundamental basis for motoric behavior, particularly whole-body movements, by continuously monitoring the direction of the force of gravity and other forces of acceleration affecting movement. It also provides a reflex mechanism that serves both to prevent us from losing our balance and to contribute to our sense of the upright in the environment.

Chapter 9 / *Language and the Nonverbal Hemisphere*

Recent research has established that the two hemispheres in the human brain carry responsibility for somewhat different functions. The left hemisphere is usually specialized for language and other symbolic operations, while the right excels in nonverbal information processing. The evidence derives from (1) cases of damage to one or the other hemisphere; (2) commissurotomized subjects; (3) intact normal brains, using sophisticated devices to test the skills of each hemisphere separately; and (4) evoked potential studies of the hemisphere's response to verbal and nonverbal stimuli. Apparently the two hemispheres tend in most people to be anatomically distinct from birth. The larger and differently structured auditory association cortex atop the temporal lobe on the left may be related to lateralization of the language function, which becomes more pronounced throughout childhood. Other evidence suggests that the two hemispheres are subtly different in their innate neural organization, producing a more focal and discrete form of information processing in the left hemisphere, a more global and diffuse form in the right. The former has proven better adapted to the task of verbal recognition.

Members of many animal species communicate with one another, signalling in such a way as to facilitate adaptive response. Communication occurs among insects that live in large communities, such as ants, termites, and bees, and in fishes that travel in schools and birds that flock together. Among mammals, communication is particularly notable among the primates. This intraspecies communication — a system of gestures and vocalizations, largely unlearned, with specific meanings for other individuals — is language. What is unique about human language is that, in addition to communication by gesture and vocalization (for example, "ouch"), we assign a particular agreed-on vocalization pattern (a word) to each kind of thing perceived in the environment, allowing it to be referred to at will and unambiguously. With such a vocabulary, a **195** baby can unambiguously declare "Doggie gone!" or "I'm gonna smack you," or "I'd like some more toast, please."

The great advantage of possessing such an arbitrary agreed-on vocabulary is apparent in a comparison of the behavior of a chimpanzee and a human being in a given situation. A wild chimpanzee who finds a cache of bananas tries to communicate this fact to his troupe by jumping up and down, screeching, and pulling at them, until at long last some of the others follow their excited companion to the prize. If the chimpanzee had a human-type language, he would only have to say, "Hey, you guys, bananas!" and the whole troupe would come running. One might ask how it happens that such a marvelously adaptive kind of communication evolved only in the human species, and not in any other life form. (It is speculated that whales may communicate comparably specific messages, but the question is still open.)

Two possible answers suggest themselves: because our brains are larger, containing extra neurons not used in basic survival functions, or because our brains are somehow differently structured. The former theory, called the *critical-mass hypothesis,* seems to be contradicted by the observations that individuals whose brains are little larger than that of the chimpanzee can speak, and that the considerable variability in the size of human brains appears not to correlate with linguistic or other skills. The hypothesis that our human brain is differently structured appears more likely. It is known that the two hemispheres of our brain have characteristic anatomical differences in the temporal-lobe speech region (Geschwind and Levitsky, 1968), with a larger auditory association area on the left (Figure 9.1). This anatomical fact might well be related to the tendency of language functions to become centered in the left hemisphere, leaving the corresponding regions of the right hemisphere free to pursue their prelinguistic functions. The human brain also has a pronounced *arcuate fasciculus* projecting from the posterior *receptive speech area of Wernicke* to *Broca's motor speech area* in the inferior frontal lobe, a tract not found in other primates. If one were designing a brain capable of learning to speak by hearing speech and trying it out on the tongue, this is precisely what one would specify in the wiring diagram (see Figure 9.2).

Arcuate fasciculus (*fa-SIK-yew-lus*)**. A fiber bundle passing from the region of Wernicke's receptive speech area to the region of Broca's motor speech area, presumed essential to the language function of the brain.**

There is other evidence of what appear to be inborn anatomical differences in the two hemispheres. The posterior portion of the lateral fissure, above the temporal lobe, turns dramatically upward in the right hemisphere while continuing posteriorly in the left, an obvious anatomical fact that surprisingly went unnoticed until recently (Rubens, 1977). Also, infants have a larger auditory evoked

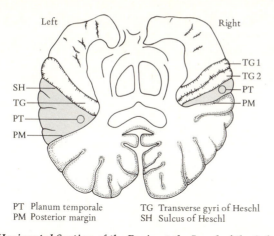

PT Planum temporale   TG Transverse gyri of Heschl
PM Posterior margin   SH Sulcus of Heschl

Figure 9.1 / *Horizontal Section of the Brain at the Level of the Sylvian Fissure (Geschwind and Levitsky, 1968).* This drawing, done from a photograph of the brain cut away just above the temporal lobe, gives a dramatic impression of the difference sometimes found in the auditory cortex of the two hemispheres. The one on the left is far more extensive, owing to the rearward angle of the posterior border of the planum temporale (PT), and contains only a single transverse gyrus of Heschl (TG), representing the auditory projection cortex. In this brain the sulcus intermedius of Beck (SI) separating the two transverse gyri on the right is barely visible on the left, while the sulcus of Heschl (SH) slopes forward more sharply. It may be that this newly discovered structural difference between the two hemispheres is significantly related to the tendency of language functions to become centered in the left hemisphere.

potential over the left hemisphere for speech sounds and over the right for noises or tones, suggesting that even at birth one hemisphere is better adapted to the kind of sound-wave transformations characteristic of speech (Molfese, Freeman, and Palermo, 1975). Another study of infants found that brain waves in the 4 Hz range are reduced over the left hemisphere when speech sounds are presented (Gardner, Schulman, and Walton, 1973). If we assume that this four-per-second wave band in the three-month-old infant is the forerunner of the alpha wave (8–13 Hz) in adulthood, this finding corresponds to a finding of reduced alpha-wave activity over the left hemisphere in adults occupied in verbal-symbolic information processing (Morgan, McDonald, and MacDonald, 1971). More recently, too, the difference found by Geschwind and Levitsky in the adult temporal lobe association cortex has been found to be already present in the neonatal stage (Wada, 1973; Witelson and Pallie, 1973), which seems to rule out a structural change due to learning.

Is it possible, then, that the evolution of verbal speech depends

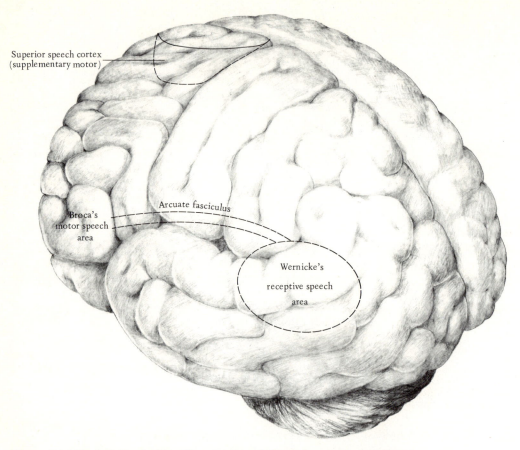

Figure 9.2 / *The Left Hemisphere Showing Speech Areas.* Language functions, usually centered in the left hemisphere, are critically important to human life. Damage to either the frontal portion (Broca's motor speech area) or the rear portion (Wernicke's receptive speech area) can sometimes permanently block the ability either to use expressive language or to understand it.

on structural arrangements in the human brain that do not exist in the brains of other species, and which themselves evolved as the capacity of verbal language matured? This question will be discussed further in Chapter 13. Here we shall take for granted the human capacity for speech. Instead, we shall concern ourselves with the interesting fact that, by the time we reach adulthood, most of us devote a large portion of one hemisphere to processing language and languagelike material, while the other hemisphere specializes differently, and appears largely unconcerned with language, as well

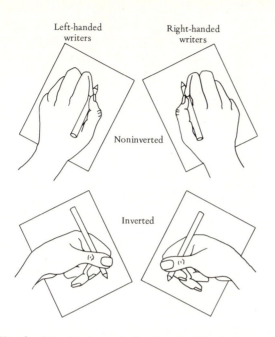

Figure 9.3 / *Handwriting Postures Indicating the Hemisphere Dominant for Language.* A recent finding appears to make it possible to identify those individuals whose language dominance is in the right hemisphere, rather than the left, as is more usual in both right-handed and left-handed persons. Left-handed individuals with normal left-hemisphere language dominance write with the upside-down posture, with the writing implement pointing down toward them rather than up and away. When left-handed individuals do not use this "hooked" posture, they are found to have right-hemisphere language dominance. The same is true of right-handed individuals who *do* use the "hooked" handwriting posture.

as incompetent at verbal-symbolic functions such as logical argument (Figure 9.3).

Effects of Left-Hemisphere Lesions

Study of damage to the left hemisphere — the "language hemisphere" — is closely associated with the name of Alexander Luria, who devoted the bulk of his professional life to working with Russian soldiers with penetrating head wounds in an effort to rehabilitate them (Luria, 1966, 1969). On the basis of his observational studies, Luria speculated about the nature of the neural mechanisms underlying language function. In cases of damage to the frontal speech area (Broca's), in which ability to articulate is impaired but understanding of language remains normal, Luria was impressed with the importance of "verbal kinaesthesias," sensory input arising from *subvocal speech* in the process of thought formation. If damage to Broca's area was sufficiently severe, Luria found that patients sometimes declared, on questioning, that no thoughts at all came into their head. In cases of less severe damage, asking the patient to hold his tongue between his teeth (thus disrupting subvocal speech) might make even the simplest consecutive thought process impossible. In all such cases Luria found unimpaired ability to understand the speech of others.

Typically, patients with lesions in Broca's area lack initiative to speak, and tend to remain silent. When they do speak, it is apt to be telegraphic, with all connecting words omitted. Their preference is to answer a question with a single word. Luria's finding that these individuals have exactly the same difficulty expressing themselves in writing demonstrates that theirs is a defect in the verbal thought mechanism itself, not merely an articulatory difficulty. (Luria emphasizes that subvocal speech mechanisms are importantly involved in writing.)

Luria's noteworthy observation that such patients retain their ability to sing songs, showing no apparent difficulty with the words, suggests that their difficulty involves the production of new and original verbal constructions, as opposed to old, well-rehearsed word sequences.

When cortical damage occurs in the posterior portion of the left-hemisphere language system, the symptoms are strikingly different. Speech is fluent and articulate, but apt to be quite meaningless. It is long-winded, filled with qualifying phrases and circumlocutions, but never gets to any point. In many cases the individual is incapable both of emitting a meaningful verbal thought and of understanding spoken or written language, even though the auditory and visual channels remain intact. Grammatical construction is apt to be entirely normal, as is vocal intonation and phrasing, but the words themselves appear to bear no meaning for the person and are often garbled. This syndrome contrasts directly with the speech associated with damage to the motor speech area, in which only the most meaningful, specifically denotative words are used, and in a slow, effortful fashion.

These observations suggest that the grammatical rules of sentence structure are learned by the motor regions of the frontal lobe, while words' referential meanings are learned by the perceptual cortex of the more posterior portions of the brain. Such a functional differentiation within the speaking hemisphere presumably reflects the fact that language consists of two kinds of operations, understanding the speech of others and constructing meaningful utterances. Young children begin to understand speech well before the ability to speak intelligibly emerges, though the two kinds of language learning appear to occur concurrently thereafter, as do the perceptual and motor mechanisms involved in reaching, grasping, and manipulating objects under the guidance of visual input.

It is of interest that Broca's motor speech area of the cortex is quite restricted in size, only a small portion of the posterior inferior frontal gyrus in a structure identified as the *pars triangularis* (Figure 9.2). Wernicke's receptive speech area is, by contrast, quite extensive; it comprises not only the posterior portion of the superior temporal gyrus, but much of the general association cortex to the rear and above, including the parietal structures known as the angular gyrus and the supramarginal gyrus (see Figure 9.2). Lesions in any portion of this large cortical region are apt to result in some form of *aphasia*, the technical term for language difficulty of organic origin. Since the language function in literate people includes not only speaking and hearing, but also reading, writing, and working with other symbolic systems (such as calculating), the various forms of aphasia are quite numerous, and appear to correlate with the site of the lesion. Thus a particular lesion may result in such bizarre-seeming phenomena as a patient's inability to read something he or she has just finished writing.

Effects of Right-Hemisphere Lesions

If the human brain is damaged in the right hemisphere opposite Broca's motor speech area in the left, no specific deficit is likely to appear; speech usually remains unimpaired. However, lesions in the parietal lobe of the right hemisphere, in areas corresponding to Wernicke's receptive speech area in the left, may result in a wide range of symptoms, all suggesting that this portion of the brain is normally preoccupied with functions of a quite different sort. Speech, however, is likely to be unimpaired, as in the case of right frontal-lobe lesions.

More than two decades ago it was established that right parietal lesions tend to leave the patient functionally impaired in operations that require a normal orientation of self to surroundings, as well as in a sense of the spatial relations between things. Such spatial skills are required, for example, in using a map, or assembling blocks according to a given pattern, or copying a design, or knowing left from right (Critchley, 1953; Semmes, Weinstein, Ghent, and Teuber, 1955). A somewhat subtler right-hemisphere function has been found more recently. Patients who have suffered extensive damage to the posterior portions of the right temporal-parietal region, or the cortex underlying them, tend to have great difficulty with *physiognomic memory*, the ability to remember or recognize the unique appearance of a familiar face, as seen in snapshots (De Renzi and Spinnler, 1966; Benton and Van Allen, 1968; Tzavaras, Hécaen, and Le Bras, 1970; Yin, 1969, 1970).

Physiognomic memory. **Memory for faces or, by extension, for individuals.**

Evidence is accumulating that recognition of individuals is a very special kind of perceptual function, different from generic object perception (recognition of a thing or material) and specifically dependent on an intact posterior cortex in the right hemisphere. Unlike perception of houses, trees, dogs, and the like, physiognomic memory is severely disturbed by inversion. Upside down, a familiar face is apt to be quite unrecognizable even to the normal adult. (Curiously, children under 8–10 years of age are much less affected than adults by inversion of a facial portrait, as are the mentally retarded. This phenomenon is examined further in Chapter 14.) But right parietal-lesion patients have difficulty recognizing people by their facial features in the upright position as well.

Yin (1969, 1970) studied this phenomenon by exposing normal subjects to snapshots of unfamiliar faces, then showing each again paired with another, and asking the subjects which of the two they had seen before. It is highly significant that those who did best on this facial-recognition task did poorest on another part of the test in which the faces were presented upside-down. It was also found, paradoxically, that patients with right temporal-parietal lesions were less disturbed by this inversion than were patients with lesions in other cortical areas — a difference that was not found when the snapshots were of familiar *things*. These findings suggest that there is a special mode of perception, which gradually matures during childhood, for recognition of the human face in the normal upright position, and that such recognition is dependent on normal function of the posterior portions of the nonverbal hemisphere (Carey and Diamond, 1977). The loss of this facial-recognition capacity in right-parietal patients was noticed many years ago (Bodamer, 1947) and termed *prosopagnosia*.

Prosopagnosia. **Loss of ability to recognize familiar people by their facial appearance.**

Hans Lucas Teuber has reported a bizarre extreme of this difficulty in a patient with right temporal-lobe damage who had difficulty recognizing even the faces of his own family, and who misinterpreted an obvious line drawing of a face as an apple (and the eyes as worm holes). Yet this same patient recognized outline drawings of inanimate objects such as houses without difficulty.

To complete the picture, Doehring and Bartholomeus (1971) found patients with right temporal-lobe damage to have a similar difficulty recognizing individuals by their voices. For what specific kind of perception, then, does the right hemisphere seem especially important? What is the difference between recognition of faces and voices and recognition of classes of things, such as trees, houses, and dogs? Is the latter mode of perception distinctively a left-hemisphere mode — a "language mode" — and the former a right-hemisphere mode, corresponding to things that do not fall into verbal categories?

Studies of Commissurotomized Patients

When the two hemispheres are isolated from each other by severing the corpus callosum and anterior commissure (see Figure 9.4), it is possible to study each hemisphere's response to visual and tactile input. The right hemisphere's visual operations can be studied by very briefly projecting visual stimuli to the left of the foveal fixation point in a tachistoscope (see Figure 9.5). (Recall that there is complete crossover of the visual half-fields, right and left, due to crossover of fibers from the nasal half of each retina.) The right hemisphere's tactile functioning can be studied by having the subject manipulate objects out of sight behind a screen with the left hand, since there is complete crossover of tactile stimuli from the hand to the opposite hemisphere. The left hemisphere's unique manner of functioning can be studied by sending visual or tactile stimulation to it in a similar manner.

The results are consistent. In tasks involving spatial visualization, as opposed to verbal processing, the right hemisphere tends to be greatly superior; without its assistance, the left hemisphere proves astonishingly inept. A study of seven patients who underwent commissurotomy as a last desperate (and successful) effort to control epileptic seizures found that the left hemisphere alone was unable to remember even for a moment the felt shape of a bent wire (Milner and Taylor, 1972). By contrast, the right hemisphere (using the left hand) could in all cases remember such unfamiliar shapes for as long as fifteen seconds, and four of the seven retained memory of such nonsense patterns for more than two minutes. In a parallel tactile study, Nebes (1971) asked commissurotomized patients to match a block representing a segment of a circle with the corresponding

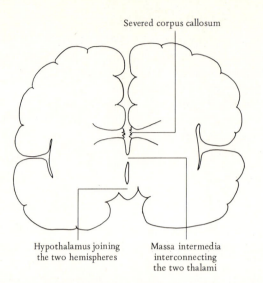

Severed corpus callosum

Hypothalamus joining
the two hemispheres

Massa intermedia
interconnecting
the two thalami

Figure 9.4 / *The Brain with the Corpus Callosum Severed.* This diagram shows the surgical operation that disconnects the two hemispheres, producing the apparent behavioral phenomenon of two persons in the same body. In the intact brain, each portion of the cortex is in direct communication with its opposite region through commissural fibers. The evidence suggests that when this intercommunication is blocked through disconnection, each hemisphere is capable of full operation, but independently of its partner. The fact that only one of them is capable of verbal communication makes it necessary to use nonverbal means to observe the operation of the silent hemisphere.

whole circle. Here again, with regard to part-whole relationship perception, the right hemisphere (left hand) proved greatly superior. When such patients are presented a visual stimulus in the tachistoscope such that each hemisphere receives input from one half of a *chimeric figure* (the two halves of the face representing different individuals), each hemisphere "fills in" the other half of the visual field to correspond with the half it sees. If the left hemifield in the tachistoscope shows half the face of a clock, the other half of the clock face is automatically perceptually assumed, and "seen" by the subject, even though the stimulus presented in the other half of the picture (seen by the other hemisphere) is entirely different. The question then is: which hemisphere will prove superior in selecting the object it saw from among an array of possible candidates?

A very interesting test case presents a stimulus composed of two mismatched halves of the human face. In the case of a commissurotomized patient viewing such a stimulus in the tachis-

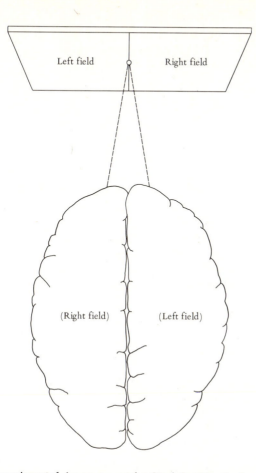

Figure 9.5 / *Experimental Arrangement for Studying Hemispheric Function in the Intact Brain Through Visual Stimuli.* When different stimuli are presented simultaneously to the two eyes separately in the tachistoscope, the left half of the visual field projects to the right hemisphere exclusively, and vice versa. Under these conditions, verbal material is recognized more quickly when presented in the right half-field of the tachistoscope, nonverbal material more quickly when presented in the left half-field (that is, to the right hemisphere). Thus, the same hemispheric difference in verbal and nonverbal skills is demonstrated in the intact brain through visual stimuli.

toscope, eyes fixed on the midline, each hemisphere sees a different whole face, the subject appearing not to notice that only half the face is exposed. Under these conditions, the right hemisphere (left hand) is far superior in its ability to select the face it saw from a group of photographs (Levy, Trevarthen, and Sperry, 1972). Thus the right hemisphere again demonstrates superiority in physiognomic perception. In another study, however, the right hemisphere was also found to be superior at matching any such unfamiliar stimuli, or indeed matching one visual pattern with another, even if the pattern was a printed word, so long as the question of its meaning was not involved (Umiltá *et al.* 1973).

Patients with this *disconnection syndrome* report seeing nothing when a stimulus is presented tachistoscopically only to the left half of their visual field: the message, transmitted to the nonspeaking right hemisphere, is not relayed by the corpus callosum to the speaking left hemisphere. Behaviorally, it is as if the stimulus had not been seen. The patient can neither describe nor name it. The same thing is true of objects manipulated behind a screen with the left hand, which is connected almost entirely with the right hemisphere. However, an object seen in the left visual half-field or palpated with the left hand can be readily selected from an array of objects. The right hemisphere cannot indicate its functioning except by nonverbal means. Whenever this opportunity is presented, however, the right hemisphere proves itself superior to the left (speaking) hemisphere in a wide range of tasks involving visual-spatial functioning, such as reconstruction of Necker cubes, block design

Roger Sperry (1913–

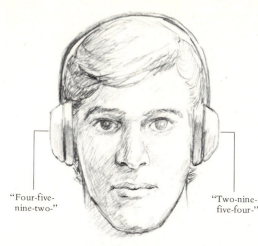

"Four-five-
nine-two-"   "Two-nine-
                                                        five-four-"

Figure 9.6 / *Experimental Arrangement for Studying Hemispheric Function in the Intact Brain Through Auditory Stimuli.* When different stimuli are presented simultaneously to the two ears through earphones, the left ear, which has closest connections with the right hemisphere, is found less competent than the right ear (left hemisphere) in discriminating a series of numbers, but more competent with musical materials. Thus, in the intact brain we can observe the same hemispheric specialization found in split-brain cases.

problems, and the like. On the other hand, the right hemisphere tends to be extremely deficient at numerical calculation, even as easy an operation as subtracting 2 from 9 (Sperry, 1968).

Studies of the Intact Hemispheres

That the specialized functions of the two hemispheres can be studied in the normal individual is the discovery of Kimura (1961), who made use of the Broadbent dichotic-listening technique (Broadbent, 1954) whereby the subject listens to two messages simultaneously, one through each earphone (see Figure 9.6). She found the left ear, which projects the bulk of its auditory input to the right hemisphere, inferior to the right ear when the task is to remember a spoken series of numbers (a verbal task), but superior to the right ear (left hemisphere) when the task is recall of snatches of musical passages. This finding was reversed, however, when the subject was known (by means of injected sodium amytal) to have language

Doreen Kimura (1933–   )

centered in the right hemisphere. Thus by forcing the subject to listen to two stimulus patterns simultaneously, one in each ear, Kimura demonstrated the specialization of the two hemispheres for verbal and nonverbal information processing in the intact brain.

In further studies using this method, Kimura (1964) found the right hemisphere to be more accurate in perceiving melodies. Interestingly, this left-ear effect has also been demonstrated in dichotic presentation of such environmental sounds as a dog barking, a clock ticking, and the like (Curry, 1967; Knox and Kimura, 1968). Even more interesting is the discovery by Kimura and Folb (1968) that speech sounds played backward, like normal meaningful speech, are more accurately identified by the *right* ear. This finding strongly suggests that the features of speech to which the left hemisphere particularly responds are aspects of its sound structure, unrelated to the meaningfulness, familiarity, or conceptual content of the sound stream.

The superiority of the left hemisphere for verbal information and the right for nonverbal has also been verified in normal subjects by presenting different stimuli to the left and right sides of the point of

visual focus, too briefly for the eyes to shift to see the image presented on the other side. Similar findings have resulted from measurement of averaged evoked potentials in the brain waves of the
left and right hemispheres: both the intensity and the wave form of
the averaged potentials detected on stimulus presentation are different, depending on whether the stimulus is of a verbal or nonverbal character (see Figure 9.7). A great deal of exciting research is

Figure 9.7 / *Differential Potentials over Broca's Area in Verbal and Nonverbal
Utterances.* Here is an electroencephalographic demonstration that it is the
region of Broca's area, the left inferior frontal convolution (LiF), that is
involved in language production. For both subjects there is an upward
deflection of the baseline EEG immediately prior to uttering the word (arrow).
The negativity averages −10.0 and −2.8 microvolts, which is outstanding
when compared with the other three areas tested (left precentral
gyrus — LpC; right precentral gyrus — RpC; and right inferior frontal
gyrus — RiF). For each subject the next highest upward deflection was in
the left precentral gyrus, the motor region in the tongue area (LpC −5.9 and
−0.9). Interestingly, the cough also shows a negative deflection of the
baseline in anticipation of the act over Broca's area and the related motor
area for the tongue.

Subject C.U.

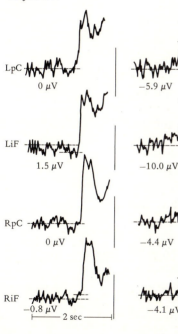

Subject M.K.

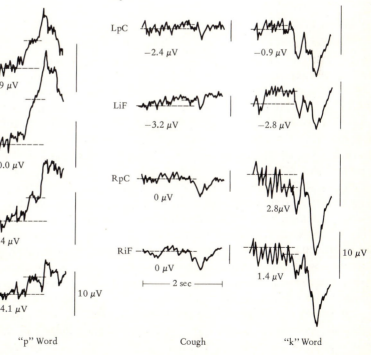

currently being done on the character of the information-processing difference between our two hemispheres. Eventually it will lead to a much more sophisticated understanding of whole-brain operations than in the past, when it was assumed that the left hemisphere, with its language dominance, took care of everything.

Summary

Study of the effects of brain lesions restricted to a single hemisphere of the brain confirm that human beings have, in effect, two brains in one head, in the sense that we make use of one hemisphere principally for language functions and the other hemisphere for nonverbal functions. These studies have also shown that the defect differs when the damage is to Broca's area or to Wernicke's area. When Broca's motor speech area of the frontal lobe is lesioned, the patient understands spoken and written language perfectly well, but has difficulty speaking. Such a patient finds speech of any kind burdensome, uses a telegraphic style, and prefers to answer questions with a single word. A contrasting syndrome is found when Wernicke's receptive speech area is damaged: the verbal production sounds entirely normal, with good sentence structure and verbal facility, but meaning is absent.

These observations suggest that the grammatical structure of language is the province of the frontal lobe speech mechanism, while the referential meaning of words is a function of the posterior language-interpretive cortex. Thus the anatomical structures responsible for syntax and semantics respectively are quite distinct.

Luria's studies also suggest that thought is organized by the speech mechanism of the frontal lobe. If it is sufficiently severely damaged, no thoughts at all appear to come into the individual's head; in less severe cases, complete inability to carry through the simplest consecutive thought process results if the motor speech mechanism is interfered with, such as by holding the tongue between the teeth. That such individuals can sing the lyrics of familiar songs without difficulty illustrates that it is the formulation of original utterances (or, perhaps, thoughts themselves) that is impaired.

When the right hemisphere is damaged, notably in the posterior region opposite Wernicke's receptive speech area, speech is unimpaired but a wide range of symptoms all point to difficulty in processing pattern information, as in the visual-spatial skills used in drawing or reading a map. Such patients have a peculiar difficulty recognizing faces, but no corresponding difficulty recognizing objects. This finding suggests that recognition of individuals is handled differently by the brain than recognition of things that can be categorized, such as houses and trees. Moreover, face recognition is peculiarly susceptible to disruption through inversion of the picture, but oddly, not so for children or brain-damaged individuals. Children under 8–10 years of age are much less affected by inversion of a picture of a person. Very interestingly, right-hemisphere damage also impairs recognition of individuals by their voices.

The functional difference between the two hemispheres has been further clarified by study of patients whose two hemispheres have been separated by cutting the corpus callosum and anterior commissure. Since each hemisphere deals with only half the field of vision, a tachistoscope can be used with such patients to observe the perceptual responses of each hemisphere to briefly presented visual stimuli. Tactile perception in the two hemispheres can be studied in the same way, since each hemisphere receives tactile input only from the opposite hand. The results of such studies consistently show one hemisphere to be specialized for verbal processing of information, while the other specializes in strictly nonverbal operations. In these cases the nonspeaking right hemisphere consistently proves far superior to the left in dealing with patterned information — even the pattern of printed words, provided verbal meaning is not involved. It also proves superior at recognition of faces. Yet the right hemisphere is grossly inferior, indeed incompetent, when asked to deal with language in any form.

The lateralization of specific functions in the human brain has been confirmed for normal subjects with the tachistoscopic and with dichotic listening techniques. The finding that music is recalled better by the right hemisphere confirms that musical recognition belongs in the nonverbal sphere. However, aphasic patients with left-hemisphere damage have no difficulty singing songs, though they are unable to speak. This suggests that the difficulty is one of production of original verbal sequences, or thoughts.

Part III / *The Major Functional Systems*
B. The Ancient Subcortical Systems

To this point we have considered only the functions of the modern brain — the portion of the brain that evolved only in the mammals, consisting of the neocortex and the thalamus. In Part III the spotlight shifts to the older portions of the brain, which comprised the entire brain prior to the development of the thalamocortical system. Though buried beneath the neocortex, their functions have by no means been eclipsed by this recent addition to the brain. Instead, mammals have developed a new kind of brain, a greater whole, in which the more recently evolved structures have been integrated into the ongoing functions of the older regions. These ancient systems have themselves continued to expand, both in size and in the scope of their functions, during the evolution of the primates and the human. As we have seen, new systems were evolved for handling visual, auditory, and tactile perception and voluntary behavior. All the remaining functions still lie within the province of the ancient subcortical systems, which may be conveniently viewed as consisting of three major system complexes associated respectively with the limbic structures, the medial forebrain bundle, and the brainstem.

Chapter 10 / *The Limbic System: The World of Feeling and Remembrance*

The limbic system is an older structure of the brain consisting of the septal nuclei, the hippocampal formation, and the amygdala, along with their associated cortical regions and connecting fiber pathways. Many of its structures appear to be importantly involved in the evaluation of experience and the control of behavioral choice based on it. The limbic system appears to be responsible for emotional expression and mood states, as well as the consolidation of experience in lasting memory form. That lesions in different portions of the limbic system produce very similar behavioral deficits suggests the existence of interlocking circuitries including within their scope such structures as the olfactory bulbs, the caudate nucleus, the prefrontal granular cortex, and the orbital cortex, along with their associated thalamic nucleus, the dorsomedial.

From a number of points of view, the limbic system is the most fascinating portion of the brain. It deals with something deeper and more subtle than perception, planning, or skilled performance, namely our feeling responses to our experiences. The essence of life is joy and sorrow, worry and frustration, hope and despair, loves and hatreds. The thalamocortical system alone, for all its intellectual power, can provide us none of these. Without its integration with the limbic system, it is essentially cold.

When we consider that the limbic brain represents the highest level of integration of neural systems prior to expansion of the neocortex, it is apparent that it must be inherently capable of a wide range of functions. We are thus prepared to find in it a much greater complexity of structures than in the thalamocortical system. Until now its complexity, as well as the difficulty of gaining access to these interior structures, has largely defeated our efforts at analysis. Yet we are on the verge of understanding, and that is the point where science is most interesting. The nature of the limbic system is such that its operations appear to be performed by a number of distinct subsystems in an intricate interlocking fashion, each structure carrying on several functions simultaneously; one subsystem is nested within another, and operations overlap. The more we learn about this portion of the brain, the more intriguing the picture becomes, inviting active speculation on the role of this or that structure in the total scheme. In the past such speculation has been far wide of the mark. We can be certain the same thing will be said about our present understanding, but this chapter will be devoted to a survey of our current knowledge and the hints it provides about the grand scheme of the organization underlying limbic functions.

The Limbic Lobe

It was Paul Broca who gave the term *limbic lobe* to the continuous sheet of cortical tissues circling the brainstem structures on the medial surfaces of the brain (see Figure 10.1). The limbic lobe begins in the septal region of the frontal lobe, swings forward around the *genu* (knee) of the corpus callosum, and passes just above that commissure as the *cingulate gyrus*. It then turns downward around its posterior enlargement (splenium) to form the medial surface of the temporal lobe, where the *hippocampus* and *amygdala* are found, and terminates in the *uncus,* the structure in which the *amygdaloid nuclei* reside. The cortical tissues involved are generally of a more primitive type, called *paleocortex,* somewhat thinner than the neocortex and containing fewer or less distinct layers. The hippocampal formation was long ago recognized to be the most primitive cortex of all (*archicortex*), consisting essentially of just two layers.

As we shall see in Chapter 13, three principal structures of the limbic lobe, the septum, amygdala, and hippocampus, were present in primordial form in the most primitive vertebrates (such as the lamprey *Petromyzon*) and are found in all higher forms (sharks, amphibians, reptiles, birds, and mammals), essentially unchanged in their interrelationships. We must assume from this startling fact that the limbic lobe has fulfilled some very fundamental brain function throughout evolution, and that it continues to fulfill such a function in our brain. The question is: what function?

The expansion of the neocortex has changed the relative positions of these three structures, pushing the hippocampus progressively to the rear until it came (in the primates) to lodge in the temporal lobe. The amygdala moved laterally to its present location in the temporal lobe just anterior to the hippocampus. There is still no direct fiber

Cingulate gyrus. **That portion of the medial surface of the hemispheres that lies immediately above the corpus callosum.**

Paleocortex. **That portion of the cerebral cortex that evolved prior to the neocortex and exhibits a somewhat simpler laminar structure.**

Archicortex (ARK-ee-kor-tex). **The type of cortex found in the hippocampus.**

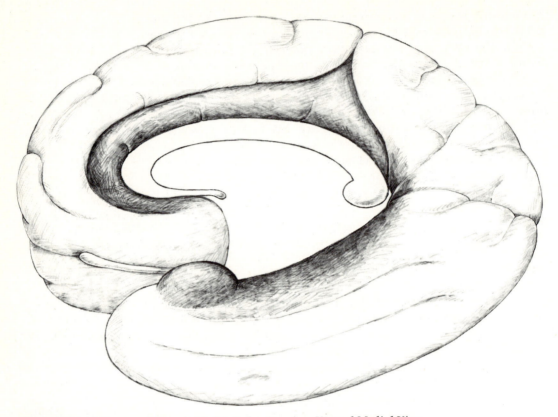

Figure 10.1 / *Diagram of Broca's Limbic Lobe, Seen in a Ventral Medial View of the Right Hemisphere.* Broca's early conception of the limbic system consisted only of the cortical regions immediately surrounding the corpus callosum and subcortical nuclei on the medial surfaces of the brain. Later work was to expand this concept of the ancient cerebral system now overlain by the massive thalamocortical system.

connection between the two; the original fiber bundles connecting hippocampus and amygdala to the septum are still found in the human brain in the *fornix* and *stria terminalis* respectively. Thus we may justifiably say that the basic organization of the limbic lobe has not changed in any fundamental way over the entire course of vertebrate evolution. (The same may also be said of our brainstem structures and the spinal cord.) It is not too rash to speculate that these three structures serve a very important survival function in the vertebrates, and that the key to their function probably lies in the close relationship that amygdala and hippocampus have always

Fornix. **The fiber bundle forming the major output pathway of the hippocampal formation passing to the mammillary bodies of the hypothalamus.**

Stria terminalis. **A fiber pathway from the amygdala to the septal area and anterior hypothalamus.**

borne to the septum. This preliminary conceptual framework may make it easier to keep our bearings as we explore deeper into the complexities of the older brain hidden beneath the neocortical mantle.

The limbic system encompasses somewhat more than just the limbic lobe as Broca defined it (see Figure 10.1). The entire *circuit of Papez* is included (Figure 10.2), running from the hippocampal area via the fornix to the hypothalamus in the region of the *mammillary bodies,* via the mammillothalamic tract to the *anterior thalamic nucleus,* up to the cingulate gyrus, posteriorly in the cingulum bundle down into the entorhinal cortex of the temporal lobe, and finally over the *perforant pathway* into the hippocampus again. The *ventral amygdalofugal pathway* carries signals from amygdala to hypothalamus (Figure 10.3), while the *diagonal band of Broca* interconnects amygdala and septum (Figure 10.4), and these, too, are limbic structures. Many investigators now include in the limbic system the *orbital cortex* of the frontal lobe, as well as its massive interconnection with the *dorsomedial nucleus* of the thalamus, with which the amygdala is also in communication (Figure 10.5). In that the Papez circuit involves neither amygdala nor septum, it is conceptually useful to treat the limbic system as consisting of at least two independent circuitries, (1) the hippocampal and (2) the more anterior system involving the two nuclear structures, septum and amygdala. That both limbic systems have enlarged, rather than diminished, over the course of evolution is perhaps best symbolized by the surprising finding that the human fornix contains more fibers, proportionally, than that of any other mammal, indeed more than either optic nerve or pyramidal tract! (Sarnat and Netsky, 1974, p. 244).

The larger conception of the limbic system outlined above is shown diagrammatically in Figure 10-6.

Circuit of Papez (Pa-PAY). **A complex neural circuit in the limbic system, proceeding from hippocampal formation to mammillary bodies, to anterior thalamic nucleus, to cingulate gyrus, to entorhinal cortex, and back to the hippocampus.**

Orbital cortex. **The cerebral cortex underlying the frontal lobe.**

The Rhinencephalon

The limbic system was once known as the *rhinencephalon* or "nosebrain," since early neuroanatomists, who worked with primitive species heavily dependent on the sense of smell, traced fibers from the olfactory tracts to many of the limbic structures. The term is still in common use (as are such derivative terms as *entorhinal cortex,*) even though it is recognized that dependence on olfactory stimuli has greatly decreased in many species, such as the primates, even as the limbic structures were growing larger. The seeming paradox would appear to imply that these structures are being used in the

Rhinencephalon. **That part of the limbic system receiving olfactory input.**

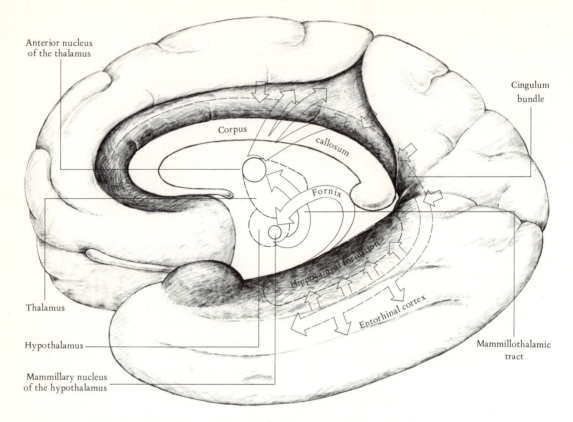

Anterior nucleus
of the thalamus

Cingulum
bundle

Corpus

callosum

Fornix

Hippocampal formation

Entorhinal cortex

Thalamus

Hypothalamus

Mammillary nucleus
of the hypothalamus

Mammillothalamic
tract

Figure 10.2 / *Diagram of the Circuit of Papez* (*the Hippocampal Circuit*). The circuit of Papez, originally conceived to function as the basis of emotional expression, is now recognized to be more importantly involved in memory functions and orientation in space. It projects from the hippocampal formation via the fornix to the mammillary bodies, thence via the mammillothalamic tract to the anterior nucleus of the thalamus, thence to the cingulate gyrus, which projects into the entorhinal cortex via the cingulum bundle. The entorhinal cortex in turn projects into the hippocampal formation over the perforant pathway to complete the circuit. The circuit of Papez is thought to be continually operative during waking hours, when we are recording memories of our moment-by-moment experiences. It ceases to function during much of our sleep time, which may account for the fact that it is so difficult to remember dreams.

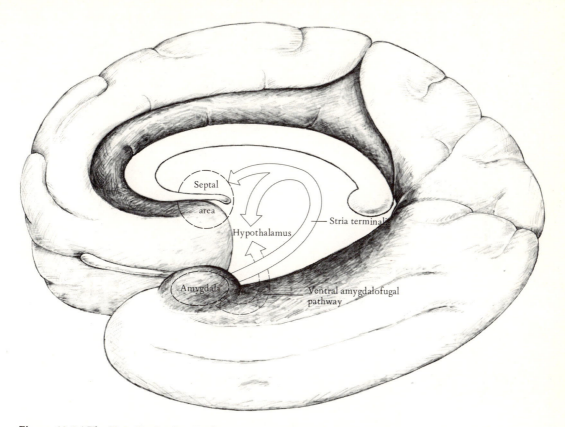

Figure 10.3 / *The Two Projection Pathways from the Amygdala to the Hypothalamus.* Two pathways serve the amygdalar control of hypothalamic functions. One is the ancient stria terminalis system, shown here, whose course parallels that of the fornix. The other is a more diffuse and more recently evolved route, the ventral amygdalofugal pathway, passing more directly to the hypothalamic centers. The specific functions of these two pathways are not yet firmly established.

human brain for functions of a similar sort but based on other than olfactory input, or else that they have now been taken over for use in other functions entirely. Some suggestions as to the answer will appear in what follows.

It is of great interest that, with better methods of tracing axonal fibers — even small, unmyelinated ones — we are finding the ramifications of the olfactory-tract fibers in mammals far more extensive than had previously been thought. In effect a revolutionary new

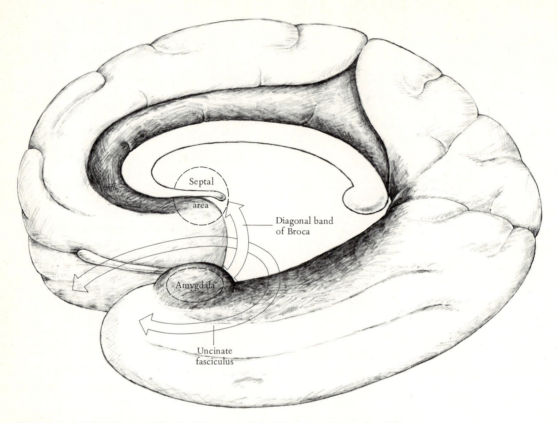

Figure 10.4 / *The Diagonal Band of Broca and the Uncinate Fasciculus.* The amygdala and its surrounding cortex are in close intercommunication with both the septal region and the orbital cortex, via the diagonal band and the uncinate fasciculus (passing through the uncus). The uncus, the bulbous projection from the medial surface of the temporal lobe, houses the amygdaloid nuclei. Unlike the stria terminalis and ventral amygdalofugal paths to the hypothalamus, these two fiber bundles reciprocally interconnect their regions. Thus, the temporal lobe tip (frontotemporal cortex) is in intimate intercommunication with the frontal lobe.

look is being taken at the functions of the limbic system in evolutionary perspective. The apparently paradoxical enlargement of limbic structures in species whose olfactory distance sense was becoming less dominant — even moribund, as in the aquatic mammals — is now recognized as not paradoxical at all. The trend is toward attributing great importance to the olfactory-system structures, if not the olfactory sense itself, in the human brain (Wenzel,

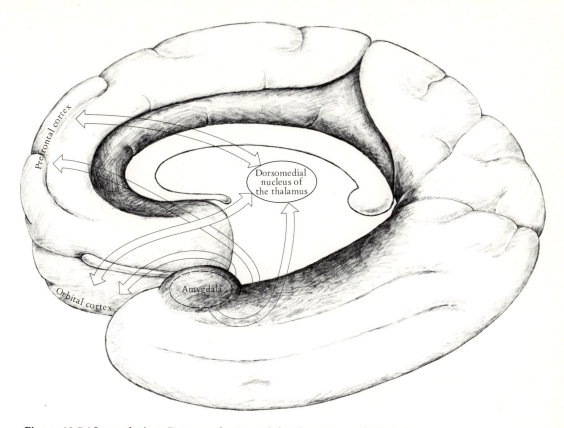

Figure 10.5 / *Interrelations Between the Amygdala, the Dorsomedial Nucleus of the Thalamus, and the Prefrontal and Orbital Cortices.* The dorsomedial nucleus of the thalamus is a massive nucleus occupying the central medial portion of that body. It is in intimate intercommunication with the prefrontal granular cortex and with the orbital cortex. The amygdala, in turn, projects directly to these two cortical regions and to the dorsomedial nucleus of the thalamus. These various pathways provide a direct "upward" projection — presumably concerned with the evaluation of experiences encountered as good or bad — from the limbic system to the thalamocortical system.

1974). While there is room for speculation, their importance may well involve the most fundamental and primitive of characteristics of behavior, namely selectivity in response — also known as behavioral choice or action decision.

Behavioral choice, and the evaluative mechanism on which it is based, are both vividly demonstrated by some of the most primitive life forms, protozoa consisting of a single living cell. One large class

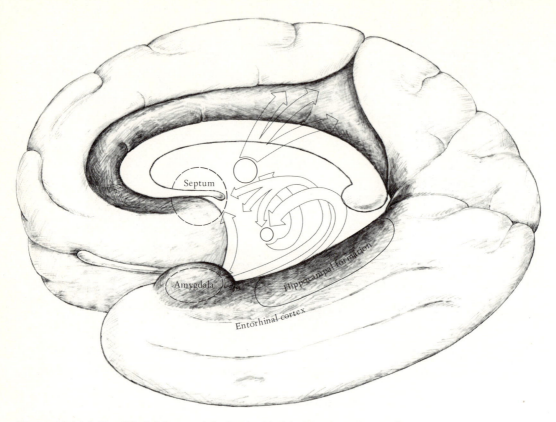

Figure 10.6 / *A Simplified Schema of the Entire Limbic System as Currently Understood.* The limbic system is seen to be comprised of two relatively independent subsystems: (1) the Papez circuit and (2) the more anterior system involving the two nuclear groups, septum and amygdala, which appear not to be involved in the Papez circuit in any important way.

of protozoa, the ciliates, employ hairlike projections from their surface membrane, either to propel themselves through the water or to create a vortex in the water that sucks floating food particles toward them while they remain anchored to some stationary object. Our favorite *Vorticella*, already mentioned in Chapter 8, is of the latter type. Observed in a tiny microaquarium on the stage of a microscope, *Vorticella* rejects the vast majority of particles in the incoming stream, which are allowed to pass by on one side or the other. Occasionally, however, the stream contains a desired edible particle (usually, in *Vorticella*'s case, a much smaller ciliate), which is selected out as it comes swiftly forward, and can be seen to pop into the animal's gullet. There it swirls for a moment in a tiny internal whirlpool while its desirability is further evaluated, after which it is either ingested or ejected again into the passing stream (see Figure 10.7).

This single-celled animal obviously has a fully functional mechanism for evaluation and choice of behavioral alternatives. It is no doubt a chemical mechanism, like our senses of smell and taste, and has perhaps consistently been so throughout the long evolutionary history of multicellular animals. Even in our highly sophisticated nervous system it is still largely through these chemical senses that we decide whether we like something or not. We invoke them to symbolize pleasure and disgust, and much of our enjoyment of life involves food. It would be counterintuitive to assume that brain

Figure 10.7 / Vorticella *Feeding: Selectivity of Response in a Single-Celled Animal.* Purposive behavior is dramatically illustrated in this common pond-water animalcule. Though it has no brain, it exercises critical judgment in its selection of particles as food. The selection process involves two stages, one of capturing the prospective food particle and one of savoring it as it swirls in a tiny whirlpool in the *Vorticella's* mouth, before being ingested or spit out into the passing stream.

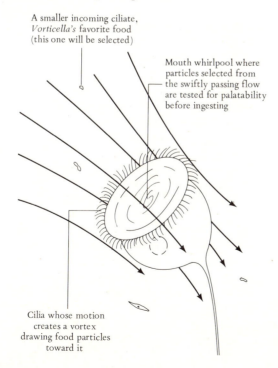

A smaller incoming ciliate, *Vorticella's* favorite food (this one will be selected)

Mouth whirlpool where particles selected from the swiftly passing flow are tested for palatability before ingesting

Cilia whose motion creates a vortex drawing food particles toward it

structures originally evolved for this purpose have totally lost their ancestral function. This fully justifies giving consideration to the olfactory system in the human, despite notions of its minimal usefulness to our species.

The Olfactory System

We are capable of discriminating countless distinctive odors, and of identifying the sources of an enormous number of them. In what sense, then, is it justifiable to regard the olfactory system as inferior to those of vision, touch, and hearing? It is nondirectional, often ineffective at distances of more than a few feet, and useless for spatial orientation in humans (though not to the more sensitive noses of bloodhounds and other animals), but these are poor justifications for its disparagement. The sense of smell is possibly the most ancient of all sensory systems for identification and, prior to that, evaluation of external objects and substances. It is also still the most mysterious. While we have the beginnings of rational understanding of visual, auditory, and tactile perception, we have none whatever of olfactory perception.

Olfactory epithelium. **The nasal tissue sensitive to odors.**

The *olfactory epithelium,* the receptor surface for odors, is a patch of membrane about the size of a postage stamp deep in the nasal passages, where inspired and expired air circulates high up near the base of the skull at the roof of the nasal cavity. The receptor cells are bipolar; the receptor extension passes to the surface of the olfactory epithelium, where its cilia lie within the mucous secretion covering the surface. It is presumed that odorous gases and particles in the air have to dissolve in the mucous secretion to be effective. Olfactory perception of fatty substances, which will not dissolve in water, was long a puzzle, but there is now reason to believe that part of the mucous secretion of the olfactory glands is lipid in nature, allowing lipid-soluble substances to penetrate the secretion and induce olfactory perception (Frisch, 1967). The axons of the bipolar cells gather into bundles and penetrate the *cribriform plate* of the *ethmoid bone* forming the base of the skull, to synapse with the single dendrites of the large *mitral cells* in the olfactory bulb. The axons of these mitral cells form the main constituents of the lateral olfactory tract running in part to *pyriform* cortex and the medial nucleus of the amygdala.

Cribriform plate. **The bony structure immediately above the nasal passages.**

Ethmoid bone. **The bone underlying the frontal lobes of the brain.**

Mitral cells. **Second-order neurons of the olfactory system with a curious cross-shaped configuration.**

Some of the fibers from the mitral cells go to what appears to be the ancient olfactory cortex, on which all animals heavily depended before the evolution of the thalamocortical system, variously called

Pyriform. **Pear-shaped, referring to the cortex forming the basal surface of the temporal lobe in the region of the hippocampus.**

the *anterior perforated substance*, the *substantia innominata* (substance without a name), or the *olfactory tubercle*. It forms the basal surface of the brain in the region just above the optic chiasma. Little was known about this region of the brain until very recently, when it was found, surprisingly, that it projects axons into all regions of the cortex (Kievit and Kuypers, 1975). Here is one example, then, of a strong projection "upward" from the limbic system to the thalamo-cortical system, presumably concerned with the evaluation of the goodness or badness of things encountered and with behavioral choice. But most of the olfactory fibers are apparently confined to the limbic system.

Substantia innominata. **The ancient olfactory cortex at the base of the brain immediately anterior to the hypothalamus in the anterior commissure region.**

The Effect of Lesions in the Olfactory Bulbs

Early in the course of brain research the interesting observation was made that rats whose olfactory bulbs had been removed exhibited a curious stereotypy of behavior characterized by compulsive, aimless running, as distinguished from normal exploratory behavior. The experimenter conjectured, "Possibly the olfactory lobes have functions other than that of receiving olfactory stimuli" (Liggett, 1928, p. 52). Herrick, in 1929, came to the considered judgment that "At all stages of cortical elaboration an important function of the olfactory cortex, in addition to participation in its own specific way in cortical association, is to serve as a nonspecific activator for all cortical activities" (Herrick, 1963, p. 14), including, significantly, *affective* (emotional-evaluative) reactions.

That brilliant early intuition was not followed up until many years later. In 1968, Wenzel and her colleagues at the Brain Research Institute at UCLA raised the interesting question of whether an essentially nonolfactory function might have been responsible for the preservation of the olfactory structures over evolutionary time in animals no longer dependent on them for strictly olfactory functions. They chose to study one such species, the pigeon. In a series of experiments Wenzel and her associates found that lesions to the olfactory bulb or olfactory tract in the pigeon interfered with learning a visual-discrimination habit presumed unrelated to olfactory cues. The task was learning to peck one of two illuminated keys, depending on whether they were both red or both green. The lesioned birds made far fewer correct responses than did pigeons with equivalent lesions in other portions of the brain. Curiously, the birds also withdrew from the food hopper, rather than approaching, when they heard it become available to them (a startle

Affective. **Designating an emotional response associated with distinctly positive or negative feelings.**

response), and their heart rate persisted in accelerating when a light was turned on, rather than habituating to it as did the control pigeons (Wenzel *et al.*, 1969).

More recently a number of studies of the rat have confirmed that lesioning the olfactory bulbs produces animals that act as if they fail to become normally habituated to their experiences, continuing to explore a maze with undiminished energy time after time, or continuing to be just as upset by a flash of light or a tone as they were the first time (Richman *et al.*, 1972; Sieck, 1972). In both the pigeon and the rat, failure of habituation after olfactory-bulb lesions might be interpreted as failure to remember on subsequent exposure that the stimulus had been encountered before and found to be of no consequence or interest. Could it be that this basic memory function involves the olfactory bulbs at some point in its grand neural circuit?

Both pigeons and rats with olfactory-bulb lesions exhibit a related characteristic: quicker learning of an escape response in the *two-way active avoidance* situation (Thomas, 1973). In this experimental paradigm, very commonly used with readily available small animals (pigeon, rodent, cat), the animal must run or jump into an adjoining cage to escape a shock delivered in the first, and then back into the first cage to flee a similar shock in the second. That these lesioned animals learn the trick quicker than control animals might mean that they are unable to recall that they were just shocked in the first cage, and hence flee fearlessly into it, while the controls are reluctant to do so. This implies a memory deficit, as does failure of habituation. Another possible explanation is that they are unable to refrain from making the response even though they are fully aware of the dangers lurking in the first cage. The latter would be a deficit in response withholding — a performance variable rather than a learning variable. We shall see that it is frequently difficult to differentiate between these two kinds of explanatory principle.

In a very different kind of experimental situation, the animal must learn to avoid making some response, such as stepping off a small platform onto an electrified grid, or eating from an electrified food cup that delivers a frightening shock on each attempt. Both pigeons and rats with olfactory-system lesions are deficient in the required behavioral withholding (a *passive avoidance deficit*). These animals fail not only to become habituated to familiar innocuous stimuli, but also to avoid getting burned twice by touching the same hot stove! Is this a failure to remember the shock, or perhaps an abnormal absence of fear? A recent experiment by Mollenauer *et al.* (1974) demonstrated that bulbectomized rats will explore freely around a confined cat, exhibiting none of the fear shown by the

Passive avoidance deficit. **Failure of an animal to learn to avoid a punished response.**

control animals. It is conceivable, however, that the smell of the cat is the trigger to fear in normal animals, a trigger missing in the experimentals.

Evidence such as this suggests that the olfactory mechanism of the brain, presumably involved in evaluative functions since earliest evolutionary times, has also been involved in the adaptive response to danger and pain, and in remembering a painful experience when the same situation is encountered again. It may be justifiable to say that the olfactory system not only identifies sensory stimuli but also "thinks": when the olfactory bulbs are removed, the animal's behavior is less intelligent. Perhaps it is for their usefulness in this way that they have been preserved even in species that make little use of them as a perceptual system per se.

The Effect of Lesions in the Septal Nuclei

What is known as the *septum* in the brain consists of clumps of gray matter in the midline, in the immediate vicinity of the *anterior commissure* (Figure 10.8). This gray matter receives input from the *hippocampus* via the *precommissural fornix*. The *medial septal nucleus*, in turn, projects back to the hippocampus, appearing to control the characteristic hippocampal *theta wave*, a highly regular type of brain wave, similar to the alpha wave recorded over the posterior neocortex but slower (4–7 Hz rather than 8–12 Hz). The septal nuclei also receive input from the hypothalamus via the medial forebrain bundle, and via the same bundle project fibers into the hypothalamic region and beyond, as shown in Figure 10.9 Also shown is septal input from the *orbital cortex* of the frontal lobe and projection into the head of the *caudate nucleus*.

Although there are no known projections directly to the septal nuclei themselves from the olfactory bulbs, there are many olfactory fibers running to the septal region, and secondary fibers of olfactory significance running into the septal nuclei. It is not surprising, then, that lesions in the septal nuclei produce symptoms largely parallel to those resulting from ablation of the olfactory bulbs.

It was Petsche *et al.* (1962) who discovered that the medial septal nucleus contains the *pacemaker cells* for the hippocampal theta rhythm. Donovick (1966, 1968) found that lesions in these nuclei that tend to block the theta rhythm correlate with a peculiar inability on the part of the animal to alter its behavior adaptively. The generic term for this phenomenon is *perseveration* (persevering abnormally). It is manifested in the animal by inability to learn a task requiring either reversal of its response or alternation of responses

Septum. **A region in the midline of the brain immediately above the anterior commissure.**

Medial septal nucleus. **One of two septal nuclei projecting to the hippocampus and containing the pacemaker cells that control the hippocampal theta wave.**

Pacemaker cells. **Neurons in the medial septal nucleus presumed responsible for regulating hippocampal rhythms, such as the theta wave.**

Perseveration. **Persistence of a learned response after it is no longer rewarded, or even punished.**

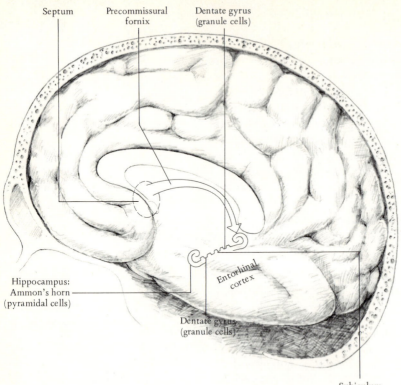

Septum   Precommissural   Dentate gyrus
          fornix   (granule cells)

Hippocampus:
Ammon's horn
(pyramidal cells)

Entorhinal
cortex

Dentate gyrus
(granule cells)

Subiculum

Figure 10.8 / *The Precommissural Fornix Pathway.* The medial septal nucleus has "pacemaker cells" that control the hippocampal theta wave, and hippocampal function, via a fiber projection passing posteriorward through the fornix. Other fibers in this pathway project from the hippocampus to the septal area.

to two different stimuli, or to unlearn a response that is no longer rewarded (*failure of response extinction*). It may mean inability to withhold a learned response even when it is punished. The common factor in these instances is best described as a loss of normal adaptive plasticity or flexibility in the face of changed circumstances (Ellen, Wilson, and Powell, 1964; Douglas and Raphelson, 1966; Schwartzbaum and Donovick, 1968).

Lesions in the *lateral septal nucleus*, though they do not impair the hippocampal theta rhythm, produce the same curiously quick learning of the two-way active avoidance response seen in animals with olfactory lesions. Beatty and Schwartzbaum (1968) found another quite different effect of septal lesions in rats. They became more finicky about food — more rejecting of unpalatable food (water

Lateral septal nucleus. **One of two major septal nuclei, projecting heavily into the head of the caudate nucleus.**

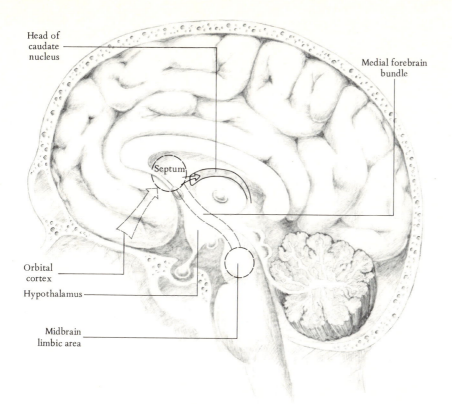

Figure 10.9 / *Input to the Septal Nuclei from the Hypothalamus.* The septal nuclei, particularly the lateral septal nucleus, project via a ventral route into the hypothalamus. Other fibers project from the same hypothalamic regions into the septal area. These fibers form the anterior portion of the medial forebrain bundle, which extends posteriorward into the midbrain limbic area. Orbital and caudate connections are also shown.

adulterated with quinine) and more voracious in their appetite for tasty food (water sweetened with saccharin). As we shall see in Chapter 11, this behavior parallels that of rats with lesions in the ventromedial hypothalamus; it is of interest that there are important fiber bundles interconnecting these two regions in the medial forebrain bundle.

Thus there appear to be two sets of symptoms corresponding to the two septal nuclei, one intimately involved with hippocampal functioning, the other independent of hippocampal functions but possibly more closely related to hypothalamic hunger and fear mechanisms. But now the picture of septal functions suggested by septal lesions must be expanded further. It is known that in monkeys the orbital cortex projects principally to the septal sector known to contain the pacemaker cells for the theta rhythm. Damage to the orbital cortex itself results in the same perseveration described above in connection with loss of the hippocampal theta wave (Butters and Rosvold, 1968). This situation is similar to what we found with regard to the olfactory bulbs, which project to the septal region. Thus medial septum and orbital cortex appear to participate in the same hippocampal system.

One further curious complication must be added. The orbital cortex is also known to project strongly into the head of the caudate nucleus, which lies just lateral to the septal area but belongs to the basal ganglia system. Lesions to this region of the head of the caudate nucleus produce the same perseverative phenomena in an *object-reversal task*. Projecting into a slightly different sector of the caudate head are fibers from the prefrontal cortex, where lesions have been found in the monkey to produce deficits in delayed response and delayed alternation learning. Lesions in this portion of the caudate nucleus produce similar learning deficits (Mishkin, 1964). It seems, then, that these two regions of the frontal-lobe cortex must be included within the septal system, whose destruction produces a range of specific learning deficits, some of which appear to involve the caudate nucleus as well.

What might we expect to find, then, in the case of damage to the hippocampus, which seems so importantly involved in some of these deficits?

Object-reversal task. **An experimental arrangement in which the subject is required to select one of two objects, having first learned to choose the other.**

The Effect of Hippocampal Lesions

Almost all the lesion studies that have been done on the hippocampal formation appear to apply specifically to the *septo-hippocampal* or precommissural portion of the overall system.

Briefly, the effects of such lesions appear largely to parallel the effects of septal lesions, which in turn overlap those of lesions of the olfactory bulbs, orbital cortex, prefrontal granular cortex, and caudate nucleus. In addition we have findings gathered from human patients who have suffered damage to (or removal of) the hippocampal region, which indicate the very specific importance of the hippocampus in the consolidation of event memory (what happened last time) for long-term storage.

We have already seen in our discussion of hemispheric specialization that people with hippocampal damage have a specific kind of memory deficit, depending on the hemisphere affected — loss of musical memories in right temporal-lobe ablations, loss of recent verbal memory in left temporal-lobe lesions. It has long been recognized that bilateral hippocampectomy of the human produces a permanent disruption of memory of newly acquired experience (Ojemann, 1966; Milner, 1972). In such cases it is characteristic for short-term memory and general intelligence to remain intact, but the patient has no recollection whatever of experiences that were the focus of attention just a short time before. The moment the attention shifts to something else, the experience of the moment before is lost to recall, like a dream from which we awake with no recall.

No doubt certain aspects of the deficits associated with experimental hippocampal lesions in animals can be explained as the result of failure to remember recent experiences. A common deficit is inability to suppress dominant responses, innate or the result of training, when they are no longer rewarded, or even when they are punished (McCleary, 1961, 1966; Ellen, Wilson, and Powell, 1964; Douglas and Raphelson, 1966; Kimble, 1968). Others are perseveration, specifically of a position habit (Orbach, Milner, and Rasmussen, 1960; Fischman and McCleary, 1966); poor performance in learning a complex maze (Kimble, 1963; Bender, Hostetter, and Thomas, 1968); the passive avoidance deficit (Kimura, 1958; Kimble, Kirkby, and Stein, 1966; Blanchard and Fial, 1968); failure to learn an alternating bar-press response task (Gross, Chorover, and Cohen, 1965); and faster learning in the two-way shuttlebox avoidance learning task (Green, Beatty, and Schwartzbaum, 1967). It has also been observed that hippocampal damage in animals interferes with habituation (Roberts, Dember, and Brodwick, 1962; Douglas and Isaacson, 1964; Raphelson, Isaacson, and Douglas, 1965). One interesting aspect of the animal research has indicated something quite different and apparently unrelated to memory deficit, namely a curious imperviousness to distraction from the goal pursuit (Wickelgren and Isaacson, 1963, for rats; Douglas and Pribram, 1969, for monkeys). We shall examine this subject further below.

The Effect of Hippocampal Removal in the Human

It has long been declared that memory consolidation involves a grand feedback loop called *Papez' circuit,* presumed to pass from the hippocampus to the *mammillary bodies* via the fornix, then to the *anterior nucleus of the thalamus* via the *mammillothalamic tract,* thence to the cingulate gyrus, and via the *cingulum bundle* back down to the

Mammillothalamic tract. A fiber bundle leading from the mammillary bodies to the anterior nucleus of the thalamus as part of Papez' circuit.

Cingulum bundle. A stout fiber bundle passing through the cingulate gyrus beneath its cortical layer and continuing around the posterior end of the corpus callosum and into the entorhinal cortex of the temporal lobe.

temporal lobe in the *entorhinal cortex*, from which fibers feed back into the hippocampus (refer to Figure 10.2). This circuit, we know today, begins instead in the *subiculum*. In a recent study, Swanson and Cowan (1975) established that the postcommissural fornix fibers arise not in the hippocampus but in the subicular cortex adjacent to it, which receives information just processed through the hippocampal–dentate gyrus system. (See Figures 10.10 and 10.11.)

More challenging to the Papez-circuit theory, however, is the finding that bilateral destruction of the fornix does not impair memory functions or learning ability in the human (Clark, Beattie, Riddoch, and Dott, 1938; Cairns and Mosberg, 1951). Moreover, *fornical agenesis* (congenital lack of a fornix) is reported not to be associated with memory defect in humans (Nathan and Smith, 1950). This finding is puzzling, since the mammillary bodies, which are the major target of postcommissural fornix fibers, are frequently found damaged in *Korsakoff syndrome* patients, who suffer from severe memory-consolidation deficit.

Milner, who has done the classic research on the effects of temporal-lobe ablation (Milner, 1966), found a dissociation between the kind of memory defect we have been discussing and a different kind unrelated to recalled evaluations of previous experience. Her most famous case, H. M., at age 27 underwent bilateral removal of the medial temporal lobe, including the hippocampi, as a drastic measure to relieve an intractable epileptic condition. When he recovered from the surgery, it became apparent that he had total lack of recall of things that happened just moments before, and was unable to remember even the way to the bathroom in the hospital ward. Except for this profound loss of ability to store experiential memories, H. M. appeared completely normal, in full possession of knowledge and skills acquired before the operation, and unimpaired in all other aspects of intelligence.

Among the tests Milner employed in examining her patient was one that taps motor learning of a special sort: the subject is required to follow the outline of a figure (a star) with a pencil while observing his progress in a mirror. This is exceedingly difficult at first, but with practice normally becomes quite easy. H. M.'s performance on this learning task was entirely normal, becoming almost perfect after twenty-one trials on the second day of testing. Astonishingly, this was true though he had no recollection of ever having performed the task before, and had to have the problem explained over and over again in the course of the testing.

The dissociation here appears to be between memory of experienced events — which is a kind of "one-shot" learning, since events

Entorhinal cortex. **The limbic system cortex on the medial and basal surfaces of the temporal lobe in the vicinity of the amygdala and the hippocampal formation.**

Subiculum. **A paleocortical region within the hippocampal formation to which the hippocampally processed information projects for output via the fornix to the mammillary bodies.**

Fornical agenesis. **(*a-JEN-i-sis*). Failure of the fornix to form during gestation.**

Korsakoff syndrome. **A degenerative neurological disorder afflicting long-term chronic alcoholics and characterized by loss of short-term memory consolidation into long-term memory storage.**

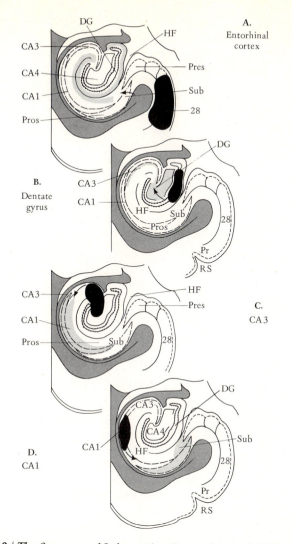

Figure 10.10 / *The Sequence of Information Processing in the Hippocampus.*
As shown in this important study using autoradiographic technique and
fiber degeneration tracing, a stepwise sequence of intrinsic hippocampal
efferents goes from the entorhinal cortex (28) to the entire dentate gyrus
and hippocampal pyramidal cell regions. The dentate gyrus (DG) projects to the hippocampal pyramids of the CA4 and CA3 regions. CA3 projects massively into CA1, while injection of radioactive amino acids here
results in radioactive labeling throughout the subiculum (Sub), which is
the take-off point for efferents into subcortical regions via the fornix as well
as into several limbic cortical areas adjacent to neocortical association areas
in the frontal and parietal lobes. (HF, hippocampal fissure; Pros, prosubiculum; Pres, presubiculum; RS, rhinal sulcus; CA, cornu Ammonis,
Ammon's horn)

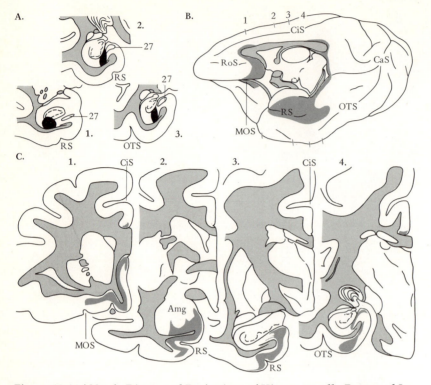

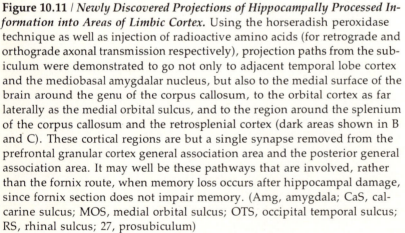

Figure 10.11 / *Newly Discovered Projections of Hippocampally Processed Information into Areas of Limbic Cortex.* Using the horseradish peroxidase technique as well as injection of radioactive amino acids (for retrograde and orthograde axonal transmission respectively), projection paths from the subiculum were demonstrated to go not only to adjacent temporal lobe cortex and the mediobasal amygdalar nucleus, but also to the medial surface of the brain around the genu of the corpus callosum, to the orbital cortex as far laterally as the medial orbital sulcus, and to the region around the splenium of the corpus callosum and the retrosplenial cortex (dark areas shown in B and C). These cortical regions are but a single synapse removed from the prefrontal granular cortex general association area and the posterior general association area. It may well be these pathways that are involved, rather than the fornix route, when memory loss occurs after hippocampal damage, since fornix section does not impair memory. (Amg, amygdala; CaS, calcarine sulcus; MOS, medial orbital sulcus; OTS, occipital temporal sulcus; RS, rhinal sulcus; 27, prosubiculum)

in their uniqueness are only experienced once — and memory resulting from training through repeated similar experiences. We commonly call the latter knowledge, or acquired skill, or concept attain-
ment, or perhaps "semantic" memory (Tulving, 1972). One might
have thought that the development of a given skill would make use
of the mechanism through which event memory is consolidated,
but the evidence here suggests otherwise. Thus we are forced to
sharpen our thinking about the phenomenon we have loosely called
memory, if we are to employ the concept properly in our efforts to
understand brain functions.

We will have more to say about the hippocampus in our discussion of learning processes in Chapter 16.

The Effect of Amygdalar Lesions: Physiological Emotion

Recent studies by McGaugh and his associates have shown that
low-level electrical stimulation of the amygdala in rats disrupts
memory of electroshock (Gold, Macri, and McGaugh, 1973). Even
more recently there has been discovered a system within the amygdala, based on the neurotransmitter norepinephrine, which is involved in the memory mechanisms with regard to aversive experiences (Gallagher *et al.*, 1977). If a chemical blocking the effect of
norepinephrine is injected immediately following footshock as the
animal steps into a dark compartment, the rat is significantly less
reluctant to step into the compartment again the next day than are
control animals. (This is the classic passive avoidance deficit.) Thus
there is evidence that the amygdala too may be involved in circuits
mediating retention of information relevant to behavioral choice, or
perhaps mediating only the ability to utilize such information in
the adaptive control of behavior. Ursin (1966) and McNew and
Thompson (1966) both found amygdalar lesions to result in a deficit
in active avoidance learning as well (in the one-way situation).
Curiously, Ursin reported that his animals failed to escape the
shock by leaping away despite evident emotional response to the
warning signal. This finding suggests that the information was
available to the animals, but that its utilization was interfered with.

The lesions in this instance were in a portion of the amygdala
that an earlier study (Ursin and Kaada, 1960) implicated in fear
responses. That study found that stimulation of the anterior portions of the amygdala in the cat produces flight or fear responses,
while stimulation of the more caudal regions of the amygdalar complex result in defensive rage responses. Ursin and Kaada have suc-

cessfully established the concept of a division of the amygdala into two functionally different nuclear groups: the *basolateral* group associated with fear and rage responses, more anterior, and projecting to the hypothalamus via the *ventral amygdalofugal fibers;* and the *corticomedial* group, a phylogenetically more ancient structure, situated more posteriorly and projecting to the hypothalamus over the stria terminalis pathway.

It is now well established that complete bilateral ablation of both portions of the amygdala is associated with a taming effect in a wide variety of animals (Goddard, 1964). Thus a ferocious tiger can be dramatically transformed into a big affectionate pussycat, neither fearful nor prone to anger. Perhaps the adaptive significance of this close association in the amygdala of such behaviorally distinct phenomena as fear and rage is to be seen in the well-documented capacity of mammals to shift very dramatically from one to the other. A cornered rat, fleeing in terror but finding no escape route, characteristically switches to the attack mode with amazing abruptness, only to switch back to flight the moment an escape avenue presents itself. It is as if the amygdala represents a flip switch in the brain governing these two modes of expressing recognition of danger: fear (flight or freezing) and ferocity (when attack appears to be the best or only remaining mode of defense).

Fear and rage can also be elicited by stimulating the hypothalamus, into which the two divisions of the amygdala project, but the response differs. When the amygdala is stimulated, the current must be left on for a second or two before the response becomes full-blown; response to hypothalamic stimulation is instantaneous and in full force from the start. Also, response to amygdalar stimulation subsides more gradually, while hypothalamic stimulation ends immediately when the current is cut off. Apparently the function of the amygdala here is to modulate or control the release and behavioral expression of hypothalamic survival mechanisms of a reflex sort, which, left to themselves, might be maladaptive. Such pre-wired response processes may be called *physiological emotions,* involving as they do high-level activation of the sympathetic nervous system and preparation of the organism for maximum energy release (Isaacson, 1974).

Physiological emotion. **The change in bodily state associated with such emotions as rage and fear, representing activity of the sympathetic nervous system.**

The Effect of Amygdalar Lesions: Mood States

Fonberg, a highly imaginative researcher, recently introduced a new look at the functional division of labors within the amygdala. Long ago it had been found that lesions in the region of the lateral hypothalamus may cause rats to lose all appetite for food (Hetherington and Ranson, 1942; Anand and Brobeck, 1951). In her experiments on dogs, Fonberg (1976) found that an identical syndrome is produced by lesions in the dorsomedial amygdalar region, lasting only five to ten days but followed by persistent poor appetite, finickiness, vomiting, and decrease in bodily weight. More dramatic, however, is her finding that dorsomedial amygdalar lesion produces behavioral symptoms in the dog that closely resemble human clinical depression:

Their outlook and behavioral patterns were completely changed. They were generally apathetic and motionless, did not explore the surroundings as they used to do before the operation; they stood motionless, mostly in one spot, and were not responsive to most of the external signals. They lost their friendly relations with technicians who fed them, seemed not to recognize well-known persons, did not come when called by name, and abandoned all their previous skills and habits. The technicians also judged the dog as "not the same one." On the other hand, these dogs were not completely unreactive. They withdrew from the food bowl, resisted feeding, ran away quickly, even through obstacles, and with great force opposed being led by leash or other manipulations, and showed this negativistic attitude in most instances. (E. Fonberg, in D. Novin, W. Wyrwicka, and G. Bray (Eds.), *Hunger: Basic Mechanisms and Clinical Implications*, Raven Press, New York, 1976, pp. 62–63)

Since these changes in feeding behavior resemble those associated in other species with lateral hypothalamic lesions, it was decided to perform this operation too. The lateral hypothalamic lesions produced symptoms identical in all respects to those of the dorsomedial amygdalar lesions, such that one could not guess which dogs had which operation. In both instances the most striking symptoms (unlike rats, presumably) were "changes in the general emotionality and behavioral signs of apathy, indifference, and . . . negativism" (p. 63), rather than loss of appetite.

However, lesions in the region of the lateral amygdala produced a dramatically different syndrome:

The dogs became hyperphagic, voracious, interested in food and in all objects in the environment. They were running around and sniffing the area. They were, in general, very lively and mobile. They became more affectionate toward the technicians: jumping on them, licking their faces, asking for petting and for play. (p. 64)

Fonberg proposed that the similarity of symptoms produced by dorsomedial amygdalar and lateral hypothalamic lesions (aphagia and depression of behavioral response) reflects the strong anatomical connections between the amygdala and the hypothalamus, and that the dorsomedial amygdala may normally facilitate the activity of the lateral hypothalamic neurons while inhibiting the (inhibitory) ventromedial hypothalamic neurons. Lesions of the dorsomedial amygdala would thus be expected to cut off the facilitatory influences on the lateral hypothalamus while releasing the inhibitory *ventromedial nucleus* from suppression. The lateral amygdala, on the other hand, might normally inhibit the lateral hypothalamus through its fiber projections, while facilitating the activity of the ventromedial inhibitory neurons. Lesions in the lateral amygdala might then be expected to release the lateral hypothalamic centers from direct inhibitory influences, while blocking the inhibition normally arising from the ventromedial nucleus. (These relationships will be discussed in Chapter 11.)

Ventromedial nucleus. **A nucleus near the midline of the hypothalamus, medial to the hunger centers, into which it projects laterally-running inhibitory fibers.**

There may also be feedback fibers from the hypothalamus to the amygdala regulating this activity. Thus the question is posed whether the dorsomedial amygdalar neurons play a general facilitatory role in normal living, while the lateral nucleus exercises a general inhibitory role influencing many functions (defensive, alimentary, sexual, general activity level, responsiveness to external stimuli, and the like). In short, perhaps emotional tone is primary, behavioral changes and motivational level secondary!

Two more points about Fonberg's important study deserve mention. First, the dogs' depression and changes in emotional expression following dorsomedial amygdalar lesions were "cured" by subsequent lesions in the lateral amygdalar nucleus. And the same cure was effected by the drugs imipramine and amytriptyline, which are frequently effective in the treatment of human psychotic depression.

Unipolar depression. **Endogenous depression, without manic symptoms as found in the manic-depressive disorder.**

Thus it appears that, just as there is a flip switch in the amygdala for the behavioral expression of physiological emotion (fear or rage), there is also such a switch for euphoria and depression (mood swings). To our knowledge, no one has yet followed up this intriguing suggestion that the manic-depressive syndrome in the human may be a function of a shifting imbalance between two portions of the amygdala. Perhaps it is just as well, since the antidepressant drugs that mimic "cure" of depressed spirits in the dog are often quite ineffective with the manic-depressive patient. (See Chapter 15 for a fuller discussion of this question.) The depression involved here is probably the kind commonly called *unipolar* or *endogenous,* which does respond to these medications. Still, it is intriguing to note the close resemblance to the human manic disorder of the dog with lesions in the lateral amygdaloid nucleus.

Endogenous (en-DOJ-i-nus). **Referring to depressions which appear to be unrelated to present life circumstances, hence arising presumably from some altered conditions within the brain.**

There is a most interesting recent finding, using the new horseradish peroxidase technique, of projections from the amygdala to the region of the cortex of the cat corresponding to our prefrontal granular cortex. Heretofore only the amygdala's frontal connections with the orbital portion had been known, directly and through relay via the dorsomedial thalamic nucleus. The new evidence, however, implicates the amygdala in the operations of the entire frontal lobe, including perhaps even areas 4 and 6 of the motor cortex, though fewer fibers were found passing to this region (Llamas, Avendaño, and Reinoso-Suárez, 1977). The authors say:

In conclusion, the amygdala has been considered as the site of evaluation of the motivational significance of stimuli from the environment and from the internal milieu, exerting its influence by modulating hypothalamic drive mechanisms. To this one should add that it has a double influence on the frontal cortices: indirectly through a thalamic relay and directly by way of the paths identified here. (p. 706)

There is thus increasing justification for inclusion of these high-level associative regions of the cortex in the operations of the limbic system. This finding represents another instance of "upward" communication to the thalamocortical system from more ancient structures below.

Summary

Analysis of the limbic structures through lesion studies suggests that their functions are heavily concerned with the evaluation of experience as rewarding or punishing, and with retaining memory of that evaluation as a control of adaptive behavior in subsequent encounters with a similar stimulus situation. In addition to the classic limbic structures — the hippocampus, the septum, the amygdala, the cingulate and entorhinal cortices — other structures, including the olfactory bulbs, the prefrontal and orbital cortices, and the head of the caudate nucleus, also participate in this global functional system. Many aspects of the limbic-lesion syndrome, for example, are found after removal of the olfactory bulbs in the experimental animal, including failure to habituate to nonrelevant stimuli, failure to respond appropriately to situations previously accompanied by punishment, and apparent inability to withhold natural or trained responses when they are no longer rewarded, or even when they are punished. Similar deficits are found after septal lesions, as well as lesions in prefrontal and orbital cortical areas projecting into the septal region. Perseveration — inability to alter or withhold behavior adaptively — is particularly evident after frontal-lobe lesions, as well as lesions to the caudate sectors to which they project.

Similar effects are produced by lesions or removal of the hippocampus, which intimately intercommunicates with the septum via the precommissural branch of the fornix. However, we have evidence from studies of human patients who have suffered damage to or loss of the hippocampi that memory functions are particularly closely associated with this structure. Specifically, the human hippocampal syndrome is inability to remember recent experience. The moment attention shifts to something else, the experience of the preceding moment is lost to recall. In view of the close link between septum and hippocampus, a similar deficit may largely account for the behavior of the lesioned animal, whatever the limbic structure affected.

In the case of the amygdala, however, deficits resulting from lesions are less readily attributed to a memory deficit. Removal of the amygdala results in a dramatic taming effect, as well as evidence of failure of normal fear and rage responses. That these emotions can be readily produced by stimulating the animal in one or another portion of the amygdala suggests the existence there of a flip switch mediating sudden behavioral shift from flight to fearless attack as a defensive maneuver. Also found in the amygdala of dogs are distinct regions whose balance appears to control mood. Removal of the lateral amygdala produces a lively, apparently euphoric animal; removal of the dorsomedial portion produces a contrasting syndrome reminiscent of human pyschotic depression. It is believed, in light of recent evidence, that these effects are mediated through paths projecting to the hypothalamus as well as to the prefrontal and orbital cortices.

Chapter 11 / *The Medial Forebrain Bundle System: Inborn Drive and Response Mechanisms*

The medial forebrain bundle system as here defined includes the hypothalamus as well as the fiber bundles coursing through the lateral hypothalamus between the brainstem and the septal region. These fiber bundles are interspersed with numerous small nuclei which are involved in such motivational mechanisms as hunger, thirst, sex, fear, and rage. Nuclei in the medial hypothalamus appear to be inhibitory to those motivational mechanisms through laterally running fibers. The medial forebrain bundle fibers consist in part of ascending fibers from the brainstem supplying the forebrain with the neurotransmitters norepinephrine, dopamine, and serotonin. A temperature-regulation mechanism is situated in the hypothalamus. The hypothalamus also exercises control over the subjacent pituitary gland as well as the autonomic nervous system through fibers descending to the brainstem. Moreover, the medial forebrain bundle system is importantly involved in mechanisms of reward and punishment: electrical stimulation of many points along its course causes the animal intense pleasure; other points cause pain.

Coursing through the base of the brain along the midline, from the septal area through the lateral hypothalamic region and into the *limbic midbrain area* at the top of the brainstem, lies a system of nerve fibers, interspersed among which are the neural cell bodies of a number of small nuclei. This system, together with the other nuclei of the hypothalamus, will be discussed here as the *medial forebrain bundle system* (Figure 11.1). It is related to but distinguishable from the limbic system. Along its length are points that elicit striking results when electrically stimulated in the experimental animal. The widely-publicized "pleasure centers" of the brain are most densely concentrated here, as are points whose stimulation can cause an animal who has just eaten to begin eating again voraciously, or one who has just drunk its fill to begin drinking as if intensely thirsty. Stimulation of other regions instantly produces sexual behavior

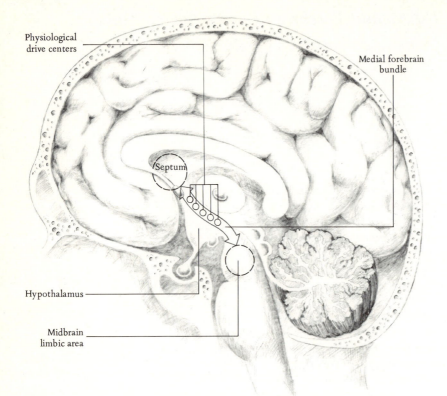

Figure 11.1 / *The Medial Forebrain Bundle and its Connections.* This short fiber bundle passing through the lateral hypothalamus between the septal region and the midbrain limbic area of the brainstem plays an enormously important role in human brain function. In addition to providing a pathway for many important projection systems, it contains numerous small nuclei concerned with such basic motivational mechanisms as hunger and thirst, sexual urge, rage and fear, and pleasure and pain (reinforcement mechanisms). These are played upon and regulated by overlying limbic system structures such as the amygdala and lateral septal nucleus. More medial to the bundle lie inhibitory nuclei serving as governors of the excitability of the motivational neurons.

(mounting or ejaculation in the male, adoption of the *lordosis posture* by the female), or a violent rage response, or panic.

Loosely speaking, we are discussing the functions of the *hypothalamus*, a tiny mass of neural tissue at the base of the brain below the two thalami, which joins the two hemispheres below the third ventricle (Figures 11.2 and 11.3). The motivational regions just mentioned lie in its more lateral part, along the bundle; medial to them,

Lordosis posture. **A typical sexual presentation posture of the female mammal, inviting sexual contact and facilitating intromission.**

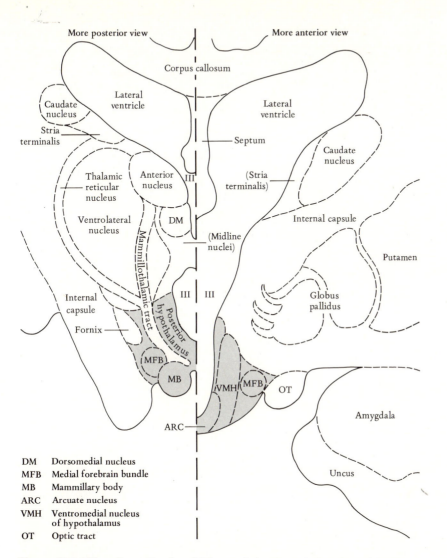

More posterior view

More anterior view

Corpus callosum

Caudate nucleus

Lateral ventricle

Lateral ventricle

Stria terminalis

Septum

Caudate nucleus

Thalamic reticular nucleus

Anterior nucleus

III

(Stria terminalis)

Ventrolateral nucleus

DM

Internal capsule

(Midline nuclei)

Putamen

III   III

Globus pallidus

Internal capsule

Posterior hypothalamus

Mammillothalamic tract

Fornix

MFB

MB

VMH

MFB

OT

Amygdala

ARC

Uncus

DM	Dorsomedial nucleus
MFB	Medial forebrain bundle
MB	Mammillary body
ARC	Arcuate nucleus
VMH	Ventromedial nucleus of hypothalamus
OT	Optic tract

Figure 11.2 / *Two Cross-Sectional Views of the Hypothalamus and Its Surrounding Structures.* In the left half of the figure the hypothalamus (darkened portion) is seen lying immediately below the thalamus and bordering the third ventricle (III), with the bulbous mammillary body forming its base. On the right, more anteriorly in the brain, the thalamus is no longer in evidence but the basal ganglia (caudate nucleus, putamen, and globus pallidus) are shown. Note that the medial forebrain bundle (MFB) in both views lies in the lateral portion of the hypothalamus. The prominent ventromedial nucleus (VMH) is an important inhibitory nucleus blocking action of more laterally situated motivational mechanisms through laterally running fibers.

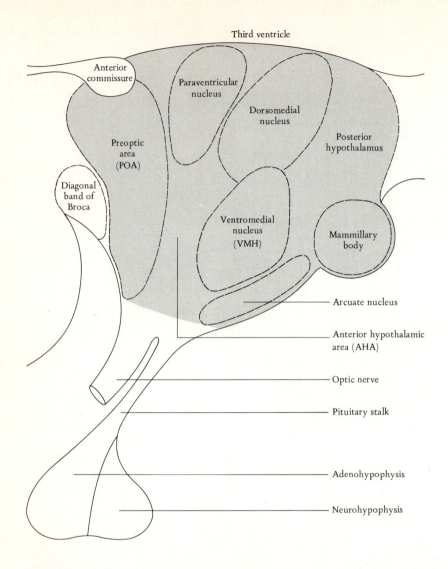

Third ventricle

Anterior commissure

Paraventricular nucleus

Dorsomedial nucleus

Posterior hypothalamus

Preoptic area (POA)

Diagonal band of Broca

Ventromedial nucleus (VMH)

Mammillary body

— Arcuate nucleus

— Anterior hypothalamic area (AHA)

— Optic nerve

— Pituitary stalk

— Adenohypophysis

— Neurohypophysis

Figure 11.3 / *A Sagittal Section of the Hypothalamus, Showing Prominent Nuclear Areas.* This enlarged view of the hypothalamus shows the relative positions of the major nuclei in the medial hypothalamus. The medial forebrain bundle (not shown) lies just lateral to the ventromedial nucleus and the anterior hypothalamic area. The anterior commissure and the diagonal band of Broca mark the anterior extent of the hypothalamic region, while the mammillary bodies mark its most posterior extent. The third ventricle lies above, and the pituitary gland below.

along the centerline, are nuclei that appear to exert an inhibitory control over them through laterally running fibers. Both the excitatory and the inhibitory nuclei are modulated in their functioning by neural circuits of the limbic system associated with the hippocampus, septum, and amygdala, as already described in Chapter 10. Those circuits in turn are modulated by ongoing activities in the overlying thalamocortical system. Here we see clearly the downward cascade of neural influences, so characteristic of the mammalian brain, from more recently evolved structures into the older, more primitive structures that handle basic survival mechanisms.

But the medial forebrain bundle itself is composed of longitudinally running fibers, some of which form the major pathway along which certain neurotransmitters travel by axoplasmic flow from their cell bodies of origin in the brainstem into forebrain sites. As we shall see, there is evidence that these chemical substances may also be importantly involved in the activities of the motivational and emotional circuits within the bundle itself.

Three Psychogenic Neurotransmitter Systems

The vast majority of studies of the neurochemistry of the brain have focused on just three of the many neurotransmitter substances known or suspected to be involved in its functioning: norepinephrine, dopamine, and serotonin (Figure 11.4). Interest has centered on these three because, though they represent only a small fraction of the neurochemicals employed by the brain, they have been found to be critically involved in such psychological phenomena as motivational states and moods, as well as waking and sleeping. That is, they are involved in certain conscious phenomena and their associated behaviors. A prime illustration is the apparent relationship between the neurotransmitter norepinephrine and the experience of pleasure.

Norepinephrine is manufactured only in certain brainstem nuclei, particularly one called the *locus coeruleus* for its curiously bluish color when the brain is examined in the fresh state. It has been discovered, astonishingly, that neurons in these brainstem nuclei project their axons to all areas of the neocortex in a highly systematic manner, probably innervating each and every cortical column (Morrison, Molliver, and Grzanna, 1979). The pathway enters the medial forebrain bundle at the midbrain level and projects all the way through the septal region, under the *rostrum* of the corpus callosum into the frontal lobe. Here the fibers turn caudally

Locus coeruleus (ser-ROO-lee-us). **A brainstem nucleus (of bluish color in the fresh state), the source of much of the norepinephrine in the brain.**

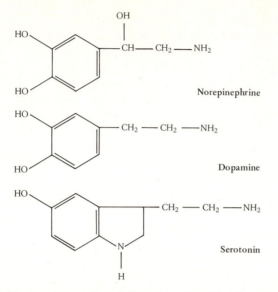

Figure 11.4 / *Structural Formulas of Three Important Psychogenic Neuro-*
transmitters in the Brain. In these structural diagrams of the three important monoamines we can note a number of similarities. They are relatively
small molecules. (Protein molecules, by comparison, are enormously large.)
They all have an amine group (NH_2) at one end and an ethyl group in
the middle (CH_2—CH_2). And norepinephrine differs from dopamine only
in having the carbon in the beta position hydroxylated. The first two of
these neurotransmitters are called catecholamines in recognition of the di-
hydroxylated phenyl group on the left, while the last, serotonin, is called an
indole amine for its somewhat different group on the left.

to travel in parallel ranks all the way to the occipital lobe (Figure
11.5); along the way they send out collaterals to invade every region
of the neocortex. This innervation is obviously nonspecific, carrying
no particular sensory information, and its function in the cortex is
presently unknown. Nor is it known whether its terminals synapse
on particular cortical neurons or diffusely release their norepinephrine as a *neurohormone* within the extracellular space.

   This new finding appears to correct an earlier speculation that
norepinephrine-containing fibers project laterally into the cortex
after reaching the cingulate gyrus. It is interesting that the study
found very little evidence of *noradrenergic* innervation of the anterior cingulate gyrus (Brodmann's area 24, now thought to be
associated with the reticular system), but an extremely heavy innervation of the posterior cingulate and the *retrosplenial* region
(Brodmann's areas 23 and 29), which — curiously enough — has

Neurohormone. A
hormone released
by neurons into in-
tracellular space
rather than into the
synaptic cleft, thus
exercising a diffuse
rather than discrete
influence.

Noradrenergic
(nor-a-dre-NUR-jik).
Said of neurons or
neural systems
making use of the
neurotransmitter
norepinephrine.

Retrosplenial. Be-
hind the splenium,
or posterior end of
the corpus cal-
losum.

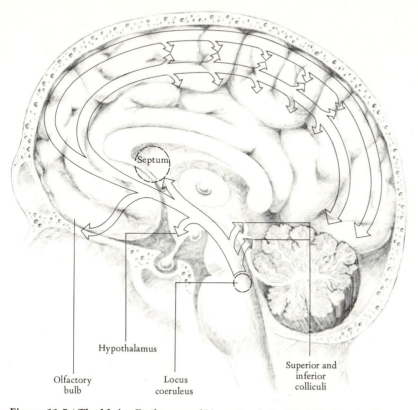

Hypothalamus

Olfactory
bulb

Locus
coeruleus

Superior and
inferior
colliculi

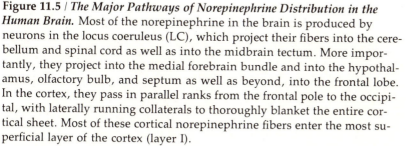

Figure 11.5 / *The Major Pathways of Norepinephrine Distribution in the Human Brain.* Most of the norepinephrine in the brain is produced by neurons in the locus coeruleus (LC), which project their fibers into the cerebellum and spinal cord as well as into the midbrain tectum. More importantly, they project into the medial forebrain bundle and into the hypothalamus, olfactory bulb, and septum as well as beyond, into the frontal lobe. In the cortex, they pass in parallel ranks from the frontal pole to the occipital, with laterally running collaterals to thoroughly blanket the entire cortical sheet. Most of these cortical norepinephrine fibers enter the most superficial layer of the cortex (layer I).

been found to be a strong projection area of neurons in the olfactory cortex of the *substantia innominata.* (The olfactory system as a whole appears to be importantly noradrenergic.)

In the lateral convexity of the neocortex it was found that norepinephrine fibers terminate in layers IV and V, but that the heaviest projection is into layer I, where the fiber branches turn both anteroposteriorly and mediolaterally to blanket the entire hemispheres. This heavy projection into the surface layer of the cortex — which also receives terminals from other cortical regions and the reticular formation, as well as the dendritic extensions of the apical dendrites of the cortical pyramidal cells — strongly suggests a noradrenergic role in the control of general cortical integration, of the sort recorded electrographically from the scalp as brain waves. These neural activities will be discussed further in Chapter 12.

Dopamine-containing neurons originate higher in the brainstem, principally in the midbrain region, in the darkly pigmented structures called the *substantia nigra* near the ventral surface of the midbrain (Figure 11.6). From here an orderly fiber bundle projects along with the norepinephrine fibers through the lateral hypothalamic region, following the course of the medial forebrain bundle, then branches, sending its major projection into the *striatum* (the nigrostriatal pathway) while other fibers continue into the anterior portions of the brain, including particularly the olfactory bulb and cortex and the medial surface of the frontal lobe neocortex. Another more local source and pathway originates in the *tuberal* region of the hypothalamus and projects only a short distance to the stalk of the pituitary gland and (from somewhat more dorsal hypothalamic regions) into the anterior hypothalamus.

Tuberal region. **The basal portion of the hypothalamus immediately above the pituitary stalk.**

The third psychogenic neurotransmitter coursing through the medial forebrain bundle from the brainstem is *serotonin* (5-hydroxytryptamine). Serotonin is synthesized in neurons in a number of small nuclei lying along the midline of the brainstem, in a structure called the *median raphé* (seam), from the medulla to the midbrain. The two largest are the dorsal and medial raphé nuclei high up in the midbrain region. Serotonergic terminals are found along the medial forebrain bundle from the hypothalamus to the septal region, with a pronounced concentration in the *suprachiasmatic nucleus* (just above the optic chiasma) where, as will be seen, a forebrain "sleep center" makes use of this neurotransmitter. Another path projects to the basal ganglia, and a more anterior projection follows the route of the norepinephrine fibers into the neocortex. There is a widespread ramification of terminals in the neocortex as well as in the archicortex of the hippocampus and the adjoining amygdalar nuclei in the temporal lobe. Figure 11.7 depicts these pathways, for comparison with those of the norepinephrine system.

Median raphé. **A structure in the midline of the brainstem, the location of nuclei producing serotonin.**

Suprachiasmatic nucleus. **A small nucleus above the optic chiasma, anterior to the hypothalamus proper.**

Briefly, then, all three systems have terminals in the hypothalamus and septum. Norepinephrine and serotonin both project into the hippocampus and amygdala as well, while a distinct dopaminergic pathway goes to the basal ganglia (the nigrostriatal path). All three are thought to be usually inhibitory in their influence —

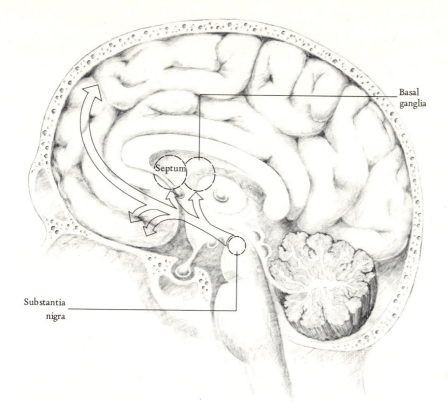

Figure 11.6 / *The Major Dopamine Pathways in the Human Brain.* Most of the brain's dopamine is produced by neurons in the substantia nigra (SN), which project their axons into the medial forebrain bundle. Most then follow the nigrostriatal pathway into the basal ganglia, but others pass to the septal area and into the medial surface of the frontal lobe. Another source of dopamine (not shown) is within the hypothalamus, serving only local hypothalamic regions. Still another (conjectural) may be the medial surface of the frontal lobe neocortex.

although, in a more general sense, whether a neurotransmitter is excitatory or inhibitory at a particular synapse depends on what receptors are present in the postsynaptic membrane.

The Hypothalamic Lesion Syndrome

Because of its inaccessibility at the base of the brain, the hypothalamus came under experimental investigation relatively late.

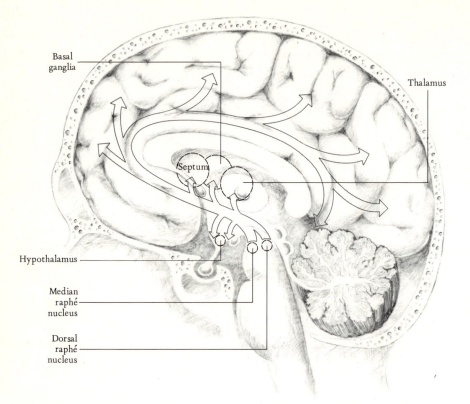

Basal
ganglia

Thalamus

Septum

Hypothalamus

Median
raphé
nucleus

Dorsal
raphé
nucleus

Figure 11.7 | *The Major Pathways of Serotonin Distribution in the Human Brain.* Serotonin is produced in the raphé nuclei of the brainstem, the most prominent being the median and dorsal raphé nuclei in the midbrain region. Their neurons project widely within the neocortex, but also heavily into the septum, basal ganglia, anterior thalamus, and hypothalamus, as well as into the cerebellum and midbrain tectum.

Back in 1940, however, a classic study demonstrated that damage to the medial region of the hypothalamus produces striking *hyperphagia* (overeating) in rats, which overate day after day until they became grotesquely obese. It was as if they no longer knew when they had eaten their fill (Hetherington and Ranson, 1940). Eleven years later came another dramatic finding: if more lateral regions of the hypothalamus are destroyed, both rats and cats cease eating entirely and die of starvation if left to themselves, despite the availability of familiar and nutritious food (Anand and Brobeck, 1951). These findings suggested what appeared to be a satisfying theory of hunger regulation, based on *interoceptors* in the lateral

Hyperphagia (hie-per-FAY-jee-a). **Abnormally large food intake, associated with obesity.**

Interoceptors. **Sensory receptors within the body and registering its internal conditions rather than environmental events.**

hypothalamus signalling a low nutritional state in the blood, and a "satiety center" in the medial hypothalamus that would inhibit these lateral hypothalamic "motivational" neurons when the nutritional state returned to normal, thereby blocking the hunger drive.

The picture became more complicated and intriguing, however, with the surprising discovery by Teitelbaum (1955) that rats with lesions in the ventromedial hypothalamus were, though hyperphagic and obese, actually more finicky about their food than normal rats, refusing to eat food laced with a bit of quinine, or otherwise made less palatable, that normal rats ate without hesitation. This combination of overeating and finickiness about the taste and freshness of the food came to be known as the *ventromedial hypothalamic syndrome.* The interpretation seemed unavoidable that without their satiety center the rats became controlled not by hunger, properly speaking, but by the incentive value of the food and its sensory qualities as a stimulus — in other words, by appetite. Stimulus-bound, they behaved as if controlled externally rather than internally.

Two years later came the next finding, anticipated by what had gone before. Anderson and Wyrwicka demonstrated in 1957 that electrical stimulation of the lateral hypothalamus in rats that have already eaten and drunk their fill causes them to eat and drink voraciously. Five years later it was finally shown that electrical stimulation of the *ventromedial nucleus* of the hypothalamus inhibits the hunger drive (Hoebel and Teitelbaum, 1962; Margules and Olds, 1962). The story unfolded further when it was found that an injection of *glucose* (blood sugar, the brain's food) into the ventromedial nucleus decreases the activity of neurons in the lateral hypothalamic hunger centers. This finding is what might have been expected if the hunger drive were indeed controlled by glucostatic receptors in the ventromedial nucleus, monitoring the concentration of sugar in the blood (Oomura *et al.*, 1964).

There were complications, however. Ungerstedt (1971) pointed out that the lateral hypothalamic hunger centers are the site of transmission fibers of the medial forebrain bundle system from the substantia nigra, and that hunger-destroying lesions in most such experiments had interrupted axons carrying dopamine to the basal ganglia. After destroying their neurons of origin in the substantia nigra by injecting the neurotoxin *6-hydroxydopamine,* Ungerstedt found the symptoms of the lateral hypothalamic syndrome (*aphagia* and *adipsia,* or cessation of eating and drinking), suggesting that these dopaminergic paths are essential to normal hunger and thirst mechanisms. Countering this argument, Stricker and Zigmond

Ventromedial hypothalamic syndrome. **The effects of ablating the ventromedial nucleus of the hypothalamus, including hyperphagia and obesity, finickiness, and apparent absence of true hunger drive.**

Aphagia. **Lack of normal hunger.**

Adipsia. **Lack of normal thirst.**

(1976) found that both aphagia and adipsia can be produced by lateral hypothalamic lesions that do not disrupt the nigrostriatal pathway fibers.

Other studies suggested that norepinephrine, rather than (or in addition to) dopamine, might be involved (Grossman, 1960, 1962; Ahlskog and Hoebel, 1973; Gold, 1973). As a result of these studies, doubt was cast on the concept that there are specific neurons in the lateral hypothalamus whose activation turns on the hunger drive, and the very notion of "drive centers" began to come into disrepute. It had been shown that rats with lateral hypothalamic lesions kept alive through force-feeding for a few weeks would survive, and that some of their hunger drive would return. In 1978, however, by injecting into the lateral hypothalamus the chemical *kainic* acid, which destroys cell bodies without interfering with fibers in passage through the region, Grossman and his colleagues definitively demonstrated the existence of motivational neurons in that region, since both aphagia and adipsia were produced (Grossman *et al.*, 1978).

One of the most fascinating outgrowths of these studies of the ventromedial hypothalamic syndrome is the finding by Schachter (1971) that a subgroup of obese people appear to suffer from symptoms closely paralleling those of the rat with a lesion in the ventromedial nucleus of the hypothalamus. Despite overeating, they are much more finicky about their food than most people. Their problem seems to be that they are responding to appetite (the anticipated reward value of the food, the pleasure of eating) rather than true hunger, the felt need for food. Schachter found that these individuals may experience no hunger as such at all, and could easily go for days without eating if no appetizing food were presented to them. If the food is delicious, however, they are helpless to resist the temptation to eat, and to continue eating.

But that is not all. Schachter discovered that hyperphagic rats are more intelligent in some ways than normal rats, and that the same thing is true of these obesity-prone people. Presented a stimulus card illustrating many unrelated items and allowed to study it for a brief period, they recall significantly more items than their normal peers; a comparable superior perceptual scanning ability was found in the hyperphagic rat. Could it be that normal individuals, whose effectively functioning satiety center inhibits appetite after consumption of a normal amount of food, pay a price in a global inhibition that affects even their perceptual scanning skill? Further investigations of this marvelous finding will be followed with great interest.

Further Studies of the Hunger Mechanism

Oomura and his group, who demonstrated the existence in the ventromedial nucleus of glucostatic receptors that monitor the level of blood sugar, also made the surprising finding that *free fatty acids,* which increase in quantity in the blood when we are hungry, directly activate the lateral hypothalamic "hunger neurons" and simultaneously disinhibit them by reducing the level of activity of the ventromedial "satiety" neurons. It is of particular significance here that the level of free fatty acids begins to fall shortly after the onset of eating, more dramatically than changes in the concentration of glucose or insulin. The free fatty acids are thus a very plausible candidate for the mechanism whereby the hunger drive is turned off, as well as for the trigger mechanism by which it is turned on (Oomura *et al.,* 1969). Further support comes from the finding that injection of free fatty acids can induce food intake in the rat. Furthermore, obese people, as well as diabetics (who tend to be hyperphagic), are known to have high levels of free fatty acids in their blood (Nisbett, 1972). Also noteworthy is the discovery that lesions in the ventromedial nucleus of the hypothalamus increase the level of free fatty acids in the blood.

Conjecture about the hunger-control mechanisms has been stimulated by the observation that the body weight of even the ventromedial-lesioned rats tends to level off. Instead of swelling up like balloons and bursting, they appear to reach a plateau and thereafter stay at that weight by eating just enough to maintain it. They now appear controlled in their eating, much like normal rats, but as if they are "defending" a higher *set point* for body weight (using the analogy of a thermostat). It has also been observed that when rats with lesions in the lateral hypothalamic "hunger center" are kept alive through forced feeding until they recover, they too appear to defend a new set point, but a lower one than before.

A plausible resolution of the confusion caused by varying results in such studies is the "dual lipostat model" of body-weight regulation proposed by Sclafani and Kluge (1974): one *lipostat* controlling the hunger drive would come into play when weight loss below the set point threatens; the other, controlling appetite (responsivity to highly palatable foods), would come into play when weight approaches an upper limit. A later version of the model (Sclafani, 1976) depicted body weight as determined by two factors, set point and the palatability of the available food. If the food is unpalatable, body weight falls until, at some point below the normal set point, the excitatory output of the set-point mechanism (hunger instigator)

Free fatty acids. **Breakdown products of triglycerides, which build up in the blood when we have not eaten recently and quickly diminish shortly after eating has begun.**

Set point. **The level toward which the body tends to gravitate as normal, as with reference to fat storage.**

Lipostat. **A hypothetical mechanism in the hypothalamus setting the level of fat deposition the animal will seek to maintain.**

balances the effect of the low palatability of the food, and the animal begins to eat more. If the food is particularly tasty, the animal will eat until the inhibitory effect of the set-point mechanism increases to the point of balancing the appetitive drive.

According to this theoretical model, the set point is not raised in the hyperphagic rat; instead, the inhibitory output of the upper lipostat is reduced. Such reduction in the upper-level inhibitory output of the lipostat makes the sensory qualities of the food a more important factor in how much the animal (or, perhaps, the obesity-prone person) will eat. Lateral hypothalamic damage is thought to lower the set point, thus comparably lowering the upper and lower limits of weight resulting from differences in palatability. Other theoretical models that do not make use of the concept of set point have also been proposed (Peck, 1976). In view of the evidence that overweight is a health hazard, shortening life span in the statistical average, this is important theoretical work that may soon have practical application in the solution of "America's number-one health problem" (see Chapter 21).

Studies of the Mechanism of Thirst

Twenty-five years ago it was shown that injection of common table salt into the anterior preoptic region (anterior to the hypothalamus) produced what appeared to be compulsory drinking in the goat (Andersson, 1953). A second important finding about thirst mechanisms was Grossman's demonstration that, whereas norepinephrine injected into the hypothalamus results in eating, *carbachol* (a chemical that mimics the effect of acetylcholine but is less easily deactivated) injected into the same region produces drinking (Grossman, 1960). Two years later it was found that carbachol elicits drinking when injected into many areas of the forebrain (Fischer and Coury, 1962). Thus began scientific study of the phenomenon of thirst.

Our body is by weight about two-thirds water. About two-thirds of that water is in the *cellular phase* (contained within the body's cells); the remaining one-third is in the *extracellular phase* (in the blood stream, in the lymphatic system, and in the intercellular space surrounding the living cells). This "internal sea"— that part of the primordial ocean that multicellular animals carry about in their bodies today — has approximately the same salinity as present-day sea water, equivalent to about a teaspoonful of salt in a glass of water. It is of vital importance that body water be main-

Carbachol (KAR-ba-kol). A substance mimicking the effect of acetylcholine but not as quickly deactivated.

tained. While we can store food in our fat cells, and thus go without eating for an extended period, we cannot store water. Body water is continually being lost, and unless it is replaced by drinking we will die — hence the enormous power of the thirst drive when our body begins to become desiccated. But how does the threat of dangerous water loss communicate itself to the brain, to initiate and maintain drinking or the search for water? This is equivalent to asking how the experience of thirst is generated.

Though we tend to associate thirst with dryness in the mouth, thirsty dogs quickly stop drinking when water is introduced directly into the stomach, leaving the mouth dry. In fact, removal of the salivary glands in the dog, which makes the mouth permanently dry, does not lead to increased drinking. Thus we can reason that, though dry mouth plays a role in signalling that the body is becoming desiccated (the salivary glands stop secreting when the water content of the blood decreases), this peripheral mechanism is not a sufficient explanation of either the initiation or cessation of drinking.

In the anterior hypothalamic region of the brain lies an apparently more central mechanism whereby neurons respond to an excessive concentration of salt in the blood or in the extracellular space around them. When the water content of the body is reduced, its salt concentration increases, and water flows out through body-cell membranes to dilute the extracellular fluids — the mechanism artificially triggered by Andersson in his goats. There appear to be interoceptors along the medial forebrain bundle system specifically responsible for generating water-seeking behavior (and presumably thirst) whenever the salinity of the blood increases above normal (Fitzsimons, 1971). These *thirst receptors* are on a par with the hunger receptors. The *osmosensitive zone* of the hypothalamus, whose receptors respond to cellular dehydration, appear in the rat and the rabbit to lie in the lateral preoptic region.

Another mechanism involves blood-pressure receptors in the walls of the veins, which respond to a fall in blood pressure. In the rat, tying off the *vena cava* in the abdomen, which lowers blood pressure, produces prolonged drinking. It is not yet known how this signal is transmitted to the brain.

A third and better-known mechanism involves production of the enzyme *renin* by the kidneys when blood volume or pressure falls. (The venous blood pressure receptors described above may achieve their effect by firing to the kidneys to signal renin release.) The renin causes a plasma protein called *angiotensinogen* to be converted into the peptide *angiotensin I,* which is in turn altered by circulating

Osmosensitive zone. **A region in the lateral preoptic area where neurons are sensitive to cellular dehydration, triggering the thirst mechanism.**

Vena cava. **A large vein emptying into the right atrium of the heart, the main venous trunk draining blood from the lower portion of the body.**

Renin. **The enzyme released by the kidneys that transforms the blood plasma protein angiotensinogen into angiotensin.**

enzymes to produce *angiotensin II*, the most powerful *dipsogenic* (thirst-producing) chemical known, far more potent than salt or carbachol. This chemical's point of action has been found in the rat not in the lateral preoptic region, but in a nearby region called the *subfornical organ* (below the fornix), a structure difficult to locate in the human brain. Angiotensin II reaches this point through blood circulation. Though it will not cross the *blood brain barrier,* the barrier is absent at this point, permitting it to reach the neurons in the brain. Three major arterial systems have overlapping fields of irrigation in this region, making it a likely spot for a peripherally circulating chemical to affect the neurons of the brain.

Thirst operates in conjunction with a second mechanism of body-water control that has nothing directly to do with thirst or with motivational mechanisms. When blood pressure falls, the posterior pituitary gland, under control of the anterior hypothalamus, releases *antidiuretic hormone (ADH),* which stimulates the kidneys to reduce their excretion of water into the urine.

Studies of the Sexual Urge

The bulk of the research on the sexual urge and sexual behavior has been done with laboratory animals (rat, rabbit, cat, and monkey). It may be that many of the findings of these studies do not bear directly on our human sexual motivation and behavior, since our species has escaped completely from the mammalian domination by the cyclic estrus phenomenon. Removal of a woman's ovaries does not appear to affect her sexual interest or responsiveness, while the same operation on a laboratory animal quite abolishes sexual behavior. A review of the findings of animal studies will nevertheless provide a preliminary basis for the discussion of human sexuality.

As is true of hunger and thirst mechanisms, it now appears that regions within the hypothalamic area, along the medial forebrain bundle, are critically important in the organization of biologically adaptive behaviors involving reproduction. It is clear from observation of animals that quite complete specification of behavior patterns can be genetically coded. In the case of sexual behavior, there is a complex behavior pattern characteristic of the female and another quite different one for the male; these patterns are species-specific. Critically important in such patterns is the preferential direction of sexual congress — that is, whether the beast seeks out a member of the opposite sex, or one of its own, as mate.

There were few cues to the nature of the neural mechanisms un-

Subfornical organ. **An organ found in some mammals, such as the rodents, immediately below the fornix in the preoptic area.**

Blood brain barrier. **A barrier formed by glial cells which prevents all but a few blood substances from entering the brain tissues.**

Antidiuretic hormone (an-ti-dye-you-RETT-ik). **ADH, also called vasopressin; a hormone secreted by the neurohypophysis, causing the kidneys to reduce water loss in the urine and causing the smooth muscles of the arteries to contract.**

derlying sexual behavior until twenty years ago, when Phoenix and his associates (1959) injected the male hormone *testosterone* into pregnant guinea pigs and found that their female offspring in adulthood exhibited the male sexual pattern (mounting other females, rather than presenting in *lordosis* position to males). Later studies by the same laboratory showed that there was a critical period for testosterone injection if the effect was to occur. This finding strongly suggested that, long after the fetus had developed normal female genitalia, the presence of testosterone in the fetal circulation (passed through the placenta) could turn the female animal's motivational mechanisms in the inappropriate male direction. This stimulus set in motion a great many laboratory studies seeking to clarify the situation.

Testosterone. **The male sex hormone secreted by the testes.**

In 1967, Whalen and Edwards reported an important study in which female rat pups were injected with testosterone shortly after birth (rats are born prematurely, if viewed in terms of human gestation) (Whalen and Edwards, 1967). In adulthood these females did not display sexually receptive behavior when injected with estrogen, as do normal female rats. Apparently they were *defeminized* by the inappropriate presence of testosterone during the sensitive period shortly after birth. It was later found (Clemens, 1973) that, while postnatal injection of testosterone into female pups does not yield masculine mounting behavior in later life, prenatal exposure to testosterone does appear to. When there are male pups in the litter, the females next to them in the uterus tend to be affected in a masculine direction, in that when adult they tend to display mounting behavior when injected with testosterone. This does not happen in all-female litters.

Defeminized. **Rendered incapable of feminine sexual response by the presence of testosterone in the blood of the fetus at a critical period of hypothalamic maturation.**

Debold and Whalen (1975) found that injection of as little as 100 micrograms (millionths of a gram) of testosterone into female hamster pups at birth blocked female sexual behavior in adulthood, and that masculine behavior is elicited by testosterone injection in those animals. In fact, injection of even a hundredth of this amount at birth can effectively defeminize the animal, though it is not sufficient to produce the masculine behavior pattern in the adult.

Beach *et al.* (1973) found that female dogs given testosterone prenatally and shortly after birth are both masculinized and defeminized; that is, when grown to adulthood they exhibit masculine behavior when injected with testosterone and do not display female behavior even when given estrogen. This finding suggests that this exposure to androgens at the sensitive period effectively changes the organization of their brain from the normal female pattern of response to the normal male pattern.

The opposite result — turning a genetically male animal into a behaviorally female one — has been demonstrated in rats, and a similar sensitive period is involved. If male rats are castrated before day ten after birth, their sexual orientation and behavior in adulthood is in the female pattern, inviting sexual congress by presenting to males in the female lordosis position. Administration of the missing testosterone at any later time fails to alter this established orientation. Meanwhile, their female littermates who are administered testosterone at day five exhibit the full male sexual orientation as adults. They mount other females and will have nothing to do with males who approach (Grady *et al.*, 1965). In each case it is the presence or absence of testosterone at the critical stage in the maturation of the brain that controls whether the neural structures mediating sexual preference and behavior will differentiate according to the male or female pattern, irrespective of the genetic sex or genital structures of the animal. In the normal course of events male pups, whose testes are producing small amounts of testosterone at that time, are blocked from developing in the female pattern and become organized as behavioral males, while their female littermates continue in the female direction.

Just where in the brain these critical events take place has been a subject of intensive investigation. The brain sites governing the female sexual pattern appear to be located in regions where injected estrogens concentrate — the preoptic area, the ventral hypothalamus, the limbic midbrain area, and the amygdala. These are also the sites where electrical stimulation is most apt to elicit sexual behavior in the female rat.

In the male rat the posterior hypothalamus appears to be the principal site for stimulation of the sexual urge. Herberg (1960) found that stimulation of that region produces ejaculation, and Caggiula and Hoebel (1966) found that it also elicits lever-pressing to obtain access to a receptive female, followed by copulation. Similar results were observed in the monkey by MacLean and Ploog (1962). Thus there appear to be different sites for the establishment of male and female sexual potential and behavior.

Curiously, it seems to be the *androgens* — the male sexual hormones — that determine the degree of the sexual urge in both males and females. When adult males, human or animal, are castrated, the normal supply of testosterone in their blood is eliminated; their sexual drive thus diminishes, dramatically in lower animals, much more gradually in a man. Men whose testes are removed for medical reasons are restored to normal levels of sexual urge by administration of testosterone (replacement therapy). Nor

Androgen. **Male sex hormone.**

when women undergo a comparable operation, removal of the ovaries, does such loss of sexual urge occur. Women are supplied with androgens via the adrenal gland, the most important of such hormones being *androstenedione*. Women whose adrenal glands are removed as a treatment for cancer, cutting off their supply of androgens, characteristically report a dramatic reduction in sexual urge.

Androstenedione (an-droh-steen-DYE-own). **An androgen secreted by the adrenal cortex, the principal androgen present in the female.**

It is noteworthy that, though testosterone replacement therapy of the castrated male animal restores normal sexual activity, additional testosterone does not increase such activity beyond the precastration level, nor does testosterone administered to the human male operate as an aphrodisiac. It appears that hormonal influences operate only to maintain a normal level, not to increase it.

The Question of Human Homosexuality

As we have just seen, animal studies clearly suggest that the direction of sexual preference is established at a very early point in development, corresponding in human beings to a period before birth. There is a specific critical period in which the hypothalamus becomes permanently organized on a male or female pattern which becomes manifest only later.

The issue of human homosexuality has been much clouded by studies that are essentially off the point. One of the most outstanding researchers in the field of sexuality, John Money (1965), for example, has proposed seven criteria by which to distinguish maleness and femaleness, ranging from genetic constitution to *gender identity*, our sense of ourselves as male or female. Not one of these criteria, however, is sexual preference in a mate, same sex or opposite, which is the central concern in homosexuality. Clinical observations confirm animal studies in suggesting that one's natural sexual orientation, when so defined, is unlikely to change over the course of life. This is true even though under abnormal circumstances one's sexual *behavior* might belie such natural orientation, as in men in a prison setting.

Gender identity. **One's sense of oneself as masculine or feminine.**

Obligate heterosexuals. **Individuals whose preference for a mate of the opposite sex is exclusive.**

Those of us who have been exclusively heterosexual in our feelings from our earliest days are properly designated *obligate heterosexuals*. We find it difficult to understand any other sexual orientation. Those of us whose sexual preference has been equally strongly homosexual from the start are properly termed *obligate homosexuals,* and find heterosexuality equally incomprehensible. There is clinical evidence of all degrees along the continuum between these two ex-

Obligate homosexuals. **Individuals whose preference for a mate of the same sex as themselves is exclusive.**

tremes, including a great many individuals of bisexual orientation, able to respond to either a male or a female as a sexual partner. The term *facultative homosexual* is used for those whose sexual preference is for a mate of the same sex, but who are not exclusively so disposed. Sexual preference is apparently quite independent of self-identity as male or female, and of masculinity or femininity in everyday behavior and physical appearance.

The American Psychiatric Association has at long last removed homosexuality from its latest Diagnostic and Statistical Manual describing the mental disorders to which human beings are vulnerable, in acknowledgment that it is not a "mental illness" as previously understood. That organization has not, however, clarified its position as to whether homosexuality is something learned or an inborn tendency discovered, as it were, as sexual maturation proceeds. When the latter view becomes accepted, perhaps much of the phobic quality of our cultural reaction to homosexuality may disappear.

Facultative homosexuals. **Homosexuals who prefer a sexual partner of the same sex but who may also function sexually with a partner of the opposite sex.**

Studies of Fear and Aggression

As we saw in Chapter 10, stimulation of the cat's brain in the region of the basolateral nuclei of the amygdala could produce either attack or escape behavior, depending on the location of the electrode. The fear response was the standard alarm reaction characteristic of mammals, a frantic effort to escape from the cage and flee. The rage response was the "halloween cat" syndrome: arched back, fur standing on end, snarling and hissing and spitting, teeth bared and claws unsheathed, and attack characteristically executed with rapid strikes of the front paw, rather than the teeth. The climactic expression of this defensive rage in the cat is a sudden shrill scream and alternating swift strikes with both front paws while standing on hind legs.

Such rage behavior is readily distinguished from predatory attack, in which the animal silently approaches the prey in crouching position and administers a series of quick bites to its neck. The two serve quite different adaptive purposes. In most instances mammalian rage behavior is pure bluff, very seldom resulting in serious harm. This violently threatening behavior warns the other animal that it has invaded someone else's territory, or frightens an intruder away from the young, or a scavenger away from a fresh kill. The bull elephant makes use of a dramatic rage display to drive an interloper away from the herd, charging ferociously for a short distance and then stopping to see whether its display has achieved the desired purpose. The baboon about to be seized by a leopard suddenly wheels and attacks its attacker in a desperate last-minute effort to escape, and just as quickly resumes its flight the moment the leopard, awed by its flashing canines, draws back. Another classic demonstration of rage behavior without intent to kill is the sparring for supremacy of males of the deer family. The purpose is not to kill but to best the enemy in an antler wrestle. To kill, deer use not their antlers but their feet, stamping the enemy into the ground or kicking with the hind legs. But a good deal of rage behavior among mammals is the flip side of fear, and ceases the moment the threat is removed.

Jules Masserman (1941) long ago demonstrated that the behavioral expression of rage can be dissociated from any true emotional arousal. Masserman found that stimulation of a region in the hypothalamus of the cat could produce *sham rage*, with all of the outward appearances of anger, but in conjunction with many indications that the animal was not emotionally upset — purring, lapping milk, allowing itself to be petted, and the like. More recent studies (Flynn, 1967; Flynn *et al.*, 1970) have shown that all the behavioral manifestations of rage can be elicited without any autonomic-nervous-system arousal by stimulating the central gray area of the midbrain; stimulation of the hypothalamus, meanwhile, can produce real rage, accompanied by autonomic arousal.

The same investigators showed that this *affective attack* could be replaced by the other kind of aggression, predatory *biting attack* with clear intent to kill, by slightly changing the location of the stimulating electrode in the hypothalamus. At times the two responses were intermingled, which is what we ourselves sometimes experience. Students of human aggression have failed to distinguish consistently between these two forms of aggression so clearly demonstrated in the mammals.

When sham rage is replaced by true rage (affective attack), a dramatic change occurs in the physiology of the organism. The heart begins to beat faster, the blood pressure increases, blood circulation is altered to shunt blood out of the internal organs and into the striped skeletal musculature, and blood chemistry is altered by the release into it of hormones and additional sugar, among other changes, all of which serve to prepare the body for maximal emergency energy expenditure. Once these autonomic nervous system responses have begun, it is impossible to suddenly resume a calm, pleasure-seeking mode of behavior. Most mammalian rage appears to be of the sham variety, demonstrated by the fact that the

Sham rage. Behavioral manifestation of rage without the physiological response normally accompanying it.

Affective attack. Attack with a distinctively emotional basis, such as fear or rage.

Biting attack. Attack designed to kill rather than to frighten away, characteristic of carnivores in food gathering.

moment the emergency is over the animal resumes feeding, grooming, tending to its young, or whatever, as if nothing had happened.

True rage is seen in the cornered rat or baboon, in the rogue elephant, in the irritable rage of the grizzly wounded by a trophy hunter, and in the bull bred for this very proclivity in the bullring. In true rage, fear is totally inhibited, and courage is complete. A field mouse will attack a mountain lion without the slightest sign of trepidation. It is a craziness, but it must frequently have survival value or the capacity for it would not be "wired in" to our mammalian hypothalamus. Very interestingly, the true rage response has been found to be reduced or blocked in the animal by administration of the common human tranquilizer drug chlordiazepoxide (Librium) (Horovitz *et al.,* 1966; Panksepp, 1971).

Stanley Schachter, the researcher who discovered the hyperphagic-rat syndrome in a subgroup of obese humans, has shown that once the physiological response of rage or fear is initiated in the human organism, cognitive factors play a decisive role in determining the emotional feelings we experience and hence the direction we take in behavioral expression (Schachter and Singer, 1962). By injecting *epinephrine* (adrenalin) into the bloodstream of naive volunteer subjects, it was demonstrated that the resulting bodily feelings could be alternatively interpreted as anger, euphoria, fear, or amusement, depending on suggestions provided by the social context (a stooge who simulated these emotions in the presence of the real subject). Control subjects, who were told to expect the physiological symptoms (pounding heart, shaking hands, warm and flushed face), failed to experience the emotions reported by the uninformed subjects, whose feelings corresponded exactly to those manifested by the stooge. The lesson that must be drawn from this unequivocal demonstration — which today's ethical standards for human research would prohibit — is that the physiological phenomenon is the same whether we are angry or frightened or bursting with enthusiasm, and that it is our perception of the feeling that controls both our behavioral expression and the subjective experience attending such physiological upset.

The Hypothalamus and Emotional Response

Both the hormonal systems of the body and the autonomic nervous system are under the control of the medial forebrain bundle — and, more specifically, the hypothalamus — and both are involved in the physiological response of emotion. The *neuroendocrine* system is di-

Neuroendocrine system. **The system governed by the pituitary gland under the stimulation of the hypothalamus.**

rectly governed by secretions of the *pituitary gland* (also known as the *hypophysis*), which lies directly below the hypothalamus in a small hollow in the base of the bony skull called the *sella turcica*. The pituitary is the master gland of the system. Its major (anterior) portion manufactures hormones, several of which pass into the bloodstream and reach other glands, causing them to secrete their own hormones. Thus the *thyrotropic hormone* stimulates the *thyroid gland* to release thyroxine and other hormones into the bloodstream, encouraging the body cells to burn more fuels for energy. The *adrenocorticotrophic hormone* (ACTH), when so released by the pituitary, causes the *adrenal gland*'s cortex to secrete *cortisol* and other *steroid hormones,* preparing the body for stress. The *gonadotrophic hormones* similarly activate the *gonads,* the ovaries and testes, to secrete their hormones, estrogen and testosterone. The posterior portion of the pituitary releases other hormones that are actually manufactured in the anterior hypothalamic region.

When we become emotionally aroused, as in fear or true rage, the physiological response is triggered by the hypothalamus in two ways. First, neurons in the hypothalamus secrete hormones into the anterior pituitary, causing it to release two of its hormones in particular, ACTH and thyrotropic hormone, which activate the adrenal cortex and the thyroid gland. Second, it sends signals to various brainstem nuclei governing the activity of the autonomic nervous system, whose sympathetic branch prepares the body in innumerable subtle ways for emergency response. Among other things it causes the *adrenal medulla* to secrete adrenalin into the blood, producing many of the symptoms of emotional arousal.

Figure 11.8 depicts the autonomic nervous system. Note that there are two separate branches that counterbalance each other; most of the organs in the body receive fibers from both systems. The *sympathetic branch,* when activated, excites us; the *parasympathetic branch* works in an opposing fashion to restore the body to a tranquil state. Note that the first-order fibers of both divisions have their cell bodies of origin within the brainstem. In the case of the sympathetic system, these fibers project principally to second-order neurons situated in the sympathetic ganglia strung out along the vertebral column in its thoracolumbar region. The parasympathetic fibers project to the cranial and sacral regions of this ganglionic system, as well as to some outlying plexuses within the viscera. The first-order fibers of both systems are *cholinergic* (making use of acetylcholine). Second-order fibers project to various organs and glands of the viscera; those of the parasympathetic branch are also cholinergic, while those of the sympathetic branch are *adrenergic* (making use of norepinephrine).

Thyrotropic hormone. A pituitary hormone activating the thyroid gland.

Adrenocorticotrophic hormone. ACTH, one of the trophic hormones released by the anterior pituitary gland; it activates the adrenal cortex to release its own hormones.

Gonadotrophic hormones. Pituitary trophic hormones whose target is the ovaries or testes.

Adrenal medulla. The endocrine gland forming the core of the adrenal gland.

Sympathetic branch. One of the two branches of the autonomic nervous system; its influence is to prepare the body for emergency energy expenditure.

Parasympathetic branch. That branch of the autonomic nervous system concerned with preparing the body for peaceful pursuits, such as eating and exploration.

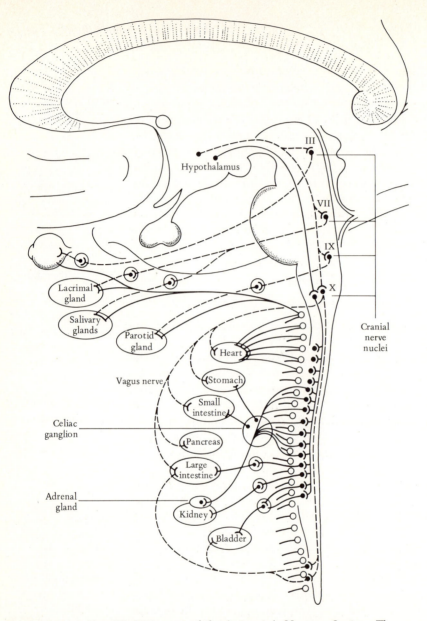

Figure 11.8 / *A Simplified Diagram of the Autonomic Nervous System.* The sympathetic branch of the autonomic system is represented here by solid lines, the parasympathetic by dashed lines. Both systems are activated by fibers descending from the hypothalamus into the brainstem, where the first-order neurons are stationed. These project into the spinal cord in the case of the sympathetic branch, and also into the nuclei of the third, seventh, ninth, and tenth cranial nerves in the case of the parasympathetic. Most of the visceral organs are innervated by second-order fibers of both branches, counterbalancing each other, sympathetic innervation tending to prepare the body for emergency, parasympathetic for relaxation and calm.

By means of the hormonal secretions of the neuorendocrine system (see Table 11.1) and the autonomic nervous system, the hypothalamus can very quickly bring about a state of physiological
emotion, which we then interpret and express, as well as experience, depending on the situation and our past experience of similar
situations. It then takes some time for the body to be restored to
normal so we can return to peaceful pursuits and relaxation. The
parasympathetic system returns to a balance with the sympathetic
branch, while the bloodstream is gradually cleared of its excess
thyroxin and blood sugar, the adrenalin released from the adrenal
medulla, the insulin released from the pancreas, and the like.

Studies of the Pleasure Mechanisms of the Brain

Strange as it may seem, it was unknown until the 1950s that the
brain has a neural mechanism of reward, or pleasure. Motivation
tended to be dealt with in psychological theory in terms of "drive
reduction" rather than pleasure-seeking; curiously, the latter concept was considered unscientific, and banned from theoretical dis-
course. Then came the discovery of a region in the brain which,
when stimulated, appeared to produce pleasure (Olds and Milner,
1954). A rat with a stimulating electrode in its brain was observed
to return continually to the portion of its cage where it was triggering its own stimulation. On one of the marvelous scientific hunches
that overturn conventional notions, the experimenters arranged for
the rat to activate the stimulation by pressing a lever. The result
was an eye-opener. The animal not only repeatedly stimulated its
own brain in this manner, but was willing to work at learning
tasks, and to cross an electrified grid that other rats would not cross
for any reward, just for the opportunity to obtain that intracranial
electrical stimulation.

The site where the electrode produced self-stimulation was in the
septal region of the medial forebrain bundle. Subsequent studies
showed, however, that there are points all along that bundle, from
the septum to the midbrain, as well as in the amygdala, where similar results can be obtained. The most intensely rewarding spots appear to be in the lateral hypothalamus all along the medial forebrain
bundle. This is the region already found to contain neurons related
to the hunger drive; for the animal world as a whole, if not for the
human, food is the most prominently sought-after source of pleasure, preoccupying many species continually throughout their waking hours.

Table 11.1 / *Some Important Hormones*

Hormone	Source	Action
Psychogenic hormones involved in activation of the sympathetic nervous system		
1. Epinephrine (adrenalin) and norepinephrine	Synthesized and released by the adrenal medulla under sympathetic nervous system stimulation	Increases heart rate, elevates blood pressure, stimulates breakdown of sugars and glycogen for production of muscular energy, enhances effect of sympathetic stimulation
2. Thyroxine and triiodothyronine	Released by the thyroid gland under stimulus of thyrotropic hormone (TSH) from the anterior pituitary gland	Causes faster burning of sugars by the cells, i.e., an increase in metabolic rate
3. Glucagon	Secreted by the *alpha* cells of the islets of the pancreas	Brings about the breakdown of liver glycogen, thus increasing the concentration of blood sugar
Reproductive hormones		
4. Estrogens	The ovaries	Necessary to the development of female secondary sexual characteristics at puberty and to maintenance of the condition of the uterus and birth canal
5. Progesterone	The corpus luteum	Necessary to the maintenance of the condition of the uterus
6. Testosterone	The testes	Organizes fetal hypothalamus in the male pattern; maintains male reproductive motivation
7. Follicle-stimulating hormone (FSH)	The adenohypophysis	Stimulates follicle maturation in the ovaries (in preparation for release of an egg) and sperm production in the testes
8. Luteinizing hormone (LH)	The adenohypophysis	Stimulates ovulation, corpus luteum formation, and secretion of testosterone in the male

Table 11.1 (*cont.*)

9. Prolactin	The adenohypophysis	Stimulates milk production after birth
10. Oxytocin	The neurohypophysis	Stimulates contraction of smooth muscle, such as in the birth process
11. Relaxin	The ovary	Allows for separation of pelvic bones in the birth process
Trophic hormones		
12. Adrenocorticotropin (ACTH)	The adenohypophysis	Stimulates the adrenal cortex to release its special hormones (glucocorticoids), some of which prepare for stressful experience (faster blood clotting); for this reason it tends to be secreted concurrently with activation of the adrenal medulla by the sympathetic nervous system. (Recent evidence suggests that ACTH may also be involved in brain activities, such as learning.)
13. Thyrotropin (thyroid-stimulating hormone, TSH)	The adenohypophysis	Causes the thyroid gland to secrete thyroxine and triiodothyronine; involved in the breakdown of fats for energy use
Other		
14. Somatotropin (growth hormone, GH)	The adenohypophysis	Stimulates growth of tissues, such as in the long bones; mobilizes stored fats for use in energy production; involved in the metabolism of proteins; inhibited by somatostatin released from the hypothalamus
15. Vasopressin (antidiuretic hormone, ADH)	The neurohypophysis	Stimulates the kidneys to preserve water, under conditions of dehydration

Later studies have shown that some of these "hot spots" of pleasure in the brain are also related to the drives of thirst and sex. Self-stimulation in these areas ceases when the animal is sated with food or drink or has just copulated, depending on the location of the electrode; it also ceases if the animal is rendered hypophagic or is castrated. It is increased when the animal is very hungry or thirsty. However, there are other rewarding points that appear to be unrelated to any known specific biological drive. There are also some curious aspects to electrical self-stimulation behavior. At some stimulation sites the animal will continue lever-pressing at an astonishingly high rate until it drops from exhaustion, all along spurning food or water or sex. At others the animal will stop when it has "had enough," thereafter appearing to find stimulation aversive, and perhaps painful. Also, self-stimulation at some points requires priming: the animal has to be stimulated by the experimenter a few times before the self-stimulation drive begins, reminiscent of an alcoholic responding to a first drink.

Studies of self-stimulation in human beings have yielded less clear findings. Often there is merely a generalized feeling of well-being, a "high" with no particular drive component. However, the feeling frequently has sexual overtones — particularly when the electrode is in the lateral septal region, curiously enough. Since such electrodes can be implanted in the human brain only for sound medical reasons, and not for purposes of psychological research, progress toward understanding may be expected to be slow.

Summary

The medial forebrain bundle system includes not just the hypothalamus but a more extensive system, running from the septal region at the anterior end to the midbrain limbic center at the rear, composed of many axonal fibers interspersed with clumps of neural cell bodies. Many of the fiber bundles are ascending tracts through which the brain is supplied with such neurotransmitters as norepinephrine, dopamine, and serotonin. Others carry signals in the reverse direction from more anterior regions into the midbrain and lower brainstem. The entire system receives massive input from such limbic structures as the septal nuclei, the amygdala, and the hippocampal circuit, and appears to operate as a final common path through which emotional and motivational functions are expressed. Though tiny, this system in the very center of the brain is thus exceedingly important.

Damage to this region tends to be expressed in behavioral alterations suggesting dysfunction of such basic motivational systems as hunger, thirst, and sexuality, or in such basic physiological emotions as rage and fear. However, it is improper to speak of "centers" for such functions in the hypothalamus, since the neurons involved are undoubtedly only part of a larger neural circuitry. What has been firmly established is that destruction of certain regions in the lateral hypothalamus, through which the fibers of the medial forebrain bundle run, may effectively block all interest in food, water, or a mate, as the case may be, even for a starved or thirsty or sexually active animal. If the same regions are stimulated with an electric current, rather than destroyed, the hunger, thirst, or sex drive may be dramatically increased, causing the animal to eat or drink voraciously immediately after completing a meal, or to display sexual behavior shortly after copulation. There is also a region in the medial hypothalamus, in or near the ventromedial nucleus, whose stimulation blocks the hunger drive through laterally running inhibitory fibers. When this region is ablated, normal satiety mechanisms are interfered with, causing the animal to overeat to the point of grotesque obesity.

The hypothalamus also controls three other distinct functions: temperature regulation; the neuroendocrine system, via its influence on the immediately subjacent pituitary gland; and the autonomic nervous system, via fibers descending to the brainstem. Thus the hypothalamus may be viewed as the point where activities in the thalamocortical and limbic systems are brought to bear on reflex bodily mechanisms involving internal regulation and preparation of the body for either emergency response or peaceful pursuits.

The medial forebrain bundle system is also importantly involved in mechanisms of reward and punishment. Many regions along its course appear to produce intense pleasure for the animal when electrically stimulated, as indicated by its avid pursuit of self-stimulation if it is made possible. Other points appear to be aversive, the animal carefully avoiding stimulating itself in that region a second time. Some rewarding self-stimulation points are closely associated with the drives of hunger, thirst, and sex; others appear to be more generalized in their effect. The discovery of this phenomenon discredited earlier drive-reduction theories of animal motivation and demonstrated that the organization of the brain for learning is *hedonic,* as common-sense intuition suggests.

Chapter 12 / *Ancient Brainstem Mechanisms*

The brainstem consists of many distinct nuclei concerned with such vegetative functions as digestion, circulation of the blood, breathing, and the vestibular functions of balance. The reticular system running through its core serves as an integrative center for many bodily functions, and monitors both incoming bodily sensations as well as descending motor signals. In addition to the descending influences on sensory and motor functions, including first-order neurons of the autonomic nervous system, the brainstem contains the principal sources of the brain's norepinephrine and serotonin — the locus coeruleus and the raphé nuclei respectively. Another ascending function of the reticular formation is control of waking and sleeping, as well as alerting the organism to environmental danger and opportunity. Ascending fibers pass to the thalamic reticular nuclei and then ascend, with or without synapse, to the cortex, which they prepare for reception and processing of incoming signals from the environment. Sleep is induced in conjunction with thalamic and hypothalamic nuclei. Normally several periods of slow-wave sleep are interspersed with periods of rapid-eye-movement sleep (REM sleep) during which organized dreams occur.

To live we must breathe, ingest food and drink, digest and eliminate, maintain circulation for delivery of nutrients and oxygen to the living cells of body and brain, control the volume and pressure and chemical composition of the blood, maintain body temperature within narrow tolerances, and perform many other functions. Meanwhile our attention is directed toward entirely different things going on in our external environment. The mechanisms governing these functions are built-in reflexes, automatic and mostly unconscious in their operation, largely controlled by nuclei situated in the brainstem. Except for automatic temperature control, all are inherited from our ancient ancestors in the premammalian world.

But the brainstem contains something else, an integrative center   270 called the *reticular formation,* which appears to keep track of both sensory signals passing up through the brainstem and motor signals passing down to the spinal motor centers. As we shall see, the reticular formation appears designed to perform three fundamental operations: (1) to prepare the forebrain for the reception of the incoming signals, (2) to modulate the effect of the down-streaming motor influences in the light of information received from cerebellum and vestibular system, and (3) to control sleep and waking. With regard to the first operation, the reticular system appears to be particularly involved in alerting us to danger and to novel and interesting stimuli (the arousal response) and, in conjunction with its forebrain extension in the thalamus, to exercise more detailed and refined control of attention shift and holding.

In this chapter we will deal first with the basic survival mechanisms that have been incorporated in reflex responses, and then discuss what is currently known of the reticular formation and its role in brain functioning.

Reflex Responses

If we cross our legs and tap the tendon just below the kneecap of the free-swinging leg, a knee jerk (the *patellar reflex*) results. The tap stretches the large extensor muscles above the knee; the sensors within them, and in the tendons, in turn signal to the alpha motor neurons in the lower spinal cord to activate the muscles in opposition. Their contraction produces the kick. This obviously unthinking and mechanical operation is an example of the very simplest reflex mechanism in the body — the *spinal reflex.* (Its specific function is to prevent the knees from buckling when we stand.)

Most reflex circuits involve many more nerve cells in the chain, as well as other complications. If we hold our breath long enough, for example, we will feel an increasingly insistent urge to breathe again, that eventually proves irresistible however hard we try. The neural circuitry here is fairly complicated. Sensors in the respiratory centers in the brainstem, as well as in the arteries carrying blood to the brain (the carotid sinuses), are responsive to increasing concentrations of carbon dioxide in the blood. They send signals to the diaphragm and the muscles of the ribcage to contract which increases the rate and depth of breathing in a simple reflex-arc fashion. There is also obviously an associated neural circuit running to higher centers in the brain, providing the conscious sensation of suffocation and arousing an emotional response to the emergency of the

Patellar reflex (pa-TELL-er). **The knee-jerk reflex, an example of the simplest form of spinal reflex.**

Spinal reflex. **A simple reflex consisting essentially of only two neurons, one transmitting signals into the spinal motor centers from the periphery, the other transmitting signals to the muscles to cause contraction.**

situation. Moreover, though breathing is normally reflexly controlled, such side loops to higher brain centers afford the possibility of voluntary control, overriding (within limits) the reflex servomechanisms.

Similar reflexes are the withdrawal response (if a hand is held over a flame, for instance) and the scratching of an itch. Some are far subtler and more difficult to trace through the nervous system, though equally automatic and reflexive. When we see somebody smile, yawn, or laugh, we may experience an ungovernable tendency to do likewise. If we pass someone who represents a very adequate releaser stimulus to the sexual urge in us, we may be aroused automatically, even if we manage to inhibit all overt expression of the impulse. Many of our highly overlearned response patterns, such as riding a bicycle or driving a car, are not innate, but nevertheless take on much of the unthinking character of the automatic reflexes, and are handled largely by brainstem (and cerebellar) mechanisms.

Reflexes of a similar sort govern breathing, swallowing, defecation and urination, and totally unconscious mechanisms such as those that keep our stomach churning, our intestines moving food along (peristalsis), our heart beating, and our blood pressure within normal range. These fundamental survival functions are organized by our brainstem nuclei, especially in the medulla, and were there from birth, pre-wired. It has recently been discovered that these unconscious processes can to some degree be manipulated through down-running signals from the cortex by such tricks as hypnosis and biofeedback training, but getting our bodies under conscious control is by no means an unmixed blessing. As Lewis Thomas suggests in *The Lives of a Cell* (Thomas, 1974), we are probably much better off leaving these arrangements alone, because they are probably smarter than we are, and know what they are doing.

The Reticular Formation

Running through the deep interior of the brainstem, forming its core, lies a longitudinally organized neural tissue whose axons and dendrites are woven into an intricate network, or *reticulum;* hence the name of the system as a whole. Many of the nuclei governing the reflex mechanisms we have been discussing lie embedded within the reticular formation, along with the vestibular nuclei. Running through the dorsal portion is the central canal, which continues down the center of the spinal cord, and this is surrounded with a tissue of nerve cells called the *central gray*. As we saw in our discussion of the sensory systems, the somatosensory fibers following the spinothalamic tract (the ancient "protopathic" signals) send collaterals into the reticulum as they ascend in the medial lemniscus; auditory fibers do the same ascending in the lateral lemniscus. Visual signals appear to reach the reticular formation of the brainstem from the cortex or the superior colliculus, rather than from the optic tract. These relations are illustrated in Figure 12.1.

The functions of the reticular formation appear to be characteristically integrative, rather than relay; it brings influences from many sources to bear on all the forebrain structures: neocortex, thalamus, basal ganglia, and the limbic and medial forebrain bundle structures. In this respect, the reticular system — perhaps the oldest structure in the brain, phylogenetically — may be considered the regulator of the functions of the entire brain. In view of the complexity of this role, it is not to be expected that the reticular system is yet well understood. Nor is it easily described. It will be discussed here from the standpoint of several of its outstanding functions, namely its control of sleep and waking; its participation in the mechanism of attention focus, shift, and habituation; and its role in the production and dissemination of the three important brain neurotransmitters, norepinephrine, dopamine, and serotonin.

The Reticular Activating System

Thirty years ago Moruzzi and Magoun (1949) found that electrical stimulation of the brainstem reticular system could immediately change the brain wave pattern recorded from the cortex from that of somnolence (spindles, slow delta waves, regular 8–12 Hz alpha waves) to an arousal pattern of high-frequency, low-amplitude beta waves (Figure 12.2). It had previously been demonstrated that transection of the brainstem of the cat at the level of the midbrain (the *cerveau isolé* preparation) produced a permanent state resembling normal sleep, including typical electroencephalographic patterns. Such sleep was first thought to be a consequence of the interruption of major sensory input from the body, since it was known that these lemniscal pathway fibers ascend through the midbrain lateral to the reticular system. However, the Moruzzi and Magoun study demonstrated that the reticular system itself might be responsible for the effect, and the concept of the *ascending reticular activating system* was born.

Support for this concept arose from the finding that lesions in the

Central gray. A region of the brainstem immediately surrounding the cerebral aqueduct and continuing into the spinal cord surrounding the central canal, composed of gray matter.

Cerveau isolé (ser-VO ee-so-LAY). A preparation in which the brainstem has been severed at the level of the midbrain colliculi.

Ascending reticular activating system. ARAS; a massive, nonspecific fiber system ascending from the brainstem reticular formation through the thalamus and into the cortex, serving to arouse the organism, alert attention, and maintain the waking state.

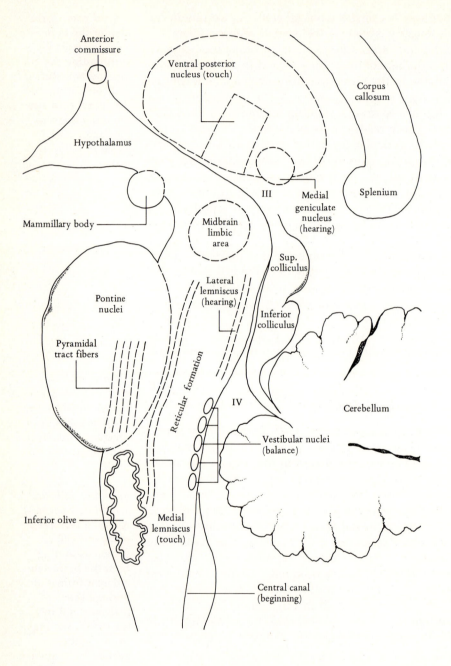

Anterior
commissure

Ventral posterior
nucleus (touch)

Corpus
callosum

Hypothalamus

Splenium

Mammillary body

III

Medial
geniculate
nucleus
(hearing)

Midbrain
limbic
area

Sup.
colliculus

Pontine
nuclei

Lateral
lemniscus
(hearing)

Inferior
colliculus

Pyramidal
tract fibers

Reticular formation

Cerebellum

IV

Vestibular nuclei
(balance)

Inferior olive

Medial
lemniscus
(touch)

Central canal
(beginning)

midbrain reticular formation that do not destroy the ascending sensory pathways produce the same continuous sleep state in the cat as does complete brainstem transection, while severing the ascending sensory pathways alone does not (Lindsley, Bowden, and Magoun, 1949). Further support came from the observation that stimulation of the region by means of implanted electrodes in the freely moving animal produces behavioral alerting, attentional focus, and search for the stimulus, simulating normal arousal by an external stimulus.

Two years later it was found that evoked potentials could be recorded from the brainstem reticular formation in the monkey by stimulating any sensory system at all (French, Van Amerongen, and Magoun, 1952). Moreover, these stimuli interacted in their effect; for example, a visual flash stimulus masks an immediately subsequent tactile stimulus effect, reducing the amplitude of the evoked potential the latter elicits. Thus the system appears to be responsive in the same region to a variety of types of stimulus (nonspecific response). Finally, it was demonstrated that a reticular arousal response pattern could be produced by stimulation of the cortex, suggesting a reciprocal relationship between cortex and brainstem activating system (Bremer and Terzuolo, 1954; French, Hernandez-Peon, and Livingston, 1955).

The essential concept of the reticular activating system, studied extensively by the Russians under the leadership of Sokolov, was that, if not for continual ascending stimulation, the brain would lapse into somnolence, and hypersynchrony in the firing of its cortical neurons would give rise to the characteristic "sleep spindles" and large-amplitude slow waves of the sleeping brain. It was this notion that sleep represented a state of relative quiescence of the neocortex that was to be fundamentally altered by later research.

Figure 12.1 / *Major Sensory Signal Pathways in Relation to the Brainstem Reticular Formation.* In this sagittal section of the brainstem we can see the relationship between many of the structures we have been discussing. Ascending pathways for somatosensory input (medial lemniscus) and auditory input (lateral lemniscus) project collaterals into the reticular formation in the brainstem core on their way to the thalamus. The descending pathway, the pyramidal tract, lies more ventrally (pyramidal tract fibers), also projecting collateral fibers into the reticulum. Within the formation itself are found many embedded nuclei, such as those concerned with postural reflexes (vestibular nuclei) and the nuclei governing the respiratory, circulatory, and digestive functions (not shown). Thus, the reticular formation is ideally situated to fulfill a basic integrative function for the brain, lying athwart both incoming and outgoing information channels.

Excited (beta waves)

Sleep spindles

Relaxed

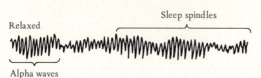

Alpha waves

Drowsy

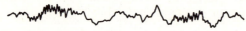

Asleep

Deep sleep (delta waves)

Figure 12.2 / *Types of Brainwave Patterns Recorded Under Different Conditions of Somnolence and Arousal.* Deep sleep is characterized by two dramatically different kinds of brainwave patterns, which distinguish slow-wave sleep (SWS) from rapid-eye-movement sleep (REMS). The waves produced during REM sleep are indistinguishable from those found in arousal and waking attention. SWS waves are called delta waves, while REMS waves are called beta waves. Between these two extremes are many other distinguishable characteristic patterns. In going to sleep we progress through a highly regular 8–12 Hz alpha wave stage, followed by a transitional stage characterized by a mixture of alpha waves, sleep spindles, and delta waves, followed by a pattern dominated by the slow, hypersynchronous delta waves. After about an hour and a half, this pattern is suddenly interrupted by the commencement of the REM stage, with its high-frequency, low-amplitude beta waves, followed later by a gradual return to delta waves, still later by a sudden return to beta waves, and so forth through the night.

The Discovery of REM Sleep

Following Berger's (1929) discovery of a consistent change in brain waves on passing into the sleep state, careful studies of EEG patterns during sleep were conducted by many investigators (Loomis, Harvey, and Hobart, 1937; Davis *et al.*, 1939; Blake, Gerard, and Kleitman, 1939). While great variations in the electroencephalogram

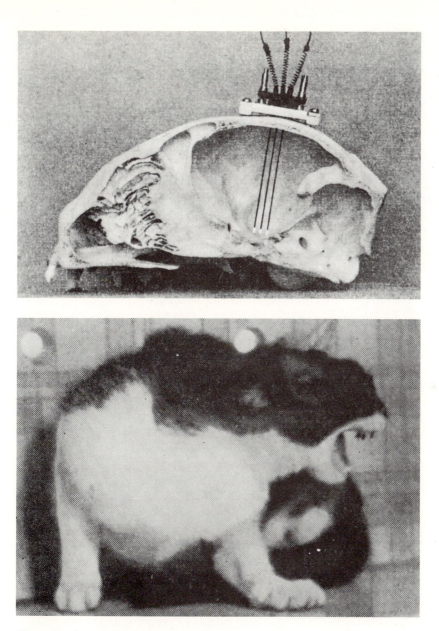

Electrodes have been implanted in the brain of this cat to induce a state of arousal. The upper photograph shows, using a halved skull, how the electrodes are mounted.

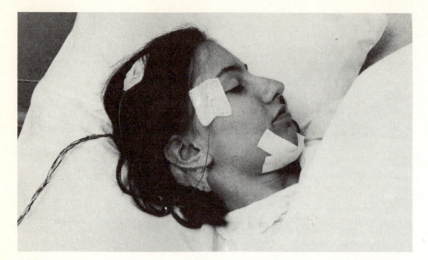

The electrodes attached to this subject's scalp, temples, and chin allow sleep researchers to monitor brain waves, rapid eye movements, and muscle tonus. These electrodes are applied externally to the subject's skin and held in place with adhesive tape.

during sleep were found, it is curious in retrospect that the dramatic phenomenon now recognized as *rapid-eye-movement (REM) sleep* was not reported until more than a decade later.

In 1953 Aserinsky and Kleitman published an epoch-marking article in *Science* entitled "Regularly Occurring Periods of Eye Motility, and Concomitant Phenomena, During Sleep" (Aserinsky and Kleitman, 1953). Based on the systematic monitoring of the electroencephalogram in sleeping normal human adults, they reported the regular occurrence of curious jerking eye movements during sleep episodes characterized by high-frequency, low-amplitude brain waves, similar to those of the waking state. Subjects awakened during these bouts of saccadic eye movements were apt to report that they had been dreaming. This very exciting discovery led to intense investigation of the phenomenon in many laboratories. The observation of a characteristic cyclic shift during the course of the night between REM episodes and episodes dominated by spindles and slow waves (*slow-wave sleep,* or *SWS*) led to the concept of a "basic rest–activity cycle" (Dement and Wolpert, 1958; Kleitman, 1963) involving a swing from light sleep to deep sleep and return.

In 1959 Dement found that REM periods also occur in the cat, which led to similar investigations of sleep in the laboratory animal. This finding led in turn to the next remarkable discovery, by

Rapid-eye-movement (REM) sleep. **A sleep stage characterized by jerking movements of the eyes, flickering of the eyelids, loss of muscle tonus, and the occurrence of dreams.**

Slow-wave sleep (SWS). **A stage of sleep characterized by the large, hypersynchronous, slow brain wave oscillations (delta waves).**

Jouvet and Michel (1959), that when REM episodes are well underway, muscle movement, and indeed muscle tonus, is *totally suppressed* throughout the body. The reason this finding proved so
surprising was that muscular activity had been assumed to increase
when the brain waves pass (abruptly) from the *hypersynchronous*
SWS to the fast activity of REM sleep, until that time considered to
represent a "lighter stage." The strange disappearance of muscular
tone, especially in the region of the neck, observed in the cat during
REM episodes was later demonstrated in the human (Berger, 1961),
and it began to become clear that there are two quite distinct states
of sleep that all human beings experience every night of their lives.

Hypersynchronous.
**Said of brain waves
during slow-wave
sleep (delta waves),
representing the
synchronous firing
of great numbers of
neurons.**

How could something so easily observed — indeed, so dramatic
— as the periodic jerking of the eyeballs under closed or half-
open lids, occurring for extended periods every night in all people,
have escaped notice until the middle of the twentieth century? It
would appear that notice of significant phenomena is not automatic, but requires priming of a sort. One is reminded of the fact
that Aristotle, the great observer of nature, taught that women have
fewer teeth than men, even though he had two wives with whom
he might have checked (and corrected) his facts. Occasions for noticing this eyeball flickering and complete loss of muscle tonus have
obviously been myriad over time, yet the phenomenon remained
unknown to science until well after the careful study of brain waves
in sleep had begun! It was a discovery that, like many others, came
in by the back door!

This discovery inaugurated a new era of understanding. Jouvet's
careful analysis of a great deal of research based on continuous
monitoring of sleep phenomena in the human with the electroencephalogram, the electromyogram (which records changes in muscle
tension), and the electrooculogram (which records eye movements)
appeared in 1962, and the modern discipline of sleep research was
firmly established.

Undoubtedly the technological development of convenient means
of continuously recording events occurring in the sleeper over the
course of a night led to the belated recognition of sleep as an active
phenomenon, rather than a mere resting state of the brain, and to
the realization that we all dream a good deal every night, contrary
to popular belief. Presumably we do not usually remember our
dreams because the brain's mechanism for consolidating our stream
of consciousness into lasting impressions is normally nonfunctional
until some moments after we awake.

One result of these developments was research focusing on the
reticular formation, where a mechanism involved in sleep and wak-

ing was already known to exist. In 1960 it became known that, in addition to the midbrain "sleep center" where a lesion could produce a permanent sleeping state in the cat, there is a lower brainstem region where low-frequency stimulation produces in the electroencephalogram the large slow waves and spindle bursts characteristic of the sleeping animal. Then it was found that stimulation in the preoptic area of the hypothalamus elicits SWS — both its brain wave pattern and its behavioral manifestation — in the cat. In that forebrain locus, either high- or low-frequency stimulation produces this result (Sterman and Clemente, 1962). It was even found that the cat could be put to sleep by a tone or other signal conditionally associated with the stimulation (Clemente, Sterman, and Wyrwicka, 1963). Here, then, was the discovery of a forebrain "sleep center" whose activation produces normal sleep.

What would happen if this anterior hypothalamic region were bilaterally destroyed? The result, as expected, was the opposite effect — suppression of sleep patterns in the brain waves and continuous wakefulness with hyperactivity (Sterman *et al.*, 1964; McGinty and Sterman, 1968).

Much subsequent research has focused on elucidating the mechanisms of the cyclic shift during sleep between the slow (delta) wave sleep mode and the REM state in which the brain waves are predominantly fast (beta) waves (Figure 12.2). Two questions were posed: What mechanism produces the hypersynchrony of SWS, and what is the mechanism underlying the phenomena observed in REM sleep?

Research on the Mechanism of REM Sleep

Once it was recognized that two distinct states of sleep alternate during the night, a number of questions crowded in on one another. What is the function of these states? Do we have a specific need for a certain amount of each state every night? Why does SWS characteristically precede REM sleep? Why does SWS set in gradually, both at the beginning of sleep and after each of the several REM episodes, whereas REM episodes begin abruptly as full-blown cortical desynchronization — a brain wave indistinguishable at a glance from the waking brain wave? (Refer to Figure 12.2.)

Before the discovery of REM sleep as a distinctive stage of sleep, efforts to study the function of the sleep mechanism confounded the two stages, particularly with regard to the effects of sleep deprivation. Then efforts were made to study REM sleep alone. In the belief that the "function" of REM sleep must have something to do with the dreaming that occurs during its tenure, many laboratories undertook to examine the effect of waking the subject each time the electroencephalogram indicated the start of a new REM episode, inquiring whether a dream was in progress, and allowing the subject to return to (SWS) sleep again. Thus the subject was deprived of normal amounts of REM sleep for the night.

These studies regularly observed, after several nights of this treatment, a *postdeprivation rebound* characterized by greatly increased portions of the night spent in REM sleep. This finding justified the presumption that some specific need is normally satisfied by the REM sleep process, and perhaps another need by SWS. However, cats were deprived of REM sleep in this manner for two months with no serious consequences other than the rebound tendency afterward, casting doubt on the hypothesis that the REM stage fulfills some necessary function for the brain. A more promising hypothesis has to do with the function of REM in the process of memory formation or learning.

Many experiments have now shown that learning performance is impaired in animals that have been deprived of REM sleep (Pearlman and Becker, 1973, 1974; Pearlman and Greenberg, 1973; Greenberg and Pearlman, 1974). Other experiments have shown that REM-sleep deprivation prolongs the period during which new memories are susceptible to disruption by electroshock or other brain insult (Fishbein, McGaugh, and Swarz, 1971). Still other evidence supporting the notion that REM sleep is somehow important in the learning or memory-consolidation process comes from the finding that an increase in REM sleep characteristically occurs after intensive learning (Paul and Dittrichova, 1975). Young animals and human beings experience more REM sleep than older ones, and it has been suggested that this correlates with the amount of new experience with which the organism must deal.

REM sleep can be suppressed by many drugs. The class of antidepressants known as monamine oxidase inhibitors (Chapter 15), if given in sufficient quantity over several days, can completely abolish REM sleep, as do many of the tricyclic antidepressants. The common sleeping pills (barbiturates) likewise suppress REM sleep, thus producing an abnormal night's sleep. In most such instances a REM sleep rebound occurs on withdrawal from the medication, often overshooting the mark. That is, REM sleep may be greatly increased in proportion to SWS time for several weeks after a single administration of a sleeping pill.

The *locus coeruleus* nuclei of the brainstem are, as we have said, the primary source of norepinephrine in the brain. Bilateral destruction of these nuclei completely abolishes REM sleep, demonstrating that norepinephrine is in some way importantly involved in this sleep stage. Administration of a drug (alpha methyl paratyrosine) that inhibits synthesis of norepinephrine also effectively abolishes REM sleep. A REM sleep rebound follows withdrawal from the drug, and this is associated with an increased turnover (brain use) of norepinephrine (Pujol *et al.,* 1968). As long ago as 1964 (George, Haslett, and Jenden) it was found that an injection of acetylcholine into the locus coeruleus of the cat will trigger REM sleep, suggesting that this neurotransmitter may regularly operate as the triggering mechanism in that nucleus.

In his careful study of all the experimental findings to date, Jouvet (1969) concluded that the mechanism of production of REM sleep is complex, serotonin from the *raphé nuclei* priming the locus coeruleus to release norepinephrine (Figure 12.3). (Recall that REM sleep normally follows an extended period of SWS, which, as we shall see, is associated with serotonin.)

Raphé nuclei. A group of nuclei along the midline of the brainstem that produce serotonin.

More recently, Hobson, McCarley, and Wyzinski (1975) have proposed a more specific theory involving a group of very large neurons in the brainstem (the *FTG cells*), an increase in whose firing correlates with the onset and continuation of REM sleep. Their evidence suggests that the function of norepinephrine, as an inhibitory neurotransmitter, is to hold the FTG cells in check during SWS, and that the locus coeruleus cells actually diminish their firing at the onset of REM sleep. A recent finding supporting the hypothesis that the FTG cells are the final pathway in the production of REM sleep phenomena — perhaps including dreams — involves their production of the excitatory neurotransmitter acetylcholine. Injection of a chemical (physostigmine) that acts to enhance the effect of acetylcholine at cholinergic synapses induces REM sleep (Sitaram *et al.,* 1976). Low-dose injections at the onset of REM sleep wake the subject, as do higher doses during SWS. In keeping with this finding is the observation that more acetylcholine is released from the cortex during REM sleep than during SWS (Jasper and Tessier, 1971).

FTG cells. Giant cells in the midbrain tegmentum whose increased firing rate is correlated with onset and continuation of REM sleep.

Research on the Mechanism of Slow-Wave Sleep

Once it became recognized that sleep is not mere lack of brain activity but a specific kind of brain functioning, theories about the

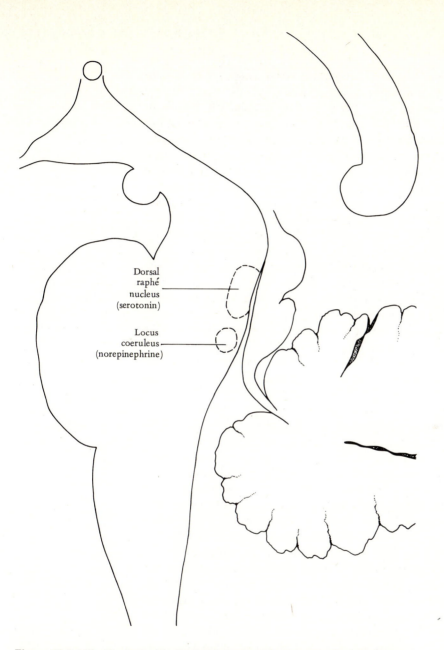

Dorsal raphé nucleus (serotonin)

Locus coeruleus (norepinephrine)

Figure 12.3 / *The Brainstem in Sagittal Section, Showing the Relationship of Major Sources of Norepinephrine and Serotonin.* Both norepinephrine and serotonin appear to be crucially important in the regulation of sleep and waking, as well as the shift from slow-wave sleep (serotoninergic) to REM sleep (noradrenergic). There is evidence that the dorsal raphé nucleus and locus coeruleus, closely juxtaposed in the brainstem, exert a mutual influence upon each other in their control of these functions.

mechanism underlying this active process were sought. Why do we go to sleep at night, and what is sleepiness?

One possible active factor in the production of sleep had already been discovered by Pavlov in his work with dogs at the turn of the century. Having trained an animal to salivate in response to a *conditioned stimulus,* such as a bell, associated with the arrival of tasty food, Pavlov observed a curious phenomenon, which he termed *internal inhibition,* if he continued to present the stimulus in the absence of further food. Not only did salivation decrease, and eventually cease altogether, during this *extinction* process, but the animal also characteristically became drowsy. As the once-significant signal continued to be presented, the eyes closed, the head began to droop, and the animal at length fell into sound sleep — put to sleep by the incessant presentation of the stimulus!

One is reminded of hypnotists putting people to sleep by focusing their attention on the monotonous (meaningless) movement of a bauble, and of the repetition of a mantra (a meaningless word) in the practice of transcendental meditation. Apparently not mere boredom but an active process that serves to turn off the attention mechanism is thus brought into play; pushed to its limits, it can produce sleep.

Some forty years after Pavlov's discovery of this apparent neural mechanism for turning on sleep, it was discovered that a cat could be put to sleep by low-frequency stimulation of its thalamus (Hess, 1944). Much later it was discovered that this procedure is associated with large-amplitude slow waves and spindle bursts in the electroencephalogram (Hess, Koella, and Akert, 1953; Akimoto *et al.,* 1956). There thus appeared to be a hypnogenic center in the thalamus whose stimulation could put an animal or human to sleep through its induction of these hypersynchronous neural activities in the cortex. Shortly thereafter, experimental studies revealed the existence of two distinct portions of the thalamus acting as part of the reticular system. One portion relays brainstem reticular activating influences to the cortex (this involves the *reticular nucleus,* forming the exterior surface of the thalamus); the other relays such influences to the intralaminar and midline nuclei (refer to Figure 2.11), which are responsible for SWS (Tissot and Monnier, 1959; Monnier, Kalbere, and Krupp, 1960).

The following year, a hypothalamic mechanism seeimgly capable of driving this thalamocortical mechanism that generates SWS was found. When food is injected into the stomach of a hungry dog, or glucose injected into its bloodstream, the characteristic arousal pattern of the brain wave immediately becomes indistinguishable from

Conditioned stimulus. A stimulus which through training has become effective in producing a given response.

Extinction. The process through which a given stimulus, through repetition in the absence of reinforcement, loses its power to evoke a conditioned response.

SWS, and the animal often quickly falls asleep. Could it be that the inhibitory satiety mechanism of the ventromedial hypothalamus, which turns off hunger, and which when ablated leaves the rat smarter than before (Chapter 11), is able to suppress wakefulness itself? It might be speculated that a similar mechanism in the hypothalamus is responsible for postorgasmic sleepiness in the human. A languid torpor with cortical spindle bursts has been found in the female rabbit following coitus (Sawyer and Kawakami, 1959).

We have already seen that a hypothalamic hypnogenic center was found by Sterman and Clemente (1962). Electrical stimulation of the preoptic region of the hypothalamus of the cat elicits both the typical brain wave pattern and behavioral manifestations of SWS. The same effect could be elicited by a tone or other signal conditionally associated with the electrical stimulation (Clemente, Sterman, and Wyrwicka, 1963). Bilateral destruction of the same region of the hypothalamus produces suppression of sleep patterns in the brain waves and wakefulness with hyperactivity (Sterman *et al.*, 1964; McGinty and Sterman, 1968). Perhaps the ventromedial nucleus satiety center operates in conjunction with the preoptic hypnogenic center.

It is of interest that the earliest experimental research on sleep mechanisms focused on the hypothalamus (von Economo, 1929), where a "waking mechanism" was discovered. Lesions in the posterior hypothalamus were reported to produce a lethargic syndrome, a finding later confirmed by Ranson (1939) in the monkey. Von Economo also located a "sleep center" in the preoptic region, presumably the same one studied by Sterman and Clemente at a later date. Nauta (1946) confirmed the existence of these two hypothalamic centers — the anterior one capable of putting the animal to sleep, the posterior one capable of arousing it to wakefulness — and contributed the new discovery that simultaneous ablation of both areas results in an approximately normal sleep–wakefulness balance.

Early interest in the thalamus began with the discovery of the cortical *recruiting response* (Dempsey and Morison, 1942, 1943). Stimulating the thalamus of the cat with 8–12 Hz electrical pulses, they reported, results in brain waves curiously similar to the spontaneous spindling of SWS (see Figure 12.2). More significantly, Dempsey and Morison found that destruction of those regions of the thalamus from which recruiting responses are elicited in the cortex (now recognized as the intralaminar and midline nuclei) abolishes spontaneous sleep spindles, implicating these nuclei in the production of the brain waves associated with SWS.

Recruiting response. **A brain wave similar to sleep spindles produced by 8–12 Hz stimulation of the thalamus.**

The most recent route of inquiry into the mechanism of SWS induction, however, is biochemical. Jouvet (1967) demonstrated that reduction of both serotonin and norepinephrine in the cat brain by injection of the drug reserpine suppresses sleep of both types for 12 to 24 hours. If, on the other hand, 5-hydroxytryptophan, the chemical precursor of serotonin, is injected (thus indirectly increasing the quantity of serotonin and restoring normal brain levels), SWS is immediately resumed. If dopamine, the precursor of norepinephrine, is injected, this is turned into norepinephrine in the brain, restoring normal levels of that neurotransmitter, and REM sleep is produced. This classic experiment provided strong support for the thesis that the mechanism of SWS is dependent on serotonin, and that of REM sleep on norepinephrine.

It now began to make sense that the preoptic region in the anterior hypothalamus is a hypnogenic center, as Clemente had found, since this region is connected via the medial forebrain bundle to the brainstem raphé, where the neurons generating serotonin are found. Another region of the brain that appears to exercise control over the raphé serotonergic neurons is the orbital cortex, whose stimulation has been found to produce slow-wave sleep (Clemente, 1968). The strongest evidence, however, was the finding that destruction of the raphé nuclei abolishes sleep altogether. A significant correlation was also found between the amount of the raphé system destroyed and the degree of insomnia. No drugs have been found that have the effect of increasing the amount of SWS above normal (Hartmann, 1974).

These and similar studies represent a strong basis for the belief that the processes of sleep are very intimately involved with the two neurotransmitters serotonin and norepinephrine, which appear to act in a reciprocal fashion and in connection with the excitatory neurotransmitter acetylcholine. Research in this field of the neurosciences is becoming very active in view of the prospect that exploration of the sleep mechanism will elucidate some very fundamental biochemical mechanisms of the brain, including the memory process itself.

Summary

The brainstem, extending from the midbrain above through the pons and the medulla below, contains numerous small nuclei involved in such reflex functions as balance (the vestibular nuclei), swallowing, digestion, breathing, heart rate, and blood pressure. Such basic survival mechanisms are normally self-operating, requiring no conscious attention on the part of the individual. Some, such as swallowing and breathing, can be overridden by voluntary motivation; it has recently been discovered (as Eastern religious traditions have long known) that others normally beyond voluntary control can be brought under control through training if the subject has some means of monitoring them.

The brainstem also contains in its core the reticular formation, which appears to serve as an integration center for many of the functions of the organism. The reticular formation receives collaterals from ascending sensory fibers, as well as descending motor fibers. Composed in large part of small short-axon neurons, it also contains embedded nuclei composed of larger neurons whose axons may descend into the cord or ascend into various structures of the forebrain. Among the latter are the neurons of the locus coeruleus, the primary source of norepinephrine, and the raphé nuclei, the primary source of serotonin in the brain. Of the neurons projecting into the spinal cord, many constitute the first-order fibers of the autonomic nervous system; others are the vestibular neurons concerned with postural control and balance.

Two major functions of the reticular formation appear to be control of sleep and waking, in conjunction with neurons in the hypothalamus and thalamus, and alerting the organism to danger or opportunity in the environment. Ascending fibers from the reticular formation pass to the thalamic reticular nuclei, and from there (with or without synapse) to the neocortex, which they prepare for the reception and processing of stimulus information. The same pathways appear to be involved in waking us from sleep and in the production of REM sleep, characterized by a waking-type brain wave, inhibition of muscular tonus, and a characteristic jerking movement of the eyeballs under partially closed lids. Dreams during this stage tend to be organized dramatic scenarios, in contrast to the mental processes characteristic of slow-wave sleep. The biological function of REM sleep is unknown, as is its psychological function (if any) in the production of dreams.

Research indicates that the sleep mechanism involves serotonin-mediated mechanisms producing slow-wave sleep in counterbalance with norepinephrine-mediated mechanisms producing REM sleep, both in conjunction with mechanisms utilizing acetylcholine. The normal sleep period consists of several abrupt shifts from slow-wave sleep into REM sleep, followed by gradual returns to slow-wave sleep again. This pattern suggests that some process occurring during slow-wave sleep is a precursor to REM sleep, which can only persist for ninety minutes or so before the process must be renewed. When a person or animal is waked repeatedly at the onset of REM sleep, preventing its occurrence for several nights, a subsequent rebound occurs in which extended time is devoted to REM sleep. The proportion of time spent in REM sleep is greatest in infancy, diminishing gradually with age.

Part IV | *Four Perspectives on the Brain*

To this point we have discussed the brain and its functions in general terms as the machinery of the mind, the biological basis of behavior, thought, and feeling. In the four chapters to follow we will focus on the same structures, but from four special vantage points: that of the anthropologist interested in the origins of the human brain over the broad span of biological evolution (phylogenesis); that of the child development specialist concerned with the evolution of the individual personality in the formative years (ontogenesis); that of the clinician concerned with things that can go wrong with the functioning of the brain (mental health); and that of the learning theorist concerned with achieving maximum actualization of the potentialities inherent in the brain (functional intelligence).

Each chapter is a concise treatment of the neurosciences as viewed by one of four disciplines whose ways of thinking do not always interpenetrate. For this very reason they together provide a wide-spectrum view of their mutual field of study, the human brain, and its product, the human mind.

Chapter 13 / *The Evolutionary Perspective: How Our Brain Came to Be*

The evolution of the human brain may be described in terms of a number of significant emergent developments, beginning with the evolution of the neuron and then the ganglionic system of neural organization. There followed the emergence of the central nervous system in the vertebrates. The forward end of the spinal cord eventually differentiated into the major structures of the brain, as seen in fish, amphibians, reptiles, and birds. The mammalian evolutionary advance represents a significant development in the emergence of the overriding thalamocortical system, which in advanced forms of life has come to overshadow the earlier-evolved but still-existing limbic and brainstem structures. The evolution of the primate brain involved an increase in size relative to body size, and an alteration in structure involving a progressively expanding temporal lobe. The human brain is a very recent evolutionary emergent featuring a vastly increased brain volume and a structural differentiation of the two hemispheres; the latter apparently underlies our ability to use language.

If Earth solidified around 4.7 billion years ago, as appears to be the case, mammals did not make their appearance until approximately 97 percent of Earth time to date had already elapsed. We are thus all latecomers in the geological scheme of things, our own species (the most recent of the mammals to evolve) having emerged perhaps less than 2 million years ago. It is important to try to grasp the immense stretches of time that have elapsed since the beginning of life — perhaps 3.5 billion years ago, according to the geological evidence — when we speculate about how something as complex as the human brain could have come into existence (Figure 13.1).

Ours is a mammalian brain, sharing many structures and functions with the beasts of forest and field, jungle and savannah. The first mammals appear in the fossil record in rock formations dating from the Jurassic Period, some 150 million years ago, when dino-

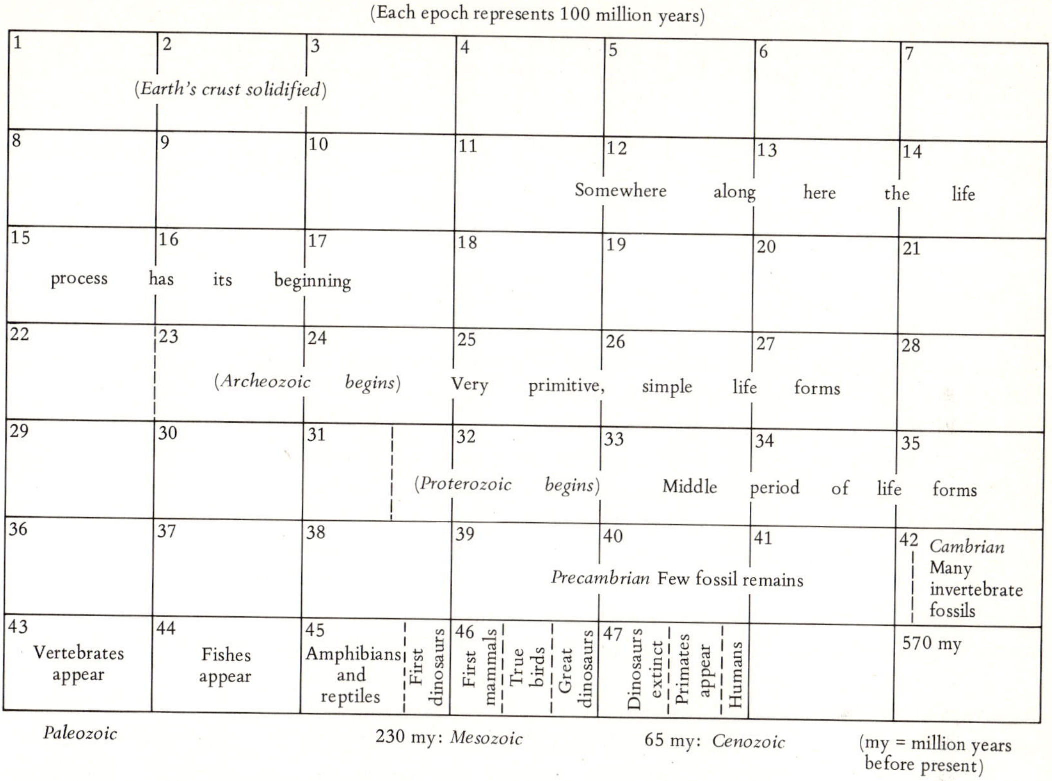

(Each epoch represents 100 million years)

1	2	3	4	5	6	7
	(Earth's crust solidified)					
8	9	10	11	12	13	14
				Somewhere along here the life		
15	16	17	18	19	20	21
process has its beginning						
22	23	24	25	26	27	28
		(Archeozoic begins) Very primitive, simple life forms				
29	30	31	32	33	34	35
			(Proterozoic begins) Middle period of life forms			
36	37	38	39	40	41	42 *Cambrian* Many invertebrate fossils
			Precambrian Few fossil remains			
43 Vertebrates appear	44 Fishes appear	45 Amphibians and reptiles / First dinosaurs	46 First mammals / True birds / Great dinosaurs	47 Dinosaurs extinct / Primates appear / Humans		570 my

Paleozoic   230 my: *Mesozoic*   65 my: *Cenozoic*   (my = million years before present)

Figure 13.1 / *Earth Calendar.* Geologists tell us the earth cooled some 4.7 billion years ago. Dividing the time since that event into epochs of 100 million years each, we have a convenient calendar showing the time-scale of the evolution of life forms. The mammals only began their amazing development during the last (47th) of our epochs, with the sudden mysterious extinction of the dinosaurs, who had held them in check for more than a hundred million years. The human species emerged from earlier humanoid creatures only a few million years ago. The human species is, so far as we know, the very latest species to evolve in the animal kingdom.

saurs dominated much of the land mass of Earth during the daylight hours, but left the nocturnal world open for exploitation. It was the mammals that perfected warm-bloodedness (internal temperature control) to capitalize on this opportunity. One can gain an excellent impression of what these early mammals might have been like by studying the common opossum (*Didelphis virginiana*). If driving through a forest preserve you should come across a freshly killed one along the roadside (a frequent occurrence), it would be highly worthwhile to take it home for dissection at your leisure. You will be the proud owner of a specimen of a Cretaceous mammal, little changed since the days when dinosaurs roamed North America.

Once you have decapitated it and removed the enormously tough, leathery hide covering the skull, you will discover that its head is almost all muscle. After cutting away the massive muscles that cross over the top of the skull to clamp the jaws shut in a viselike grip (beware of those jaws in the live animal), there is a remarkable discovery to be made: the entire forward portion of the skull above the jaws is an enormous nasal cavity; the cranium, housing a tiny brain, is about the size of a marble, far to the rear, where the skull connects to the spinal column (Figure 13.2).

Should you find it possible to saw through the cranium without destroying the brain inside, you will discover it to be composed largely of olfactory structures. The early mammals, like many of their successors, were heavily dependent on their sense of smell (*macrosmatic*). Tiny and primitive as it is, this opossum brain, or something very much like it, was the forerunner of modern mammalian brains, and was in its time the most advanced biocomputer extant. It had evolved a neocortex, but not hemispheres connected by a corpus callosum. Its two sides were dependent on the anterior commissure for communication, and most of its cortex was of the more primitive type (*paleocortex*) still found in our limbic system, where it is still interconnected by the anterior commissure. The

Macrosmatic. **Said of animals largely dependent on the olfactory sense.**

Paleocortex. **That part of the cerebral cortex that evolved prior to the neocortex and exhibits a somewhat simpler laminar structure.**

Figure 13.2 / *An Opossum Skull, Showing Tiny Cranium at Rear.* The present-day opossum is little changed since the time of its Cretaceous ancestors of a hundred million years ago. Its brain is probably very representative of the brains of the earliest mammals. Note the size of the cranium in comparison with the olfactory structure in this macrosmatic animal. The opossum depends largely on the sense of smell for locating and evaluating food and mate.

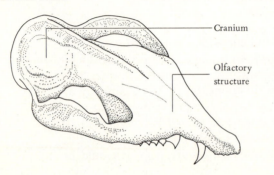

Cranium

Olfactory structure

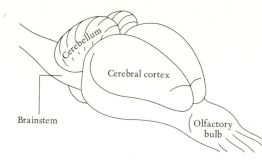

Figure 13.3 / *The Brain of the Opossum, a Living Fossil from Cretaceous Times.* The tiny bony cranium, whose walls are so thick and hard it is almost impossible to extract the contents, contains an even tinier brain. The cerebral cortex is devoted almost exclusively to the olfactory sense, receiving information already highly processed in the olfactory bulb. Behind the hemispheres is the optic tectum, which receives visual and auditory signals, and behind that are the cerebellum and brainstem. By comparison, human olfactory bulbs are minuscule, and our olfactory cortex is only a patch of tissue at the base of the brain, the olfactory tubercle.

great modern thalamocortical system had just evolved in rudimentary form. Figure 13.3 is a rough approximation of the most advanced brain that existed some 75 million years ago. But let us start at the beginning, which was very much earlier.

The Evolution of the Neuronal System

Biologists are in almost total agreement that all existing life forms belong to the same family of life, related to a single common ancestral species. For one thing, we all share the same genetic mechanism. For another, we all have the same plasma membrane surrounding our cells, characterized by maintenance of an internal negativity of electrical potential relative to surrounding fluids. Such a polarity is capable of being disturbed, with the disturbance traveling as a wave across the membrane surface. As soon as multicellular organisms reached a critical size, cells specialized for this membrane responsiveness — the first neurons — evolved as a means of integrating the functions of the whole colony of cells.

In the simplest multicellular animals, such as *Hydra*, a primitive coelenterate (hollow-intestined creature), we find a *nerve net* organization, in which the neurons pass their membrane impulses along

Nerve net. A type of primitive neural organization in which the nerve fibers transmit their excitation in either direction.

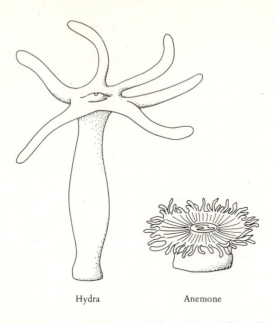

Hydra   Anemone

Figure 13.4 / *Two Nerve-Net Organisms Whose Nerve Fibers Signal in Either Direction, Communicating Only Excitation.* The coelenterates (hollow-intestined) are simple, radially symmetrical animals representing the second great evolutionary advance since the evolution of the neuron itself. They have survived perhaps a billion years.

their fibers in either direction, depending on the source of the predominant stimulation. A wave of excitation passes through the organism, and a slow muscular contraction produces movement of the animal's trunk or arms (Figure 13.4). A similar network of interconnecting nerve cells is found in the sea anemone. For hundreds of millions of years in the early seas, creatures such as these represented the most advanced forms of nervous system. The nerve-net system was eventually superseded in other animal forms by a more advanced piece of neural engineering known as the *ganglionic system.*

This new type of nervous system made use for the first time of a new kind of nerve cell, which transmitted its signal in only one direction and produced its effect at its terminal through release of a neurotransmitter or an electrical contact. One-way transmission made possible a more sophisticated organization of the nervous system involving chains of successive nerve cells, and providing for more specific and controlled effects through the muscles of the ani-

Ganglionic system. **A primitive neural system found among many invertebrates in which semi-autonomous clumps of neurons carry on special functions.**

mal. In the early sea worms, the ganglionic structure took the form of a ladder, each rung being responsible for the activities of its segment of the body. The neurons of each segment were connected with those in front and behind by fibers running lengthwise along each side of the body. The freshwater flatworm *Planaria*, a common pond dweller, is a familiar example of this stage of neural evolution (Figure 13.5). Now it was possible for something far more complex than a mere wave of excitation to produce the animal's movement. We need only compare the rhythmic contractions of the swimming jellyfish with the subtle, controlled swimming of the graceful planarian to appreciate the improvement in performance wrought by this more advanced technology of nerve-muscle integration.

Still later in biological time, the directionally firing neuron with chaining capabilities was adapted to even more sophisticated purposes in the ganglionic systems of the advanced invertebrates. Characterized by a *head ganglion* loosely controlling all the rest — a primitive brain — this system is exemplified by the insects and

Head ganglion. **A term applied to the hypothalamus in relation to the autonomic nervous system.**

Figure 13.5 / *A Primitive Ganglionic Nervous System in "Ladder" Form, as Seen in the Early Worms.* This more advanced stage of neural organization is illustrated by the pond-water swimmer, *Planaria*, a flat worm. It has a bilaterally symmetrical arrangement, with a primitive brain at the head end and cross-fibers at each segment (the ladder rungs) integrating activities of the two sides of the animal.

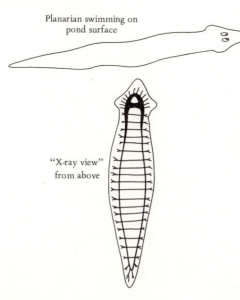

Planarian swimming on
pond surface

"X-ray view"
from above

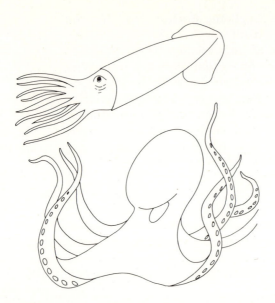

Figure 13.6 / *Squid and Octopus, Representing the Most Advanced Form of the Ganglionic Nervous Organization.* The octopus is perhaps the most intelligent and most complexly organized of the invertebrates. It exhibits a far more human-like personality than the frog or lizard, yet makes use of the same primitive ganglionic form of nervous system found in the insects and other lowly creatures.

spiders, the lobsters, shrimps, and crabs, and reaches its most magnificent development in the squid and the octopus (Figure 13.6).

The genius of the ganglionic nervous system is the relative autonomy of its functional groups of neurons, which may independently perform some quite complex information-processing operations and motor control with minimal supervision. Each ganglion tends to be loosely interconnected with the other ganglia, creating a system resembling a northern European feudal society in medieval times. Some central authority exists, but each ganglion performs its appointed role in the ensemble with a minimum of dictation. We retain this early ganglionic type of neural system in our autonomic nervous system, which controls such vegetative functions as operation of our digestive tract and circulatory system. Such a neural mechanism has inherent limitations, however, and it is doubtful that a very high level of intelligence would ever have evolved on Earth had the ganglionic system not been superseded by a still more advanced type of neural organization.

The Evolution of the Vertebrate Central Nervous System

The next great technological advance was the evolution of a spinal cord, a centralized column of neural tissues with sensory fibers leading into it at many stations along its length, and motor fibers issuing from it at every station as well. The ground plan on which all higher animal organisms are designed, the spinal cord came into existence with the *Chordata,* the ancestors of the vertebrates, and has remained essentially unchanged through the rise of the fishes, amphibians, reptiles, mammals, and ourselves.

The living species that perhaps best represents the early chordates is the lancelet (*Amphioxus*), shown in Figure 13.7 in semidiagrammatic form. The lancelet has a primitive spinal cord (hence its classification as a chordate), but no bony vertebral column enclosing and supporting it, as do the more advanced true vertebrates. A flexible structure called a *notochord* runs the length of the two-inch translucent, flattened body; just above it, running its full length, is a *dorsal nerve cord* tapered at both ends, forming a simple first central nervous system. Some species similar to this one was presumably the progenitor of all the vertebrates living today. Some 600 million years ago, even though small and inconspicuous, it no

Notochord. A flexible structure, the precursor of the vertebral column, found in the primitive chordates.

Dorsal nerve cord. The precursor of the spinal cord in evolution, found in the prevertebrate chordates.

Figure 13.7 / *A Chordate and a True Vertebrate, Presumed Similar to the First Vertebrates to Evolve. Amphioxus* is classed as a chordate, not having a true vertebral column but having something like a spinal cord, its dorsal nerve cord. *Petromyzon* is far more advanced, having a true spinal cord and surrounding protective (though cartilaginous) vertebrae. Out of similar toothless, eel-like fishes, presumably all of the present-day vertebrates — fishes, amphibians, reptiles, birds, and mammals — evolved.

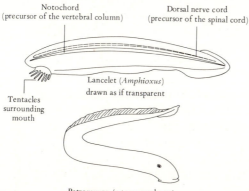

Notochord
(precursor of the vertebral column)

Dorsal nerve cord
(precursor of the spinal cord)

Lancelet (*Amphioxus*)
drawn as if transparent

Tentacles
surrounding
mouth

Petromyzon (a true vertebrate)

doubt represented the most highly advanced form of life. Since it had no bony skeleton, this hypothetical ancestor of us all left no fossil remains yet discovered.

The dorsal nerve cord of *Amphioxus* and the other living chordates is a neural tube consisting of a number of segments strung together longitudinally. In our own bodies it is represented by the *spinal cord,* its central canal filled with cerebrospinal fluid, with its dorsal sensory roots and its ventral motor roots at each segment. There are 28 such segments in the human spinal nervous system, divided for purposes of discussion into 8 cervical, 12 thoracic, 5 lumbar, and 3 sacral segments. As is true of all the vertebrates, our spinal cord is enclosed within the *vertebrae,* a segmented column of intricately structured bony pieces, each with a hole through the center to accommodate the cord and channels for the entrance and exit of the segmental nerves, as shown in Figure 13.8.

Figure 13.8 / *Cross-Sectional View of the Human Spinal Column in the Thoracic Region.* Here we can see the relationship of the bony vertebrae and the spinal cord nestled within its protection, with nerve roots, dorsal (sensory) and ventral (motor), leading away at each segment.

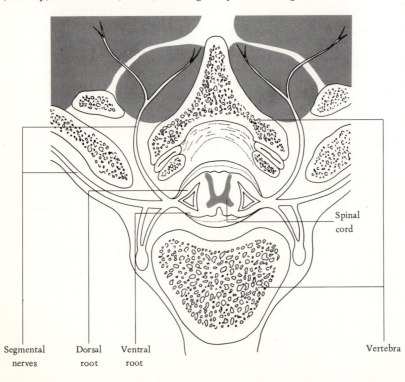

Segmental   Dorsal   Ventral   Vertebra
nerves   root   root

The most primitive of the true vertebrates living today is an eel-like, jawless freshwater fish, the lamprey *Petromyzon*, in whom the head end of the spinal cord has a conspicuous enlargement not found in the chordates — the first true brain (Figure 13.9). A step further in the elaboration of the brain is found in the cartilaginous fish — the sharks, rays, and skates — whose brain has differentiated into a conspicuous forebrain structure, a midbrain behind it, and a hindbrain, on the plan of all the more advanced vertebrates. The forebrain, the precursor of the hemispheres, is concerned in the fishes primarily with the sense of smell, which in some species (sharks, salmon) is exquisite. It exhibits a true cortex, whose remnants are still to be found in the olfactory cortex of the human brain, the anterior perforated substance or substantia innominata, at the base of the olfactory bulbs.

The structure behind the forebrain hemispheres, the optic lobe, is also covered with cortical tissue and serves the principal function of vision. Behind the optic lobe is the cerebellum, which in the fishes has been likened to an inertial guidance system, governing muscular tension and relaxation of the two sides of the animal to change its position in the water and to propel it forward. Below the cerebellum is the medulla, connected to the ancient spinal cord, of which the structures described above are enlargements, outpocketings, and elaborations.

Both the optic lobes and the cerebellum became relatively diminished in size and importance in the amphibians (frogs, toads, salamanders), while the olfactory forebrain expanded. At this point in evolution the brain is much more than a mere enlargement at the forward end of the cord. The amphibian brain is an intricately organized system of systems to handle all incoming sensory signals from the body (previously handled reflexly at the segmental level in the cord) and to direct all extended, nonreflex motor activities. The diminished size of the cerebellum appears to reflect lack of need for an inertial guidance system anymore, as in the fishes. Frogs out of water rest on their bellies and make their way over the terrain by a series of not-too-well-coordinated hops, often with a tumble at the end.

As Figure 13.9 shows, the amphibian forebrain contains a primordial hippocampus intimately connected by fibers to a septal area. There is also a region that will become the amygdala in more advanced brains, as well as a primitive thalamus and striatum. At the next level of life, these structures become more clearly differentiated and enlarged, and it is in the brain of the reptiles that we can begin to see the emerging outlines of the mammalian brain to come.

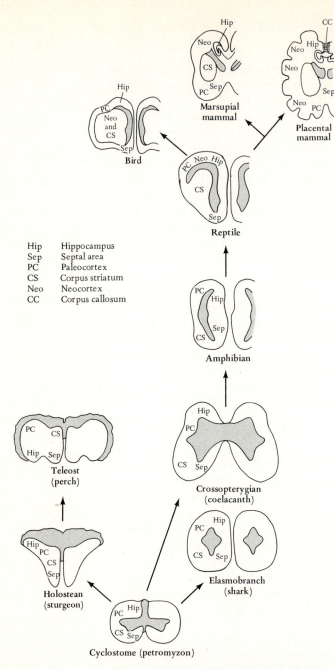

Hip — Hippocampus
Sep — Septal area
PC — Paleocortex
CS — Corpus striatum
Neo — Neocortex
CC — Corpus callosum

Figure 13.9 / *Hippocampal-Septal Relations Throughout the Evolution of the Vertebrates.* Examining these diagrammatic sketches, progressing up the phylogenetic scale from a simple cyclostome, such as *Petromyzon,* to the human, it can be seen that a similar close relationship between septum and hippocampus has remained constant throughout. This ages-old persistence of septal-hippocampal interconnection suggests that it fulfills a most important survival function today as in the past. What is that function?

With the evolution of the reptiles, who walk rather than hop and tumble, the vestibular system and the closely related cerebellum both re-emerge as important brain structures. In the lizards, snakes, turtles, and crocodilians, the brain of the typical land-living, air-breathing animal was for the first time fully established. The enlarged cerebellum is accompanied by a much enlarged striatum, and the two structures are now in a position to govern varied and agile forms of behavior. A primordial neocortex also emerges. I like to think that this is functionally related to a kind of behavior new in the reptiles — an emergent deliberateness, almost thoughtfulness, in behavior, perhaps most vividly apparent in the lizards. Whereas a frog sits stolidly impervious until an insect passes, when its tongue flicks out suddenly to capture it in a swift reflex action, lizards are much more mobile, even curious, in their behavior. One has the impression that here is the beginning of the world view so strikingly evident in the mammals. It is as if motor programs are not mere reflex jerks but scenarios played out on the stage of an environment of which the animal is fully cognizant, peopled with objects of more or less interest to it. It is an even higher form of psychological existence when the true neocortex appears in the mammals.

The reptiles apparently emerged very shortly after the amphibians shifted to an air-breathing, land-living mode. Unlike the amphibians, the reptiles escaped the watery environment entirely; the rest of the vertebrates remained at least partially water-borne. Thus reptiles had little use for the fishes' device for hearing underwater, the *lateral line system,* a series of hair-cell receptors situated at points along the side of the animal, responsive not only to underwater vibrations but also to its own movement through the water. What was required was an entirely new system of auditory reception, based not on underwater vibrations but on air waves. The vibrations of gaseous molecules carry far less force than do vibrations in water, which is incompressible, and a more delicate receptor system was called for.

The evolutionary adaptation to this new need was quite remarkable. Three small *articular bones* that had joined the lower jaw to the skull were found dispensible; they happened to lie near the head end of the lateral line system, whose receptors were retained. These receptors in the fishes had specialized for analysis of a wide range of sounds, including pitch discrimination. (In the laboratory, fish learn to come for food at the sound of a particular whistle.) The receptors formed the lining of an auditory tube leading to the air at the side of the head, the progenitor of our auditory meatus. In time

Lateral line system. A system of acoustic receptors strung along the sides of certain fishes, the evolutionary precursor of the auditory system in mammals.

Articular bones. Three small bones at the point of articulation of the jaw bone and the skull in reptiles, to be transformed into the ossicles of the middle ear in mammals.

this auditory tube curled into the cochlear tube, as we know it in the mammals, and a vibratile eardrum was formed, closing off the tube from the middle ear cavity, into which the articular bones migrated to form the three tiny interconnecting ossicles. As we saw in Chapter 5, these ossicles greatly magnify the force of the sound waves entering the ear canal as their vibrations are transmitted to the oval window of the cochlea.

The reptiles, with only a primordial neocortex, do not have a corpus callosum; their two hemispheres are still joined by the anterior commissure. They do have a well-developed hippocampus, situated in the midline at the top of the hemispheres; it has developed from a mere group of neurons with appropriate connections with the septal region and anterior hypothalamus, as in the amphibians, into a very large and distinctive infolded cortical structure. At the same time the paleocortex adjacent to it has differentiated into what will become in the mammals the subiculum and entorhinal cortex and the cingulate cortex of the limbic system. It is out of the cingulate cortex that the neocortex was eventually to emerge as mammalian evolution progressed. With the emergence of neocortical tissues, the corpus callosum began to form in the anterior portion of the brain to interconnect them.

The Evolution of the Mammalian Brain

An enormous evolutionary leap separates the mammals from any of their predecessors about whom we have solid information (Figure 13.10). In terms of brain structure, the outstanding innovation appears to be the emergence of the thalamocortical system. Neocortex and thalamus developed in tandem, simultaneously with the increasing size and rearward extension of the corpus callosum. There were also less externally visible changes. A new internal temperature-control mechanism evolved in the hypothalamus, to govern such autonomic reflex mechanisms as panting and the shunting of the blood from internal regions into the skin for more efficient radiation of excessive heat (perspiration appears to have been a relatively recent development), and shivering and piloerection to keep the body warm, under the control of a thermostat sensitive to blood temperature changes. Externally, the mammals could be differentiated from other animals by their possession of fur; all the reptiles had scaly skin, the amphibians a naked skin, and the birds and their dinosaurian progenitors evolved feathers. Fur and feathers apparently evolved early as methods of internal temperature regula-

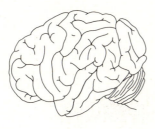

Shark   Frog   Turtle   Pigeon

Opossum   Rabbit   Cat   Macaque

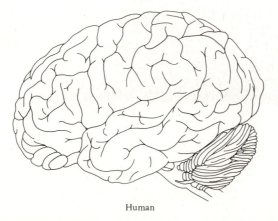

Chimpanzee

Human

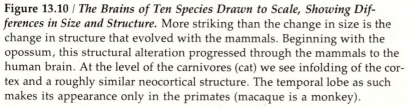

Figure 13.10 / *The Brains of Ten Species Drawn to Scale, Showing Differences in Size and Structure.* More striking than the change in size is the change in structure that evolved with the mammals. Beginning with the opossum, this structural alteration progressed through the mammals to the human brain. At the level of the carnivores (cat) we see infolding of the cortex and a roughly similar neocortical structure. The temporal lobe as such makes its appearance only in the primates (macaque is a monkey).

tion. Not until later was it found that wing feathers make an excellent airfoil for flying; with only fur to adorn them, the mammals (except for the bats) remained earthbound.

Of the three types of mammals — monotremes (one hole), marsupials (pouch-bearing), and placentals (developing a placenta and thus able to carry their young to full term internally) — only the placental mammals succeeded in carrying brain development much further. When the demise of the great reptiles made the daytime world available to exploitation, the mammals abandoned their furtive nocturnal, tree-dwelling, and ground-boring habits for a life in the open and the daylight. Relatively quickly thereafter, they grew in size and in the size of their brains. Throughout much of the world, the monotremes and marsupials became extinct, unable to compete successfully with the more advanced placentals. Many environmental niches were open for occupancy, and the placental mammals spread over the earth from the tropics to the polar regions and began their differentiation into many different types. The browsers and grazers evolved into two major groups, the perissodactyls with a single hoof (horses, rhinoceroses) and the artiodactyls with two hooves or a double, cloven hoof (cattle, sheep, deer). The carnivores who preyed on them evolved into the pack hunters (dogs, wolves, hyenas) and the stalking hunters (cats). The seed eaters evolved into the rodents, and the fruit eaters into the primates (and bats). The omnivores evolved into the weasels and skunks and badgers and wolverines and (a very late comer) the bears, while the fish eaters evolved into the otters, the seals, and the toothed whales. All these types evolved, apparently, from the same primitive insectivore, whose mode of existence is still to be found in some of the most primitive mammalian forms, such as the hedgehog and the opossum, which closely resemble their ancient insectivore ancestors.

If we follow the brain development of the placental mammals in their evolution from that early ancestral type, we find a common trend in every developmental direction: a tendency toward an increase in size, partly correlated with increased body size. (Recall the tiny cranium of the opossum, whose thick walls house a much smaller brain.) Careful study of *endocasts* of the brain case of fossil Mesozoic animals suggests that before the Cenozoic era, when the great *mammalian radiation* began, increased brain size could be entirely explained by such a correlation. About 40 million years ago, however, at the end of the Eocene epoch, an increase in brain size *in proportion to body size* began to occur in many mammalian lines. Moreover, a second great surge in relative brain size occurred in

Endocast. A reproduction of the interior form of the cranium, especially of fossil remains.

Mammalian radiation. The rapid development of different types of mammals after the disappearance of the dinosaurs.

many mammalian lines in the Miocene epoch about 20 million years ago. At that time the brains of the hoofed animals and carnivores had reached about half their modern dimensions (Jerison, 1973).

Since the sensory projection areas of the cortex in all modern species occupy only a small cortical expanse, it is reasonable to speculate that these increases in brain size — which occurred in parallel in many mammalian species — largely represented an expansion of the association cortex lying between the projection areas. Also, when more recently evolved species are compared with those whose lines appeared earlier, it seems clear that much of the increase in brain volume must have been due to expansion of cortical area and the volume of the white matter beneath, rather than in brainstem and subcortical forebrain nuclear structures. This increase appears to have characterized the paleocortex as well as the neocortex, and the cerebellum — particularly its lateral hemispheres — whose growth was closely associated with the growth of the neocortex.

An argument can also be made that a relative increase in brain size was necessitated by the development of the modern visual system today enjoyed by the carnivores, the hoofed animals, and the primates. (Some large modern mammals, such as the elephant and rhinoceros, have notoriously poor eyesight.) During the Cenozoic radiation, many mammalian lines appear to have evolved a highly sophisticated new visual system, which put the primitive visual capacities of early mammals like the opossum to shame. This new system, based on the neocortex, might well have required an increased cranial volume in predator and smaller prey animals for whom the more sophisticated visual system was prerequisite to survival (Figure 13.11).

Developments of the Brain Over the Primate Series

The earliest primates appear to have been insectivores who, unlike their cousins, took to a life in the trees, and became specialized for climbing and living in trees, probably before the close of the Cretaceous period and the disappearance of the dinosaurs. The lemur of Madagascar is very similar in structure to an early Eocene primate, *Notharctus*. Lemurs are nocturnal, tree-dwelling insectivores and frugivores (fruit eaters) with small brains and undifferentiated cortex — a model, perhaps, of the generalized primate brain at the time the primate order became distinct. Lemurs, like opossums, are

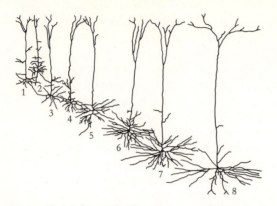

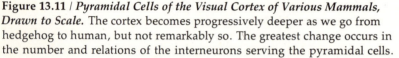

Figure 13.11 / *Pyramidal Cells of the Visual Cortex of Various Mammals, Drawn to Scale.* The cortex becomes progressively deeper as we go from hedgehog to human, but not remarkably so. The greatest change occurs in the number and relations of the interneurons serving the pyramidal cells.

"living fossils" that would probably long ago have become extinct had their island, Madagascar, not broken away from mainland Africa very early during the mammalian radiation; no large carnivores ever developed there or arrived from the mainland.

Tracing the progressive development of more advanced forms of primates, in fossil remains and in living examples, we observe that expansions of the hemispheres of the brain are accompanied by a progressive change in their shape, undoubtedly of great significance but not well understood. In primitive forms, the central fissure is far toward the front, and the frontal lobe is minuscule. With expansion of the neocortex of the frontal lobe, the central fissure was pushed progressively further back until, in the great apes, it lies rearward of the vertex (center top of the cranium). Meanwhile, the parietal-lobe cortex also expanded equally dramatically and was pushed backward, appearing in the primates to have progressively pushed the temporal lobe downward and forward as a distinct cerebral lobe. In the process, the visual cortex, originally at the top of the brain, was pushed back into the occiput, and the auditory cortex was buried from sight atop the massive temporal lobe.

The rearward progression of the expanding neocortex was accompanied by a corresponding rearward migration of the posterior extension of the corpus callosum. In the process the hippocampus was thrust from its original position, in the midline at the top of the brain, into its primate location in the medial temporal lobe close to the amygdala. This migration of the anterior dorsal structures rearward and downward into the temporal lobe is marked in the modern human brain by the shape of the limbic system fiber bundles, the fornix, the stria terminalis, and the cingulum.

It is of interest that these expansions of the primate brain thrust the projection areas for the three thalamocortically organized sensory systems into deep fissures, as if pushed there by the expanding association cortex between them. Thus we find the primary projection cortex for tactile sensation mostly in the postcentral gyrus deep within the central fissure, the visual signals reaching the brain principally deep in the calcarine fissure on the medial surface of the occipital lobe, and the auditory cortex largely out of sight within the lateral fissure atop the temporal lobe. However, there is some controversy over whether these primary projection cortices are primitive or, alternatively, differentiated out of the more diffusely organized association cortices with which they are now associated, and thus representing a more advanced phylogenetic phenomenon.

There is a noteworthy contrast between, on the one hand, the great stability over evolutionary time of the calcarine fissure and the two other important fissures of the medial surface of the brain, the parieto-occipital sulcus and the cingulate sulcus, which remain almost unchanged over the primate series and show little individual variation, and, on the other hand, the convolutions of the lateral surfaces of the brain which tend to be highly variable from individual to individual, especially in the great apes and in our own brain. Perhaps this is related to a greater expansion, phylogenetically, of the dorsolateral convexity of the brain.

The Emergence of the Human Brain

There has been extensive speculation as to the selection pressures that might have been responsible for the dramatic latter-day increase in brain size with the emergence of our own species. A brief review of some relevant information is all we will attempt here.

The human brain does not differ greatly in shape from that of the great apes, the chimpanzee, the gorilla, and the orangutan (whose forehead bulge is even more spectacular than ours). Its major distinction appears to be its vastly increased volume, which represents the fastest evolutionary increase in brain mass ever to occur in any species. Our brain essentially doubled in volume over the brief span of some millions of years, while that of the great apes showed little change over the same period. The question is: Why?

The best-known possible early progenitor of the human species is

Australopithecus (southern ape), who lived in Africa about 5 million years ago. The more *gracile* form of this animal, *Australopithecus africanus,* stood upright and had apparently adopted an omnivorous diet, including meat, while its forest-dwelling relatives remained vegetarian (like the great apes of today). Though a small animal, perhaps four feet tall, its brain was about the size of a large ape's, something less than a pound and a half in weight. We know that Australopithecus made simple tools of pebbles chipped to form a sharp edge. It appears to have become extinct in the neighborhood of 2 million years ago.

The great leap forward in brain volume occurred between Australopithecus, whose brain had apparently reached a plateau, and the appearance in the fossil record of *Homo erectus* (the generic term for many upright human species, including Peking man) a million years ago or more. At that stage, as seen in Neanderthal man (*Homo Neanderthalensis*), the brain weighed more than twice that of Australopithecus — at least three pounds. Homo erectus not only walked upright, but spread far beyond the confines of Africa and manufactured much more refined stone tools. They knew how to use fire, and appear to have included meat in their diet. They had become hunters and gatherers, like many primitive peoples today. Some graves from this era contain the remains of flowers.

A number of possible factors in the sudden explosive expansion of the human brain's volume (perhaps 3.5 pounds today) and intelligence have been suggested. The life of a predatory hunter presents challenges a simple vegetarian escapes, which possibly explains why the apes did not experience parallel brain growth. This was also the period of the great glaciers. Slowly changing climates might have forced adaptation to cold and a changing fauna, especially for an adventurous animal seeking to exploit environmental niches far from its origins in tropical Africa. (Except for the continents of North and South America and Australia, the entire landmass of Earth appears to have been invaded by these peoples.) Already possessing one of the highest brain-body ratios among living animals, these early hominids grew larger, and their brain volume increased in parallel with their body size. Whatever the relevant factors, a point was reached when increased brain volume became highly advantageous, and the evolutionary trend was greatly speeded.

The emergence of our present brain was accompanied by such subtle structural changes as those apparently underlying language competence; our harmonic ear, capable of appreciating the subtlest of musical tone clusters; our ability to appreciate rhythmic complexes of equal subtlety; and our capacity to distinguish between beauty and ugliness and, perhaps, right and wrong. These structural uniquenesses of the human brain have only recently begun to capture the interest of neuroscientists.

Summary

The human brain is the product of gradual evolution over the course of much of the span of Earth time. When the first multicellular animals evolved, there must have been a selective advantage for development of a cell specialized for signalling over a distance, in order to coordinate the movements of the organism. Thus the first nerve cells came into being. In the most primitive living animal forms in which signalling occurs, such as the jellyfish and the coelenterate *Hydra,* the fiber extensions of these specialized cells transmit their signals in either direction. At a more sophisticated level we find chaining of neurons; signals pass only in one direction, each neuron activating the next through the release of a chemical substance at point of contact, or through direct electrical stimulation. At this level we find groups of neurons (ganglia) rather autonomously governing certain functions or parts of the organism. Our peripheral nervous system retains examples of such organization from very early evolutionary times; in the brain, it was superseded by more complex types of neural organization.

Ganglionic systems today characterize the nervous systems of invertebrates, such as the crustaceans and the insects, the most sophisticated examples being the octopus and squid. With the evolution of the early vertebrates, the ganglionic system was essentially replaced by the central nervous system, represented by the spinal cord, with an increasing enlargement at the head end that became the brain. In the evolution of the fishes, the structures of the brain enlarged and became differentiated into a forebrain corresponding to our cerebrum, a midbrain devoted to sensory integration, and a hindbrain (brainstem and cerebellum) devoted principally to motor functions. This basic differentiation has been retained in the more recently evolved brains of amphibians, reptiles, birds, and mammals, in conjunction with a progressive ascendancy of the forebrain.

The mammalian brain represents a significant departure from previous evolutionary lines leading to the great dinosaurs, who dominated the major land masses of Earth for the enormously long reign of some hundred million years. A new system, involving integrated functioning of neocortex and thalamus, was eventually to take primary control over the still-retained older brainstem and limbic forebrain structures. It was to feature a more sophisticated auditory, visual, and tactile sensory system and a more efficient and flexible voluntary motor system (the pyramidal system) with more direct access to spinal motor centers.

The primate order (to which we belong), which evolved for life in the trees, eventually developed a larger brain relative to body size than most mammalian lines. Its structure too was unique, featuring an expanding temporal lobe. Much of the expansion of the primate brain occurred in the thalamus and neocortex, which in the more recently evolved forms completely covers and hides from external view the older, more primitive brain structures that evolved with the fishes, the amphibians, and reptiles. The human brain represents a very recent evolutionary development: the brain size more than doubled in the course of just a few million years. Over the same period, apparently, it also evolved a differential structure in the left and right hemispheres, and a quite distinctive mode of information processing in the left based on the language function.

Chapter 14 / *The Developmental Perspective: How Our Brain Grew*

In the ontogenetic development of the brain, genetically coded structures and connectivities come about through the proliferation and migration of neuroblasts to their appointed stations, followed by the projection of their axons, sometimes over long distances, in search of their appropriate target cells. Many more neuroblasts are formed than will be found in the brain at time of birth; those that fail to contact appropriate targets, and those that fail to be contacted, die off. Most of the neurons are formed by the time of birth, but only those in certain essential structures are functionally mature by that time. The neurons continue to elaborate their basic connectivities in more recently evolved portions of the brain, partly under the influence of developmental learning experiences, until well into adolescence. There also appear to be critical periods for given types of learning, such as language functions, after which such learning proves considerably more difficult. Whether environmental challenge can completely overcome deficiencies in early experience or nutrition is not yet well understood.

A human life begins, amazingly, as a single cell, when the egg (ovum) in its descent down the Fallopian tube toward the uterus encounters sperm cells, one of which manages to penetrate its protective coating and enter its cytoplasm. Both egg and sperm have only a single copy of each of the 23 chromosomes. Shortly after penetration (*fertilization*), the nuclear membranes of both sperm and egg break down, permitting the mating of the 23 pairs and thus establishing the blueprint for the organism-to-be. Shortly thereafter, each of the 46 chromosomes begins to undergo the process of *replication*, whereby each of its *genes* — the chemical structures carrying the genetic code — is duplicated through a copying of its molecules, one by one, into a new chromosome. The original cell is

Gene. A segment of DNA containing the code for a specific biologically active protein.

311

then ready to divide in two (*mitosis*), each part containing an exact copy of the original gene complex. So accurate is this process that an error is made only about once in 100 million duplicated genes. Each of the billions of living cells that will form the body of the new person will thus contain the same genetic information coded in its genes (barring mutations). Each will be, in effect, genetically identical to all the rest, and unlike any in the body of any other individual who ever lived, or ever will — with the one exception of identical twins.

Sometimes the fertilized egg (zygote), upon dividing, splits into two separate zygotes, rather than adhering together to form parts of the same organism. Thus identical twins are formed, each developing on the same set of genetic instructions. Shortly they begin a second replication of their genes in preparation for a second division. This process of cell multiplication continues until the baby is fully formed.

The genes strung along the chromosomes are molecules of *deoxyribonucleic acid* (*DNA*), each containing the code for the manufacture of a specific protein molecule; many are *enzymes* governing specific chemical processes that occur in the cell's cytoplasm. The DNA itself remains enclosed within the cell's nucleus except when the cell is undergoing mitosis. The DNA code in the gene is *transcribed* into a complementary code in a second molecule, the *messenger*, composed of *ribonucleic acid* (*RNA*), which is then released from the chromosome. It passes out through a pore in the nuclear membrane into the cytoplasm, where it attaches itself to a structure (a *ribosome*) capable of using its code to form a protein molecule, a process called *translation*. Once this occurs, the *messenger RNA* (*mRNA*) breaks down into its component ribonucleic acids, ready for reuse inside the nucleus to produce another messenger molecule.

The translation process, whereby the code in the mRNA is "read out" to produce a specific protein molecule, is not nearly as errorfree as the replication process at insuring accurate duplication of the genetic material during cell multiplication. Translation errors occur when a "wrong" amino-acid molecule is inserted into the chain of amino acids composing the protein molecule. The resulting protein may be ineffective or less effective, as an enzyme, but that is of much less concern than an error in duplication of the original genetic material, which would result in the continuing production of faulty proteins in all of that cell's progeny. It has been estimated for bacteria that translation errors may occur in one amino acid out of 10,000. This is still, of course, a remarkable success ratio, speaking well for the precision of a very complex manufacturing process

Mitosis. **Cell division in which the two daughter cells have the same number of chromosomes as the mother cell.**

Deoxyribonucleic acid. **DNA, the chemical substance containing the genetic code.**

Transcription. **The copying onto messenger RNA of the genetic code contained in the DNA.**

Ribonucleic acid. **RNA, the chemical that carries the genetic code transcribed from the nuclear DNA for translation into protein molecules.**

Translation. **The process through which the genetic code transcribed in the messenger RNA is copied into the manufactured protein molecule at the ribosome.**

Messenger RNA. **mRNA, the RNA transcribed directly from the DNA in the nucleus, carrying the code for the production of a biologically important protein.**

at the ribosome. Under the control of specific enzymes, small pieces of ribonucleic acid called *transfer RNA (tRNA)*, one for each of the 20 types of amino acids, bring their attached amino acid to the site at the proper times so they may all be strung together sequentially to form the new protein molecule, according to the specifications of the mRNA molecule that happens to be inserted in the ribosome at the moment.

Transfer RNA. tRNA, small segments of RNA responsible for bringing appropriate amino acids to the ribosomes to be linked to form the required protein molecule.

As the newly forming organism is wafted down the tube toward the uterus, its cells continue to undergo mitosis, continually doubling, from two to four to eight to sixteen and so on. Yet it grows very little larger in the process; its component cells become progressively smaller (the mulberry stage). Meanwhile the organism is nourished by an excretion of the lining of the tube called uterine milk. Before reaching the uterus, however, the new organism begins to expand into the hollow-ball stage (*blastocyte*) with the tiny embryo situated along one wall. It is at this stage that the organism enters the uterus and implants itself in the already prepared, highly vascularized, spongy tissue, usually on the rear wall of the forward-tilted uterus. Immediately the exterior wall of the blastocyte begins to produce a spongy tissue of its own, to form its part of the placenta — the marvelous innovation that permits the young to be nourished within the body of the mother until well formed, in some mammals almost until the point of independent viability. (But not quite: all placental mammals continue to nourish their young through their milk after birth.)

Blastocyte. The forming organism at the hollow-ball stage, reached shortly before implantation in the uterine wall.

The growing organism can obtain nourishment from the mother's blood stream (though the two circulatory systems never make direct contact) through the close apposition of its own placental circulation to the capillaries of the mother's placental circulation. Thus, though totally dependent on the mother, the young embryo is from the beginning an independent organism, never a part of the mother. It has its own life to live and she hers, but until birth it accepts board and lodging in the warmth of her hospitality.

More significantly, it has within its genes complete instructions for its own development, in the minutest detail. These instructions are carried out quite autonomously, without the mother's assistance other than provision of her life-support system. In the course of *gestation*, the growing organism will go through many developmental stages in sequence and on time, under the guidance of a developmental schedule characteristic of our species and contained within the genetic blueprint. A significant feature of that developmental program is the gradual growth and maturation of the central nervous system, which will be the focus of this chapter.

Gestation. The process of fetal development; the period from conception to birth.

Development to the Neural Tube Stage

As cell proliferation within the tiny embryo continues, what was originally a ball of apparently identical cells becomes an organized structure, with a head end and a tail end, a dorsal and a ventral layer, a left and a right side. Cell *differentiation* has begun. Cell division that produces two identical daughter cells is called *cloning*, and the group of cells so produced a *clone*. (In this process the mother cell at each step becomes one of the indistinguishable daughters.) In the course of cell proliferation, however, there comes a point when the two daughter cells are no longer the same. One has become subtly different, and is now the progenitor of a new clone, all of whose members will harbor the same difference. What has happened is that some of the genes that were suppressed in the original clone are being expressed in the new clone, while others in the genetic complex are now being suppressed, no longer producing their kind of protein molecules. Thus the chemistry of the two groups of cells differs now, and so will that of their daughter cells. Probably only a very small fraction of the total genetic complex contained within the chromosomes is expressed at any one stage of cell differentiation.

Cloning. **The process of cell multiplication in which daughter cells do not differentiate into new cell types.**

One of the first major differentiations that takes place in the formation of the embryo (*morphogenesis*) is between cells destined to become epidermal cells and nervous tissue, which form the dorsal layer of the early embryo, and those destined to line the visceral cavities, which form the ventral layer of the embryo. The former are called *ectodermal,* the latter *endodermal* cells. Between these two layers there forms a third differentiated layer of cells, called the *mesoderm,* whose cells are destined to become, among other things, muscle and bone. In this early three-layered stage, the tiny organism is already beginning to specify which cells are to become what in the final structure.

Morphogenesis. **The complex process through which the zygote is transformed into the fully formed embryo.**

As soon as this sandwich of three types of tissue is formed, a groove begins to appear down the middle of the back (ectodermal layer) of the organism. This groove quickly deepens, its sides turning up and over to form a hollow tube called the *neural tube;* the process is called *neurulation.* The cells lining the lumen or interior wall of the neural tube are destined to become the nerve cells and glial cells of the central nervous system. Where the two walls of the tube arch over and join, there forms a *neural crest* whose cells are — to oversimplify somewhat — progenitors of the peripheral nervous system (see Figure 14.1).

Neurulation. **The process of formation of the neural tube during embryogenesis.**

At this point in development, differentiated cells have already

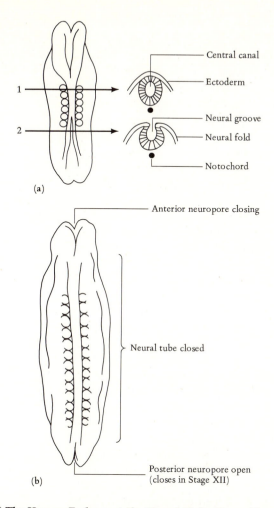

Central canal

Ectoderm

Neural groove

Neural fold

Notochord

(a)

Anterior neuropore closing

Neural tube closed

Posterior neuropore open
(closes in Stage XII)

(b)

Figure 14.1 / *The Human Embryo at the Neural-Tube Stage.* Shortly after implantation in the uterine wall, the embryo undergoes a rapid process of metamorphosis, of which two stages are shown here. In the upper figure, a groove forms along the surface of the embryo, its walls curve in as it deepens, and they close to form the neural tube, which then elongates as the embryo expands lengthwise. The neural tube becomes the source of the many billions of neurons that will form the central nervous system.

begun to travel, or *migrate,* from their place of origin in the clone to their appointed position within the rapidly enlarging structure. Most of them will continue the process of cell proliferation, yielding clones and further differentiating cell lines at their new station. The most significant questions here for the theoretical biologist are: how do they know (a) which direction to go in their migration and (b) when they have found their appointed place within the evolving total structure? This matter has been very intensively studied in the case of the *neuroblasts,* immature neurons that differentiate close to the germinal epithelial tissue lining the lumen of the neural tube, and that, once differentiated, will never undergo cell division again.

Many years ago F. C. Sauer (1935), studying the formation of neuroblasts in the lining of the neural tube of the chick embryo, made a number of important discoveries. Sauer found that the cells undergoing mitosis in this region are separate cells, bounded by their own plasma membranes, and not a *syncytium* of interconnected cells as had been thought. He also found that the germinal cells are columnar in form, with slender extensions connecting the cell body with the inner and outer surfaces of the neural tube proper. Most curiously, Sauer observed that in the course of mitosis the cell soma moves away from the lumen after cell division, attaching to the outer surface of the tissue layer toward which it migrates, then moves back toward the lumen, rounding up there at the time of cell division. At this point, one of the daughter cells might migrate into the overlying mantle layer, while its sister continues the mitotic cycle. (Presumably those migrating away have differentiated into neuroblasts, and begun their migration through the tissues toward their predestined station.) Sauer's early findings have since been confirmed by study of the process under the electron microscope (Fisher and Jacobson, 1970). Although the significance of the soma's to-and-fro movement during mitosis is unknown, it is apparently common in embryonic tissues with such a columnar epithelial form (Zwaan, Bryan, and Pearce, 1969).

The neural tube closes first in the middle, then progressively further toward each end as the embryo elongates and grows in size. As it does so, out-pouchings occur toward the head end, the most dramatic being the two lateral ventricles, whose interior surfaces will continue to germinate additional neuroblasts until about the time of birth, when cloning stops and essential differentiation is complete. The neurons that form the forebrain hemispheres arise from these neuroepithelial germinal tissues, continuing to migrate outward to form the cortex and subcortical nuclei in the course of the fetal stage.

Migration. Movement of cells from point of origin to final destination in the embryo in the process of morphogenesis.

Neuroblasts. Immature neurons during their formation and migration to their ultimate stations.

Syncytium. A hypothetical interconnected network of fibers once thought to be the basic structure of the brain, now disproved.

Establishing the "Wiring Diagram" of the Brain

Somehow all the neurons in the brain manage to find their way to their appropriate nuclei or region of the cortex with remarkable precision. Such a thing was once believed impossible, and it was thought that quasi-randomly distributed migrating neurons achieved their final functional determination by the use to which they were put after arrival (a belief that coincided with the heyday of the environmentalist school of child development). This theory has now been abandoned due to repeated demonstrations that maturational factors alone appear to be responsible for completing the original structural relationships within the brain before functional connections between neurons have been established. The question remains: how is such an improbable feat accomplished?

First let us distinguish between differentiation and determination. *Differentiation* is the differential gene expression that results in the final form and function of the cell; *determination* is the progressive reduction in the potential directions of development open to a given cell. The degree or stage of determination of portions of the developing nervous system has been studied by grafting small portions into other regions to see if they take on the function of their new environment or retain their already determined developmental course, out of keeping with their surround. Such methods reveal that it all depends on the time at which the grafting is done. The principle is summarized by Jacobson (1970, pp. 94–95):

Differentiation. **The change in gene expression which determines the type and function of a given cell.**

Determination. **The change in the complement of functional genes that occurs during embryo formation to restrict the different types of cells that a given cell may become.**

The first phase of neural determination consists initially of repression of genes that support differentiation of non-neural tissue. The second phase of neural determination consists of the expression of the activity of genes that support differentiation of specific types of neurons. We may think of neural determination as a process that becomes progressively more restrictive during development. At first the general relationships between parts of the nervous system are determined; later in development, particular relationships such as the synaptic connections between nerve cells are determined.

The Migration of the Cortical Neurons

Several general principles of morphogenesis of the brain provide some insight into the underlying strategy. In general, the larger *transmission neurons* of any region of the cortex appear to arrive at their stations first. The smaller neurons arrive later at their more

Transmission neurons. **Neurons whose axons leave the vicinity of the soma to innervate distant regions of the brain.**

superficial stations, passing between the larger neurons. The pyramidal cells, in general, arrive at their stations first relative to the granule and stellate *interneurons* that later come to heavily populate
layers IV, II, and I, perhaps in the course of their invasion establishing the columnar associations that will later be observed
functionally. This pattern is equally characteristic of the pyramidal
cells of the hippocampus and the large Purkinje cells of the cerebellum. It is conceivable that these early-arriving neuroblasts actually
travel very short distances in a straight line from their point of origin in the neuroepithelial germinal layer bordering the lumen of the
ventricular wall, and in their migration leave a *chem-trail* for the
later-arriving neurons with which they are to be associated. There
is some evidence that neuroblasts generated at the same location in
the germinal layer tend to be functionally related in the later stages
of morphogenesis.

> *Interneurons.* Small neurons whose axons terminate in the vicinity of the cell body.

> *Chem-trail.* A hypothetical chemical pathway laid down by migrating neurons and later followed by others.

A second principle to be borne in mind is that many more
neuroblasts are formed through cell proliferation than are to be
found in the brain of the child at birth. In some regions of the
brain, it appears, the dying-off of neuroblasts is common; many
more are available than are needed, a great percentage never matur-
ing and in time vanishing from the tissues as the process of morphogenesis continues. Perhaps the overall process of formation of
the brain can be largely ascribed to this dying-away of immature
neurons found to be unnecessary because others have reached their
appointed posts before them. Thus some selectivity among candidate neurons at the end of their trek through the neural tissues
may play a role in the ultimate structural relations. It is well established that many neurons fail to mature and begin sending out
dendritic processes until their axons successfully contact a target
neuron or muscle (or gland) cell.

The researcher principally responsible for the overthrow of the
early "neural plasticity" theory was R. W. Sperry, whose elegant experiments on the amphibian optic tract and other nerve-end organ
relations suggested a meticulous inborn blueprint for the vast and
intricate interconnections throughout the brain, apparently established partly through the use of chemical markers. His conclu-
sions are worth quoting (Sperry, 1968, pp. 30–31):

In brief, as we now see it, the complicated nerve fiber circuits of the brain
grow, assemble, and organize themselves through the use of intricate
chemical codes under genetic control. Early in development the nerve cells,
numbering in the billions, acquire individual identification tags, molecular
in nature, by which they can be recognized and distinguished one from
another.

As the differentiating neurons and their elongating fibers begin to form functional interconnections to weave the complex communication networks of behavior, the outgrowing fibers become extremely selective about the molecular identity of other cells and fibers with which they will associate. Lasting functional hookups are established only with cells to which the growing fibers find themselves selectively matched by inherent chemical affinities. In many cases the proper molecular match may be restricted further to particular membrane regions of the dendritic tree or soma of the target neuron.

The outgrowing fibers in the developing brain are guided by a kind of probing chemical touch system that leads them along exact pathways in an enormously intricate guidance program that involves millions, in the higher mammals presumably billions, of different, chemically distinct brain cells. By selective molecular preferences expressed through differential adhesivity the respective nerve fibers are guided correctly into their separate channels at each of the numerous forks or decision points which they encounter as they travel through what is essentially a three-dimensional Y-maze of possible channel choices.

Each fiber in the brain pathways has its own preferential affinity for particular prescribed trails in the differentiating surround. Both pushed and pulled along these trails, the probing fiber tip eventually locates and connects with certain other neurons, often far distant, that have the appropriate molecular labels. The potential pathways and terminal connection zones have their own individual biochemical constitution by which each is recognized and distinguished from all others in the same half of the brain and cord. Indications are that the right and left halves are chemical mirror maps.

Maturation of the Cortical Neurons

Study of the lineages of neurons has been largely limited to invertebrates, and it would be unwise to extrapolate from these studies to assumptions about neural lineages in the mammals. However, it is now generally recognized that all types of neural and glial cells arise from a common type of stem cell in the lumen of the neural tube, or from corresponding epithelial tissues in the walls of the ventricles, once formed. As the young embryo rapidly increases in size, the lumen of the neural tube elongates, increasing in area and "following" the expanding periphery. The out-pouchings of the tube at the head end, forming the ventricles, again keep the neuro-epithelial germinal layer within striking distance, apparently, of the most remote portions of the expanding brain. Indeed, if one were today to ask the question that so intrigued the early students of the brain — "What is the function of the ventricles?" (see Chapter

1) — the answer might be "to facilitate the migration of neurons and glia during morphogenesis"! In fact, no other function, and no function at all in connection with the mature brain, has yet been suggested.

When neuroblasts have migrated to their stations (and sometimes before), they are indistinguishable from somatic cells; very quickly, however, they start to project an axon filament. In the case of the large neurons, such as the cortical pyramidal cells, a definite polarity with a top and bottom is clearly present from the start, since the axon appears regularly to be projected from the base and to move into deeper tissues, then turning toward some biologically determined target. Dendrites regularly appear only after the axon has formed a synaptic contact. Some "signal" gets back to the soma to begin the maturation of the cell into a full-fledged neuron. If no appropriate contact is made, the cell appears to shrink and die.

The polarity of these neuroblasts is demonstrated when, as occasionally happens, a pyramidal cell is formed lying in an aberrant position, such as sideways or upside down. The apical dendrites then extend in that direction, rather than conforming to the orientation of their surround, and the axon typically leaves from the base. However, the axon in such a case is regularly found to change its course after leaving the soma, even doubling back if necessary to adopt a normal direction. This is evidence that the basic polarity is intrinsic to the neuron, but the direction of axonal course is eventually under the control of factors in the cell's environment.

The tip of the out-growing axon, called the *growth cone*, was first observed by Ramón y Cajal, who likened it to a living battering ram pushing its way between obstacles in its path. That the axon is characterized by *amoeboid movement*, projecting and withdrawing *pseudopods*, is illustrated in Figure 14.2, which shows a growing axon tip in tissue culture. This axon's not unusual rate of elongation is about a micron per minute. The drawings in the figure, of a cell from the ectodermal layer of a frog embryo, were done with the aid of a *camera lucida*. Note that one pseudopod projected to the right is eventually withdrawn after considerable elongation. The oval structure is a red blood corpuscle, which remains stationary. Many axons grow at a much faster rate. (See also Figure 14.3.)

Figure 14.4 shows the developing terminal arborization of an axon seen through the transparent tail fin of a living tadpole. The specific *telodendria* are indicated by numbers. It is apparent that the growing tips have amoeboid processes extending forward from the growth cone. Careful study of this remarkable observational report can give one a good feel for the essential character of brain develop-

Growth cone. The formation at the growing tip of an elongating axon.

Amoeboid movement (a-MEE-boyd). A distinctive type of cellular progression characterized by the sending out of extensions (pseudopods) into which the cytoplasm subsequently flows.

Telodendria. Terminal branches and tips of axons.

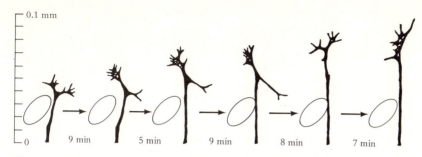

Figure 14.2 / *Six Stages in Axon-Tip Growth in the Ectodermal Layer of a Frog Embryo.* In these remarkable drawings we can observe the actual process of growth of the axon tip in its search for its appropriate target cell. The oval outlines a red blood corpuscle, marking a fixed point. Note that the amoeboid pseudopods sometimes grow quite long before being retracted as a result of poor choice of direction.

ment. C. C. Speidel, who made an intensive study of this preparation, described the process as a continuous one, involving terminal branching, projection of collaterals, halting of extension in some branches while others continue to grow, and retraction of filaments that have begun extending (Speidel, 1941).

It is known that axons characteristically branch before reaching their target zones, and that such branching is part of the mechanism through which appropriate synaptic contacts are established. Many more branches are commonly formed than are required at the moment, and those telodendria that are found unnecessary characteristically atrophy. (Further branching and synaptic contacts will be formed later as the brain matures). However, it is noteworthy that many transitory synaptic contacts may be made by immature neurons in first establishing their target connections, suggesting that it is the zone that is recognized at first, rather than the specific target cell. Shifts of synaptic contact to other portions of the cell surface, and withdrawal of synaptic contacts, appear to be a normal part of the delicate adjustment of neural connectivities. In the words of Ramón y Cajal (1937, p. 278):

There is no doubt that, at first, many imperfect connections occur. But these incongruences are progressively corrected, up to a point, by two parallel methods of rectification. One of these occurs in the periphery, and is the atrophy through disuse of superfluous and parasitic ramifications, in combination with the growth of congruent sprouts. The other occurs in the ganglia and spinal centers; by this there would be a selection, due to the

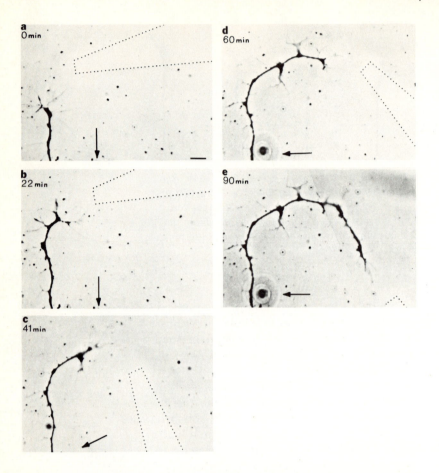

Figure 14.3 / *Growth of an Axon Tip Influenced by the Stimulus of Nerve Growth Factor.* This is another example of growth of the axon tip, this time influenced by a microinjection into its vicinity of a chemical substance stimulating neural growth. Again the quasi-random extension of pseudopods and their retraction is evident.

atrophy of certain collaterals and the progressive disappearance of disconnected or useless neurons, of the sensory-motor fibers capable of being useful.

When the tendency of neural extensions, such as axons, to extend and arborize during growth is viewed in light of the theory of a *chemoaffinity* between nerve terminals leading to synaptic junction, we can begin to grasp the nature of the mechanism by which the genetically prescribed "wiring diagram" of the brain is put into ef-

Chemoaffinity. **The hypothesis that some chemical signal attracts neural extensions and leads to the formation of appropriate synaptic junctions.**

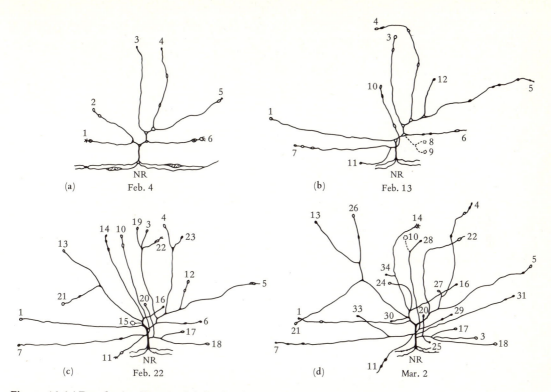

Figure 14.4 / *Developing Terminal Arborization of an Axon in a Transparent Tadpole Tail.* Drawn with the aid of a camera lucida, this figure shows the progressive elaboration of the branches of an axon terminal forming synaptic contacts with other neurons at the places numbered.

fect. Moreover, adjustment of connections in the course of development — observable in the continual replacement of neural connections as well as collateral sprouting of axon terminals when adjacent muscle or nerve cells have been *denervated* — suggests the possibility of continuing repair, correction, and creatively innovative adjustment of the grand wiring diagram in the course of experience. Whether this form of plasticity in the nervous system is implicated in the mechanisms of learning will be discussed in Chapter 16.

Denervation. Severing of neural input to a neuron or muscle cell.

As we have mentioned, dendritic growth does not begin for some time after development of the axon, and presumably not until the axon has become functionally determined by establishing synaptic contact (Figure 14.5). Thus for a while the developing neural tissues consist of immature neural cell somas and their axonal extensions. (Glial cells do not migrate until much of the neuroblast migration has been completed.) The appearance of dendrites therefore

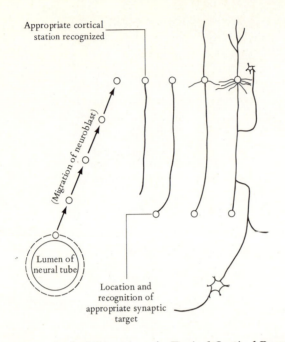

Appropriate cortical
station recognized

(Migration of neuroblast)

Lumen of
neural tube

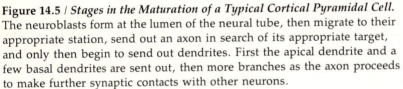

Location and
recognition of
appropriate synaptic
target

Figure 14.5 / *Stages in the Maturation of a Typical Cortical Pyramidal Cell.*
The neuroblasts form at the lumen of the neural tube, then migrate to their
appropriate station, send out an axon in search of its appropriate target,
and only then begin to send out dendrites. First the apical dendrite and a
few basal dendrites are sent out, then more branches as the axon proceeds
to make further synaptic contacts with other neurons.

suggests that the neuroblast has established its right to live, and
that maturation into a true neuron can begin. The first dendrites
tend to be short and thick, with few branches. Though the pattern
of dendritic growth appears to be under the control of internal factors, there seems to be some external influence as well: observations
suggest the differentiation of dendritic branches on approach of axonal *telodendria*. For example, dendrites of the principal neurons of
the lateral geniculate nucleus appear precisely at the time of arrival
of axons of the retinal ganglion cells.

The dendritic processes appear to have growth cones and amoeboid *filopodia* at their tips similar to those on the telodendria of the
growing axon. Synapses between axons and dendrites appear regularly to be the first formed, and to continue to increase in numbers
in the mammalian cortex, even after birth, as the dendritic branches
grow larger; this process is most easily observed in the case of the
large pyramidal cells. Axosomatic synapses appear to form much

Filopodia.
Amoeboid exten-
sions of the grow-
ing tip of either an
axon or a dendrite.

later, representing a more mature stage of development of the cortical tissues. These growth changes in the cortex are reflected in correlated changes in the electroencephalogram and in cortical evoked potentials.

The mechanisms determining synaptic contact are unknown. As for the synapses formed by later-appearing granule and stellate cells in the cortex, synaptic contact is usually established eventually with those earlier-arriving, larger neurons between which the smaller neurons must push, so to speak, to reach their more superficial stations; perhaps a determining "scent" is picked up in the process. The synapses of many of these smaller neurons with short axons are formed upon the somas of the pyramidal cells.

In the absence of synaptic contact, dendrites seem to fail to achieve their full development, as in the case of stellate cells in layer IV of the striate cortex of cats reared in the dark (Coleman and Riesen, 1968). Another study (Valverde and Esteban, 1968; Valverde, 1968) found removal of the mouse's eyes at birth to lead not only to degeneration in the lateral geniculate nucleus, but also to a radical change in orientation of the dendrites of stellate cells. In the absence of visual afferent axons in layer IV of the visual cortex, the normal dendritic arborizations in this region were conspicuously absent. The investigators concluded that the dendrites of stellate cells that would normally have been found in layer IV grew instead into layers II and III to make synaptic contact with recurrent collaterals of pyramidal cell axons in those layers, and into layer V to make synaptic contact with the horizontal collaterals of deep-lying pyramidal neurons (Figure 14.6).

It is of interest here that there is a specific preference for the formation of synaptic contacts between afferent sensory axons and the central three-fifths of the apical dendritic shafts of the pyramidal cells in the primary projection cortices. Meanwhile, axons arriving from cortical neurons, whether of local stellate or granule cells or of pyramidal cells crossing from the opposite hemisphere, characteristically synapse upon the laterally extending dendritic branches of the apical shafts or upon the basal dendrites (Globus and Scheibel, 1966). Further, Colonnier (1968) found two types of synapses in the cat's visual cortex: one type, containing spheroidal synaptic vesicles and presumed to be excitatory, synapses only upon dendritic spines of the pyramidal cells; the other, containing flattened synaptic vesicles and presumed to be inhibitory, synapses not upon spines, but principally upon the soma and occasionally upon the surface of dendrites. Thus the spine structure appears to be specifically associated with excitatory synapses, and the spine itself may represent part of the mechanism of synaptic determination.

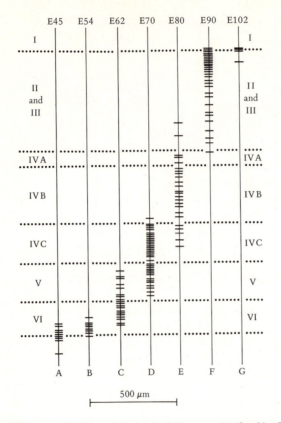

Figure 14.6 / *Differential Time of Arrival of Neurons in the Six Cortical Layers.* This figure shows actual counts of neuroblasts arriving to take up stations in the various layers of the cortex at different developmental stages. Neurons of the lower layers arrive first, followed by neurons to take up progressively higher stations. The last to arrive populate layers I and II.

Maturation of the Neural Systems of the Brain

Once the essential connectivities of the brain have been established, apparently, neural connections continue to be elaborated for many years after birth (Figures 14.7 and 14.8). At the same time the basic modifiability of functional connections decreases in many respects; this is apparent at the level of the individual neuron, whose differentiation probably involves many stages of determination, with progressive restriction of its potential. At the other end of the developmental continuum is the well-known loss of plasticity of the language structures of the brain. After a certain point, language

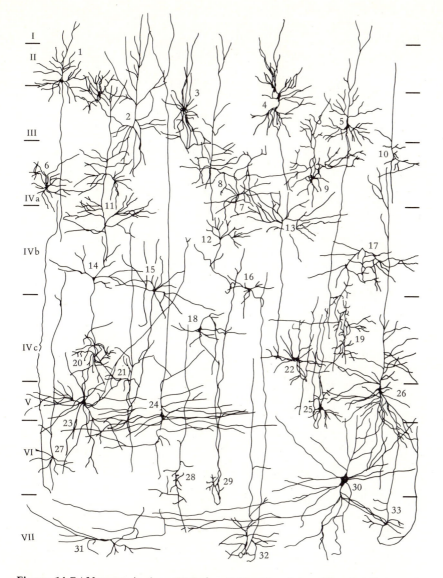

Figure 14.7 / *Neurons in Area 17 Before 6 Months of Age, Showing Extent of Development.* This figure shows the very considerable development of the cortex of the human infant in the primary visual area. Other parts of the cortex, such as the prefrontal granular cortex, are not nearly so advanced. Indeed, they will continue to develop, remaining partially immature, into early adolescence.

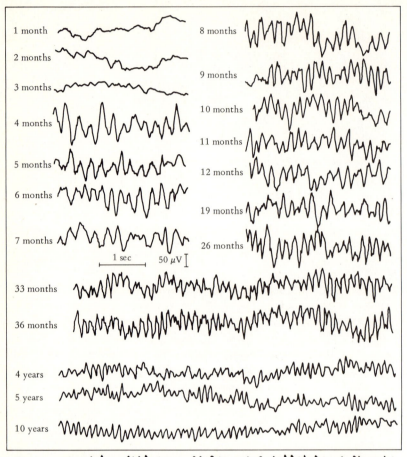

Figure 14.8 / *EEG Records from the Same Child from One Month of Age to 21 Years, Showing Alpha Wave Development.* Using the maturation of the alpha wave as an index of functional development of the cortex, this figure shows that the final adult brainwave patterns, representing mature organization of the brain, emerge only gradually. By age 10, however, the pattern has begun to assume an adult-like appearance.

learning becomes far more difficult, and damage to the language hemisphere that might earlier have been overcome results in severe and irreparable aphasia.

Between these two extremes, environmental circumstances appear to influence the quality of the brain's functioning in maturity. One such environmental factor is, of course, adequate nutrition, specifically during the third trimester of gestation, during the neonatal period, and in the first two years after birth, when brain growth is rapid. (After age three, surprisingly, malnutrition's effects operate primarily on the body; the brain is largely spared.) Not only inadequate intake of protein (and hence of essential amino acids), but also deficiencies in calories during the early period of brain growth may result in impaired maturation and myelination of neurons. Frank reduction in the number of viable cells may occur if the deprivation is severe and prolonged. Adequate vitamins and minerals are also essential to the normative development of the brain.

On the other hand, much sociological evidence suggests that early experience, particularly with regard to language, may constitute a significant factor in the quality of functioning (and, by inference, the quality of the neural connectivities formed) in adulthood. Children deprived of communicative opportunities compare unfavorably in their capacity for cognitive operations with children who have enjoyed a rich linguistic environment in their early years. If this hypothesis proves to be the case, it would seem to imply that the brain depends in some important respects on appropriate environmental challenge to reach its optimum neural organization. Whether early experiential deprivation can be overcome through later enrichment of experiential opportunity has not yet been adequately tested.

Summary

Early in the development of the embryo, a neural tube corresponding to the spinal cord is formed. The cells lining its walls and roof, which constitute a part of the ectodermal layer, differentiate into neuroblasts (immature neurons) and glial cells, and then migrate away from the wall of the tube to take up their genetically designated positions within the developing central nervous system. Eventually the head end of the tube enlarges to form the two lateral ventricles, which in turn become the source of the cells that form the two hemispheres. Neurons continue throughout the gestation period to multiply and migrate to their ultimate stations, ceasing to multiply at about the time of birth.

At birth, however, only certain essential neural structures have matured to a functional level. Much of the brain establishes its functional relations only gradually during infancy. Most brain structures do not become functional until their neurons have developed myelinated axons, and myelination occurs only after synaptic contact has been made with other neurons. At that point, dendritic processes quickly begin to sprout. If axonal contact with appropriate target neurons is not established, a neuron dies off. Thus many more neuroblasts are formed and migrate than are actually required, or are present in the mature brain. In cortical tissues the larger pyramidal cells migrate first, establishing the basic "wiring diagram" of the brain; the smaller neurons of the more superficial cortical layers take up their stations later.

The mechanisms underlying neural migration, and the projection of axons to their appropriate targets, are the subject of a good deal of highly sophisticated research. Of particular interest is the process by which the axon makes its way past countless inappropriate target cells and eventually recognizes its appointed target cell. Target neurons that fail to be found in this process also die off.

After the essential connectivities of the brain have been established (largely before birth), neural connections apparently continue to be formed until well into adolescence, partly under the influence of developmental learning experiences. During this ripening of the brain, there appear to be critical periods for certain functions, after which learning may prove considerably more difficult. In general, the plasticity of the brain appears to diminish over the childhood years, and environmental challenge becomes less effective as a molding force. Whether or not deficits resulting from early experiential or nutritional deprivation can be overcome in later years is still under investigation.

Chapter 15 / *The Clinical Perspective: What Can Go Wrong with the Brain?*

The psychotic disorders are functional rather than organic, in that their origin appears to be biochemical rather than a matter of structural damage. Both schizophrenia and the psychotic depressions appear to have a strong genetic component, and to be treatable with medication in the absence of psychotherapy. The psychotic depressions are now thought to consist of several subgroups involving differing neurochemical defects and appropriate chemical treatments. The manic disorder is considered distinct in its behavioral manifestation and its treatment, but it too seems to have a strong genetic component. The organic disorders include the epilepsies; neurological dysfunctions due to brain damage suffered before, during or after birth; and more subtle dysfunctions that may reflect neural loss due to brain poisoning of environmental or drug-related origin. Organic disorders may have a wide spectrum of behavioral manifestations, from hyperactivity to a variety of forms of mental retardation. It is not clear to what extent defects resulting from early trauma or nutritional deficiency can be overcome through later interventions.

Our growing knowledge of the brain has begun to shed light on some of the psychological difficulties we as humans are heir to, and on the bodily impairments that can ensue when unfortunate circumstances are too severe in their psychological impact. It is accepted today that mind and body are mutually interpenetrating and interacting entities: disorders of the body or the brain can severely disturb normal adaptive behavior, while difficulties in our emotional lives can significantly disturb bodily functions and even produce organic impairment.

This chapter will explore current knowledge, ongoing research, and theory concerning the major psychological disturbances which apparently afflict the human species alone. This massive topic will be broken down into several areas. We will look first at the major psychoses — schizophrenia and the psychotic mood disorders of depression and mania. Next we will consider the organic difficulties, in which neurological impairment or defect can result in psychological impairment and behavioral limitation or distortion. Our third area of concern will be the psychosomatic disorders. Finally we will discuss the relation of brain function to such more specifically mental afflictions as the psychological addictions (to eating, gambling, and other forms of emotional dependency), the phobias, the obsessions and psychological compulsions, paranoia, and uncontrollable aggression.

The Major Psychoses

It is one thing to understand difficulties that arise from known brain damage; it is quite another when there is no evidence of structural damage or brain malformation. Since its inception psychiatry has struggled with this problem, especially with regard to schizophrenia, which causes people of perfectly clear mind (awareness of who and where they are, and the date and time) to behave in ways that are bizarre and incomprehensible to normal people. The very incomprehensibility of schizophrenics' disordered behavior led in the past to accusations of witchcraft or demonic possession. Today we are beginning to understand that schizophrenia's cause is not in the overt physical structure or connectivities of the brain, but in its chemistry, its metabolic processes, its functioning. Hence the term *functional psychosis* for this type of disorder.

Another functional disorder with no overt basis in organic impairment causes some people to become unaccountably depressed, or so euphorically energetic that they embarrass others and frequently exhibit extremely poor judgment. The former condition is known as *endogenous depression* signifying that the mood state appears to arise from within, often suddenly, on the basis of no apparent change in life circumstances. The second condition, *mania,* frequently shifts unaccountably to its diametric opposite, a depressive mood behaviorally indistinguishable from endogenous depression.

Other comparable functional disorders are infantile and early childhood autism, certain cases of childhood hyperactivity that appear to be ameliorated by amphetamines, psychotic conditions resulting from nutritional deficiency (such as pellagra, now recognized as a niacin deficiency) or toxic substances, and the like. All these functional disorders are beginning to be understood as both chemical in etiology and eventually successfully treatable with medications.

Functional psychosis. A psychosis which appears to have no tangible neurological defect as its basis; differentiated from organic disorders.

Endogenous depression (en-DOJ-i-nus). A depression which appears unrelated to present life circumstances, hence arising presumably from some altered conditions within the brain.

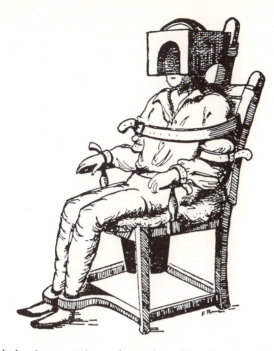

The bizarre behavior sometimes shown by schizophrenics often led in the past to barbarous treatments, all in the effort to be helpful. Today we have begun to understand the nature of the brain malfunction involved, and to adopt a more sophisticated approach to treatment.

The prospects are not so favorable for the true psychological disorders, the frank organic disorders, or the deleterious effects of our way of life.

The Schizophrenic Disorder

At least 1 percent of the population of every society in the world is recognizably afflicted with schizophrenia (Snyder, 1975). Many more people may suffer from the disorder in subthreshold form, whose characteristic manifestations are too minor to call attention to themselves. Let us look briefly at the characteristic manifestations of schizophrenia before considering its relation to brain dysfunction.

There appear to be two differentiable populations of schizophrenics. One form of the disorder appears early in life and gradually worsens after middle adolescence, unresponsive to all known remedies; the other tends to strike later in life (seldom before late adolescence) and characteristically comes on rather suddenly, though preceded by telltale warning symptoms. In cases of the latter type, *spontaneous remission* (disappearance of symptoms without treatment) is common, and the effect of medical treatment is in many instances seemingly miraculous; the patient can leave the hospital and return to normal life, with or without ongoing self-administered medication. The symptoms of the two forms of the disorder in its florid (full-blown) manifestation are very similar, and current thinking attributes both to faulty brain chemistry, rather than organic impairment or such *exogenous* (external) factors as early psychic damage inflicted by a "schizophrenogenic mother."

The most characteristic manifestation of schizophrenia is simply the disappearance of something we ordinarily take so for granted (like the air we breathe without noticing it until it is absent) that it passes unnoticed. That something is normality, the broad spectrum of behaviors we have come to regard as normal, expressive of normal thought and feeling, without bothering to define the concept further. It is the unexpectedness of the schizophrenic's deviation from such normality — the bizarreness, unaccountability, and irrationality of the things schizophrenics occasionally do and say —that calls immediate attention to them as suffering from a mental disorder. It is as if the principles that typically guide behavior, as well as habitual and conventional modes of speaking, thinking, and feeling, are oddly absent, permitting behavior and expressed thoughts whose abnormality or unconventionality the patient is not in the least aware of. Schizophrenics thus "don't make sense" to other people (and their odd behavior helps us identify just what it is that we deem normal).

On investigation, it often becomes apparent that what has happened is that the schizophrenic has been following a private train of thought, unrelated to the present circumstances; thus the resulting behavior is out of context, and often seems bizarre only because it is out of place. At other times the fantasy or train of thought is itself frankly irrational. Nevertheless, self-awareness is fully intact, as are the general mental faculties measured by IQ tests. Schizophrenics' intelligence is employed on behalf of a fantasy rather than the shared reality others perceive.

There were once thought to be as many different types of schizophrenia as there were major symptom categories. More recently we have come to realize that the symptoms are often interchangeable. For example, a patient may slip unaccountably from a *catatonic state* of stuporous waxy immobility into hyperalert paranoia, and thence into other manifestations, suggesting that they all represent the same disease process. It is also noteworthy that many of the symp-

Spontaneous remission. Disappearance of psychotic symptoms in the absence of treatment.

Exogenous (*ex-OJ-i-nus*). Referring to factors in the environmental circumstances, rather than within the organism, as the source of difficulty.

Catatonic state. A schizophrenic symptom characterized by bodily rigidity and immobility in which peculiar postures may be held for hours.

toms may be not at all evident. Many schizophrenics are difficult to characterize as such, seeming perfectly normal most of the time. Thus, unless the doctor asks, a patient may give no hint that he or she is at the moment hearing voices (*auditory hallucination*).

The issue is well illustrated in an experimental study conducted by Rosenhan (1973), who managed to have eight subjects, all perfectly normal people, admitted to various mental hospitals across the country (both state institutions and small private university hospitals). On admission, all eight indicated only the vague complaint that they had been experiencing auditory hallucinations. After admission they acted entirely normal and did nothing to further indicate psychosis. In every instance they found themselves diagnosed schizophrenic, a diagnosis accepted by the entire hospital staff. Moreover, they found themselves trapped by their own ploy, since most of them found it difficult to secure discharges; and when they finally were released, it was with medical records reading "schizophrenia, in remission."

Involuntary commitment to a mental hospital used to be a simple matter, if one wanted a relative "put away." Exposure of this circumstance to public attention has recently led to the belated passage of new statutes seeking to protect the rights of the person for whom commitment is sought. However, commitment can still be obtained in some states merely on the word of a physician. No such problem would present itself if schizophrenia were as infallibly diagnosed as measles or cancer; but it is not as yet. One result is that many people have been diagnosed schizophrenic in the past who were actually suffering from other disorders, thus vastly confounding attempts to study the disorder.

The World Health Organization recently sponsored a transcultural pilot study of 1202 psychiatric patients in Colombia, Czechoslovakia, Denmark, India, Nigeria, China, the Soviet Union, the United Kingdom, and the United States, seeking to lay the groundwork for international epidemiological studies of schizophrenia and other disorders. Analysis of data from these nine countries revealed nine criteria universally employed in the diagnosis of schizophrenia, as distinguished from other psychiatric disorders:

1. Absence of normal emotional response (called "flattened affect" in the United States)
2. Poor insight
3. The delusion that one's thoughts are being read by others
4. Withdrawal from personal contacts (difficulty on the part of the interviewer in establishing rapport with the patient)

Auditory hallucination. The hearing of voices in their absence.

5. Incoherent though fluent speech (called "word salads" in the United States)

6. Providing information of doubtful credibility

7. Bizarre delusions, incomprehensible to the interviewer

8. Widespread delusions, affecting many aspects of the patient's life

9. "Nihilistic delusions" that parts of the body are missing, decaying, or dead (Carpenter, Strauss, and Bartko, 1973)

There was also found to be consensus that three negative criteria — elation, depression, and early waking in the morning — rule out a diagnosis of schizophrenia, tending instead to characterize the affective psychoses.

The authors of the study state that these criteria constitute not a definition of schizophrenia, but a useful method of identifying "patients who would be commonly considered schizophrenic in many centers." This method can be rendered more or less stringent for experimental purposes by requiring more or fewer criteria to be satisfied by those selected for study. In view of the absence of any clearly defined organic pathological indices, it may seem remarkable that there is even this much diagnostic consensus across widely differing cultures with different medical and psychiatric traditions. This list of criteria is not necessarily ideal (note that it omits the single most easily assessed criterion, auditory hallucinations). It nevertheless demonstrates considerable cross-cultural agreement that schizophrenia is a psychiatric disorder clearly differentiable from the manic-depressive syndrome and the endogenous depressions.

In the search for causative factors, it was hoped for a while that some psychotogenic chemical would be found in the urine or body fluids of schizophrenics. Many such substances have been reported, in fact, only to prove to have been false hopes. New findings, including reports that blood cleansing through hemodialysis (the artificial-kidney machine) ameliorates the symptoms of schizophrenia, suggest that such a substance may yet be found. It appears, meanwhile, that certain chemical substances attack the symptoms at their source in the brain, while others can quickly exacerbate the symptoms of schizophrenia and bring on florid schizophrenic breakdowns in patients in remission. These substances appear to be the best clue thus far to exactly what is wrong with the functioning of the brain in schizophrenics. (See Figure 15.1 for some basic neurochemistry.)

Eugen Bleuler (1911) distinguished two types of symptoms in

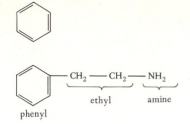

This is six carbon atoms in a benzene ring, with a hydrogen atom (not shown) attached to each. Altogether it is a phenyl group ("*fee*-nil").

phenyl — CH₂ — CH₂ — NH₂ (ethyl, amine)

This is *phenylethylamine*, a likely neurotransmitter in the brain. C = carbon, H = hydrogen, N = nitrogen. Phenyl + ethyl + amine (3 groups).

HO, HO catechol — CH₂ — CH₂ — NH₂

This is *dopamine*. OH (or HO) is a hydroxyl group. A phenyl group with two hydroxyl groups replacing the hydrogen atom is a catechol group.

HO, HO — CH — CH₂ — NH₂ (OH)

This is *norepinephrine*. The carbon in the beta position has been hydroxylated. Dopamine is the chemical precursor of norepinephrine.

— CH₂ — CH — NH₂ (CH₃)

This is *amphetamine*, a dangerously addicting drug, a stimulant to the brain and hunger suppressant. CH₃ is a methyl group. The carbon in the alpha position has been methylated.

CH₃O, CH₃O, CH₃O — CH₂ — CH₂ — NH₂

This is *mescaline*, a drug that produces colorful visual hallucinations. CH₃O is a methoxy group. The phenyl group has been tri-methoxylated.

HOOC — CH₂ — CH₂ — CH₂ — NH₂

This is GABA (gamma-aminobutyric acid), an important inhibitory neurotransmitter in the brain.

HOOC — CH₂ — CH₂ — CH — NH₂ (COOH)

This is glutamic acid, a very prevalent excitatory neurotransmitter in the brain.

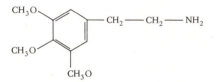

Figure 15.1 / *A Short Course in Neurochemistry*. A careful study of this chart will familiarize you with some important basic neurochemistry. Organic molecules are so amazingly various because molecules can be built from simple building blocks, such as the phenyl group, whose hydrogen atoms can be readily replaced (through appropriate enzymes) with a large number of substitutes, such as NH_2, CH_3, CH_3O, COOH, and simple OH, the hydroxyl group. Once one is familiar with this principle, and with the many building blocks of this sort, the long chemical names, such as gamma-aminobutyric acid, can be readily translated into a structural formula.

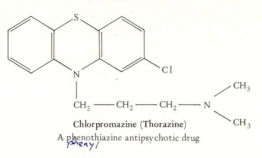

Chlorpromazine (Thorazine)
A phenothiazine antipsychotic drug

Figure 15.2 / *Structural Formula of Chlorpromazine.* Here is the structural formula for the "miracle drug" that was found to specifically block the symptoms of schizoprenia, rather than merely sedating the patient. It was the first of a long series of such antipsychotic drugs and has done much to bring about a breakthrough in our understanding of this neurological disorder.

schizophrenics: fundamental symptoms and accessory symptoms. The fundamental symptoms Bleuler identified are thought disorder, blunted affect, withdrawal from human contact, and autistic behavior; the accessory symptoms — often more spectacular, though not always present — are hallucinations, paranoid ideation, grandiosity, and belligerence. A careful double-blind study sponsored by the National Institutes of Mental Health and the Veterans Administration (Klein and Davis, 1969) compared the effects on a large number of schizophrenics from many hospitals of a class of drugs called *phenothiazines* (see Figure 15.2), and, on the other hand, sedatives such as phenobarbital and such antianxiety drugs as diazepam (Valium) and chlordiazepoxide (Librium). The study found that the phenothiazines specifically ameliorate schizophrenic symptoms, which the other drugs do not, and that the phenothiazines are more efficacious against fundamental symptoms than against accessory symptoms.

Of the drugs that tend to bring on schizophrenic symptoms, and to exacerbate them when present, the most striking examples are the *amphetamines* (called "speed" by those who purchase them on the street). Ingested in large doses over several weeks, these substances produce a condition indistinguishable from paranoid schizophrenia (Ellinwood, 1967), which disappears within a few days if the drug ingestion is stopped. It had been argued that this represented the triggering of a latent schizophrenia through the activating effect of amphetamines. To test this notion, Angrist and Gershon (1970) and Griffith, Cavanaugh, Held, and Oates (1972) administered progressively larger doses of amphetamines to volunteer subjects selected for absence of any evidence of schizophrenia or schizoid tendencies. All the subjects became floridly psychotic after one to four days. The same drugs also reliably precipitate schizophrenic breakdown in patients whose symptoms are in remission, suggesting that the effect of amphetamines results from their action on the true chemical substrates of the disease.

These two pieces of evidence — that certain chemicals protect against the symptoms of schizophrenia, while others appear to produce them — enormously encouraged research into the chemical basis of the schizophrenic disorder. Something was clearly going on in the brain of the schizophrenic that was not going on in the normal person, or in the schizophrenic in remission. Identifying that something has been the focus of research efforts ever since, but the final answer is not yet in. Investigation has centered on the neurotransmitters (dopamine, norepinephrine, serotonin, and acetylcholine. The activity of the first two has been found to be directly affected by the antischizophrenic drugs and (in an opposite direction) by the amphetamines. (See Figures 15.3 and 15.4)

The specific action of the antischizophrenic drugs on the neurotransmitters is unknown. However, those phenothiazines that are effective in treating schizophrenic symptoms increase the amounts of certain metabolites of dopamine and norepinephrine (available) *because of blocking* at brain centers, while those that are ineffective against schizophrenic symptoms do not. Another antischizophrenic drug, the butyrophenone haloperidol (which is effective at much lower doses) is even more effective at raising the level of these metabolites, indicating increased brain turnover of the neurotransmitters (Figure 15.5). This suggests that the antischizophrenic drugs block the postsynaptic receptor sites of these two catecholamines, thereby causing more neurotransmitters to be called up via a feedback loop to the cells manufacturing them. These cells fire faster, thus synthesizing more of the substance and resulting in the production of more metabolites. This suggestion is supported by the finding that the antischizophrenic drugs do accelerate the synthesis and turnover of dopamine in the rat in proportion to their effectiveness in reducing schizophrenic symptoms in the human being (Nyback, Borzecki, and Sedvall, 1968).

Another finding that seems to implicate dopamine in schizophrenia is the discovery that the phenothiazines, when taken in massive doses over time, tend to produce *extrapyramidal* side effects, specifically the symptoms of Parkinson's disease (resting tremor of hands and arms, difficulty in initiating movement, masklike immobility of facial features, scarcely audible and slow speech,

Extrapyramidal. Referring to the older motor systems of the brain that handle highly overlearned, automated behavior such as walking.

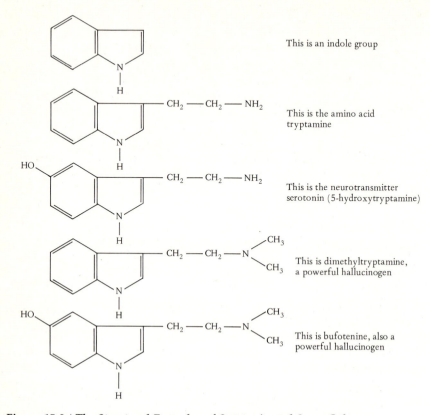

This is an indole group

This is the amino acid
tryptamine

This is the neurotransmitter
serotonin (5-hydroxytryptamine)

This is dimethyltryptamine,
a powerful hallucinogen

This is bufotenine, also a
powerful hallucinogen

Figure 15.3 / *The Structural Formulas of Serotonin and Some Other*
Indoleamines. Serotonin is based on the indole group, rather than the
catechol group, as are norepinephrine and dopamine. LSD, the powerful
hallucinogenic drug, appears to achieve its effects by blocking serotonin
activity. It is interesting, then, to observe that two other powerful hallucinogens, dimethyltryptamine and bufotenine, have formulas very similar to serotonin (5-hydroxytryptamine).

and the like). These symptoms are alleviated by treatment with the
dopamine precursor L-Dopa. (Dopamine itself has difficulty crossing the blood-brain barrier.) It is accepted that Parkinsonism directly reflects an absence of sufficient dopamine in the caudate and
putamen, headwaters of the extrapyramidal motor system cascade.
If the phenothiazines and butyrophenones block the action of dopamine (in the striatum and elsewhere), Parkinsonian effects presumably might be expected. This dopamine theory of schizophrenia
is also supported by the finding that L-Dopa brings on

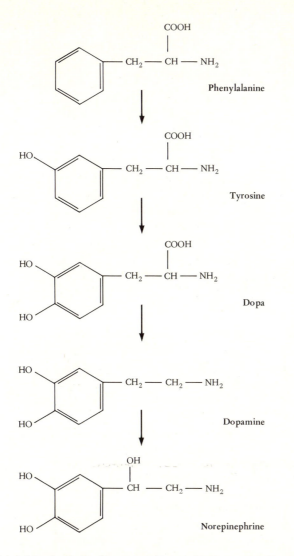

Figure 15.4 / *A Metabolic Pathway Leading to Dopamine and Norepinephrine.* For each step in this chemical pathway there is a different specific enzyme catalyzing the change from one chemical substance to the next.

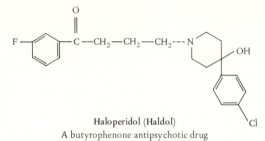

Haloperidol (Haldol)
A butyrophenone antipsychotic drug

Figure 15.5 / *The Structural Formula for Haloperidol, a More Potent Antipsychotic than Chlorpromazine.* The butyrophenones, including haloperidol, are a newly discovered class of drugs blocking schizophrenic symptoms and requiring very much smaller doses to achieve the same result.

schizophrenia-like symptoms in some Parkinsonism patients (Yaryura-Tobias, Diamond, and Merlis, 1970).

The action of the amphetamines is thought to be of two kinds: (1) increasing the amount of norepinephrine and dopamine released at adrenergic synapses and (2) interfering with the re-uptake of the released transmitter. Both serve to increase the amount available at the synapses and potentiate the activity of the systems — exactly the opposite of the effect now thought to be produced by the antischizophrenic drugs. Differing effects on different kinds of behavior in the rat have been associated with the two *stereoisomers* of amphetamine, dextro- and levo-amphetamine. Careful studies have demonstrated that the dextroisomer is ten times as effective as its levo counterpart, l-amphetamine, in stimulating locomotor activity, but only about twice as effective in producing compulsive gnawing. This difference corresponds nicely with the tenfold greater capacity of d-amphetamine to block catecholamine re-uptake at norepinephrine terminals; at the dopamine terminals, meanwhile, the effects of the two amphetamine isomeric forms differ very little. These studies suggest that compulsive gnawing behavior is dopamine-related, while the general activation effect is norepinephrine-related.

In the human, d-amphetamine (Dexedrine) is about five times more potent than l-amphetamine as a central stimulant (Prinzmetal and Alles, 1940), again suggesting that the activating effect of this drug is related to its action at norepinephrine terminals in the brain. If it is assumed that the alerting response is associated with the activation of the cortex, this finding makes sense "because the cerebral cortex is extensively innervated by norepinephrine fibers

Stereoisomers. Alternate structural forms of a given organic molecule.

but receives no dopamine innervation" (Snyder, 1975, p. 729). (There is some dispute over the latter point.) This reasoning also leads us to suspect that, in producing psychosis, the amphetamines exert their primary effect on dopaminergic neurons somewhere other than the cortex.

Interestingly, comparisons of these two isomers of amphetamine in the treatment of hyperactive children with "minimal brain dysfunction" (Wender, 1971) found little difference in effect (Snyder and Meyerhoff, 1973; Arnold, Wender, McClosky, and Snyder, 1972), apparently implicating dopamine rather than norepinephrine neurons in this disorder. On the other hand, Gilles de la Tourette's syndrome, characterized by compulsive scatological language and facial tics, is greatly accentuated by d-amphetamine and not at all by l-amphetamine, suggesting a norepinephrine dysfunction. Confounding the picture somewhat is the discovery that this curious disorder is most effectively treated by the potent antischizophrenic drug haloperidol. which

Another type of evidence points to a hyperactive dopamine system as the critical factor in schizophrenia. Wise and Stein (1973) examined the brains of schizophrenic patients shortly after death and found a significant deficiency in the enzyme that catalyzes the transformation of dopamine into norepinephrine (dopamine beta hydroxylase). A deficiency in this enzyme would appear to lead to an abundance of dopamine, the norepinephrine precursor, and thus might be a significant factor in the disorder. (The validity of this study was later questioned (Wyatt, Schwartz, Erdelyi, and Barchas, 1975), but Wise and Stein's reply appears convincing.) It is of great interest that three patients diagnosed as paranoid schizophrenics, all of whom committed suicide, showed no deficiency in this enzyme, a finding that casts doubt on the validity of treating paranoid cases just like cases of chronic, undifferentiated schizophrenia.

If antipsychotic drugs were to produce their effect by blockading dopamine receptors in the brain, they would presumably do so by attaching to the dopamine receptors in the postsynaptic membrane, making these sites unavailable to dopamine. Horn and Snyder (1971) demonstrated that the preferred conformation of the effective phenothiazines, as determined by X-ray crystallography, can be largely superimposed on the preferred conformation of dopamine (Figure 15.6). The chlorine atom shown on one of the side rings of the phenothiazine molecule in the case of chlorpromazine appears to tilt the side chain toward it. Those phenothiazines that have little or no antischizophrenic action lack this feature, and hence presumably have a fully extended side chain and less effectively mimic the

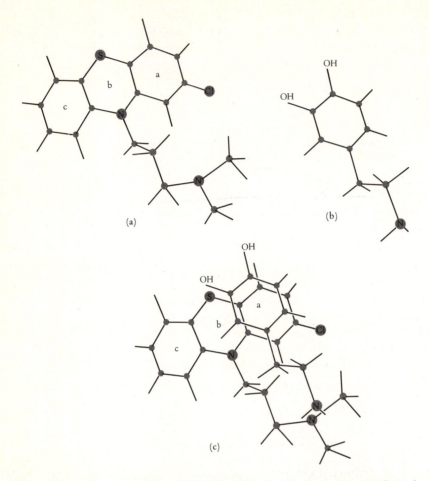

Figure 15.6 / *Superimposition of the Phenothiazine Conformation on that of Dopamine.* The phenothiazine drugs appear to achieve their result in blocking schizophrenic symptoms by interfering with the brain's dopamine circuits, perhaps by replacing dopamine at its receptor sites in the postsynaptic membrane. It is interesting that when the conformations of the two drugs are superimposed, they are in part almost identical in structure.

dopamine conformation (Snyder, 1975). Moreover, the therapeutically effective phenothiazines have three carbon atoms separating the ring system from the nitrogen of the amine radical (as in Figure 15.2). Phenothiazines with two-carbon side chains prove ineffective as antipsychotic agents. Thus some support is gained for the theory of the proposed action of these drugs at the molecular level in the brain.

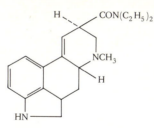

Figure 15.7 / *The Structural Formula of d-Lysergic Acid Diethylamide* **(LSD).**
When the astonishing power of LSD to produce strange psychological
phenomena became known, it gave strong impetus to the theory that
schizophrenic symptoms are the result of some such chemical in the blood.
On sober reflection, it was realized that the LSD symptoms do not correspond to those of schizophrenia.

The Psychotogenic Substance Theory

The discovery of the astonishing psychotogenic power of the drug
LSD (Figure 15.7) raised the interesting possibility of an endogenous hallucinogenic substance in the brains of schizophrenics
directly responsible for some schizophrenic symptoms. However, a
careful study of the effects of psychedelic drugs such as LSD and
mescaline shows them to be clearly differentiable from those of
schizophrenia (Hollister, 1962); furthermore, schizophrenics receiving these drugs report the experience as quite different from the
symptoms of their disorder (Chloden, Kurland, and Savage, 1955).
However, the observation that the structural formula of mescaline — perhaps the oldest known hallucinogen — is quite similar to
that of the catecholamines (Figure 15.8) made the notion of the
schizophrenic as a walking hallucinogen factory quite persuasive.
As we have noted, many early reports of substances found in the
urine or body fluids of schizophrenics turned out on further study
to be false hopes, attributable to treatments the patients had been
undergoing or to other conditions. Still, there is no way of easily
explaining the schizophrenic's ability to hallucinate voices, and the
hallucinogen theory has by no means been ruled out.

Almost twenty years ago it was reported that a substance similar
to bufotenine, a powerful hallucinogenic drug, could be found in
the urine of schizophrenics but not that of normals. (This substance
is a derivative of serotonin, an indoleamine, and not of the
catecholamines.) More recently it has been found that normals excrete small amounts of bufotenine in their urine, while untreated
schizophrenics excrete considerable amounts (Sirex and Marini,

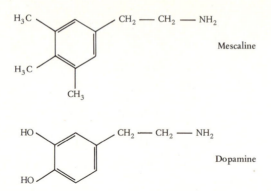

Figure 15.8 / *The Structural Formulas of Mescaline and Dopamine Compared.* Another suggestion that schizophrenic symptoms might represent the presence of endogenous hallucinogens in the blood came from the striking structural similarity of mescaline and dopamine. However, the hallucinations produced by mescaline are almost exclusively visual, while those of schizophrenia are almost exclusively auditory (voices).

1969). Changes in diet were found not to affect the amount excreted.

Further research has revealed that when *monoamine oxidase* (MAO) *inhibitor* is administered, other serotonin-related compounds appear in high concentrations in the urine of schizophrenics shortly before or during florid symptom outbreaks, and decline in concentration with the amelioration of the symptoms. Moreover, changes in thought content were found to correlate with variations in the concentration of these compounds (Himwich, Narasimhachair, Heller *et al.*, 1970). Treatment of normals with MAO inhibitors produced no psychotic symptoms. These and other studies lend support to the hypothesis that the *methylation* of serotonin, blocking its effective action at receptor sites, may play a role in schizophrenia (Marczynski, 1976). Also supportive is the finding that methysergide, a powerful and specific serotonin antagonist, markedly aggravates the symptoms of autistic and schizophrenic children (Fish, Campbell, Shapiro *et al.*, 1969).

More recently, interest has turned to the peptide substances known as *endorphins* or *enkephalins.* When the blood of schizophrenics is cleansed by means of dialysis they may become symptom-free with no other treatment. When the dialysis fluid from these patients is analyzed, there is found a very large decrease in leucine endorphin (one of two major types of endorphin), as well as a decrease in tryptophan, the precursor of sero-

Monoamine oxidase inhibitor. A chemical substance that interferes with the normal breakdown of the monoamine neurotransmitters, resulting in their buildup and thus accentuating their synaptic effect.

Methylation. The chemical transformation resulting from replacement of a hydrogen atom (H) by a methyl group (CH_3).

Endorphins. Peptide substances (chains of linked amino acids too short to be classed as proteins) which appear to be natural opioid substances mediating analgesia and euphoria.

Enkephalins (en-KEFF-a-lins). Very small peptide substances which appear to have opioid activity and may be the basic substances used by the brain to control the pain response.

tonin, which supports Marczynski's theory of serotonin deficiency. *[handwritten, circled: dopamine excess]*

Wheat gluten has recently been proposed as a possible pathogenic factor in schizophrenia on the grounds that children suffering from celiac disease, a chronic digestive disturbance caused by improper absorption of fats, are intolerant of wheat gluten and exhibit schizophrenia-like personalities (inwardness, negativism paranoia, stereotyped and repetitive behavior). Eliminating gluten from the diets of these children diminishes such behavioral characteristics. The pathogenicity of gluten was recently tested by administering a special gluten drink to 14 schizophrenic patients; others were given a placebo containing soy flour. The "gluten challenge" was introduced only after treatment with antipsychotic medication had begun to reduce symptoms (Singh and Kay, 1976). The result was significant exacerbation of symptoms during the period the patients were being fed gluten. The authors concluded that wheat gluten is pathogenic in schizophrenia, though individual susceptibility may vary: the effect was more marked in the more seriously ill patients with less favorable treatment outcomes. How gluten might contribute to the schizophrenic process is unknown.

A Proposed Theory of Schizophrenia

Building on the hypothesis that the antischizophrenic action of the phenothiazines, the butyrophenones, and other major tranquilizers is to blockade dopamine receptors (the most promising current hypothesis), Steven Matthysse of Massachusetts General Hospital has suggested a very provocative, though speculative, way of understanding what occurs in the brain in schizophrenia. First, the *nigrostriatal system*, which sends dopamine to the basal ganglia, is presumed to function normally in the selective disinhibition of "motor commands" continually arriving from the cortex, thus transforming them into action (which is then modulated and subjected to sensory feedback control by the motor cortex). Too much dopaminergic activity in the basal ganglia allows such motor commands more unrestricted access to motoric expression, as exemplified by the *choreiform movements* that may be accentuated by l-Dopa administration. When there is too little dopaminergic activity, as in Parkinson's disease, voluntary movement decisions are difficult to put into action. In keeping with this view, it has been observed that neurons in the caudate nucleus that are ordinarily hyperpolarized and unresponsive to cortical stimulation undergo spontaneous depolarizing shifts of as much as 5 millivolts, lasting several

[handwritten margin note: dopamine excess / serotonin deficiency]

Nigrostriatal system (ni-grow-strye-ATE-al). **The dopamine system projecting from the substantia nigra to the striatum.**

Choreiform movements (kor-REE-i-form). **Involuntary movements of the limbs and facial muscles due to a neurological disorder.**

minutes, during which they do respond to cortical stimulation (Ernst, 1965; Iversen, 1975). High-frequency stimulation of the substantia nigra produces similar depolarizing shifts in caudate neurons, resulting in increased firing rates. Thus there appears to be a mechanism in the basal ganglia that selects from among subthreshold motor commands those that are to be implemented; all the rest remain suppressed, and dopamine is the means of their disinhibition.

Matthysse's radical new idea is that dopamine plays a similar role with respect to ideation and feelings. It is evident that maintenance of the unity and focus of the attention field requires massive inhibition of extraneous thoughts, which presumably remain preconscious until and unless they are "disinhibited" to the point of reaching the threshold of awareness. Matthysse suggests that "preconscious thoughts and fantasies are like subthreshold motor commands; that some structure, analogous to the basal ganglia, releases them to enter the stream of consciousness; that dopamine neurons regulate the threshold for emergence of ideas, as they do the emergence of actions; that this disinhibitory system is overactive in schizophrenia; and that neuroleptic drugs increase 'repression' of distracting ideas by blocking dopamine synapses" (Matthysse, 1975, p. 734).

The brain region, analogous to the basal ganglia, where dopaminergic disinhibition of thoughts and feelings might take place could be the *nucleus accumbens,* which forms a forward extension of the basal ganglia into the septal region and has important dopaminergic innervation (Ungerstedt, 1971). Its major afferent input, however, is from widespread regions of the limbic system, rather than the neocortex.

Nucleus accumbens. **A nucleus in the septal region considered to function in connection with the limbic system.**

If schizophrenic symptoms are less motor than ideational and emotional, the antischizophrenic drugs may not be having their effect in the basal ganglia at all, but in some other region where parallel disinhibitory processes take place. If antischizophrenic drugs with a more regionally selective effect could be developed, the Parkinsonian side effects of phenothiazine on the basal ganglia neurons could be avoided. Such a discovery might also suggest a more intuitively acceptable locus of origin of schizophrenic symptoms.

Evidence has recently been found — contrary to earlier belief — that there are dopaminergic terminals in the cortex. Thierry, Blanc, and Sobel (1973) destroyed norepinephrine pathways to the rat cortex both surgically and chemically, and still found evidence of the synthesis of dopamine from tyrosine, indicating the presence of

dopaminergic terminals in the cortex. The cell bodies of these dopaminergic neurons have not been located, but cortical dopamine
levels do not seem to be affected by lesions of the medial forebrain
bundle in the lateral hypothalamus, severing the nigrostriatal tracts.
The possibility has not been ruled out that the terminals found are
those of dopaminergic interneurons within the neocortex. Should
this prove to be the case, it would coincide well with our intuitive
sense that the ideational disturbances in schizophrenia must have a
cortical counterpart to their limbic-system emotional-responsive
and evaluative component.

A search is underway for dopaminergic pathways other than
those originating in the substantia nigra and terminating in the
striatum, of interest not only to those working on schizophrenia but
also to those investigating the brain dysfunction underlying the endogenous depressions. According to Hockman and Bieger (1976, p.
280):

There is growing interest in projections to the limbic system regions, e.g.,
the "paleocortical" gray of the forebrain, the fundus striati, the interstitial
nucleus of the diagonal band, the nucleus centralis of the amygdala, and
the cingulate cortex. . . . Thus investigations into the pathobiology of
brain DA neurons now form an important part of research strategies aimed
at establishing a neurochemically based, unifying nosology of mood disorders. The desirability of such attempts is all the more apparent if one con-
siders the large diagnostic vacillations between the so-called undifferentiated subcategories of schizophrenia and manic-depressive syndromes.

The Affective Disorders

There appear to be three major groups of mood disorders: (1) the endogenous depressions, (2) the manic-depressive disorder, and (3)
the neurotic depressions. The first two appear to have a strong (if
not exclusive) genetic component; the third appears to have none,
and is perhaps best thought of as specifically developmental in origin, the product of life experience or "environment." It is the first
two that are of primary interest to the physiological psychologist,
since they appear to represent specific brain dysfunctions or primary neurological disorders, even though their manifestations appear to arise from biochemical rather than structural defects.

Differentiating the cyclic manic-depressive dysfunction from the
depressive syndrome proper has been greatly facilitated by the discovery that the manic-depressive condition is very effectively

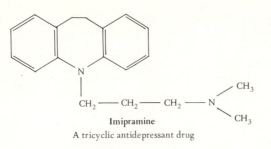

Imipramine
A tricyclic antidepressant drug

Figure 15.9 / *The Structural Formula of the Tricyclic Antidepressant Imipramine.* The endogenous depressions are known to represent a quite different class of disorder from schizophrenia and appear to respond not to chlorpromazine, but to another class of drugs. Yet if the formula for imipramine, used in treating psychotic depression, is compared with that of chlorpromazine, a striking similarity will be noted (see Figure 15.2).

treated with lithium carbonate; by contrast, the endogenous depressions are unresponsive to lithium, but responsive to the tricyclic antidepressants (Figure 15.9) and the monoamine oxidase inhibitors, which in turn are ineffective in manic-depression. The so-called neurotic depressions are unresponsive to either type of medication (and possibly should not be considered disease entities at all), but respond well to certain supportive kinds of psychotherapy — to which the others, the true mental diseases, are quite impervious and unresponsive. (It is apparently as dangerous to attempt to help a person afflicted with endogenous depression psychotherapeutically, without the use of medication, as it is to attempt to help a neurotic depressive with medication alone.)

Before the discovery of the tricyclic antidepressant drugs, the only known effective treatment for endogenous depression was "shock treatment" — a convulsive seizure induced by administering insulin or metrazol, or by projecting an electric current through the head (electroconvulsive therapy). This brutal, primitive, purely empirical treatment for depression has since been largely abandoned. While the therapeutic effect of seizure treatments remained completely unexplained throughout their extended history, there is some evidence now that such treatments might produce their effect by altering the patient's brain chemistry, specifically by increasing levels of amines, particularly of norepinephrine.

This finding lends the support to Schildkraut's classic theory (1965) of the endogenous depressions to the effect that psychotic depression is due to a deficiency of norepinephrine in the brain. While early studies pointed to deficiency in amine synthesis or, alternatively, receptor sensitivity to the amines, a later publication (Schildkraut, 1973) laid the problem specifically at the door of norepinephrine, whose metabolites were viewed as criteria for classifying the depressive disorders. The major support for this hypothesis is that the tricyclic antidepressants, which appear to be particularly helpful in depression of the unipolar endogenous type, were thought to exert their effect by inhibiting norepinephrine re-uptake at the synapse, thus permitting a buildup of the transmitter substance in the brain and potentiating its effect.

Schildkraut also recognized, however, that a parallel buildup of serotonin in the brain by these drugs might be involved, and suggested the possibility that the therapeutic response depends on the relationship between the two. It had been suggested by Carlsson, Corrodi, Fuxe, and Hökfelt (1969) that a buildup of norepinephrine due to interference with its re-uptake mechanism might be responsible for the specific energizing effect of the tricyclic antidepressants, while inhibition of serotonin re-uptake might be responsible for alleviating the depressive mood.

It has been suggested more recently that there may in fact be two types of endogenous depression, one based on a deficiency of norepinephrine, the other on a deficiency of serotonin; the low-serotonin disorders would thus constitute a subgroup within the affective disorders. Low concentrations of serotonin had frequently been reported in the brains of suicide victims — but only some and not others. It had also been discovered that tryptophan, the precursor of serotonin, is an effective antidepressant for some patients but not for others. Recently, Asberg, Thoren, Traskman, Bertilsson, and Ringberger (1976) reported a significantly higher percentage of suicide attempts among depressive patients with low concentrations of the serotonin metabolite 5-hydroxy indoleacetic acid than among those with normal or high concentrations, presumably reflecting a disturbance in serotonin turnover in the suicide-prone. Within the low-serotonin subgroup, the severity of the depression was found to correlate with the concentration of the metabolite.

A quite new approach to affective disorder biochemistry was recently suggested by Sabelli and his co-workers (Sabelli, Mosnain, and Vasquez, 1974), who questioned the validity of the time-honored *Dale's principle* that each neuron makes use of one and only one neurotransmitter at the synapse. The basis for this change of opinion is mounting evidence that there are numerous biologically active chemical compounds in the brain ("false neurotransmitters,"

Dale's principle. The notion, now abandoned, that each neuron makes use of only one neurotransmitter.

"neuromodulators") that might conceivably modify or regulate synaptic transmission across synapses mediated by the recognized neurotransmitters. In short, it is proposed that a multiplicity of chemicals may act at each synaptic site. Thus neurons might well synthesize and release a pool of one main neurotransmitter and several metabolically related "co-transmitters," which in combination determine the effect on the postsynaptic membrane. The actual content of the transmitter–co-transmitter pool might vary over time due to hormonal action, circadian rhythms, and the like, altering the relative proportions of the co-transmitters available at the synapse. The neuromuscular junction is thought of as a "limiting case" in which only one chemical, acetylcholine, is involved. Another possibility is that metabolically related compounds with antagonistic effects, such as glutamic acid (excitatory) and gamma aminobutyric acid (GABA) (inhibitory) might be present in varying quantities at the same synaptic site.

This broadened concept of neurotransmitter function is supported not only by many instances in which the opposing single-transmitter hypothesis appears not to explain findings, but also by the logic of the situation. Contained within the norepinephrine neuron is its precursor dopamine, along with the enzyme dopamine beta hydroxylase, which converts dopamine to norepinephrine. But dopamine is itself an established neurotransmitter, and could well participate in the synaptic process in such neurons. On the other hand, the *nonhydroxylated* analogs of both dopamine and norepinephrine, *phenylethylamine* and *phenylethanolamine* (note the logic of these terms: the six-carbon-ring structure is the phenyl radical, the two CH_2's constitute the ethyl radical, and the NH_2 is the amine radical), are known to be biologically active neuroamines, even though they do not meet all the criteria for classic neurotransmitters. But many other metabolites of both the catecholamines and serotonin may be suspected of biological activity in connection with neural mechanisms, whether at the synapse or elsewhere.

Of particular interest with regard to the affective disorders is phenylethylamine (Figure 15.10), which is found throughout the body and brain, and readily crosses the blood-brain barrier since it is lipid-soluble. Phenylethylamine is thought to be derived from the amino acid phenylalanine (see Figure 15.4) through its *decarboxylation*, since administration of that amino acid increases urinary excretion of phenylethylamine in the human, as well as phenylethylamine levels in the brains of laboratory animals. It has recently been found that antidepressive agents increase the level of phenylethylamine in human urine and in the animal brain, while

Phenylethylamine (*fee-nil-ETH-il-a-meen*). The chemical substance whose structure is that of dopamine without the two hydroxyl groups on the phenyl group, considered a possible neurotransmitter.

Phenylethanolamine (*fee-nil-ETH-a-nol-a-meen*). The chemical substance whose structure is that of norepinephrine without the two hydroxyl groups on the phenyl group, recently found to be an effective hunger suppressant.

Decarboxylation. Enzymatic removal of a carboxyl group (COOH) from an organic compound.

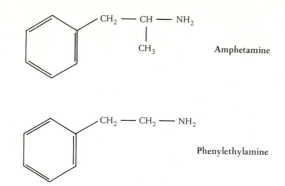

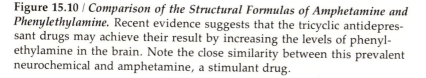

Figure 15.10 / *Comparison of the Structural Formulas of Amphetamine and Phenylethylamine.* Recent evidence suggests that the tricyclic antidepressant drugs may achieve their result by increasing the levels of phenylethylamine in the brain. Note the close similarity between this prevalent neurochemical and amphetamine, a stimulant drug.

drugs that induce depression reduce it. Specifically, brain levels of phenylethylamine are increased by pargyline and imipramine as well as by electroshock, and reduced by reserpine. Interestingly enough, its levels in the brain are not affected by the phenothiazines, which are antischizophrenic drugs. Phenylethylamine is also known to have a stimulating effect on the behavior of animals. Together these observations suggest that the "neuromodulator" phenylethylamine plays a significant role in endogenous depression. Significantly, an increase in phenylethylamine excretion also occurs in manic states, suggesting that this substance may be implicated in both endogenous depression and the manic-depressive disorder.

The facts that (1) administration of phenylethylamine induces amphetamine-like stimulant effects, while DOPA, the precursor of the catecholamines, is ambiguous in this regard; (2) imipramine increases brain levels of phenylethylamine but not of catecholamines; and (3) monoamine oxidase, which is inhibited in its action by many antidepressant drugs, preferentially metabolizes phenylethylamine rather than the catecholamines, all suggest that phenylethylamine is more closely associated with endogenous depression in its absence, and with recovery when restored to normal levels, than is norepinephrine. Both may, however, be significantly involved. Meanwhile it is suggested by these studies that the stimulant effect of the amphetamines may not be due to their power to release dopamine and norepinephrine at synaptic sites, but rather that they mimic the action of phenylethylamine (compare the two structural formulas in Figure 15.10).

With regard to the manic-depressive disorder, it is still poorly understood why lithium effectively blocks the manic phase while simultaneously preventing ensuing depressions. If the patient begins treatment with lithium carbonate during the manic phase of the cyclic disturbance — typically characterized by an overabundance of energy, euphoria, a mind racing with original ideas, and enormous pleasure in the most trivial things — the effect is not counteractive, as are depressive drugs (such as barbiturates), but seems merely to permit a return to normalcy, as if a deficiency in the brain were being compensated for. However, it is accepted that lithium — a simple element, third after hydrogen and helium in the table of elements, belonging to the group containing sodium and potassium — is the agent responsible. Jones, Maas, Dekirmenjian, and Fawcett (1973) traced one manic-depressive patient's rate of urinary excretion of a catecholamine metabolite over time, and found it significantly decreased during depressive stages and increased during manic phases. The latter increase began as much as four days before the onset of a manic episode, demonstrating that it was not merely a result of greater energy expenditure during the manic phase. This finding lent support to earlier studies that had found urinary excretion of both norepinephrine and epinephrine to increase during the manic phase, appearing to implicate norepinephrine metabolism directly in the mood shift.

Organic Problems

As we have seen, schizophrenia occurs in something over 1 percent of the population in all human societies, and is thought to have a genetic basis. The manic-depressive disorder is only about half as prevalent in the world, but its genetic basis is even more firmly established. If these disorders are eventually understood as to their specific neurochemical basis, they will be considered *organic disorders* — disorders whose biological or neural basis is known. At present, the most dramatic instance of a clearly neurological brain disorder is epilepsy, which also appears in many instances to be genetically determined.

Three major types of epilepsy may be distinguished, each characterized by particular brain-wave patterns and behavioral expressions. *Grand mal* seizures are characterized by loss of consciousness; a *tonic* phase of muscular rigidity and absence of breathing; a *clonic*

Organic disorder. A neurological disorder with demonstrable impairment of brain structure; differentiated from functional disorders.

phase of rhythmic shaking of the entire body, lasting a minute or two; and a *post-ictal* phase of drowsiness, confusion, and headache, of variable duration. *Petit mal* seizures are characterized principally by momentary loss of consciousness, during which the patient does not fall down but remains motionless, then abruptly returning to normal. Its characteristic brain waves are not the violent, high-amplitude, stormy waves of the grand mal seizure (Figure 15.11) but a curiously consistent "spike-and-wave" pattern (Figure 15.12) thought to represent abnormal neural activity in the subcortical structures of the brain. Petit mal epilepsy is a brain disease of chil-

Tonic phase. Muscular rigidity preceding the jerking (clonic) phase in grand mal epileptic seizures.

Clonic phase. A jerking of the body musculature characterizing an early stage of a grand mal epileptic seizure.

Post-ictal phase. The phase following cessation of an epileptic seizure, characterized by drowsiness, confusion, and headache.

R.O.

R.A. Eshock 8 sec prior

R.F. Tonic phase   Clonic phase

EKG

|1 sec| 200 µv

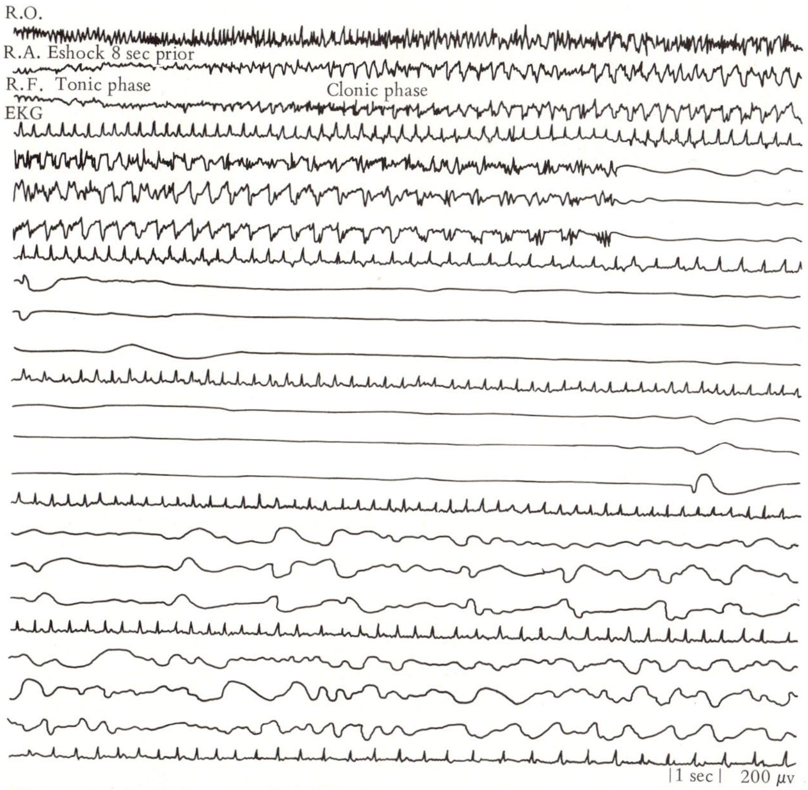

Figure 15.11 / *EEG Record Produced by Electroconvulsive Shock.* This record illustrates the phases characteristic of the grand mal seizure electroencephalogram: tonic phase, high voltage fast activity (patient falls unconscious); clonic phase, 3-per-second waves slowing to 1 per second (muscular jerking). Following the flat isoelectric period the large slow waves of deep sleep develop, and the patient sleeps. (The lower line of each set of four is an electrocardiogram.)

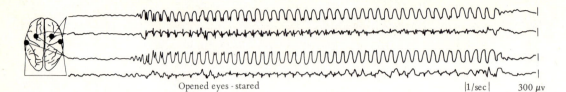

Opened eyes - stared |1/sec| 300 μv

Figure 15.12 / *EEG Record of a Petit Mal Seizure.* This record shows the characteristic "spike-and-slow-wave" sequence associated with momentary "absences" during which the individual loses consciousness but does not fall down. This seizure lasted about 14 seconds. Note the similarity of the waves in the two hemispheres.

dren, and tends to clear up within a few years; it is rare in individuals over age fifteen.

The third category is *psychomotor* seizures, which appear to involve abnormal firing of limbic-system neurons, often in structures of the temporal lobe (amygdala, hippocampus, and uncus). Behaviorally, these seizures are characterized by strange subjective experiences, automatic repetitive behaviors (lip-smacking, chewing, gagging, swallowing) or more complicated quasi-purposive impulsive behaviors of an inappropriate sort, as well as bizarre postures. Often the patient's memory of events during the seizure is absent or distorted, though consciousness is characteristically not lost. *Fugue states* — extended episodes of behavior which the person later cannot recall — sometimes occur. It is of particular interest to the psychologist and the public that psychomotor seizures rarely but occasionally take the form of outbursts of aggressive, violent behavior. Encephalograms of psychomotor seizure states tend to show clear spiking, especially in temporal leads (Figure 15.11).

The psychologist's interest in the epileptic phenomenon also stems from studies suggesting that a schizophrenia-like syndrome may be significantly associated with the psychomotor type of epilepsy. In one study, 80 percent of psychotic epileptics were found to have histories of psychomotor seizures and/or temporal lobe spiking in the electroencephalogram. The typical case had had epileptic seizures for fourteen years before the onset of psychotic symptoms. A low incidence of schizophrenia in the first-degree relatives of these patients strongly suggests that they were not suffering from classic schizophrenia, though their symptoms were similar. Other studies of psychotic epileptics (Flor-Henry, 1969, 1973) support the contention that abnormal firing in temporal-lobe neurons and other limbic structures tends over time to predispose the individual to a schizophrenia-like syndrome.

Psychomotor. Referring to a type of epilepsy characterized by loss of memory for one's behavior but not loss of consciousness.

Fugue state. A pathological state characterized by loss of memory for behavior and frequently bizarre behavior.

Abnormal Brain Activity and Violence

In addition to a relationship between epilepsy and a schizophrenia-like behavioral syndrome, violent behavior appears to be associated with abnormal electroencephalographic phenomena. Specifically, some individuals are prone to be provoked to violence by very minimally provocative stimuli. One study of such cases found that males predominate nine-to-one over females, and that the propensity for violence begins early in childhood, declining after age 30. In a study of habitual aggressors, Williams (1969) found that out of 1250 prisoners in jail for crimes of aggression, 57 percent of those convicted of repeated aggressive attacks had abnormal encephalograms, while only 12 percent of those convicted of a solitary aggressive crime had such abnormality. (Mentally retarded, epileptic, and head-injury cases were excluded from the study.)

In another study of more than 400 violent prisoners in a large penitentiary, half had symptoms of epileptic phenomena, a third had abnormal electroencephalograms, but fewer than 10 percent had frank temporal-lobe epilepsy (Mark and Ervin, 1970). Very interestingly, the latter inmates tended to have histories not only of multiple aggressive attacks, but also of attempted rape, traffic violations, serious automobile accidents, and a peculiar response to alcohol known as *pathologic intoxication.* It is recognized that alcohol tends to precipitate episodes of violence in certain violence-prone individuals. Though violent disposition is relatively rare among brain-damaged individuals, one study found 90 percent of pathologic-intoxication cases to be associated with brain damage, epilepsy, retardation, or psychosis. Another found electroencephalographic changes to be associated with episodes of pathologic intoxication.

Pathologic intoxication. An abnormal response to alcohol characterized by impulsively violent behavior.

Whether the result of genetic defect, early life experience, or cerebral insult or deficiency, no means has yet been found to alter a pattern of episodic violence in some individuals (Hartelius, 1965).

The Nature of the Epileptic Process

The epileptic process may be viewed more generally as any abnormally high rate of firing beginning in a group of neurons anywhere in the brain. The symptoms differ depending on the brain region or circuits affected. An epileptic focus in a cortical region may frequently be detected by scanning the brain with the electroencephalograph, where it shows up as a region producing hypersynchronous delta waves while the rest of the cortex exhibits normal beta waves of the waking state. When epileptic spiking occurs, it appears to represent a failure of normal inhibitory influences, permitting a small "electrical storm" to begin. The general nature and causative agency of the phenomenon is only poorly understood, but scar tissue from a cerebral accident is sometimes involved. The many medications effective in controlling (preventing) the onset of such runaway neural processes all appear to act by supporting neural inhibitory influences.

Effects of Cerebral Accidents

Brain damage that renders a portion of the brain inoperative is manifested as the disappearance of some function, behavioral or intellectual, or, in the case of motor regions of the brain, disinhibition of motor circuitries (chorea, spastic paralysis). As we saw in Chapter 9, damage in the left hemisphere is apt to produce deficits in language function, while similar damage to the right hemisphere tends to produce non-language-related deficits. Most particularly, damage to Broca's motor speech area in the inferior frontal convolution (pars triangularis) of the left hemisphere is apt to impair the production of speech, leaving understanding of the meaning of language intact; damage to Wernicke's receptive speech area in the left temporal-parietal region usually produces more profound verbal-symbolic deficits. Lesions in the right-hemisphere region corresponding to Broca's motor speech area in the left typically produce no detectable defect at all, while those in the right-hemisphere region corresponding to Wernicke's area in the left are apt to impair spatial visualization and produce certain forms of apraxia (such as difficulty dressing oneself or copying a simple pattern or object arrangement). More extensive types of apraxia may result from damage to the left parietal cortex, especially in the region of the supramarginal gyrus (Figure 15.13). Lesions in the left posterior temporal or occipital region may result in inability to recognize familiar objects or pictures of such objects visually — a form of agnosia. Curiously, lesions in the right parietal region are apt to impair recognition of the faces of familiar individuals. (On a number of grounds, recognition of individuals appears to be a special form of perception, independent of the ability to recognize generic objects.)

Apraxia. A neurological disorder characterized by inability to perform familiar goal-oriented behavioral sequences.

Gerstmann's syndrome — inability to name the fingers and distinguish between right and left, in conjunction with loss of ability to write and to calculate — was once thought to be associated with lesions of the left parietal lobe (angular gyrus). It is now known that lesions in this area can also produce *dyslexia* (inability to read). Deficits in reading, writing, and calculating can also result from left

Dyslexia. Difficulty in learning to read.

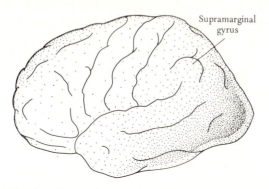

Supramarginal
gyrus

Figure 15.13 / *The Left Hemisphere, Showing the Supramarginal Gyrus.*
Damage to this region, though closely associated with language functions,
may produce profound disturbances in motor performance (aparaxia).

temporal-lobe lesions; reading and writing deficits from left oc-
cipital-lobe lesions, and deficits in calculating ability from lesions
in the right hemisphere (Hécaen, 1962).

It has already been mentioned that damage to the hippocampus
bilaterally produces severe loss of the ability to consolidate a permanent memory of recent events, though old event memories remain unimpaired. It is noteworthy here that bilateral destruction of
the fornix — the major efferent pathway from the hippocampus —
produces some difficulty in recall of recent events but not a total
deficit, as does bilateral hippocampal destruction (Ojemann, 1966).
Moreover, bilateral destruction of the dorsomedial nucleus of the
thalamus, which has massive reciprocal relations with the prefrontal granular and orbital cortices, and of the pulvinar, which is massively interconnected with the posterior association cortex, produces severe deficits in event-memory consolidation even though
the hippocampi remain intact. Korsakoff's syndrome, which is associated with prolonged alcoholism, and one of whose major symptoms is this curious loss of recent memory, has traditionally been
attributed to damage to the hippocampus, fornix, mammillary bodies, and/or dorsomedial nucleus of the thalamus (Barbizet, 1963;
Lewis, 1961; Rosenbaum and Merritt, 1939). However, a recent
study by Victor and his associates (1971) found damage to the locus
coeruleus nucleus of the brainstem, including cell loss and depig-
mentation, in over two-thirds of the Korsakoff patients studied —
an incidence considerably higher than the incidence of damage to

the hippocampus. The locus coeruleus is, of course, the principal source of norepinephrine in the brain, directly innervating the hippocampus.

Damage to the prefrontal granular cortex produces a wide variety of symptoms whose common denominator is difficult to conceptualize. There may be inappropriate responses, out of keeping with the circumstances, which appear to arise not from an ongoing organized fantasy, as in the case of the schizophrenic, but from a loss of controls governing normal behavior. As in the case of prefrontal lobotomy, there is apt to be poor capacity for understanding the consequences of behavior, as well as difficulty in orienting behavior on behalf of future goals, and passive acceptance of circumstances, as if motivational functions had been impaired.

Delirium, with loss of awareness of who or where one is, or the time of day, or loss of memory, is not a characteristic of chronic brain conditions, but may occur in connection with recent brain damage of any sort. There may be stupor, or visual hallucinations, or panic states, or irritability. The cause is more frequently a metabolic or toxic disorder, such as hypoglycemia on the one hand or metal poisoning, sedative drugs, hallucinogens, or alcohol on the other. Such disorders are sometimes misdiagnosed as schizophrenia in the absence of more specific information. In the very elderly the likelihood is that this condition is a form of senility, a progressive deterioration of the brain in many cases due to dietary and circulatory deficiencies.

Neurological Disorders of Childhood

The syndrome known as early childhood autism has puzzled psychologists and neurologists ever since its description as a disease entity by Kanner (1957). Often manifested before age one in feeding difficulty and screaming, autism's primary symptoms are a peculiar inability to relate to people, severe social withdrawal, and marked retardation in language development. Often neurological impairment is strongly suspected, but autopsy (infrequently conducted, oddly enough) reveals no evidence of brain defect. It has nevertheless been estimated that as many as half of those who suffer from autism have electroencephalographic abnormalities and/or a history of epileptic seizures (Kolvin, Ounsted, and Roth, 1971; Kolvin, Humphrey, and McNay, 1971). Autism is four times as prevalent in boys as girls, and appears not to be heritable: only 7 out of 521 families of autistic children were found in one study to have more than one afflicted child.

Most baffling of all is the fact that some autistic children, though generally of low-grade intellect, can perform prodigious feats of calculation (involving, for example, calendar dates), memory, or musical ability, the phenomenon for which the term *idiot savant* was coined. Unusual artistic talent is also sometimes present. There is still uncertainty as to whether autism represents a true organic syndrome and whether, if so, its origin is congenital or environmental. It appears to be more prevalent in the families of well-educated professionals.

The same question has been raised about the phenomenon widely characterized as *hyperactivity* in children of school age. Like autism, hyperactivity predominantly affects boys, and involves a seriously impaired attention span that interferes with normal learning processes. Some children who exhibit the signs of hyperactivity (primarily restlessness) are very dramatically helped by amphetamines, which — in contrast to their effect on adults — quiet them and allow for the return of "normality." Reminiscent of the effect of lithium on the manic condition, amphetamines appear in these instances to make up for a chemical deficiency in the brain. A number of questions remain. One careful study has shown that the differential effect on adults and children is not as paradoxical as was thought, since d-amphetamine administered to normal children produces a parallel quieting effect on them for five hours, after which there follows the activating and euphoric effect the adult experiences. This activating and euphoric effect had also been observed in the hyperactive children, but was commonly attributed to the "wearing off" of the drug's effect. A study of the effect of methylphenidate (Ritalin), an amphetamine analog, found improved learning to occur in hyperkinetic children at a dosage level far below that required for behavioral calming, and actual deterioration in learning at doses widely employed to achieve the desired behavioral result, suggesting a distinction between two effects once thought to be related (Sprague and Sleator, 1977). In the meantime, many contributory factors have been proposed, from toxic food additives to fluorescent lighting. The widespread and interesting phenomenon of hyperactivity is generally believed to be of relatively recent origin, but it may be merely a matter of recently having been brought to attention by the discovery of the dramatic effect of amphetamines.

A good deal more serious is minimal brain damage in children, often confused with hyperactivity. Such children are apt to be hy-

Idiot savant (ee-dee-OH sa-VANH). An autistic child exhibiting very remarkable abilities in a narrow field but grave deficiency in many others.

perkinetic, "driven" in their behavior, constantly on the move and touching and manipulating objects in a compulsive fashion. Attention span tends to be short, shifting constantly from one thing to another without apparent selectivity. Behavior is apt to be impulsive, perhaps involving aggression and tantrums in response to anxiety-provoking situations such as misunderstood demands and changes in routine or familiar surroundings. Learning disability in the three Rs may be present, and difficulty with abstractions may mark a developmental lag. The incidence of such organic difficulties among schoolchildren is now beginning to be recognized, and special learning situations and teaching methods appropriate to their needs have proven helpful.

One way of viewing minimal brain damage in children is to consider all of us as belonging in the same category, some merely more deeply embedded in it than others. Towbin (1969) concluded his analysis of over 600 fetal and neonatal brains by rejecting the widespread opinion that few, if any, brain changes could be attributed to *hypoxia* in the prenatal period. According to Towbin, the occurrence of such damage to the neonatal brain has been underestimated. Using improved techniques of histopathologic examination, he found damage from anoxia in the premature fetus and newborn to be consistently localized in the brain interior, in the germinal matrix lining the walls of the ventricles (see Chapter 14), rather than the cortex as is more often true of the mature fetus or newborn. Such interior damage is easy to underestimate, since it is difficult to detect by cursory examination.

Hypoxia. **Absence of normal oxygen supply.**

Prenatal hypoxia occurs most commonly due to placental disorders, such as premature detachment from the uterine wall (Towbin, 1969). During the prenatal period the highly vascularized germinal tissues, where neurons are differentiating and beginning their migration to outlying regions of the cerebrum, are apparently particularly vulnerable to oxygen deficit, which leads to devitalization and necrosis of tissue, often as the result of interference with local circulation (obstruction of either arterial inflow or venous outflow). With the stoppage of circulation, venous infarction occurs and the lesion hemorrhages. The result is the destruction of neuroblasts and a reduction in the number of neurons that reach their appointed posts in the cortex and the subcortical nuclei. Near full term, vulnerability shifts to the cortical tissues, where lack of oxygen may produce the same necrosis of tissues. If the destruction occurs in the precentral region, spastic cerebral palsy may result. If the process sweeps forward into the prefrontal region, mental defect may result. In the deep cerebral structures, such as the basal ganglia, *athetosis*

Athetosis. **A neurological disorder characterized by involuntary writhing movement of limbs and torso.**

and other forms of *dyskinesia* result. Often there are *epileptogenic* scars as well.

Towbin (1969, pp. 159–160) puts it eloquently:

Dyskinesia. Impairment of normal muscular function.

Epileptogenic scars. Scar tissue producing abnormal neural firing.

The processes of gestation and birth expose the fetus to many hazardous complications. The maternal-placental-fetal organization is delicately balanced; the placenta has a narrow margin of safety; pathologic changes such as premature detachment and infarction of the placenta, contravening oxygen exchange, may cause fetal death or render the fetus hypoxic for prolonged periods. During gestation and delivery, the fetus is subjected to rapid, often turbulent alterations in its environment and is required to make complicated changes in circulation, respiration and other systemic functions. Particularly the premature, unready and fragile, born through a physiologically unprepared, unrelaxed birth canal, is highly vulnerable to hypoxic and mechanical damage.

The fetal and neonatal period has a death rate greater than any other time of life. The frequency of sublethal damage — the organic attrition suffered by the fetus and newborn — often escapes consideration. The broad, varied spectrum of diseases which affect the fetus includes most of the organic disorders which occur in the adult. Many latent pathologic processes in the nervous system and other organs initiate their damage in the fetus and manifest their effects in the adult.

Although all organs of the fetus and newborn are vulnerable to hypoxia, the most sensitive register of such damage proves to be the brain. For the fetus, during its marginal existence *in utero* and as it is pistoned down the birth canal and separated, some degree of hypoxic and mechanical damage to the nervous system is inescapable. Gestation and birth form an inexorable leveling mechanism; with the brain blighted at birth, the potential of mentation may be reduced from that of a genius to that of a plain child, or less. The damage may be slight, imperceptible clinically; or, it may spell the difference between brothers, one a dexterous athlete, the other "an awkward child." Substantially, it is said, all of us have a touch of cerebral palsy and mental retardation, some more, some less — the endowment pathologically of gestation and birth.

Manifestly, fetal and neonatal hypoxic cerebral damage results not only in the reduction but also in distortion of nervous system function. The child with cerebral palsy exhibits spastic paralysis and often the abnormal motor activity of athetosis. Clinically, in addition to the three generally recognized sequels of neonatal hypoxic cerebral damage — cerebral palsy, epilepsy and mental retardation — attention is being increasingly directed to a fourth category, reflecting the high incidence of behavioral disorders in children with a history of complicated birth and prematurity.

Note that five-sixths of all mental retardation is genetic, environmental, or illness-related in origin and of moderate severity; Towbin's remarks apply only to the one-sixth attributable to damage during gestation and birth.

The Psychosomatic Disorders

When a human or animal is under stress, a polypeptide hormone is discharged from the hypothalamus and passes via the portal circulation into the anterior pituitary, which it stimulates to release ACTH into the blood stream. This hormone in turn stimulates the adrenal cortex to secrete hormones, such as cortisol or corticosterone, which have a variety of generalized effects — production of glycogen as a ready source of energy to the muscles, suppression of immune responses and inflammation — that prepare the body for such emergencies as physical combat. Simultaneously, a neural pathway from the hypothalamus stimulates activity in the sympathetic branch of the autonomic nervous system, causing the *chromaffin cells* of the adrenal medulla to release epinephrine (adrenalin) into the blood stream. Epinephrine forms glucose from glycogen stores throughout the body, thus supplying energy directly to the muscles, and changing triglycerides stored in fatty tissues into free fatty acids, the form in which the body can utilize them for energy. It also increases both pulse rate and blood pressure, increasing blood supply to the skeletal muscles, and accelerates the coagulation of the blood if wounds are sustained. This process was discussed in Chapter 10 in connection with "physiological emotion."

This adaptive response to stressful conditions is adaptive only for short periods, during the alarm stage of the general adaptation syndrome (Selye, 1976). If stress is sufficiently prolonged without relief, it can impair normal bodily functioning. We should remind ourselves that throughout the long evolution of the human structures stress was always a momentary phenomenon. Once a confrontation is over, organisms in the natural state revert quickly to a condition of internal quiet and go about their business as if nothing had happened. Clearly, things are not this way anymore for our species, at least in urban societies. We are not genetically prepared in our physiological capacities for chronic anxiety and frustration and rage, which prolong the body's alarm reaction over many hours, even weeks and months, allowing little opportunity for true relaxation.

Chromaffin cells (KROH-ma-fin). **Cells in the adrenal medulla that act as second-order neurons of the sympathetic nervous system, secreting epinephrine into the bloodstream during sympathetic system arousal.**

Among the conditions that can be demonstrated in animals to result from prolonged, unrelieved stress are gastrointestinal disorders (peptic ulcers, ulcerative colitis), cardiovascular disorders (hypertension, heart disease), numerous metabolic disorders (diabetes, hypoglycemia, thyroid disease, hyperinsulinism), damage to pancreas and kidneys, and skin disorders. In the human we can add dental caries, constipation, headache, backache, and indigestion.

Students of stress, such as Hans Selye, have emphasized the general nature of long-term stressors, including such psychological conditions as chronic worry, hostility that must be suppressed, ego-deflating experiences, disappointment, and the like. On the other hand it has been recognized that each individual has an optimal stress level: some people thrive in situations whose psychological pressures would quickly put other people in the hospital. Moreover, we now recognize that the part of the bodily system that suffers first under the strain of chronic stressful conditions differs with different individuals, some seeming to "favor" gastrointestinal disorders, circulatory conditions, and the like. Often recommended as treatment are such "counterstressors" as vigorous physical exercise, moderate use of alcohol (Coopersmith, 1964), and psychotherapy.

Pathological Psychological Conditions

It would be tempting to apply this formula of environmentally induced disorder to the wide variety of psychological dysfunctions we humans are subject to. Indeed, attempts have repeatedly been made to associate schizophrenia and the endogenous depressions with life-experience factors. The argument is much more convincing in the case of such neurotic problems as obsessive-compulsiveness, which can persuasively be ascribed to early childhood circumstances that cause the toddler, still unconvinced he or she is truly loved and secure, to take overly to heart the many do's and don't's inherent in the early socialization process. Yet even disorders such as these hint of biological proclivities. (Compulsive overeaters, for example, are difficult to explain purely on the basis of life-experience determinants.) The possibility of genetically determined differences in hypothalamic hunger-control mechanisms is readily suggested by animal experiments on hunger and satiety. Other apparently pure psychological compulsions, such as alcohol consumption to excess, have not yet been clearly disengaged from possible innate proclivities. Nor has the final word been said about such addictions as gambling and such compulsive behaviors as sexual self-exposure, transvestism, pyromania, and the like.

A great many cases of abnormal behavioral tendencies are nevertheless easy to attribute to developmental circumstances that have affected the structure and function of the growing brain, sometimes irreversibly, leading to adaptive difficulties in later life. Chapter 16 will propose that it is through the learning process that the more recently evolved portions of the brain achieve their adult organization. Many theories of human development have emphasized very early learning experiences as particularly determinative of the later personality. It is therefore hypothesized that such inexplicable phenomena as phobic responses refer to long-forgotten and no longer retrievable life experiences or circumstances, now effectively embedded in the functional organization of the brain. A similar explanation might be proposed for the curiously stereotypic phenomenon of paranoid suspicion, which accompanies many diverse behavioral and neurological dysfunctions.

With regard to the *dyscontrol syndrome* Mark and Ervin (1970) identified (see page 357), the researchers warn that not all instances of impulsive violence involve traditional temporal-lobe epilepsy, though many of the violent prisoners they studied gave evidence of seizure activity, such as altered states of consciousness or warning states preceding impulsive violent attacks. Interestingly, a large percentage of such patients voluntarily sought psychiatric help because of their uncontrollable rage, and many freely admit that they are dangerous drivers, using their vehicles to relieve tension and work out aggression. Whether their behavior reflects overt neurological abnormality or the subtle "functional" effect of life experience (nearly half of Mark and Ervin's hospital patients with dyscontrol syndrome had histories of enuresis (bedwetting) beyond age seven, half had histories of cruelty to animals, and one-fourth histories of pyromania), the most characteristic aspect of the syndrome is a history of repeated offenses against other individuals, and the uncontrollability of their responses to their violent feelings.

Such individuals' seizures can often be effectively treated with medications if their brain abnormality is recognized. Others can control their behavior with the help of tranquilizer drugs. No such remedies have been found, however, for the *psychopathic personality*, whose orientation to life is frankly to take advantage of people (especially the trusting and gullible), who is constitutionally incapable of loyalty and friendship, and whose selfishness and predatory impulses know no restraint. These baffling individuals are not known to exhibit any overt brain abnormality, nor are they known to have experienced abnormal developmental circumstances. All efforts to change such individuals have proved unavailing.

Summary

The major psychoses — schizophrenia and psychotic depression — are functional disorders, as distinguished from organic disorders arising from some tangible brain defect or malfunction. Schizophrenia and the endogenous depressions (as opposed to depressions induced by unfortunate life experiences or circumstances) appear now to be not structural but biochemical. The strongest evidence for such a conclusion is that their symptoms are in many instances abolished, or controlled, by appropriate medication entirely in the absence of psychotherapeutic intervention. Current research efforts are focusing on discovering improved medical treatments, chemicals that are more reliably effective and with fewer untoward side effects.

The evidence is convincing that some individuals are genetically at risk of these disorders, which often run in families. The evidence for the hypothesis that these psychoses are the consequence of unfortunate life experiences is considerably weaker. Confusion has arisen through failure to differentiate psychotic depressions (which are unaccountable, often occurring abruptly without any precipitating occurrences) from neurotic depression, which is lifelong in onset and readily understandable in terms of unfortunate circumstances during the developmental years.

The manic-depressive disorder, characterized by periods of manic excitement and enthusiasm alternating with depressive episodes, is a distinct subcategory of the psychotic depressions, with a strong genetic component. Recent evidence suggests that the monopolar (noncyclic) endogenous depressions may also have subcategories with differential responses to medical treatment, suggesting that somewhat different biochemical malfunctions are involved. While the manic disorder responds well to lithium, the true psychotic depressions may respond well to any of a large number of tricyclic antidepressant drugs or to the monoamine-oxidase inhibitors, which potentiate the effect of the neurotransmitters norepinephrine, dopamine, and serotonin in the brain. Schizophrenia is effectively treated in an opposing manner with the phenothiazines and butyrophenones, whose effect appears to be partly to block the activity of dopamine.

The human brain is subject to many organic disorders. To oversimplify, we may say that there are two types of epileptic disorders, one affecting the neocortex and often resulting in the classic grand mal seizure, the other affecting the limbic structures (psychomotor or temporal-lobe epilepsy), and characterized by strange subjective experiences, automatisms, and quasi-purposive impulsive behaviors inappropriate to the situation, often accompanied by bizarre postures. Such patients frequently have no memory of their experiences during a seizure, even though they do not lose consciousness. On rare occasions, such seizures may result in outbursts of aggressive violence. In addition to the epilepsies, which represent brain malfunctions, frank brain damage may result in the disappearance of some function, intellectual or behavioral, or in abnormal motoric expression (chorea, spastic paralysis, and the like). Damage to language areas may produce aphasia; damage to the nonspeaking hemisphere in the parietal or temporal region may produce various forms of agnosia or apraxia (failure to recognize objects or persons, or inability to perform simple learned behaviors).

Prenatally or during the birth process, brain damage results relatively frequently from anoxia and consequent loss of neural tissue. More often brain defects due to environmental poisons or drugs administered to the mother may result in the many shades of mental retardation and behavioral abnormalities (hyperactivity syndromes) affecting children, conditions more common than has previously been realized.

Chapter 16 / *The Learning Perspective: How Our Brain Is Structured Through Experience*

Learning, defined as change in the functional organization of the brain as a result of experience, provides for progressively more flexible adaptation to the specific demands of a given environment as we move from very primitive, almost completely genetically programmed invertebrates toward the organisms of highest neural complexity, mammals and humans. At the human level, specifically, adaptive flexibility through learning involves (1) significant erasure of early learning by more adaptive later learning, (2) building on earlier learning, rather than erasure, as in the elaboration of such scientific disciplines as biology, and (3) continued learning throughout life, without significant decline. The concept of the engram is now deemed poorly descriptive of the change that occurs in learning, which appears to involve the establishment of a new and subtly different pattern of firing in widely distributed brain regions. A beginning has been made at identifying the neural basis of learning at a very primitive level in Aplysia with respect to habituation and sensitization, and, less specifically, at the level of the brainstem and cord, the hippocampus, the limbic pleasure and drive circuits and amygdala, and the neocortex.

Plants have complete genetic instructions on how to grow and reproduce, and the same thing is largely true of animals below the level of the mammals. Yet even very simple animals can modify their behavior in some respects in response to their experience, and this is learning. The capacity for such adaptive modification becomes progressively more evident as we move up the phylogenetic scale toward the human being. Nevertheless, for insects, or even for rodents, behavioral instructions for most occasions are pre-wired in the connectivities of the nervous system. These coded instructions specify, in effect, "If such and such happens, do this!"

Insects inherit instructions that are marvelously complex and complete, anticipating all the circumstances the organism is apt to encounter in its lifetime — but in a sense they are too complete, making no allowance for changes in instructions to adapt behavior to new environments or unforeseen circumstances. Such changes in instructions are possible, however, in species with more complex nervous systems, capable of adopting new behaviors for which their original neural connections are not specifically preadapted. This is in a sense a new kind of brain, in which some instructions are left loose and permissive, open-ended, suggesting rather than dictating. The advantages of greater adaptive flexibility are most evident in those species whose young take a long time to mature, since adaptive flexibility tends in many species to be lost upon reaching adulthood. As we shall see, this is not necessarily true of our species — in this respect, as in so many others, our species is unique in the animal kingdom.

As we saw in Chapter 14, the human infant is born in a highly immature state with respect to brain development: the great majority of its cortical neurons have not yet reached a functional level of maturation at birth. It is left for postnatal experience to dictate, in part, the connectivities that will be formed. Thus the human brain is structured in very significant measure through learning experience. Another feature, of the human brain in particular, is that early learnings can be largely superseded by later learnings, erasing the earlier effect. Human beings are far better able than other animals to overcome the effects of an abnormal or traumatic early experience (neurotic behavior in the apes is notoriously difficult to overcome).

Still more remarkable, in view of the totality of life forms, is the fact that at the human level of cerebral organization it is possible progressively to build huge systems of knowledge and understanding, such as the science of biology, through facility in the acquisition and manipulation of concepts. In the human brain — a third-generation biological computer — one learning can build on, rather than erase, another or can function in parallel with prior learnings. The process of intellectual organization thus afforded may apparently proceed indefinitely. Not so in the chimpanzee or, needless to say, in the housefly or ant.

In this chapter we will examine the remarkable ability of the human brain to become progressively better adapted, apparently in whatever milieu it finds itself, by capitalizing on the significance of its experiences from infancy on. We will also examine the way animals learn, methods we can also employ, and by which we may be shaped more than we know. Of the thousand-and-one questions that press for answers, we can deal here with only a few. How do we develop complex skills and elaborate skill systems, such as those involved in driving in city traffic or performing in a ballet or on a basketball court? How do we acquire and retain for future use factual information relevant to our purposes? How are our perceptions of the world altered, new perspectives gained and old misconceptions abandoned? How do we form likes and dislikes, and become committed emotionally to a system of values that guides our behavior? What we have learned about the brain to date is at least an initial foundation for an understanding of these momentous questions.

The Search for the Engram

The search for the *engram*, the supposed neural repository of the products of learning experience, has thus far proven futile, and may well represent a faulty phrasing of the question. The alteration that learning brings about in the brain may not be the formation of a new set of neural connections, as the concept of the engram tends to suggest, but instead a subtle shift in the functioning of an already-existent system which was given in the genetic instructions for the forming of the kind of brain we have (John, 1972). Such a system change in neural functions is not adequately suggested by the familiar notion of "memory" somehow deposited in the brain, of which the engram is a physiological reification. A more modern view suggests instead a subtle change in the pattern of firing of the neurons involved, which might be highly local (such as in the experimental conditioning of spinal motor neurons) or extended over literally billions of neurons. Moreover, we might be well advised to entertain the notion that more than one learning process at the neuronal level may be involved.

Engram. The presumed neural substrate of a memory.

The amount of experimental work on the learning process performed to date in the neurophysiological laboratory is mountainous. For one thing, much of what we know about brain functioning in general has been learned from studies involving learning mechanisms, since behavior change as the result of controlled experiences provides a convenient window into brain operations. A good deal of this research has focused on the mechanism of classical conditioning (particularly in the Soviet Union) and aversive conditioning, most frequently employing mild electroshock as the aversive stimulus. Much work has been done on *retrograde amnesia,* after-the-fact disruption of learning due to some subsequent treatment of the animal, which corresponds to human loss of memory of events preceding brain concussion or therapeutic electroshock treat-

Retrograde amnesia. Loss of memory for occurrences during a period prior to some event, such as a brain concussion.

ments. Other studies have implanted electrodes in the "pleasure centers" of the brain to produce rewarding experience in the interest of studying positive reinforcement effects. In addition to behavioral changes, shifts in brain-wave patterns have been charted in the course of learning, as well as changes in electrical evoked potentials when sensory stimuli are applied. Through these studies we have learned a great deal about the brain, but no clear concept of memory, or the nature of the learning product, has emerged.

In what follows, we will not be looking for a substance created by the learning process and capable of being injected into another brain to produce the same result — this notion has been one result of the fallacious reification of the concept of the engram — nor for a reverberating circuit such as D. O. Hebb (1949) suggested to account for the temporary holding of the message of experience. For our purposes we shall define learning as *some change in the functional organization of the brain resulting from exposure to environmental experience* (or from internal analysis of that experience after the fact). This broad definition encompasses everything from the simplest cellular learning to the most complex thoroughgoing shift in the manner in which the brain looks at the world and responds to it.

Learning at the Most Primitive Level

The arousal or alarm response probably exemplifies the most primitive form of learning we know. When a deer browsing in the forest hears a sound it cannot make out as familiar and posing no threat, its brain is instantly put on alert. The deer turns its head toward the sound and stands perfectly still, searching with its eyes and listening, prepared to flee if called for. This is the classic picture of attentional focus. It might last half a minute, after which, if there is no further indication of danger, the animal abruptly returns to its browsing. This highly organized reaction pattern — variously called alerting, arousal, orienting, alarm, and simple curiosity — is found in all animals, from the simplest jellyfish to the human being. It is as common a denominator of animal life as the ingestion of food.

The response has *habituated*, we say, when the stimulus that originally aroused it is repeated, and the animal no longer attends to it. The same noise enters the deer's auditory system, and electrodes on its scalp would show that the signal continues to reach its cortex, but it continues to browse undisturbed as if it no longer heard. The *brain* still hears, but the *animal* actually may not, because its attention is focused on its browsing. Here for the first time we must ask who is the animal that no longer hears. Let us skirt the issue for the present by answering conditionally that it is the attending or responding animal, or perhaps, in the human, the self.

We are, of course, under continual bombardment by stimuli we pay no attention to, via our exteroceptors and via the interoceptors that signal the state of the body. The miracle of our attention mechanism is that out of this rain of stimulation impinging upon us from all quarters, moment by moment, we quite automatically *configurate* only one small segment for consideration at any given time. All the rest are somehow simultaneously inhibited. Little is contributed to our understanding of this process by merely pointing to the reticular activating system of the brain as the mechanism that produces shifts of attention. Curiously, this question has largely escaped the attention of researchers in the neurosciences as well as in psychology. The attention phenomenon is so familiar, like the air we breathe, that we have tended to be unaware of it as a phenomenon. Yet it is a fundamental fact of our brain.

The key to the brain's feat of inhibiting thousands of stimuli at once, while retaining the ability to shift the spotlight of attentional focus to any of them in an instant, appears to be that the very act of configurating one portion of the stimulus rain in our attention field blocks the rest from being configurated. But this conjecture takes us far beyond our present level of sophistication about brain mechanisms.

What is so remarkable about the habituation process — until recently largely overlooked — is that it implies that some form of template is left in the brain by means of which a stimulus is recognized the next time it occurs. In focusing on the fact of behavior change (on the deer's continuing to browse rather than attending), the perceptual aspect of the learning process involved has been largely ignored. Yet habituation would be impossible, even for a simple sea anemone alarmed by a drop of water falling on the aquarium's surface, unless some "image" of the stimulus were retained. The reduced intensity of the sea anemone's response (sudden withdrawal of its feeding tubes) to a second drop of water means that learning has taken place — that a memory was formed somewhere in the organism's nervous system. By extension, this means that even so simple an animal has a "memory image" of many of the salient features of its surroundings — bubbles that rise to the surface of the tank, fish that swim by, the people who stop to admire its beauty. The question is: where does such a simple nervous system store all these memories?

This question is easier to answer for the deer or the human being, whose brains contain hundreds of billions of neurons. However, it is more difficult in the case of a complex brain to find out how learning occurs. Thus very simple organisms, with fewer neurons, often provide clues to learning processes in more complex organisms.

Learning at the Neuronal Level

Eric Kandel (1979) has summarized some fascinating recent work on the mechanisms of habituation in the sea hare (*Aplysia*), a large mollusk without a shell that travels swiftly over the sea floor (hence its name) in search of prey — a fast snail. In simple invertebrates, particular identifiable neurons, found in all members of the species, synapse with specific other neurons. The specific neurons involved in *Aplysia*'s gill-retraction response have been identified. When *Aplysia*'s siphon is touched, specific sensory neurons make contact with the six motor neurons in the gill (as well as with some interneurons), which cause the extended gill to draw in out of harm's way, much as the sea anemone's feeding tubes retract. But after this happens 10 to 15 times in a single training session, the withdrawal reflex ceases to occur: the response has habituated. The investigators can now research the question of how habitation happens. By stimulating a single such sensory neuron so as to produce only a single action potential, a large excitatory postsynaptic potential is produced in the motor neuron across the synapse. Subsequent stimulations produce progressively smaller potentials in the postsynaptic membrane. It has been determined that this is a consequence of fewer *quanta* of the neurotransmitter (acetylcholine, in this case) being released into the synaptic cleft, rather than a change in the sensitivity of the postsynaptic membrane. (A similar mechanism has been implicated in other animals.)

This finding supports a longstanding theoretical hypothesis that learning must involve a change in the effectiveness of synaptic transmission, wherever in the brain the learning occurs. In the case of habituation, fewer and fewer synaptic vesicles of neurotransmitter are released with successive stimulations (at least in *Aplysia*). The second aspect of habituation — the fact that it is short-lived — can be explained by revival, after a rest period, of the stimulated neuron's capacity to release a full load of transmitter substance. What has not yet been explained is how, over the course of repeated training sessions, habituation becomes much longer-lasting. The experimenters found that, on first stimulation of the siphon in untrained *Aplysia,* over 90 percent of the sensory neurons impinging on a particular motor neuron for the gill-retraction response made highly effective synaptic contact. After long-term training, however, a large percentage of these sensory neurons became functionally inactive and remained so for more than a week. This finding suggests that, at least in the case of habituation, short-term and long-term memory can both occur at the same locus — the synapse leading to the motor response — and both result from depression of the effectiveness of the synapse. (*Long-term memory* here means only a week or two.)

The opposite of habituation is *sensitization,* enhanced response to strong or once-meaningful stimuli. If the browsing deer discovers that a given sound to which it oriented was in fact not innocuous — if it was the sound of a predator on the prowl — that sound will be remembered and brought to focal attention the moment it occurs, rather than being eventually ignored. A special mechanism underlying the phenomenon of sensitization to stimuli was found in *Aplysia.* A noxious stimulus to the head of the animal activates *sensitizing neurons* that synapse upon the sensory neurons described above — not on their dendrites or cell soma, but on their synaptic terminals. (Recall the *presynaptic inhibition* discussed in Chapter 8, in which an inhibitory effect is produced by a subthreshold depolarization of the presynaptic membrane before the action potential arrives, reducing both the amplitude of the subsequent depolarization and the amount of neurotransmitter released.) In this case the sensitizing neurons release serotonin (usually inhibitory in its effect), which through a three-stage chemical chain within the synaptic terminal increases the amount of neurotransmitter released.

It is very interesting that, at least at this simple level of neuronal organization, both habituation and sensitization can result from modification of the amount of neurotransmitter released at the activating neuron's synaptic terminal. Further complexities will be found in the mechanisms of synaptic operation (new neurotransmitter substances, the effect of neurohormones in the bathing intercellular fluids, and the like) at more complex levels of neural organization, yet an exciting beginning has been made at the task of reducing brain operation to "mere mechanism," with the emphasis upon neurochemistry.

Sensitization. The tendency to increased alerting response to a stimulus found to be biologically significant.

Sensitizing neurons. Neurons found in some invertebrates which increase response to a stimulus found to be biologically significant.

Presynaptic inhibition. The inhibitory effect of a subthreshold activation of the axon terminal before arrival of the action potential, whose amplitude of effect is thereby decreased.

Learning at the Brainstem and Cord Level

Habituation may be defined as a diminishing response with repetition of an unchanging and inconsequential stimulus. But the change that occurs is more appropriately described as ceasing to attend, after a while, to a monotonously recurring signal to which no meaning attaches. The more technical definition, however, covers those instances in which conscious awareness is not involved, as in the case of habituation of a spinal reflex.

Richard Thompson and his colleagues have demonstrated in the case of the withdrawal reflex to skin shock in the *spinal cat* that the afferent signal from the skin to the cord does not decrease with repeated shocks, nor is the decrease in response attributable to muscle fatigue, neuromuscular junction change, or responsiveness of the motor nerve. Habituation to repeated application of the shock stimulus appears therefore to result from changes in the activity of the interneurons within the gray matter of the cord (Spencer, Thompson, and Neilson, 1966; Groves, Glanzman, Patterson, and Thompson, 1970). Further research suggests that two different types of interneurons in the cord are responsible for habituation and its opposite, sensitization. In the frog and invertebrates, meanwhile, habituation appears to result from changes in the effectiveness of neural transmission (synaptic depression) in monosynaptic reflexes; in higher animals, habituation appears to occur through the mediation of interneurons.

At the cortical level, habituation in connection with the arousal response, as detected by changes in the electrocorticogram, has been intensively studied. An early study (Sharpless and Jasper, 1956) found that the sleeping cat's brain switches to a waking-type brain wave at the sound of a brief tone. With repetition, however, the arousal response becomes shorter and shorter and eventually disappears entirely. The brain continues to sleep unperturbed. If after a period of no stimulation the tone is sounded again, the arousal response returns in full. This phenomenon, called *spontaneous recovery*, is universally reported in habituation studies. Habituation normally proceeds more rapidly the second time. If the tone's pitch is changed after habituation, the brain may respond as if to a new signal. In Sharpless and Jasper's study, this occurred with a change from a 500 Hz to a 1000 Hz tone, but not to a 600 Hz tone.

A later study (Glickman and Feldman, 1961) found habituation of cortical arousal in response to electrical stimulation of the midbrain reticular formation by implanted electrodes, demonstrating that ha-

Spinal cat. **A cat whose cerebral forebrain structures have been surgically removed.**

Spontaneous recovery. **Return of the arousal response after habituation, when the stimulus has not occurred for a period of time.**

bituation of the arousal response occurs somewhere in the central nervous system, not in the receptors. The brainstem reticular formation appears to be importantly involved. Here, in contrast to habituation in the simple invertebrates, enormous numbers of neurons are available, acting in concert (Figure 16.1).

Extensive research on habituation of the arousal response in the human has been performed in the Soviet Union by Sokolov and his co-workers. This form of learning may be thought of as one aspect of the fundamental inhibitory mechanisms governing the brain's

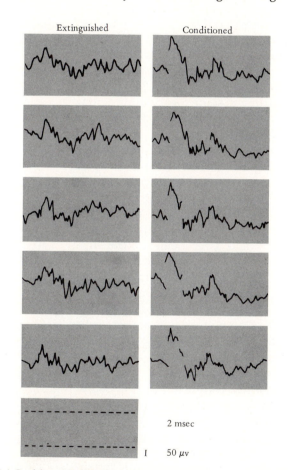

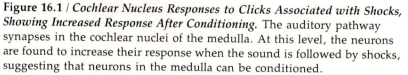

2 msec

I   50 μv

Figure 16.1 / *Cochlear Nucleus Responses to Clicks Associated with Shocks, Showing Increased Response After Conditioning.* The auditory pathway synapses in the cochlear nuclei of the medulla. At this level, the neurons are found to increase their response when the sound is followed by shocks, suggesting that neurons in the medulla can be conditioned.

activities, reflected, for example, in the unitary quality of the subjective content of the attention field at any given moment. However, the transitory character of habituation suggests that its mechanisms are not identical to those underlying the more lasting
changes in the functional organization of the brain usually considered to characterize true learning processes.

Learning at the Hippocampal Level

Thus far we have discussed only the most primitive — in the sense
of early-evolving — kinds of learning mechanisms. Habituation
and sensitization have to do principally with attentional control —
whether or not one alerts to and orients toward a given stimulus —
and with reflex withdrawal out of harm's way in case the stimulus
signals danger. Implied in such learning is some means of recognizing the stimulus the next time it occurs, but we have little evidence
of the nature of that neural trace as yet.

   In 1972 James Olds and his colleagues designed an extremely
well-controlled experiment to distinguish between two theories of
hippocampal function, one considering it as involved primarily in
motor mechanisms, the other conceiving it as a more general information processor that also influences perceptual functions (Segal,
Disterhoft, and Olds, 1972). Twelve rats had electrodes implanted in
the dentate gyrus and in the CA3 and CA1 fields of the hippocampus proper. It was found that, in the course of conditioning,
the dentate gyrus neurons (granule cells) increase their rate of firing
(into the CA3 pyramidals) when the tone signal is paired with the
conditioned stimulus of food, and reduce their rate of firing when
the conditioned stimulus is a shock. One might say that these cells
(or the circuits of which they are an integral part) "learn" to increase or decrease their rate of firing in response to the stimulus cue
as a result of conditioning. That the brain of the animal is now differently structured, for the duration of the conditioning, is apparent
in its altered behavior. Thus the neuroscientist can find altered behavior in the brain neurons paralleling the altered behavior of the
animal. This is not to say, of course, that the changed behavior of
the dentate granule cells causes the changed behavior of the animal. The former merely partakes of the changed functional organization of the brain that the conditioning process produces.

   A change in the behavior of the hippocampal pyramidal cells was
also found. Unlike the dentate cells, the pyramidal cells of *Ammon's
horn* apparently learn quickly to respond with increased firing (per-

Ammon's horn. **The
hippocampus
proper, distin-
guished from the
dentate gyrus with
which it constitutes
the hippocampal
formation; charac-
terized by large
pyramidal cells.**

haps only reflecting their input from the dentate granule cells) when food is the unconditioned stimulus, and persist in their increased firing rate when shock follows the tone. Thus the hippocampal pyramidal cells, or the circuits of which they are an integral part, seem to "learn" to increase their rate of firing in response to the tone, whether it is food or shock that is signalled. This finding may imply their participation in an alerting circuitry, rather than a circuitry differentiating between reward and punishment. With regard to these cells as well, we may say that the brain is now subtly altered in its functional organization as a consequence of experiencing tones associated with food and shock.

Richard Thompson and his colleagues investigated a somewhat different hippocampal functional alteration during conditioning, this time of the classical Pavlovian variety. Rabbits were conditioned to blink their *nictitating membrane* (their protective second eyelid) in response to a tone repeatedly paired with a puff of air directed to the face. Electrodes implanted to record multiple-unit activity in Ammon's horn and in the dentate gyrus revealed an increase in rate of firing preceding the nictitating response (Figure 16.2). In effect, increased hippocampal neuronal activity came to predict the puff of air. Of this remarkable finding, the authors say "The marked increase in hippocampal activity that develops early in training is dependent only upon the paired CS-UCS conditioning procedure. Since it develops within a very few trials of training, it is likely to be the earliest, or certainly one of the earliest, neuronal indications that learning is occurring. In this sense it might be considered an initial process in the formation of the 'engram' " (Berger, Alger, and Thompson, 1976, p. 485).

Nictitating membrane. A second eyelid in some mammals forming a translucent sheath over the cornea as protection.

As we noted in our discussion of habituation, reduction in the intensity of the alerting response when the stimulus proves innocuous and of no significance to the animal implies some form of memory of the stimulus, even in a simple jellyfish or mollusk. In time the animal becomes accustomed to many stimuli, somehow managing to remember them as having no relevance, so that they may not even come to attention at all. There is much research evidence suggesting that, at the mammalian level at least, the hippocampus is instrumental in the process of forming the memory traces that must underlie nonattendance to stimuli in the normal course of things. One clue, already mentioned, is that the animals whose hippocampi have been removed no longer habituate to stimuli on which they have fixed, even if irrelevant to their goal. It is as if they are no longer able to turn their attention and interest off — as if normal boredom and lack of interest with repeated exposure to

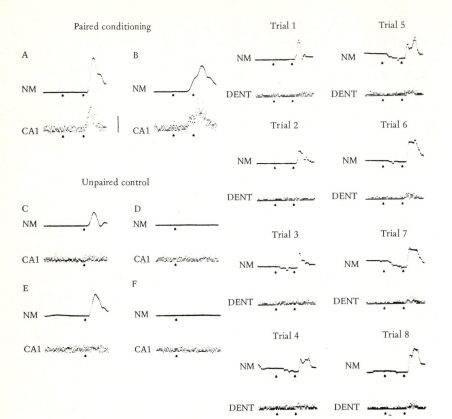

Figure 16.2 / *Conditioning of the Nictitating Response in Rabbits and Correlated Change in Hippocampal Firing.* Note the marked increase in hippocampal cell firing (CA1) when the signal tone is paired with an air puff. With further conditioning, the air puff begins to precede the onset of the signal (second dot). No such change occurs when the two stimuli are unpaired. On the right, note that with successive trials (Trial 1 to Trial 8) the dentate gyrus neural response increases. This is a remarkably rapid process of functional change, signifying neural learning at the cortical level. (NM= nictitating membrane, CA1= CA1 field of the hippocampus, DENT= dentate gyrus.)

meaningless stimuli no longer affects them. In short, it is as if no template had consolidated in their brain by which to recognize the stimulus as familiar.

On the basis of findings such as these, Douglas and Pribram (1966) proposed a model of limbic functioning whereby the hippocampus is specifically involved in a mechanism directing attention *away from* a once-rewarded stimulus that is no longer rewarded. This is not to suggest, of course, that the memory traces whose establishment is dependent on a normally functioning set of hippocampi are actually retained in these structures. The role of the amygdala in this theory is quite the opposite. On the basis of a study in which both hippocampi and amygdalae were removed in monkeys, Douglas and Pribram proposed that the amygdala functions to help the animal "lock on" to a stimulus that has proved significant, whether associated with reward or punishment (Douglas and Pribram, 1969; Pribram, Douglas, and Pribram, 1969).

Still another type of hippocampal learning has to do with spatial orientation to surroundings. There is change of functioning during the conditioning process, a very simple form of learning. But another study found learning of quite a different order to take place through the mediation of hippocampal-cell function. Studying rats with electrodes implanted in the hippocampus, O'Keefe and Dostrovsky (1971) found some 10 percent of the cells increased their discharge rate when the animal was in a particular location (relative to surrounding environmental landmarks) and facing in a given direction. This remarkable observation has implications not yet well studied: it suggests that place learning — orientation to familiar surroundings — is also mediated by hippocampal circuitries.

Learning at the Hypothalamic Level

Various brain regions and circuits associated with fear and pain have been discussed in earlier chapters, as have regions and circuits that appear to partake in the reward systems of the brain. These structures lie along the medial forebrain bundle extending from the midbrain limbic area through the hypothalamus and into the septum, apparently with outlying related regions in the amygdala and hippocampus. These are areas of the brain in which intracranial self-stimulation occurs if a stimulating electrode is implanted in a laboratory animal, and the animal is allowed to operate it.

The most dramatic example of operant conditioning is the response of such an animal upon discovering that pressing a lever produces raw pleasure. The likelihood of the animal's repeating the performance is very high, and the instrumental response is very quickly established, presumably because the reward and the operant behavior are very closely associated in time. The degree of the pleasure sensation may also be a factor. Other kinds of rewards (patting a dog on the head, giving a bear a lump of sugar), by contrast, may elicit learning of the required response very slowly indeed.

Rats receiving electrical stimulation of the hypothalamic region known as the pleasure center preferred this stimulation to food, when given a choice. Rats with electrodes implanted in other brain regions preferred the food reward.

In human terms, the learning of a self-stimulation procedure involves learning, so to speak, to "press lever for kicks," and might well be thought of as a species of know-how. As a result of a repeated rewarding experience, the brain is now so structured that a specific behavioral target (pressing the lever) is formulated in the brain matter. That the rat will seek the goal by another means if the original one is blocked demonstrates that it is no mere reflex motor program that is learned. Whatever behaviors are effective in producing the reward take on a new value and saliency in the animal's behavioral repertoire.

While the speed of most appetitive learning is less impressive than this, the character of the reward-related learning appears to be much the same. If we ignore any signal learning associated with operant conditioning and consider only the increased tendency to respond or, better, to *act* in a particular manner associated with rewarding experience, we might logically look for the underlying change in functional organization within the evaluative structures comprising the limbic system and in the motivational structures within the medial forebrain bundle system. The brain seems specifically designed in these areas to acquire information from the environment about what sort of behavior yields a satisfying state, and to employ this *hedonic* criterion as the basis of behavioral choice. One of the questions confronting the neurophysiologist is how the reward systems of the brain interface with the motivational (energy-releasing and behavior-organizing) systems. In the simplest terms, this problem can be stated: how do we learn not to want to touch a hot stove a second time, and how do we learn to want to do those things that produce satisfaction?

Hedonic. **Based on the pleasure-pain principle.**

The "pleasure centers" in the brain are found intimately mingled with those nuclei that appear to be critical for motivational direction and emotional response. From an engineering point of view, this makes eminently good sense. When an animal discovers food in a given location, or obtains it through some activity, the experience automatically becomes memorable — energized by the reward system, so to speak — and the location or activity is "valued" in a way it was not before, presumably in the interaction of these two systems so closely associated in the center of the brain.

Olds, Allen, and Briese (1971) did a careful mapping of self-stimulation sites, using microelectrodes to detect responses to stimulation of discrete small regions of the hypothalamus. In brief, they found pure self-stimulation sites along the course of the medial forebrain bundle whose stimulation does not elicit hunger, thirst, or sexual drive. The regions that produce hunger, thirst, and sexual drive were found to be separate, though closely intermingled with pure self-stimulation sites: thirst nuclei more anteriorly; compulsive eating mediated by nuclei somewhat above the optimum self-stimulation sites in the middle region; and nuclei associated with copulation again more anteriorly. Sites that appeared to produce both pleasure and hunger were found in the middle lateral region *between* the upper hunger sites and the somewhat lower medial forebrain bundle optimum self-stimulation centers.

Thus motivational systems can apparently be differentiated from the reward system, justifying the notion that the two are not identical in neural terms, and that the reward system exists as an independent learning mechanism through which the direction of drive energies may be reoriented through experience on behalf of adaptive success.

Some experimental results will help to clarify the relationship between these two systems. If an electrode is implanted in a pure self-stimulation site (reward system), the animal will continue to self-stimulate, even if hungry and choice food is available, often to the point of starvation (Routtenberg and Lindy, 1965). If, on the other hand, the electrode is implanted in the lateral hypothalamic hunger region (drive system), weak electrical stimulation might produce eating — but if the food is withdrawn, the animal might drink instead; if the water is withdrawn, it might gnaw on a piece of wood; and if that is withdrawn, it might copulate with a receptive female, all as the result of the same weak stimulation of a "drive center" (Valenstein, Cox, and Kakolewski, 1970).

Such results appear to argue against the long-popular drive-reduction theory of positive reinforcement, since stimulation of the reward system is clearly not drive-reducing in its effect. On the other hand, they appear to support the notion that there is such a thing as generalized drive that may find various forms of expression. Both these findings comport well with our subjective experience of what might be termed pure "drive states." Boredom, for example, does not serve any specific goal or bodily need, and can be relieved by many alternative activities. On the other hand, we are quite capable of compulsive bouts of eating so minimally hunger-driven that one can consume peanuts by the handful during a challenging conversation or good TV show right after a full meal.

Species Differences in Reward-Induced Learning

Numerous experimental efforts have been made to analyze the process by which reward systems become instrumental in the formation of new behavioral tendencies, with some interesting differences across *phyletic* levels (see Bitterman, 1975, for an excellent summary). More sophisticated animals (such as rats and human beings) work less well for rewards, and are slower to learn in connection with reinforcement, if the quantity or quality of the reward is reduced after the start of the experiment. Not so with goldfish: they appear entirely unaffected when their rations are reduced from 40 to 4 *Tubifex* worms for making the correct behavioral choice. Such simple brains appear not to notice a discrepancy between currently offered rewards and those previously encountered. The *depression effect* of lowered reward in more advanced animal forms is difficult

Phyletic. Pertaining to evolutionary levels.

Depression effect. A response of mammals to the reduction in quantity or quality of the reward during conditioning.

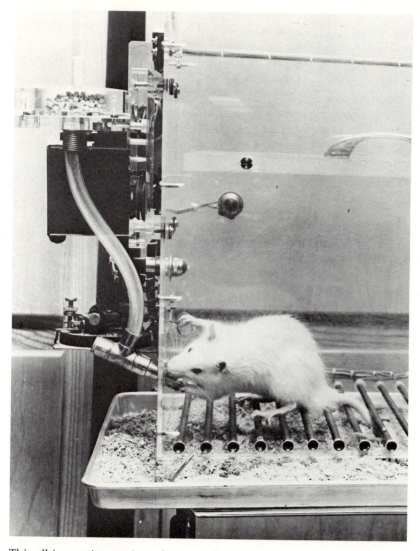

This albino rat is pressing a lever to obtain food as part of a behavioral research program. Experimentation with rats such as this one has shed light on mechanisms of human behavior.

to explain on the basis of simple mechanistic assumptions, though the finding makes good intuitive sense to a human being.

Also, if rats and more sophisticated animals are trained with large rewards for correct responses, their behavior extinguishes more quickly when the behavior is no longer rewarded than if the rewards were small. Not so with goldfish or turtles. The bigger the reward, the longer they will continue trying to get it through re-peated unrewarded trials. In pigeons, on the other hand, the in-verse relation between size of reward and resistance to extinction is the same as in most mammals. Pigeons seem to have the brain ca-pacity to equate the frustration of nonreward (following a large reward) with an aversive stimulus.

If fishes, turtles, or pigeons are randomly rewarded for choosing one or the other of two stimuli, 70 percent of the time for one choice, 30 percent for the other, it is found that they eventually come to choose one or the other discriminative stimulus in ratio ap-proximating 70–30. If the reward schedule is then shifted so that each stimulus is rewarded equally often, their pattern of choice quickly comes to approximate a 50-50 ratio. Interestingly enough, mammals do not adopt this sensible adaptation when confronted with a similar discrimination problem. In fact, the simple random matching behavior of more primitive species has never been dem-onstrated in a mammal. Instead, one of a number of more complex "strategies" tends to be adopted. Confronted with the 70–30 reward schedule, most mammals tend to *maximize* — that is, to respond consistently to the more frequently rewarded stimulus. Sometimes they choose other systematic approaches, such as selecting the choice rewarded on the immediately preceding trial, or system-atically choosing the other stimulus, or apparently "playing hunches," much as human beings do in a gambling situation when the odds are indeterminate.

It is clear from such studies that some changes have occurred in the course of evolution, beginning roughly with the birds and mammals, in the manner by which the reward system is imple-mented in the control of learning and behavior. While a simple mechanistic relationship between reward and learned behavior ap-pears to explain the behavior of simpler forms, more intelligent (perhaps thoughtful) animals use what appear to be hypotheses derived from their experience to attempt to predict the reward, and behave accordingly, thus vastly complicating a simple connectionist process. The mammals appear to insist on *interpreting the meaning* of their experience, even if their interpretations sometimes mislead them into quite unrewarding behavior, rather than permitting themselves to be unthinking passive recipients of environmental manipulation.

The phenomenon of *extinction* also illustrates an interesting dif-ference between the learning processes of primitive and more ad-vanced brains. Extinction of a response occurs when the behavior is no longer rewarded. In mammals, cessation of reward appears to generate an emotional response, reminiscent of our own experience of disappointment. This emotional response seems to militate against repetition of the behavior, as if the behavior were now punished (*frustrative nonreward* is the term usually used). The effect of sudden cessation of an expected reward tends to be quite abrupt. If the reward continues intermittently, however, the extinction process takes much longer: the animal continues to respond, like a gambler hoping to hit the jackpot, a phenomenon known as the *partial reinforcement effect.*

Fishes and turtles exhibit such an effect only in connection with massed trials. If the trials are spaced out, extinction occurs as abruptly as if the reward had consistently appeared in every previous trial. Not so with birds and mammals. Unless the reward is insignificant, rats continue to respond long after the cessation of rewards if those rewards had been intermittent, even when the training trials are spaced over considerable intervals.

There is some question about whether the principle of reinforcement operates in human beings primarily on the basis of the medial forebrain bundle reward system revealed by intracranial self-stimulation experiments. Subjectively, we seem to acknowledge a dual theory of human rewards when we say we do not live by bread alone. Hunger and sex are powerful motivators in the human, as well as in other mammals, but even the lowly rhesus monkey will work hard at learning a task for the reward of merely being permitted to look out a window of its cage at other monkeys at play. How much more important such nonsensual gratifications may be to human beings is subject to argument, but the effectiveness of their capacity to elicit learning is undoubted.

A reasonable hypothesis to account for the seeming duality of human reward systems is that they both operate through the same neurochemical system, the drive-related rewards achieving their effect through one part of the system, the hypothalamus, while the more specifically mood-related rewards achieve their effect in the amygdalar region, where Elsbieta Fonberg discovered a remarkable counterbalancing of high- and low-morale mechanisms in the dog (see Chapter 10). This might be a sound starting-point for speculation that a less "earthy" reward system has grown increasingly important in more recently evolved brains, in view of the vast growth in recent evolutionary time of the basolateral portion of the amygdala and its connections with the prefrontal granular cortex, on whose medial surface a possibly related self-stimulation site has been found (Mora and Myers, 1977). This portion of the cortex has recently been discovered to receive projections from the amygdala

Frustrative non-reward. **The emotional effect of disappointment at finding an expected reward not forthcoming, quickly extinguishing the learned response.**

Partial reinforcement effect. **The tendency of animals to continue a learned response after it is no longer rewarded when the rewards during learning trials were intermittent and unpredictable.**

(Llamás, Avendaño, and Reinoso-Suárez, 1977). The latter researchers comment (p. 796):

In conclusion, the amygdala has been considered as the site of evaluation of
the motivational significance of stimuli from environment and the internal
milieu, exerting its influence by modulating hypothalamic mechanisms. To
this one should add that it has a double influence on the frontal cortices:
indirectly through a thalamic relay and directly by way of the paths identified here. In this way, possibly the higher the evolutionary stage, the connections between neocortex and limbic system increase in complexity,
allowing progressively more complex and finely adjusted patterns of
behavior.

Learning at the Cortical Level

Perceptual learning — learning to discriminate a significant stimulus — appears to occur in mammals at the cortical level, in those
posterior regions of the cortex devoted to sensory registration and
analysis. The development of object perception in children appears
to begin as gradual familiarization with the kinds of cues the environment supplies in its invariant relationships and transforms. Lesion studies point to the dependence of such perceptual learning on
an intact sensory projection cortex, but just how the perceptual
brain is altered in its functional organization upon acquisition of a
new pattern recognition has until very recently been quite mysterious. Some experimental findings have now begun to shed light
upon the question.

> **Perceptual learning.**
> Learning to recog-
> nize things through
> repeated sensory
> exposure.

   In one study, electrical activity in a single polymodal cell in area
18 of the cat visual cortex in response to a flash of light was recorded. Then the response of the same neuron to a click stimulus
was recorded. When the two stimuli were presented together, there
occurred a third pattern of firing that was not a mere combination
of the two separate responses. After 40 such pairings, the combined
response was elicited by the light stimulus alone. This appears to
be an unmistakable example of neural association of two previously
unassociated stimuli. Perhaps it is such shaping of neural responses — no doubt in the context of their widespread neural connectivities — on which perceptual learning is dependent.

   The portion of the primate brain cortex where lesions most se-
verely interfere with visual learning is the inferotemporal region
(Gross, Bender, and Rocha-Miranda, 1975). As we discussed in
Chapter 4, Hubel and Wiesel have described a hierarchy of feature-

detection mechanisms in the visual cortex such that the neurons at each successive level respond to increasingly specific stimuli, but over increasingly broad regions of the visual field. This hierarchy moves progressively from the striate cortex into areas 18 and 19 and into the inferotemporal region, where there are neurons with exceedingly specific trigger stimuli (recall the "monkey's hand" cell) and receptive fields limited only by the field of retinal acuity. We might speculate that it is especially within this region that neural association of invariantly related stimulus features reaches its culmination in establishment of the neural basis of recognition of familiar objects.

Once we understand the neural basis of pattern discrimination, and how it is formed through experience, we shall presumably not be far from a theory of how concepts are acquired, perhaps a theory implicating the very same neural tissues utilized in the formation of our perceptual discriminations.

Finally, language learning must be addressed in any discussion of change in the functional organization of the human brain. Language learning appears, to begin with, to represent both a highly specialized discrimination of auditory patterns (spoken words the child hears) and an intimately associated stereotyped motor program for their pronunciation. Aphasia studies suggest that in early childhood (like most other sensorimotor integrations) both hemispheres participate in this learning process, after which it becomes sequestered in (usually) the left hemisphere, where adult verbal learning presumably continues to occur. Very little research into the neural aspects of the process of verbal learning is being conducted at present, partly because experimentation involving language cannot be conducted on laboratory animals. In view of the fact that motor skills are involved in such learning, both the cerebellum and the basal ganglia might eventually be expected to be found crucially important, though once learning has taken place their participation may be minimal.

The acquisition of motor skills is addressed in Chapter 8 in the discussion of the voluntary motor system.

Studies of the Memory Mechanism

Analysis of the memory process through studies of laboratory animals has been plagued with difficulties, now being overcome with sophistication born of past errors. One such problem concerns the difference between learning and performance. The animal might under certain circumstances "know the answer" but refuse, or be unable, to demonstrate that knowledge in adaptive behavior. Monkeys and other intelligent animals frequently exhibit what appears to be willful noncompliance with the experimenter's all-too-obvious efforts to manipulate them by carrot or stick, giving the impression of being more stupid than they are. In another situation it may be difficult to detemine whether a chemical injected into a rat blocked the memory of shock or the ability to withhold the habitual behavior that elicited the shock. A parallel problem in the analysis of human memory mechanisms concerns the difference between storage and retrieval processes. Did we forget the answer, or did we fail to learn it in the first place? Has the trace of the experience disappeared from the brain, or has something gone wrong with the ability of the brain to reactivate it? What we wish to understand is really two things: how the brain forms a record of our experience, and how that record is "accessed," to use computer terminology, either voluntarily or involuntarily at some later time.

Lesion studies have been particularly fraught with problems of interpretation (Figure 16.3). As Isaacson (1976) has pointed out, the effect of the lesion itself — apart from any effect on learning or

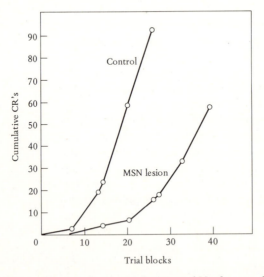

Figure 16.3 / *Effect of Lesions to the Medial Septal Nucleus on Conditioning of the Nictitating Response.* Lesions to the medial septal nucleus, which controls the hippocampal theta wave and presumably therefore its normal functioning, can be seen in this experiment to severely retard the conditioning process.

memory — may influence perception, motivation, arousal, or motor activity. A similar caution is necessary in interpretating the effects of neurologically active chemical substances on memory or learning. A somewhat more straightforward interpretation may be made of the results of injecting substances that improve learning or retention, especially when they are administered *after* the learning trials to rule out effects on attention or perception during training. The same rule applies to studies of *retrograde amnesia* (failure, presumably, of long-term memory storage) when the experimental variable is introduced after training trials and tested after their behavioral effects can be presumed to have worn off.

The earliest studies of animal memory loss induced by treatments following training trials examined the curious effect of an electric current passed through the animal's head (in the case of rats or hamsters or mice, with electrodes clipped to their ears) (Duncan, 1949; Gerard, 1949). The experiment itself is very simple. The animal is given a simple learning task allowing for very quick acquisition, such as learning not to step down from a pedestal onto an electrified grid floor, or not to go through a hole into a dark compartment where it has received a shock. Some time after training, a brief electroconvulsive seizure is produced in the animal by passing a current through the brain, and it is then tested for retention of the training experience. If the electroshock is administered shortly after the training trial(s), the training seems to be totally forgotten: the animal unhesitatingly does what it did the first time, and is again punished with a shock. Control animals not treated to the post-training electroshock treatment scrupulously avoid repeating the initial behavior. It has been plausibly hypothesized that the post-training treatment somehow interferes with consolidation of the memory into a lasting form or, alternatively, with the animal's ability to retrieve the memory of the dreadful experience. The punchline to all such experiments is that the longer the time lapse between training trials and post-training treatment, the more likely it is the memory will remain intact. If the interval between training and electroshock treatment is brief, forgetting is apt to be quasi-permanent. The animal can be put through the training-treatment cycle time after time, and each time it is as if it had never had the training experience before. If the intensity of the electroshock current is increased, the same effect can be produced when the treatment is delayed as much as an hour (Gold, Bueno, and McGaugh, 1973). The gradient of retrograde amnesia depends on the dose, duration, and number of electroshock treatments as well as the time elapsed since training trials.

Other studies have shown that the retrograde amnesia effect is not dependent on convulsive seizures as such. Subseizure levels of electrical stimulation of subcortical structures (caudate nucleus, substantia nigra, hippocampus, amygdala, and midbrain reticular formation) can also produce amnesia for immediately prior experiences (McGaugh and Gold, 1976; Kesner and Wilburn, 1974). This finding should not, of course, be interpreted as indicating that memory processes occur uniquely in those regions of the brain, since their stimulation undoubtedly has widespread effects within the brain. Surprisingly, electrical stimulation of the reticular formation in the midbrain region after training sessions has also been found to facilitate learning (Bloch, 1970); under certain conditions the same is true of stimulation of the amygdala (Gold and McGaugh, 1975; Gold, Macri, and McGaugh, 1973). We are not yet in a position to interpret these findings definitively. Parallel findings of improved memory of a visual-discrimination task in mice have been demonstrated with either pre- or post-training administration of such chemical stimulants as strychnine, picrotoxin, pentylenetetrazol, and amphetamines (McGaugh and Herz, 1972). Again, the memory-improving effect of such drugs is greatest if they are administered very shortly after the training sessions.

A great deal of research has sought to ascertain the biochemical correlates of memory. Emphasis has centered on drugs that interfere with either RNA or protein synthesis. A number of these (such as puromycin, cyclohexamide, acetoxycyclohexamide and anisomycin) can be shown to interfere with retention in a wide variety of animal species (rodents, goldfish) when given near the time of training. However, it is impossible to say whether these chemicals disrupt memory through their inhibitory effect on RNA or protein synthesis, or through some other effect on brain processes. The hypotheses about the importance of RNA and/or protein synthesis in memory consolidation merit further research to clarify their role.

A number of researchers are exploring the role in memory consolidation of norepinephrine and various pituitary hormones, with results that, though intriguing, are still confused and indeterminate.

Summary

The mammalian brain, unlike the brains of more primitive life forms, is not completely specified by genetic instructions, allowing for an adaptive flexibility not found in the insect or in other more completely "prewired" neural systems. For mammals, and especially for the primates and ourselves, the functional organization of the brain takes its shape in significant measure as a consequence of the experiences the organism meets after birth, and this shaping of the brain's functional organization is the process of learning. In human beings, this process may well continue throughout life.

Another feature of the human brain in particular is that early learnings can be largely superseded, and to some degree erased, by later learnings. Thus, under appropriate circumstances, the effects of abnormal or traumatic early experience can be overcome in human beings by later normative experiences. In other species, even the great apes, neurotic behavior is notoriously difficult to correct. An even more important feature of the human brain's special learning capacities is its ability to build progressively larger and more complex systems of knowledge and understanding through its facility at the acquisition of facts and the manipulation of abstract concepts. Thus one learning can build on another, rather than erase it, or function in parallel with it, exemplified by the building of the science of biology. In this respect the human capacity for learning appears to be categorically different from that of lower life forms.

The concept of the engram as the outcome of the learning process appears now to be misleading, since the alteration that occurs in the brain through the learning experience is more likely a distinctively functional change, probably represented simultaneously in many portions of the brain. All efforts thus far to identify a unique change in neural tissue associated with a particular memory have proven futile, and appear to represent a faulty assumption about the nature of the learning change. What happens in learning is more probably the establishment of a subtly different *pattern of firing,* perhaps in widely dispersed regions of the brain, which might be quite difficult to demonstrate through neurophysiological techniques.

The study of learning at the neuronal level has begun with an effort to understand the process of habituation in simple invertebrates. The gill-retraction reflex of the sea hare, *Aplysia,* has been found to diminish in intensity with the repetition of a meaningless stimulus as the effect of running out of neurotransmitter in the activating neurons; another set of neurons governs sensitization to dangerous stimuli, overriding the habituation effect. Similar experiments have demonstrated the mechanisms of learning at the level of the spinal cord and brainstem, and at the cortical level in the case of hippocampus. Learning through reward systems of the brain has been demonstrated in many animal species. In mammals such learning presumably involves the reward systems of the medial forebrain bundle, where James Olds discovered pleasure centers. One very significant finding is that fishes and turtles, representing primitive forms, appear to learn by a somewhat different operant-conditioning process than do the more advanced species represented by birds and mammals. Learning in the human again differs in that the character of the reward is often not physiological pleasure but an emotional response or mood of euphoria associated with amygdalar, rather than hypothalamic, functioning.

Studies of the memory mechanism in laboratory animals have been plagued by the problem of distinguishing between deficits in learning and deficits in performance resulting from experimental interventions. Thus drugs may block consolidation of the memory of a training experience, or merely interfere with later accessing (recall), or perhaps alter the animal's perception, or motivation, or state of arousal, or motoric activity, thus interfering with its performance. In an effort to focus specifically on the memory function itself, a great deal of experimentation has been done on the effect of administering treatments after training trials are completed (presumably after learning has taken place). The earliest such studies found that electroshock can apparently completely block the animal's memory for an immediately preceding aversive stimulus (retrograde amnesia). The longer the elapsed time between training trials and the electroshock treatment, the more likely the animal is to recall the previous experience. This finding suggests that memory is a time-dependent function, becoming less vulnerable to obliteration over time.

Surprisingly, other studies have demonstrated that electrical stimulation of the midbrain reticular formation may facilitate learning when administered after training trials are completed. The same appears to be true under certain conditions for stimulation of the amygdala. A parallel finding is that either pre- or post-training administration of such chemical stimulants as strychnine, amphetamine, picrotoxine, and pentylenetetrazol improves memory for a visual-discrimination task. Here too, the effect on memory is greatest when the drugs are administered close to the time of training sessions.

Much research has focused on the possible role of RNA and protein synthesis in the formation of stable memory traces, and that of norepinephrine and various pituitary hormones and the recently discovered endogenous opioid substances, the endorphins. The results are still confusing and indeterminate.

Part V / *Current Issues in the Neurosciences*

This survey has so far examined what is known about the brain and how it produces the varied phenomena of the psychological sciences. Neuroscientists and psychologists inspired by these discoveries are now beginning to probe vast new domains of understanding that promise to dwarf in importance what has thus far been established. The new fields of research opening before us hold the promise of solutions to theoretical and human problems thus far untouched by the discoveries of the past.

Part V will introduce in a preliminary way some of these exciting new directions of exploration on which brain scientists have now embarked. The materials we will discuss are still largely speculative in their implications, and should be viewed not as solid fact to be stored away in our fund of understanding, but as findings whose full significance is not yet known, as is always the case at the forefront of scientific research.

The neurosciences' quest has in recent years acquired a number of new features that promise to become even more pronounced in the future. One is the growing emphasis on neurochemistry. The previous emphasis was upon neuroanatomy and the "wiring diagram" of the brain — its overt physical structure and relations of parts — and upon the neuron as a quasi-electrical signalling system between those parts. But the structures of the brain are now increasingly being viewed as arenas where the biochemical processes of the several neurotransmitter systems act out their distinctive roles in a great pageant — and the number of distinct chemical systems of the brain is growing as our knowledge increases. Meanwhile the neuron itself is beginning to be recognized as the site of enormously complex and subtle interactions, with its neighbors and with its surrounding chemically rich fluids. Micro-region activities are beginning to overshadow in importance the signalling properties of the axon. The synapse, once viewed as a fairly straightforward chemical switch, is being revealed as a highly intricate system involving many chemical substances, often in chained sequences.

Another important feature of recent developments is growing appreciation that brain and body are one — that what goes on in the body affects the mind, and what happens in the mind affects the body. We have traditionally sought to separate the two, the medical doctor operating on the physical corpus as if it were a mechanical thing, the spiritual doctor, (psychotherapist, shaman, religious leader) operating on the soul as if it were independent of the body. Yet ancient folk wisdom has always been there to remind us that the separation is artificial. The depressed man, rejected by his beloved, suffering searing disappointment in life, brings himself out of his despair by hard physical labor, and the man sick unto death is restored to vigorous health when hope of future is regained, when there is something worth living for at last. We are now in a position to begin to understand, as we were not just a few decades ago, the intimate interplay between consciousness and its substrate, the physical self.

A third feature of recent developments is a team approach to the creative work of scientific discovery in the neurosciences, and an increasingly interdisciplinary character to scientific research. The psychologist is becoming thoroughly dependent on the work of the biochemist and the neurophysiologist for effective response to the challenge of human problems, and the neurophysiologist has long since invaded the psychologist's once-sacred territory of learning and thought, motivation and emotion. Librarians are having difficulty deciding where biology ends and psychology begins. The following chapters will provide graphic illustration of these developments.

Chapter 17 / *The Enkephalins: The Brain's Own Narcotics*

The search for the mechanisms of pain, and for means of bringing it safely under control, is one of the most pressing issues confronting the neurosciences. Pain is universally recognized as a vitally important function, alerting the animal to bodily harm and its threat, much as does fear, but there are times when we could devoutly wish it would go away and leave us in peace. It is easier to accept the sharp pain of injury, such as when we are pricked with a pin or stub our toe, than the other kind, the slow burning pain that may reach its peak much later, after the warning signal has been obeyed, and that tends to linger on and on. We can readily understand the necessity to survival of the initial warning pain, but a headache, or the stinging pain of a burn, or the intractable pain of a wrenched lower back, or of terminal cancer, seems more difficult both to understand and to tolerate.

Until the nineteenth century, a shot of whiskey might be the sufferer's only protection against the fearful pain of a tooth-pulling, or even an amputation. In 1798 Humphry Davy discovered the miraculous anaesthetic properties of nitrous oxide, and at last the cruel suffering of past eras began to prove more manageable. Five years later morphine was introduced into medical practice; it soon acquired great popularity, both for its ability to deaden chronic pain and its ability to produce euphoria. Morphine's addictive properties were not recognized until long after indiscriminate use had rendered countless people hopelessly dependent on it. Later modifications, such as heroin in the 1890s and Demerol in the 1940s, were introduced as nonaddictive pain killers but also proved addictive. The golden dream of a nontoxic, nonaddictive pain reliever seemed ever to elude our grasp.

Today the goal appears close at hand, thanks to a remarkable series of research findings that began only about a decade ago, and continues with ever-greater intensity today. In 1969, David 397

Reynolds of the Stanford Research Institute in Menlo Park, California, published a brief article in *Science* describing surgical operations on the rat simulating human abdominal surgery, using electrical stimulation of a region in the brainstem as the only analgesia (Reynolds, 1969). Three animals, with electrodes implanted in an effective spot just lateral to the midbrain central gray region, underwent the operation, and none showed any aversive reaction to the procedures. It was demonstrated that the animals were not paralyzed, and pain sensitivity returned within five minutes after brain stimulation ended.

It had already been known that electrical stimulation of the animal's whole brain with external scalp electrodes could render it insensitive to pain or other sensations. But here for the first time was a specific location in the brain where electricity could block pain without impairing sensitivity to other kinds of sensory input. In 1971 a second study more thoroughly exploring the matter, this time by workers in John Liebeskind's laboratory at UCLA (Mayer *et al.*, 1971), appeared in *Science*. The effective points were located in the dorsal and ventral tegmentum of the midbrain, as well as the dorsal medial thalamus and the far posterior hypothalamus. Some of the points also proved to be reward-producing, some only when pain was inflicted. The regions in which analgesia was produced only partially overlapped self-stimulation sites. One interesting finding was that rats quickly learn to self-stimulate at a spot that produces analgesia but no self-stimulation when painful electric shocks are applied to their tails, demonstrating that reinforcement can derive from pain reduction as well as pleasure.

The researchers theorized that brain stimulation at these locations attenuates pain by activating neural systems that function under normal circumstances to block pain. Morphine, they proposed, may activate a neural pathway that releases neurotransmitters whose normal function is to inhibit pain perception — pathways located in the hypothalamus, the midbrain central gray, and the more posterior periventricular regions where electrical stimulation was found effective. In view of the finding that a high transection of the spinal cord abolishes the inhibitory effect of morphine on ascending pain signals, they also postulated a descending inhibitory pathway capable of blocking pain, arising in those brain regions activated by morphine, now stimulated electrically to produce analgesia.

Two years later there came another impressive breakthrough in the unfolding story of the mechanisms of pain. Candace Pert and Solomon Snyder at the Johns Hopkins University School of Medicine reported a direct demonstration of the existence of opiate receptors in nervous tissue, and a method of rapidly determining the relative potencies of potential narcotic drugs and their antagonists.

It had long been assumed that opiates achieve their effect much as do neurotransmitters and neurohormones in general, by binding to specific receptor sites on their target cell membranes, into which they fit like a key in a lock. Now the existence of such binding sites, and a method of locating them in the brain, was established. The method makes use of the specific opiate antagonist naloxone, which appears to compete with opiates to occupy opiate receptor sites. The brain tissues of rats, mice, and guinea pigs were homogenized and incubated for a time with naloxone that had been rendered radioactive. After careful washing to remove all unbound naloxone, the radioactivity of the whole brain homogenate was measured to estimate the number of binding sites. The same procedure can be used to compare binding in different brain regions. This technique revealed in the rat the heaviest binding (and thus the heaviest concentration of opiate receptors), surprisingly, in the corpus striatum. No opiate receptor binding at all was found in the cerebellum, and relatively little in the cerebral cortex.

By treating homogenized neural tissue with a glucose solution, it has been found that the synaptic structures tend to condense out separately from other neural tissues, which makes it possible, using such devices as the centrifuge, to isolate them for special study. The several fractions of neural tissues from the brains of these animals were separately treated with radioactive naloxone and tested for radioactivity. The fraction containing the most bound naloxone was found to be the synaptic structures; the least naloxone was found in the fraction containing the cell nuclei (within the soma), and the soluble (liquid) portion contained none. This finding clearly demonstrates that the opiate receptors are closely associated with synaptic sites.

The existence of opiate receptors in the brain was simultaneously and independently demonstrated by two other laboratories, that of Eric Simon at the New York University School of Medicine and that of Lars Terenius at Uppsala University in Sweden. The time was ripe for the breakthrough, a finding with significant implications. Since opiates such as morphine do not occur naturally in the brain, it seemed evident that there must be some naturally-occurring endogenous substances, perhaps operating as neurotransmitters, whose activity is similar to that of the opiates. The search for such a substance was on.

The Discovery of the Enkephalins

John Hughes and Hans Kosterlitz, at the University of Aberdeen in Scotland, had been studying the effects of morphine on involuntary muscle, in preparations of guinea-pig intestine and mouse vas deferens (the tube that carries semen from the testes), which contract under electrical stimulation. This contraction is suppressed by morphine and, they discovered, also by extracts of brain tissue. Morphine suppression is inhibited by its antagonist, naloxone, which was also found to inhibit the effect of the extract of brain tissue. This finding meant that, whatever the substance in the brain, it was clearly binding to opiate receptors, and constituted the sought-for endogenous opioid, or at least one such. Hughes and Kosterlitz were able to isolate the factor from pig brains: it consists of two *peptides* (short chains of amino acids, not long enough to be called proteins), each containing only five amino acids. They called these peptides *enkephalins* ("in the head").

If enkephalins were to prove to be neurotransmitters, they were certainly the largest such molecules yet found. Most known and suspected neurotransmitters were much smaller, similar in size to a single amino acid. Both of the enkephalins were found to consist of the sequence tyrosine, glycine, glycine, phenylalanine, and either methionine or leucine; hence the designations *methionine enkephalin* and *leucine enkephalin* (see Figure 17.1).

The evidence is now substantial that enkephalins are, indeed, neuromodulators in the brain. Moreover, they appear to be trans-

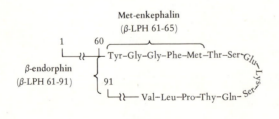

Met-enkephalin
(β-LPH 61-65)

β-endorphin
(β-LPH 61-91)

Tyr–Gly–Gly–Phe–Met–Thr–Ser–Glu–Lys–Ser–Gln–Thy–Pro–Leu–Val

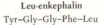

Leu-enkephalin
Tyr–Gly–Gly–Phe–Leu

Figure 17.1 / *Formulas of the Enkephalin Peptides.* Both leucine enkephalin and methionine enkephalin consist of just five amino acids linked in a chain. As such, they are the largest molecules yet suspected of being neurotransmitters. They appear to be specifically associated with an ancient system governing pain and euphoria. Their discovery was one of the most exciting developments in recent neuroscience.

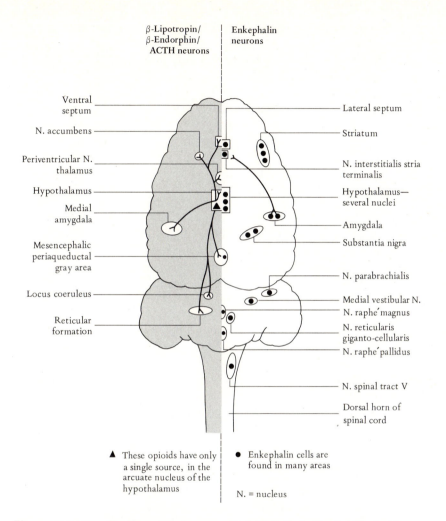

Figure 17.2 / *Localization of Endogenous Opioid Cells in the Rat Brain.* Note in the right half of the figure the many brain regions where the enkephalins may be found, but only in regions below the modern thalamocortical system.

mitter substances specifically associated with neural pathways mediating pain and emotional response. They are found distributed in the brain in concentrations closely paralleling the distribution of opiate receptors (Figure 17.2), and in the spinal cord as well. There is also evidence that they are confined to the region of synaptic nerve terminals, as neurotransmitters would be expected to be. However, they appear to function as neurotransmitters in a somewhat different fashion. They are, like morphine, inhibitory in their effect. But unlike such other inhibitory neurotransmitters as gamma-aminobutyric acid, they appear to hyperpolarize the membrane of the postsynaptic cell by blocking the channels in its membrane through which sodium ions normally flow under the influence of arriving depolarizing (excitatory) impulses. Theory has it that morphine acts in a similar manner.

But, to complicate matters, there is now evidence suggesting that opiate receptors are to be found not only on the postsynaptic membranes of target cells, but also on nerve terminals. Snyder has proposed that neurons that release enkaphalin synapse upon the terminals of excitatory neurons. The enkephalin would bind to the opiate receptors on the postsynaptic membrane and increase the conductance of sodium across it, partially depolarizing it. Then when a nerve impulse reached the terminal, there would be a decreased amount of excitatory transmitter release. This would be another example of presynaptic inhibition, such as was discussed in connection with motor functions.

The next chapter in this unfolding saga concerns the work of Avram Goldstein of Stanford University, director of the Addiction Research Foundation. In 1975 Goldstein's co-workers reported opioid activity in extracts of the pituitary gland, especially the posterior neurohypophysis. A pituitary hormone of unknown function called beta-lipotropin, isolated long before, was later found to be a peptide, 91 amino-acid residues in length. Its specific sequence was published eleven years later. It was then noticed that the sequence of amino acids 61–65 was the same as that of methionine enkephalin. Goldstein and Li tested the entire beta-lipotropin peptide and its fragment 61–91 for opioid activity. The entire peptide is apparently devoid of activity, but the 61–91 fragment was found to have about the same potency as methionine enkephalin, and was designated *beta-endorphin* (endogenous morphine). Later, Roger Guillemin's group at the Salk Institute in La Jolla, California, was to show that the fragment 61–76 is also about as potent an opioid as methionine enkephalin and to designate it alpha-endorphin.

The next question to arise was whether the enkephalins are products of the cleaving of the larger peptide by enzymes. One problem with this hypothesis was that there was no known pathway from the pituitary into the brain, and thus no way for the larger peptide to get in. Beta-lipotropin itself has never been found in the brain (the pituitary is, properly speaking, not part of the brain), and beta-endorphin is present only in small amounts. The method of production of the two enkephalins in the brain is still in question, and the likelihood is that the two endorphins, beta and alpha, although they have similar effects when injected into the brain, are not a natural part of the brain's pain-control system. At the moment there is speculation that there may be a pathway from pituitary to brain after all.

The Role of Substance P

Almost 50 years ago, while looking for acetylcholine in extracts of brains and intestinal tissues, the biochemists Ulf von Euler and John Gaddum happened on a substance that acted like acetylcholine, causing intestinal contractions and dilating blood vessels to lower blood pressure, but turned out to be a peptide instead. Somewhat arbitrarily, they designated it *substance P*. Its amino-acid sequence was worked out only in 1970, when Susan Leeman and Michael Chang of Brandeis University found a substance that stimulates salivation in animals. Having worked out its sequence of eleven amino acids, Leeman and Chang then demonstrated it to be the long-forgotten substance P. Substance P had been difficult to study because its structure was unknown, and preparations were impure. Once its structure was known, however, it could be produced in pure form in large quantities, and it has been the object of intensive research ever since. Substance P is now known to exist in both the brain and spinal cord and in the autonomic nervous system. The question is: what is it doing there?

One clue appeared when Fred Lembeck, of the University of Graz in Austria, discovered that there is ten times more substance P in the dorsal roots of the spinal ganglia (sensory fibers from the periphery) than in the ventral roots (motor fibers from the cord), suggesting that substance P is a neurotransmitter used by the sensory neurons. The suggestion was confirmed by Masanori Otsuka's group at the Tokyo Medical and Dental Center, who not only found the same substance-P concentration in the dorsal roots, but also showed it to be an excitatory neurotransmitter activating neurons in the spinal cord.

Further clarification was offered by Tomas Hökfelt of the Karolinska Institute in Sweden, who found that many of the small-diameter fibers of the dorsal horn of the spinal cord, long assumed to be pain-transmission fibers, contain substance P, as do the nerves of the tooth pulp. It was later found that substance P is concentrated in the nerve terminals of those neurons. Furthermore, tying off the dorsal roots was found to cause a buildup of substance P on the side toward the cell body, indicating axon transport of the substance from cell soma to terminals, and disappearance of the materials from the dorsal horn. Finally, when substance P is injected in the region of spinal sensory neurons, including those that mediate pain, it proves to be excitatory. Given all these independent pieces of evidence, it appears highly likely that substance P is an excitatory neurotransmitter — perhaps *the* excitatory transmitter — within the pain pathways to the brain.

At this point it must have seemed evident that the mechanism of pain sensation was finally coming clear. What remained to complete the picture was the question of how the opiates — or our endogenous opiates, the enkephalins — block the pain impulses from reaching the brain and consciousness. The answer was shortly forthcoming from the laboratory of Leslie Iversen in Cambridge, England. Methionine enkephalin was found to block the release of substance P from neurons of the *trigeminal nucleus* of the brainstem, a region richly supplied with pain nerve terminals and substance P. To complete the picture, the inhibitory effect of the enkephalin was found to be blocked by naloxone, the opiate antagonist.

But what brings the enkephalins into play to block pain pathways by preventing the release of substance P? How might stimulation of the *periaqueductal gray* region of the midbrain produce analgesia? Liebeskind and his colleagues have now found strong evidence of a fiber tract, using the neurotransmitter serotonin, that descends from this midbrain region to the spinal sensory centers. Stimulation of its neurons produces analgesia, and the pain-killing effect is blocked by naloxone, which identifies it as a part of the opiate system. What is suggested is that enkephalin neurons in the cord, activated by the descending pain-suppressing pathway, suppress the release of substance P to achieve their effect.

Trigeminal nucleus (tri-JEM-i-nal). **The nucleus of the trigeminal nerve (the fifth cranial nerve) in the brainstem which is interconnected with the facial region.**

Periaqueductal gray. **The gray matter immediately surrounding the cerebral aqueduct leading from the third to the fourth ventricle.**

Relieving Slow Pain in the Human

Surgeons in wartime have often been astonished by the apparent stoicism of soldiers brought back from the front lines with horrible wounds, many of whom do not even request treatment for their pain, but respond with normal aversive reaction to injection of an antibiotic. It also appears that some individuals can face suffering much better than others. Do such individuals have a more efficient endogenous pain-killer system?

Recent reports provide new insight. Human patients with intractable chronic pain have been effectively treated by stimulating the brain with implanted electrodes in the periaqueductal midbrain region and in the walls of the third ventricle. The resulting pain relief specifically alleviates "slow pain" of the fine-fiber type; it does not affect the acute pain of a pinprick. Moreover, this pain suppression is immediately reversible by naloxone, demonstrating that the system involved is the one affected by the opiates. But it was also found that such stimulation dramatically increases the quantity of *beta-endorphin* in the ventricular fluid, with no enkephalin of the leucine variety.

The same researchers report that there are cell bodies containing beta-endorphin in the basal hypothalamus (immediately above the pituitary) with long fiber projections into the midbrain periaqueductal gray matter, where they found a high concentration of beta-endorphin fibers in the rat. They also report the highest concentration of beta-endorphin to be in the anterior part of the rat hypothalamus, unmistakably establishing the presence of this larger peptide in the brain, with dense concentrations of the fibers around the wall of the third ventricle. Hosobuchi and his colleagues postulate this forebrain portion of the pain-suppressive opiate system to have been stimulated *antidromically* (in reverse direction along the axon) in their patients by stimulation of the midbrain region. The existence of this anterior extension of the opiate system offers a vast new basis for speculation about the mechanisms of pain control, suggesting that under certain psychological circumstances pain can be momentarily alleviated.

Recall that methionine enkephalin is in fact a segment of beta-endorphin, and could be cleaved from it enzymatically. Perhaps the two substances are employed by the brain in two independent pain-control systems. Guillemin and his group have recently isolated another substance, designated *anodynin,* whose structure is quite unlike the endorphins, but which also blocks pain. Cohn, Cohn, and Taylor (1978) report that another substance, dibutyryl cyclic GMP, apparently blocks pain by a nonopiate system, since it is not reversed in its effect by naloxone, and has none of the depressive effects of the opiates and opiate-like peptides. Astonishingly, dibutyryl cyclic GMP was found to protect rats from burn trauma fatal to morphine-treated rats. It appears that pain research has only just begun. Perhaps we can look forward shortly to much more satisfactory methods for the control of pain.

Many years ago the Chinese found pain to be effectively treated by inserting needles into certain points on the body surface and stimulating the tissue by twirling them. It is a later refinement to pass a mild electric current through the needles. This method, known in the West as acupuncture, was for many years discounted as at best an exploitation of the power of suggestion. No longer. Acupuncture analgesia has been unequivocally demonstrated to be effective in the laboratory animal, as well as the human sufferer. The prevailing theory is that such stimulation causes the release of enkephalins in the nervous system (it often takes about 15 minutes to begin to work), and the phenomenon is under intensive research. The most dramatic evidence for the enkephalin-release theory of acupuncture is the fact that its effect is almost instantly abolished by administration of the opiate antagonist naloxone.

Chapter 18 / *New Light on Drugs and Addiction*

Addiction may be broadly defined as a physiological or psychological dependence that develops over time through repeated exposure to something. This very broad definition allows one to speak of addiction to a person, a trusty blanket, golf or chess, gambling, certain foods, cigarettes, alcohol, sleeping pills (barbiturates), wake-up pills (amphetamines), anxiety-reducing pills (Librium, Valium), cocaine — even marijuana, which, like a trusty blanket, apparently has no physiological addicting powers. Though the most dangerously addicting drugs are the opium derivatives, dependence on nicotine can be just as complete, and cigarettes, unlike heroin, cause cancer. Some people simply cannot stop smoking. It is as if the will were powerless to decide against the temptation where the addictions are concerned, even if the behavior is known to be life-threatening.

How can we explain this strange human vulnerability to certain kinds of self-indulgences and compulsive habits, even when they are known to be self-destructive? Curiously, it is easier to understand in the case of the physiological addictions, where neuroscientists have begun to develop some sophisticated theory concerning the addictive process.

When a given drug proves addicting, in the sense that the individual repeatedly exposed to it becomes dependent on a continued supply to "feel normal," sudden withdrawal of the supply produces distinctive symptoms characterized as the *withdrawal syndrome*. This syndrome signifies that the body's chemistry (more specifically, its neurochemistry), has changed in accommodation to the substance and that lack of the substance is now felt as abnormal. The body must readjust to what was once its normal mode of functioning, and in this process of readjustment the addict suffers. In the case of alcoholism, the symptoms of withdrawal are known as *delirium tremens* and include the shakes, convulsions, and frequently horrifying visual hallucinations. In the case of heroin addiction, the

Withdrawal syndrome. **The distressing effects of ceasing intake of a drug to which the body has become addicted.**

Delirium tremens. **A quasi-psychotic state representing one of the withdrawal symptoms in alcoholism, characterized by frightening hallucinations.**

407

symptoms may include severe depression, stomach cramps, sleeplessness, diarrhea, dilated pupils, gooseflesh, and generalized physical discomfort. (The term *cold turkey* refers to the gooseflesh.) The withdrawal symptoms of other drugs, such as barbiturates (downers), amphetamines (speed), and the benzodiazepines (Librium and Valium), are equally unpleasant and psychologically stressful.

For reasons not yet fully understood, delirium tremens can be relieved by barbiturates or benzodiazepine antianxiety drugs as well as by another shot of booze. This phenomenon is known as *cross-tolerance*. Heroin withdrawal symptoms are similarly alleviated by other opiates, such as methadone, but there is no cross-tolerance between, on the one hand, alcohol, the barbiturates, and the antianxiety drugs, and, on the other, the narcotic alkaloids.

Tolerance is best defined as the need to administer ever-higher doses of a drug in order to achieve an effect equivalent to that of the original dose. This phenomenon is characteristic of many drugs, both addicting and nonaddicting, but is of particular concern where, as in the case of the opiates and barbiturates, as well as the amphetamines, the required dose reaches toxic levels. Researchers have begun to unravel the mechanism of the tolerance phenomenon. One aspect of it appears to be that the drug, as a foreign substance in the body, stimulates the liver to increase the quantity of the enzymes that will metabolize it, thus more quickly eliminating it from the system. Another, and subtler, aspect known as *cellular tolerance*, which all known addictive drugs exhibit, is not yet understood. It is as if the cells themselves have altered their internal processes to make use of the substance, and now require it.

This chapter will discuss some recent directions of research in this important field.

Is Alcoholism an Opiate Addiction?

Alcoholism is our most prevalent form of drug addiction. Not until recently, however, was it recognized as a true addiction. For one thing, many people who drink, even in large quantity, never seem to become truly "hooked" in the sense of forming a physiological dependence on alcohol. For another, unlike heroin, which elicits a beginning tolerance in a single application and a physiological dependence very quickly, alcoholism is usually very slow in developing. Yet a number of clues have now begun to suggest that heroin addiction and alcoholism may have a common biochemical basis.

Cross-tolerance. The tendency of different addictive drugs to produce the tolerance phenomenon for each other.

Tolerance. The tendency for certain drugs to require increasing dosage to obtain the same effect.

Cellular tolerance. That aspect of physiological addiction in which the body's need for more of the addictive substance to produce the same effect is not the result of more efficient elimination of the substance from the body.

One is the similarity of their withdrawal symptoms. A more important clue is the discovery of a metabolic pathway through which, in the presence of alcohol, the neurotransmitter dopamine can lead to the production of narcotic alkaloids in the brain under certain circumstances (that is, in some individuals).

In the opium poppy (*Papaver somniferum*), the requisite intermediate in the biosynthesis of morphine is a complex molecule called *tetra-hydro-papaveroline*. It has now been found that this substance could be produced in the brain when alcohol interferes with the normal metabolic destruction of dopamine. The primary metabolic product of *ethanol* (drinking alcohol) is the chemical *acetaldehyde*, which competes with the normal enzyme metabolizing the monomine neurotransmitters at the synaptic terminals. When that happens, it may form the beginning of an alternative metabolic chain leading to the production of *tetrahydropapaveroline* (*THP*), which could then be transformed to morphine as it is in the opium poppy.

Experimental tests by Virginia Davis and Michael Walsh at Baylor University in Houston have demonstrated the feasibility of such a chemical pathway. Rat brainstem homogenates were incubated with dopamine and either ethanol or acetaldehyde. When a cofactor, nicotinamide adenine dinucleotide (NAD), was added, the formation of THP was virtually abolished; but in the limited supply of this cofactor naturally present in the homogenate, THP remained the predominant metabolite. The addition of either ethanol or acetaldehyde, in short, was found to significantly increase the synthesis of THP in the brainstem through inhibition of the normal metabolic breakdown path of dopamine and its diversion into the THP pathway.

Davis and Walsh also demonstrated that the final step in conversion of THP to morphine-like alkaloids could also occur. After injecting radioactive THP into rats, they found the radioactive urine excreted by these animals to contain such alkaloids as normorphine, morphine, norcodeine, and codeine.

In further support of the hypothesis that alcoholism is a true addiction that may involve the biogenesis of morphine-like alkaloids in the brain, Davis and Walsh cite several observations. Rats habituated to alcohol seem to form a tolerance to morphine, since a dose lethal to rats not habituated to alcohol is not lethal to them. A relationship between alcoholism and opiate addiction has long been suspected, since opiate addicts may substitute alcohol — as much as a quart of whisky a day — during periods of abstinence, and many were previously alcoholics. While THP itself may produce analgesia and dependence, as similar alkaloids have been shown to

Acetaldehyde (ass-et-AL-di-hyde). The first metabolic breakdown product of alcohol.

Tetrahydropapaveroline (tet-ra-hy-droh-pa-PA-ver-oh-leen). THP, the chemical substance produced by the opium poppy which is turned into morphine and other opiates.

do, Davis and Walsh find it a more intriguing possibility that dopamine may under certain circumstances progress down a metabolic pathway similar to that taken in the opiate poppy (see Figure 18.1). They also suggest that other addictive drugs of the hypnotic type, such as chloral hydrate and paraldehyde, which also potentiate THP synthesis, might involve a similar path and addictive mechanism.

An interesting sidelight on alcohol addiction very recently came to light. It has long been suspected from informal observation and anecdotal reports that some individuals are more prone to alcohol addiction than others, and, more generally, that there are great individual differences in physiological response to alcohol. But systematic studies, especially studies focusing on differences in physiological response, have been few. Recently, however, Schuckit and Rayses (1979) reported in *Science* that acetaldehyde concentrations are significantly higher after a single dose of alcohol in the blood of healthy young men with an alcoholic parent or sibling than in the blood of matched control subjects without family histories of alcoholism.

Previous studies had found a similarly high acetaldehyde concentration in the blood of abstinent alcoholics, but it might have been the cumulative result of long, heavy exposure to alcohol. Schuckit and Rayses' study specifically discounted such an explanation by eliminating heavy drinkers from the experimental subjects, and by matching them with their controls for amount of alcohol consumption. The study thus clearly suggests that there are different familial patterns in the ability to metabolize alcohol safely, without excessive buildup of acetaldehyde, and that healthy people with family histories of alcoholism may unknowingly be at risk of developing an opiate-like addiction to a substance others can safely enjoy. Schuckit and Rayses conclude, "This study demonstrates the potential importance of carrying out prospective investigations into the possible causes of alcoholism and the need to carefully test children of alcoholics" (Schuckit and Rayses, 1979, p. 55).

Is Susceptibility to Alcoholism Inherited?

The discovery of individual biochemical differences in efficiency of acetaldehyde metabolism, in conjunction with the demonstrated ability of such a deficiency to lead to the production of THP, and potentially to morphine in the brain, inevitably raises the question of whether the disease of alcoholism, or the proclivity toward it, is something we inherit. The evidence is impressive. Studies have

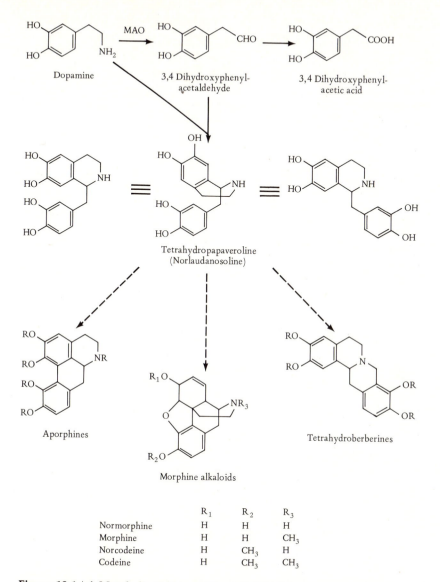

	R_1	R_2	R_3
Normorphine	H	H	H
Morphine	H	H	CH_3
Norcodeine	H	CH_3	H
Codeine	H	CH_3	CH_3

Figure 18.1 / *A Metabolic Pathway Through Which Dopamine Might be Turned into an Opiate Compound in the Presence of Alcohol.* Recent evidence suggests that alcoholics may suffer from a true opiate addiction as a result of lack of an appropriate enzyme in their blood to properly metabolize alcohol, allowing the abnormal buildup of acetaldehyde. It has been suggested that offspring of alcoholics might be tested for absence of the enzyme to warn them that they are at risk for alcoholism if it is found lacking. Perhaps only those who are genetically lacking in this respect are at risk for the disease of true alcoholism.

shown a 25–50 percent lifetime risk of alcoholism in sons and brothers of severely alcoholic men, but this could be explained on grounds other than an inherited trait. However, other studies have found a concordance rate for alcoholism in twins (if one is alcoholic, is the other?) that clearly supports the genetic hypothesis: 55 percent for identical twins compared to 28 percent for same-sex fraternal twins. More impressive are studies of children separated from their biological parents shortly after birth and raised without knowledge of their parents' drinking problems. The incidence of alcoholism among such people in adulthood is three- to fourfold greater than in similar children whose biological parents were not alcoholic. Interestingly enough, children whose biological parents were not alcoholic, but whose adoptive parents were, had relatively low rates of alcoholism.

Since the children in these studies, conducted in Scandinavia and the United States, had no opportunity to be inducted into alcoholism by their alcoholic parents, the genetic hypothesis is strongly supported. Other evidence of genetic differences in response to alcohol were found in a study aimed at a quite different question: why the incidence of alcoholism is significantly lower in some cultures than others, specifically among certain Oriental populations. The observation that many Orientals exhibit pronounced flushing of the face and signs of mild-to-moderate intoxication after drinking amounts of alcohol that leave Caucasians apparently unaffected led Peter Wolff of Children's Hospital Medical Center in Boston to question the common anthropological assumption that population differences in behavior are determined by cultural variables.

To study the question Wolff systematically compared the flushing response in young American men and women of Caucasian ancestry with young people of comparable age in Japan, Taiwan, and Korea. His results are dramatic. Wolff found that 83 percent of Oriental adults flushed after drinking, both visibly and as detected by optical densitometry of the earlobe, while only 2 of 34 Caucasians did so with a greater quantity per body weight of 5 percent beer. Flushing began 2–7 minutes after drinking, which corresponds closely to the time when alcohol can first be detected in the blood, and reached its peak at 30–37 minutes, corresponding to the point in Caucasians when blood concentrations reach a peak after a single dose of alcohol on an empty stomach. At that time the strong flushers reported pounding sensations in their heads; relative increases in blood pressure were observed in 74 percent of the Orientals and only one Caucasian (3 percent). The Orientals also reported significantly more symptoms of intoxication.

These results suggest that ethnic differences in response to alcohol may have a genetic basis, and that ethnic groups with significantly low incidences of alcoholism may avoid large amounts of alcohol owing to their greater autonomic responsiveness, which tends to be experienced as unpleasant.

To control for differences in history of alcohol consumption and other postnatal environmental factors, Wolff also compared the flushing responses of healthy, full-term Caucasian infants and Japanese and Taiwanese infants. Even though the Caucasian infants received more alcohol per body weight than the Orientals, the results paralleled those for the adults. Of the Oriental infants tested, 74 percent responded with a pronounced flush, while only one of the 20 Caucasian babies exhibited a visible flush and a measurable densitometer reading. Thus dietary and cultural factors can be safely ruled out as responsible for the physiological response differences observed.

What Is the Biochemical Mechanism of Dependence?

Discovery of the mechanism whereby brain cells are altered by exposure to an addicting substance, rendering them dependent on its continued supply, should lead to better means of preventing addiction and of freeing individuals from addiction. Several lines of current work seem to point to an early answer to the problem. Ever since Wei and Loh demonstrated that methionine enkephalin and beta-endorphin can cause morphine-like physical dependence in rats, the search for the addicting process has focused on administration of these drugs to experimental animals. The simple model proposed by Solomon Snyder assumes that under resting conditions the brain's opiate receptors are exposed to a continuing level of enkephalins, some of the receptors remaining unoccupied. When an exogenous opiate, such as morphine, is administered, it binds to these unoccupied receptors, potentiating the pain-resistant effect of the system as a whole. With sustained treatment (repeated "fixes"), neurons receiving the opioid effect find themselves overloaded, and by some feedback mechanism convey to the enkephalin neurons to stop firing (and releasing their enkephalin), which leaves the receiving cells exposed only to the exogenous drug (e.g., heroin). With the natural supply of the body's own opiates thus inhibited, a continuing supply of the artificial stimulant is necessary to avoid withdrawal symptoms.

Snyder's model is supported by research indicating that other neurotransmitters in the brain have means of controlling their quantity at the site of their action through feedback mechanisms, shutting down the supply when the target cells become overloaded. Assuming the enkephalins to operate as regular neurotransmitters in the brain, the enkephalin neurons might be expected to have a similar controlling mechanism within the opiate-receptor system. Two chemical mechanisms have already been suspected of involvement in such an inhibitory governor mechanism in the case of the opiate receptors: one involves sodium ions and the other involves *cyclic nucleotides*, specifically *guanosine monophosphate*, a substance activated within the neuron soma to alter its firing characteristics. It is known that the opiates and enkephalin elevate the amount of cyclic guanosine monophosphate in brain tissue slices.

> *Cyclic nucleotides.* Chemical compounds which serve as internal regulators of a neuron's firing rate in the case of some neurons.

   The biochemical mechanism underlying physiological dependence on the barbiturates through continued use is unknown, as is also true of the amphetamines, and the newly discovered danger of dependence on the benzodiazepines, Valium and Librium. Withdrawal symptoms are similar to those associated with opiate and alcohol dependence, and a similar mechanism might be involved. It was once assumed that the distress of withdrawal symptoms, and the fear of them, was the major factor in continuing use of an addictive drug, but that is now recognized to be a misconception. In the case of the opiates, there is also a strong craving for the drug. In the case of nicotine, the craving for another cigarette is equally strong though the withdrawal symptoms are by no means as pronounced. Research into the nature of that craving has just begun. What little evidence there is appears to suggest that the craving, as distinguished from the withdrawal symptoms, may be closely associated with the familiar environment surrounding drug use, to which the habit has become conditioned.

The Effect of Drugs on the Unborn

The discovery of the disastrous effects of thalidomide opened up a new field of investigation: the field of *teratology*. For a number of years concern focused solely on the possibility that drugs taken by a mother during pregnancy might produce physical deformities in the child. More recently it has been recognized that some drugs produce behavioral defects (behavioral teratology) rather than physical deformities — or, most disturbing of all, intellectual or emotional abnormalities that might not manifest themselves until years later, and hence not be recognized as related to the prenatal drug

> *Teratology.* The study of the disastrous effects of some medications or conditions on the development of the fetus.

administration. Intense new research interest in this possibility within the past few years has begun to yield some disturbing findings.

It has recently been established that children are more likely to be mentally retarded if their mothers took thalidomide during pregnancy, even when no physical deformity resulted. The same thing is true of the anticonvulsant drugs hydantoin and trimethadione. It is now well established that the drinking of alcohol by a pregnant mother can produce a severely retarded child with a characteristic deformity of facial features — a syndrome that went entirely unrecognized until very recently. Even more serious is the fact that some obstetric medications are still being routinely administered as hospital policy or on specific standing orders of doctors as routine procedure for their patients, in some cases long after their effectiveness has been disproved, and in some cases even after their ability to produce teratological defects has been demonstrated. Yvonne Brackbill of the University of Florida has estimated that medications are given during labor and delivery in 95 percent of all cases in this country, often on the physicians' standing orders rather than tailored to the specific needs of the situation.

In a study of 3500 healthy full-term babies selected for having experienced the most uncomplicated deliveries, Brackbill and her colleague Sarah Broman of the National Institute of Neurological and Communicative Disorders and Stroke found that obstetric medication affected the children's behavior at least through seven years of age, a finding consistent with the results of many smaller-scale cross-sectional studies done by others. These effects were found to be dose-related, the greatest effects being suffered by children whose mothers had received inhalant anesthetics or the strongest drug doses. The effects were especially apparent in cognitive functioning and gross motor ability, where such children lagged significantly in development relative to children born with little or no drug medications.

Brackbill and Broman point out that obstetric medications have long-lasting deleterious effects on children because (1) such medications cross the placenta rapidly and reach the fetus' brain easily, since the blood-brain barrier is still immature, (2) they are only slowly eliminated from the newborn's body, since its liver and kidneys are not yet fully functioning, and (3) such important brain regions as the hippocampus (cognitive function) and cerebellum (motor function) are not fully developed at birth. If the effect of such drugs is at all deleterious, therefore, the neonate is particularly vulnerable to their influence.

The opiate narcotic drugs have long been suspected to be behavioral teratogens. But because addicted mothers also present other potentially deleterious conditions, such as poor nutrition, heavy cigarette smoking, and often abuse of other drugs, it has been difficult to assess the matter. It is also common for babies born to heroin addicts to be treated for some time after birth with barbiturates, antipsychotic drugs such as chlorpromazine, or narcotics to alleviate their withdrawal symptoms. It is nevertheless established that children born to these mothers exhibit a wide range of symptoms typical of drug withdrawal (tremors, excessive high-pitched crying, abnormally strong reflex responses, irritability, failure to gain weight despite a voracious appetite) and later tend to be hyperactive with short attention spans. Donald Hutchings of the New York State Psychiatric Institute (who notes that some 3000 such babies are born each year in New York City alone), after testing adult rats exposed to methadone, concludes that narcotics are implicated in childhood hyperactivity.

The dangers posed by the possibility of behavioral teratology are only now becoming apparent, and efforts to detect more human teratogens are underway. The United Kingdom and Japan now require that new drugs be tested on laboratory animals before being approved for obstetrical use, though it is recognized that effects in the human are often subtle, and might not be revealed in standard laboratory tests of animal intelligence.

Chapter 19 / *New Light on Madness*

Anyone who observes a full-blown schizophrenic episode, whether of catatonic stupor or paranoid terror or any of the many other dramatic manifestations of this neurological disorder, must recognize that a serious derangement of the brain's functioning is taking place. The person we knew prior to the episode is now entirely different, out of communication with us, somehow not human, having apparently taken leave of his or her senses. Yet the brains of schizophrenics examined after death are often perfectly normal in appearance, giving no hint of disorder. Moreover, the abruptness with which a schizophrenic episode can occur, turning a sane and sober individual into someone whose behavior is incomprehensible, suggests that some catastrophic occurrence, such as an epileptic seizure, is taking place in the brain — but there is no evidence of such an event. That is the puzzling thing, and the frightening thing, about human madness, which has led in the past to accusations that the insane are possessed of devils. Today we know that such a derangement of normal functioning is a medical problem, an affliction to which the fantastic bionic computer in our skulls is vulnerable. We can even cause it at will, in the laboratory, for research purposes.

Perhaps it is unreasonable to expect such a massive system of interconnected living cells in constant interaction with one another to be entirely stable. In fact, human brain function is from certain points of view a remarkably fail-safe operation. But just what it is that goes so weirdly wrong with its operations at times, such as after heavy ingestion of amphetamines, or in severe niacin deficiency (pellagra, whose symptoms are similar to those of schizophrenia), or ergotism resulting from poisoning by fungus-infected grain (possibly the cause of the madness that led to the Salem witchcraft trials), or ingestion of a tiny amount of LSD, is still unknown. New evidence is beginning to suggest that what we call schizophrenia is merely a common symptomatology shared by **417** many causative agents, substances and conditions that set the vast machinery reeling into disorder. A wide variety of brain disorders, for example, express themselves in the curiously stereotyped behavior of paranoia, and nobody knows why. Perhaps we should remind ourselves that pneumonia was believed fairly recently to be a single disease with a single causative agent; now we know that many agents may produce the same symptom pattern. If we can isolate different factors that produce the symptomatology of schizophrenia, we may move swiftly toward a more rational clinical approach to its prevention and cure.

The same remarks appear to pertain to the depressions. There is now strong evidence of distinct subsets of depression for which treatment must be specific if it is not to be useless or contraindicated. The manic-depressive form of depression is responsive to lithium carbonate medication, and endogenous psychotic depressions to one or another of the tricyclic or monoamine oxidase-inhibitor antidepressant drugs, while neurotic depression is unaffected by either but responsive to intensive, supportive human contact with a caring person, preferably in a nondrugged state. Suicide prevention thus requires us to be aware of such differences, and calls for some sophistication in our therapeutic efforts. We will briefly survey some of the exciting routes research into the phenomenon of madness is taking.

Is Schizophrenia an Environmental Disorder?

Recent research has begun to question the validity of the long-accepted assumption that the incidence of schizophrenia is uniform all over the globe, approximately 1 percent of any given population. The new evidence has to do with locales where the prevalence of schizophrenia is unusually high — often small regions within a single country, whose other regions exhibit the classic one-in-a-hundred incidence. The peninsula of Istria, jutting into the Adriatic Sea from northwestern Yugoslavia, is one such area: schizophrenia is about three times as prevalent there as in the rest of Yugoslavia, according to a ten-year study of the problem, and interviews with the inhabitants suggest that this has been the case for generations. Are the inhabitants of this region genetically uniform with a high risk of schizophrenia in their family lines, or is there something in the Istrian soil that is poisoning their brains?

Another such region is the west of Ireland. The high prevalence of schizophrenia in this rural area has been long recognized, and used to be attributed to the emigration to America of the healthier stock, leaving the families at risk behind. This hypothesis has been disproven however, by a study showing that emigrants from western Ireland are also unusually prone to schizophrenia, a finding that seems to cast doubt on the environmental explanation of the disorder. Another such region of high incidence in northern Sweden has been studied for 26 years. In the United States, New England has long had a reputation for a high prevalence of insanity. During the period from 1922 to 1960, the rate of first admissions for schizophrenia in Massachusetts, Connecticut, and New York was found to be two-and-a-half times that of Kansas, South Dakota, and Idaho.

From 1934 to 1937 the anthropologist-psychologist Meyer Fortrex studied the Talensi people of northern Ghana, and found an exceedingly low prevalence of schizophrenia, approximately one case in 5000 people. Fortex returned in 1963, and in the same villages, even the same families, found the prevalence of schizophrenia to have risen sharply — 13 cases where 27 years before there had been only one. A baffling discovery.

Relatively low rates of schizophrenia have been found in other regions: Formosa, among the aborigines and Chinese immigrants to the region; Papua, New Guinea; and some African countries.

In the United States, England, Japan, Norway, and Ireland, the prevalence of schizophrenia is apparently higher among the lower socioeconomic groups and the least well educated. It has been argued that such findings reflect the "downward drift" of individuals at risk for schizophrenia. In India, however, studies since 1930 have found a higher prevalence among the best-educated and most Westernized sector of the population, making the "downward drift" hypothesis less convincing.

Most puzzling of all the demographic findings is the evidence that a disproportionate number of schizophrenics are born in late winter and spring. This conclusion is attested to by studies of more than 125,000 patients in nine northern-hemisphere countries; studies of South Africa, Australia, and New Zealand also show a tendency for a higher proportion of schizophrenics to be born in the cooler months. A *secular trend* has recently been identified in such figures: the peak months for births of schizophrenics appear to be shifting toward later in the year in America. In Missouri in the 1920s the peak month was February; in the 1930s it was March and April; in the 1940s, April and May were the months of highest risk. These findings are highly significant, both statistically and for our understanding of the nature of the disorder, but what they mean is still unknown. They may suggest the effects of such things as envi-

Secular trend. A trend of change over time.

ronmental poisons (such as lead or other heavy metals), or nutritional differences, or perhaps viral infections with long latency periods (true schizophrenia does not manifest itself until late in the second decade of life). Perhaps the conditions surrounding pregnancy are different for children born in early spring than for those born during the warm months — a different diet for the mother, differential prevalence of infectious disorders — leading to a greater chance of some subtle brain deformity or defect that later manifests itself in an "at-risk" personality. More research will undoubtedly soon bring more clarity to this very puzzling and fascinating series of findings.

One clue that may prove relevant is the recent finding by Singh and Kay (1976) that wheat gluten in the diet may be a precipitating factor in schizophrenia-prone individuals. After studying the progress of schizophrenics maintained on a grain-free and milk-free diet, they replaced a special drink containing soy flour with one containing wheat gluten, on a double-blind basis. The result was a dramatic exacerbation of the schizophrenic process and diminishing response to drug treatment. When the wheat gluten challenge ended, the course of improvement under the same medication regimen resumed. Singh and Kay note that schizophrenic exacerbation in response to wheat gluten was particularly marked in the more seriously ill patients with poorer therapeutic prognoses.

Is Schizophrenia an Organic Disorder?

Organic disorders are characterized by tangible evidence of brain abnormality, such as loss of neurons or abnormal firing patterns (epilepsy). Schizophrenia and the endogenous depressions have classically been defined as functional disorders, because of a presumed absence of any such neurological evidence. Yet there are accumulating indications that a subset of schizophrenics have brains that are anatomically different, as detected by computerized X-ray tomography, and that others have neurological "soft signs" indicative of minor neural abnormalities. Many schizophrenics' heads deviate from normal bilateral symmetry, or have other characteristics suggestive of a congenital deformity. There may be kinds of subtle brain damage that manifest themselves only in late adolescence and are capable of producing the kinds of behavioral abnormalities we speak of as schizophrenia.

In a quantitative study of the brains of ten schizophrenics and ten controls at autopsy, only one measurement that consistently and significantly differentiated the two groups was found: a greater thickness of the schizophrenic corpus callosum. This anatomical difference is difficult to interpret, since so little is known about the function of this massive sheet of nerve fibers interconnecting the two hemispheres. Because the corpus callosum is poorly myelinated in early life, infants are functionally equivalent to individuals whose hemispheres have been surgically separated. This finding implies that the two hemispheres come into integrated contact only gradually over the course of childhood, and that lateralization of functions, such as speech and spatial visualization, occurs gradually in the course of the early developmental years. Might an abnormally thick corpus callosum be related to faulty development of this hemispheric interaction, which in turn later results in schizophrenic phenomena?

In a search for early signs of children later to become schizophrenic, Theodore Blau observed that children with academic and behavioral difficulties tend to draw circles clockwise, while the more common manner is counterclockwise. (A corresponding tendency in handwriting toward rightward spiraling is thought to be associated with personality peculiarities.) Blau wondered whether this tendency represented a neurological *soft sign* indicative of abnormal development of the lateralized brain, possibly associated with schizophrenic developments. In a longitudinal study of matched groups of children, Blau found a significantly greater number of the right-circlers diagnosed schizophrenic by the time they reached age 21 — 2 percent versus 21 percent (Blau, 1977). Thus one more curious finding is added to our knowledge of schizophrenia.

Soft sign. A symptom of neurological disorder which is mild or not obviously related to the problem.

Schizophrenia: The New LSD Connection

Ever since it was noticed that mescaline bears a remarkably close resemblance structurally to dopamine, the notion of the schizophrenic as a producer of endogenous hallucinogens has been intriguing. The discovery of LSD as a derivative of the ergot fungus, and recognition of its family resemblance to serotonin, gave rise to another wave of enthusiasm for the notion of the schizophrenic as a "walking LSD factory." This hypothesis lost favor, however, when it became apparent that LSD symptoms are quite different from those of schizophrenia, even in its acute, florid manifestation. (Hallucinations elicited by LSD and mescaline are primarily visual, while schizophrenic hallucinations appear to be almost exclusively auditory, and usually verbal, akin to the way we "hear" our own thoughts.)

A new route of research recently evolved when Michael Trulson and his colleagues at Princeton developed an "animal model" of the action of LSD by observing dose-response relationships in the cat. The most pronounced and reliable of the cat's behavior signs under the influence of LSD were limb-flicking (as if to shake something off its paw) and abortive grooming (orienting to some part of its body as if to begin biting, licking, or scratching, but not completing the act or completing it in midair). Others included hallucinatory behavior (visually tracking, hissing at, batting, or pouncing on nonexistent objects) and investigatory behavior (pawing in corners, sniffing at objects). None of these behaviors were observed in response to other classes of psychoactive drugs, but all were observed in cats whose brains were depleted of serotonin by inhibiting its synthesis. Since it had already been established that LSD inactivates brain serotonin systems by directly depressing the activity of the serotonin neurons of the raphé nuclei, it was hypothesized that it is this action of LSD that is responsible for the symptoms.

To test the generality of the animal model for LSD, the investigators administered psilocybin, another hallucinogen derived from the sacred mushrooms of Central America. Psilocybin has a chemical structure similar to that of LSD, and similarly depresses raphé-nucleus activity, cutting the brain's supply of serotonin. The symptoms were the same. On the other hand, delta 9-tetrahydrocannabinol, the active substance in marijuana, was found to be without effect. Like the effect of LSD in humans, the effects of psilocybin were lasting — up to eight hours after administration — and resulted in the tolerance phenomenon (more of the drug was needed on succeeding trials to produce an equivalent effect).

More recently, Trulson and Jacobs (1979) studied the effect on cats of long-term amphetamine use in light of their animal model. It has long been known that long-term use of amphetamine is capable of producing classic symptoms of paranoid schizophrenia. Amphetamine has also been shown to release both norepinephrine and dopamine at the synapses of the neurons that make use of them, an important finding in support of the dopamine theory of schizophrenia. However, another researcher had reported both limb-flicking and abortive grooming in cats treated for 11 days to high doses of amphetamine, suggesting that serotonin, in addition to norepinephrine and dopamine, is depleted by amphetamine.

Trulson and Jacobs undertook a careful study to test this new hypothesis. They found short-term amphetamine administration to produce only small decreases in serotonin, in conjunction with large decreases in norepinephrine and dopamine. Long-term administration of the drug, however, produces large decreases in serotonin (40 to 67 percent) in all brain regions examined — a new finding. The limb-flicking and abortive grooming characteristic of central nervous system depletion of serotonin also appeared, increasing to statistical significance (in comparison with controls) by day 5 and reaching *asymptote* (the point at which further doses fail to increase the rate of occurrence of the signs) by day 8. Since a single injection produced no such symptoms, it appears that the serotonin content of the brain decreases only with repeated administration, and that depletion of brain serotonin is progressive with continued exposure to amphetamine.

These results reopen the question of whether the hallucinogenic effects of depleted serotonin stores may be significantly involved in the production of schizophrenic symptomatology, not only in amphetamine abuse but in acute schizophrenia as well. A competing "serotonin theory" of schizophrenia must now be considered. Maybe some manifestations of schizophrenia are indeed produced by the same mechanism through which the brain poison LSD operates.

Two very recent studies point the way to the future. Postmortem examination of the brains of long-standing paranoid schizophrenics found above-normal levels of norepinephrine at four loci in the limbic system, but no deviation from normal in any other parts of the brain, even the hypothalamus and preoptic areas, known to be rich in norepinephrine innervation. The most conspicuous abnormalities were in the *ventral septum,* where the values were three times normal, and in the adjacent bed nucleus of the *stria terminalis,* where there was double the normal amount of norepinephrine. In the *nucleus accumbens* (also adjacent to the septum) and the mammillary bodies, the level was approximately 50 percent higher than normal. These unusually high levels of norepinephrine clearly suggest a specific neurochemical feature of this form of schizophrenia.

With respect to the dopamine hypothesis, an even more recent study suggests that the antipsychotic drugs used to treat schizophrenia act in restricted regions of the brain, specifically area 24 of the *anterior cingulate gyrus,* the *orbital cortex* (area 12), and the region of the temporal lobe tip (Brodmann's area 38); they do *not* act in the putamen and nucleus accumbens, targets of the nigrostriatal and mesolimbic dopamine pathways respectively. This is the first evidence suggesting that schizophrenic symptomatology does not arise in the basal ganglia (despite their heavy use of dopamine), but in regions concerned with cognitive and affective functions — that is, in cortical rather than subcortical nuclear tissues.

All three of the familiar neurotransmitters — dopamine, norepinephrine, and serotonin — appear now to have been implicated in schizophrenia. Reports that naloxone, the opiate antagonist, can block schizophrenic hallucinations suggest that the enkephalins may yet prove to be involved as another neurotransmitter substance. (Beta-endorphin injected into the periaqueductal gray of rats produces symptoms resembling catatonia.) The excitement of the pursuit grows even as the problem appears more and more complex.

Chapter 20 / *New Light on Mind-Body Relations*

In 1946, Caroline Thomas began an epidemiological study of Johns Hopkins Medical School students in an effort to identify any psychological traits associated with the development of coronary heart disease, hypertension, mental disorders and suicide. Cancer was included as a purely physiological condition, unrelated to psychological factors. Thirty years later, 48 of the subjects had developed cancer. Thomas found their psychological profiles, based on psychological tests on entrance to medical school and yearly questionnaires about their health and living habits, to be strikingly similar to those of subjects who had committed suicide. Despite the growing body of evidence that there are environmental factors of purely nonpsychological significance associated with cancer, this study has aroused interest in the possibility that cancer, like many other illnesses, may be related to psychological state and life experiences.

Psychological factors of a different sort were found to be associated with eventual development of coronary heart disease, high blood pressure, and mental illness. The cancer and suicide cases tended to be "low-gear" people, outwardly unemotional, who had had relatively distant and cold relationships with their parents. Those who developed heart disease, hypertension and mental illness tended to be rated high in anxiety and tension, and anger under stress. How could a relationship between personality variables and "chosen mode of death" be rationalized?

A more fundamental question about the relationship between mental state and bodily functioning must also be asked: is it possible that our morale, our fundamental joy in living and hope for the future, is in some sense a prerequisite to our continued life? Do we become less able to fend off disease, as well, perhaps, as personal tragedy, under certain kinds of emotional conditions? Were the Ancients right in suggesting that a healthy mind produces a healthy body, and are some kinds of life experience, through the mental states they produce in us, dangerous to our health?

The history of medicine is replete with dramatic anecdotal descriptions of something of the sort. Typical is the story of a woman dying of tuberculosis in a sanatorium who fell in love with a newly admitted patient. Suddenly her disease process was reversed, and she became progressively better as the relationship between the two of them deepened. They planned to marry as soon as they were discharged, but her lover was discharged first, and on leaving broke off their relationship. Her health then took a precipitous plunge, her disease process greatly intensified, and she died of tuberculosis very shortly thereafter. A slight variant on this classic tale is that of a man whose prostatic cancer was being closely monitored in the hospital (the growth and retreat of prostatic cancer can be readily followed through urine samples). When another patient dying of cancer was admitted as his roommate, the first patient's prostatic cancer suddenly began to grow rapidly. When the roommate died and the patient was again alone in the room, his cancer abruptly ceased its rapid expansion, returning to its prior nearly stable condition.

Many doctors can relate tales of a similar sort from their own practices. Nevertheless, it is very difficult to put the almost self-evident proposition that the mind affects the body to controlled test, and as a consequence its full implications for medical practice, and for human understanding, have been slow in becoming accepted. Now the neuroscientists are joining the medical practitioners in actively pursuing this new frontier of knowledge.

The Mystery of Hypnosis

Throughout the history of science, observation of something that defies understanding has been the springboard to that curiosity out of which great new scientific discoveries have arisen. It is curious, then, that the phenomenon of hypnosis, so dramatic and so readily demonstrable, has been all but ignored by the science of psychology. In fact, numerous attempts to deny its existence or significance dot the literature. Whatever the explanation for this apparently willful blindness on the part of science to a fact about the human brain pregnant with suggestive possibilities, we have today not a shred of a theory about how hypnosis works, nor what it implies about the structure of the mind. A breakthrough in this area may well revolutionize our theories of brain function, shedding fresh light on the two most ill-understood phenomena: the attention mechanism and conscious awareness.

Yet hypnosis has been widely accepted as an effective substitute for local anesthetics in such minor surgery as dentistry, and Paul Sacerdote, associated with Montefiore Hospital in New York, maintains that one cancer patient in four will respond well to hypnotherapy for relief of chronic pain. Under hypnosis a good hypnotic subject can be stuck with a pin and not feel it (nor respond with the most primitive of reflexes, the withdrawal response). The effect seems to involve a different pain-gating system from that utilized by the enkephalins and the narcotic alkaloids, but we have no knowledge of how such a system might work.

But it is not merely pain-killing of which hypnosis is capable. Supernormal muscular strength, presumably based on an abnormally high level of activation of spinal motor units, is a common demonstration of the powers of hypnotic suggestion. Another remarkable effect of hypnosis is to render the autonomic nervous system completely amenable to control by thought: subjects in stage demonstrations can be made to switch suddenly from tears of grief to violent outrage, and again to placid calm or uproarious mirth in response to suggested thought processes. Perhaps the most bizarre bodily effect of the hypnotic mental state is its ability to cause wheals to form on the skin of a subject informed that he has been burned, and to remove warts by the mere force of the suggestion that they will go away.

In one study, 14 patients with warts on both sides of the body were hypnotized and given the suggestion that the warts on one side of the body would go away. In 9 of the 14 cases, all or nearly all the warts on that side vanished in several weeks, while the warts on the other side were as plentiful as ever. Another subject made a mistake, or misunderstood the instructions, and the warts on the other side disappeared. In an identical study at Massachusetts General Hospital, the warts on both sides disappeared even though the subjects had been instructed that only those on one side would disappear. No doubt different presentations of the suggestion are responsible for the discrepancy.

It may be easier to accept the proposition that hypnosis can produce amnesia (forgetting of events that occurred during the hypnotic state), since this is an effect of mind upon mind. But to emphasize such phenomena would be to miss the major point. Hypnotic suggestion has been demonstrated to produce specific effects on the body as well, and no one has yet explored the range of its powers to alter bodily function. There are, for example, anecdotal reports of its effectiveness in the treatment of Parkinsonism. When adequate tests are run, we may discover a wide variety of bodily disorders that will respond to this remarkable capacity of the brain to receive and act on hypnotic suggestion. To date, sober scientists have been reluctant to explore this area of knowledge, so sullied with quackery and mysticism, so unreliable in its implementation, and apparently requiring special talent in its application.

Trained hypnotists claim that it is possible to teach almost anybody to become a hypnotic subject in a few trials, after which the subject can hypnotize himself or herself as necessary, such as in controlling chronic pain. If this is true, it appears to behoove psychologists and neuroscientists, as well as medical practitioners, to take this aspect of the mind-body relationship more seriously. The discovery of the eighteenth-century physician, Franz Anton Mesmer, deserves to become a legitimate and avidly investigated scientific topic.

The Effect of Psychological Stress

In discussing hypothalamic mechanisms, we saw that an intricate and widespread system, both neural and chemical, prepares the body in many ways to meet emergency — the condition of *physiological emotion*, usually registered subjectively as some form of fear or of anger. Its adaptive function is clear. When activated, the sympathetic branch of the autonomic nervous system causes the heart to beat faster, the blood pressure to increase, and the circulatory system to alter so that blood is shunted out of the viscera and into the skeletal musculature in preparation for vigorous physical exertion in fighting or fleeing an enemy. In nature, among mammals, fear tends to be highly momentary, and rage usually sham or bluff. Emergency situations are soon over, and the animal goes back to its business as if nothing had happened.

Physiological emotion. The change in bodily state associated with such emotions as rage and fear, representing activity of the sympathetic nervous system.

This is frequently not the case among human beings, perhaps particularly in urban settings, where close contact with others not only causes emotional upset but often requires us to suppress overt expression of our feelings. Heavy responsibilities combined with uncertainties about the future may keep many of us in a chronic state of anxiety, which is unnatural in the sense that we were not preadapted for it in our prehistory or in the makeup of our nervous system. Many have asked what portion of our physical ills may be the direct result of the unrelieved stress inherent in our way of life, so different from the life of the peasant, or the nomadic hunters and gatherers, or even the average American a hundred years ago. During the 1960s, *psychosomatic medicine* emerged as a field of inquiry into those diseases, such as gastrointestinal ulcers, hypertension, and arteriosclerosis, likely to be stress-related in origin.

Hans Selye (1976) has carefully analyzed the characteristic physiological process that occurs in the rat under conditions of prolonged stress, whether its origin is repeated tail pinches, dunking in cold water, or loud noises. The response, which Selye calls the *general adaptation syndrome,* has a sequence of stages, beginning with the sympathetic nervous system response described above and ending in death if the stress is sufficiently protracted. When we speak of human stress, we are usually referring to the first stage. But Selye has shown that prolonged stress can lead to serious physiological disorganization, one aspect of which is an increasing susceptibility to infections and other disorders. In the penultimate stage of the general adaptation syndrome, the stressed animal enters a state we would describe in the human as despair. In the end, loss of hope appears to be the killer.

Two observations deserve mention here. One is that individuals differ in their responses to stressful circumstances; some people tolerate, even demand, a level of stress that others would find disorganizing. And, second, once one has become adjusted to a given level of stress, its sudden disappearance is as dangerous to health as an intolerable increase in its intensity. That is, a sudden change in life style or circumstances, either greatly increasing or greatly reducing stress, is disorganizing to the body. The startling regularity with which men who have worked under stress all their lives fall apart and quickly die after retirement should remind us that we must remain active and engaged when we retire from the "rat race" to live the good life. Though the human organism is apparently able to adjust to a level of stress that would quickly destroy a wild animal, it is simultaneously vulnerable to changes in its level of intensity, either up or down, once having become adjusted to the pace.

No one who is familiar with the intricate feedback mechanisms of the neuroendocrine and autonomic nervous systems should be too surprised that prolonged intense stress can bring about physiological disorganization, or that an abrupt shift in level of stress can do the same. To the medical practitioner and the neuroscientist, this means that environmental conditions can indeed very radically alter the state of our physical health. When this occurs, it does so through the effect of those conditions on the mind, which is the interface between the two. It is via our perceptions of our environment that we experience stress. It makes a great difference whether the rat has a technique for turning off the electric shock or whether

Psychosomatic medicine. Treatment of illnesses caused by environmental stress and other psychological conditions.

General adaptation syndrome. A sequence of behaviors or states representing a universal response to severe or prolonged stress.

it has none, and must endure whatever comes (learned helplessness). It is the latter state of affairs that can carry the general adaptation syndrome through to its end-point in the death of the animal. In the human being, meanwhile, it appears to be the sense of helplessness and hopelessness that correlates with high risk of psychosomatic disorders.

Stress and Hypertension

Though clinical observation convinces most physicians that stress can cause high blood pressure, it is quite another thing to prove it in carefully controlled observational studies. Indeed, a recent conference on stress research held at Boston University School of Medicine concluded that epidemiological studies have thus far failed to prove the connection, and that it is therefore premature to advise people to seek to avoid stress as a means of preventing hypertension. Once the condition has become established, however, the evidence is clear. Stress can further elevate hypertensives' already-high blood pressure, risking serious blood-vessel damage or even stroke (the bursting of blood vessels in the brain, causing subsequent damage to neural tissue). What is in question is whether prolonged stress can bring on the disease in the first place.

Members of the lower socioeconomic classes appear to be more vulnerable than other people to the development of chronic high blood pressure, but it is unclear why. They tend to be more overweight, under more stress, and to get poorer medical care. Obesity is very strongly correlated with risk of high blood pressure, but several factors are confounded here and the evidence on the effect of stress is unclear. Some researchers suggest that stress is not involved, and that obesity and too much salt in the diet are sufficient to produce the condition. When hypertensive patients lose weight, their blood pressures drop. However, if stressful life circumstances lead people to overeat, and perhaps to ingest more salt with their meals, stress could still be the indirect cause of hypertension.

An increase in blood pressure is one of the ways the sympathetic nervous system prepares the organism for emergency response. In the case of people whose circumstances tend to elicit a chronic low-level emergency response from their autonomic nervous systems, the hypothesis that stress is a direct cause of hypertension has a *prima facie* quality that is difficult to deny. One reason why epidemiological studies seeking a relationship between chronically stressful circumstances and high blood pressure fail to find clear evidence of it may be that such studies routinely fail to investigate the psychological effect on the subjects of the circumstances in question, preferring to focus on the environmental circumstances themselves. As Richard Lazarus of the University of California at Berkeley has insisted, stress is not just an environmental condition but an interaction between a particular environmental circumstance and a particular kind of individual. That is, such studies have been apsychological, treating the subjects as physical bodies from whom uniform responses to treatments can be expected, rather than as people with quite varying perceptions of their world.

Psychological Correlates of Cancer

Spurred by Caroline Thomas' study of medical students suggesting a link between suicidal tendencies and vulnerability to cancer, a number of researchers have attempted to determine whether there is such a thing as a cancer-prone individual. Are certain psychological factors predictive of the disease?

Nicholas Rogentine, an immunologist with the National Cancer Institute, has noted that among patients suffering from malignant melanoma (a dark-pigmented skin cancer), those who relapsed after successful surgery tended to be those who minimized their illness, failing to take it seriously. D. M. Kissen of the University of Glasgow found a similar phenomenon among industrial workers suffering from various lung ailments (all of whom were smokers). Those subsequently found to have lung cancer were judged to be those who repressed their emotions and had poor outlets for emotional discharge. The theory that associates cancer-proneness with denial and repression of emotions is also supported by a study by Leonard Derogatis and Martin Abeloff of Johns Hopkins Medical School of 35 women suffering from breast cancer. Those women who were pliant and cooperative fought their disease significantly less well than did those who expressed anger, both toward the disease and toward their doctors. It appeared that the ability to externalize negative feelings correlated with a better prognosis. Another study at Kings College Hospital in London reported the somewhat equivocal finding that in women who visited physicians for examination of breast lumps, malignancy correlated with an inappropriate mode of coping with anger, whether suppression or extremely overt expression.

The findings of William Greene of the University of Rochester, who studied patients with leukemia and Hodgkin's disease, point in a somewhat different direction. In nine cases out of ten, according to Greene, the disease develops at a time when the person feels alone, helpless, and hopeless. A similar finding is reported by Arthur Schmale of the University of Rochester, who ten years ago undertook an effort to predict which women examined for suspicious cell changes in the cervix would turn out to be suffering from malignancy. Using interviews and the Minnesota Multiphasic Personality Inventory, a personality test, Schmale looked for signs of hopelessness; on that basis he correctly predicted the cervical cancer patients in 36 cases out of 51. Lawrence LeShan, a New York psychotherapist, studied more than 400 cancer patients and found that 72 percent had suffered a loss of a significant personal relationship from one month to eight years prior to the onset of the disease. Only 10 percent of those in psychotherapy for other reasons had suffered a similar loss. LeShan found that most of the cancer patients, unlike the controls, experienced a profound sense of despair, futility, and personal isolation (which of course might reflect their knowledge of their cancerous condition).

Jerome Frank of Johns Hopkins reports a case illustrating the potential effect of emotional state on the progress of pre-existing cancer. A patient dying of lymphoma, a cancer of the lymphatic system, heard about Krebiozen, a drug some claim to cure cancer, and demanded to be treated with it. Two days after the first injection his tumors began to shrink visibly, and ten days later he was discharged from the hospital as an apparently miraculous cure. A few months later, the patient read reports discounting the worth of the drug and suffered a relapse. Reassured by his doctor that the reports were unreliable, and offered a new, super-refined form of Krebiozen (he was actually given distilled water), the patient's spirits revived and the symptoms vanished. Two months later he read another highly authoritative report describing Krebiozen as useless, and his faith in his treatment was destroyed. It no longer proved effective, and the patient died two days later.

The *placebo effect* attests to the mind's ability, when convinced of the efficacy of a treatment, to affect the course of a disease for the better. It appears that confidence and hope, however generated, can greatly assist the body in its efforts to fight off disease and restore normal health.

Placebo effect (pla-SEE-boh). **The beneficial effect of a substance taken as a medicine which in fact has no true medicinal value.**

Miracle Cures: The Healing Power of Faith

How is it that faith in the treatment, in the doctor, in oneself powerfully abets the efforts of the body to repair and restore and defend itself against insult? Is genuinely wanting to live a precondition of continued living? The question is clearly not whether faith heals but how it heals. There seems to be a link somewhere in the organism — perhaps via the route of the hypothalamus — between the mechanisms designed to preserve the body and the mental processes of the brain, whereby the one can influence the other. Suicide is historically most prevalent among the aged who no longer wish to live. Perhaps some disease processes are subtler forms of suicide.

On the other side of the picture is the demonstrable power of hope, confidence, and the will to live to help the body regain vigorous health. One widely accepted hypothesis is that cancer cells are continually being formed in the body, but are detected and destroyed as long as the individual's natural immune system is effective, never becoming established as a tumor. Perhaps many other things in the body tend to slip into disarray but are continually monitored and corrected by bodily systems, not yet identified, whose function is to keep the vast machinery in good working order. Might disease in general — even infections, whose immediate cause is a demonstrable virus or bacterium — on a deeper level reflect failure of the body's maintenance systems, in turn influenced by the person's state of mind? This kind of speculation is spreading in the health-maintenance fields, from molecular biology to psychiatry, and is the basis of the *holistic* approach to healing.

Holistic. **Emphasizing the relationship of all relevant factors within a dynamic system.**

Faith healers appear to operate on the same implicit assumption. Magic rituals and the laying on of hands, so curiously uniform throughout the world, appear to represent a folk discovery of long standing that healing can be fostered by building hope and confidence. Religious shrines such as Lourdes, which draws over 2 million pilgrims each year seeking help after unsuccessful medical treatments, report many instances of surprisingly rapid improvements in their visitors. Such cures were once regarded as spurious, or as genuine only in cases of hysteria, in which the illness is all in the mind. But modern medicine is now taking a more serious look at them. One might argue that the successful healing rituals of faith healers and religious shrines alike are ideally designed to strengthen the individual's sense of self-worth, to replace a sense of isolation with a feeling of belonging, and to build confidence and hope in the future, psychological states found in other contexts to be conducive to the body's successful maintenance and recovery of health.

We must thus ask to what degree modern medicine, presumed to depend on the specific effects of treatments on parts of the body, in fact depends on the patient's faith in the scientific basis of the treatment. Many patients regard doctors as a species of miracle worker, dispensers of chemical substances the patient does not understand but implicitly believes will work and lead to cure. The treatment is fortified in the patient's mind by the assumption that it has been thoroughly laboratory-tested by the awesome methods of modern science.

Studies have shown that the placebo effect often correlates closely with the effect of an active medication. In a double-blind experiment — one in which the doctor never knew who was receiving Stellazine and who a placebo — psychiatric patients were evaluated for their degree of improvement. The degree of improvement of those who received Stellazine was rated 32 percent; that of those receiving the placebo was 35 percent. In a second study with different patients, the amount of both drug and placebo was doubled. Those receiving Stellazine were judged 67 percent improved, those receiving the placebo 72 percent better. In addition to faith in the doctor and the medication, the size of the placebo is apparently also a significant factor in placebo effects.

Controlling the Autonomic Nervous System

As its name suggests, the autonomic nervous system was once considered autonomous in its activity, uninfluenced in any direct manner by the central nervous system (brain and spinal cord) governing voluntary behavior. Although practitioners of yoga had repeatedly demonstrated voluntary control of heart rate, blood pressure, and the like, the eyes of scientific psychologists were closed to this phenomenon, as they were to hypnosis. The psychologist to whom we owe our understanding of this phenomenon is Neal Miller, whose work at Rockefeller University in New York inaugurated a wave of subsequent research, as well as a new mode of psychotherapy called behavior modification, which makes use of techniques such as biofeedback.

Miller and his co-worker, Alfredo Carmona, found that salivation could be controlled in thirsty dogs merely by rewarding them with water whenever they emitted a spontaneous burst of salivation (an autonomically controlled process) or, alternatively, when a certain period of time elapsed without a burst of salivation. In the one case the dogs were trained to increase their salivation; in the other, to reduce it.

In all attempts to condition autonomic responses directly, it is possible that the response is mediated through the voluntary nervous system. Activating the skeletal muscles, for example, may in turn produce the autonomic response. It proved impossible to test this possibility in the case of salivation, since treatment with curare to paralyse dogs' skeletal muscles produces copious salivation. However, the curare treatment was applicable in a second experiment by the same researchers, the attempt to condition a faster or slower heartbeat (another autonomically controlled process). Rats were used, and electrical brain stimulation in reward areas was the mechanism of reinforcement. Using the technique of *shaping*, whereby the animal is rewarded at first for slight increases (or decreases) in spontaneous heart rate, and later only for larger changes, it proved possible within 90 minutes to produce changes averaging 20 percent in either direction. Since the animals were paralyzed during the training, the change could not have been produced by greater or less exertion of the voluntary musculature.

They also discovered that rats can be trained to respond with a faster or slower heartbeat to a flashing light and tone signal, demonstrating that autonomic learning of visceral responses shares an important feature with learning of voluntary responses through conditioning — namely association of the response to a conditioning signal. Further experimentation demonstrated that curarized rats could be conditioned to increase or decrease their heart rate in response to conditioned stimuli signalling the advent of an electric shock, thus illustrating that aversive conditioning, as well as reward reinforcement, is effective with autonomic processes. Moreover, the learned response was still elicited by the signal two weeks later in a noncurarized state.

These successes surprised the community of psychologists working on learning theory, who had assumed that their operant conditioning procedures were applicable only to functions mediated by the central nervous system. Confirmations were to follow involving other autonomically mediated processes: contractions of the lower bowel, rate of urine formation by the kidneys, amount of blood in the stomach wall, vasodilation and vasoconstriction in specific peripheral regions, blood pressure as independent of heart rate, even alterations in brain waves. (See Miller, 1969, for an excellent summary of these discoveries and their possible implications as seen at that time.)

The technique Miller and his co-workers used in all these demonstrations of training of autonomic responses consisted of moment-to-moment recording of the autonomic response, and provision of an immediate reward (or reprieve from punishment) for changes in the desired direction — at first for all changes, however small, and later only for substantial changes. It is but a small step from this laboratory procedure to the biofeedback method. In the case of the human being, the opportunity to monitor one's own visceral responses from moment to moment, by technological means, is sufficient to bring the process under voluntary control. No reward is necessary since, according to Miller, a movement of the monitoring recording signal in the desired direction constitutes an implicit reward. Others prefer to say that, at the human level of functioning, the relevant factor is not reward but the information itself. If we wish to increase or decrease the rate of a given visceral process, and we have moment-to-moment access to that process, we can experiment until we find some means of consistently influencing the process in the desired direction. To call success at this endeavor a reward may be seen as an unwarranted importation into human functioning of a principle more applicable to a dumb animal, who cannot deliberately choose to pursue such a goal.

It now begins to appear as if feedback is all that is necessary to make brain waves, blushing, heart rate, blood pressure, and the like amenable to voluntary manipulation, at least to some degree. Under hypnosis, the range of voluntary control appears to be considerably enlarged, for reasons not yet understood. How the person exerts voluntary influence over the process is not always clear. One tries this and that, until one discovers what works: the adoption of a particular attitude, or envisioning a particular kind of scene, or putting thoughts out of one's mind, or whatever. By this means, and with a suitable continuous-recording device, individuals with hypertension have been able to lower their blood pressure voluntarily, with fairly lasting effects in some cases.

One important aspect of this methodology is its application to relaxation under conditions of abnormal chronic tension. Some people appear to derive significant therapeutic benefit from brief periods of quiet relaxation interspersed throughout the day, whether spent in meditation, prayer, daydream fantasies, or a "time out" in which one tries to think of nothing. Tension, psychological as well as muscular, tends to correlate with dominant activation of the sympathetic branch of the autonomic system, which keeps us in a chronic state of readiness for emergency. One simple technique of altering the imbalance in the direction of parasympathetic dominance is merely to become aware of muscle tension, and deliberately seek to relax, perhaps one muscle system after another, until the whole body is limp. Another technique is to monotonously repeat a word or brief phrase, whether it be "Hail Mary, full of grace!" or a nonsense word (a mantra) as is recommended by some Oriental religious traditions, in order to expel thoughts from the mind. Transcendental Meditation, with its thousands of devotees, is not the first cult to take advantage of this principle, nor will it be the last.

Chapter 21 / *New Light on Obesity*

Approximately 30 percent of the American population is obese, and the prevalence of obesity in the United States is apparently increasing. Adults examined in 1960–1962 weighed less, on the average, than those examined in the period 1971–1974. One estimate is that some 10 to 30 percent of Americans weigh at least 30 percent more than their ideal weights. Yet the health hazards of being overweight are well known, and cultural pressure toward slimness is pervasive and powerful. How can we understand this apparent paradox? What keeps us eating more calories than our bodies can consume?

The answer is not that we are too affluent as a society, since poor people are more apt than affluent people to be obese. It is not that people do not care about their figures or their health. Diet fads are rampant (though none appear to be any more effective than the others), and health-and-slimness-through-exercise is a multi-million-dollar industry. Saul Genuth of Mt. Sinai Hospital in Cleveland is reported to have stated that cure of obesity is virtually unheard of, and even control is achieved only rarely (Kolata, 1979). It sounds as if he were talking about heroin addiction.

In addition to hypertension, obese people are at risk of gallbladder disease, strokes, diabetes, heart disease, and damage to the weight-bearing bones. Though overweight women are prone to menstrual disorders and endometrial cancer, obesity appears to pose the greatest danger to men. Women carry their excess weight principally in subcutaneous fat on the exterior of the body, while men are more prone to carry it interiorly, around the heart and liver and other viscera. A man putting on weight is thus apt to be fooled by the solidity of the muscles over his belly even as it protrudes further each month. The buildup of interior stores puts an extra strain on the heart and other internal organs, compresses the urinary bladder so that the man must awaken at night to relieve himself, and diminishes the capacity of his lungs. But a distinction must be made between a man with a "pot belly" or "rubber tire" and an equally overweight football player. The one is obese, the other a magnificent specimen of health. It is apparently all a matter of eating more than the body needs. But what goes wrong in humans with the self-regulatory mechanisms that keep mammals in the natural state slim and trim?

The answer seems to be complex. There appear to be different kinds of obesity, as there are different kinds of cancer. Research is focusing on identifying the several apparently independent factors underlying what doctors now frankly call the disease of obesity.

Recent studies have debunked a number of long-accepted beliefs about obese people. As a whole, obese people are not psychologically distinguishable from nonobese people. Some fat people and some lean people eat under stress, to relieve tension, but others in both groups do not. Fat people as a group are no more likely than lean people to be at the mercy of the sight and smell of delicious food. Some gobble their food and some eat slowly. Some fat people are jolly, but others are anxiety-ridden and depressive. There appears to be no style of life or eating behavior that differentiates obese people from slim people, or at least none that has yet been discerned. The one thing that is fairly certain is that, relative to their energy expenditure, fat people eat more. The question is: why are they so hungry or such compulsive unconscious nibblers, and why do they avoid muscular exertion, which is frequently a pleasure for slender people?

In a study done many years ago at the University of Chicago Laboratory School, it was observed that obese children tend to move languidly in everything they do, as if concerned to expend as little effort as possible, while their nonobese playmates use much more energy than necessary, apparently for the sheer joy of it. Though most evident on the playground, this energy-conservation tendency was also apparent in the classroom.

Four distinct factors have been identified as possibly relevant to overeating. One is the visceral sensations of discomfort, commonly known as "hunger pangs," which we know from experience are readily relieved by eating. Another is the incentive value of the food stimulus — the sight and smell of tasty food, discussion of food, thoughts of food, food displayed in magazines and television advertisements — coming to us through our exteroceptors. A third factor, much researched in the past 20 years, is the satiety mechanism of the brain or stomach or intestine, which normally produces a diminished interest in eating long before any significant absorption of nutrients can have occurred. This mechanism seems not to be operative in some individuals, who continue to eat with pleasure when their slimmer companions have become sated. Fourth, there is strong evidence that some people eat as a means of relieving tension — a motivation irrelevant to hunger, which serves the same purpose as would lighting a cigarette, flipping on the television set, or any of the thousand and one activities people engage in for the same purpose. Such eating is goaded by a nonspecific motivational urge, whether nervous tension, psychological stress, generalized physical discomfort, boredom, depression, or avoidance of painful thoughts.

Each of these four potential factors in obesity has been the subject of intensive research, which we shall briefly review.

The Hunger Factor

One common-sense theory of obesity postulates that some people simply have a stronger hunger drive than others. While there may well be genetic differences between individuals in this regard, as there appears to be in the sexual urge, we noted in Chapter 11 that some obese people seldom experience hunger as such. They are motivated instead by appetite, the incentive value of the food stimulus and the anticipation of pleasure in eating. Such people report that they could go for days without eating if they were not exposed to the external stimulus. Such testimony suggests that they are motivated by external rather than internal stimuli, and that they have little will power when confronting such external stimuli as the sight of a chocolate cream pie or a juicy steak. It would apparently be misleading to describe such individuals as suffering from an abnormally strong hunger drive.

Another phenomenon that appears to rule out an abnormally strong hunger drive as an explanation of obesity in general is the tendency of some adolescents to experience a spectacular increase in their hunger drive, and their food intake, without putting on excess weight. It is commonly observed, furthermore, that some people can eat plentifully without gaining weight while others must control their intake very carefully if they are not to become fat. It must be assumed that some of us have much more efficient intestinal nutrient-absorption and fat-deposition processes than others. That is, some obesity cannot fairly be attributed to overeating at all, when the usual norms of caloric intake are applied. Such individuals' hunger is abnormal, if at all, only relative to their own bodies' food requirements.

Nevertheless, there do appear to be individuals whose hunger drives are peculiarly strong and persistent. Such people report that they are hungry all the time. It is not the pleasure of eating well-prepared foods but true hunger — feelings of discomfort in the stomach region (and perhaps other internal receptor indicators) — that impels them to overeat. They are hungry again shortly after finishing a meal, and quiet that hunger by constant snacking.

Curiously enough, research has failed to clarify the nature of the perceptual experience of hunger. It is unknown whether the neural signals of hunger reach the neocortex; it may be that the interoceptors in general find only limbic representation, though we may be fully conscious of them and capable of imaginal representation of them.

Presumably foods acquire their incentive value through associative learning processes. Why some individuals take great pleasure in food, while others with apparently comparable experiential opportunities never care much about eating, is also unknown. Some people live to eat, while others eat only to keep alive (Figure 21.1).

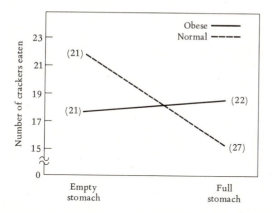

Figure 21.1 / *Effects of Preliminary Eating on the Amounts Eaten during an Experiment by Normal and Obese Subjects.* There is evidence that many obese individuals are controlled in their eating not by hunger cues, signifying the body's need for food, but by the incentive value of the food as stimulus — its tastiness, appetizing appearance, etc. In one experiment, obese and normal subjects were asked to rate the tastiness or flavor of five types of crackers before and after eating a full meal. The results are shown in the accompanying graph. The normal controls ate far fewer crackers in the course of tasting them on a full stomach, as might be expected, while the obese individuals actually ate somewhat more on a full stomach than on an empty one.

It is also largely a mystery why some people's bodies are much more efficient than other's at nutrient absorption and fat deposition, though research has begun. Some people have more fat cells, others have larger fat cells, and some have both large and numerous fat cells waiting to be inflated from their collapsed state into spherical fat vesicles. There is suggestive evidence that this bodily characteristic is reflected in how much fat one is apt to carry. In lean individuals, the number of fat cells apparently increases up to age two, after which there is a long hiatus during which the number of fat cells remains constant; additional proliferation of fat cells occurs from age 10 to 16. In obese people, on the other hand, the number of fat cells appears to increase continuously throughout childhood and adolescence. Whether or not this phenomenon is a function of childhood overeating is not firmly established.

The Satiety Factor

More than a decade ago, discovery of a hormone that inhibits eating was reported. The substance, *enterogastrone,* is obtained from the wall of the small intestine, and had been known for years to reduce stomach secretions and motility. Improved purification methods made possible an experiment in which mice, having fasted for 17 hours, were injected subcutaneously with either enterogastrone or another substance, such as glucagon, secretin, glucose, or bovine albumin. Control mice were injected with saline (salt water), presumed to have no effect. Only enterogastrone was effective: it reduced or totally inhibited food intake for up to an hour. The mice in question appeared healthy, active, and quite normal in every respect except that they had no interest in eating after 17 hours of starvation. Of particular interest was the observation that neither glucose nor glucagon injections, intravenously or subcutaneously, inhibited food intake, though these substances are known to reduce gastric hunger contractions in both rats and mice under similar circumstances. It appeared that enterogastrone, secreted by the small intestine, specifically activates a satiety center in the hypothalamus, though how it acted there was unknown.

More recently enterogastrone has been found to be a complex substance, an important constituent of which is the peptide *cholecystokinin.* Straus and Yalow (1979), reasoning from other studies that had found a similar substance to affect satiety in the rat when injected into the brain ventricles, hypothesized that genet-

*Cholecystokinin (koh-lee-sis-toh-*KYE-*nin*). A chemical substance found in the lining of the upper intestine which, when injected into an animal, powerfully suppresses its hunger.

ically obese mice would be found to have a lower brain content of cholecystokinin than normal mice. Indeed, they found the brains of the genetically obese strain of mice to contain only one-fourth as much of this presumed satiety-inducing substance as those of normal mice. This finding lends support to the argument that cholecystokinin is a chemical substance normally involved in turning off hunger shortly after one begins eating. Whether a deficiency in this substance also occurs in the gut of mice with un-restrained appetites has yet to be tested.

The potential importance of this finding for obese people is obvious. If it turns out that merely increasing the quantity of cholecystokinin in the blood stream is sufficient to reduce an abnormal level of hunger drive, the problem of obesity might be near solution. The implications of this finding for our understanding of the normal hypothalamic satiety mechanism are also of great theoretical interest.

Another line of research aimed at understanding the normal satiety mechanism has been pursued at Princeton University by Eric Ahlskog and Bartley Hoebel. In 1973 these investigators reported that destruction of the ventral norepinephrine bundle supplying the hypothalamus produces hyperphagia in rats, implying that this bundle normally mediates suppression of feeding (Ahlskog and Hoebel, 1973). Two years later the same investigators presented evidence that this satiety mechanism is independent of the classical hypothalamic mechanism controlling food intake. In short, localized lesions in the ventromedial hypothalamus produce hyperphagia quite independently of the newly discovered ventral-norepinephrine-bundle hyperphagia phenomenon. The evidence was clear-cut. Loss of norepinephrine causes overeating in rats (though only at night, that nocturnal animal's normal mealtime). Also, ventral hypothalamic lesions produce hyperphagia without depletion or norepinephrine. Furthermore, the two mechanisms are additive: when both mechanisms are destroyed, the rats eat at least as much as the sum of the two effects would account for. The investigators also found that the hyperphagia induced by destruction of the ventral norepinephrine bundle is not associated with finickiness, as is ventral hypothalamic hyperphagia (Ahlskog, Randall, and Hoebel, 1975).

At this point it had been established that at least two independent satiety mechanisms operate in the normal brain. (Perhaps the cholecystokinin peptide is involved in one of them.) In the following year the same group of investigators reported evidence that another neurotransmitter, serotonin, is also implicated in the satiety mechanisms of the brain. When serotonin stores in the brain are depleted following injection of the chemical p-chlorophenylalanine into the ventricles, rats become hyperphagic, but primarily in the daytime, when rats usually eat very little. In this experiment the levels of norepinephrine and dopamine in the brain were not altered. The rats' food intake doubled during the light period (corresponding to daytime).

The authors note three implications of their findings. They suggest, first, that hypothalamic lesions found to produce hyperphagia, particularly in the daytime, may interrupt serotonin supplies to the hypothalamus. Second, human obesity might be due to genetic or environmentally induced damage to essential serotonin neurons that normally participate in the control of food intake. Finally, in view of evidence that serotonin depletion also produces hyperactivity and hyperreactivity in rats, serotonin may represent an integrated system in the brain that suppresses behavior in general.

Serotonin, unlike most other neurotransmitters, depends directly on dietary factors vulnerable to malnutrition. It is the availability of the amino acid tryptophan, the precursor of serotonin, that controls the amount present in the brain. While concentrations of dopamine and norepinephrine are regulated by a feedback mechanism, no such regulatory control of serotonin appears to exist. Thus it seems particularly appropriate for serotonin to be used as a satiety indicator by the brain.

The Stress Factor

In 1975, Seymour Antelman and his associates at the University of Pittsburgh made a remarkable observation. Rats subjected to a steady mild tail pinch almost immediately begin to eat, if food is present, and continue eating as long as the pressure on the tail is maintained. Gnawing and licking may also occur, but by far the most common response is normal, unhurried eating. Observation suggests that the pinch produces mild discomfort but not pain. Tail-pinching is a common experimental technique to simulate environmental stress with rats.

Since norepinephrine and dopamine had been linked to control of eating, their roles in this pinch-induced eating were investigated. Dopamine, but not norepinephrine, was found to be a critical factor. When dopamine-blocking agents were administered, the eating response to tail pinch could be completely blocked in the presence of food. In the presence of dopamine the response pattern appears to be determined by the stimulus object available in the environment, and is always normal and appropriate to those objects, eating being the most usual response. The authors concluded that the nigrostriatal dopamine system might be importantly involved in regulating the animal's responsiveness to a wide variety of environmental stimuli.

In the following year Rowland and Antelman reported further research in this area. In the presence of milk, rats were subjected to six daily tail-pinch sessions (10–15 minutes each) spaced throughout the 24-hour cycle, for up to five consecutive days. All 24 animals became hyperphagic and obese, ingesting a mean 181 kilocalories per 24-hour period compared to 71 for the control animals. The experimental animals exhibited marked and rapid weight gain.

The researchers point out that their results are in complete accord with those reported on obesity induced by electrical stimulation of the lateral hypothalamic region. Like electrical stimulation, tail pinch does not abolish weight-regulation mechanisms but only temporarily overrides them. According to Rowland and Antelman, such nonspecific stress-induced overeating may be a more realistic model for the study of some kinds of nongenetic obesity in humans than experimental results involving brain damage. In support of this view, they note that many obese people eat when they are emotionally tense or experiencing other unpleasant states, such as depression or boredom. Some degree of finickiness is usually apparent: particularly desirable foods stimulate the hyperphagia. When food is not available, or when dieting, such individuals exhibit enhanced reactivity to other goal objects. Studies show a higher incidence of smoking and other oral behaviors, as well as an increase in sexual activity under such circumstances, suggesting that for such individuals hyperphagia may be a food-directed manifestation of a more general hyper-responsivity to environmental stimuli.

Thus dopamine appears to be linked not with hunger, in the sense of a specific drive motivation, but perhaps with a generalized need to "do something." Rats whose tails are being pinched behave surprisingly like humans who eat to take their minds off besetting troubles. Either rats have "minds" similar to ours, or what we interpret as a need for distractions is in reality a biochemically governed behavior.

Another Interpretation: Obesity as a Hibernation Response

David Margules of Temple University, working in another theoretical direction, has found that naloxone, the opiate antagonist, injected into hibernating hamsters dramatically increase heart and respiratory rates, induces shivering, and eventually awakens the animal. This finding indicates what appears to be a powerful link between the opioid systems of the brain and hibernation, suggesting that the endorphins may be critically important in the hyperphagia that precedes hibernation. Is it possible that nonhibernating animals, such as rats and humans, retain a similar *endorphinergic* system, designed to prepare adaptively for a coming food shortage, and that such a mechanism underlies human obesity?

Margules suggests that this may be the case, and that an opposing system based on naloxone (or similar opiate antagonists) normally keeps this mechanism in check by signalling that the body has plenty of food stored and conservation is unnecessary (Margules, 1979). Thus dominance by the endorphinergic system might be expected to lead to obesity and other addiction-like attachments, while the "endoloxonergic" system would stimulate activities that use energy rapidly (and keep us lean and trim). While no endoloxones have yet been isolated in the brain, genetically obese rodents are found to have much more beta-endorphin in their pituitaries and blood streams than do lean animals, and obese rats immediately stop eating and drinking when injected with small doses of naloxone. (The same dose has no effect on lean animals.) Also, beta-endorphin lowers the body's normal rate of heartbeat, respiration, and thyroid hormone activity, thereby reducing energy expenditure. Pain arouses the sympathetic nervous system less after beta-endorphin injections, and body temperature is reduced.

All these endorphinergic responses are, of course, in precisely the direction of the hibernation response, which in some animals leads to almost total cessation of energy expenditure. The suggestion that nonhibernating animals have in their bodies a similar system, which normally does not act to such an extreme, is highly plausible. Now that the idea has been proposed, and evidence marshalled in its support, we can expect further findings, and perhaps a demonstration of another entirely independent mechanism underlying human obesity.

Present evidence suggests that there are three kinds of obese people: those whose lipostat is set too high, and who thus constantly suffer from hunger; those who seldom suffer hunger pangs, but cannot resist the temptation to eat, and to continue eating inordinately, when challenged with their favorite foods; and emotional eaters, who eat to relieve their tensions. The solution may be easiest for the first type: the use of hunger-suppressant medication, now available in a nonaddicting form. The second type needs merely to avoid temptation, but that is not easily accomplished in our food-oriented society. Perhaps the solution for the third type, the emotional eater, lies in awareness of the tendency, and — like the pinched rats when no food was present — finding some other behavioral expression of emotional discomfort.

Appendix A / *Brodmann's Cortical Areas*

Since the numbered areas in Brodmann's chart are sometimes difficult to distinguish, this redrawing has been done to improve its usefulness to the beginning student of the brain. Over time it has been demonstrated that these numbered areas are very helpful in discussions of cortical function and in conceptualizing the integrated functioning of the neocortex. They form a map of the terrain which would be difficult to explore without it.

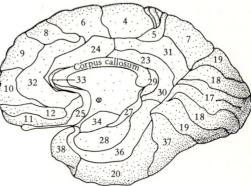

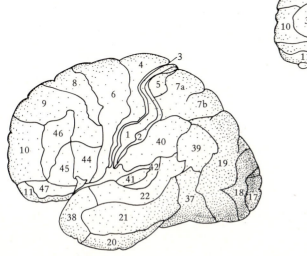

Appendix B / *Brain Atlas*

The purpose of a brain atlas is to make possible the development of a mental image, in three dimensions, of the brain's major structures. While the convolutions of the cortex over the lateral convexity of the brain differ in each individual, interior structures tend to be quite uniform. In this series of diagrams, those uniformities are emphasized. Figures 1 through 4 depict the hemispheres as seen from outside, but indicating major fiber bundles interconnecting various regions. Figures 5 through 12 represent coronal sections through the whole brain, each succeeding section revealing interior structures successively further toward the rear. Figures 13 through 16 show successive slices through the brain beginning with the sagittal section and moving laterally, revealing what a neuroanatomist might expect to see. Figure 17 represents the brain as it might appear if sectioned horizontally through the major subcortical nuclei. Study of these figures will serve to familiarize the beginning student with the interior structure of the brain.

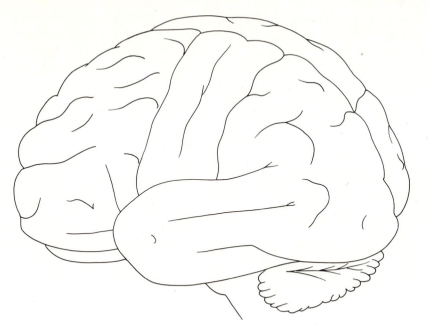

Figure 1.
A View of the Lateral Convexity of the Cortex

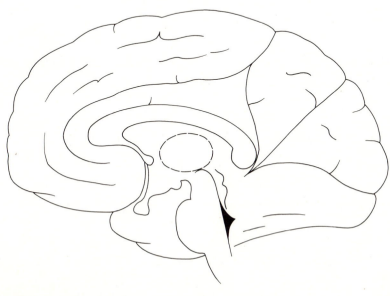

Figure 2.
A Sagittal-Section View of the Brain

Superior longitudinal fasciculus

Arcuate fasciculus

Figure 3.
**Major Fiber Bundles
of the Neocortex**

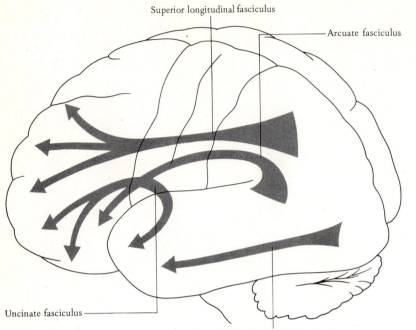

Uncinate fasciculus

Inferior longitudinal fasciculus

Cingulum bundle

Figure 4.
**Major Fiber Bundles
of the Medial Sur-
faces of the Brain**

Fornix

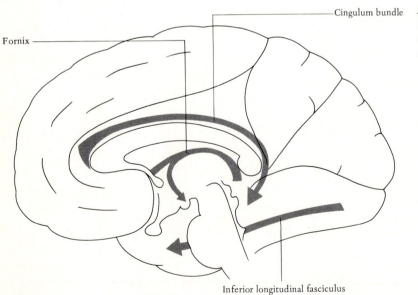

Inferior longitudinal fasciculus

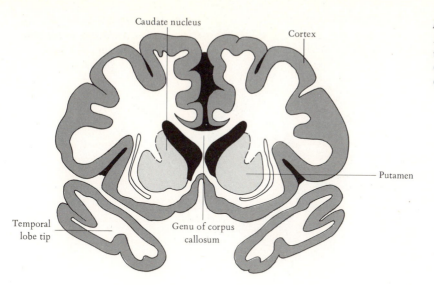

Caudate nucleus

Cortex

Putamen

Temporal
lobe tip

Genu of corpus
callosum

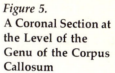

Figure 5.
**A Coronal Section at
the Level of the
Genu of the Corpus
Callosum**

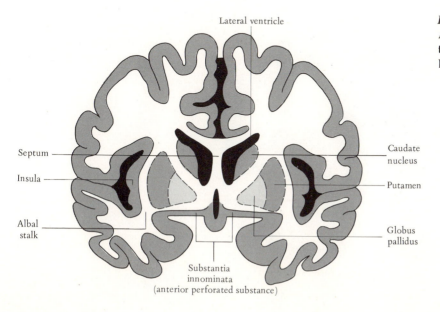

Lateral ventricle

Septum

Insula

Albal
stalk

Caudate
nucleus

Putamen

Globus
pallidus

Substantia
innominata
(anterior perforated substance)

Figure 6.
**A Coronal Section at
the Level of the
Basal Ganglia**

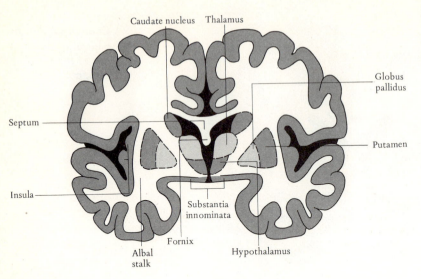

Caudate nucleus   Thalamus

Globus
pallidus

Septum

Putamen

Insula

Substantia
innominata

Fornix

Hypothalamus

Albal
stalk

Figure 7.
**A Coronal Section
through the Anterior
Hypothalamus**

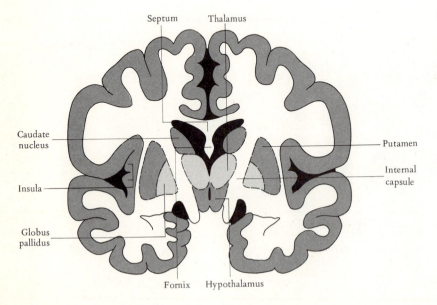

Septum   Thalamus

Caudate
nucleus

Putamen

Internal
capsule

Insula

Globus
pallidus

Fornix   Hypothalamus

Figure 8.
**A Coronal Section
through the Middle
Hypothalamus**

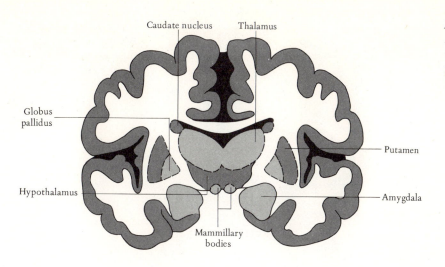

Caudate nucleus   Thalamus

Globus
pallidus

Putamen

Hypothalamus

Amygdala

Mammillary
bodies

Figure 9.
**A Coronal Section
through the Mam-
millary Bodies**

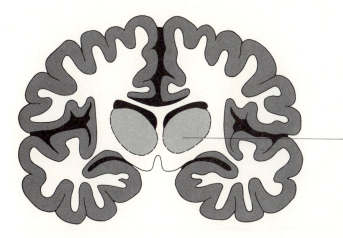

Thalamus

Figure 10.
**A Coronal Section
through the
Thalamus, to the
Rear of the Basal
Ganglia**

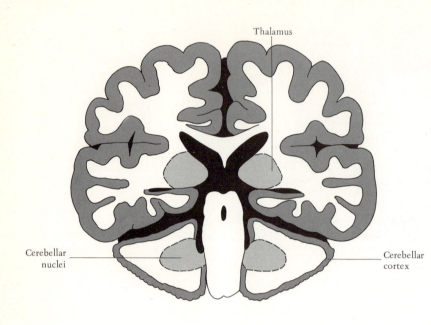

Figure 11.
A Coronal Section through the Mid-brain Region of the Brainstem

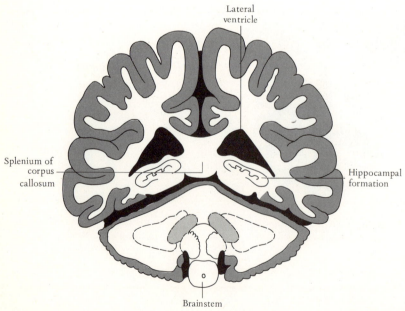

Figure 12.
A Coronal Section through the Splenium of the Corpus Callosum

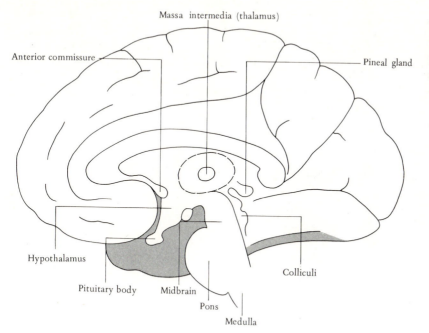

Massa intermedia (thalamus)

Anterior commissure

Pineal gland

Hypothalamus

Pituitary body

Midbrain

Pons

Medulla

Colliculi

Figure 13.
The Medial Surface of the Right Hemisphere of the Brain before Longitudinal Sectioning

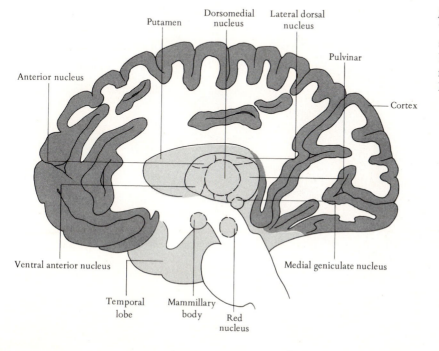

Putamen

Dorsomedial nucleus

Lateral dorsal nucleus

Pulvinar

Anterior nucleus

Cortex

Ventral anterior nucleus

Medial geniculate nucleus

Temporal lobe

Mammillary body

Red nucleus

Figure 14.
The Same Hemisphere with a First Layer of Tissue Removed, Showing the Medial Thalamus

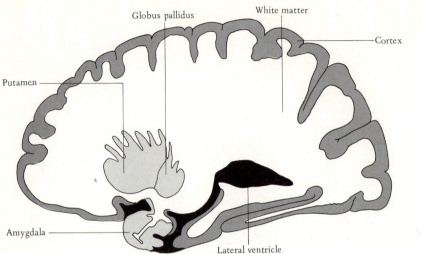

Globus pallidus

White matter

Cortex

Putamen

Amygdala

Lateral ventricle

Figure 15.
The Same Hemi-sphere with a Second Layer of Tissue Removed, Showing the Amygdala and White Matter

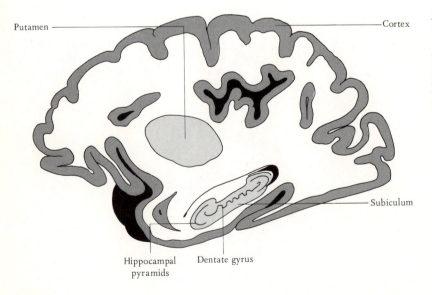

Putamen

Cortex

Subiculum

Hippocampal pyramids

Dentate gyrus

Figure 16.
The Same Hemi-sphere with a Third Layer of Tissue Removed, Showing the Hippocampal Formation

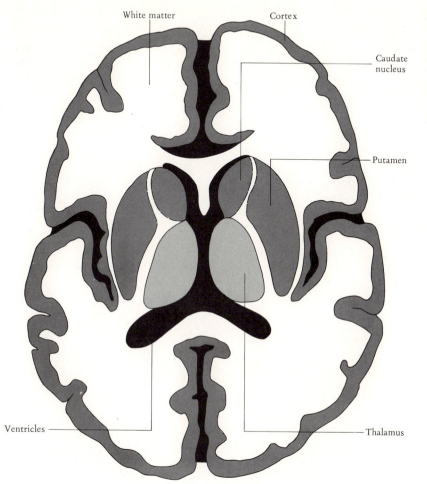

White matter

Cortex

Caudate nucleus

Putamen

Ventricles

Thalamus

Figure 17.
A Horizontal Section Showing Basal Ganglia, the Two Thalami, and the Genu and Splenium of the Corpus Callosum

Glossary

acetaldehyde. The first metabolic breakdown product of alcohol.

acetylcholine. A major neurotransmitter in the brain and the body, excitatory in the brain and at the neuromuscular junction, and as first-order fiber neurotransmitter in the autonomic nervous system; also used by second-order neurons of the parasympathetic branch of that system.

action potential. The nerve impulse, also called the spike potential.

adduction. Turning of a member toward the main axis of the body. Opposite of abduction.

adenohypophysis. The anterior portion of the pituitary gland, distinguished from the neurohypophysis at the rear.

adenosine triphosphate. The chemical used by the cells to store and release chemical energy for metabolic processes.

adenylate cyclase. Cyclic adenosine monophosphate, a chemical important as an intracellular messenger; controls the firing rate in the case of some neurons.

adipsia. Lack of normal thirst.

adrenal gland. An endocrine gland situated atop the kidneys (the renal glands). It secretes a number of essential hormones from its cortex (outer portion), and adrenalin (epinephrine) from its medulla (central portion).

adrenal medulla. The endocrine gland forming the core of the adrenal gland. It secretes adrenalin under stimulation of the sympathetic nervous system.

adrenergic. Designating neurons that make use of norepinephrine or adrenalin.

adrenocorticotrophic hormone (ACTH). One of the trophic hormones released by the anterior pituitary gland. It activates the adrenal cortex to release its own hormones.

affective. Designating an emotional response associated with distinctly positive or negative feelings.

affective attack. Attack with a distinctively emotional basis, such as fear or rage; differentiated from biting attack, which is based on a food-gathering instinct and is essentially unemotional.

afferent. Said of neural signals incoming to a given neuron or neural region.

agnosia. Failure to recognize familiar objects.

alpha-endorphin. The endorphin consisting of beta-lipotropin amino acid residues 61–76; functions as an analgesic.

alpha motor neurons. The large neurons in the spinal motor centers whose axons synapse on muscle cells, causing the skeletal muscles to contract.

amacrine cells. Neurons lacking axons, found particularly in the inner plexiform layer of the retina.

Ammon's horn. The hippocampus proper, distinguished from the dentate gyrus with which it makes up the hippocampal formation. It is characterized by large pyramidal cells.

amoeboid movement. A distinctive type of cellular progression characterized by the sending out of extensions (pseudopods) into which the cytoplasm subsequently flows.

amygdala. A cluster of nuclei located beneath the medial surface of the temporal lobe in the region of the uncus, anterior to the hippocampal formation.

androgen. Male sex hormone.

androstenedione. An androgen (male sex hormone) secreted by the adrenal cortex; the principal androgen present in the female.

angiotensin I. The precursor of angiotensin II.

angiotensin II. A powerful stimulus to the urge to drink.

angiotensinogen. A precursor of angiotensin I, acted on by renin to produce angiotensin I.

angular gyrus. A region of the cortex at the posterior end of the superior temporal sulcus, forming a confluence of visual and auditory information processing. Lesions here often produce dyslexia.

annulospiral ending. A sensory receptor within the muscle spindle of skeletal muscles. It registers muscle stretch and causes the associated motor neuron to increase its firing rate, producing muscle contraction and relieving the stretch, and thus forming a regulating feedback loop.

anosognosia. Failure to recognize one's functional impairment due to brain lesion.

anterior commissure. A fiber bundle interconnecting the two hemispheres with respect to limbic-system structures, principally of the basal and medial temporal lobes. It is situated below the massive corpus callosum in the region of the septal nuclei.

anterior perforated substance. The ancient olfactory cortex, also called the substantia innominata and olfactory tubercle. It is situated at the basal surface of the brain immediately anterior to the hypothalamic region.

anterior thalamic nucleus. The nucleus situated at the anterodorsal region of the thalamic mass, properly belonging not to the thalamocortical system but to the limbic system. It receives input from the mammillary bodies and projects to the cingulate gyrus.

antibodies. Cells generated in response to foreign substances that invade the bloodstream, serving to engulf and/or destroy them.

antidiuretic hormone. ADH, also called va-sopressin; a hormone secreted by the neurohypophysis, causing the kidneys to reduce water loss in the urine and the smooth muscles of the arteries to contract.

antidromically. In reverse direction along the axon.

antigen. Foreign substances which, on entering the bloodstream, cause the formation of antibodies that subsequently eliminate them.

aphagia. Lack of normal hunger.

aphasia. A neurological disorder characterized by impairment of the ability to speak or understand language.

apical dendrite. A stout dendrite extending from the apex, or upper point, of the pyramidal cell.

apraxia. A neurological disorder characterized by inability to perform familiar goal-oriented behavioral sequences.

arachnoid tissue. A spongy tissue surrounding the brain and forming a cushion between it and the bony cranium.

archicortex. The type of cortex found in the hippocampus, the simplest and perhaps most ancient type of cortical tissue.

arcuate fasciculus. A fiber bundle passing from the region of Wernicke's receptive speech area to the region of Broca's motor speech area, presumed essential to the language function of the brain.

articular bones. Three small bones at the point of articulation of the jawbone and the skull in reptiles, transformed in mammals into the ossicles of the middle ear.

ascending reticular activating system (ARAS). A massive, nonspecific fiber system ascending from the brainstem reticular formation through the thalamus and into the cortex, serving to arouse the organism, alert attention, and maintain the waking state.

asteriognosis. A neurological disorder characterized by impairment of the ability to recognize familiar objects by their form.

astrocyte. A type of glial cell characterized by many dendritic extensions.

asymptote. The point at which further doses

fail to increase the rate of occurrence of the signs.

athetosis. A neurological disorder characterized by involuntary writhing movements of the limbs and torso.

auditory hallucination. The hearing of imaginary voices, often associated with the schizophrenic disorder.

autism. A neurological disorder characterized by failure to learn to speak, abnormal attentional focus, absence of social interaction, and extreme compulsive ritualism. The underlying condition is unknown.

autoradiography. The process whereby tissue slices rendered radioactive produce a photographic image showing the location of the radioactivity; used to trace neural pathways and points of chemical concentrations in the brain.

axoaxonic synapse. A synapse formed between two axons, often close to the terminal of one of them.

axodendritic synapse. A synapse of an axon terminal upon a dendrite, the most common type of neural connection.

axon. The single output fiber of a neuron, often coated along its length with an insulating sheath of myelin.

axosomatic synapse. A synapse of an axon terminal upon the soma (cell body) of another neuron.

basal dendrite. The dendritic extensions found at the base of the pyramidal cell soma, extending laterally.

basal ganglia. Collective designation of a group of subcortical nuclei involved in motor functions, usually the caudate nucleus and putamen (collectively known as the corpus striatum) and their common output nucleus, the globus pallidus.

basilar membrane. The structure within the cochlea upon which the auditory receptors (hair cells of the organ of Corti) ride, and whose movement causes their stimulation.

basolateral nuclei. A group of nuclei in the amygdala implicated in the control of fear and rage responses.

beta-endorphin. The endorphin consisting of beta-lipotropin amino acid residues 61–91. It functions in the control of pain.

Betz cells. Giant pyramidal cells found in the motor cortex, presumed to project via the pyramidal tract to the spinal motor neurons.

bipolar cells. Neurons whose input structures extend from one end and output structures from the other; found prominently as second-order neurons in the sensory systems.

biting attack. Attack designed to kill rather than frighten away, characteristic of carnivores in food-gathering; differentiated from affective attack.

blastocyte. The forming organism at the hollow-ball stage reached shortly before implantation in the uterine wall.

blood-brain barrier. A barrier of glial cells that prevents all but a few blood substances from entering the brain tissues.

bouton. An axon terminal.

brainstem. The oldest part of the brain, consisting of midbrain, pons, and medulla.

C fibers. Slender, unmyelinated nerve fibers of ancient origin. An example is the sensory fibers mediating slow "burning" pain, originating in the free nerve endings in the skin.

calcarine fissure. A deep fissure on the medial surface of the hemispheres, the site of arrival of visual signals in the cortex of the occipital lobe.

camera lucida. A device designed to facilitate the careful drawing of things observed under the light microscope.

cannula. A slender tube for injecting minute amounts of liquid substances into discrete regions of the brain.

carbachol. A substance mimicking the effect of acetylcholine but less quickly deactivated.

catatonic state. A schizophrenic disorder characterized by bodily rigidity and immobility, in which the individual may hold peculiar postures for hours while appearing unaware of the surroundings.

catecholamine. Collective designation of norepinephrine, dopamine, and similar neurotransmitters characterized by possession of the catechol group.

caudate nucleus. One of the basal ganglia nuclei which, together with the putamen, forms the striatum.

cell theory. The now-substantiated theory that the body is composed of tiny individual living units (cells).

cellular phase. Fluids contained within the cells, rather than in the extracellular space or vascular system.

cellular tolerance. The aspect of physiological addiction (the body's need for increasing amounts of the addictive substance to produce the same effect) that does not result from more efficient elimination of the substance from the body.

central canal. The continuation of the cerebrospinal fluid system down the center of the spinal cord.

central fissure. Fissure of Rolando; a deep fissure crossing the lateral convexity of the cortex and forming the line of division between the frontal and parietal lobes.

central gray. A region of the brainstem immediately surrounding the cerebral aqueduct and continuing into the spinal cord surrounding the central canal; composed of gray matter.

central nervous system. The brain and spinal cord collectively, distinguished from the peripheral nervous system.

cerebellum. A massive structure (little brain) below the occipital lobe and behind the brainstem, involved in motor functions.

cerebral cortex. The gray matter that composes the surface tissues of the brain.

cerveau isolé. A preparation in which the brainstem has been severed at the level of the midbrain colliculi.

chemoaffinity. The hypothesis that some chemical signal attracts neural extensions, leading to the formation of appropriate synaptic junctions.

chem-trail. A hypothetical chemical pathway laid down by migrating neurons and later followed by others.

cholecystokinin. A chemical substance found in the lining of the upper intestine which, when injected into an animal, powerfully supresses its hunger.

cholinergic. Said of neurons or neural systems making use of the neurotransmitter acetylcholine.

chorea. A neurological disorder characterized by uncontrollable movements of the limbs and facial muscles (St. Vitus' dance).

choreiform movements. Involuntary movements of the limbs and facial muscles due to a neurological disorder.

chromaffin cells. Cells in the adrenal medulla that act as second-order neurons of the sympathetic nervous system, secreting epinephrine (adrenalin) into the bloodstream during sympathetic-system arousal.

cilia. Tiny fiber extensions from the hair cells of the cochlea, whose motion due to contact with the overlying tectorial membrane is thought to generate the receptor potential.

cingulate gyrus. That portion of the medial surface of the hemispheres that lies immediately above the corpus callosum. It is an important part of the limbic system, separated from the overlying thalamocortical cortex by the cingulate sulcus.

cingulum bundle. A stout fiber bundle passing through the cingulate gyrus beneath its cortical layer and continuing around the posterior end of the corpus callosum and into the entorhinal cortex of the temporal lobe. It is an important structure in the limbic system.

circuit of Papez. A complex neural circuit in the limbic system, proceeding from hippocampal formation to mammillary bodies, anterior thalamic nucleus, cingulate gyrus, entorhinal cortex, and back to the hippocampus.

climbing fibers. Fibers entering the cerebellum from the inferior olivary nucleus, each synapsing upon the dendritic tree of a single Purkinje cell and powerfully activating it; differentiated from mossy fibers.

clone. A group of cells of identical ancestry and chemical constitution.

clonic phase. An early stage of a grand mal epileptic seizure characterized by a jerking of the body musculature.

cloning. The process of cell multiplication in which daughter cells do not differentiate into new cell types.

cochlea. A spiraling hollow tube in the temporal bone housing the auditory receptor mechanism.

cochlear microphonic. A response of the entire cochlea to incoming sound waves, capable of registering their pattern apparently without dependence on neural receptors.

cold turkey. Breaking of an addictive dependency without the assistance of medication.

colliculi. Small nuclei forming four rounded protuberances (little hills) from the roof of the midbrain, serving visual and auditory reflexes.

commissural. Referring to fibers passing between the two hemispheres.

complex cells. Neurons in the visual cortex that respond preferentially to a particular orientation of a linear stimulus as it moves across their retinal fields.

concentric organization. A characteristic of the retinal field of a ganglion cell such that its center responds to stimulation in a manner opposite to that of its immediate surround.

conditioned stimulus. A stimulus that has through training become effective at producing a given response.

cone cells. Receptor cells, particularly in the central regions of the retina, that are differentially responsive to colors.

convergence. Input to a single neuron of signals originating in many other neurons, and often many other brain regions.

corpus callosum. A broad band of commissural fibers interconnecting the neocortex of the two hemispheres.

corpus striatum. The caudate nucleus and putamen collectively.

cortex. A type of neural tissue consisting of distinct layers forming a continuous sheet, as at the surface of the brain.

cortical layers. Distinguishably different layers in the cortex with different cell-type compositions.

corticofugal. Designating fibers passing out of the cortex.

corticomedial nuclei. A group of amygdalar nuclei of ancient origin, characterized by a significant olfactory input and projecting to the hypothalamus via the stria terminalis pathway.

cortisol. A hormone secreted by the adrenal cortex that has numerous and complex effects, including regulation of carbohydrate metabolism.

cribriform plate. The bony structure immediately above the nasal passages.

critical mass hypothesis. The notion that the large size of the human brain can explain its superior intelligence, and particularly its capacity for language.

cross-modal response. Responsiveness to sensory input of different types, such as auditory and visual; said of some neurons in the posterior general association cortex.

cross-tolerance. The tendency of different addictive drugs to produce the tolerance phenomenon for each other.

cryogenic. Making use of cold to deactivate neurons temporarily.

cuneate nucleus. A nucleus at the base of the medulla that serves as the lemniscal system's first relay station from the upper regions of the body. It lies lateral to the gracile nucleus, which handles similar information from lower regions.

cupula. A structure at the junction of the semicircular canals and the utricle, containing the vestibular receptors.

cutaneous. Referring to the skin.

cyclic guanosine monophosphate. cGMP or guanylate cyclase; a chemical important as an intracellular messenger controlling the firing rate of some neurons.

cyclic nucleotides. Chemical compounds that serve as internal regulators of the firing rate of some neurons, including cyclic adenosine monophosphate and guanosine monophosphate.

cytoplasm. The semi-liquid material within the cell, exclusive of nucleus and organelles.

Dale's principle. The notion, now abandoned, that each neuron makes use of only one neurotransmitter.

decarboxylation. Enzymatic removal of a carboxyl group (COOH) from an organic compound.

defeminized. Rendered incapable of feminine sexual response by the presence of testosterone in the fetal blood at a critical period of hypothalamic maturation.

delirium tremens. A quasi-psychotic state that sometimes characterizes withdrawal in severe alcoholism, often involving frightening hallucinations.

dendrite. A neural extension designed to receive input — usually excitatory — from other neurons.

denervation. Severing of neural input to a neuron or muscle cell.

dentate gyrus. The portion of the hippocampal formation characterized by numerous closely packed granule cells, partially surrounded by the hippocampus proper (Ammon's horn) containing pyramidal cells.

dentate nucleus. An important subcortical nucleus within the cerebellar white matter whose neurons project to the thalamic motor nuclei.

dentatorubrothalamic tract. The fiber bundle passing from the dentate nucleus of the cerebellum through the red nucleus of the midbrain (rubro) and into the thalamic motor nuclei.

deoxyribonucleic acid (DNA). The chemical substance containing the genetic code; found only in the cell nucleus, strung out along the chromosomes.

depolarized. Designating a region of neural membrane when its normal polarity is lost or reduced.

depression effect. A response on the part of mammals to reduction in the quantity or quality of the reward during conditioning.

dermatome. An area of skin served by sensory neurons at a particular segmental level of the spinal cord.

determination. The change in the complement of functional genes that occurs during embryo formation to restrict the different types of cells that a given cell may become.

diazepam. Valium; a benzodiazepine drug, useful as an anxiety suppressant but highly overprescribed and capable of leading to addiction in some individuals.

diencephalon. The thalamus and hypothalamus collectively.

differentiation. Technically, the change in gene expression that determines the type and function of a given cell.

dipsogenic. Causing thirst.

disconnection syndrome. The result of severing the corpus callosum to functionally isolate the two hemispheres.

discontrol syndrome. Uncontrollable rage or impulsive violent behavior, often associated with temporal-lobe epilepsy.

disinhibition. Liberation of a neuron or nucleus from inhibitory control. Inhibitory neurons slow the firing rate of those neurons acting as inhibitory controls.

divergence. The output of a single neuron to many other neurons, often in widely separated brain regions, through the many terminal branches of its axon.

dopamine. One of the major neurotransmitters in the brain, especially prominent in the basal ganglia.

dorsal. Situated above (in the brain) or to the rear (in the brainstem and spinal cord).

dorsal funiculus. The mass of ascending fiber bundles in the dorsal (rear) portion of the spinal cord.

dorsal nerve cord. The evolutionary precursor of the spinal cord, found in such prevertebrate chordates as *Amphioxus.*

dorsomedial nucleus. A major nucleus of the thalamus, situated medially and in massive intercommunication with the prefrontal granular cortex and orbital cortex.

dura mater. A tough fibrous covering of the brain outside the spongy arachnoid tissue.

dyskinesia. Impairment of normal muscular function.

dyslexia. Difficulty in learning to read.

dysphasia. Impairment of fluent speech.

echolocating. Orienting to surrounding objects through the sounds they reflect (echoes).

ectodermal. Designating the tissues that compose the dorsal layer of the embryo, the source of the neurons, epidermal skin cells, and other cells.

electrocorticogram. A record of brain waves recorded from the surface of the cortex.

electroencephalogram. A record of brain waves recorded from the scalp.

electromyogram. A record of neural activity in the muscles.

electrooculogram. A record of movements of the eyeball.

electrophoresis. The technique of injecting a tiny controlled amount of a chemical substance into a specific brain region by applying low electrical voltage to a hollow electrode containing the substance.

electrotonic. Designating a traveling wave of polarity change over the surface of a neuron when no action potential is generated. Unlike the axon's nerve impulse, the electrotonic propagation is slow and diminishes in amplitude and speed.

encephalization. Transfer of a brain function to the cortex from more primitive structures over the course of evolution.

end bulbs of Krause. Sensory receptor structures in the skin, once thought to respond exclusively to cold.

endocast. A reproduction of the interior form of the cranium, especially of fossil remains.

endodermal. Designating the tissues that compose the ventral surface of the embryo, the source of cells lining the walls of the viscera, as well as others.

endogenous. Designating depressions that appear to be unrelated to present life circumstances, and hence to arise from some altered conditions within the brain. Arising from within.

endolymph. The fluid investing the structures of the inner ear (cochlea and vestibular apparatus).

endoplasmic reticulum. A system of membrane-bound channels and cisternae occupying much of the cell's cytoplasmic space.

endorphinergic. Referring to neurons or neural systems presumed to employ endorphins as their neurotransmitter.

endorphins. Peptide substances (chains of linked amino acids too short to be classed as proteins) which appear to be natural (endogenous) opioid substances mediating analgesia and euphoria.

endplate. Motor endplate. The equivalent of the postsynaptic membrane at the neuromuscular junction.

engram. The presumed neural substrate of a memory.

enkephalins. Very small peptide substances, containing only five amino acids, which appear to function as opioids and may be the basic substances used by the brain to control the pain response.

entorhinal cortex. The limbic-system cortex on the medial and basal surfaces of the temporal lobe in the vicinity of the amygdala and the hippocampal formation.

enzyme. A protein whose biological activity is to catalyze a specific chemical reaction without itself being altered; the basic metabolic mechanism whereby reactions take place rapidly that would otherwise occur only slowly or not at all.

epicritic. Designating the more recently evolved lemniscal sensory system characterized by fast-firing, highly specific sensory registration; differentiated from the older protopathic system making use of the spinothalamic pathway.

epidermis. The superficial layer of the skin.

epileptogenic scars. Scar tissue producing abnormal neural firing.

epinephrine. A hormone secreted by the adrenal medulla under sympathetic-system activation; also called adrenalin.

ethanol.   Ethyl (grain) alcohol, C_2H_5OH.

ethmoid bone.   The bone underlying the frontal lobes of the brain.

evoked potential.   An electrical response recorded from the cortex in response to sensory stimulation.

exocytosis.   The process in which unwanted substances are excreted by the cell into the surrounding medium.

exogenous.   Designating factors in the environment, rather than within the organism (endogenous), as the source of difficulty.

expectancy wave.   Contingent negative variation (CNV); a sustained baseline negativity in the electroencephalogram recorded from the scalp over the frontal lobes when the subject is alertly expectant of a forthcoming signal to respond.

external auditory meatus.   The outer ear canal leading into the eardrum.

extinction.   The process by which a given stimulus, through repetition in the absence of reinforcement, loses its power to evoke a conditioned response.

extracellular phase.   The portion of the body's fluids that is not contained within the cells, including that in the extracellular space and in the circulatory system.

extrafusal fibers.   The large skeletal muscle fibers involved in bodily movement; distinguished from intrafusal fibers within the embedded muscle spindles.

extrapyramidal.   Designating the older motor systems of the brain that handle highly overlearned automated behavior, such as walking.

facultative homosexuals.   Homosexuals who prefer a sexual partner of the same sex, but who may also function sexually with a partner of the opposite sex; differentiated from obligate homosexuals.

feed-backward inhibition.   Inhibition of neural firing through local inhibitory neurons activated by collaterals of the axon of the inhibited neuron.

feed-forward inhibition.   Inhibition of neural firing through local inhibitory neurons activated by collaterals of incoming fibers to the inhibited neuron.

fertilization.   Penetration of the egg (ovum) by a sperm cell (spermatocyte), bringing about fusion of the nuclear materials of the two and the beginning of a new life process.

filopodia.   Amoeboid extensions of the growing tip of either an axon or dendrite.

fissure of Rolando.   Central fissure; a major fissure descending from behind the vertex diagonally forward across the lateral convexity of the brain, forming the posterior extent of the frontal lobe.

flocculo-nodular lobe.   The older midline portion of the cerebellum concerned with such reflex functions as balance and postural control.

flocculus.   The midline portion of the cerebellum concerned with postural reflexes.

follicle-stimulating hormone (FSH).   One of the two gonadotrophic hormones affecting both ovaries and testes.

fornical agenisis.   Failure of the fornix to form during gestation.

fornix.   The fiber bundle that serves as the major output pathway of the hippocampal formation, passing to the mammillary bodies of the hypothalamus, and carrying signals from septum to hippocampus.

fovea.   Fovea centralis; the portion of the retina providing central vision, with maximum visual acuity.

free fatty acids.   Breakdown products of triglycerides, which build up in the blood when one has not eaten recently, and quickly diminish shortly after eating has begun; perhaps involved in the regulation of food intake.

free nerve endings.   A type of ancient sensory nerve ending in the skin and other bodily organs, thought to be especially involved in the sensation of slow "burning" pain.

frontal lobe.   That portion of the brain anterior to the central fissure (of Rolando) and containing the motor cortex, the frontal eye fields, the prefrontal granular cortex, and the orbital cortex.

frustrative nonreward. The emotional effect of "disappointment" when an expected reward does not appear: quick extinction of the learned response, especially among higher mammals.

FTG cells. Giant cells in the midbrain tegmentum whose increased firing rate is correlated with the onset and continuation of REM sleep.

fugue state. A pathological state characterized by loss of memory for behavior, and frequently by bizarre behavior.

functional psychosis. The major psychoses — schizophrenia, endogenous depression, and the manic-depressive disorder — which appear to have no tangible neurological defect as their basis; differentiated from organic disorders, in which such a neural basis is demonstrable, and thought to represent a chemical and metabolic disorder rather than a structural defect.

fusiform. Spindle-shaped.

gamma-aminobutyric acid (GABA). One of the major inhibitory neurotransmitters in the brain.

gamma efferent loop. A feedback loop whereby muscle tension may be "set" to accommodate different task requirements.

gamma efferent neuron. The motor neuron projecting to the muscle spindle — a sensory receptor mechanism within the skeletal muscles — rather than to the muscle cells proper.

ganglion cells. Third-order fibers of the retina, whose axons form the optic nerve.

ganglionic system. A primitive neural system found among many invertebrates in which semiautonomous clumps of neurons have special functions.

gender identity. One's sense of oneself as masculine or feminine.

gene. A segment of DNA containing the code for a specific biologically active protein.

general adaptation syndrome. A sequence of behaviors or states representing a universal response to severe or prolonged stress.

geniculate. Bent; designating either of two sensory-relay nuclei (visual or auditory) of the thalamus.

geniculate bodies. The lateral and medial geniculate nuclei of the thalamus, relaying visual and auditory signals respectively.

geniculocalcarine system. The visual perceptual system involving the optic radiation projecting from the lateral geniculate nucleus to the region of the calcarine fissure in the occipital lobe.

genu. Knee; the anterior pole of the corpus callosum.

gestation. The process of fetal development (the period from conception to birth).

glabrous. Smooth, nonhairy; said of skin.

glial cells. Nonneural cells, which greatly outnumber the neurons whose functioning they serve.

globus pallidus. One of the three nuclei of the basal ganglia, serving as their common outlet.

glucose. Blood sugar, the brain's sole energy source.

glycine. An inhibitory neurotransmitter in the spinal cord, replacing GABA.

Golgi apparatus. A portion of the endoplasmic reticulum devoted to the packaging of cellular products in membrane-bound vesicles.

gonadotrophic hormones. Pituitary trophic hormones whose target is the ovaries or testes, stimulating their hormone production and responsible for their development and maintenance in a functional state.

gonads. The primary sexual organs, ovaries and testes.

gracile nuclei. Nuclei at the base of the medulla serving as the first relay station of the lemniscal system from lower regions of the body. They lie medial to the cuneate nuclei serving upper regions of the body.

grand mal seizure. The most dramatic form of epileptic seizure. It begins with tonic rigidity and loss of consciousness, followed by spasmodic jerking and frothing at the mouth, a short sleep, and the regaining of consciousness.

granule cells. Tiny neurons, such as those

found in the dentate gyrus of the hippocampal formation, the cerebellar cortex, and the prefrontal granular cortex.

growth cone.   The formation at the growing tip of an elongating axon.

habituation.   Cessation of attendance to a meaningless stimulus after repeated exposure.

hair cells.   Receptor cells in the inner ear, both the cochlea and the vestibular apparatus, characterized by protruding cilia which may be the triggers to the generation of the receptor potential.

haptic perception.   Perception mediated by touch.

head ganglion.   The hypothalamus characterized in relation to the autonomic nervous system.

hedonic.   Based on the pleasure-pain principle.

hemifield.   Half of the visual field to the right or left of the point of fixation of the gaze.

hemiretina.   Half of the retina to the right or left of the foveal region.

hemispheres.   The two massive structures of the thalamocortical system, including their embedded nuclei, the basal ganglia, thalamus, amygdala, and septum. The two are separated by the longitudinal fissure and connected by the corpus callosum and anterior commissure.

higher-order complex cells.   Neurons of the visual cortex that respond preferentially to linear stimuli forming an angle of a specific orientation approaching a right angle.

hippocampal formation.   The hippocampus proper (Ammon's horn) and the dentate gyrus collectively.

hippocampus.   The hippocampal formation, a major structure of the limbic system and part of Papez' circuit, involved in memory formation.

holistic.   Emphasizing the relationship of all relevant factors within a dynamic system.

homeostasis.   Maintenance of constancy in the internal conditions of the organism, necessary to the continued life of the cells.

hominid.   Bipedal primates, including ourselves and our immediate progenitors among ancestral hominoids.

homologous.   Having the same relative position or structure.

homunculus.   A little man; used to designate the map of bodily areas along the fissure of Rolando.

horizontal cells.   Neurons without axons, found especially in the outer plexiform layer of the retina.

horseradish peroxidase.   An enzyme used in tracing the course of nerve fibers.

6-hydroxydopamine.   A nerve poison destructive to dopaminergic and adrenergic neurons and neural systems.

hypercomplex cells.   Neurons in the visual cortex that respond maximally to linear stimuli of a given orientation, but only if the stimulus terminates within their receptive field.

hyperphagia.   Abnormally large food intake, associated with obesity.

hyperpolarize.   To move the polarity of the membrane in a direction opposite to depolarization, resulting in increased polarity and inhibition of firing; said of neural plasma membranes.

hypersynchronous.   Said of brain waves during slow-wave sleep (delta waves), characterizing the synchronous firing of great numbers of neurons.

hypophysis.   The pituitary gland.

hypothalamus.   The brain region immediately below the thalamus, responsible for such basic life-supportive systems as hunger, thirst, and temperature control; also controls the neuroendocrine system and the autonomic nervous system.

hypoxia.   Absence of normal oxygen supply.

idiot savant.   An autistic child who exhibits very remarkable abilities in a narrow field and grave deficiencies in many others.

imipramine.   One of the tricyclic antidepressant drugs used in the treatment of endogenous depressions.

incus.   One of the three ossicles of the middle

ear, which transmit sound waves from the eardrum to the oval window of the cochlea.

inferior longitudinal fasciculus. A transcortical fiber bundle interconnecting the occipital- and temporal-lobe cortices.

inferior olivary nuclei. Large nuclei situated in the ventral brainstem below the pons, the source of the climbing fibers that enter the cerebellum.

inferotemporal lobe cortex. The inferior portion of the temporal lobe neocortex, roughly consisting of Brodmann's areas 37 and 21; the site of high-level visual-perceptual information processing.

internal capsule. A massive fiber bundle interconnecting the neocortex and lower structures, passing between the thalamus medially and the putamen laterally, and separating the head of the caudate nucleus from the putamen.

internal inhibition. An inhibitory phenomenon noted by Pavlov, whose dogs were put to sleep by repeated presentation of a conditioned stimulus without further reinforcement (during the conditioning process).

internal medullary lamina. A sheet of gray matter and nerve fibers running through the thalamus and separating the lateral nuclei from the dorsomedial nucleus; considered a part of the reticular system.

interneurons. Small neurons whose axons terminate in the vicinity of the cell body, often inhibitory in function; differentiated from transmission or projection neurons, whose axons travel to distant regions.

interoceptors. Sensory receptors within the body that register its internal conditions, rather than environmental events.

intralaminar nuclei. Nuclei embedded within the internal medullary lamina, a sheet of neural tissue coursing through the thalamus and representing part of the reticular system.

invagination. An infolding of the plasma membrane to engulf a particle, as in pinocytosis.

ion. An atom carrying a positive or negative charge as a result of having lost or gained one or more electrons.

ionic pump. A mechanism within the plasma membrane that moves ions through it. In the case of the sodium pump, sodium ions (Na^+) are continuously caused to flow out into extracellular space.

ipsilateral. On the same side of the head; differentiated from contralateral.

kainic acid. A neural poison that destroys nerve cell bodies without destroying axonal fibers passing through the region.

Korsakoff's syndrome. A degenerative neurological disorder afflicting long-term chronic alcoholics, characterized by failure to consolidate short-term memory into long-term memory storage.

l-dopa. Levo-dopa, the precursor of dopamine; used in the treatment of Parkinson's disease. Unlike dopamine itself, l-dopa readily crosses the blood-brain barrier.

lateral fissure. Sylvian fissure; the deep fissure separating the mass of the temporal lobe from the frontal and parietal lobes.

lateral inhibition. Inhibition of surrounding neurons by neural activity in certain sensory receptor fields or cortical stations, serving to sharpen the signal.

lateralization. Specialization of the two hemispheres for different functions, particularly language and nonverbal functions.

lateral lemniscus. A fiber bundle passing upward through the brainstem and carrying auditory-system fibers among others.

lateral line system. A system of acoustic receptors strung along the sides of certain fishes; the evolutionary precursor of the auditory system in mammals.

lateral septal nucleus. One of two major septal nuclei, projecting heavily into the head of the caudate nucleus.

lemniscal system. The more modern of the two somatosensory systems, characterized by large, fast-firing neurons and discrete representation of stimuli; differentiated from the older spinothalamic system.

leucine enkephalin. One of the two known enkephalin peptide molecules apparently involved in control of the pain response.

limbic lobe. Broca's concept of the limbic system, consisting of the cortical regions that line the medial surfaces of the brain, encircling the subcortical nuclei and brainstem structures.

limbic system. An older system of the brain, largely buried beneath the thalamocortical system in mammals; concerned with such functions as emotional response, mood states, and consolidation of event memory.

lipid. Referring to fatty substances.

lipostat. A hypothetical mechanism in the hypothalamus setting the level of fat deposition the animal will seek to maintain.

locus coeruleus. A brainstem nucleus (of bluish color in the fresh state), the source of much of the norepinephrine in the brain.

lordosis posture. A typical sexual presentation posture of the female mammal, inviting sexual contact and facilitating intromission.

luteinizing hormone (LH). One of two gonadotrophic hormones secreted by the pituitary gland and affecting both ovaries and testes.

lysergic acid diethylamide (LSD). A powerful hallucinogenic substance.

lysis. A process by which unwanted or dangerous substances are destroyed in the cell, as by the lysosomes.

macrosmatic. Said of animals largely dependent on the olfactory sense.

malleus. One of the three ossicles in the middle ear transmitting sound waves from the eardrum to the oval window of the cochlea.

mammalian radiation. The rapid development of many types of mammals after the extinction of the dinosaurs.

mammillary bodies. Nuclei at the base of the hypothalamus, the major target of fibers from the hippocampal formation via the fornix.

mammillothalamic tract. A fiber bundle leading from the mammillary bodies to the anterior nucleus of the thalamus as part of Papez' circuit.

massa intermedia. A structure connecting the two thalami across the third ventricle in some brains.

maximization. The tendency of most mammals to choose consistently the most frequently rewarded of two stimuli.

mechanoreceptors. Sensory receptors responsive to deformation of the sensory nerve tip, as in many cutaneous receptors.

medial. Toward the midline of the brain.

medial forebrain bundle system. The system of nuclei and their connections associated with the medial forebrain bundle coursing through the lateral hypothalamus.

medial lemniscus. A fiber bundle passing upward through the brainstem carrying signals of the somatosensory system.

medial septal nucleus. One of two septal nuclei projecting to the hippocampus and containing the "pacemaker cells" controlling the hippocampal theta wave.

median raphé. A structure in the midline of the brainstem (its seam); the location of nuclei producing serotonin.

medulla. The lowest of the three structures composing the brainstem, located immediately above the spinal cord.

Meissner's corpuscles. A type of rapidly adapting nerve ending in the skin, lying just below the epidermis and sensitive to touch.

meninges. Membranes such as the dura mater and pia mater, surrounding the brain and spinal cord.

Merkel's discs. A complex type of nerve ending in the skin, situated within the epidermis and exquisitely sensitive to touch.

mesoderm. The tissue forming the middle layer of the embryo, the source of muscle and bone and other tissues.

messenger RNA (mRNA). The RNA transcribed directly from the DNA in the nucleus, carrying the code for the production of a biologically important protein.

metabolite. An organic compound resulting from a metabolic process in the cell.

methionine enkephalin. One of the two known enkephalin peptide molecules apparently involved in the control of pain response.

methylation. The chemical transformation resulting from replacement of a hydrogen atom (H) by a methyl group (CH_3); an important enzymatically controlled process in organic chemistry.

midbrain. The uppermost of the three structures composing the brainstem.

midbrain limbic area. A region in the midbrain with important connections to the medial forebrain bundle and limbic system.

migration. Movement of cells in the embryo from point of origin to final destination in the process of morphogenesis.

mitochondria. Organelles within the cytoplasm responsible for producing useful chemical energy for its metabolic processes.

mitosis. Cell division in which the two daughter cells have the same number of chromosomes as the mother cell.

mitral cells. Second-order neurons of the olfactory system with a curious cross-shaped configuration.

monoamine oxidase (MAO). The major enzyme responsible for breakdown of norepinephrine, dopamine, and serotonin (the monoamine neurotransmitters) once they are released into the synaptic cleft.

monoamine oxidase inhibitor. Chemical substances that interfere with the normal breakdown of the monoamine neurotransmitters, resulting in their buildup and thus accentuating their synaptic effect.

morphogenesis. The complex process through which the zygote is transformed into the fully formed embryo.

mossy fiber. One of two types of fibers entering the cerebellum; differentiated from climbing fibers. Arising from various sources, they project to the granule cells of the cerebellar cortex, which in turn project the parallel fibers through many Purkinje cell dendritic trees.

motoneurons. Motor neurons; the large neurons in the spinal motor centers projecting to the skeletal muscles. They form the final common pathway for all brain activity.

motor homunculus. The map of the regions of the motor cortex associated with movement in various regions of the body; parallels the sensory homunculus in the postcentral gyrus.

motor nuclei. Any of various nuclei involved in the initiation and control of bodily movement.

motor program. The neural basis of a particular skilled motor performance.

motor unit. The group of skeletal muscle cells activated by a particular motor neuron, together with that motor neuron.

mulberry stage. The developmental stage immediately following formation of the zygote, when the new organism is descending to the uterus, growing in number of cells but scarcely increasing in size.

muscle impulse. The wave of depolarization of the muscle-cell plasma membrane, which initiates the cell's contraction; corresponding to the nerve impulse passing along the axon.

muscle spindles. Sensory receptor systems embedded within the skeletal muscles, registering muscle extension.

myelin sheath. A fatty sheath surrounding many axons, formed by multiple wrappings of the endfeet of a specialized type of glial cell, the oligodentroglia (sparsely branching glia).

myelinated. Provided with a myelin sheath; said of most of the larger axons in the brain when functionally mature.

myoneural junction. Neuromuscular junction; the synapse formed by the spinal motor neuron on the muscle cell.

necrosis. Tissue death.

nerve net. A type of primitive neural organization in which the nerve fibers transmit excitation in either direction.

neural crest. A ridge of tissue formed at the point of closure of the neural tube in embryogenesis; the source of neurons of the peripheral nervous system.

neural tube. The earliest form of the central nervous system in embryogenesis. It is created when a deepening neural groove in the dorsal surface of the embryo closes and sinks into the ectodermal layer.

neuroblasts. Immature neurons during formation and migration to their ultimate stations.

neuroendocrine system. The system governed by the pituitary gland under the stimulation of the hypothalamus. It includes both the adenohypophysis and its target glands and the neurohypophysis.

neuroglia. Glial cells; supporting cells surrounding the neurons and forming the blood-brain barrier.

neurohormone. A hormone released by neurons into extracellular space rather than into the synaptic cleft, thus exercising a diffuse rather than discrete influence.

neuromuscular junction. Myoneural junction; the synaptic contact of a motor neuron with a muscle cell.

neuron. A nerve cell.

neuron doctrine. The hypothesis, now substantiated, that the fibers composing the various nerves are in fact the cytoplasmic extensions of individual neural cells.

neurotransmitter. A chemical substance released into the synaptic cleft from the axon terminal upon the arrival of a nerve impulse, influencing the firing rate of the postsynaptic (target) neuron.

neurulation. The process of formation of the neural tube during embryogenesis.

nictitating membrane. A second eyelid in some mammals forming a translucent protective sheath over the cornea.

nigrostriatal system. The dopamine system projecting from the substantia nigra to the striatum.

nodes of Ranvier. Points between successive lengths of myelin sheath where the axon is bare, providing for saltatory transmission.

nonopponent excitators. Lateral geniculate neurons that do not respond in opposing ways to opposite colors, but increase their firing rate over the middle range of the spectrum.

nonopponent inhibitors. Lateral geniculate neurons that do not respond in opposing ways to opposite colors, but decrease their firing rate over the middle range of the spectrum.

noradrenergic. Said of neurons or neural systems that make use of the neurotransmitter norepinephrine.

norepinephrine. One of the important neurotransmitters in the brain.

notochord. A flexible structure, the precursor of the vertebral column, found in the primitive chordates.

nucleus. In neurological terms, any group of neurons that together fulfill a particular brain function. In the peripheral nervous system, such neural clusters are called ganglia.

nucleus accumbens. A nucleus in the septal region thought to function in connection with the limbic system.

nystagmus. Involuntary jerking of the eyeball.

object constancy. The tendency to continue to perceive objects as constant in shape even though the retinal pattern they present changes when they are viewed from different positions.

object-reversal task. An experimental arrangement in which the subject is required to select one of two objects, having first learned to choose the other.

obligate heterosexuals. Individuals whose preference for a mate of the opposite sex is exclusive.

obligate homosexuals. Individuals whose preference for a mate of their own sex is exclusive.

occipital lobe. The rear portion of the brain, behind the parietal-occipital sulcus.

occiput. The rear pole of the brain, or of the cranium.

ocular dominance columns. Columns in the visual cortex selectively responsive to input from the two eyes — which differs owing to the lateral displacement of the eyeballs — and correlated with object distance; differentiated from columns selectively responsive to a particular angle of orientation of the linear stimulus.

off responses. Cessation of firing of retinal ganglion cells when a light stimulus strikes their retinal field.

olfactory epithelium. The nasal tissue sensitive to odors.

olfactory tubercle (also **substantia innominata** or **olfactory tubercle**). The ancient olfactory cortex of the brain situated anterior to the hypothalamus, forming the base of the brain in the region of the anterior commissure.

on responses. Increased firing of retinal ganglion cells when a light stimulus strikes their retinal field.

opponent color cells. Lateral geniculate nucleus cells differentially responsive to yellow and blue light.

opsin. A protein molecule attached to the retinal molecule to form a visual pigment, and temporarily detached therefrom in response to an appropriate light stimulus.

optic chiasma. The crossover point of the optic nerve fibers from the nasal half of each retina.

optic disc. The point on the retina where the ganglion-cell axons plunge through to form the optic nerve, causing a blind spot.

optic nerve. Axons of the retinal ganglion cells passing to the optic chiasma.

optic tectum. In primitive mammals and pre-mammalian forms, the structure receiving major visual input; homologous with the superior colliculi in the human brain.

optic tract. Retinal ganglion-cell fibers after they have passed the optic chiasma.

orbital cortex. The cerebral cortex underlying the frontal lobe.

organelles. Small organs in the cell cytoplasm responsible for specific functions (such as the mitochondria and lysosomes).

organic disorder. A neurological disorder caused by demonstrable impairment of brain structure; differentiated from functional disorders.

organ of Corti. The complex structure in the cochlea responsible for auditory registration.

orientation columns. Cortical columns in the visual cortex selectively responsive to a particular angle of orientation of the visual stimulus; differentiated from ocular dominance columns.

osmosensitive zone. A region in the lateral preoptic area where neurons are sensitive to cellular dehydration, triggering the thirst mechanism.

ossicles. Three small interconnected bones of the middle ear transmitting vibration from the eardrum to the oval window of the cochlea.

otolith. A particle of calcium carbonate embedded in a gelatinous matrix in the utricle of the vestibular system, registering head position and movement.

oval window. The cochlear apperture receiving sound stimulation from the eardrum via the ossicles.

oxytocin. One of the major endocrine hormones secreted by the neurohypophysis.

pacemaker cells. Neurons in the medial septal nucleus presumed responsible for regulating hippocampal rhythms, such as the theta wave.

Pacinian corpuscles. Sensory structures in the deeper layers of the skin and other regions responsive to deep pressure.

paleocortex. The portion of the cerebral cortex that evolved prior to the neocortex and exhibits a somewhat simpler laminar structure. It is associated with the limbic system.

parallel fibers. Axons of the cerebellar granule cells that ascend to the level of the Purkinje cell dendrites, then bifurcate to pass in parallel with others through the array of such dendrites.

parasympathetic branch. The branch of the autonomic nervous system concerned with preparing the body for peaceful pursuits, such as eating and exploration.

parietal lobe. The cortical lobe immediately behind the central fissure, between the frontal lobe and the occipital lobe.

parieto-occipital sulcus. A deep fissure on the medial surface of the hemispheres separating the parietal and occipital lobes.

pars triangularis. The posterior portion of the inferior frontal convolution containing Broca's motor speech area on the left.

partial reinforcement effect. The tendency of

animals to continue a learned response after it is no longer rewarded if the rewards during learning trials were intermittent and unpredictable.

passive avoidance deficit.   Failure of an animal to learn to avoid a punished response.

patellar reflex.   The knee-jerk reflex, an example of the simplest form of spinal reflex.

pathologic intoxication.   An abnormal response to alcohol characterized by impulsively violent behavior.

peptides.   Short chains of amino acids.

perceptual learning.   Learning to recognize things through repeated sensory exposure.

perforant pathway.   The major input pathway to the hippocampal formation, originating in the entorhinal cortex.

periaqueductal gray.   The gray matter immediately surrounding the cerebral aqueduct leading from the third to the fourth ventricle.

perilymph.   The fluid investing the cochlea and the vestibular system.

peripheral nerves.   Bundles of nerve-cell axons outside of the central nervous system; collectively the sensory, motor, and autonomic nerve fibers.

perseveration.   Persistence of a learned response after it is no longer rewarded, or even punished.

petit mal.   A type of epilepsy characterized by momentary lapses of consciousness and lip-smacking, but not falling.

phenothiazines.   A group of drugs useful in treating the symptoms of schizophrenia.

phenylethanolamine.   The chemical substance whose structure is that of norepinephrine without the two hydroxyl groups on the phenyl group; recently found to be an effective hunger suppressant.

phenylethylamine.   The chemical substance whose structure is that of dopamine without the two hydroxyl groups on the phenyl group; considered a possible neurotransmitter.

phospholipid molecules.   Molecules composed of a phosphate group and a fatty (lipid) group; component elements of the plasma membrane.

phosphorylation.   The process through which an organic substance is changed by addition of a phosphate group.

phyletic.   Pertaining to evolutionary levels.

physiognomic memory.   Memory for faces and, by extension, for individuals through any sensory modality.

physiological emotion.   The change in bodily state associated with such emotions as rage and fear, representing activity of the sympathetic nervous system.

pia mater.   The delicate translucent membrane immediately covering the brain tissue.

pinna.   The external ear.

pinocytosis.   Cell drinking; the process in which the cell takes in particles or substances by means of a local invagination and pinching-off of its plasma membrane.

pituitary gland.   Hypophysis; the major endocrine gland, suspended below the hypothalamus and responsible for the activities of other endocrine glands through the secretion of trophic hormones.

placebo effect.   The beneficial effect of a substance, taken as a medicine, that has no actual medicinal value.

planum temporale.   The structure immediately behind the auditory projection area (Heschl's gyri) atop the temporal lobe, constituting part of the auditory association cortex.

plasma membrane.   The membrane immediately surrounding the cytoplasm of the cell.

plexiform layers.   Layers of neural interaction between the receptors and bipolar cells and between the bipolars and ganglion cells of the retina, occupied by horizontal cells and amacrine cells respectively.

polarity.   Electrical charge differential on two sides of the plasma membrane.

pons.   The middle of the three structures of the brainstem, between the midbrain above and the medulla below.

postdeprivation rebound.   The tendency to experience more REM sleep on nights following REM sleep deprivation.

post-ictal.   Designating the period immediately following an epileptic seizure.

postsynaptic potentiation. An increase in synaptic effect resulting from the increasingly rapid arrival of nerve impulses, and unrelated to the amplitude of the impulses.

potential (electrical). Electrical charge.

precommissural fornix. That part of the fornix interconnecting the hippocampus and the septal region.

prefrontal granular cortex. The frontal lobe general association cortex.

presynaptic inhibition. The inhibitory effect of a subthreshold activation of the axon terminal before arrival of the action potential, whose amplitude of effect is thereby decreased.

primary motor cortex. Brodmann's area 4, receiving the major input from the ventrolateral nucleus of the thalamus.

primary somatosensory cortex. Brodmann's areas 3, 1, and 2 in the postcentral gyrus, which receive input from the ventral posterior nucleus of the thalamus.

projection areas. Entry stations in the cortex for visual, auditory, and tactile-somatosensory input.

projection neurons. Neurons that transmit over long distances; differentiated from interneurons, which have only a local effect.

proprioceptive. Pertaining to sensory input from the muscles and joint receptors, which ordinarily does not reach the level of conscious representation.

prosopagnosia. Loss of the ability to recognize familiar people by their facial appearance.

protopathic. The more ancient of the two major ascending somatosensory pathways, registering temperature sensations and slow "burning" pain, among other feelings; differentiated from epicritic.

pseudopods. Amoeboid extensions into which the cytoplasm flows in cell movement, as in migration, in embryogenesis, and in dendritic and axonal extension.

psychomotor. Designating a type of epilepsy characterized by loss of memory for one's behavior, but not loss of consciousness. The epileptic focus is frequently in the temporal lobe.

psychosomatic medicine. Treatment of illnesses caused by environmental stress and other psychological conditions.

pulvinar. A large association nucleus at the rear of the thalamus interconnected with the posterior general association cortex.

punctate. Produced by a point, or affecting only a very local region.

Purkinje cells. The large cells characteristic of the cerebellar cortex, inhibitory in their effect upon the subcortical cerebellar nuclei.

putamen. One of two large nuclei forming the striatum of the basal ganglia. It fulfills motor functions.

pyramidal cells of Betz. Large neurons in the motor cortex projecting via the pyramidal tract.

pyramidal motor system. The voluntary motor system taken as a whole, including some extrapyramidal structures (such as the basal ganglia).

pyramidal tract. The fiber bundle passing directly from the cortex into the spinal motor centers; active in voluntary behavior.

pyriform. Pear-shaped; designating the cortex forming the basal surface of the temporal lobe in the region of the hippocampus.

raphé nuclei. A group of nuclei along the midline of the brainstem that produce serotonin.

rapid eye movement sleep (REMS). A stage of sleep that recurs for extended periods throughout the night, characterized by jerking eye movements, flickering of the eyelids, loss of muscle tonus, and dreams.

receptive field. The sensory field to which a portion of the receptor apparatus, or the sensory cortex, responds.

receptive speech area of Wernicke. The portion of the posterior temporal lobe and surrounding cortex where lesions result in impaired understanding of language.

recruiting response. A brainwave similar to sleep spindles, produced by 8–10 Hz stimulation of the thalamus.

red nucleus. An important motor nucleus in

the midbrain region, forming a relay station for extrapyramidal pathways to the spinal motor neurons.

reentrant circuits. Neural circuits forming continuous loops that are more extensive than local feedback loops.

refractory period. The period following propagation of an action potential when the neuron is momentarily incapable (or less capable) of propagating another.

Reissner's membrane. A thin membrane in the cochlea separating the perilymph immediately surrounding the organ of Corti from the rest of the perilymph in that portion of the cochlear canal.

renin. The enzyme released by the kidneys that transforms the blood plasma protein angiotensinogen into angiotensin.

Renshaw cells. Small inhibitory interneurons surrounding the motor neurons in the spinal motor centers.

replication. Duplication of the genetic code in the process of mitosis.

resting potential. The polarity normal for a plasma membrane when not under stimulation, or for an axon when not propagating a nerve impulse.

reticular formation. The structure in the brainstem core consisting of a network of neural cell bodies and their short axons, the basis of the reticular system function.

reticular nucleus. A thin sheet of neural tissue surrounding the thalamus, representing an upward extension of the brainstem reticular system.

reticular system. An ancient neural system that controls arousal, attention focus, and states of consciousness, as well as the various stages of sleep.

reticulum. Network.

retina. The photosensitive tissue lining the interior of the eyeball.

retinal. The aldehyde of retinol (Vitamin A). In association with an opsin, it forms the visual pigment.

retinol. Vitamin A.

retrograde amnesia. Loss of memory for a period immediately prior to some event, such as brain concussion.

retrograde transmission. Transmission of a nerve impulse in a direction opposite to normal, or of a substance through the axon in the direction of the cell body.

retrosplenial. Behind the splenium, or posterior end of the corpus callosum.

rhinencephalon. "Nose brain." The part of the limbic system receiving olfactory input.

rhodopsin (visual purple). The visual pigment responsible for night vision.

ribonucleic acid (RNA). The chemical that carries the genetic code transcribed from the nuclear DNA for translation into protein molecules.

ribosomes. Manufacturing stations within the cytoplasm where translation of the genetic code into proteins takes place.

rods. The retinal receptors responsible for night vision and detection of motion in peripheral vision.

rough endoplasmic reticulum (Nissle substance). The portion of the endoplasmic reticulum whose walls are lined with ribosomes.

round window. A second membrane-covered opening in the cochlea, permitting flow of the perilymph through the cochlear canal.

Ruffini ending. A sensory structure in the skin, once thought to be exclusively responsive to heat.

saccade. A sudden swift movement of the eyeball in fixing upon a target; differentiated from smooth pursuit movement in following of the target.

saltatory transmission. A rapid mode of transmission, characteristic of myelinated axons, in which the action potential leaps from one node of Ranvier to another.

scanning electron miscroscope. A modification of the electron miscroscope permitting vivid three-dimensional visualization of microscopic structures.

scotoma. Loss of vision in some portion of the visual field, often resulting from lesions in area 17 of the visual cortex.

second messenger. A substance, such as cAMP, that operates inside the neuron to control its responsivity to stimulation.

secular trend. A trend of change over time.

sella turcica. The bony receptacle in which the pituitary gland rests.

semicircular canals. The portion of the vestibular system consisting of three slender tubes in which the perilymph flows during head-turning.

sensitization. The tendency to an increased alerting response to a stimulus found to be biologically significant.

sensorimotor cortex. The sensory and motor cortices considered together.

sensory adaptation. The tendency of sensory receptors to diminish their response to repeated or continuous stimuli.

sensory association areas. Those cortical areas adjoining the sensory projection areas, into which the latter project.

sensory homunculus. The map of the regions of the somatosensory cortex associated with sensations in various regions of the body.

septal nuclei. The two major nuclei of the septal region (medial and lateral) constituting important elements of the ancient limbic system.

septohippocampal. Passing from the medial septal nucleus to the hippocampus; designating the functions they together serve.

septum. A region in the midline of the brain immediately above the anterior commissure.

sequential processing. A cortical activity uniquely associated with the auditory and motor regions in which the firing pattern produced is necessarily sequential, rather than simultaneous as in the visual cortex.

serotonin. 5-hydroxytryptamine, an important neurotransmitter in the brain.

servomechanism. A feedback circuit controlling the intensity of a given function.

set point. The level toward which the body tends to gravitate as normal, such as with reference to fat storage.

sham rage. Behavioral manifestation of rage without the physiological response that normally accompanies it.

simple cells. Neurons in the visual cortex selectively responsive to a particular linear orientation of the stimulus within their small receptive field.

simultaneous processing. A cortical activity uniquely associated with the visual regions, in which the firing pattern is characteristically simultaneous rather than sequential.

slow-wave sleep (SWS). A stage of sleep characterized by large, hypersynchronous, slow brain-wave oscillations (delta waves).

smooth endoplasmic reticulum. The portion of the endoplasmic reticulum that contains no ribosomes lining its membranes.

smooth pursuit system. The eye-movement control system employed in the visual tracking of a moving target.

sodium pump. An enzymatic mechanism through which sodium ions are continuously excreted by the cell against the electrical gradient.

soft sign. A symptom of neurological disorder that is mild and/or not obviously related to the overt problem.

soma. The cell body proper.

somatosensory association cortex. The cortical region immediately posterior to the somatosensory projection cortex, into which the latter projects.

somesthesis. Bodily sensation

spike potential. See **action potential.**

spinal cat. A cat with cerebral forebrain structures removed.

spinal ganglia. Sensory nuclei located within the vertebral column alongside the spinal cord. They contain the unipolar cell bodies of the somatosensory system.

spinal reflex. A simple reflex consisting essentially of only two neurons, one transmitting signals into the spinal motor centers from the periphery, the other transmitting signals to the muscles causing contraction (for example, many postural reflexes).

spinothalmic system. The more ancient of the two major ascending pathways for somesthetic input; differentiated from the lemniscal system.

spiny stellate cell. A type of neuron in the

sensory projection areas of the cortex, thought to receive incoming sensory signals for transmission to the local pyramidal cells.

spontaneous recovery.   Return of the arousal response after habituation, when the stimulus has not occurred for a sufficient time.

spontaneous remission.   Disappearance of psychotic symptoms in the absence of treatment.

stapedius muscle.   A tiny muscle in the middle ear that prevents damage to the cochlea from loud noises by restricting the amplitude of movement of the ossicles.

stapes.   One of the three interconnected ossicles transmitting sound vibration from the eardrum to the oval window.

stellate cells.   Star-shaped neurons prevalent in many regions of the brain.

stereoisomer.   An alternate structural form of a given organic molecule.

steroid hormones.   A type of endocrine hormone, including cortisol, produced particularly by the adrenal cortex.

stria terminalis.   A fiber pathway from the amygdala to the septal area and anterior hypothalamus.

striatum.   Corpus striatum; the caudate nucleus and putamen considered together.

subfornical organ.   An organ found in some mammals, such as the rodents, immediately below the fornix in the preoptic area.

subiculum.   A paleocortical region within the hippocampal formation to which the hippocampally processed information projects for output via the fornix to the mammillary bodies.

substantia innominata.   Olfactory tubercle; anterior perforated substance; the ancient olfactory cortex at the base of the brain, immediately anterior to the hypothalamus in the anterior commissure region.

substantia nigra.   A large dark-colored nucleus in the midbrain, the major source of the brain's dopamine.

sulcus.   A fissure between two convolutions of the surface of the cortex.

superior olivary nuclei.   Nuclei in the medulla

that receive third-order fibers of the ascending auditory pathway.

suprachiasmatic nucleus.   A small nucleus above the optic chiasma, anterior to the hypothalamus proper.

supramarginal gyrus.   A region of the brain immediately surrounding the posterior end of the fissure of Sylvius, where lesions to the left hemisphere tend to impair the ability to read.

Sylvian fissure.   Lateral fissure; the deep fissure separating the temporal lobe from overlying structures.

sympathetic branch.   One of the two branches of the autonomic nervous system, whose influence is to prepare the body for emergency energy expenditure.

synapse.   The structure mediating the effect of a nerve impulse upon its target cell.

synaptic cleft.   The narrow space between the pre- and postsynaptic membranes, into which neurotransmitter is released to activate receptors of the postsynaptic membrane.

syncytium.   A hypothetical interconnected network of fibers once conceived to be the basic structure of the brain; now disproved.

tachistoscope.   A mechanism for presenting very brief exposures to visual stimuli.

tectorial membrane.   A membrane, immediately overlying the auditory hair cells, whose movement is thought to activate them.

tectum.   Roof; the midbrain structure supporting the colliculi.

telodendria.   Terminal branches and tips of axons.

temporal lobe.   The ventrolateral portion of the mass of the hemispheres.

tensor tympani.   One of two small muscles of the middle ear restricting the ossicles' amplitude of movement.

teratology.   The study of the disastrous effects of some medications or conditions on the development of the fetus.

testosterone.   The male sex hormone secreted by the testes.

tetrahydropapaveroline. The chemical substance produced by the opium poppy, which is turned into morphine and other opiates.

thalamic reticular nucleus. A thin sheet of tissue surrounding the thalamus and constituting an upward extension of the brainstem reticular system.

thalamocortical system. The modern system of the brain consisting of the major thalamic nuclei, their neocortical regions of association, and the corpus callosum.

thalamus. A group of subcortical nuclei intimately associated with the neocortex.

theta wave. A characteristic regular 7–10 Hz brain wave recordable in the hippocampus during the waking state.

thirst receptors. Hypothalamic nuclei responsive to excessive salt concentrations in the blood.

thyrotropic hormone. A pituitary hormone activating the thyroid gland.

timbre. The quality of a sound based on its unique combination of component pitches.

tolerance. The tendency in the case of certain drugs to require increasing dosages to obtain the same effect.

tonic stage. Muscular rigidity preceding the jerking (clonic) stage in grand mal epileptic seizures.

tonotopic. Mapped onto the auditory projection cortex systematically in relation to pitch.

transcortical. Projecting from one local cortical region to another without thalamic relay.

transcription. The copying onto messenger RNA of the genetic code contained in the DNA.

transduction. The process through which the physical energy of the stimulus is translated into neural energy by the receptor cell.

transfer RNA (tRNA). Small segments of RNA responsible for bringing appropriate amino acids to the ribosomes to be linked to form the required protein molecule.

translation. The process through which the genetic code transcribed in the messenger RNA is copied into the manufactured protein molecule at the ribosome.

transmission electron micrograph. An electron microscopic picture produced by projecting electrons through a very thin slice of tissue.

transmission neurons (projection neurons). Neurons whose axons leave the vicinity of the soma to innervate distant regions of the brain; in the cortex, used principally to describe the pyramidal cells.

trigeminal nucleus. The nucleus of the trigeminal nerve (the fifth cranial nerve) in the brainstem; interconnected with the facial region.

tuberal region. The basal portion of the hypothalamus (tuber cinerium) immediately above the pituitary stalk.

tympanic membrane. The eardrum.

U fibers. Transcortical fibers dipping below a fissure.

uncus. A bulbous portion of the medial temporal lobe containing the amygdala.

unipolar depression. Endogenous depression, without the manic symptoms that characterize the manic-depressive disorder.

utricle. A hollow structure in the vestibular system containing receptors responsive to movement of tiny particles of calcium carbonate embedded in a gelatinous matrix (the otoliths or ear stones).

vena cava. A large vein emptying into the right atrium of the heart; the main venous trunk draining blood from the lower portion of the body.

ventral amygdalofugal pathway. A major fiber pathway leading from the basolateral group of amygdaloid nuclei to the hypothalamus.

ventral posterior thalamic nucleus. A large nucleus in the lateral thalamus immediately posterior to the ventrolateral nucleus. It forms a relay station for somatosensory input to the cortex.

ventricles. A system of interconnected hollow

fluid-filled cavities within the two hemispheres, between the two thalami (the third ventricle) and between the brainstem and cerebellum (the fourth ventricle).

ventromedial hypothalamic syndrome. The effects of ablating the ventromedial nucleus of the hypothalamus, including hyperphagia and obesity, finickiness, and apparent absence of true hunger drive.

ventromedial nucleus of the hypothalamus (VMH). A nucleus near the midline of the hypothalamus, medial to the hunger centers, into which it projects laterally running inhibitory fibers.

verbal kinaesthesia. The motoric component of subvocal speech in the process of thought.

vertex. The midpoint at the top of the brain.

vesicle. A membrane-bound sack.

vestibular system. The inner-ear mechanism, consisting of semicircular canals and utricle, responsible for the sense of balance and acceleration.

vestibulo-ocular reflex. The effect upon eyeball-turning caused by turning the head in the course of fixing the gaze upon a target. Head-turning is registered by the vestibular system.

visual agnosia. A neurological disorder characterized by inability to recognize familiar objects by sight.

Wallerian degeneration. The progressive degeneration of a severed nerve fiber.

Wernicke's receptive speech area. The posterior portion of the left-hemisphere language area situated in the posterior superior temporal gyrus and overlying regions.

withdrawal syndrome. The distressing effects of ceasing intake of a drug to which the body has become addicted.

zygote. The single cell formed by the fusion of egg and sperm at conception.

References

Adrian, E. D. Double representation of the feet in the sensory cortex of the cat. *Journal of Physiology,* 1940, *98,* 16.

Ahlskog, J., & Hoebel, B. Overeating and obesity from damage to a noradrenergic system in the brain. *Science,* 1973, *182,* 166–169.

Ahlskog, J., Randall, P., & Hoebel, B. Hypothalamic hyperphasia. Dissociation from hyperphagia following destruction of noradrenergic neurons. *Science,* 1975, *190,* 399–401.

Akimoto, H., Yamogushi, N., Okabe, K., Nakagawa, T., Nakamura, I., Abe, K., Torii, H., & Masahashi, K. On the sleep induced through stimulation of the dog thalamus. *Folia Psychiatrica et Neurologica Japonica,* 1956, *10,* 117–146.

Anand, B. K., & Brobeck, J. R. Hypothalamic control of food intake in rats and cats. *Yale Journal of Biological Medicine,* 1951, *24,* 123–140.

Andersson, B. The effect of injections of hypertonic NaCl solutions into different parts of the hypothalamus of goats. *Acta Physiologica Scandinavica,* 1953, *28,* 188–201.

Angrist, B., & Gershon, S. The phenomenology of experimentally induced amphetamine psychosis: Preliminary observations. *Biological Psychiatry,* 1970, *2,* 97–107.

Arnold, L., Wender, P., McCloskey, K., & Snyder, S. Levoamphetamine and dextroamphetamine: Comparative efficacy in the hyperkinetic syndrome: Assessment by target symptoms. *Archives of General Psychiatry,* 1972, *27,* 816–822.

Asanuma, H., & Rosén, I. Topographical organization of cortical efferent zones projecting to distal forelimb muscles in monkey. *Experimental Brain Research,* 1972, *14,* 243–256.

Asberg, M., Thoren, P., Traskman, L., Bertilsson, L., & Ringberger, V. "Serotonin depression" — a biochemical subgroup within the affective disorders. *Science,* 1976, *191,* 478–480.

Aserinsky, E., & Kleitman, N. Regularly occurring periods of eye motility, and concomitant phenomena during sleep. *Science,* 1953, *118,* 273–274.

Barbizet, J. Defect in memorizing of hippocampal-mammillary origin: a review. *Journal of Neurology, Neurosurgery and Psychiatry,* 1963, *26,* 127–135.

Beach, F. A., Keuhn, R. E., Sprague, R. H., & Anisko, J. J. Coital behavior in dogs. XI. Effects of androgenic stimulation during development on masculine mating response in females. *Hormones and Behavior,* 1973, *3,* 143.

Beatty, W. W., & Schwartzbaum, J. S. Commonality and specificity of behavioral dysfunctions following septal and hippocampal lesions in rats. *Journal of Comparative and Physiological Psychology,* 1968, *66,* 60–68.

Beatty, W. W., & Schwartzbaum, J. S. Enhanced reactivity to quinine and saccharin solutions following septal lesions in the rat. *Psychonomic Science,* 1968, *8,* 483–484.

Békésy, G. von. *Experiments in Hearing.* New York: McGraw-Hill, 1960.

Bender, R. M., Hostetter, G., & Thomas, G. J. Effects of lesions in hippocampus-entorhinal cortex on maze performance and activity in rats. *Psychonomic Science,* 1968, *10,* 13–14.

Benton, A., & van Allen, M. Impairment in facial recognition in patients with cerebral disease. *Cortex,* 1968, *4,* 344–358.

Bergeijk, W. A. van, Pierce, J. R., & David, E., Jr. *Waves and the Ear.* Garden City, N.Y.: Doubleday, 1960.

Berger, H. Über das Elektroenkephalogramm des Menschen. *Archiv für Psychiatrie und Nervenkrankheiten,* 1929, *87,* 527–580.

Berger, R. J. Tonus of extrinsic laryngeal muscles during sleep and dreaming. *Science,* 1961, *134,* 840.

Berger, T. W., Alger, B., & Thompson, R. Neuronal substrate of classical conditioning in the hippocampus. *Science,* 1976, *192,* 483–485.

Berry, S., & Thompson, R. Medial septal lesions retard classical conditioning of the nictitating membrane response in rabbits. *Science,* 1979, *205,* 209–211.

Bieger, D., & Hockman, C. H. On the physiology and pharmacology of cerebral dopamine neurons. In *Chemical Transmission in the Mammalian Central Nervous System,* edited by C. H. Hockman and D. Bieger. Baltimore: University Park Press, 1976.

Bitterman, M. The comparative analysis of learning. *Science,* 1975, *188,* 699–709.

Bizzi, E. The coordination of eye-head movements. In *Recent Progress in Perception: Readings from Scientific American,* edited by B. Held and W. Richards. San Francisco: W. H. Freeman, 1976, 115–121.

Blake, H., Gerard, R., & Kleitman, N. Factors influencing brain potentials during sleep. *Journal of Neurophysiology,* 1939, 48–60.

Blanchard, R. J., & Fial, R. A. Effects of limbic lesions on passive avoidance and reactivity to shock. *Journal of Comparative and Physiological Psychology,* 1968, *66,* 606–612.

Blau, T. H. Torque and schizophrenic vulnerability: As the world turns. *American Psychologist,* 1977, *32,* 997–1005.

Bleuler, E. *Dementia Praecox or the Group of Schizophrenias* (1911). Translated by J. Zinkin. New York: International Universities Press, 1950.

Bloch, V. Facts and hypotheses concerning memory consolidation. *Brain Research,* 1970, *24,* 561–575.

Bodamer, J. Die Prosopagnosie. *Archiv Psychiatrie Z. Psychologie,* 1947, *179,* 6–54.

Bower, T. G. R. *Human Development.* San Francisco: W. H. Freeman & Co., 1979.

Brady, J., & Nauta, W. Subcortical mechanisms in emotional behavior: affective changes following septal forebrain lesions in the albino rat. *Journal of Comparative and Physiological Psychology,* 1953, *46,* 339–346.

Bremer, F., & Terzuola, C. Contribution à l'étude des méchanismes physiologiques du maintien de l'activité vigile du cerveau. Interaction de la formation réticulée et de l'écorce cérébrale dans le processus du réveil. *Archives of International Physiology,* 1954, *62,* 157–178.

Broadbent, D. The role of auditory localization in attention and memory. *Journal of Experimental Psychology,* 1954, *47,* 191–196.

Brodmann, K. *Physiologie des Gehirns.* In *Die Allgemeine Chirurgie der Gehirnkrankheiten, Neue Deutsche Chirurgie.* Stuttgart: F. Enke, 1914.

Brooks, V. B., & Stoney, S. D., Jr. Motor mechanisms: The role of the pyramidal system in motor control. *Annual Review of Physiology,* 1971, *33,* 337–392.

Brown, P. K., & Wald, G. Visual pigments in single rods and cones of the human retina. *Science,* 1964, *144,* 145–151.

Butters, N., & Rosvold, H. E. Effect of septal lesions on resistance to extinction and delayed alternation in monkeys. *Journal of Comparative and Physiological Psychology,* 1968, *66,* 389–395.

Caggiula, A., & Hoebel, B. Copulation-reward site in the posterior hypothalamus. *Science,* 1966, *153,* 1284–1285.

Cairns, H., and Mosberg, W. H., Jr. Colloid

cyst of the third ventricle. *Surgery, Gynecology and Obstetrics,* 1951, *92,* 545–570.

Carey, S., and Diamond, R. From piecemeal to configurational representation of faces. *Science,* 1977, *195,* 312–313.

Carlsson, A., Corrodi, K., Fuxe, T., & Hökfelt, T. Effect of antidepressant drugs on the depletion of intraneuranal brain 5-hydroxytryptamine stores caused by 4-methyl 2-ethylmetatyramine. *European Journal of Pharmacology,* 1969, *5,* 357.

Carpenter, W., Strauss, J., & Bartko, J. Flexible system for the diagnosis of schizophrenia: Report from the WHO international pilot study of schizophrenia. *Science,* 1973, *182,* 1275–1278.

Chloden, L., Kurland, A., & Savage, C. Clinical reactions and tolerance to LSD in chronic schizophrenia. *Journal of Nervous and Mental Disease,* 1955, *122,* 211–221.

Chomsky, N. *Language and the Mind.* New York: Harcourt Brace Jovanovich, 1968, rev. ed. 1972.

Clark, W., Beattie, J., Riddoch, A., and Dott, N. *The Hypothalamus.* Edinburgh: Oliver and Boyd, 1938.

Clemens, L. G. Neurohormonal control of male sexual behavior. In *Reproductive Behavior,* edited by W. Montagna and W. Sadler. New York: Plenum Press, 1973, 23–53.

Clemente, C. D. Forebrain mechanisms related to internal inhibition and sleep. *Conditioned Reflex,* 1968, *3,* 145–174.

Clemente, C. D., Sterman, M. B., & Wyrwicka, W. Forebrain inhibitory mechanism: conditioning of basal forebrain induced EEG synchronization and sleep. *Experimental Neurology,* 1963, *7,* 404–417.

Clemente, C. D., Sterman, M. B., & Wyrwicka, W. Post-reinforcement EEG synchronization during alimentary behavior. *Electroencephalography and Clinical Neurophysiology,* 1964, *16,* 355–365.

Cohn, M. L., Cohn, M., & Taylor, F. H. Guanosine 3',5' = monophosphate: A central nervous system regulator of analgesia. *Science,* 1978, *199,* 319–322.

Colemen, P., & Riesen, A. Environmental effects on cortical dendritic fields: I. Rearing in the dark. *Journal of Anatomy,* 1968, *102,* 363–374.

Colonnier, M. Synaptic patterns on different cell types in the different laminae of the cat visual cortex. An electron microscope study. *Brain Research,* 1968, *9,* 268–287.

Coopersmith, S. Adaptive reactions of alcoholics and non-alcoholics. *Quarterly Journal of Studies of Alcoholism,* 1964, *25,* 262–278.

Corkin, S. Tactually-guided maze learning in man: Effects of unilateral cortical excisions and bilateral hippocampal lesions. *Neurophysiologia,* 1965, *3,* 339–351.

Cowan, W., Raisman, G., & Powell, T. The connexions of the amygdala. *Journal of Neurology, Neurosurgery and Psychiatry,* 1965, *28,* 137–151.

Critchley, M. *The Parietal Lobes.* London: Edward Arnold, 1953.

Curry, F. A. A comparison of left-handed and right-handed subjects on verbal and nonverbal dichotic listening task. *Cortex,* 1967, *3,* 343–352.

Darwin, C. Ear differences and hemispheric specialization. In *The neurosciences—third study program,* edited by F. Schmitt and F. Worden. Cambridge, Mass.: MIT Press, 1974, 57–63.

Davis, H. Enhancement of evoked potentials in humans related to a task requiring decision. *Science,* 1964, *145,* 182–183.

Davis, H. A model for transducer action in the cochlea. *Cold Spring Harbor Symposium on Quantitative Biology,* 1965, *30,* 181–190.

Davis, H., Davis, P., Loomis, A., Harvey, N., & Hobart, G. Electrical reactions of human brain to auditory stimulation during sleep. *Journal of Neurophysiology,* 1939, *2,* 500–514.

Davis, V. E., Walsh, M. J., & Yamanaka, Y. Augmentation of alkaloid formation from dopamine by alcohol and acetaldehyde in vitro. *Journal of Pharmacology: Experimental Therapy,* 1970, *174,* 401–412.

Debold, J. F., & Whalen, R. E. Differential sensitivity of mounting and lordosis control systems to early androgen treatment in male and female hamsters. *Hormones and Behavior,* 1975, *6,* 197–209.

Dement, W., & Wolpert, E. A. The relation of eye movements, bodily motility, and external stimuli to dream content. *Journal of Experimental Psychology,* 1958, *55,* 543–553.

Dempsey, E. W., & Morison, R. S. The production of rhythmically recurrent cortical potentials after localized thalamic stimulation. *American Journal of Physiology,* 1942, *135,* 293–300.

Dempsey, E. W., & Morison, R. S. The electrical activity of a thalamocortical relay system. *American Journal of Physiology,* 1943, *138,* 283–396.

Denny-Brown, D., & Chambers, R. The parietal lobe and behavior. *Research Publications of the Association for Research in Nervous and Mental Diseases,* 1958, *36,* 35–117.

De Renzi, E., & Spinnler, H. Facial recognition in brain-damaged patients. *Neurology,* 1966, *16,* 145–152.

Desmedt, J. E. Neurophysiological mechanisms controlling acoustic input. In *Neural Mechanisms of the Auditory and Vestibular Systems,* edited by G. L. Rasmussen and W. F. Windle. Springfield, Ill.: Charles C Thomas, 1960, 152–164.

DeValois, R., & Pease, P. Contours and contrast: response of monkey lateral geniculate nucleus cells to luminance and color figures. *Science,* 1971, *171,* 694–696.

DeValois, R. L., & Jacobs, G. Primate color vision. *Science,* 1968, *162,* 533–540.

Doehring, D., & Bartholomeus, B. Laterality effects in voice recognition. *Neuropsychologia,* 1971, *9,* 425–430.

Donovick, P. J. Effects of localized septal lesions on hippocampal EEG activity, and avoidance and spatial behavior. Unpublished doctoral dissertation, University of Wisconsin, 1966.

Donovick, P. J. Effects of localized septal lesions on hippocampal EEG activity in behavior in rats. *Journal of Comparative and Physiological Psychology,* 1968, *66,* 569–578.

Douglas, R. J., & Isaacson, R. L. Hippocampal

lesions and activity. *Psychonomic Science,* 1964, *1,* 187–188.

Douglas, R. J., & Pribram, K. H. Learning and limbic lesions, *Neuropsychologia,* 1966, *4,* 197–220.

Douglas, R. J., & Pribram, K. H. Distraction and habituation in monkeys with limbic lesions. *Journal of Comparative and Physiological Psychology,* 1969, *69,* 473–480.

Douglas, R. J., & Raphelson, A. C. Spontaneous alternation and septal lesion. *Journal of Comparative and Physiological Psychology,* 1966, *62,* 320–322.

Dowling, J. & Werblin, F. Organization of the retina of the mud puppy *Necturus maculosus.* I. Synaptic structure. *Journal of Neurophysiology,* 1969, *32,* 315–354.

Duncan, C. P. The retroactive effect of electroshock on learning. *Journal of Comparative and Physiological Psychology,* 1949, *42,* 32–44.

Eccles, J. C. *The Understanding of the Brain.* New York: McGraw-Hill, 1973.

Economo, C. von. Schlaftheorie. *Ergebnis der Physiologie,* 1929, *28,* 312–339.

Ellen, P., Wilson, A. S., & Powell, E. W. Septal inhibition and turning behavior in the rat. *Experimental Neurology,* 1964, *10,* 120–132.

Ellenwood, E. J. Amphetamine psychosis: I. Description of individuals and process. *Journal of Nervous and Mental Disease,* 1967, *144,* 273–283.

Ernst, A. Relation between the action of dopamine and apomorphine and their O-methylated derivatives upon the CNS. *Psychopharmacologia,* 1965, *7,* 391–399.

Evarts, E. Brain mechanisms in movement. In *Progress in Psychobiology: Readings from Scientific American,* edited by R. Thompson. San Francisco: W. H. Freeman, 1976, 216–223.

Fischer, A., & Coury, J., Cholinergic tracing of a central neural circuit underlying the thirst drive. *Science,* 1962, *138,* 691–693.

Fischman, M., & McCleary, R. A. A patterned

perseverative deficit following fornicotomy in the cat. Cited by R. A. McCleary, *Progress in Physiological Psychology*, Vol. I., New York: Academic Press, 1966.

Fish, B., Campbell, M., Shapiro, T., *et al.* Schizophrenic children treated with methysergide (Sansert). *Diseases of the Nervous System*, 1969, *30*, 534–540.

Fishbein, W., McGaugh, J. L., & Swarz, J. R. Retrograde amnesia: electroconvulsive shock effects after termination of rapid eye movement sleep deprivation. *Science*, 1971, *172*, 80–82.

Fisher, S., & Jacobson, M. Ultrastructural changes during early development of retinal ganglion cells in *Zenopus*. *Zeitschrift für Zellforschung und Microskopische Anatomie*, 1970, *104*, 165–177.

Fitzsimmons, J. T. The physiology of thirst: a review of the extraneural aspects of the mechanisms of drinking. In *Progress in Physiological Psychology*, edited by E. Stellar and J. M. Sprague. New York: Academic Press, 1971, 119–201.

Flor-Henry, P. Psychosis and temporal lobe epilepsy: A controlled investigation. *Epilepsia* (Amsterdam), 1969, *10*, 363–366.

Flor-Henry, P. Psychiatric syndromes considered as manifestation of lateralized temporal-limbic dysfunction. In *Surgical Approaches in Psychiatry*, edited by L. V. Laitinen and K. C. Livingston. Baltimore: University Park Press, 1973, 22–26.

Flynn, J. The neural basis of aggression in cats. In *Neurophysiology and Emotion*, edited by D. Glass. New York: Rockefeller University Press, 1967, pp. 40–60.

Flynn, J., Vanegas, H., Foote, W., & Edwards, S. Neural mechanisms involved in a cat's attack on a rat. In *The Neural Control of Behavior*, edited by R. Whalen, M. Thompson, M. Verzeano, and N. Weinberger. New York: Academic Press, 1970.

Fonberg, E. The normalizing effect of lateral amygdalar lesions upon the dorsomedial amygdalar syndrome in dogs. *Acta Neurobiologiae Experimentalis*, 1976, *33*, 449–466.

Fonberg, E. The relation between alimentary and emotional amygdalar regulation. In *Hunger: Basic Mechanisms and Clinical Implications*, edited by D. Novin, W. Wyrwicka, and G. Bray. New York: Raven Press, 1976.

French, J. D., Hernández-Peón, R., & Livingston, R. B. Projections to cephalic brain stem (reticular formation) in monkey. *Journal of Neurophysiology*, 1955, *18*, 44–55, 74–95.

French, J. D., Van Amerongen, F. K., & Magoun, H. W. An activating system in the brain stem of the monkey. *Archives of Neurological Psychiatry*, 1952, *68*, 577–590.

Frisch, D. Ultrastructure of mouse olfactory mucosa. *American Journal of Anatomy*, 1967, *121*, 87–119.

Galambos, R. Suppression of auditory nerve activity by stimulation of afferent fibers to cochlea. *Journal of Neurophysiology*, 1956, *19*, 424–437.

Galambos, R. Studies of the auditory system with implanted electrodes. In *Neural Mechanisms of the Auditory and Vestibular Systems*, edited by G. Rasmussen and W. Windle. Springfield, Ill.: Charles C Thomas, 1960, 137–151.

Galambos, R., & Davis, H. The response of single auditory-nerve fibers to acoustic stimulation. *Journal of Neurophysiology*, 1943, *6*, 39–58.

Gallagher, M., Kapp, B., Musty, R. E., & Driscoll, P. A. Memory formation: Evidence for a specific neurochemical system in the amygdala. *Science*, 1977, *198*, 423–425.

Gardner, M. F., Schulman, C., & Walton, D. O. Facultative EEG asymmetries in infants and adults. In *Cerebral Dominance*. B.I.S. Conference Report no. 34, 1973, 37–40.

Gazzaniga, M. S., Steen, D., & Volpe, B. T. *Functional Neuroscience*. New York: Harper & Row, 1970.

George, R., Haslett, W., & Jenden, D. A cholinergic mechanism in the brain stem reticular formation: induction in paradoxical sleep. *International Journal of Neuropharmacology*, 1964, *3*, 541–552.

Gerard, R. W., Physiology and psychiatry. *American Journal of Psychiatry,* 1949, *106,* 161–173.

Geschwind, N. Language and the brain. In *Recent Progress in Perception: Readings from Scientific American,* edited by R. Held and W. Richards. San Francisco: W. H. Freeman & Co., 1976, 238–245.

Geschwind, N., & Levitsky, W. Human brain: Left-right asymmetries in temporal speech region. *Science,* 1968, *161,* 186–187.

Gibson, J. J. *The Senses Considered as Perceptual Systems.* Boston: Houghton Mifflin, 1966.

Glickman, S. E., & Feldman, S. M. Habituation of the arousal response to direct stimulation of the brain stem. *Electroencephalography and Clinical Neurophysiology,* 1961, *13,* 703–709.

Glickstein, M., & Gibson, A. R. Visual cells in the pons of the brain. *Scientific American, 235,* No. 5, 90–98, 1976.

Glickstein, M., & Whitteridge, D. Degeneration of layer III pyramidal cells in area 18 following destruction of callosal input. *Brain Research,* 1976, *104,* 148–151.

Globus, A., & Scheibel, A. Loss of dendrite spines as an index of presynaptic terminal patterns. *Nature,* 1966, *212,* 463–465.

Goddard, G. Functions of the amygdala. *Psychological Bulletin,* 1964, *62,* 89–109.

Gold, D., Macri, J., & McGaugh, J. Retrograde amnesia gradients: effects of direct cortical stimulation. *Science,* 1973, *179,* 1343–1345.

Gold, P. E., Bueno, O. F., & McGaugh, J. L. Training and task-related differences in retrograde amnesia thresholds determined by direct electrical stimulation of the cortex in rats. *Physiology and Behavior,* 1973, *11,* 57–63.

Gold, P. E., & McGaugh, J. L. A single-trace, two-process view of memory storage processes. In *Short Term Memory,* edited by D. Deutsch and J. A. Deutsch. New York: Academic Press, 1975, 355–378.

Goldstein, M. H., Jr., Hall, J. L., & Butterfield, B. L. Single-unit activity in the primary auditory cortex of unanesthetized cats. *Journal of the Acoustic Society of America,* 1968, *43,* 444–455.

Gordon, B. The superior colliculus of the brain. In *Recent Progress in Perception: Readings from the Scientific American,* edited by B. Held and W. Richards. San Francisco: W. H. Freeman, 1976, 85–95.

Gordon, H. Hemispheric asymmetry and musical performance. *Science,* 1975, *189,* 68–69.

Gouras, P. Color opponency from fovea to striate cortex. *Investigative Opthalmology,* 1972, *11,* 427–432.

Grady, K. L., Phoenix, C. H., & Young, W. C. Role of developing rat testes in differentiation of the neural tissue mediating mating behavior. *Journal of Comparative and Physiological Psychology,* 1965, *59,* 176–182.

Green, R. H., Beatty, W. W., & Schwartzbaum, J. S. Comparative effects of septohippocampal and caudate lesions on avoidance behavior in rats. *Journal of Comparative and Physiological Psychology,* 1967, *64,* 444–452.

Greenberg, R., & Pearlman, C. Cutting the REM nerve: an approach to the adaptive role of REM sleep. *Perspectives in Biology and Medicine,* 1974, *17,* 513–521.

Griffith, H., Cavanaugh, J., Held, N., & Oates, J. Dextroamphetamine: evaluation of psychomimetic properties in man. *Archives of General Psychiatry,* 1972, *26,* 97–100.

Gross, C., Bender, D., & Rocha-Miranda, C. Visual receptive fields of neurons in inferotemporal cortex of the monkey. *Science,* 1969, *166,* 1303–1306.

Gross, C., Rocha-Miranda, C., & Bender, D. Visual properties of neurons in inferotemportal cortex of the macaque. *Journal of Neurophysiology,* 1972, *35,* 96–111.

Gross, C. G., Bender, D. B., & Rocha-Miranda, C. E., Inferotemporal cortex: A single-unit analysis. In *Central Processing of Sensory Input.* The Neurosciences Research Program, Cambridge, Mass.: M.I.T. Press, 1975, 229–238.

Gross, C. G., Chorover, S. L., & Cohen, S. M. Caudate, cortical, hippocampal and dorsal thalamic lesions in rats: alternation and Hebb-Williams maze performance. *Neuropsychologia,* 1965, *3,* 53–68.

Grossman, S. Effect of adrenergic and cholinergic blocking agents on hypothalamic mechanisms. *American Journal of Physiology,* 1962, *202,* 1230–1236.

Grossman, S. P. Eating or drinking elicited by direct adrenergic or cholinergic stimulation of hypothalamus. *Science,* 1960, *132,* 301–302.

Grossman, S. P., Dacey, D., Halaris, A., Collier, T., & Routtenberg, A. Aphagia and adipsia after preferential destruction of nerve cell bodies in hypothalamus. *Science,* 1978, *202,* 537–539.

Groves, P., Glanzman, D., Patterson, M., & Thompson, R. Excitability of cutaneous afferent terminals during habituation and sensitization in acute spinal cat. *Brain Research,* 1970, *18,* 388–392.

Hartelius, H. Study of male juvenile delinquency. *Acta Psychiatrica Scandinavica,* 1965. *40,* 7–17.

Hartmann, E. L. *The Function of Sleep.* New Haven, Conn.: Yale University Press, 1974.

Head, H. *Studies in Neurology.* London: Oxford University Press, 1920.

Hebb, D. O. *The Organization of Behavior.* New York: Wiley, 1949.

Hécaen, H. Clinical symptomatology in right and left hemispheric lesions. In V. Mountcastle, Interhemispheric Relations and Cerebral Dominance. Baltimore: *Journal of Comparative and Physiological Psychology,* 1963, *56,* 872–876.

Held, R., and Hein, A. Movement produced stimulation in the development of visually guided behavior. *Journal of Comparative and Physiological Psychology,* 1963, *56,* 872–876.

Helmholtz, H. von. *Handbuch der Physiologischen Optik,* 3rd ed. Leipzig: Voss, 1911. Published in English as *Treatise on Physiological Optics,* translated by J. P. C. Southall. 3 vols. Rochester, N.Y.: Optical Society of America, 1924, 1925.

Herberg, L. Hunger reduction produced by injecting glucose into the lateral ventrical of the rat. *Nature,* 1960, *187,* 245–246.

Herrick, C. *The Brain of the Tiger Salamander, Ambystoma tigrinum.* Chicago: University of Chicago Press, 1948.

Herrick, C. *Brains in Rats and Men.* Chicago: University of Chicago Press, 1929; New York: Harper and Row, 1963.

Hess, R., Jr., Koella, W. P., & Akert, K. Cortical and subcortical recordings in natural and artificially induced sleep in cats. *Electroencephalography and Clinical Neurophysiology,* 1953, *5,* 75–90.

Hess, W. R. Das Schlafsyndrom als Folge diencephaler Reizung. *Helvetica Physiologica et Pharmacalogica Acta,* 1944, *2,* 305–344.

Hess, W. R. *Das Zwischenhirn.* Basel: Schwabe, 1949.

Hetherington, A. N., & Ranson, S. W. The spontaneous activity and food intake of rats with hypothalamic lesions. *American Journal of Physiology,* 1942, *136,* 609–617.

Himwich, H., Narasimhachair, N., Heller, B., *et al.* Comparative behavioral and urinary studies on schizophrenics and normal controls. In a *Biochemistry of Brain and Behavior,* edited by R. Bowman and S. Datta. New York: Plenum Press, 1970, 207–221.

Hobson, J., McCarley, R., & Wyzinski, P. Sleep cycle oscillation: reciprocal discharge by two brainstem neuronal groups. *Science,* 1975, *189,* 55–58.

Hockman, C. H., & Bieger, D., (Eds.). *Chemical Transmission in the Mammalism Central Nervous System.* Baltimore: University Park Press, 1976.

Hodgkin, A. L., & Huxley, A. F. A quantitative description of membrane current and its application to conduction with excitation in nerve. *Journal of Physiology,* 1952, *117,* 500–544.

Hoebel, B., & Teitlebaum, P. Hypothalamic control of feeding and self-stimulation. *Science,* 1962, *135,* 375–376.

Hollister, L. Drug-induced psychoses and schizophrenic reactions — a critical comparison. *Annals of the New York Academy of Sciences,* 1962, *96,* 80–88.

Horn, A., & Snyder, S. Chlorpromazine and

dopamine: conformational similarities that correlate with the anti-schizophrenic activity of phenothiazine drugs. *Proceedings of the National Academy of Sciences,* 1971, *68,* 2325–2328.

Horovitz, A., Piala, J., High, J., Burke, J., & Leaf, R. Effects of drugs on the mouse-killing (muricide) test and its relationships to the amygdaloid formation. *International Journal of Neuropharmacology,* 1966, *5,* 405–411.

Hubel, D., & Wiesel, T. Receptive fields and functional architecture in two nonstriate visual areas (18 and 19) of the cat. *Journal of Neurophysiology,* 1965, *28,* 290–299.

Hubel, D., & Wiesel, T. Receptive fields and functional architecture of monkey striate cortex. *Journal of Physiology,* 1968, *195,* 215–243.

Hubel, D. H., & Wiesel, T. N. Receptive fields of single neurons in the cat's striate cortex. *Journal of Physiology,* 1959, *148,* 574–591.

Hubel, D. H., & Wiesel, T. N. Receptive fields, binocular interaction and functional architecture in the cat's visual center. *Journal of Physiology,* 1962, *160,* 106–154.

Hubel, D. H., & Wiesel, T. N. Shape and arrangement of columns in cat's striate cortex. *Journal of Physiology,* 1963, *165,* 559–568.

Hubel, D. H., & Wiesel, T. N. Laminar and columnar distributon of geniculocortical fibers in the macaque monkey. *Journal of Comparative Neurology,* 1972, *146,* 421–450.

Humphrey, D. R., & Rietz, R. R. Cells of origin of corticorubial projections from the arm area of primate motor cortex and their synaptic actions in the red nucleus. *Brain Research,* 1976, *110,* 162–169.

Hutton, R., Wenzel, B., Baker, T., and Homuth, M. Two-way avoidance learning in pigeons after olfactory nerve section. *Physiology and Behavior,* 1974, *13,* 57–62.

Iggo, A., & Muir, A. R. The structures and function of a slowly adapting touch corpuscle in hairy skin. *Journal of Physiology,* 1969, *200,* 763–796.

Isaacson, R. *The Limbic System.* New York: Plenum Press, 1974.

Isaacson, R. L. Experimental brain lesions and memory. In *Neural Mechanisms of Learning and Memory,* edited by M. R. Rosensweig and E. L. Bennett. Cambridge, Mass.: MIT Press, 1976, 521–543.

Iversen, L. L. Dopamine receptors in the brain. *Science,* 1975, *188,* 1084–1089.

Jacobson, M. *Developmental Neurobiology.* New York: Plenum Press, 1970.

Jasper, H., & Tessier, J. Acetylcholine liberation from cerebral cortex during paradoxical (REM) sleep. *Science,* 1971, *172,* 601–602.

Jerison, H. J. *Evolution of the Brain and Intelligence.* New York: Academic Press, 1973.

John, E. *Mechanisms of Memory.* New York: Academic Press, 1967.

John, E. Switchboard versus statistical theories of learning and memory. *Science,* 1972, *177,* 850–864.

John, E., Chesler, P., Bartlett, F., & Victor, I. Observation learning in cats. *Science,* 1968, *159,* 1489–1491.

John, E., Karmel, B., Corning, W., et al. Neurometrics: Numerical taxonomy identifies different profiles of brain functions within groups of behaviorally similar people. *Science,* 1977, *196,* 1393–1410.

Jones, E. G., Burton, H., & Porter, R. Commissural and cortico-cortical "columns" in the somatic sensory cortex of primates. *Science,* 1975, *190,* 572–574.

Jones, E. G., Coulter, J. D., Burton, H., & Porter, R. Cells of origin and terminal distribution of cortico-striatal fibers arising in the sensory motor cortex of monkeys. *Journal of Comparative Neurology,* 1977, *173,* 53–80.

Jones, E. G., & Powell, T. An anatomical study of converging sensory pathways within the cerebral cortex of the monkey. *Brain,* 1970, *93,* 793.

Jones, E. G., & Wise, S. P. Size, laminar and columnar distribution of efferent cells in the sensory-motor cortex of primates. *Journal of Comparative Neurology,* 1977, *175,* 391–438.

Jones, F., Maas, J., Dekirmenjian, H., & Fawcett, J. Urinary catecholamine metabolites during behavioral changes in a patient with manic-depressive cycles. *Science,* 1973, *179,* 300–302.

Jones, W. H. S. *Hippocrates,* Vol. 2. New York: Putnam, 129.

Jouvet, M. Recherches sur les structures nerveuses et les mécanismes responsables des différentes phases du sommeil physiologique. *Archives italiennes de Biologie,* 1962, *100,* 125–206.

Jouvet, M. Neurophysiology of the states of sleep. *Physiological Review,* 1967, *47,* 117–177.

Jouvet, M. Biogenic amines and the states of sleep. *Science,* 1969, *163,* 32–41.

Jouvet, M., & Michel, F. Correlations électromyographiques du sommeil chez le chat décortiqué et mésencéphalique chronique. *Compte Rendu Societé de Biologie,* 1959, *153,* 422–425.

Kaada, B., Rasmussen, E., & Kveim, O. Impaired acquisition of passive avoidance behavior by subcallosal, septal, hypothalamic and insular lesions in rats. *Journal of Comparative and Physiological Psychology,* 1962, *55,* 661–670.

Kaas, J. H., Nelson, R. J., Sur, M., Lin, C., & Merzenich, M. Multiple representations of body within the primary somatosensory cortex of primates. *Science,* 1979, *204,* 521–523.

Kandel, E. R. Small systems of neurons. *Scientific American,* 241, No. 3, 66–85, 1979.

Kanner, L. *Child Psychiatry.* Springfield, Ill.: Charles C Thomas, 1942.

Kanner, L. Problems of nosology and psychodynamics of early infantile autism. *American Journal of Orthopsychiatry,* 1949, *19,* 416–426.

Katsuki, Y. Neural mechanisms of auditory sensation in cats. In *Sensory Communication,* edited by W. A. Rosenblith. New York: Wiley, 1961.

Kesner, R. P., & Wilburn, M. W. A review of electrical stimulation of the brain in the context of learning and retention. *Behavioral Biology,* 1974, *10,* 259–293.

Kievit, J., & Kuypers, H. Basal forebrain and hypothalamic connections to frontal and parietal cortex in the rhesus monkey. *Science,* 1975, *187,* 660–662.

Kimble, D. P. The effects of bilateral hippocampal lesions in rats. *Journal of Comparative and Physiological Psychology,* 1963, *56,* 273–283.

Kimble, D. P. Hippocampus and internal inhibition. *Psychological Bulletin,* 1968, *70,* 285–295.

Kimble, D. P., Kirkby, R. J., & Stein, D. G. A response perseveration interpretation of passive avoidance deficits in hippocampectomized rats. *Journal of Comparative and Physiological Psychology,* 1966, *61,* 142–143.

Kimura, D. Effects of selective hippocampal damage on avoidance behavior in the rat. *Canadian Journal of Psychology,* 1958, *12,* 213–218.

Kimura, D. Some effects of temporal lobe damage on auditory perception. *Canadian Journal of Psychology,* 1961, *15,* 154–165.

Kimura, D. Left-right differences in the perception of melodies. *Quarterly Journal of Experimental Psychology,* 1964, *16,* 355–358.

Kimura, D. Cerebral dominance and the perception of verbal stimuli. *Canadian Journal of Psychology,* 1969, *15,* 166–171.

Kimura, D., & Folb, S. Neural processing of backwards speech sounds. *Science,* 1968, *161,* 395–396.

Klein, D., & Davis, J. *Diagnosis and Drug Treatment of Psychiatric Disorders.* Baltimore: Williams & Wilkins, 1969.

Kleitman, N. *Sleep and Wakefulness.* Chicago, Ill.: University of Chicago Press, 1963.

Knox, C., & Kimura, D. Cerebral processing of nonverbal sounds in boys and girls. *Neuropsychologia,* 1968, *6,* 1–11.

Kolata, G. B. Sex hormones and brain development: what goes on early in development when sex hormones act on the brain. *Science,* 1979, *205,* 985–987.

Kolvin, I., Humphrey, M., & McNay, A. Cognitive factors in childhood psychoses. *British Journal of Psychiatry*, 1971, *118*, 415–419.

Kolvin, I., Ounsted, C., & Roth, M. Cerebral dysfunction and childhood psychoses. *British Journal of Psychiatry*, 1971, *118*, 407–414.

Kornhuber, H. H. Cerebral cortex, cerebellum, and basal ganglia: An introduction to their motor functions. In *Central Processing of Sensory Input Leading to Motor Output*, edited by E. V. Evarts. Cambridge, Mass.: MIT Press, 1975, 267–280.

Kuffler, S. W. Discharge patterns and functional organization of mammalian retina. *Journal of Neurophysiology*, 1953, *16*, 37–68.

Kuhn, T. *The Structure of Scientific Revolutions*, 2nd ed. Chicago: University of Chicago Press, 1970.

Levy, J., Trevarthen, C., & Sperry, R. Perception of bilateral chimeric figures following hemispheric deconnexion. *Brain*, 1972, *95*, 61–78.

Lewis, A. Amnesic syndromes: the psychopathological aspect. *Proceedings of the Royal Society of Medicine*, 1961, *54*, 955.

Lewis, R., & Brindley, G. S. The extrapyramidal cortical motor map. *Brain*, 1968, *88*, 397–406.

Liggett, J. R. An experimental study of the olfactory sensitivity of the white rat. *Genetic Psychology Monograph*, 1928, *3*, 1.

Lindsley, R. B., Bowden, J., & Magoun, H. W. Effect upon EEG of acute injury to the brainstem activating system. *Electroencephalography and Clinical Neurobiology*, 1949, *1*, 475–586.

Llamás, A., Avendaño, C., & Reinoso-Suárez, F. Amygdaloid projections to prefrontal and motor cortex. *Science*, 1977, *195*, 794–796.

Llinás, R. The cortex of the cerebellum. In *Recent Progress in Perception: Readings from Scientific American*, edited by B. Held and W. Richards. San Francisco: W. H. Freeman, 1976, 122–133.

Loomis, A. L., Harvey, E. N., & Hobart, G. Electrical potentials of the human brain. *Journal of Experimental Psychology*, 1936, *19*, 249–279.

Lund, J. S., Lund, R. D., Hendrickson, A. E., Bunt, A. H., & Fuchs, A. F. The origin of efferent pathways from the primary visual cortex, area 17, of the macaque monkey as shown by retrograde transport of horseradish peroxidase. *Journal of Comparative Neurology*, 1975, *164*, 287–304.

Luria, A. *Higher Cortical Functions in Man*. New York: Basic Books, 1966.

Luria, A. *Human Brain and Psychological Processes*. New York: Harper & Row, 1969.

Luria, A. The functional organization of the brain. In *Recent Progress in Perception: Readings from Scientific American*, edited by R. Held and W. Richards. San Francisco: W. H. Freeman, 1976, 230–237.

Luria, A. R. Symposium on brain research and human behavior. *International Journal of Psychology*, 1968, 317–319.

MacLean, P. D., & Ploog, D. W., Cerebral representation of penile erection. *Journal of Neurophysiology*, 1962, *25*, 30–55.

Marc, R. C., & Sperling, H. G. Chromatic organization of primate cones. *Science*, 1977, *196*, 454–456.

Marczynski, T. Serotonin and the central nervous system. In *Chemical Transmission in the Mammalian Central Nervous System*, edited by C. Hockman and D. Bieger. Baltimore: University Park Press, 1976, 349–429.

Margules, D. L. Obesity and the hibernation response. *Psychology Today*, October 1979, p. 136.

Margules, D. L., & Olds, J. Identical 'feeding' and 'rewarding' systems in the lateral hypothalamus in rats. *Science*, 1962, *135*, 374–375.

Mark, V., & Ervin, F. *Violence and the Brain*. New York: Harper & Row, 1970.

Marks, H., Remley, N., Seago, J., & Hastings, D. Effects of bilateral lesions of the olfactory bulbs of rats on measures of learning and motivation. *Physiology and Behavior,* 1971, *7,* 1–6.

Marks, W. B., Dobelle, W. H., & MacNichol, E. F. Visual pigments of single primate cones. *Science,* 1964, *143,* 1181–1183.

Masserman, J. H. Is the hypothalamus a center of emotion? *Psychosomatic Medicine,* 1941, *5,* 3–25.

Matthysse, S. Dopamine and the pharmacology of schizophrenia: the state of the evidence. *Journal of Psychiatric Research,* 1974, *11,* 107.

Mayer, D. J., Wolfe, T. M., Akil, H., Carder, B., and Liebeskind, J. C. Analgesia from electrical stimulation of the brainstem of the rat. *Science,* 1971, *174,* 1351–1354.

McCleary, R. A. Response specificity in the behavioral effects of limbic system lesions in the cat. *Journal of Comparative and Physiological Psychology,* 1961, *54,* 605–613.

McCleary, R. A. Response modulating functions of the limbic system: initiation and suppression. In *Progress in Physiological Psychology,* edited by E. Stellar and J. M. Sprague. Vol. I. New York: Academic Press, 1966.

McEwen, B. Interactions between hormones and nerve tissue. *Scientific American, 235,* No. 1, 48–67, 1976.

McGaugh, J. L., & Gold, P. E. Modulation of memory by electrical stimulation of the brain. In *Neural Mechanisms of Learning and Memory,* edited by M. R. Rosenzweig and E. L. Bennett. Cambridge, Mass.: MIT Press, 1976, 549–560.

McGaugh, J. L., & Herz, M. J. *Memory Consolidation.* San Francisco: Albion, 1972.

McGinty, D. J., & Sterman, M. B. Sleep suppression after basal forebrain lesions in the cat. *Science,* 1968, *160,* 1253–1255.

McNew, J., & Thompson, R. Role of the limbic system in active and passive avoidance conditioning in the rat. *Journal of Comparative and Physiological Psychology,* 1966, *61,* 173–180.

Miles, F., & Fuller, J. Visual tracking and the primate flocculus. *Science,* 1975, *189,* 1000–1002.

Miller, G., Galanter, E., & Pribram, K. *Plans and the Structure of Behavior.* New York: Holt, Rinehart & Winston, 1960.

Miller, N. E. Learning of visceral and glandular responses. *Science,* 1969, *163,* 434–445.

Milner, B. Amnesia following operation on the temporal lobes. In *Amnesia,* edited by C. W. M. Whitty and O. L. Zangwill. London: Butterworths, 1966. 112–115.

Milner, B. Disorders of learning and memory after temporal lobe lesions in man. *Clinical Neurosurgery,* 1972, *19,* 421–446.

Milner, B., & Taylor, L. Right-hemisphere superiority in tactile pattern-recognition after cerebral commissurotomy: Evidence for nonverbal memory. *Neuropsychologia,* 1972, *10,* 1–15.

Mishkin, M. Perseveration of central sets after frontal lesions in monkeys. In *The Prefrontal Granular Cortex and Behavior,* edited by J. M. Warren and K. Akert. New York: McGraw-Hill, 1964, 219–237.

Molfese, D. L., Freeman, R. B., Jr., & Palermo, D. S. The ontogeny of brain lateralization for speech and nonspeech stimuli. *Brain and Language,* 1975, *2,* 356–368.

Mollenauer, S., Plotnik, R., & Snyder, E. Effects of olfactory bulb removal on fear response and passive avoidance in the rat. *Physiology and Behavior,* 1974, *12,* 141.

Molliver, M. E., Grzanna, R., Morison, J. H., & Coyle, J. T. Immunohistochemical characterization of noradrenergic innervation of the rat neocortex: A regional and laminar analysis. *Neuroscience Abstracts,* 1977.

Money, J. Psychosexual differentiation. In *Sex Research: New Developments,* edited by J. Money. New York: Holt, Rinehart & Winston, 1965, 3–23.

Money, J., & Ehrhardt, A. A. *Man and Woman, Boy and Girl.* Baltimore: Johns Hopkins University Press, 1972.

Monnier, M., Kalbere, M., & Krupp, P. Functional antagonism between diffuse reticular and intralaminar recruiting projections in the medial thalamus. *Experimental Neurology,* 1960, *2,* 271–289.

Mora, F., & Myers, R. Brain self-stimulation: direct evidence for the involvement of dopamine in the prefrontal cortex. *Science,* 1977, *197,* 1387–1389.

Morgan, A. H., McDonald, P. J., & MacDonald, H. Differences in bilateral alpha activity as a function of experimental task with a note on lateral eye movements and hypnotizability. *Neuropsychologia,* 1971, *9,* 459–469.

Morrison, J. H., Molliver, M. E., & Grzanna, R. Noradrenergic innervation of cerebral cortex: widespread effects of local cortical lesions. *Science,* 1979, *205,* 313–316.

Moruzzi, G., & Magoun, H. W. Brain stem reticular formation and activation of the EEG. *Electroencephalography and Clinical Neurophysiology,* 1949, *1,* 455–473.

Motokawa, K., Taira, N., & Okuda, J. Spectral response of single units in the primate visual cortex. *Tohoku Journal of Experimental Medicine,* 1962, *78,* 320–337.

Mountcastle, V. B. Some functional properties of the somatic afferent system. In *Sensory Communication,* edited by W. A. Rosenblith. New York: Wiley, 1961.

Mountcastle, V. B. An organizing principle for cerebral function: the unit module and the distributed system. In *The Mindful Brain,* edited by G. M. Edelman and V. B. Mountcastle. Cambridge, Mass.: MIT Press, 1978, 7–50.

Mountcastle, V. B., & Powell, T. P. S. Central neural mechanisms subserving position sense and kinesthesis. *Johns Hopkins Hospital Bulletin,* 1959, *105,* 173–200.

Mountcastle, V. B., & Powell, T. P. S. Neural mechanisms subserving cutaneous sensibility, with reference to the role of afferent inhibition in sensory perception and discrimination. *Johns Hopkins Hospital Bulletin,* 1959, *105,* 201–232.

Nathan, P. W., & Smith, M. C. Normal mentality associated with a maldeveloped "rhinencephalon." *Journal of Neurology, Neurosurgery and Psychiatry,* 1950, *13,* 191–197.

Nauta, W. J. H. Hypothalamic regulation of sleep in rats: an experiméntal study. *Journal of Neurophysiology,* 1946, *9,* 285–316.

Nebes, R. Handedness and the perception of part-whole relationships. *Cortex,* 1971, *7,* 350–356.

Neville, H. J. The development of cerebral specialization in normal and congenitally deaf children: An evoked potential and behavioral study. Unpublished doctoral dissertation, Cornell University, 1975. Reported in Neville, H. J. The functional significance of cerebral specialization. In *The Neuropsychology of Language,* edited by R. W. Rieber. New York: Plenum Press, 1976, 195–227.

Nisbett, R. Hunger, obesity and the ventromedial hypothalamus. *Psychological Review,* 1972, *79,* 433–453.

Nyback, H., Borzecki, Z., & Sedvall, G. Accumulation and disappearance of catecholamines formed from tyrosine-C in mouse brain: Effect of some psychotropic drugs. *European Journal of Pharmacology,* 1968, *4,* 395–402.

Ojemann, R. Correlation between specific human brain lesions and memory changes: a critical survey of the literature. *Neuroscience Research Program Bulletin* (Supplement), 1966, *4,* 1–70.

O'Keefe, J., & Dostrovsky, J. The hippocampus as a spatial map. Preliminary evidence from unit activity in the freely-moving rat. *Brain Research,* 1971, *34,* 171–175.

O'Keefe, J., & Nadel, L. *The Hippocampus as a Cognitive Map.* London: Oxford University Press, 1974; Clarendon, N.Y.: Oxford University Press, 1978.

Olds, J., Self-stimulation of the brain. *Science,* 1958, *127,* 315–323.

Olds, J. Learning and the hippocampus. *Review of Canadian Biology,* 1972, *31* (Supplement), 215–238.

Olds, J., Allen, W., & Briese, E. Differentiation of hypothalamic drive and reward centers.

American Journal of Physiology, 1971, *221*, 368–375.

Olds, J., & Milner, P. Positive reinforcement produced by electrical stimulation of the septal area and other regions of the rat brain. *Journal of Comparative and Physiological Psychology*, 1954, *47*, 419–427.

Oomura, Y., Kimura, K., Ooyama, H., Maeno, T., Iki, M., & Kuniyoshi, M. Reciprocal activities of the ventromedial and lateral hypothalamic area of cats. *Science*, 1964, *143*, 484–485.

Oomura, Y., Ono, T., Ooyama, H., & Wayner, M. Glucose and osmosensitive neurons of the rat hypothalamus. *Nature*, 1969, *222*, 282–284.

Orbach, J., Milner, B., & Rasmussen, T. Learning and retention in monkeys after amygdala-hippocampal resection. *AMA Archives of Neurology*, 1960, *3*, 230–251.

Pandya, D., & Kuypers, H. Corticocortical connections in the rhesus monkey. *Brain Research*, 1969, *13*, 13–36.

Panksepp, J. Drugs and stimulus-bound attack. *Physiology and Behavior*, 1971, *6*, 317–320.

Paul, K., & Dittrichova, J. Sleep patterns following learning in infants. In P. Levin and W. Koella (Eds.), *Sleep, 1974. Proceedings of the 2nd European Congress on Sleep Research, Rome, 1974*. Basel: Karger, 1975.

Pasik, P., Pasik, T., & Schilder, P. Extrageniculostriate vision in the monkey: Discrimination of luminous flux-equated figures. *Experimental Neurology*, 1969, *23*, 421–437.

Pearlman, C. A., & Becker, M. Brief posttrial REM sleep deprivation impairs discrimination learning in rats. *Physiological Psychology*, 1973, *1*, 373–376.

Pearlman, C. A., & Becker, M. REM sleep deprivation impairs serial reversal and probability maximizing in rats. *Physiological Psychology*, 1974, *2*, 509–512.

Pearlman, C. A., & Greenberg, R. Posttrial REM sleep: a critical period for consolidation of shuttlebox avoidance. *Animal Learning and Behavior*, 1973, *1*, 49–51.

Pearlman, C. A., Sharpless, S. K., & Jarvik, M. E. Retrograde amnesia produced by anesthetic and convulsant agents. *Journal of Comparative and Physiological Psychology*, 1961, *54*, 109–112.

Peck, W. Situational determinants of the body weights defended by normal rats and rats with hypothalamic lesions. In *Hunger: Basic Mechanism and Clinical Implications*, edited by D. Novin, W. Wyrwicka, and G. Bray. New York: Raven Press, 1976, 297–311.

Penfield, W., & Jasper, H. *Epilepsy and the Functional Anatomy of the Human Brain*. Boston: Little, Brown, 1954.

Petsche, H., Stumpf, C., & Gogolak, G. The significance of the rabbit's septum as a relay station between the midbrain and the hippocampus: I. The control of hippocampus arousal activity by the septum cells. *Electroencephalography and Clinical Neurophysiology*, 1962, *14*, 202–211.

Pettigrew, J. The neurophysiology of binocular vision. In *Recent Progress in Perception: Readings from Scientific American*, edited by R. Held and W. Richards. San Francisco: W. H. Freeman, 1972, 55–66.

Phoenix, C. H., Goy, R. W., Gerall, R. A., & Young, W. C. Organizing action of prenatally administered testosterone propionate on the tissues mediating behavior in the female guinea pig. *Endocrinology*, 1959, *65*, 369–382.

Powell, T. P. S. Sensory convergence in the cerebral cortex. In *Surgical Approaches in Psychiatry*, edited by L. Laitinen and K. Livingston. Baltimore: University Park Press, 1973.

Pribram, K. H., Douglas, R. J., & Pribram, B. J. The nature of nonlimbic learning. *Journal of Comparative and Physiological Psychology*, 1969, *69*, 765–772.

Prinzmetal, M., & Alles, G. The central nervous system stimulant effects of dextroamphetamine sulphate. *Journal of the American Medical Association*, 1940, *200*, 665–673.

Pujol, J., Mouret, J., Jouvet, M., & Glowinski, J.

Increased turnover of cerebral norepinephrine during rebound of paradoxical sleep in
the rat. *Science*, 1968, *159*, 112–114.

Raisman, G., & Field, P. M. Sexual dimorphism
in the neuropil of the preoptic area of the rat
and its dependence on neonatal androgen.
Brain Research, 1973, *54*, 1–29.

Ramón y Cajal, S. *Recollections of My Life*, translated by H. Craigie. Memoirs of the American
Philosophical Society, Vol. 8. Philadelphia:
the Society, 1937.

Ranson, S. W. Somnolence caused by hypothalamic lesions in monkeys. *Archives of Neurological Psychiatry*, 1939, *41*, 1–23.

Raphelson, A. C., Isaacson, R. L., & Douglas,
R. J. The effect of distracting stimuli on the
runway performance of limbic damaged rats.
Psychonomic Science, 1965, *3*, 483–484.

Raphelson, A. C., Isaacson, R. L., & Douglas,
R. J. The effect of limbic damage on the reten-
tion and performance of a runway response.
Neuropsychologia, 1966, *4*, 253–264.

Rasmussen, G. L. The olivary peduncle and
other fiber projections of the superior olivary
complex. *Journal of Comparative Neurology*,
1946, *84*, 141–219.

Razran, G. *Evolution of Mind*. Boston: Houghton
Mifflin, 1971.

Reynolds, D. V. Surgery in the rat during electrical analgesia induced by focal brain stimulation. *Science*, 1969, *164*, 444–445.

Richman, C., Gulkin, R., and Knoblock, K. Effects of bulbectomization, strain, and gen-
tling on emotionality and exploratory behavior in rats. *Physiology and Behavior*, 1972, *8*,
447.

Rimland, B. *Infantile Autism: The Syndrome and
Its Implications for a Neural Theory of Behavior.*
Englewood Cliffs, N.J.: Prentice-Hall, 1964.

Rimland, B. Inside the mind of the autistic savant. *Psychology Today*, August 1979, p. 69.

Rizzolatti, G., Umiltá, D., & Berlucchi, G. Opposite superiorities of the right and left cerebral hemispheres in discriminative reaction
time to physiognomical and alphabetical
material. *Brain*, 1971, *94*, 431–442.

Roberts, W. W., Dember, W. N., & Brodwick, M. Alternation and exploration in rats
with hippocampal lesions. *Journal of Comparative and Physiological Psychology*, 1962, *55*,
695–700.

Rodieck, R. W., & Stone, J. Analysis of receptive fields of cat retinal ganglion cells. *Journal
of Neurophysiology*, 1965, *28*, 833–849.

Rosén, I., & Asanuma, H. Peripheral inputs to
the forelimb area of the monkey motor cortex:
Input-output relations. *Experimental Brain
Research*, 1972, *14*, 257–273.

Rosenbaum, M., & Merritt, H. H. Korsakoff's
syndrome. *American Medical Association Archives of Neurology and Psychiatry*, 1939, *41*,
978–983.

Rosene, D., & Van Hoesen, G. Hippocampal efferents reach widespread areas of cerebral
cortex and amygdala in the rhesus monkey.
Science, 1977, *198*, 315–317.

Rosenhan, D. On being sane in insane places.
Science, 1973, *197*, 250–258.

Routtenberg, A., & Lindy, J. Effects of the
availability of rewarding septal and hypothalamic stimulation in bar pressing for
food under conditions of deprivation. *Journal
of Comparative and Physiological Psychology*,
1965, *60*, 158–161.

Rubens, A. B. Anatomical asymmetries of the
human cerebral cortex. In *Lateralization in the
Nervous System*, edited by S. Harnad. New
York: Academic Press, 1977, 429–448.

Sabelli, H., Mosnain, A., & Vasquez, A.
Phenylethylamine: Possible role in depres-
sion and antidepressive drug action. In
Neurohumoral Coding of Brain Functions,
edited by R. Myers and R. Drucker-Colin.
New York: Plenum Press, 1974, 331–357.

Sarnat, H. B., & Netsky, M. G. *Evolution of the
Nervous System*. New York: Oxford University Press, 1974.

Sauer, F. Mitosis in the neural tube. *Journal of
Comparative Neurology*, 1935, *62*, 337–405.

Sawyer, C. H., & Kawakami, M. Characteristics
of behavioral and encephalographic after-
reactions to copulation and vaginal stimula-

tion in the female rabbit. *Endocrinology,* 1959, *65,* 622–630.

Scalia, F. A review of recent experimental studies on the distribution of the olfactory tracts of mammals. *Brain, Behavior, Evolution,* 1968, *1,* 101–123.

Schachter, S. Some extraordinary facts about obese humans and cats. *American Psychologist,* 1971, *26,* 129–144.

Schachter, S., & Singer, J. E. Cognitive social and physiological determinants of emotional state. *Psychological Review,* 1962, *69,* 379–399.

Schilder, P. The role of the monkey superior colliculus in eye movement and vision. *Investigative Opthalmology,* 1972, *11,* 451–459.

Schilder, P., Pasik, P., & Pasik, T. Extrageniculostriate vision in the monkey: III. Circle vs. triangle and 'red' vs. 'green' discrimination. *Experimental Brain Research,* 1972, *14,* 436–448.

Schildkraut, J. Norepinephrine metabolites as biochemical criteria for classifying depressive disorders and predicting responses to treatment. *American Journal of Psychiatry,* 1973, *130,* 695–699.

Schuckit, M. A., & Rayses, V. Ethanol ingestion: Differences in blood acetaldehyde concentrations in relatives of alcoholics and controls. *Science,* 1979, *203,* 54–55.

Schwartzbaum, J., & Donovick, P. Discrimination reversal and spatial alternation associated with septal and caudate dysfunction in rats. *Journal of Comparative and Physiological Psychology,* 1968, *65,* 83–92.

Sclafani, A. Appetite and hunger in experimental obesity syndrome. In *Hunger: Basic Mechanisms and Clinical Implications,* edited by D. Novin, W. Wyrwicka, and G. Bray. New York: Raven Press, 1976, 281–295.

Sclafani, A., & Kluge, L. Food motivation and body weight — Level I. Hypothalamic hyperphagic rats: A dual lipostat model of hunger and appetite. *Journal of Comparative and Physiological Psychology,* 1974, *86,* 28–46.

Scoville, W. B., & Milner, B. Loss of recent memory after bilateral hippocampal lesion. *Journal of Neurology, Neurosurgery and Psychiatry,* 1957, *20,* 11–21.

Segal, M., Disterhoft, J., & Olds, J. Hippocampal unit activity during classical, aversive and appetitive conditioning. *Science,* 1972, *175,* 792–794.

Selye, H. *The Stress of Life.* New York: McGraw-Hill, 1976.

Semmes, J., Weinstein, S., Ghent, L., & Teuber, H. L. Spatial orientation in man after cerebral injury. I: Analyses by locus of lesion. *Journal of Psychology,* 1955, *39,* 227–249.

Semmes, J., Weinstein, S., Ghent, L., & Teuber, H. L. *Somatosensory Changes after Penetrating Brain Wounds in Man.* Cambridge, Mass.: Harvard University Press, 1960.

Sharpless, S., & Jasper, H. H. Habituation of the arousal reaction. *Brain,* 1956, *79,* 655–680.

Sherrington, C. S. *The Integrative Action of the Nervous System.* New Haven, Conn.: Yale University Press, 1906.

Sieck, M. The role of the olfactory system in avoidance learning and activity. *Physiology and Behavior,* 1972, *8,* 705.

Sieck, M. Selective olfactory system lesions in rats and changes in appetitive and aversive behavior. *Physiology and Behavior,* 1973, *10,* 731.

Sieck, M., & Gordon, B. Anterior olfactory nucleus or lateral olfactory tract destruction in rats and changes in aversive and appetitive behavior. *Physiology and Behavior,* 1972, *10,* 1051.

Simmons, F. B. Monaural processing. In *Foundations of Modern Auditory Theory,* edited by J. V. Tobias. Vol. 1. New York: Academic Press, 1970, 343–379.

Singh, M., & Kay, S. Wheat gluten as a pathogenic factor in schizophrenia. *Science,* 1976, *191,* 401–403.

Sirex, D., & Marini, F. Bufotenine in human urine. *Psychiatry,* 1969, *1,* 189–191.

Sitaram, N., Wyatt, R., Dawson, S., & Gillin, J. REM sleep induction by physiostigmine infusion during sleep. *Science,* 1976, *191,* 1281–1283.

Snyder, S. *Madness and the Brain.* New York: McGraw-Hill, 1975.

Snyder, S., & Meyerhoff, J. How amphetamine acts in minimal brain dysfunction. *Annals of the New York Academy of Science,* 1973, *205,* 310–320.

Speidel, C. C. Adjustments of nerve endings. *The Harvey Lectures,* Series 36. New York: Academic Press, 1941.

Spencer, W. A., Thompson, R. F., & Neilson, D. R., Jr. Response decrement of flexion reflex in acute spinal cat and transient restoration by strong stimuli. *Journal of Neurophysiology,* 1966, *29,* 221–239.

Sperry, R. Mental unity following surgical disconnection of the cerebral hemispheres. *The Harvey Lectures,* Series 62. New York: Academic Press, 1968.

Spoendlin, H. The innervation of the cochlear receptor. In *Basic Mechanisms in Hearing,* edited by A. R. Meller. New York: Academic Press, 1973.

Sprague, R., & Sleator, E. Methyl phenidate in hyperkinetic children: Differences in dose effects on learning and social behavior. *Science,* 1977, *198,* 1274–1276.

Sterman, M. B., & Clemente, C. D. Forebrain inhibitory mechanisms: Cortical synchronization induced by basal forebrain stimulation. *Experimental Neurology,* 1962, *6,* 91–102 and 103–117.

Sterman, M. B., Knauss, T. K., Lehmann, D., & Clemente, C. D. Alteration of sleep patterns following basal forebrain lesions. *Federal Proceedings,* 1964, *23,* 209.

Straus, E., & Yalow, R. S. Cholesystokinin in the brains of obese and nonobese mice. *Science,* 1979, *203,* 68–69.

Stricker, E., Bradshaw, W., & McDonald, R., Jr. The reninangiotensin system and thirst: a reevaluation. *Science,* 1976, *194,* 1169–1171.

Stricker, E., Rowland, N., & Zigmond, M. Trigeminal lemniscal lesions and the lateral hypothalamus syndrome. *Science,* 1975, *190,* 694–695.

Stricker, E., & Zigmond, M. Brain catecholamines and the lateral hypothalamic syndrome. In *Hunger: Basic Mechanisms and Clinical Implications,* edited by D. Novin, W. Wyrwicka and G. Bray. New York: Raven Press, 1976, 19–32.

Swanson, L., & Cowan, W. Hippocampohypothalamic connections: Origin in subicular cortex, not Ammon's horn. *Science,* 1975, *189,* 303–304.

Szentagothai, J. Brain circuitry of the neocortex. *Experimental Brain Research,* Supplement 1, 1976, 282–287.

Tasaki, I. Nerve impulses in individual auditory nerve fiber of guinea pig. *Journal of Neurophysiology,* 1954, *17,* 97–122.

Tasaki, I., & Davis, H. Electric responses of individual nerve elements in cochlear nucleus to sound stimulation (guinea pigs). *Journal of Neurophysiology,* 1955, *18,* 151–158.

Teitlebaum, P. Sensory control of hypothalamic hyperphagia. *Journal of Comparative and Physiological Psychology,* 1955, *48,* 156–163.

Teuber, H. L. The riddle of frontal function in man. In *The Frontal Granular Cortex and Behavior,* edited by J. M. Warren and K. Akert. New York: McGraw-Hill, 1964, 410–444.

Thierry, A., Blanc, G., Sobel, A., Stinus, L., & Glowinski, J. Dopaminergic terminals in the rat cortex. *Science,* 1973, *182,* 499–500.

Thomas, J. Some behavioral effects of olfactory bulb damage in the rat. *Journal of Comparative and Physiological Psychology,* 1973, *83,* 140–148.

Thomas, L. *The Lives of a Cell: Notes of a Biology Watcher.* New York: Bantam Books, 1974.

Tissot, R., & Monnier, M. Dualité des système thalamique de projection diffuse. *Electroencephalography and Clinical Neurophysiology,* 1959, *11,* 675–686.

Towbin, A. Mental retardation due to germinal matrix infarction. *Science,* 1969, *164,* 156–161.

Trulson, M. E., & Jacobs, B. L. Long-term amphetamine treatment decreases brain serotonin metabolism; Implications for theories of schizophrenia. *Science,* 1979, *205,* 1295–1297.

Tulving, E. Episodic and semantic memory. In *Organization of Memory,* edited by E. Tulving and W. Donaldson. New York: Academic Press, 1972, 382–403.

Tzavarus, A., Hécaen, H., & Le Bras, H. Le

problème de la spécificité du déficit de la reconnaissance du visage humain lor des lesions hémisphériques unilatérales. *Neuropsychologie,* 1970, *8,* 403–416.

Ueki, S., & Sugano, H. *Effect of olfactory bulb lesions on behavior.* 23rd International Congress of Physiological Science, Tokyo. Abstract No. 1095.

Umiltá, C., Rizzolatti, G., Marzi, A., Zamboni, G., Franzine, C., Camarda, R., & Berlucchi, G. Hemispheric differences in normal human subjects: Further evidence from study of reaction time to lateralized visual stimuli. *Brain Research,* 1973, *49,* 499–500.

Ungerstedt, U. Stereotaxic mapping of the monoamine pathways in the rat. *Acta Physiologica Scandinavica,* 1971, *367,* 1–48.

Ursin, H. The effect of amygdaloid lesions on flight and defense behavior in cats. *Experimental Neurology,* 1966, *11,* 61–79.

Ursin, H., & Kaada, B. Functional localization within the amygdaloid complex in the cat. *Electroencephalography and Clinical Neurology,* 1960, *12,* 1–20.

Uttal, W. *The Psychobiology of Sensory Coding.* New York: Harper & Row, 1973.

Valenstein, E., Cox, V., & Kakolewski, J. Polydipsia elicited by the synergistic action of a saccharin and glucose solution. *Science,* 1970, *157,* 552–554.

Vallbo, A. Muscle spindle response at the onset of isometric voluntary contractions in man: Time differences between fusimotor and skeletomotor effects. *Journal of Physiology* (London), 1971, *218,* 405–431.

Valverde, F. *Studies on the Piriform Lobe.* Cambridge, Mass.: Harvard University Press, 1965.

Valverde, F. Structural changes in the area striata of the mouse after enucleation. *Experimental Brain Research,* 1968, *5,* 274–292.

Valverde, F., & Estéban, M. Peristriate cortex of mouse: location of the effects of enucleation on the number of dendritic spines. *Brain Research,* 1968, *9,* 145–148.

Van Hoesen, G., Pandya, D., & Butters, N. Cortical afferents to the entorhinal cortex of the rhesus monkey. *Science,* 1972, *175,* 1471–1473.

Victor, M., Adams, R. D., & Collins, G. H. *The Wernicke-Korsakoff Syndrome.* Philadelphia: F. A. Davis, 1971.

Vogt, B. A., Rosene, D. L., & Pandya, D. N. Thalamic and cortical afferents differentiate anterior from posterior cingulate cortex in the monkey. *Science,* 1979, *204,* 205–207.

Wada, J. A new method for the determination of the side of cerebral speech dominance. A preliminary report on the intracarotid injection of sodium amytal in man. *Igaku To Seibutsugaku (Medicine and Biology),* 1949, *14,* 221–222. (Japanese)

Wada, J. Sharing and shift of cerebral speech dominance and morphological hemispheral asymmetry. *Excerpta Medica International Congress Series,* 1973, *296,* 252.

Wald, G. Molecular basis of visual excitation. *Science,* 1968, *162,* 230–239.

Wei, E., & Loh, H. Physical dependence on opiate-like peptides. *Science,* 1976, *193,* 1262–1263.

Weiskrantz, L. Hindsight and blindsight. In *Neurosciences Research Program Bulletin,* edited by E. Pöppel, R. Held, and J. Dowling. Cambridge, Mass.: MIT Press, 1977, 344–346.

Weiskrantz, L., Warrington, E. K., Sanders, M. D., & Marshall, J. Visual capacity in the hemianopic field following a restricted occipital ablation. *Brain,* 1974, *97,* 709–728.

Wender, P. *Minimal Brain Dysfunction in Children.* New York: Wiley, 1971.

Wenzel, B. The olfactory system and behavior. In *Limbic and Autonomic Systems Research,* edited by L. DiCara. New York: Plenum Press, 1974.

Wenzel, B., Albritton, P., Salzman, A., & Oberjat, T. Behavior changes in pigeons following olfactory nerve section or bulb ablation. In *Olfaction and Taste III,* edited by C. Pfaffman.

New York: Rockefeller University Press, 1969, 278–287.

Wenzel, B., & Salzman, A. Olfactory bulb ablation or nerve section and pigeon's behavior in non-olfactory learning. *Experimental Neurology*, 1968, *22*, 472–479.

Werblin, F. Lateral interactions at the inner plexiform layer of vertebrate retina: Antagonistic responses to change. *Science*, 1972, *175*, 1008–1010.

Werblin, F. S., & Dowling, J. E. Organization of the retina of the mudpuppy, *Necturus maculocus.* II. Intracellular recording. *Journal of Neurophysiology*, 1969, *32*, 339–355.

Wever, E., & Bray, C. Action currents in the auditory nerve in response to acoustical stimulation. *Proceedings of the National Academy of Science*, 1930, *16*, 344–350.

Wever, E., & Bray, C. Distortion in the ear as shown by the electrical responses of the cochlea. *Journal of the Acoustical Society of America*, 1938, *9*, 227–233.

Wever, E. G. *Theory of Hearing.* New York: Wiley, 1949.

Whalen, R. E., & Edwards, D. A. Hormonal determinants of the development of masculine and feminine behavior in male and female rats. *Anatomical Record*, 1967, *157*, 173–180.

Whitfield, I. C., & Evans, E. F. Responses of auditory cortical neurons to stimuli of changing frequency. *Journal of Neurophysiology*, 1965, *28*, 655–672.

Wickelgren, B. Some receptive field properties of bimodally responsive cells. *Science*, 1971, *173*, 69–71.

Wickelgren, W. O., & Isaacson, R. L. Effect of introduction of an irrelevant stimulus on runway performance of the hippocampectomized rat. *Nature*, 1963, *200*, 48–59.

Wiesel, T. N., & Hubel, D. H. Spatial and chromatic interactions in the lateral geniculate body of the rhesus monkey. *Journal of Neurophysiology*, 1966, *29*, 1115–1156.

Williams. D. Neurological factors related to habitual aggression. *Brain*, 1969, *92*, 503–520.

Wise, C., & Stein, L. Facilitation of brain self-stimulation by central administration of norepinephrine. *Science*, 1969, *163*, 299–301.

Wise, C., & Stein, L. Dopamine-B-hydroxylase deficits in the brains of schizophrenic patients. *Science*, 1973, *181*, 344–347.

Witelson, S. Sex and the single hemisphere: Specialization of the right hemisphere for spatial processing. *Science*, 1976, *193*, 425–427.

Witelson, S. Developmental dyslexia: Two right hemispheres and none left. *Science*, 1977, *195*, 309–311.

Witelson, S. F., & Pallie, W. Left hemisphere specialization for language in the new-born: Neuroanatomical evidence of asymmetry. *Brain*, 1973, *96*, 641–646.

Woolsey, C. N. Organization of the somatic sensory and motor areas of the cerebral cortex. In *Biological and Biochemical Bases of Behavior,* edited by H. F. Harlow and C. N. Woolsey. Madison: University of Wisconsin Press, 1958.

Wooten, B., & Wald, G. Color-vision mechanisms in the peripheral retinas of normal and dichromatic observers. *Journal of General Physiology*, 1973, *6*, 125–145.

Wurtz, R. H., & Goldberg, M. E. The primate superior colliculus and the shift of visual attention. *Investigative Opthalmology*, 1972, *2*, 451–460.

Wyatt, R., Schwartz, M., Erdelyi, E., & Barchas, J. Dopamine B-hydroxylase activity in brains of chronic schizophrenic patients. *Science*, 1975, *187*, 368–369.

Yaryura-Tobias, J., Diamond, B., & Morlis, S. The action of L-dopa on schizophrenic patients. *Current Therapy Research*, 1970, *12*, 528.

Yin, R. Looking at upside-down faces. *Journal of Experimental Psychology*, 1969, *81*, 141–145.

Yin, R. Face recognition by brain-injured patients: a dissociable disability? *Neuropsychologia*, 1970, *8*, 395–402.

Zeamay, D., & House, B. J. The role of attention in retardate discrimination learning. In *Handbook of Mental Deficiency*, edited by N. R. Ellis. New York: McGraw-Hill, 1963.

Zwaan, J., Bryan, P., & Pearce, T. Interkinetic nuclear migration during the early stages of lens formation in the chicken embryo. *Journal of Embryology and Experimental Morphology.* 1969, *21*, 71–83.

Art Credits

Figures 1.1 and 1.2: "An Illustrated History of Brain Function" by Edwin Clark and Kenneth Dewhurst, Sandford OXFORD. Photograph on page 10: Santiago Ramón y Cajal, Nobel Laureate, 1906. Courtesy of Mondadori. Figure 1.4: By permission of Linda Austin, Chicago State University, Biology.

Figure 3.3: From *Fundamentals of Neurology* by Ernest Gardner, MD, 6th ed., 1975, by permission of W. B. Saunders Company. Figures 3.4 and 3.6: Harold Patterson, Chicago State University. Figure 3.8: "The Fluid Mosaic Model of the Structure of Cell Membranes," S. J. Singer and G. L. Nicolson, *Science,* Vol. 175, p. 723, Fig. 3, February 18, 1972. Copyright 1972 by the American Association for the Advancement of Science. Figure 3.9: J. C. Eccles, *The Understanding of the Brain,* McGraw-Hill, 1973. Used with permission of McGraw-Hill Book Company.

Figure 4.5: D. H. Hubel and T. N. Wiese. Shape and arrangement of columns in cat's striate cortex. *J. Physiol.,* 1963, 165:559–568. Figure 4.6: "Visual Pigments in Single Rods and Cones of the Human Retina," P. K. Brown and G. Wald, *Science,* Vol. 144, pp. 145–151, 1964. Copyright 1964 by the American Association for the Advancement of Science. Figure 4.7: R. L. DeValois, I. Abramov, and G. H. Jacobs. Analysis of response patterns of LGN cells. *J. Opt. Soc. Amer.,* 1966, 56:966–977.

Figure 5.2: From *Fundamentals of Neurology* by Ernest Gardner, MD, 6th ed., 1975, p. 269, by permission of W. B. Saunders Company. Figure 5.7: *Neurons and Interneuronal Connections of the Central Visual System* by Ekaterina G. Skol'nik-Yarros. New York: Plenum, 1971. Copyright © 1971 Plenum. Reprinted by permission of the publisher.

Figure 6.7: J. C. Eccles, *The Understanding of the Brain,* McGraw-Hill, 1973. Used with permission of McGraw-Hill Book Company.

Figure 7.4: A. Iggo and A. R. Muir. The structures and function of a slowly adapting touch corpuscle in hairy skin. *J. Physiol.,* 1969, 200:763–796. Figures 7.5 and 7.6: From *Fundamentals of Neurology* by Ernest Gardner, MD, 6th ed., 1975, by permission of W. B. Saunders Company.

Figure 8.1: Photo by P. S. Tice, from *Animals Without Backbones* by Buchsbaum. Figure 8.10: From Stephen J. DeArmond, Madeline M. Fusco, and Maynard M. Dewey, *Structure of the Human Brain: A Photographic Atlas*

(New York: Oxford University Press, 1976). Left photograph on page 188: Ellis Herwig, Stock Boston. Right photograph on page 188: Cary Wolinsky, Stock Boston. Photograph on page 189: Cary Wolinsky, Stock Boston.

Figure 9.1: *Neurons and Interneuronal Connections of the Central Visual System* by Ekaterina G. Skol'nik-Yarros. New York: Plenum, 1971. Copyright © 1971 Plenum. Reprinted by permission of the publisher. Figure 9.3: "Variations in Writing Posture and Cerebral Organization," J. Levy and M. Reid, *Science,* Vol. 194, p. 337, Fig. 1, October 15, 1976. Copyright 1976 by the American Association for the Advancement of Science. Photograph on page 206: Courtesy of Roger Sperry. Photograph on page 208: © Richard Cooley, photographer. Figure 9.7: "Language Production: Electroencephalographic Localization in the Normal Human Brain," D. W. McAdam and H. A. Whitaker, *Science,* Vol. 172, p. 501, Fig. 1, April 30, 1971. Copyright 1971 by the American Association for the Advancement of Science.

Figures 10.10 and 10.11: "Hippocampal Efferents Reach Widespread Areas of Cerebral Cortex and Amygdala in the Rhesus Monkey," D. L. Rosene and G. W. Van Hoesen, *Science,* Vol. 198, pp. 315–317, Figs. 1 and 2, October 21, 1977. Copyright 1977 by the American Association for the Advancement of Science.

Figure 12.2: From H. H. Jasper, *Epilepsy and Cerebral Localization,* ed. W. Penfield and T. C. Erikson, 1941. Courtesy of Charles C Thomas, Publisher, Springfield, Illinois. Photograph on page 277: W. R. Hess, *The Functional Organization of the Diencephalon* (Grune & Stratton, 1957). Reprinted by permission of Grune & Stratton. Photograph on page 278: From Ernest Hartmann, *The Biology of Dreaming,* 1967. Courtesy of Charles C Thomas, Publisher, Springfield, Illinois.

Figure 13.8: From *Fundamentals of Neurology* by Ernest Gardner, MD, 6th ed., 1975, p. 168, by permission of W. B. Saunders Company. Figure 13.9: From Harvey B. Sarnat and Martin G. Netsky, *Evolution of the Nervous System* (New York: Oxford University Press, 1974). Figure 13.10: J. C. Eccles, *The Understanding of the Brain,* McGraw-Hill, 1973. Used with permission of McGraw-Hill Book Company. Figure 13.11: *Neurons and Interneuronal Connections of the Central Visual System* by Ekaterina G. Skol'nik-Yarros. New York: Plenum, 1971. Copyright © 1971 Plenum. Reprinted by permission of the publisher.

Figure 14.1: Marcus Jacobson, *Developmental Neurology* (New York: Holt, 1970). Figure 14.2: From Harrison, *J. Exp. Zool.* 9:787–846 (1910). Figure 14.3: "Neuronal Chemotaxis: Chick Dorsal-Root Axons Turn Toward High Concentration of Nerve Growth," R. W. Gunderson and J. N. Barrett, *Science,* Vol. 206, p. 1080, Fig. 1, November 30, 1979. Copyright 1979 by the American Association for the Advancement of Science. Figure 14.4: C. C. Speidel, "Studies of living nerves: VII. Growth ajustments of cutaneous terminal arborizations," *Journal of Comparative Neurology,* Vol. 76, 1942, pp. 57–69. Figure 14.6: "Neurons in Rhesus Monkey Visual Cortex: Systematic Relation between Time of Origin and Essential Disposition," P. Rakic, *Science,* Vol. 183, p. 426, Fig. 2, February 1, 1974. Copyright 1974 by the American Association for the Advancement of Science. Figure 14.7: *Neurons and*

Index

507

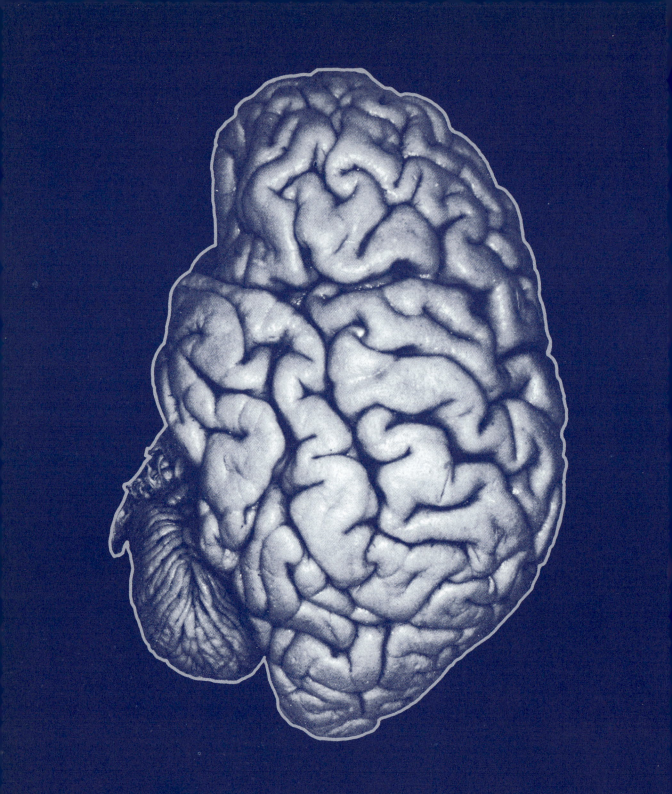

Lateral Surface of the Brain (Actual Size)